The Letters and Diaries
of
John Henry Newman

The Letters and Diaries

of

John Henry Newman

Edited at the Birmingham Oratory
with notes and an introduction

by

Charles Stephen Dessain

of the same Oratory

and

Thomas Gornall, S. J.

Volume XXIV

A Grammar of Assent

January 1868 to December 1869

CLARENDON PRESS · OXFORD

1973

Oxford University Press, Ely House, London W.1

GLASGOW   NEW YORK   TORONTO   MELBOURNE   WELLINGTON
CAPE TOWN   IBADAN   NAIROBI   DAR ES SALAAM   LUSAKA   ADDIS ABABA
DELHI   BOMBAY   CALCUTTA   MADRAS   KARACHI   LAHORE   DACCA
KUALA LUMPUR   SINGAPORE   HONG KONG   TOKYO

Nihil obstat
Mgr. H. Francis Davis

Imprimatur

Rt. Rev. Mgr. Daniel Leonard, v.g.
Birmingham, 20 October 1972

Printed in Great Britain by
Cox & Wyman Ltd,
London, Fakenham and Reading

Preface

WITHOUT the gradual building up at the Birmingham Oratory of a very full collection of Cardinal Newman's correspondence (an account of which will be found in the Introduction to Volume XI), the present work could not have been undertaken. Its aim is to provide an exhaustive edition of Newman's letters; with explanatory notes, which are often summaries of or quotations from the other side of the correspondence. Some of these letters *to* Newman, when they appear to have particular importance, or to be necessary for following a controversy, are inserted in the text. Every one of the letters written *by* Newman is included there, in chronological sequence. Should there eventually be any of his letters, whose existence is known to the editor, but of which he has failed to obtain a copy, this will be noted in its place. On the other hand, no attempt has been made to include a list of letters written by Newman and now lost, nor the brief précis he occasionally made of his reply, on the back of a correspondent's letter, although these are utilised for the annotation.

In order that the text of each letter may be as accurate as possible, the original autograph, when it still exists, or at least a photographic copy of it, has been used by the editor as his source. (The very few cases in which he has been content with an authenticated copy will be noted as they occur.) Always the text of the autograph is reproduced, or, when the autograph has disappeared, that of the copy that appears most reliable. When only Newman's draft exists, that is printed. The source used in each case is to be found in the list of letters by correspondents.

Such alterations as are made in transcribing the letters aim, without sacrifice of accuracy, at enabling them to be read with ease. Newman writes simply and has none of those idiosyncrasies which sometimes need to be reproduced for the sake of the evidence of one kind or another which they provide.

The following are the only alterations made in transcription:

ADDRESS AND DATE are always printed on the same line, and at the head of the letter, even when Newman puts them at the end. When he omits or gives an incomplete date, the omission is supplied in square brackets, and justified in a note unless the reason for it is obvious. The addresses, to which letters were sent, are included in the list of letters by correspondents. The information derived from postmarks is matter for annotation.

THE CONCLUSION of the letter is made to run on, irrespective of Newman's separate lines, and all postscripts are placed at the end.

NEWMAN'S CORRECTIONS AND ADDITIONS are inserted in their intended place. His interlinear explanations are printed in the text in angle brackets⟨⟩, after the word or phrase they explain. His erasures are given in footnotes when they appear to be of sufficient interest to warrant it. Square brackets being reserved for editorial additions; all Newman's brackets are printed as rounded ones (the kind most usual with him).

NEWMAN'S PARAGRAPHS AND PUNCTUATION are preserved, except that single quotation marks are printed throughout, and double ones for quotations within them. (Newman generally used the latter in both cases.) Further, a parenthesis or quotation that he began with the proper mark but failed to complete, or completed but did not begin, is supplied. All other punctuation marks supplied by the editor are enclosed in square brackets. Newman's dashes, which frequently do duty either for a full stop, a semicolon or a comma (especially when he is tired or writing hurriedly), are represented by a '—' with a space before and after. His spelling and use of capitals are left unchanged, but 'raised' letters are lowered in every case.

NEWMAN'S ABBREVIATIONS are retained in the case of proper names, and in the address and conclusion of each letter, since these are sometimes useful indications of his attitude at the time. In all other cases, abbreviations are printed out in full, where Newman employs them.

When he uses the initials of proper names, the full name is normally inserted in square brackets after the initials, at the first occurrence in each letter, and more often if it seems advisable in order to avoid confusion. No addition of the full name is made in the case of Newman's correspondent, whether his initials occur at the beginning of the letter or in the course of it.

When Newman uses only a Christian name, the surname is sometimes added in square brackets for the reader's convenience. The Christian names of members of the Oratory, since they are of frequent occurrence, are listed in the index of proper names and the reader is referred to surnames.

When transcription is made from a PRINTED SOURCE, typographical alterations clearly due to editor or printer are disregarded.

Sometimes Newman made HOLOGRAPH copies of his letters or of portions of them, when they were returned to him long after they had been written. In order that the reader may be able to see how much he copied and what changes he introduced, the copied passages are placed in quarter brackets ⌐⌐, and all additions of any importance included in the text in double square brackets, or, where this is impracticable, in the annotation.

Newman's letters are printed in CHRONOLOGICAL ORDER, with the name of his correspondent at the head (except that those of each day are arranged alphabetically), and, when more than one is written to the same person on the same day, numbered I, II. In the headings the name of the correspondent is given in its most convenient form, sometimes with Christian names in full, sometimes only with initials.

THE LIST OF LETTERS BY CORRESPONDENTS, at the end of each volume, shows whether the source used was an autograph, draft, printed source or copy, and in the last case, whether a holograph made by Newman later; and gives the present location of the source, as well as of any additional holograph copies or drafts. When a letter, or a considerable portion of it, has been printed in a standard work, references are given; but mistakes or omissions in these previous publications are noticed, if at all, in the annotation.

THE LETTERS WRITTEN TO NEWMAN, when inserted in the text, are printed in type smaller than that used for Newman's own letters, and headed by the name of the correspondent. These letters are not arranged in chronological order, but are placed either just before or just after the letter of Newman to which they are related. A list of them is given at the end of each volume in which they occur. These and the quotations from letters in the annotation are always, unless otherwise stated, printed from autographs at the Birmingham Oratory, and are transcribed in the same way as Newman's letters.

NEWMAN'S DIARIES COVER THE YEARS 1824 to 1879 (with a gap from July 1826 to March 1828). They are written in a series of mottled copy books, 12 × 18½ centimetres; printed for a year each, and entitled *The Private Diary: arranged, printed, and ruled, for receiving an account of every day's employment . . .*' with the exception of the four periods July 1847–May 1850, January 1854–January 1861, January 1861–March 1871, March 1871–October 1879, each of which is contained in a somewhat thicker copy book.

These diaries are printed complete for each day in which Newman has made an entry, except that the lists of people to whom he has written or from whom he has received letters are omitted, as not being of sufficient general interest. The original diaries are, of course, available for consultation. At the end of each diary book are various notes, lists of addresses, of people to be prayed for, accounts, etc. These, also, are omitted, except for occasional dated notes of events, which are inserted in their proper place. Of the rest of the notes, some are theological and will be reserved for a volume of Newman's theological papers, and others will perhaps have room found for them in any fuller edition of *Autobiographical Writings*.

Newman compiled with his own hands, on quarto sheets sewn together, a book of *Chronological Notes*, drawn largely from the diaries. Any new matter in these *Notes* is printed in italics with the appropriate diary entry. (It should be noted that the diary entries themselves were sometimes written up considerably later than the events they record.)

Each volume is preceded by a brief summary of the period of Newman's life that it covers. Summary, diaries and annotation give a roughly biographical form to the whole, and will, it is hoped, enable the ordinary reader to treat it as a continuous narrative.

THE BIOGRAPHIES OF PERSONS are collected in the index of proper names at the end of each volume, in order to simplify the annotation of the letters. Occasionally, when a person is mentioned only once or twice, and a note is required in any case, biographical details have been given in the notes, and a reference in the index. Volume XXI, being the first of a new period in Newman's life, contains an account of every person mentioned, with the exception of a few for whom a notice seemed unnecessary, and of still fewer who have not yet been identified. The indexes of Volume XXII and of subsequent volumes will contain notices of persons who appear in them for the first time, and references back, in the case of those who have been noticed in an earlier volume. (The editor will be grateful for information as to persons not identified.)

These notices have been compiled from such various sources — books of reference, letters at the Oratory, information supplied by the families or religious communities of the persons concerned, and by librarians and archivists — that the giving of authorities would be a very complicated and lengthy process. Like others faced with the same problem, the editor has decided usually to omit them. References are given, however, to *The Dictionary of National Biography*, or *The Dictionary of American Biography*, in all cases where there is an article there, and failing them, to Boase's *Modern English Biography* or Gillow's *Bibliographical Dictionary of the English Catholics*. When all the volumes of letters have been issued, a final index volume will be compiled for the whole work.

Contents

Abbreviations in Volume XXIV

THE abbreviations used for Newman's works are those listed in Joseph Rickaby, S.J., *Index to the Works of John Henry Cardinal Newman*, London 1914, with a few additions.

References to works included by Newman in his uniform edition are always, unless otherwise stated, to that edition, which was begun in 1868 with *Parochial and Plain Sermons*, and concluded in 1881 with *Select Treatises of St Athanasius*. From 1886, until the stock was destroyed in the 1939–45 war, all the volumes were published by Longmans, Green and Co. They are distinguished from other, usually posthumous, publications by having their date of inclusion in the uniform edition in brackets after the title, in the list of abbreviations below. The unbracketed date is, in every case, the date of the edition (or impression) used for giving references. (Once volumes were included in the uniform edition the pagination usually remained unchanged, but there are exceptions and minor alterations.)

Add.	*Addresses to Cardinal Newman with His Replies etc. 1879–82*, ed. W. P. Neville, 1905.
Apo.	*Apologia pro Vita Sua*, (1873) 1905.
Ari.	*The Arians of the Fourth Century*, (1871) 1908.
Ath. I, II	*Select Treatises of St. Athanasius*, two volumes, (1881) 1920.
A.W.	*John Henry Newman: Autobiographical Writings*, ed. Henry Tristram, 1956.
Call.	*Callista, a Tale of the Third Century*, (1876) 1923.
Campaign	*My Campaign in Ireland, Part I* (printed for private circulation only), 1896.
D.A.	*Discussions and Arguments on Various Subjects*, (1872) 1911.
Dev.	*An Essay on the Development of Christian Doctrine*, (1878) 1908.
Diff. I, II	*Certain Difficulties felt by Anglicans in Catholic Teaching*, two volumes, (1879, 1876) 1908.
Ess. I, II	*Essays Critical and Historical*, two volumes, (1871) 1919.
G.A.	*An Essay in aid of a Grammar of Assent*, (1870) 1913.
H.S. I, II, III	*Historical Sketches*, three volumes, (1872) 1908, 1912, 1909.
Idea	*The Idea of a University defined and illustrated*, (1873) 1902.
Jfc.	*Lectures on the Doctrine of Justification*, (1874) 1908.
K.C.	*Correspondence of John Henry Newman with John Keble and Others, 1839–45*, ed. at the Birmingham Oratory, 1917.
L.G.	*Loss and Gain: the Story of a Convert*, (1874) 1911.
M.D.	*Meditations and Devotions of the late Cardinal Newman*, 1893.
Mir.	*Two Essays on Biblical and on Ecclesiastical Miracles*, (1870) 1907,
Mix.	*Discourses addressed to Mixed Congregations*, (1871) 1909.
Moz. I, II	*Letters and Correspondence of John Henry Newman*, ed. Anne Mozley, two volumes, 1891.
O.S.	*Sermons preached on Various Occasions*, (1870) 1927.

P.S. I–VIII	*Parochial and Plain Sermons,* (1868) 1907–10.
Prepos.	*Present Position of Catholics,* (n.d. 1872) 1913.
S.D.	*Sermons bearing on Subjects of the Day,* (1869) 1902.
S.E.	*Stray Essays on Controversial Points,* (private) 1890.
S.N.	*Sermon Notes of John Henry Cardinal Newman, 1849–1879,* ed. Fathers of the Birmingham Oratory, 1913.
T.T.	*Tracts Theological and Ecclesiastical,* (1874) 1908.
U.S.	*Fifteen Sermons preached before the University of Oxford,* (1872) 1909.
V.M. I, II	*The Via Media,* (1877) 1908, 1911.
V.V.	*Verses on Various Occasions,* (1874) 1910.

*   *   *

Boase	Frederick Boase, *Modern English Biography,* six volumes, Truro 1892–1921.
Butler	Cuthbert Butler, *The Life and Times of Bishop Ullathorne,* two volumes, London 1926.
de Lisle	E. S. Purcell, *Life and Letters of Ambrose Phillipps de Lisle,* two volumes, London 1900.
D A B	*Dictionary of American Biography,* London 1928–36.
D N B	*Dictionary of National Biography,* to 1900, London, reprinted in 1937–8 in twenty-two volumes, the last being a Supplement, *D N B,* Suppl.
D N B, 1901–11	*Dictionary of National Biography,* 1901–11, three volumes in one.
D R	*Dublin Review.*
D T C	*Dictionnaire de Théologie Catholique,* Paris 1903–50.
Gillow	Joseph Gillow, *Bibliographical Dictionary of the English Catholics,* five volumes, London 1885 and later.
Harper	Gordon Huntington Harper, *Cardinal Newman and William Froude, F.R.S. A Correspondence,* Baltimore 1933.
Liddon's *Pusey* I–IV	H. P. Liddon, *Life of Edward Bouverie Pusey,* four volumes, London 1893–7.
MacDougall	Hugh A. MacDougall, *The Acton-Newman Relations,* New York 1962.
Newman and Bloxam	R. D. Middleton, *Newman and Bloxam,* London 1947.
Purcell	E. S. Purcell, *The Life of Cardinal Manning,* two volumes, London 1895.
Trevor I	Meriol Trevor, *Newman the Pillar of the Cloud,* London 1962.
Trevor II	Meriol Trevor, *Newman Light in Winter,* London 1962.
Ward I, II	Wilfrid Ward, *The Life of John Henry Cardinal Newman,* two volumes, London 1912.

Introductory Note

These two years were a calm period between two storms. During 1867 there had been the various attacks on Newman which led to the final defeat of the plan for an Oratory at Oxford. In 1870 he found himself involved against his will in the strife over the definition of papal infallibility.

The first days of 1868 saw the publication of *Verses on Various Occasions*, for which Newman was praised not only by the reviewers, but in private letters by Gladstone, F. T. Palgrave, Coventry Patmore, Sir Francis Doyle, Sir Henry Taylor and others. More important, these two years saw the republication, from their last Anglican editions, of *Parochial and Plain Sermons*, and of *Sermons on Subjects of the Day*. This, which proved to be the beginning of a uniform edition of Newman's works, was a considerable success. More than twenty thousand volumes of the *Parochial and Plain Sermons* had been sold by the end of 1869. Many Nonconformists bought them and welcomed the ethical and religious teaching which they contained. Newman thought 'the first step towards unity was a unison of feeling,' and hoped that he was helping to lay foundations for the future. He also recommended the *Sermons* to a Catholic girl, Louisa Simeon, who was thrown among unbelievers and troubled by doubts, 'I wonder how far you know what is called Tractarianism — and if you don't, whether a course of Tractarianism, so to say, would do you good.' W. J. Copeland, once Newman's curate at Littlemore, undertook the republication, and the letters between the two men reveal details about the original composition of the *Sermons*. In the *Dublin Review* of April 1869 Henry Wilberforce gave an account of the actual preaching of them in St Mary's, Oxford.

Newman's chief occupation, however, during these two years, was the completion of *An Essay in Aid of a Grammar of Assent*. He had long felt a kind of obligation laid on him to show how right and reasonable it was for men to have certitude, and especially certitude in religion. While at Glion above Geneva in August 1866 it had come home to him that he must begin by discussing assent, for 'certitude is only a kind of assent.' The work proceeded slowly. On 17 March 1868 he went out to Rednal to transcribe the first part of the *Essay*. On 27 July he wrote a long letter to Henry Wilberforce which is a kind of summary of the whole, but said, 'I despair from the difficulty of the subject and my scant time. I have begun it again and again . . . I have written my first book, it is on Assent — then would come Certitude — then Proof.' On 7 December Newman wrote to Hope-Scott that it was like tunnelling under a mountain, 'I have begun it, and it is almost too much for my strength . . . Perhaps the tunnell will break in, when I fairly get into my work.' However he persevered, and in April 1869 printing began, although much still remained to be written. At midsummer the first proofs arrived, but Newman's purposes would have been frustrated if the extreme originality of his treatment cut across the accepted Catholic philosophy of the day. As he wrote vividly to Henry Wilberforce two months later, 'What influence should I have with Protestants and Infidels, if a pack of Catholic critics opened at my back fiercely, saying that this remark was illogical, that unheard of, a third realistic, a fourth idealistic, a fifth sceptical?' To obviate this, Newman sent the proofs as they arrived, to a young Professor at Oscott College, of old Catholic stock, who had studied in Rome, Charles Meynell, for criticism. Meynell's letters are printed in full, beside those of Newman, because they throw much light on his aims and intentions — his use, for instance, of the term 'instinct' to describe an activity of the intellect, also on the importance of conscience. Meynell wrote with engaging modesty, and at one point Newman feared that his whole plan would be overturned. But they struggled on, and on 22 November 1869 Newman went out to Rednal hoping to finish the work. Not until nearly the end of January were the last pages sent back to the printer. On 11 March 1870 *A Grammar of Assent* was published, and during the year that followed Newman sent a number of letters to friends in explanation of it.

The first Vatican Council, which opened on 8 December 1869, casts its shadow over this volume. At the end of 1867 Bishop Dupanloup sent Newman, through William Monsell, an invitation to attend the Council as his theologian, an invitation which he renewed pressingly in November 1869, using Montalembert as his intermediary. In October 1868, acting on behalf of Pius IX, Cardinal Caterini, in a courteous and tactful way, asked Bishop Ullathorne to find out whether Newman would wish to be nominated a Consultor of the Council, who would sit in one of the preparatory commissions. He drew up for himself a list of the reasons for and against accepting. The latter had considerable force, for example, 'I never have succeeded with boards or committees. I always have felt out of place and my words unreal.' 'I have a warning, in the time I lost in Dublin, of what will come of my throwing myself into a work foreign to my talents and among strange persons.' When the English bishops had to nominate a Consultor to represent them in the preparatory commissions, Bishop Clifford put forward Newman's name, but he was not asked, probably because his unwillingness was known. Shortly before the Council met, Bishop Brown of Newport was urgent that Newman should go to Rome as the theologian of one of the English bishops, although none until then had invited him, but it would be hard to deny that Newman was right in maintaining that he would have been quite out of place in the Rome of 1870.

There was plenty to do at home, encouraging those who were disturbed by the claims and threats of the ultramontane party and telling them to remain calm. Again and again Newman insisted that, although he personally accepted papal infallibility as a theological opinion, and that it would not be a difficulty to him if it were defined, still it was not yet an article of faith, and if it became such it would be strictly qualified. To an enquirer he wrote on 28 September 1869, 'What you are called upon to believe is the infallibility of the *Church*. If the Church, in the ensuing Council said anything about Papal Infallibility, it will be so strictly worded, with such safeguards, conditions, limitations etc., as will add as little as is conceivable to what is *now* held.' On the other hand, Newman felt that a definition was most inexpedient and inopportune. It would start further controversies and upset the balance within the Church. To Mrs William Froude he wrote on 21 November 1869, 'If any thing could throw religion into confusion, make sceptics, encourage scoffers, and throw back inquirers, it would be the definition of this doctrine. This I shall think, even if it passes — because, though then the doctrine must be inwardly received as true, its definition may still be most unseasonable and unwise.'

Holding these views, and since he had personal experience of the harm the ultramontane campaign was doing to souls, Newman encouraged those who tried to present the other side of the question, and who had a right to be heard, such for instance as Peter le Page Renouf with his pamphlet on Pope Honorius. When the famous French Carmelite preacher, Father Hyacinth Loyson came to the Oratory at Birmingham in September 1868, Newman was much taken by him. He was an opponent of the proposed Definition, and besides having the support of Archbishop Darboy of Paris, presented a warm letter of recommendation from Montalembert. When a year later Loyson began to break with the Church, Newman used his influence gently to try to reclaim him. He approved also of the moderate line which the Jesuits as a body took, but in a letter of 29 April 1869, to Henry James Coleridge, which he did not dare to send him, he criticised the Jesuits who were influential with the Pope, and who edited the extremist *Civiltà Cattolica*. This periodical seemed to Newman 'to be hurrying on measures I cannot contemplate without pain,' and he feared that if it had its way, the Church 'should only consist of the poorer and uneducated classes, and that, as in the beginning, the talent and learning and wisdom of the world should be excluded from the divine election.'

The summoning of the Council led to correspondence with Pusey on the possibilities of corporate reunion. Pusey wondered whether he could make overtures, and Newman made the practical point that the Council might be ready to respond, if it became clear that a large body of Anglicans was involved. The Council could be expected to go out of its way for a great end, such as a reconciliation with a substantial element in the Church of England would be. On the other hand, during these two years, Newman had occasion to write half a dozen and more letters on the subject of Anglican Orders. He was thought to hold them valid, and he was obliged to state, although he found the whole controversy distasteful, that he considered them at best extremely doubtful. Anyhow, the important thing was to decide where the historic

Church was to be found. To the Anglo-Catholic F. G. Lee, he wrote, 'We rest the fact of our being the Church, not on our Orders, but on our uninterrupted visible existence, on the continuity of body, system, claim . . .'

Besides these main themes and a series of letters to enquirers, there are those to Sir Frederic Rogers on the pros and cons of inequality in wealth, to William Monsell on State education, to Edward Bellasis on the study of the lewd classics, to a student of Maynooth on how to preach, together with others of biographical interest, including correspondence with Edward Hawkins, still the Provost of Oriel, and a letter to Rogers on the fullness of satisfaction Newman felt in the Catholic religion, 'before which the neglect or the misapprehension about oneself on the part of individual living persons, however exalted, is as so much dust, when weighed in the balance.'

Summary of Events covered by this volume
1868

4 Jan.	*Verses on Various Occasions* is published.
17 March–2 April	Newman at Rednal, working on *An Essay in Aid of a Grammar of Assent*.
11 May	Death of Mother Margaret Mary Hallahan at Stone.
16 June	Newman and Ambrose St John visit Littlemore for the first time since 1846.
12–14 Sept.	The Carmelite Father Hyacinth Loyson at the Oratory.
14 Oct.	Bishop Ullathorne enquires on behalf of Pius IX whether Newman would wish to be a Consultor on the commission that was preparing the Vatican Council.
28 Nov.	Newman receives into the Catholic Church the Hon. Colin Lindsay, who had been the first President of the English Church Union.

1869

27 Feb.	Newman declines the invitation to join the newly formed Metaphysical Society, sent to him by R. H. Hutton.
15 April	The printing of *A Grammar of Assent* begins.
2 July	The first sheets of *A Grammar* are sent to Charles Meynell for criticism.
24 Oct.	John Norris and Thomas Alder Pope ordained priests at the Birmingham Oratory.
1 Nov.	Newman is appealed to by Manning, who has been accused of having withheld the former's letter of explanation to Rome after the *Rambler* delation.
10 Nov.	Newman writes to Montalembert declining Bishop Dupanloup's final invitation to attend the Council as his theologian.
22 Nov.	Newman goes out to Rednal to finish *A Grammar of Assent*.
7 Dec.	Newman returns to Birmingham and continues to work on *A Grammar* until the new year.
8 Dec.	Opening of the First Vatican Council.

The Letters and Diaries
of
John Henry Newman

WEDNESDAY 1 JANUARY 1868 snow and thaw alternating

The Oratory Bm January 1. 1868

My dear Dr Russell

Let me begin by wishing you, and all your Professors and Students a happy New Year. Every day indeed is the beginning of a new and endless term of days — but that does not make the 1st of January less awful in its associations.

But I write about Fr Ryder's out coming Pamphlet.[1] You must have thought it very ungrateful in us not to write in answer to your kind offer — and we feel also the great kindness of the friend unknown, one of your Professors, who offered with you to revise it. And we thought a good deal about it. At last we determined that it would be sure to give you a good deal of trouble, whereas the Pamphlet did not admit of being put into shape, as if it were the first. It would start from where the first Pamphlet left off. Then again we thought the worst had been said in the first Pamphlet, and all that would be said in the second would be on the side of softening the first. And further than that I felt, and always do and shall feel, tender to minorities, and desirous to defend their interests — and, though I will not, cannot speak, as we do of the American democracy, of a 'tyrant majority,' yet I think the common opinion of Catholics, of which you speak in your letter, is not sufficiently forbearing towards those who cannot in all respects follow it, and that, in the interest of conversions to the Church, it is necessary to show Protestants what they may hold when they become Catholics without being magisterially put down by the 'common opinion.' If he has said any thing he ought not to say, he is quite willing to withdraw it — meanwhile good comes even from our errors, if they are merely the effects of human frailty, and made in a docile spirit. On the other hand, if points were never discussed, much knowledge would be missed, which by discussion is attained. It is a pity indeed that the discussion should be in English — but that is Mr Ward's fault.

I think you will understand Fr Ryder's perplexities — and I sincerely trust you will not disapprove of his out come.[2]

Yours, My dear Dr Russell Affectionately John H Newman

[1] In April 1867 Ryder published *Idealism in Theology, a Review of Dr. Ward's Scheme of Dogmatic Authority,* controverting Ward's articles in *DR* on Infallibility, which had been reprinted as a separate volume. Ward retaliated with *A Letter to the Rev. Father Ryder on his recent Pamphlet,* London 1867. Ryder was now replying with *A Letter to William George Ward Esq., D.Ph. on his Theory of Infallible Instruction,* London 1868, published on 8 Jan. On 13 May 1867 Russell had written to Ryder, criticising a few points in *Idealism in Theology.*
[2] On 11 Jan. Russell wrote to Newman of Ryder's second pamphlet, 'It is exceedingly able, acute, learned and accurate; and on every point in which the 'Idealism' has left any difficulty in my mind, it entirely satisfies me.' See also Newman's remarks of 29 Jan., in *A.W.,* pp 265–6.

3

TO W. J. COPELAND

The Oratory Bm Jany 2/68

My dear Copeland

Rivington so flabbergasts me, that I think you a great man, a strong head, and a patient heart, not to be flabbergasted too.

1 Why has he set me to sign a fictitious transfer, when he said the other day I had *not* transferred to W. F. [Froude] at all?

2. Why does he supersede that second paper, in which, on the ground I need take no notice of W.F., I transferred to you directly?

3. Why has he departed from his proposal of last April 15, which you send me, and which seems very good?

4. How have you any copyright, on his showing, if you have put the work into his hands till the end of the Copyright term of years?

5 What is the good of his making an arrangement for indefinite 100s of copies, when the copyright will expire in (1834–1842) 1876–1884?

All this shows I have got into some puzzle, which it is hopeless to correct — and you must not think it worth while to attend to it. Please do what you think best. I shall be quite content, or rather much obliged to you.[1]

I return the Paper signed. All good wishes for the New Year

Yrs ever affly John H Newman

SATURDAY 4 JANUARY 1868   my Verses came out [2]

TO EDWARD BADELEY

The Oratory Birmingham Jany 5. 1868

My dear Badeley

To dedicate my book to you was so great a pleasure that it recompensed itself, even if it had not been an act of gratitude; but if it had been a step which had a right to be rewarded, I could not have received a return so purely pleasant to me than to find how acceptable it has been to you. I thank you most heartily for both your letters — which, I know, are far indeed above my deserts, but which I cannot help rejoicing to have received.[3]

[1] This letter refers to the copyright of *Parochial and Plain Sermons*, whose republication Copeland was preparing. See letter of 6 Dec. 1867 to him. John Rivington had retired from his firm after initiating negotiations about the copyright, and a different policy was now being followed. Copeland replied to Newman on 9 Jan., 'I shall simply act as trustee of the copyright, and do nothing without your full concurrence.'
[2] *Verses on Various Occasions*. In Feb. Newman issued an Appendix of twenty pages, containing eight more poems, subsequently incorporated with the rest, with the following note: 'The favour with which his Volume has been received, and the wish of friends, have led the Author to venture on the publication of the following additional compositions, which, for one reason or another, it did not enter into his mind, in the first instance, to publish. February 21, 1868.'
[3] On 3 Jan. Badeley wrote to thank for a presentation copy of *Vv.* and for the dedication to himself printed in it, 'the most beautiful, the most graceful, the most affectionate of Dedications.' For Badeley's other letter see that of 18 Oct. 1867 to him.

4

With all good wishes to you for the New Year, and assuring you that, though my prayers for you are not worth much, you have them, as I have yours,

I am, My dear Badeley, Most affectionately Yours John H Newman

E Badeley Esqr

MONDAY 6 JANUARY 1868   Fr Jones S.J. to breakfast.   Outhwaite came and slept here
TUESDAY 7 JANUARY   a cold, slight, for two days
WEDNESDAY 8 JANUARY   Ignatius's second pamphlet out

TO H. LA SERRE

The Oratory, Birmingham, Jan. 8th. 1868.

My dear M. la Serre,

You must not think I do not value your kindness in writing to me on the New Year, because I was silent when your letter came a year ago. The truth is, I have so many letters to write, and my hand gets so tired, that I put off answering from day to day, till it is too late, and the year is old instead of new.

Now let me thank you, as I do sincerely, for your most kind letters, and the affectionate wishes you express for the welfare of our Congregation and our School. Our Fathers wish me to forward the like to you with great sincerity — So also would the Masters and Boys, if they were here.

I hope soon to say Mass for you and am, My dear La Serre, Most sincerely yours in Christ,

John H. Newman of the Oratory.

A. Monsieur M. la Serre.

TO ALBERT SMITH

The Oratory Birmingham, January 8. 1868

My dear Sir,

I wish it were possible to talk with you instead of writing, for it is difficult to answer even simple questions satisfactorily on paper.

As to your first question, 'Are you indeed *one* in doctrine in the Roman Catholic Church?' the only true answer is, that we are and ever have been *one*, and that is one of the special notes of our being the True Church. It is one which has had a special effect on intellectual men not Catholics, when they have happened to become intimate with Catholics and to witness the action of the Church. Our faith is one.

This great fact, however, is quite consistent with another — viz. that in those things which are *not* of faith, there has been considerable difference of opinion, among Catholics, and often serious and bitter quarrels. I have treated of the subject in the 10th Lecture of my volume on 'Anglican Difficulties.'[1] Religion is so deeply interesting and sovereign a matter, and so possesses the whole man, when it once gains its due entrance into the mind, that it is not wonderful, that, as worldly men quarrel fiercely about wordly things, so, through the weakness of human nature, particular theologians have had unchristian disputes about Christian truths.

Such have been the quarrels of some of the religious orders with each other; and I cannot deny that, from the existing events of the day, there have arisen undue contentions about points not essential, at this time also.

But the Holy See, and the Bishops of the Church, and the School of Theologians are not committed to these extravagances.

As to your second question 'Did you ever regret leaving the Church of England?' I can answer sincerely 'Never, for a single moment.' I have been in the fullest peace and enjoyment ever since I have been a Catholic, and have felt a power of truth and divine strength in its ordinances, which exists, I believe, no where else.

Yours most truly John H. Newman

Albert Smith Esqre

TO MISS M. R. GIBERNE

The Oratory Jany 9/68

My dear Sister M Pia

I return you my most affectionate New Year and Christmas greetings. I send by this post to you a New Year's gift.

Thank you for all your prayers. I don't like to boast, but it seems as if the threatened danger had for the present passed away — perhaps for good.

I am seriously anxious about your knee — and mean to give you for some time a Mass every week. I fear your French climate tries you a good deal.

There is little news to tell you. We have been somewhat made anxious by knowing that the English Oblates are near you. They are not especially good friends of ours — and we fear that they have told you gossip, which we have carefully kept from you, because we could not tell it without telling you that a number of lies have been and are told about me, and a number of harsh and sly things have been done, which do not become the doers. This feeling spread such an uncertainty over our ideas of what you had heard and what you had not heard, that we did not know what to say and what not to say.[2]

---

[1] 'Differences among Catholics no Prejudice to the Unity of the Church,' *Diff.* I, pp. 296–329. See also letter of 6 Jan. 1869 to Smith.

[2] Miss Giberne's convent was at Autun, where the Oblates of Mary Immaculate had a house. There were three English-speaking priests living there, among them James Gubbins, who had made objections to *A Letter to Pusey*. See letters of 19 March and 7 April 1866 to him.

There are various people who think that the Oxford matter will still go on, and those who have given large sums do not like to give up the notion, but I don't expect to have to do any thing myself.

I write this to thank you for your letter — but really I have nothing to say

Ever Yours affly in Xt   John H Newman

TO WILLIAM EWART GLADSTONE

The Oratory Birmingham January 9/68

My dear Mr Gladstone,

I was glad to receive your letter, because it showed me that your late accident was less severe than the first account made it.[1]

It pleases me much to know that you and Mrs Gladstone receive so kindly the gift I have ventured to make her. Certainly, I will avail myself of your permission to present myself at your breakfast table, should any thing call me in the season to London. What chance there is of that, I do not know — for my visit to London of last year was the first I had made, except for a few hours, for — what shall I say? twenty or thirty years.

Now as to your Remarks on the Ecce Homo, which I have read with great interest. Whatever be thought of that book and its intentions, your remarks upon it have a value in themselves, and the un-known author has done a service, if in no other way, at least in eliciting them.[2]

I hope I have followed you correctly; your main proposition seems to be, that, whereas both Jew and Gentile had his own notion of an heroic humanity, and neither of them a true notion, the one being political, the other even immoral, the first step necessary for bringing in the idea of an Emmanuel into the world, was to form the human mould into which it 'might drop;'[3] and thus to supplant both the Judaic and the heathen misconception by the exhibition of the true idea. Next, passing from antecedent probabilities to history,

---

[1] On 23 Dec. 1867 Gladstone was wounded in the eye by wood that flew off a tree as it was being cut down at Hawarden. He wrote on 1 Jan. 1868, to accept a copy of *Vv.* on his wife's behalf. See letter of 18 Dec. 1867 to him.

Gladstone wrote again on 24 Jan. after the copy had arrived, 'I have been greatly delighted with the Volume. That which I may call its chief ornament indeed, I mean the Dream of Gerontius, it is not new to me. I have read it several times, and more than once aloud to friends. Opinions will form themselves independent of competency, and I own that to me it seems the most remarkable production in its own very high walk since the unapproachable Paradiso of Dante, and his less but not very much less wonderful Purgatorio. I am truly glad that now going forth with your name it will attract the attention it deserves.'

[2] Gladstone wrote on 1 Jan., 'I send you the first part of a paper I have written on Ecce Homo in a publication called Good Words. The second part will follow. The publication of such a paper is an act of daring, but I have always had my own idea about the book and have been induced to let it go forth and take its chance. Of course I remember your view of the work.' Gladstone's 'Remarks on Ecce Homo,' *Good Words*, (Jan. 1868), pp. 33–9, with two more parts n Feb. and March, was reprinted as a volume at the end of the year, and again in *Gleanings* III. J. R. Seeley published *Ecce Homo* anonymously.

[3] Cf. *Isaiah*, 45:8.

the order of succession of the Synoptical and the Fourth Gospels does in fact fulfil this reasonable anticipation.

This seems to me a *very great view*, and I look forward eagerly to what you have still to say in illustration of it.

The only objection which I see can be made to it, is, that it is a clever controversial expedient after the event for accounting for a startling fact. This is an objection, not peculiar to it, but to all explanations of the kind. Still, the question remains, — whether is it [sic] a fact that the sacred writers recognise, however indirectly, the wise Economy which you assert, or whether it is only an hypothesis? You promise us some remarks on our Lord's method of teaching; it would be a great point, if from any source you could find traces in His or His disciples' words, not of their purpose of illuminating gradually, and their general recognition of its necessity, but of the defects in the patterns of human perfection which existed in the world, and made it necessary.

Perhaps what I am asking for is a refinement; at any rate it is not necessary to make your argument most acceptable and edifying to those who are already believers. And in this day to confirm others in the faith, is more necessary perhaps that [sic] to move the unbeliever. Believers in Christianity certainly will see in your remarks a force and depth, for which they will be very grateful to you.

I have said nothing about the Ecce Homo. In truth it did not strike me so much as it did Anglicans; and it was only by deference to their opinion, that is, from a feeling that what produced so instantaneous an effect on so many minds must have something of extraordinary power in it, that I was led to spend any time upon it.[1] Accordingly as regards your Paper viewed as a defence of it, I am led to say, 'Materiam superabat opus.'[2] Your remarks are more valuable for their own sake, than as a recommendation of the Ecce Homo. If as you suggest, he writes as an inquirer, let it appear *through* his dissertation. But, in spite of his Preface, he is in his work itself dogmatical. And he imagines what our Lord *thought* — which (putting aside theological correctness) is unbecoming a severe reasoner and grave inquirer. Indeed, my own impression of the book was that it imposed a view on the Gospels, without denying there were original and deep remarks in the course of his Essay. By the bye, he did not call it an Essay, which he ought to have done if it were an inquiry.[3]

---

[1] 'Ecce Homo,' the *Month*, (June 1866), pp. 551–73; *D.A.* pp. 363–98.

[2] Ovid, *Metamorphoses*, II, 5.

[3] Gladstone replied on 24 Jan., 'With respect to my paper, or rather the first Section of it on Ecce Homo, you have expressed with an enviable felicity its leading thought. To your exposition your append a question. I fear my answer to it may be a quibling one. It is that we are not entitled to expect to find recorded by the Sacred Writers any recognition of any economy in conformity with which nevertheless their works may have been composed and arranged. Why should we? By far the larger part of the results, I apprehend, even of the most intelligent human action are not in the view of the agents. And I do not see any thing in the distinctive character of inspired writing, which should create a difference in this respect. It may be paradoxical, but [I] should almost dare to say I no more look for such recognition, than I look into the minds of Alexander and of Caesar for some trace of the vast purposes which their lives were ordained to subserve in connection with the Gospel. But indeed it appears to me that recognition in this particular case, if it found its way into the Gospels, would rather

But I have occupied your time more than I had intended to do, and therefore without more words will subscribe myself

Very sincerely Yours John H Newman

The Rt Honble W. E. Gladstone MP

MONDAY 13 JANUARY 1868   Edward went away   mild and muggy

TO HENRY JAMES COLERIDGE

The Oratory Bm Jany 12. 1868

My dear Fr Coleridge

I wish I could promise you to undertake Mr Farrar's book — but I am quite out of the subject now, not having thought of it for many years, and not knowing the progress of thought (right or wrong) which has been made in the public mind. I suppose all my axioms would have to be proved, as old world's prejudices and assumptions.[1]

I have been several times going to write to you to express my pleasure at the tone of the recent Numbers of the Month — and also to thank you personally for your kind notice of myself.[2]

As to my Verses, I suppose the 'Month' Copy was sent to you. I gave no other orders. Those Verses 'My Lady Nature' *are* mine. Now that you have mentioned them, I am almost sorry I have not included them — but I had two difficulties. 1. I thought they would scandalize some people, as too light for a grey headed man and a priest, and 2. the last stanza was obscure — and I did not know, without rewriting, [how] to set it right.[3]

Very sincerely Yours in Xt   John H Newman of the Oratory

The Revd Fr Coleridge S.J.

P.S.   I was very glad to see Fr Jones. It was very kind in him coming this way.

have impeded the attainment of the design, for it seems almost to imply some of that attempt to force the human mind, beyond what the state of its preparation and ripeness justified, which seems to me to have been so wonderfully and by so very elaborate a wisdom avoided.

I have written this very freely, and I am sensible that in the whole subject I ought to be watched and mistrusted. For I am profoundly impressed with the immense importance and significance of the anthropomorphism of the Greek mythology, which I have studied for many years, at the intervals allowed by my domineering profession, though I fear I am as yet far from master of it. An article in the present Quarterly on 'Phoenicia and Greece' represents some little corner of my work.'

[1] The book must have been *Essays on a Liberal Education*, edited by F. W. Farrar, London 1867. See the *Month*, (March 1903), p. 226.

[2] This was in a review of H. P. Liddon's *The Divinity of Our Lord*, 'Now there is one characteristic of Dr. Newman's method — we use the word in a general sense — for which we think all concerned in religious and literary discussion are bound to feel towards him a special debt of gratitude, and which we would fain hope will leave traces of itself for generations to come in the controversies of educated Englishmen. We mean of course his wonderful fairness and clearness in stating the case of his adversaries for them, often far better and more forcibly than they could do it for themselves.' The *Month*, (Nov. 1867), p. 474.

[3] *My Lady Nature and her Daughters*, written in 1829, was one of those poems added in Feb. 1868, as an appendix to the first edition of *Vv*. The poem is now in *Vv*. pp. 33–7.

TO AMBROSE ST JOHN

Jany 12/68

My dear Ambrose

Having the example of Rougement before my eyes, on receipt of your letter from London, I wrote at once (January 1 or 2) to Mr Blifeld asking him for a testimonial from France — mean while I wrote privately to France to get some confidential information.[1]

He sent me in the course of a week, January 7, several testimonials, but added that he had during the course of the week engaged himself in the Isle of Man, but wanted to know, if we would engage him for Easter or Midsummer.

What I wrote in answer (occasioned by the secret information which I received) I sent you the other day. Bring it back.

A letter has just come (January 11) from him to the effect that he is going to the Isle of Man.

I inclose you his four letters. Bring them back.

It seems to me very queer. *After* opening a negociation with you, he opens a negociation with parties in the Isle of Man — and he thinks that honour binds him to conclude an engagement with those whom he treated with second.

Is he afraid that we should be strict with him? The Terms in the Isle of Man are £10

Yrs affly JHN

TO COVENTRY PATMORE

The Oratory Birmingham Jany 14. 1868

My dear Sir,

It was a very good piece of fortune that I ventured to send you my small book, since I have gained in turn from the Author the gift of a Volume of Poetry, which stands so high in the estimation of the critical world.[2]

Thank you very much for it — and I hope you will let me take this opportunity of thanking also Mrs Patmore for a contribution she has been so kind to make to our Oxford Oratory.[3]

I am, My dear Sir, Very truly Yours
John H Newman of the Oratory

Coventry Patmore Esqr

[1] A. Rougemont was a French priest who came as mathematics master to the Oratory School in 1861, and turned out to be a thief. See index to Volume XX.

[2] In return for a copy of *Vv.*, Patmore sent *The Angel in the House*, fourth edition, London 1866, inscribed 'The Rev. J. H. Newman, with the writer's grateful regards. Jan. 10. 1868.' Only the first dozen pages have been cut.

[3] Coventry Patmore's second wife, Marianne Caroline Byles (1822–80), who had become a Catholic shortly after her husband in 1865, sent £1.

TO HENRY TAYLOR

The Oratory Birmingham Jany 14. 1868

My dear Sir,

I do not know how to express duly the great pleasure your letter has given me.[1]

You may have forgotten that years ago you were so good, at the interposition of Mr de Vere, to send me your Poems.[2] Since then I have often wished to show my sense of your kindness by some similar act on my part — but, though I have published various books, I did not think they were likely to be acceptable to you. Now, however, I thought I would run the risk, and send you the small volume I was publishing, though it was a bold step to send such a volume to a poet.

With so much diffidence did I do so, that I first put down your name in the list I sent to my publishers, then took it off, and ultimately changed my mind and restored it.

I am indeed most fortunate to have persisted in my first intention — I have gained a great and unexpected reward — both in the kind way in which you have received it, and in the words with which you have accompanied your acknowledgement.

I assure you they are not thrown away upon me, and that I am with great sincerity

Yours gratefully John H Newman

H. Taylor Esqr

TO G. P. HESTER

G P Hester Esqr   in substance

Jany 15/68

Dear Sir

I have had a conversation with Messrs Allcock and Milward on the point about which you wished them consulted and I find that through my inadvertence I have allowed you to suppose that I wished to go to law with Dr Jenkins[3]

This is far from my intention, and I have asked them to communicate with you on the subject. They will tell you that I am willing to propose to Dr Jenkins to take his fixtures instead of rent — on condition that he goes out at once, and so finishes all business transactions with me.

[1] On 12 Jan. in thanking for a copy of *Vv.* Taylor wrote, 'Although I have never seen you, yet since I read the Apologia, I have felt almost entitled to consider myself in personal relations with you . . .'
[2] See letter of 30 July 1855 to Henry Taylor.
[3] This refers to the occupier of a house on the St Aldate's site, at Oxford, who had received notice to quit at midsummer 1867. He eventually paid £20 in discharge of his obligations.

Will you be so good as to transmit this message to him, which will be put in more legal shape than I can do by Messrs Allcock and Milward.

J H N

TO G. A. COX[1]

Jan 17/68

To Revd G. A. Cox

As to a person saying that he would rather die than disbelieve the Incarnation, I do not see that it is stranger than if I said I would rather die than doubt the honour and fidelity of my long tried, my bosom friend. The word 'Incarnation' is abstract and may be called dogmatic; so are the words 'honour' and 'fidelity.' I mean to say in the latter case, that I have had long experience of a loving loyal heart, who has ever been a blessing to me. I owe him all the happiness, the moral strength, the intellectual light, which make me what I am; that I love him, not as a proposition, but as a person — that I never have had any reason whatever to doubt him — and that therefore, did I doubt, it would be an act of insane perverseness, and would carry its own punishment with it, in the utter disorganization and shattering to pieces of my mental constitution, which would ensue. Certainly I think I should have a right to say, May I rather have no mind at all than act thus against my own convictions, against my own sense of simple duty, against my own plain and essential interests!

If thus your friend in his Sermon meant to say with St Polycarp 'I have known Christ so many years and what has He done for me but good? what has He done to me that I should deny Him?' 'May my right hand rather lose its cunning, and my tongue fail, and my heart break, first!'[2] I want to know why he may not have those feelings towards his God, which we all have towards men.

All depends on this. Can a man be as sure to himself of the fact that Christ once was on earth and was God, as I that my friend is alive and is a second self to me? Catholics say that a man can; that, by the operation of grace and by natural experiences, he can apprehend the Object of faith, as men in general apprehend objects of sight. And many of them bear witness with St Polycarp that such is their own case. Though your friend is not a Catholic, I do not know why he should not be able to bear witness to the same in his own case — for tho' ordinarily the Holy Spirit acts through the Visible Church, yet it is quite certain that He vouchsafes to act beyond its boundaries — and where He implants this faith and love, and where it is improved and assimilated by due correspondence with it and persevering persevering [sic] practice of devotion, this assurance is at last received.

J H N

[1] Cox appears to be a Catholic making inquiry about the sermon of a friend who was not a Catholic.
[2] *Martyrdom of St Polycarp* 9; *Psalm* 137: 5-6.

SATURDAY 18 JANUARY 1868   Ambrose returned   glass above 60° in the morning
SUNDAY 19 JANUARY   Edward returned.

TO T. W. ALLIES

The Oratory Bm Jan. 19./68.

My dear Allies,

It is true, I have said Mass (I think weekly) for your Daughter since February. Not so much for her, since I was trying to keep her from heaven, (though indeed I said Mass for her soul as well as her bodily health) as for your wife, whose distress you told me of. I rejoice at the news you tell me and am

Yrs affly in Xt   John H Newman[1]

TO EDWARD BADELEY

The Oratory Jany 21/68

Mr dear Badeley

Your sister's letter has been a great gratification to me. You will know that, without my telling you — but I can't help writing a line to say so[2]

Ever Yrs affly   John H Newman

TO THE EDITOR OF THE SUN NEWSPAPER

The Oratory   Jany 22. 1868

Dr Newman has received from the Sun Office a copy of their Paper of the 20th, containing a Review of his Volume of Verses.

He begs to thank the Editor for the very favourable notice which is there taken of them.[3]

THURSDAY 23 JANUARY 1868   F[Francis] and A.[Alfred] Mozley called on me in their way to Oxford.

---

[1] See letter of 9 Feb. 1869 to Allies.
[2] On 18 Jan. Badeley sent a letter he had received from his sister, thanking him for Newman's copy of *Vv.*, which he had given her.
[3] The editor of the *Sun* Charles Kent, who wrote most of the reviews, replied on 25 Jan. that the words of his review 'came direct from a heart full of unaffected gratitude and of profound respect and veneration for Dr Newman's genius and character.'

TO SIR FREDERIC ROGERS

The Oratory, Birmingham. January 23rd. 1868

My dear Rogers,

I see poor Dornford's death in the paper — I have not heard about him for years and years — except one little thing which Mrs. Froude told me. It is quite possible you may know something about him, and I write to you on the chance of it.[1]

You are indeed, as your last letter shows, a great Radical — as it is the fashion to outbid, I will say on my part that I think Ireland, if the people generally ask for it, as I think they would, ought to have its own legislature, that is, for *domestic* purposes. I am told that Scotch questions are practically left to the Scotch, in Parliamentary proceedings — if Ireland were left to the Irish, perhaps it would buy off Repeal — but, as things are, Ireland will never be pacified.

Accumulations of wealth certainly are bad things; (Jan.24th.) they occasion waste, and they divide classes; but then, are there not many things which are done by rich men which cannot at all be done by poor? If combinations of men, each contributing a little, are to do these, is not this a mere appeal to the commercial spirit, the motive being gain? — and then you bring in the spirit of gambling. Is not avarice a dreadful vice to be a national one? Look at it in France where there is no primogeniture, and property is endlessly divided; is not avarice becoming the bane of the nation? It is not right to exclude morality from among the motive causes to be considered in political science — Is the political state of a country which has a low morality, to say nothing of religion, so good, so promising, as one which has a high standard and a fair average exhibition of it in fact? Several writers e.g., Trollope's authoress in his new magazine has been exposing the mercenary character of French marriages —[2] doesn't this arise, or at least is it not sanctioned by the law of subdivision of property? Or to take another side of it — does not this system of very small tenancies degrade women? they become household drudges, they even do the hard work of a farm. Some one told me, or I have read it, that it is really one cause of the stationariness of the French population, that women if they have enough to live single on, will not marry, their married life being sure to be so hard.

I am not speaking here against democracy as such — but I should like to see the contrast of the virtues of a people of large inequalities and a people of equality, in wealth, worked out. One phenomenon which I have not touched

---

[1] Joseph Dornford died on 18 Jan. He had been a Fellow of Oriel from 1819 until 1836. In 1837 he received the Oriel living of Plymtree, Devon, which he held until death. For the reply of Rogers, see letter of 2 Feb. to him.

[2] *All for Greed*, published in monthly instalments in *St Paul's*, which began in Oct. 1867. See especially chapter 2, 'The Marriage Portion,' pp. 28–35, and chapter 11, (Jan. 1868), 'Mademoiselle Félicie's Husband,' pp. 384–91. The author was Marie Pauline Rose, Baroness Blaze de Bury.

on is the effect of the acquisition without the power of arbitrary transmission, on the acquirer. Such men often spend their money on some hobby in pictures or tulips — others (as Bishops in former days) build cathedrals or drain marshes — others, as great merchants, leave their money by will for building hospitals or endowing schools — of course, if there was any definite effect here on the whole of a beneficial kind it must be put to the credit of the French system, if indeed (for I do not know) French law allows a man to divert his money by will from his family

Ever yours affectionately, John H. Newman

Sir F. Rogers Bart

P.S.   Again about taxation — you can put the screw of the Income Tax very freely on a population with a class of rich men — can you where all men are in a mediocrity of wealth.

TO HENRY SEBASTIAN BOWDEN

The Oratory Birmingham   Jany 24. 1868

My dear Harry

Thank you for your letter. I said Mass for you this morning — and pray God that He may accomplish what He has begun.[1]

Yours affectionately John H Newman of the Oratory

P.S.   If you see Fanny [Bowden], thank her for her letter about Papa.

TO HENRY ALLON

The Oratory Birmingham 25 Jan. 1868

Dear Sir,

In answer to your request, as contained in your letter of this morning, I beg to say that I have great pleasure in giving you permission to include in your Hymn Book the two compositions contained in my Volume of Verses, pp. 133 and 198.[2]

I thank you for what you say about my Hymns, and am,

Dear Sir, Yours faithfully, John H. Newman

Henry Allon Esq.

P.S.   Excuse me if I do not address you correctly.

---

[1] Bowden had just retired from the Army, in order to join the London Oratory.

[2] In the first edition of *Vv.*, 'Lead, Kindly Light,' and 'Father of mercies infinite,' the translation of the hymn for Matins on Saturday; *Vv.*, pp. 156 and 224. See letter of 28 Jan. to Allon. The two hymns were included in *Supplemental Hymns for Public Worship*, London 1868, a copy of which was sent to Newman 'with the editor's respects and thanks.'

TO EDWARD BELLASIS

January 25. 1868

My dear Bellasis[1]

It is very difficult to write to the purpose on the subject on which you wish to hear from me — that is so to write as to get others to see the matter, of which I complain, from my point of view: — to persons who do not stand where I stand, my complaint may seem frivolous. However, I will do my best to bring it home to them.

When you felt you could not safely send your boy to Oxford, on account of the religious dangers of the place, you agreed with us in thinking that, at least, at the London University, where no residence is required, those dangers whether religious or moral could not be. However, I found there was this difference between the two Universities, that, while at Oxford the books to be presented at the examinations were in great measure chosen by the candidate and thereby were submitted to the approval of his teachers or at least were books which had such claims upon the attention of all scholars as practically to involve no selection on the part of the University at all, on the other hand at the London University the student has no liberty of choice whatever, and is simply in the hands, or rather (as I am now led to say) is at the mercy of the authorities, who settle for him precisely what authors he is to present to them as the subject of his examination.

I have lately prepared youths for entrance at Oxford, and have found it enough to make them master Homer, Virgil, Cicero, great names: — to know these classics well is surely a good introduction to Latin and Greek scholarship. And again I have lately heard of youths presenting there for instance Caesar some Greek plays etc. Such is the present practice at Oxford — as far as I have come across it; as to past times, when I was Tutor there, many years ago, I lectured in College and I examined publicly in many books; but there were some I never lectured in, nor did I ever hear of any Tutor who did, nor did I ever, or scarcely ever, hear of their being taken up by candidates for

---

[1] The name has been cancelled in the source copy, which is in Bellasis's hand, corrected by Newman.

The letter was written to Bellasis in an attempt to remove a serious objection connected with the studies at London University. In Feb. it was sent privately to Lord Granville, Chancellor of the University, and was seen by members of the Senate, which was considering remonstrances from one or two Catholic colleges.

Some months later it was proposed to make public use of Newman's letter. On 21 June 1868 Bellasis wrote to Newman: 'Hope Scott and I think the time is come, when something more public may be done in relation to London University. Their annual meetings have been held, and they have done nothing to remedy the evil complained of, and we are told there is not a chance of having any thing done, unless the authorities are shamed into it.' Bellasis and Hope-Scott proposed to send Newman's letter, revised for publication, as an anonymous one to the *Pall Mall Gazette*. This could not be arranged, and on 4 July 1868 Bellasis wrote that he had sent the letter, and one of his own, as the complaining parent Newman was answering, to *The Times*. The editor sent Newman's letter to Lord Granville, who dissuaded him from inserting it. Cf. letter of 12 July 1868 to Bellasis. A further suggestion by Bellasis that the letter should be published in some Catholic periodical, Newman eventually turned down. See letter of 2 June 1869 to H. J. Coleridge.

examination; — these were Terence, Plautus, Catullus; I may even add Lucretius was uncommon. I am not against young men at College reading these authors; we cannot keep youths entering into life in glass cases — but there seems a reason why authorities should show a preference, and, thereby give their sanction to those authors who like the Epic poets, the tragedians, and Pindar, like Horace and Juvenal, like the historians Greek and Roman, like Cicero uphold the great truths of religion and the moral law, and do not praise and recommend what Christianity condemns. And if this holds even as regards young men of 19 or 22 years of age, much more does it hold in the case of poor school boys of 15 and 16, on whom a flood of temptations, intellectual and sensual, is on the point of opening.

I acknowledge Terence, and the rest I have named, to be among the greatest of classic authors, whether in point of beauty of composition or philosophical depth. For myself I knew good part of Terence by heart when I was quite a boy — and have the greatest admiration for him, as a writer. But as a boy I saw the effect upon the boys of the low standard of morality which his plays exhibit, and that as a matter of necessity, since they are representations of pagan social life, which the works of Homer, Aeschylus, Virgil, Cicero and Livy are not. He is one of the last authors whom as a whole I should put into the hands of a school boy.

Entertaining sentiments such as these, and with no suspicion that they were to be interfered with in the case of your son, you may fancy the surprise I felt, and the pain for his sake, and (to speak plainly), the insult offered to his teachers, when suddenly it broke on us that I and others were obliged to prepare him, for the examinations first in one then in another of those very authors, which in my conscience I held to be so objectionable.

I have been obliged, with an indignation at heart, (let me say it) which every now and then has burst forth into words, to teach him to construe, to master arguments, descriptions, speeches, suggestive of ideas, which I am ever bound, as a Priest, to tell boys to put away and strangle as soon as they arise, lest they lead to bad wishes and to bad acts. What bad thoughts are suggested by the tragedians, by Virgil, by great part of Horace and of Ovid, or by the historical works of Xenophon and Livy? What bad thoughts are not suggested by Terence and Plautus, and, I will add, by Lucretius? Well, these are three of the authors whom we have had to introduce to his notice.

First, I was told he must be prepared in the Adelphi of Terence.

The play is the history of two young men outwitting their father, who is over severe, with the connivance and protection of an indulgent uncle. In the opening dialogue Mitio, the indulgent uncle, lays down this maxim, 'It is not a crime (flagitium), believe me, for a young fellow to wench or to drink' and the plot of the play is worthy of this throw off. The elder of the two youths commits a rape on a young girl, promises marriage, and she, during the action of the play, is confined, I may say, on the stage. She entices his younger brother from his father's farm, secrets him at his uncle's, and carries off from

17

a trader in girls one particular girl for whom his brother has a fancy. She too is secreted at the uncle's. After the severe old father has been sufficiently hoaxed and made fun of, the play concludes with the marriage indeed of the elder brother, but with the younger being allowed by his relenting father to keep his concubine.

Well, at length we got through the odious part put upon us, and I thought it well over. But hardly had I dismissed the matter from my thoughts, when I heard of a fresh indignity which was offered to us. I was told that, willy nilly, we had to teach our London University boys two plays of Plautus, for some other examination.

Two plays of Plautus! when there are hardly more than one or two out of the whole lot which are tolerably decent, not in language merely, but in their elements.

The plays selected were not these exceptions to the rule but the Menœchmi and the Miles gloriosus.

In the former play, one of two brothers, disagreeing with his wife, keeps a mistress, paying her by means of presents of his wife's dresses and jewels. He orders a breakfast at the woman's house, but his twin brother who is so like him as to be mistaken for him, eats the breakfast instead. The plot lies in the unravelling of this mistake.

In the latter play there are two bad women. One of them, the mistress of an Athenian youth, is carried off to Ephesus by the Miles Gloriosus. She follows him and occupies the next house — then he proceeds to break a way through the party wall — by which means he has possession of his mistress, while she is under the protection of the Miles. A servant of the latter, happening to be upon the tiles, looks down through the sky-light of the next door, and sees Philocomasium 'kissing and embracing' her Athenian lover. A great deal is made of this incident, and turns upon it —[1] But I think though much more might be said, I need not proceed. I have said enough to shew what ribbald trash we, clergymen, are forced, by an imperative necessity, to teach our boys. It is a wonder we do not indignantly refuse.

Since then, I find your boy will have to get up a portion of Lucretius.

Nor can I consider it is a sufficient reply to criticisms such as I have been making on the London selection of classics, to say that all boys out of school read, and will read, everything that comes in their way, in spite of their masters, and certainly read words and poems worse than the plays of Terence and Plautus. That is no reason, be it ever so true, why a learned body should give them a sanction for doing so. That is no reason why a learned body should compel the Tutors of these boys to read bad books with them. That is no

---

[1] Newman has left the draft of a passage evidently written later and meant for insertion at this point: 'I have confined myself to the plots of the above plays; though as regards Plautus I have the gravest complaints to make of his ever-recurring indecencies in the course of the dialogues. I do not urge these lest it be said to me in answer that the literature of all countries is open to this objection; though this fact does not make it intelligible why such particular classics should not be preferred or such portions of classical authors as do not fall under it. I am not advocating an expurgated text, but a preference of one work to another.'

reason why a learned body should do in the case of a Latin, what it would not dare to do as regards an English examination. For what University would go the lengths of proposing for the subject of its examinations Cain and Don Juan, Joseph Andrews and Rodrick Random instead of such works as the Tempest, As You Like it, and Twelfth Night, Comus and Lycidas, and Sheridan's Comedies, or again (if it wished to take Byron) of Childe Harold and the Corsairs?[1]

I am, My dear — Yours affectionately

TO FRANCIS TURNER PALGRAVE

The Oratory Birmingham Jany 26. 1868

My dear Mr Palgrave

A friend had sent me the number of the Pall Mall Gazette, before your welcome letter of this morning — and I had taken the great liberty with you already, of conjecturing that the article on my volume of verses was your writing.[2]

I so fancied, first because I saw it was the writing of one who was perfectly at home in literary criticism — and next because I felt, that, did you write about me, you would be sure, like the writer of the article, to be kind to me in your notice beyond my deserts.

And now I can but pray that those who, like you, think and speak of me with interest and tenderness, may have a great reward for their goodness.

Most sincerely yours John H Newman

F. T. Palgrave Esq.

P.S.   I will not forget your kind wish, should I again come to London.

MONDAY 27 JANUARY 1868   Dr Russell called for two hours in evening, in his way to Ireland

[1] This paragraph was substituted in June, when Newman prepared his letter for publication, instead of an earlier version, which has been cancelled in the copy: 'Also *all* Horace. Now if all Horace were sent in as a candidate book at Oxford, I should know, or at least I used to know, that the examiners would not dream of putting him on in any indecent passage — but when I find, at the London University, books selected for examination which are steeped in impurity and indecency in the very dialogue, what security have I that I must not carefully indoctrinate my boys in the most horrible odes of Horace?

I should add that in the particular portion of the Memorabilia of Xenophon, beautiful work as it is, which was selected for the entrance examination, there was a passage such that I would not allow my boys to pollute their mouths with it, but construed it to them myself. It was on the subject of unnatural liberties between boys, and this to be studied by school boys!

Alas, I have heard say that Oxford is getting as bad now as other places; but God forbid that a Catholic priest should countenance such pagan teaching any where.'

[2] 'The Poetry of a Beautiful Soul,' *Pall Mall Gazette*, (23 Jan. 1868), pp. 11–12.

TO MRS WILLIAM MONSELL

The Oratory, Birmingham January 27. 1868

My dear Mrs Monsell,

I thank you for so kindly accepting my little volume, and will gladly write your name in it.

As to the set of Verses you speak of, I had hoped that my apologetic note would have made it pass, in spite of its great extravagance.[1]

A few pages before it, I say that the Creed of the Holy Roman Church is not 'sound'. If I could speak against the Church, it is not wonderful that I should speak against France; and, if good Catholics have forgiven me that great offence against the Church, I trust good Frenchmen will give me pardon for my offence against their country.

When I was reconciled to the Church, I was reconciled to France also — and France will be as generous to me, as the Church is charitable.

You will observe too, that I have *dated* it, besides putting a note. It is one of an historical series of verses, which express various states of mind.

Then again it is headed 'Apostacy.' This clearly shows *what* France I meant. I distinctly meant the France of the *revolution* — of Robespierre, and the guillotine — of desecrated Churches, murdered priests and nuns, and the Holy See insulted in the person of its Pontiffs. The word Apostacy defines exactly the *date* at which I was hating her name. You will recollect that I wrote the verses soon after the expulsion of Charles 10th; at that time the Church party in England identified the expulsion of the Bourbons with the triumph, the revival of the revolution of 1789-1792.

Now supposing a Frenchman were to write as strongly against England, as I have against France, heading it, 'Protestantism,' should I be offended, especially if he praised King Alfred, St Edward, and Oxford? I think not. Now I have not hated Catholic France, but the France which murdered its king.

Pardon me then, My dear Mrs Monsell and believe me

Most sincerely yours in Xt   John H. Newman

[1] Mrs Monsell, a Frenchwoman, when thanking for *Vv.* protested against 'Apostasy,' *Vv.*, p.190, which begins 'France! I will think of thee as what thou wast,' and ends,
'And so in silence I will now proclaim
Hate of thy present self, and scarce will sound thy name.'
In particular Mrs Monsell appealed to the example of the Frenchmen who had died fighting for the Pope.
The poem is dated 'June 26, 1833,' and in the first edition, p. 167, there was a note at the end, 'This is not the language of one who knew any thing rightly of that great Catholic and highly gifted people.' In later editions this note was omitted and instead a reference given to the note to the first line of 'The Good Samaritan,' *Vv.*, p. 153, which begins,
'Oh that thy creed were sound!
For thou dost soothe the heart, Thou Church of Rome.' This note says, 'Of course this is the exclamation of one who, when so writing, was not in Catholic Communion.'

TO WILLIAM MONSELL

The Oratory Bm Jany 27/68

My dear Monsell

I have been going to write to you every day — but something has come in the way. Now I have been just writing to Mrs Monsell, immediately on the receipt of her letter, and so I go on to write to you. I dare say she will show my letter to you. I had some doubt about printing that set of verses, but thought it illustrated what I had said in the Apologia, and therefore ought to be inserted.[1] I thought it rather reflected on me than on France — and that I was the earthen pitcher in the fable.[2] But if it is likely to hurt Montalembert and others like him, I shall be very sorry. As to Montalembert, I recollect being annoyed in 1844, at what he said about me without knowing me; and these rubs must be.[3] But the French clergy have been so generous to me, I shall be very much pained if they misinterpret those verses.

Dr Moriarty's letter is a very good one — it would be most inconsistent, as you say, for Bishops to condemn Fenianism, yet approve of the canonization of Fenian malefactors — but what is to be done about Ireland? do not the Scotch members of Parliament manage their own matters by themselves? Why should not the Irish also? Or else it must come, as Dr O'Brien says, to a Parliament *for Irish matters* in Dublin.[4]

As to my health, were it not that my case is so anomalous, I should say I was quite well — but I cannot be sure that nothing is going on wrong, and I am under a regimen both of diet and of medicine.

I have not so much to say to you as I thought I had. Have you seen Gladstone's Article in the Good Words? he sent it to me — it contains a striking view, if it could be worked out.[5]

---

[1] *Apo.*, p. 33, 'It was the success of the Liberal cause which fretted me inwardly. I became fierce against its instruments and manifestations. A French vessel was at Algiers; I would not even look at the tricolour. On my return, though forced to stop twenty-four hours at Paris, I kept indoors the whole time, and all that I saw of that beautiful city was what I saw from the Diligence.'

[2] In Aesop, where the earthen pitcher told the copper one 'bounce away from me, because if you touch me I shall break, even if it is unintentional.'

[3] See note to letter of 9 Oct. 1850 to F. W. Faber.

[4] After the execution of the Fenian 'Manchester Martyrs' on 23 Nov. 1867, Requiem Masses were said for them all over Ireland. At the beginning of Jan. 1868 Bishop Moriarty of Kerry issued a circular to his clergy, in which, while speaking with sympathy of the 'Martyrs,' he forbade such Masses and once more condemned Fenianism. On 23 Dec. 1867, after one of the Requiems, a meeting of Limerick priests, headed by Richard O'Brien, Dean of Limerick and Vicar General, issued a *Declaration*. It recited the wrongs done to Ireland, and came out in favour of the repeal of the Union as the necessary remedy. This was the beginning of the Home Rule movement. See E. R. Norman, *The Catholic Church in Ireland in the Age of Rebellion*, London 1965, pp. 121 and 345; the *Guardian*, (8 Jan. 1868), pp. 27–8.

[5] See letter of 9 Jan. to Gladstone.

Our Bishop says the quantity of things to be looked to in preparation for a Council is so great, that it is necessarily postponed. It is not wonderful[1]

Ever Yrs affly John H Newman

The Rt Honble W Monsell M P

TO HENRY ALLON

The Oratory Birmingham 28 Jan. 1868

Dear Sir,

I thank you very much for the volumes you send me, and hope you will allow me in turn to send you the small volume of my own which I have just now published. I am very glad to have your ample collection of Hymns etc with their music — and am pleased too to have the new Number of the British Quarterly Review, a work which (to judge by the specimens I have seen of it) must be interesting and welcome to every Catholic, with all its serious differences from the teaching of the Catholic Church[2].

Truth is one, but it has manifold aspects, and though the Br. Quarterly Review is not with us, as regards our Creed, yet it *is* with us in the great controversy of the day, our controversy with the spirit of infidelity — and in a missionary country like this our duty seems to fall under our Lord's rule, 'He that is not against us is for us.'[3]

I must not close my letter without thanking you, as I do most sincerely, for the very kind words you use about my writings. Whatever tends to create a unity of heart between men of separate communions, lays the ground for advances towards a restoration of that visible unity, the absence of which among Christians is so great a triumph, and so great an advantage to the enemies of the Cross. Those actual advances, and still less that restoration, cannot, alas, be reasonably expected to take place in our day, but the ground may be laid — and those who, in laying it, have 'done what they could,'

---

[1] Proposed for 8 Dec. 1868, the first Vatican Council was summonded for 8 Dec. 1869.

[2] On 27 Jan. Allon thanked Newman for his letter of 25 Jan. and sent him 'a little book of church music first published some eight years ago' containing a setting for 'Lead, kindly light.' This was presumably the *Chant Book*, 1860, of the *New Congregational Hymn Book*.

Allon also sent the *British Quarterly Review* for Jan., of which he was co-editor. It was the organ of the Free Churches. Allon wrote: 'You may be interested in seeing how we nonconformists look at Church Questions just now — and especially at the questions involved in the "Book of Common Prayer."' The *British Quarterly Review*, (Jan. 1868), pp. 69–128, contained an article on that subject, and also one on 'The Church of England in 1867,' pp. 207–30. Allon continued, 'for many years I have read your writings with great, I may say loving interest. Differing from you as on most ecclesiastical and many theological matters I do — "toto coelo —" I have never felt those differences to affect the religious response, which your books demanded, or the grateful feeling produced by their ministry to so much noble thought, and catholic religiousness . . .'

For Newman's comments on the praise he received at this time from Protestants, see *A.W.*, pp. 263–5.

[3] *Luke* 9: 50.

however small may be their work, have deep cause to thank Almighty God for having been allowed to do it. I rejoice to be accounted such.

I am, Dear Sir, Very truly Yours, John H. Newman

The Revd Henry Allon

TO ROBERT WHITTY

The Oratory Bm Jany 31. 1868

My dear Fr Whitty

Your letter, you see, is quite in time, and, please God I will not forget you on the Purification, which is the anniversary, the 20th, of the Oratory being set up in England. At Oxford it was our founder's day, and thus I have been under the shadow Mariæ Purificantis for 45 or 46 years.[1]

As to Fr Ryder's controversy, I agree with you that it would be an enormous blessing to English Catholics if Ward could be persuaded or advised to leave his dissertations out of the Dublin and publish them in Latin. Then he would be answered in Latin — but for him to write in English, and no one to answer him, is the loss, the ruin of souls.[2]

I am struck at your remark about submitting any thing I wrote to episcopal censure before publication. I have offered to do so in two instances. 1. as regards my work on Development of doctrine, when Dr Wiseman decided that it had better not be revised — 2. when I became Editor of the Rambler, I offered it to the Bishop of Birmingham for an ordinary and continual censure — and he declined my offer.[3]

It is astonishing how many works are suggested to me to undertake. I feel it a great compliment, but I ought to have the age of Metusala [sic] to do them all. Unless I took the one you suggest, first of all, it would have no chance of execution.[4] One friend wishes me to write on the Varieties of Anglicanism — his letter came just now with yours — another wishes me to give an historical exposure of the conduct of the powers of the world towards the Church — another wishes me to write a poem — another a tragedy — another a symphony for stringed instruments. They are all persons of weight whom I respect, and they give solid reasons for their suggestions.

I rejoice to hear you will be in London instead of Edinburgh. It will be

[1] Whitty, writing from the Gesù at Rome on 26 Jan., wanted Newman to know that he was to take his final vows as a Jesuit on 2 Feb. It was Founder's Day at Oriel College.

[2] In reference to Ryder's first pamphlet against W. G. Ward on papal infallibility, Whitty wrote that 'a public controversy on it cannot lead to any good and may lead to great harm.'

[3] See letters of 2 Nov. 1845 to Hope-Scott, and 16 May 1859 to Ullathorne.

[4] When urging Newman to write, Whitty remarked, 'You yourself have referred more than once to the connexion between Protestantism and wrong doctrine on the virtue of holy purity. I have often since remarked how Protestants who do not *appreciate* the angelic virtue (for the practice of it is another thing) are not on their way to the Church. Does not this connexion then explain in some way the prominence of all doctrine on our Blessed Lady as private judgment does that of the Pope's infallibility.'

better for your health. Fr St John desires his affectionate remembrances. Do not forget us at some of the Holy Shrines of Rome.

I am, my dear Fr Whitty Affectionately Yrs in Xt   John H Newman

TO BISHOP ULLATHORNE

Febry 1/68

My dear Lord

Thank you for the trouble you have taken — We could not honestly say that we require Mr Pope as a Priest for the School, considering Fr Norris stands before him and is actually engaged with the boys. And for other reasons, I think it is best to let things remain as they are — and I will tell M. Labbé, in carefully worded language, that Orders must not be hastened on a mere point of sentiment.[1]

Your Lordship's affte Servt in Xt   John H Newman

The Rt Revd The Bp of Birmingham

TO SIR FREDERIC ROGERS

The Oratory, Birmingham. Feb. 2nd. 1868.

My dear Rogers,

Pray convey my best thanks to Mr. Bartholomew (if I read his signature aright) or Canon I almost think, for his kindness in writing for me the letter you send me, which I think I have a right to keep as my own property.[2] I feel also the great kindness of what he says to you about me.[3] It is pleasant, while it is painful to me, to have left a lasting regret in the minds of such as him — yet I have reciprocated it, though my own deep wound was *before* I left them, and *in* leaving them; and it was healed, when the deed was done, as far as it was personal, and not from the reflection of their sorrow. To-day is the 20th. anniversary of my setting up the Oratory in England, and every year I have more to thank God for, and more cause to rejoice that he helped me over so great a crisis — Since Mr. Bartholomew obliges me to say it, this I cannot omit

---

[1] Before joining the Oratory, T. A. Pope had worked under M. Labbé at the Petit Seminaire at Yvetôt.

[2] In response to Newman's letter of 23 Jan. Rogers had obtained from Christopher Churchill Bartholomew, Vicar of Cornwood, Ivybridge, an account of the last years of his friend and neighbour, Joseph Dornford. Cf. letter of 7 July 1868 to H. Wilberforce.

[3] Rogers explained that Bartholomew sent him a covering letter, with that intended for Newman, 'saying what a pleasure it was to him "to be placed even indirectly in communication with one to whom I owe so much and whom I never think on sine summo desiderio". Then follow speculations as to what you would or might have done or prevented if matters had been otherwise than they are, all which I keep to myself, on the principle of "washing dirty linen at home."'

to say. I have found in the Catholic Church abundance of courtesy, but very little sympathy, among persons in high place, except a few — but there is a depth and a power in the Catholic religion, a fulness of satisfaction in its creed, its theology, its rites, its sacraments, its discipline, a freedom yet a support also, before which the neglect or the misapprehension about oneself on the part of individual living persons, however exalted, is as so much dust, when weighed in the balance. This is the true secret of the Church's strength, the principle of its indefectibility, and the bond of its indissoluble unity. It is the earnest and the beginning of the repose of Heaven.

I chose the Purification for the foundation of the English Oratory — because it was our foundation day at Oriel. I have now been 46 years under the shadow of Maria Purificans.

From what Mr. Bartholomew says of Dornford, I suppose his death must have been unexpected. A child a month old! Do I read his words aright?[1]

I have had many quarrels with poor old Joe — and have not heard about him for these 20 years, nay scarcely for all the time since 1832[7], when he took his living — yet I was more sad at seeing his death than at various other deaths, of men I have known for a longer time, and whom I never had a rub with.[2]

As to Ireland, it is a choice of difficulties. I am not certain that an Irish Parliament for Irish matters is not the least of them.

Yours affectionately John H. Newman.

MONDAY 3 FEBRUARY 1868   Audit meeting   a very fine February.   I never recollect so fine a one.

TO EMILY BOWLES

The Oratory Febry 4. 1868

My dear Child

I have read about a volume and a half of your beautiful book.[3] It is most interesting, and capitally translated. No one would dream that it was done into English. I thank you very much for it.

I trust it will have a great sale. There is much to take Protestants and Anglicans in the view which it gives of the beautiful interior of a Catholic family, which is made the more persuasive to them, inasmuch as Alexandra is

---

[1] In his letter for Newman Bartholomew wrote, 'It was a melancholy sight the 6 young children he has left behind him: the youngest scarcely a month old . . .'
[2] Dornford succeeded Keble as an Oriel tutor in 1823, and (contrary to what T. Mozley says in *Reminiscences chiefly of Oriel College and the Oxford Movement* II), was on Newman's side in the quarrel with Hawkins over the tutorship. Dornford lent Mrs Newman his cottage at Nuneham in 1828.
[3] Mrs Augustus Craven, *A Sister's Story*, translated from the French by Emily Bowles, three volumes, London 1868. Mrs Craven, daughter of Count de la Ferronnays, who had been French ambassador at St Petersburg, wrote about the wife of her brother Albert.

originally not a Catholic, and seems to be the exact double of many an Anglican lady of this day. What makes it the more valuable is, that Catholics have *not the class* of educated and refined ladies, as *a class*, — I am not speaking of course of individuals.

Of course the letters are *French* — I can hardly analyze the meaning of 'I love you, love me,' addressed by sister to sister — but I suppose, when they are separated, such expressions embody the same inward act of affection, as kissing does, when they are together — but it sounds odd to an Englishman, in print.

Our Bishop was saying the other day that the Abbé Gerbet's account of Alexandra's first communion is well known, and classical — he did not seem to know Mrs Craven's book.[1]

Thank you for sending me the Pall Mall, and for all you say. Since then I have seen the Spectator and the Saturday.[2] I wish exceedingly to turn this great providence to account, if I could — but I never have been able to write prose or verse by wishing it. The chance is, if I write any thing more, it would be on some metaphysical point, which half the world would not read, and the other half would differ from.

Ever Yrs affly John H Newman

TO HENRY CLUTTON

The Oratory Bm Febry 4. 1868

My dear Mr Clutton

I inclose a cheque for your charge on the Oxford Fund. It did not seem to me much, and you cannot charge for the zeal and anxiety you threw into your services for us.

I am sorry the payment has been so long delayed

Most sincerely Yours John H Newman

---

[1] Albert de la Ferronnays married Alexandrine, daughter of the Swedish Count d'Alopeus, Russian Minister at Berlin, and of the German Jeanne de Wenkstern, who afterwards married Prince Paul Lapoukhyn. Alexandrine was baptised and brought up a Russian Orthodox. She married Albert, who was a close friend of Montalembert, in 1834, and became a Catholic in May 1836, a month before her husband died of consumption. Alexandrine insisted on being received by Gerbet, after reading an article of his. She remained with her husband's family and eventually gave all she possessed to the poor.

[2] These periodicals contained reviews of *Vv*. For the *Pall Mall Gazette* see letter of 26 Jan. to Palgrave. And see the *Spectator* (25 Jan. 1868), pp. 102–4; and the *Saturday Review*, (1 Feb. 1868), pp. 144–6.

TO EDWARD COLERIDGE

The Oratory Bm Febry 4. 1868

My dear Coleridge

I was rejoiced to see your handwriting on the direction of one of my letters this morning. It carried me back at once to old times, as if such familiar missives, as used to be, were but of yesterday[1]

I have often thought of you amid the many and marvellous changes, which have taken place since we corresponded; and lately I tracked you, to my surprise, to Mapledurham. Not that I know Mapledurham, or that I did not know it was an Eton living, and that it came into the hands of the Premier for one of the Fitzclarences, only through Sumner being promoted from thence to the See of Chester, (is not this right?) but I had heard of the living all my life, and connected it with the family of Martha Blount, Pope's friend, and so it seemed odd to me that you should be there.[2]

Thank you very much for what you say about my Verses, which, as I felt it very bold to publish them in a volume, have been received with a general kindness and sympathy most gratifying to me.

How glad you must be to have got back for life your great friend, Bishop Selwyn! I do not forget St Simon and St Jude's day 1841, when he and his wife were kind enough to call on me at my rooms in Oriel, when they were soon to start for the Antipodes.[3]

I am, My dear Coleridge, Very affectionately Yours John H Newman

The Revd E. Coleridge.

P.S.   Are you Dr, and do I make a mistake in my Address?

[1] Coleridge wrote on 3 Feb., 'You will be surprised, no doubt, but not, I trust, offended by my expressing to you in a very few words the very great delight, with which I have read your Poems, now collected and sanctioned by your name. Many, I may say, most of them are exquisite in feeling and construction, and no one, as it seems to me, can read them without emotion and much stirring of Heart. Though not able to follow you in all your thoughts, or to agree wholly with them, I am deeply touched by the greater part of your Poems, and by many reminded of days, long past, but not forgotten, and those that were, but are no more, on earth.'

Coleridge seems last to have written on 27 Nov. 1845, when he thanked Newman affectionately for a copy of *Dev*.

[2] Coleridge became Vicar of Mapledurham in 1862, and remained there until his death in 1883. He was a Master at Eton 1825–57, and a Fellow from 1857 until death.

John Bird Sumner, Archbishop of Canterbury in 1848, became Bishop of Chester in 1828. He was succeeded at Malpedurham, which was in the gift of Eton, by Lord Augustus Fitzclarence, whose father was William IV.

Martha Blount (1690–1763), of the Blounts of Mapledurham, who always remained Catholic, first met Pope in 1700, and was his lifelong friend.

[3] George Augustus Selwyn, a Tractarian, who went out as the first Anglican Bishop of New Zealand in 1841, returned to England in 1867, and was then appointed Bishop of Lichfield.

TO FANNY MARGARET TAYLOR

The Oratory Bm Feby 4. 1868

My dear Miss Taylor

I thank you sincerely for your Translation of 'Meditations etc' which I am very glad to have.[1]

I hope all your plans are going on well.[2] Did I send you my Volume of Verses? If I did not, will you kindly take the trouble, some day that you are at Burns's to ask him to give you one of the copies which have 'From the Author' in the beginning?

I hope this is not very unceremonious, and takes away the grace of offering it to your acceptance

Most truly Yours John H Newman of the Oratory

TO CLARA L. WEBB

The Oratory Bm Febr 4. 1868

Dear Madam

I have written out and send you what you ask for. It is with true pleasure and thankfulness that I learn from you, that some of the lines which I have written have been a support to a mother in affliction.[3]

I am, My dear Madam, Most truly Yours John H Newman

Miss C. L. Webb

P.S.   I hope I address you aright.

TO MESSRS ALLCOCK AND MILWARD

The Oratory Bm Feby 5, 1868

Dear Sirs

I inclose a cheque for the amount of your account.

May I give you the trouble of telling me what the return [?] of the 'account delivered' £2.6.0 which is at its commencement, since I cannot find the paper.

[1] *Practical Meditations for every day in the Year on the life of our Lord Jesus Christ*, by a Father of the Society of Jesus, translated from the French, two volumes, London 1868.

[2] Miss Taylor was taking the first steps towards starting her order of nuns, The Poor Servants of the Mother of God.

[3] Clara Webb, of 51 Queen's Gardens, Hyde Park, although unknown to Newman, wrote on 2 Feb., for an autograph, and asked him to copy out the last verse of 'Consolations in Bereavement,' *Vv.*, p. 28. She said that the lines of that poem 'have much in them that is sweet and soothing to an almost broken Mother.'

Also can you throw any light upon the following? The sum which you paid for me on March 9 for mortgage money to Mr Hester (as representative of Chaundy) was £1025, of which £25 was interest and £1000 went against the mortgage. Now Mr Hester has charged Mr Neville with £60 as paid by him to Chaundy — making together £1060. But Mr Neville says that the purchase money agreed on was £1040 not £1060

One more question — can you tell me what has been done about Dr Jenkins's debt to me for rent?

I am, Dear Sirs   JHN

Messrs Allcock & Milward

TO HENRY JAMES COLERIDGE

The Oratory Bm Febry 6. 1868

My dear Fr Coleridge,

As to my view of Anglican orders — I cannot *conceive* that they are valid — but I could not *swear* they are not — I should be most uncommonly surprised if they were — It would require the Pope ex cathedrâ to convince me — I would not believe in them, if you or a hundred Fathers of the Society guaranteed their validity, though of course, it would be a remarkable fact; but nothing but the Church's acting on it would convince me. I don't think the Church ever will act upon it, and for this reason, that, putting them at their best advantage they are doubtful, and the Church ever goes by what is safe. How do I even know that all the Anglican Bishops who continued the succession had received valid baptism?

What can I, what need I say more? It is difficult to prove a negative — but it is not for us to prove that the Anglican orders are not valid, but for them to prove that they are. I don't think they will ever be able to prove this.

I have not written to you since the critique of my verses in the Month. I think I must find some ring of Polycrates, to make a sacrifice to fortune, else some Nemesis will come on me.[1] I am bound to read the various critiques on me for they are written by kind persons, who wish to do a thing pleasing to me, and whom I should be very ungrateful not to respond to — and they do please me — but I have been so little used to praise in my life, that I feel like the good woman in the song, 'O, cried the little woman, Sure it is not I!'[2]

---

[1] Cf. *A.W.*, p. 264. Polycrates threw a precious ring into the sea, lest his run of good fortune should come to an end.

[2] The little woman on the way to market fell asleep by the road. A pedlar cut her petticoats to the knees. On waking she says 'This is none of I.'

But if this be I
As I do hope it be,
I have a little dog at home
And he knows me;
If it be I,
He'll wag his little tail,
And if it be not I
He'll loudly bark and wail!

Do you know, if it comes to a second edition, I think of inserting that 'My Lady Nature' which you spoke of. My friends here wish it.[1]

Yrs ever most sincerely John H Newman

TO ALESSANDRO SEGNO, ARCHBISHOP OF THESSALONICA

[6 February 1868][2]

Reverendissime in Christo Pater

Amplitudini Tuae gratias relatas velim propter litteras Tuas hodie à me receptas; praesertim vero Sanctitati Suae, qui dignatus est ex sublimi loco Suo, et in mediis sollicitudinibus Suis in humilitatem meam oculos Suae benignitatis convertere, nec permittere, ut quod ad me videbatur pertinere, me inscio ad executionem perveniret.[3]

Quod autem ad eam ipsam rem spectat, quam in manibus Tuis Sanctitas Sua commendavit, profecto ad me nullo modo, (quod sciam), pertinere inveniatur. Enimvero, non solùm ex Regulâ nostrâ à S. Philippo concinnatâ, à decessore S.S. Paulo v° Pontifice Maximo comprobatâ et stabilitâ, sed etiam juxta Breve illud speciale, à S. S. Congregationi Oratorii Londinensi apud Brompton anno 1856 concessum, definitivè sancitum est ne quicquam in Congregatione supradicta jurisdictionis nec potestatis haberem.

Neque equidem, ut verum dicam, umquam audivi, donec litteras Amplitudinis Tuae perlegi, Dominam Gloag Viduam superstitem esse, nedum habere filios, aut pecunias, quae ad Congregationem Oratorii Londinensem tandem aliquando essent reversurae

Spero me satis explicuisse Amplitudini Tuae quod dicendum habui etc.

> Home went the little woman
>   All in the dark
> Up starts the little dog,
>   And he began to bark;
> He began to bark,
>   And she began to cry,
> Lawk a mercy on me,
>   This is none of I!

Iona and Peter Opie, *Oxford Dictionary of Nursery Rhymes*, pp. 427–9.

[1] See letter of 12 Jan. to Coleridge.

[2] Dated by Birmingham postmark of letter to which Newman is replying.

[3] Alessandro Segno, Archbishop of Thessalonica, of the Secretariate of the Sacred Congregation of Extraordinary Ecclesiastical Affairs, wrote on 25 Jan. from Rome. The widowed Roman mother of the London Oratorian Thomas Dominic Gloag, had been left the interest of £5000 during her lifetime. She wished this life interest to be continued for her two other children. The Pope was in favour of granting this request, but before doing so, wished to have Newman's opinion. Newman was addressed as 'Superiore della Congregazione dell'Oratorio, Brimingham'. Gloag had died in 1865, and evidently the £5000 would have gone to the London Oratory at her death.

TO GERARD MANLEY HOPKINS

The Oratory Febr 7/68

My dear Hopkins,

Thank you for your considerate note.

But you need not make up your mind till Easter comes, as we shall be able to manage matters whether you stay, or we have the mishap to lose you.[1]

Yrs most sincerely John H Newman

TO WILLIAM MONSELL

The Oratory. Febry 9/68

My dear Monsell

I suppose we are as sure that Cardinal Cullen and the Irish Hierarchy, and that Archbishop Manning and the English, will fight tooth and nail against compulsory secular Education, as of any thing as yet future. There is an Article, I am told, in the Dublin lately on the subject, recommending a union with the Anglicans and Wesleyans, to form a strong parliamentary opposition to it.[2] And you must know better than I, what nevertheless I, rightly or not, take for granted, that with so strong an expression of opinion, few Irish Catholics will decline to follow their lead. If this be so, I don't see that you have a question before you, however you may regret it. Any how you have no question to ask of such as me, who am a priest like others, and like others have never been consulted by any bishop on the subject. I suppose the bishops consult with their respective chapters.

If, however, you want to know what I think, you must recollect I have a very contracted horizon. I can but judge from the few facts I know, and, were I in the world, as you are, I might at once change my judgment, however logically drawn from those few facts.

Now you know that I, as most or all of us, am, as a matter of principle, utterly opposed to education without religion, which I suppose is the scheme which you ask me about. And I have opposed projects tending that way for the greater part of my life. But now, if I was obliged to form a political judgment, I think I should concur in it, however grudgingly, and try to make the best of it, and make terms with the promoters of it.

It is forty years this very month, that the present Lord Malmesbury, whom I was presenting for his degree, told me that the repeal of the Test and

---

[1] Hopkins was deciding his vocation. See letter of 14 May to him.
[2] 'Popular Education in England,' *DR.*, (Jan. 1868), pp. 131–65. The growing demand for universal education led to the Elementary Education Act of 1870, which, while preserving Church schools, provided state schools as required.

Corporation Act was carried (or resolved on by the Duke of W.[Wellington])[1] Ever since then the stream of opinion and legislation has been in one direction. It is cowardly to abandon a principle which you uphold as good and true, because you have suffered one or two defeats in maintaining it — but surely the time may come, after a long warfare steadily carried out in successive great reverses and uniform disappointments of your hopes, when it is as unwise and as headstrong to continue the war, as it would have been in Austria not to make peace after Sadowa. It may be very well for the Holy See, which is divinely intended to be the principle of immobility to continue its protests and to spurn the notion of concurrence or compromise; but that as little makes it its duty to forbid local hierarchies, according to their greater insight into local necessities, to act on their discretion, and as little justifies local hierarchies to refuse to political expedience what they cannot in principle originate or approve, what the Holy See cannot sanction, and must ignore, than it would have justified the Irish Hierarchy in 1829 and 1834 in refusing those concessions by which such great ecclesiastical and political advantages have accrued to Irish Catholics, the Holy See then, as it did, keeping silence.[2]

I cannot help saying I give up, after a long contest. Now here perhaps I am judging merely according to my contracted horizon, but, with this proviso, I say it seems to me as clear as day, that in a few years compulsory secular education will be the law. Some people say 'the Church of England, the Wesleyans, never will give in;' but I have been struck by the fact that the Guardian Newspaper (as it seems to me) is going round to the other side — and it says that numerous Anglicans are going round too — Moreover, it says that the orthodox dissenters have (if I understand it) gone round in a body.

Then we have the case of America — where secular education is (is it not?) the rule — and where, if you go by Fr Hecker and others, it answers so well for Catholics, that they would not alter it, if they could.[3] I know that circumstances are very different there; for we have to contend with a bigotry which does not exist there — but the question may be asked, whether these and the like great changes will not go a great way to destroy the bigotry under which we suffer.

Education is not exactly parallel to the case of Workhouses and Jails — nor is the case of London the same as that of provincial towns — but, as far as Birmingham is concerned, in spite of a bitter, active, anti-Catholic party, we have ever been treated well by the town — as in the workhouse, which was in our hands for 14 years, so in the jail, which we have still; — and, speaking under correction, I do not know why we should not also be treated well in the

---

[1] Lord Malmesbury took his degree in 1828. The repeal of the Test and Corporation Acts, decided in Feb. and passed in May 1828, marked the end of the theory that Church and State were united in England.

[2] Catholic Emancipation with limitations became law in 1829. For 1834 Newman was presumably referring to the acceptance of a national system of education in Ireland.

[3] Hecker was a champion of the view that Catholicism in America should be American, and took the side of those who wished Catholics to accommodate themselves to the state school system.

case of secular schools. And, as far as I know, the liberal feeling in Manchester and Liverpool is quite as influential.

On the other hand, we might make terms — I mean, *you*, Catholic M Ps might — there might be a provision, that some priest should be on each local board etc etc which you could not carry, if you set yourselves in opposition to a measure on which the country was set.

Moreover, to speak personally, how much we at the Oratory should be at our ease, if we had not to keep poor schools! What a load of responsibility, anxiety, nay debt would be taken off us! Of course our great effort, and an anxious one, would be to bring our children round us on Sunday for religious instruction — a very serious task and duty — and it is done at Milan, Brescia, Turin, and I don't know why we should not do it too. And other religious bodies are in the same difficulty — and, as they are sure to meet it, so shall we be.

Every yrs affly John H Newman

MONDAY 10 FEBRUARY 1868   finished adjourned Audit meeting

TO MISS M. R. GIBERNE

The Oy Bm Febry 11/68

My dear Sister Pia

Your letter has just come. I could have been quite sure that I told you Mgr Place's 100 francs came — and I beg you to thank him most sincerely for them. Are you sure you could read every word of my letter?[1]

As to H.E.M.[Manning] coming to you, it is to fish out something about me. He thinks you my confidant. Our Bishop told me some years ago, that H.E.M. never went any where but to fish out something. He is quite violent sometimes in his effort to gain secrets. He does not fish, but extorts by force. At Christmas 1857–8 he practised on *me* in this way, successfully. I was always frank with him when he called here, till the Autumn of 1863. He saw *at once* the change, tho' my manner was quite free and easy; *because* he did not get what he came for. The *reason* of my change was some unaccountable slight he put on us in an Article of his in the Dublin — which (with our Bishop's warning, that he never came except to get something) put me on my guard.[2] Lately I have found out, on his written *confession*, that he thought *I* had been already uncivil to *him*, in writing against him in the Rambler, and in taking part in a pamphlet which Renouf wrote against some Article of his. Neither accusation was true — it was mere gossip — as lately, on first hearing it, I was

___

[1] See letter of 8 Aug. 1867 to Miss Giberne.
[2] For Ullathorne's warning see letter of 7 Aug. 1862 to St John and end of Memorandum of 18 Dec. 1864. For Manning's article in *DR* see postscript to letter of 15 Aug. 1863 to St John.

able to prove to him.[1] This gossip was what he got by his prying ways. He is ever prying about — and, if he comes to you, it will be to get something out of you, to a certainty — and he may mistake *you* about me, as he mistook his informants about me in the case I have mentioned. Your best way is to say *nothing* about me.

Garside has exaggerated the case of Arnold. He was *not* our head master, nothing like it. He had only *one* class to do with, the most advanced class of course. He is a very good amiable fellow, but weak and henpecked. His wife is a Xantippe. From Australia, before he was received there, she sent me two abusive letters, and vowed he never should be a Catholic. When he was received there, she threw a brick through the Church window. When I gave him a professorship at Dublin, she was still unmitigated — and when he came to Edgbaston, she used to nag, nag, nag him, till he almost lost his senses. She preached against Catholicism to her children, and made them unmanageable. Tho' we gave him a large salary, she took care to make him feel he had nothing, and was out at elbows. He did not take enough to eat and to drink — and got ill. Then came Protestant friends and talked to him. Moreover, I always thought he had been badly instructed, and did not know his religion. He was offered splendid berths for his boys at Rugby — and they are very clever. Then he left us and went to Oxford, *not allowing* he was a Protestant — nor is he. He is a non-practising Catholic, if he is any thing. Very friendly still, and interested in our matters. He was very religious, when with us — used to delight to be before the Blessed Sacrament etc etc. And now there is nothing bitter in him; he takes pleasure in Catholic matters. I fear he *never* has had *faith*. His going has not hurt our School, nor distressed us, except on *his* account. Garside gives the London, exaggerated, view of the case.[2]

I must not say I am out of the danger of illness; but I owe a great deal to your prayers, and those of your Sisters. *Thank them from me.*

Ever Yrs affly in Xt   J H N

TO CHARLES CASOLANI[3]

To Dr Casolani Malta   Febr 12. 1868.
Dear Sir

My silence since your flattering letter addressed to me on the 4th of last month has arisen from my feeling my incompetency to deal with the question to which your letter and pamphlet relate, and were I ever so competent the

---

[1] See letter of 18 Aug. 1867 to Oakeley.

[2] Thomas Arnold was a master at the Oratory School from 1862 until April 1865. Garside was one of the priests at Somers Town.

[3] Casolani was a Maltese physician, very interested in educational and sanitary reform. The pamphlet he sent Newman must have been *Suggestions with regard to the general administration and internal affairs of Malta*, London and Malta 1867, part of which dealt with reform in education, which he held must be based on Catholic foundations, p. 7. In England the discussion which led to the Elementary Education Act of 1870 was under way.

difficulty especially at the present moment of forming an opinion on it; also, in the not unreasonable expectation that the almost daily manifestation of opinions of members of our Parliament, in prospect of the coming Session, might throw light upon it.

A great change is coming over the country as regards education. During the last 40 years the old Catholic theory, retained and maintained in a Protestant nation for near 300 years, has been gradually innovated on, undermined, and now at length is on the point of final repudiation. The State will soon recognise no religion as having any special claim upon its pecuniary support. It is said that secular schools, and those compulsory, will be soon established for primary education. As to the higher, Oxford and Cambridge are to follow the precedent of the London University. All education is to be mixed. Christian knowledge, and other knowledge professional, literary or scientific, are to be once for all separated from each other, as far as government is concerned; grants to religious denominations are to cease [?] and if Catholics wish to carry out the Catholic principle of education, they must do it by themselves, without money grants or academical degrees for their Universities, and as regards their poor at the price of a compulsory municipal school rate of which they cannot avail themselves for educational purposes, [in] addition to the heavy unshared expense of their own parochial establishments.

Such seems to be the prospect before us. If it is realized, your own true — and in Malta new principle of 'educating thro' the concurrence of the people and clergy' instead of through the government, seems impracticable; and while it does but threaten, on the other hand, it opens on us the question whether direct antagonism to it, or a compromise is best for the interests of Catholicism.

&c J H N

TO G. P. HESTER

Febry 12. 1868

My dear Sir

I hope there have been no proceedings in contemplation of a lawsuit with Dr Jenkins, since the time that, Messrs Allcock and Milward for me, and I myself wrote to you on the subject.[1]

I trouble you with this observation, because, (if I recollect rightly) since I wrote to you about it last month, you have not distinctly attended to it

As I am writing, I will add that, when I settled accounts with Mr Neville for Mr Chaundy's property, we found this difficulty, that Mr Neville had paid (through you) £60 to Chaundy and I had paid Chaundy through Messrs

---

[1] See letter of 15 Jan. to Hester.

Allcock and Milward £1000 (besides £25 interest) whereas the purchase money was £1040. Will you tell us in what way we are to receive this £20 over.[1]

J H N

TO SIR WILLIAM HENRY COPE

The Oratory Bm Febry 14. 1868.

My dear Sir William

I did not need any mention of you by Dr Russell to be acquainted with your name; you have already long had a claim upon my memory by a kind compliment which you paid me as regards some verses in one of my publications.[2]

I will gladly see you next week, as you propose — and there are no questions concerning my religious opinions which I should be unwilling to answer, when put by any one who asks in seriousness and with a practical purpose.

I must ask you to be so good as to fix the day and hour — lest otherwise I should be out of the way

Very truly yours John H Newman

Sir Wm Cope Bart

TO W. J. COPELAND

The Oratory Bm Febry 19/68

My dear Copeland

Thank you for your letter just come.

I am sure to disappoint, if I make an engagement, and therefore I never like to make one. And I had determined I must disappoint you, before your letter came, which has sustained my uneasiness. Last night and today I have not been so well as I should like — and after what happened to me in a rail carriage two years ago, I am nervous about committing myself to one, if I am in any doubt.[3]

Tell your brother that what I hope to do is to take my chance some day — if when I come he can see me, well — if not, n'importe. But I cannot make an engagement. I rejoice to hear your good account of him.

---

[1] Hester replied that the £20 was 'interest due according to the invariable custom on paying off a mortgage without giving 6 months Notice.'
Newman sent a further note, 'Febry 15/68   Dear Sir
I should very much like to have your account up to this time at once.   J H N'
[2] Cope set to music one or more pieces from *Verses on Religious Subjects*, Dublin 1853. See letter of 15 March 1859 to him.
[3] This was on 22 Dec. 1865. See letter of 31 Aug. 1867 to Church. Copeland wanted Newman to visit his brother George, at Cheltenham.

I hope you will sleep here on Friday night, that is, if you come — for I don't like your having the trouble. There is a person whom I have never seen who is coming to call on me at 1 P M on that day — therefore I do hope you will stay all the evening

Ever Yours affly With my best and kindest regards to your brother

John H Newman

TO JOSEPH EPIPHANE DARRAS

Febr. 20. 1868[1]

answered the correspondence took place in 1834 — and lasted a year — and stopped because we could not agree on some point — we each of us assumed our first principles to be the right ones. It was published by the Univers first, then by the Abbé in a volume.

N.B. I think the writer of the above, M. Darras, wished to prove the Abbé's writings had some effect on me. He (M. Jager) wished to think so himself — for in 1845 or 1846 he wrote to me to ask me whether I did not owe my conversion to him, or some such question. I was obliged to answer, No.[2]

J H N

FRIDAY 21 FEBRUARY 1868   sang High Mass   Sir Wm Cope called.   Copeland came and slept here

TO J. R. BLOXAM

The Oratory Bm Febry 21. 1868

My dear Bloxam

Thank you for your affectionate greetings on this day. The coming round of it now is very solemn, for how can I promise myself life? and certainly I cannot promise myself strength — and the loss of strength is in one sense more severe and stern a trial than the loss of life.

I am expecting Copeland here every minute from Cheltenham, where he has been seeing his brother, who you must have heard is a great invalid. Paralysis has struck every part of him but his brain, and so he has been for a year or two, able to think, but not to move.

I have nothing to tell you — And can only assure that I am, My dear Bloxam,

Very affectly Yours John H Newman

[1] Abbé Darras wrote from Paris on 16 Feb. to say that Mgr Jager had died, and that he was commissioned to write a biographical notice of him. He wanted details of the 'correspondance polémique engagée de 1840 a 1841 [sic], entre l'abbé Jager et quelques docteurs de l'Université d'Oxford sur la question de l'Anglicanisme.' See Index, under Jager.
[2] See letter at the end of 1845 to Jager, Volume XI, pp. 81–2.

The Oratory Febry 21. 1868

My dear Jemima

Thank you for your congratulations, and your beautiful mat. The one that you gave me in 1853 still lies under my inkstand, but it is the worse for wear, and, though I shall not discard it, this new one will do very nicely over it.

I have nothing to say, but thus to thank you, and am

Ever Yours affectly John H Newman

TO MRS F. J. WATT

The Oratory, Birmingham, February 21. 1868.

My dear Child,

Thank you for your affectionate letter in recollection of this day. I am glad to hear so good an account of your health; and that your husband is getting on so well. How time speeds! You have been an old lady now nearly 2 years.

There is no news to tell you from this place. You know that Mr. Pope has been trimmed down into Father Thomas. We are building an organ gallery in Church — and we have made our burying ground at Rednal twice the size it was.

My best remembrances to Mama and Mr. Watt and believe me,

Yours very affectionately in Christ, John H. Newman of the Oratory.

SATURDAY 22 FEBRUARY 1868   Copeland went
SUNDAY 23 FEBRUARY   Fine weather

TO JAMES LAURENCE SHEPHERD

The Oratory Bm Feby 23. 1868

My dear Fr Shepherd

I rejoice to hear of the success of your publication, which speaks well for the Catholic public, and is very encouraging.[1]

Your decision about the translation of the Hymns seems to me the right

---

[1] Shepherd was translating *The Liturgical Year* of Dom Prosper Guéranger, five volumes, Dublin 1867–70. The first volume 'Advent,' was published in 1867, and 'Christmas' in 1868. See letter of 8 Nov. 1868.

one. If they were for public use, then (as you say) they would naturally require to be in verse — but it is impossible to be at once literal and rhythmical, and, as you wish to bring home to the faithful the meaning exactly of the original Latin, you must sacrifice the poetical shape.

I say the same about the Antiphons. For this reason I am not quite satisfied with 'commerce' for 'commercium.'[1] It does not seem to me to convey to an unlettered reader the meaning of the Latin. No word can be graceful or elegant in the English, which exactly represents the Latin — but a faithful representation must be aimed at. The word 'intercourse' seems to me objectionable, from the unpleasant sense in which it is sometimes used — and 'commerce' is not free from this objection. I suppose the idea conveyed in the word is, that, as we (by means of Mary) gave the Divine Word humanity, so He has given us divinity. The nearest word that occurs to me is 'interchange-' 'Fellowship' also struck me, but I do not consider it so exact — for it implies something held in common (as 'si qua *societas* spiritus,' Phil. ii, 1) whereas 'commercium' implies, not a common, but a mutual action.

I wish I could say any thing more to your purpose, and am

My dear Fr Shepherd, Sincerely Yrs in Xt
John H Newman of the Oratory

The Rev Fr Shepherd OSB

TO BARTHOLOMEW WOODLOCK

The Oratory Bm   Febry 23, 1868.

My dear Rector,

I wish I could write to you anything worth reading on the anxious question which you ask me, and which is one far more likely to be answered prudently and accurately by yourself who have now so much experience of its bearings and are in the way of hearing the opinions of so many welljudging men than by me who have so long retired from work, and have had no opportunity of watching the course of public events and the changes in Catholic interests and Catholic policy. I know nothing, I may say, more than I have accidentally gathered from the incidental notices contained in your or others' able speeches and manifestos, which from time to time have appeared in Dublin papers, sent to me by the kindness of friends.

Therefore, you will understand that what I am going to say I shall say with much diffidence and under correction.

A Catholic University, recognised as such by the State, is both the right of

[1] The first antiphon for Vespers of the Feast of the Circumcision, 1 Jan.

Ireland and the normal instrument of high education and of literary and scientific proficiency within the pale of the Church. Still, as a matter of expedience, I inclined to the alternative plan, which you mention, when I was in Dublin, and do still.[1]

First, we were set up after the pattern of Louvain — and in Belgium, if I am right, there are four great bodies, popularly called Universities, two governmental, one liberal, one Catholic. The last-mentioned, Louvain, is but a College in the eyes of the State, but is bonâ fide a University, and is recognised as such by all Catholics. It gives its own theological degrees, and its degrees in philosophy and letters for its own schools etc, but, for its civil degrees it has recourse to the board of examiners to which the candidates for degrees are submitted in the other three Universities, provision being made for the protection of Catholics from unfair examination, either by the presence of Catholic examiners on the Board, or in some other way. I never heard the Belgium plan did not work well — and I suppose the answer to this question would go very far to decide the expediency of following the precedent of Louvain, one way or the other.

Then, I certainly used to think that we had a fair chance of getting Government to place us in the position of Louvain, and little chance in succeeding in gaining a State recognition of a Catholic University — but things have changed, and you tell me that the latter now is of more easy attainment.

Then again, I used to think that we had more chance of gaining endowments from Parliament, if we came before it as claimants in the shape in which the Queen's Colleges were claimants, than if Parliament were called upon directly and distinctly to give [recognition] to a formal Catholic University.

And further still, the question is to be considered, whether we should not be tided over many difficulties if we allowed ourselves to be thus indirectly and unpretendingly to gain a civil status [sic], than if we insisted on everything at once. Hitherto, high education has been in very great measure in the hands of Protestants in Ireland. Their object has been to have a monopoly of it. They have the experience in the practice of m[2]   er have much to learn. It has seemed to me that we should be relieved of the necessity of making many experiments, and of the certainty of some mistakes, if we availed ourselves for our own purposes of an existing organization, and an accumulated experience — the Church of course having a veto on all measures and acts which bore upon religion.

There would be nothing to hinder, or rather it would naturally follow, that some years later, when Catholics were well in the saddle, they might ⟨should⟩, with the consent of all parties, be placed in their true and proper place. I cannot help thinking that it would be premature now.

---

[1] The alternative plan to a Catholic university was a Catholic college in a national university. See also letter of 4 March to Woodlock. The plan of a charter that would recognise the Catholic University of Ireland was being actively pursued with Disraeli's Government at this time.
[2] Two or three words here have been obliterated by damp.

This is all I have to say — and wishing you all the success which your long anxieties and labours have merited

I am, my dear Rector, Yours most sincerely in Xt
John H Newman of the Oratory

The Very Revd Mgr Woodlock &c &c

TO MISS ELLEN FOX

The Oratory Bm Feby 25. 1868

My dear Madam

I can quite understand your state of mind — and really I do feel much sympathy in your trial. It is what many have had before you, but I cannot conceal from myself that you are at a point in your religious history when you may gain great peace and comfort or implicate yourself in much mental embarassment.

You are happy in your Priest — Father Sweeny of Downside is an excellent man and a good theologian.[1] I have some difficulty in interfering in his work — he will direct you from personal knowledge — but I am at a distance, and experience tells me that it is not well to give advice to any one who is personally a stranger.

The greatest trial a Convert has to sustain, and to women it is often greater than to men, is the strangeness at first sight of every thing in the Catholic Church. Mass, devotions, conversation, all may be a perplexity to you, so I am not at all surprised at what you say about the Mass. You must be brave and determined, and resolutely beg of God's grace to carry you through your difficulties. Every nation, every body of people, has its own ways — Catholics have their own ways — we may not at first like them — and the question is where is religious *Truth*, where is *salvation?* — not is this habit, this fashion pleasant to me or not?

Fr Sweeny does not mean that you have hitherto been a heathen, because he will give you *conditional* baptism. There is *grave* irregularity in the Baptisms of Anglican clergymen — even of the high Church party. I speak from my own knowledge. Therefore out of love to you, the Priest who baptizes you will pour water on you with the words '*If* thou art not already baptized, I baptize thee etc'. I don't see how you can scruple at that. On the contrary, I am sure, as time went on, you would be very unhappy, if you had *not* received this simple precaution.

Our Lady has nothing of her own, that is, nothing, which is not the gift of God to her. When then we ask her for any grace, we are in fact asking her to pray to God for it for us.

---

[1] James Norbert Sweeney was at this period at St John's Priory, Bath. See also letter of 9 March.

The Immaculate Conception means just this — that from the first moment of her existence she had the grace of God. You cannot surely be startled by this, when Scripture expressly tells us that even St John the Baptist had the grace of God three months before his birth.

The Temporal Power never can be made an Article of Faith.

I am, Dear Madam, Sincerely Yours, John H. Newman

TO W. J. COPELAND

The Oratory Febry 26/68

My dear Copeland

Thank you for having finished the negociation.[1]

I send by this post 96 pages. Some manifest false prints I have corrected in *ink*. The grammatical etc alterations I have put in *pencil*, that you may, if you please, use ink as regards them

Ever Yrs affly John H Newman

TO R. W. CHURCH

The Oratory Feby 27 1868

My dear Church

Rightly or wrongly, I put down to you the review of my Verses in the Guardian: — any how, they are the remarks of a friend rather than of a critic — and, as I cannot help liking kind friends better than impartial critics, I am extremely touched by a notice of me which breathes such delicate affection.[2]

I have been so little praised all through my life, (for those who loved me best, respected me too much to praise me,) that I do not know how to bear the weight of encomium which has fallen on my small volume. One thing made me blush, if an old man can blush — that about the bow of Dante.[3] I will tell you the parallel which struck me myself. Do you recollect the story of humdrum and bashful Tom Churton? how at some great Ashmolean gathering he gently breathed into something that looked like a wind instrument — and what followed?[4]

Ever yours affectly John H. Newman

The Rev. R. W. Church.

[1] i.e. with Rivingtons for the republication of *Parochial and Plain Sermons*. What follows refers to Volume I.

[2] Church was the writer of the review in the *Guardian*, (26 Feb. 1868), pp. 244-5.

[3] Towards the end, the review said of *The Dream of Gerontius*, 'Of course our thoughts go back to Dante; for it is the one attempt, since the Divina Commedia, by any competent arm, to bend his bow.' Cf. first note to letter of 9 Jan. to Gladstone.

[4] Church replied on 2 March, 'It is for me to blush, caught out in a piece of impertinence. It is very good of you to take it as it was meant — not as criticism, but as an expression of what I at any rate have a right to feel and say. . . . You must tell me some day the sequel of the story about Churton: I can only guess.'

SUNDAY 1 MARCH 1868   a little snow

TO EMILY BOWLES

The Oy Bm March 1/68

My dear Child

I have looked at the Latin Prayer carefully with our Head Master here, and we really cannot construe it — and consider we should get the character of bad scholars, if we attempted to do so. Generally the language of devotion (Latin) is very easy; what can be more simple, clear, and beautiful than the style of the Paradisus, Manuale Ordinandi, and other manuals! but we should not be honest if we said we could construe your prayer, and it is better to confess to inability than to attempt and fail.

Ever Yours affectly John H Newman

P.S.   I would gladly give any information about the Servites to Fr Morini, if I could. But 21 years is a long space of time to keep up unexercised memories.[1]

TO SIR FREDERIC ROGERS

The Oratory, March 1. 1868

My dear Rogers

I shall be very much pleased to receive your brother's book.[2] I have seen something of it in the Reviews, and supposed he was the Author. You, I deem, have no time for Authorship.

As you have done what you hesitated about, let me also. I had wished to send Lady Rogers and your Sister Mrs L.[3] my collected verses, lately published. But, when it came to the point, I could not make up my mind to send what I thought from its subject might in part be unacceptable to them. The book is coming to a second edition, having a few additions to the first. If you will take the responsibility on yourself, I will venture to offer it when printed.

Does not Disraeli's elevation show that, when you open the highest places to mere talent, you must not hope to find in them nobility of mind?[4] Napoleon I and III are other instances. Is not Gladstone too religious, and too

---

[1] The Servite, Augustine Morini in London, gave Emily Bowles a Latin prayer to translate, and also wished her to ask Newman for his recollections of the Servites when he was in Rome in 1847. Since she could not translate the prayer, she sent that to him also.

[2] Edward Rogers, *Some Account of the Life and Opinions of a Fifth-Monarchy-Man. Chiefly extracted from the writings of John Rogers, Preacher*, London 1867. Newman presented his copy, with a card in it 'From the Author,' to the library of the Birmingham Oratory. Edward Rogers (1819–95) took Orders in 1843, and was a Student at Christ Church, Oxford, 1839–76. He was Rector of Odcombe, Somerset, 1875–90.

[3] Marian, the sister of Rogers, married the Hon. Henry Legge, Vicar of Lewisham, Kent, 1831–79.

[4] Disraeli succeeded Lord Derby as Prime Minister in Feb.

conscientious to be able to compete with Disraeli? Don't you respect Lord Derby and Lord Melbourne more than you do Disraeli?

Ever Yrs affly John H. Newman

TO A STUDENT AT MAYNOOTH

The Oratory, Birmingham. March 2nd 1868

Dear Sir,

I would gladly serve you by answering the question which you ask had I anything to say which would be materially of use to you.

Also I know what able instructors you have at Maynooth, and I should shrink from interfering in a matter which requires an experience of young men which the Maynooth Professors have, and I have not. Besides, while I thank you heartily for the compliment you pay to my own mode of writing, and am truly glad if you and others have received pleasure from it, you must recollect that those who are expert in any work are often the least able to teach others; and for myself I must simply say that I have followed no course of English reading, and am quite at a loss to know what books to recommend to students such as yourselves.

As to the writing or delivery of sermons to which you refer, the great thing seems to be to have your subject distinctly before you; to think over it till you have got it perfectly in your head; to take care that it should be one subject, not several; to sacrifice every thought, however good and clever, which does not tend to bring out your one point, and to aim earnestly and supremely to bring home that one point to the minds of your hearers.

I have written some pages on the subject of preaching in a volume upon 'University Subjects' which I published when I was in Dublin.[1] It is unfortunately out of print or I would have sent it to you. One great difficulty in recommending particular authors as models of English arises from the Literature of England being Protestant and sometimes worse — Thus Hume is a writer of good English, but he was an unbeliever. Swift and Dryden write English with great force, but you can never be sure you will not come upon coarse passages. South is a vigorous writer, but he was a Protestant clergyman, and his writings are sermons.[2] All this leads me to consider that everyone must form his style for himself, and under a few general rules, some of which I have mentioned already. First, a man should be in earnest, by which I mean, he should write, not for *the sake of writing*, but to bring out his *thoughts*. He should never aim at being eloquent. He should keep his idea in view, and write sentences

[1] *Lectures and Essays on University Subjects*, London 1859, 'University Preaching,' pp. 187–220; *Idea*, pp. 405–27.
[2] Robert South (1634–1716), whose 'sermons, smart, witty and often sarcastic' (*The Oxford Dictionary of the Christian Church*), were first published at Oxford in 1679, as *Sermons Preached on Several Occasions*. There were later editions with many further sermons.

over and over again till he has expressed his meaning accurately, forcibly and in few words. He should aim at being understood by his hearers or readers. He should use words which are most likely to be understood — ornament and amplification will come to him spontaneously in due time, but he should never seek them. He must creep before he can fly, by which I mean that humility, which is a great Christian virtue, has a place in literary composition — He who is ambitious will never write well. But he who tries to say simply and exactly what he feels or thinks, what religion demands, what Faith teaches, what the Gospel promises, will be eloquent without intending it, and will write better English than if he made a study of English literature. I wish I could write anything more to your purpose, and am, dear Sir,

Faithfully Yours in Christ, John H Newman of the Oratory[1]

MEMORANDUM AS TO A NEW PERIODICAL

March 4. 1868

So far at once it is natural for me to say, that, if I go out of my way to attempt to introduce a periodical to the world, I shall choose my own subjects for my own articles, and write them in my own way. To say that other subjects would be more apposite whether in point of usefulness or interest, will be nothing to the purpose. I never have been able to write to order, and have failed, when I have attempted to do so. Any objections to what I write on the ground of its being incorrect, illogical, or shallow will be decisive, if they hold, and will be most valuable as far as they are probable — but I shall not be moved by them, if they are only to the effect that what I have written is dull, or dry, uninteresting or irrelevant at this time. This first remark has much to be weighed — for I am not sure whether the fact on which it bears may not be an extinguisher on our hope of success.

Yet of course I do not mean it to be so — and of course I hold what to me personally is a necessity, is also for the Publication the most expedient, that is, taking for granted that the object of the Publication is of a given character.

That character I conceive to be this — that there should be in the English Catholic body a witness of a freer and larger theology than appears in the Dublin, and a witness that may be generally felt. Now this object can only be obtained in a certain way. It is what gives edge to the proposed Periodical; but a weapon cannot be all edge. If the work were throughout an inculcation of its own object, it would thereby fail of impressing readers in its favour — it would not only be tiresome, but, not unreasonably, would be considered a party publication. The question is what the staple of the publication must be — and I think it would be what is sound and finished, mature, well-turned out, logical, learned, etc etc for its own sake — knowledge is always useful to some

---

[1] Newman's notes in preparation for this letter are in *Ward*, II, p. 335.

one or another. What to most men is dry is interesting to some. It would even be a great advantage, if the work only in part had reference to controversies of the day — because it then has a more solid basis — and it has a prospect of interesting those who care not for present or party controversy.

Whether it should be exclusively theological I cannot quite decide — but it should be prominently and especially so. It might embrace among its subjects the Curiosities of (theological) literature — criticism, chronology — metaphysics — as well as theology proper — controversy — history. But it must not be written ad captandum. If a subject admits of being lively and popular, well and good — but I should expect that the general character of the publication would be to be heavy and hard.

Supposing 80 pages.

TO BARTHOLOMEW WOODLOCK

The Oratory, Birmingham March 4. 1868.

My dear Dr Woodlock,

. . . .

I feel, as you do, my fourth reason is the strongest.[1] And I want to explain why — yet I cannot do it without opening my mind fully to you, and throwing myself on your confidence. It is my duty, when you, as head of the University, ask my mind, to give it, and I do so, but I don't wish what I say repeated.

There is abundance of genius, and varied talent in Ireland to make it a very safe risk indeed to accept the great venture of a real Catholic University.

There is talent in the existing body, and other talent (I know well) outside of it which might be brought into it. Men of the width of information, of the varied accomplishments and the vigour of mind, of Professor Sullivan, if not common even in Ireland, still are to be found or to be made. On the other hand it is *essential* that the Church should have a living presence and control in the action of the University. But still, till the Bishops leave the University to itself, till the University governs itself, till it is able to act as a free being, it will be but a sickly child, even though it has a charter and an endowment.

Ever yours most sincerely John H. Newman

---

[1] i.e. at the end of Newman's letter of 23 Feb., 'we should be relieved of the necessity of making many experiments, and of the certainty of some mistakes, if we availed ourselves for our own purposes of an existing organization, and an accumulated experience.'
Woodlock wrote on 3 March, arguing for 'the advantages arising from the independence and from the Catholic spirit prevading a truly Catholic University.'

The Oratory Mar 6/68

My dear Copeland

I have found the list of dates of Volume 4, and inclose it.

Did I write at the time I sent you the 96 pages of proof?[1]

You had to put into ink, some corrections of grammar which I put in pencil. G. and R. [Gilbert and Rivington] sometimes neglect to make the corrections made upon the proof. Ought you not to see the revise?

Ever Yrs affly John H Newman

Revd W J Copeland

March 8. P.S. I think it scarcely advisable to publish the dates *at once* — but, if the *eight* volumes sell well, *then* with that proof that the public is interested, they might be given with an Index, etc.[2]

Also I send an Index which, I think, Albany Christie made — or [Thomas] Meyrick — or some one else. It may assist you. It does not take in Plain Sermons. And I doubt whether it *can* be alphabetical — from the difficulty of assigning the first letter. A list of *texts* would seem to me better

The Oratory March 8. 1868

My dear Lord Denbigh

Both as losing a great pleasure, and as being unwilling to seem ungrateful to your and Lady Denbigh's kindness, I am very unwilling to say No to your very friendly invitation. Also, I do not like to miss the opportunity of making further acquaintance with your Sister, to whom you introduced me in London. However, I am obliged to decline it.

Not to mention other obstacles, I am now engaged with our School boys every day, and I could not without serious disarrangement of our plans absent myself during this week.

I am, My dear Lord Denbigh, Sincerely Yours in Xt
John H Newman of the Oratory

The Earl of Denbigh

---

[1] See letter of 26 Feb.

[2] The list of dates when sermons were first preached was inserted at the end of *S.D.*

The Oratory, March 9, 1868.

My dear Madam,

I congratulate you on your reception — and pray God to give you all the graces and all the consolations of which it is the sure earnest

Pray convey my congratulations also to Fr Sweeny and believe me to be

Yours sincerely in Xt   John H. Newman of the Oratory

To Miss Ellen J. Fox.

TO LE COMTE DE MONTALEMBERT

The Oratory Birmingham March 9. 1868

My dear Monsieur le Comte

It gives me very great pleasure to receive from such a person as yourself so kind an expression of your sympathy.[1] From whom could such an expression be so valuable to me as from one who has been himself so emphatically an example all through his life of a noble and illrequited devotion to the Catholic cause? You are one of those in an eminent way to whom a Gracious Providence has refused in this life the reward of his good deeds, that he may receive them in superabundant measure in the world to come.

And now, alas, but still in order to increase your merits, it is the good Will of God to visit you with severe illness and long-continued. I hope you will in your charity sometimes say a prayer for me. It has been for some time past my habit, when I go before the Blessed Sacrament, to remember you.

You may fancy how deeply touched I was by the inquiry of the illustrious Bishop of Orleans, to which you refer, and what gratitude I felt at his condescension.[2] At the same time I felt certain, that, if he knew me and my ways and my state of health, he would understand, that for various reasons I was right

[1] At the beginning of Jan. 1868 Monsell had sent Montalembert a copy of Ullathorne's printed *Facts and Documents relating to the Mission and contemplated Oratory at Oxford*, asking him to return it to Newman. See letter of 31 Dec. 1867 to Monsell. Montalembert sent it back on 6 March, excusing himself for the delay on the ground of illness, and 'particularly my wish to communicate with the Bishop of Orleans before writing to you.' Montalembert thanked Newman for this mark of confidence, and added 'my deepest and most respectful sympathies with you in these circumstances, as well as in every other act of your public life.'

[2] Montalembert continued, 'To the Bishop of Orleans during his last sojourn in Paris, I translated that portion of your letter to Mr Monsell, which our mutual friend had copied for me and relating to Mgr Dupanloup's wish to take you with him as his theologian to the future Council. [On 3 Jan. 1868 Monsell copied out for Montalembert the last paragraph of Newman's letter of 31 Dec.] The illustrious prelate was much affected by the terms of your letter. He abstained from all comment, reserving to himself the right of further reflection on the subject, begging me at the same time to transmit to you the expression of his most fervent wishes for your health and welfare.'

in asking him to allow me to decline his offer. Pray ask for me his Lordship's blessing, should you have the opportunity of doing so.

I have wished to offer for your acceptance a small volume of Verses which I have lately published — but I did not know where you might be — also, I had some fear of intruding upon you. I shall now venture to do so, when it comes, as it will shortly, to a second edition.

I am, My dear Monsieur le Comte, with great respect,
Your devoted Servant in J Xt
John H Newman of the Oratory

The Count de Montalembert

TO W. J. COPELAND

The Oratory Bm March 10/68

My dear Copeland

I send you by this post a sheet of Volume 2 which came to me from Rivington this morning. I have only seen 110 pages of vol 1. What is the meaning of this

Ever Yrs affly J H N

THURSDAY 12 MARCH 1868   Mr Ratcliffe came into the House   very mild and bright March

TO W. J. COPELAND (1)

The Oratory. March 13/68

My dear C

1. Will you and Messrs Rivingtons consent to the inclosed Letter being inserted in your Preface to Volume ii of the Sermons?
2. If, however, you think it would destroy the grace of the republication to insert such a protest in the *Volume*, will you and they consent to its being inserted and bound up as a *fly leaf* or *advertisement* in Volume ii?
3. If you and they decline this also, I suppose you will not mind my inserting the Letter at a proper time in the Tablet, with a few words of introduction to the effect, that I could not succeed in having it inserted in the Volume, though I do not mean to impute any blame to those, who, looking at the matter from their own point of view, have declined to comply with my wish.

You may easily understand that my object is to escape various attacks, open and concealed, of parties who are not friendly to me.

Ever Yrs affly J H N

TO W. J. COPELAND (II)

The Oratory March 13. 1868

My dear Copeland

Though my Parochial and Plain Sermons are altogether in the hands of
yourself and your Publishers, and it is, as I know, inconsistent with your plan
of publication to make any change or omission in the text, nevertheless I hope
you may be able to find me an opportunity of stating publicly, that there are
passages, as, for instance, in Sermons 21 and 31 of volume ii which I could
wish altered, and that there is one whole Sermon, that on the Intermediate
State, the last of Volume iii, which, if it were left to me, I certainly should not
republish, as it enforces doctrinal views, which I altogether disown and condemn[1]

I am, My dear Copeland, Affectionately Yours John H Newman

The Revd W. J. Copeland

SATURDAY 14 MARCH 1868   Mr Ratcliffe received, and went from the house
SUNDAY 15 MARCH   News of Badeley's illness.   Hope Scott returned *came to him* from
Hyères

TO W. J. COPELAND

The Oratory March 15/68

My dear C

I send you by this post two sheets. In 'Faith without Sight' I have suggested two alterations, which you may think transgress the rule of not altering
the sense — but you must be the judge.

1. p. 20 Line 2, I think 'truly' was *not* my meaning — but that 'severely' or
'rigidly', which latter I think the better word.

Or I might have meant this, viz. 'to use their intellect upon it, just as if
their intellect were some external instrument etc.'

I have no objection to this (second) substitution either. But I think 'truly'
an ambiguous word which suggests a false meaning.[2]

2. p. 21 line 17 'fairly probable' is surely better than 'slightly probable —' but
perhaps this *is* an alteration of sense.[3]

What I meant by a 'Collection of texts' in my last letter was a collection of

[1] See letter of 22 March to Copeland.
[2] *P.S.* II. The word 'truly' was changed: The incredulous 'find it no effort to use their
intellect upon it [Revelation] as rigidly as if it were some external instrument which could not
be swayed.'
[3] Again one word was altered: 'If it is but fairly probable that rejection of the Gospel will
involve his eternal ruin, it is safest and wisest to act as if it were certain.'

the Texts of the Sermons — People often recollect a text when they recollect nothing else — much more than they recollect the *Title* of the Sermon.

Ever Yours affly J H N.

TO JAMES HOPE-SCOTT

The Oratory ⌜March 15/68⌝

My dear Hope Scott

⌜Mrs Bellasis writes Richard word, that you are brought to London by Badeley's illness. But Bellasis, writing to Fr Ambrose by this morning's post, says indeed you have returned [[to England]], but does not give the cause. This leads me to hope that, though Badeley's state of health may be at the bottom of your coming, still there is no immediate danger to him.

Any how the news is heavy enough. Will you give me just one line about him. Perhaps he is at Chelmsford, and this will not reach you. Give him my most affectionate remembrances — I have just been saying Mass for him — and shall go on doing so, till I am made more easy⌝

Ever Yrs affly John H Newman of the Oratory

Jas R Hope Scott Esqr

TO PATRICK LEAHY, ARCHBISHOP OF CASHEL

The Oratory March 15/68

My dear Lord

It pleased me very much to receive your letter and to find you do not forget me.[1] And I felt very much the kind notice made of me by yourself and the Bishop of Clonfert in the Statement, of which you have given me a copy. Pray make my acknowledgements for me to his Lordship when you see him.

I congratulate you on the success of the long and persevering efforts which have been made to obtain a civil recognition for the University. You seem to

---

[1] Newman copied out part of Leahy's letter of 12 March, 'Feeling sure you take a deep interest in the fortunes of our Catholic University, as you had a principal part in founding it, I send you a Statement bearing upon its present position and prospects.

And I send you this, poor memento as it is, in memory of the time to which I always look back with pleasure, when I had the happiness to be associated with you as a very humble fellow worker.'

This was *A Statement on the University Question*, Dublin 1868, addressed by Archbishop Leahy of Cashel and Bishop Derry of Clonfert to the Catholic Members of Parliament. It asked for a charter and endowment for the Catholic University of Ireland, and insisted on the bishops' right of supervision of university education 'in its bearing on the faith and morals of their flocks.' The *Statement* said that the bishops could not 'set to work anew in the hope of devising a better plan of University Education than that traced out by the master hand of Dr. Newman.' p. 10.

me to have effected your object, whether the particular bill of the present Ministry is carried through the two Houses or not. There seems a general admission by all parties of the justice of your claim — they do but quarrel with each other in what way it is to be met and satisfied. It is only a question of time as to when the University is to have a charter and an endowment.

I hope you are well, and that you are less anxious about the state of Ireland than you were — and, begging your Grace's blessing,

I am, My dear Lord, Affectionately Yours in Xt   John H Newman

His Grace The Archbishop of Cashel

TO JAMES STEWART

The Oratory March 15. 1868

My dear Stewart

I am pleased at any occasion you find for writing to me — and wish you had told me something about yourself and those dear to you.[1] I wish to ask Mrs Stewart acceptance of a small book of Verses which I have lately published, and which is now coming to a second Edition.

As to the particular subject of your letter, I congratulate you on the success of the friends of the University. It is only a question of time when you get a charter and an endowment. The present Ministry's scheme may be wrecked, and I suppose it will. I don't expect much good to Ireland from Disraeli. Timeo Danaos, et dona ferentes.[2] I can't believe he is in earnest. I had rather you were in any hands but his; and shall be better pleased if you wait a year than if you gain a favor from him.

However, these feelings of mine would not hinder me complying with your request, if it were in my power to be of service to you in the way you suggest to me. But you greatly overrate my influence. I don't think I could do anything — or rather, I am sure I could do nothing. I am so absolutely out of the world, that my interference in the matter could do no good. And to interfere with effect one ought to have a confidence in self, which in this matter I have not.

Ever Yours affectly in Xt   John H Newman of the Oratory

Professor Stewart.

MONDAY 16 MARCH 1868   Woodgate called

[1] Stewart wrote on 13 March wanting Newman to write to *The Times* on behalf of a charter for the Catholic University of Ireland.
[2] *Aeneid* II, 49.

TO J. M. CAPES

The Oratory, Birmingham, March 16. 1868

My dear Capes,

I have seen your article on my Verses in the Fortnightly, and hope you will take my words as kindly as they are meant, when I say I sincerely thank you for it.[1]

Some parts of it struck me as very just. I have often been puzzled at myself, that I should be both particularly fond of being alone, and particularly fond of being with friends. Yet I know both the one and the other are true, though I can no more reconcile them than you can. You are the first, as far as I know, who have noticed an apparent inconsistency to which I can but plead guilty.[2]

I have said above that some parts of your review struck me as just, because I hardly know how to take to myself the special encomiums contained in other parts, which read more like the composition of a friend than of a critic.

I am, my dear C., Most sincerely Yours, John H Newman

J. M. Capes Esq.

TUESDAY 17 MARCH 1868   went to Rednall (with Ambrose) to transcribe first part of my Essay[3]

TO MRS MILBOURNE[4]

March 17. 1868

My dear Madam,

Since you are so kind as to say, that you have taken an interest in my writings, and so faithful an interest, extending, if I understand you, over nearly thirty five years, I seem to have a claim on you, when you open the book, in which these lines are to be inserted, for the further kindness of remembering

---

[1] The *Fortnightly Review*, (1 March 1868), pp. 342–5.

[2] Capes wrote, 'Dr Newman's plea, in justification of the publication of this volume of his verses, revised and enlarged, is to be found in the fact that he cannot live in absolute isolation from his fellow-man. The ordinary companionship of the friends and acquaintants of one who, as he told us in his "Apologia," early thought himself bound to celibacy, is not enough, even for a man whose inner resources are so varied, whose interest in human affairs is so sympathetic, and who is so penetrated with the sense, as he expresses it, that he is "solus cum Solo" in the world.'

Capes replied on 19 March, 'so far from remarking on your twofold likings as an "apparent inconsistency," which I can no more account for than you can, I have spoken of it as indicating a completeness of character which ordinary observers have not attributed to you; or at least did not attribute to you in former days.'

[3] *An Essay in Aid of a Grammar of Assent.*

[4] These three words were written by Newman at the head of this letter, which was evidently to be inserted in a copy of *Vv.*

in your good prayers one whose years and writings are now drawing to an inevitable end

Most truly Yours John H Newman

SATURDAY 21 MARCH 1868   went back to Bm [Birmingham]

TO W. J. COPELAND

The Oratory March 22/68

My dear Copeland

I thought your and Rogers' suggestion extremely good, and for that very reason (as you told me) did not write to you.[1]

Now I am led to ask whether it would be more agreeable to you and Rivington that *you* should speak altogether *instead* of me. If so, your words must be a little more in detail. I am suggesting this, not as not being more than satisfied with your sentences (which I am), but thinking you and Rivington may prefer to do *without* my letter[2]

Ever Yrs affly J H N

MONDAY 23 MARCH 1868   went out to Rednall

WEDNESDAY 25 MARCH   some cold frost   a little snow

SATURDAY 28 MARCH   back into Bm [Birmingham] late in day   Mr J. Doyle in the House

TO W. J. O'NEILL DAUNT

The Oratory Bm March 28. 1868

My dear Mr Daunt

I thank you very much for your Volume, which I shall read with great interest.[3]

[1] In order to meet the difficulty raised in Newman's letters of 13 March to Copeland, he and Rogers evidently suggested that Newman's proposed letter, disowning some of the views put forward in *P.S.*, should be inserted by Copeland in his preface to the republished volumes.

[2] Copeland agreed to this proposal and on 23 April wrote to say that it had been accepted by Rivington. Copeland's paragraph *P.S.* I, pp. viii-ix, is as follows:

'In conclusion it is right, though scarcely necessary to observe, that the republication of these Sermons by the Editor is not to be considered as equivalent to a reassertion by their Author of all that they contain; inasmuch as, being printed entire and unaltered, except in the most insignificant particulars, they cannot be free from passages which he certainly now would wish were otherwise, or would, one may be sure, desire to see altered or omitted.

But the alternative plainly lies between publishing all or nothing, and it appears more to the glory of God and for the cause of religion, to publish all, than to destroy the acceptableness of the Volumes to those for whom they were written by any omissions and alterations.'

[3] This must have been the new edition, revised and enlarged, of *Ireland and her Agitators*, Dublin 1867, which Daunt first published in 1845.

54

As you may easily believe, I am not a politican, and my opinion, if I had one, would be worth nothing — and if I have no definite political opinions, this is, from an intense consciousness which I have, that I have no right to have any.

What do I know about facts? I sit at home, and only dream about them through the information of newspapers and the like. In two great points have the English people, and I with them, been misled within this three years — one, the state of things in the United States — next the state of Germany. Our political teachers and informants were the blind leading the blind.[1]

So it is now doubtless as regards Ireland also. I can easily understand an Irishman having the best grounds possible for saying that things will never go straight in Ireland till the Union with England is repealed — but whether they will go right then, is a point which it requires greater knowledge of Ireland than I have, to determine. I thought Dean O'Brien's Address a very powerful one.[2] I suppose you would not think it enough to have an Irish Parliament for strictly *self legislation*, that is, legislation *for* itself as well as *by* itself — that is, for Irish, not for Imperial Affairs. Are they not acting on this principle now in Austria as regards Hungary?

I am, My dear Mr Daunt, Yours most truly
John H Newman of the Oratory

W. J. O'N. Daunt Esqr

SUNDAY 29 MARCH 1868   (Badeley died at ¼ past 4 P M)

TO JAMES HOPE-SCOTT

The Oratory Bm ⌐March 29/68⌐

My dear Hope Scott

Thanks for your letter — ⌐your sad news is most disappointing. I looked forward to his gradually getting better, when his mind would be his own again, and he would like to see me, and it would not seem to him forced, that I made my appearance.

What am I to do now, when he has lost his consciousness again, and not regained it, and perhaps will lose it again, *before* [[I hear that]] he has regained it? What do you advise me to do?⌐

Ever Yours affectly John H Newman

MONDAY 30 MARCH 1868   went to Rednall back   beautiful weather   I never knew so beautiful a February and March.   The hedges have been green some time and the lilac leaves are half out.

---

[1] English public opinion underestimated the strength of the Northern States and of Prussia, and was misled by Palmerston and Russell, and by *The Times*.

[2] See letter of 27 Jan. to Monsell.

Rednall March 31/68

My dear Church

Dear Badeley is taken from us. He had a stroke of some kind a fortnight ago; on Saturday last had another, and on Sunday a third, which took him off. I fancied he would get better, and put off going to see him till then. I have not seen him for nearly two years, — when his appearance somewhat alarmed me.

Hope Scott was recalled from Hyères — and was with him when he died. It is a great blow to me. To Hope Scott one of the greatest he could have — as I think you can fancy.

Henry Bowden lingers on — and now seems as if he might remain in his bedroom and sitting room for years or at least many months.

My verses have come to a second Edition — and, though it is taking somewhat of a liberty, I hope you will get it pardoned, if I venture to send a copy to Mrs Church.

Ever yours affectly John H. Newman

Rednall. March 31/68

My dear Copeland

Dear Badeley is taken from us. He had a stroke some fortnight ago — another last Saturday — a third on Sunday, which took him off. Hope Scott had been recalled from Hyères, and was at his bedside when he died It is a great blow to me, but a greater to Hope Scott

Every Yrs affly John H Newman

Rednall ⌜March 31. 1868⌝

My dear Hope Scott

⌜What a heavy, sudden, unexpected blow — I shall not see him now, till I cross the stream which he has crossed. How dense is our ignorance of the future, a darkness which can be felt, and the keenest consequence and token of the Fall. Till we remind ourselves of what we are, — in a state of punishment, — such surprises make us impatient, and almost angry, alas!

But my blow is nothing to yours, though you had the great consolation of sitting by his side and being with him to the last. What a fulness of affection he poured out on you and yours — and how he must have rejoiced to have your faithful presence with him, while he was going. This is your joy and your pain.

Now he has the recompense for that steady, well-ordered, perpetual course of devotion and obedience, which I ever admired in him, and felt to be so much above any thing that I could reach. All or most of us have said Mass for him, I am sure, this morning; certainly we two have who are here.

I did not write to you during the past fortnight, thinking it would only bother you, and knowing I should hear if there was any thing to tell. But you have been as much surprised as any one at his sudden summons. I knew it was the beginning of the end — but thought it was only the beginning. How was it his medical men did not know better?

I suppose the funeral is on Saturday

God bless and keep and sustain you⌐

Ever Yours most affectionately John H Newman

THURSDAY 2 APRIL 1868   came back to Oratory for good

TO JAMES HOPE-SCOTT

The Oratory Bm ⌐April 2. 1868⌐

My dear Hope Scott

Thank you for your letter. ⌐I had meant to have come up, unless you spoke against it — but I cannot, the hour being what it is. I have to sing High Mass here on Sunday and, as there are three Deacons of the Passion, and Deacon and Sub-Deacon of the Mass, to be provided, and Ambrose has the asthma there is no one to take my place. I hope to say Mass for dear Badeley on Saturday⌐

Ever Yours affly John H Newman

FRIDAY 3 APRIL 1868   Examinations

SATURDAY 4 APRIL   Eddy Froude came for retreat   Examinations   John [Norris] and Thomas [Pope] ordained Subdeacons at Oscott

SUNDAY 5 APRIL   Palm Sunday   I took function *of the four days*   F Coleridge came for the boys' retreat.   Towneley came for the retreat

TO MRS R. W. CHURCH

The Oratory Birmingham Palm Sunday 1868

My dear Mrs Church

If I am committing any fault against the rules of civilised society, in thus writing to you familiarly when I have not yet had the pleasure of seeing you, Richard is in fault who has sent me so kind a message from you, apropos of

57

the volume I wished to offer you, that I do not know how to let it go to you without the accompaniment of a few lines from me.

I mean to send it by this night's post, and I trust it will be the forerunner of that visit which I hope to have the pleasure of paying to you and him, as was arranged last year — but how can one look forward to the future with any security, after the loss of a friend which your husband and I are now suffering, so suddenly befalling us! Pray say every thing kind to him from me and believe me

Most truly Yours John H Newman

Mrs Church

TO ALEXANDER PENROSE FORBES, BISHOP OF BRECHIN

The Oratory Bm April 6. 1868

My dear Lord

I thank you very much for the present you have made me of your learned and important volumes.[1] Nothing but good can come from such careful investigations — though what the good and how it will come it is difficult for any one to pronounce, and still more difficult to gain any concordant judgment. A great many men will think that, in destroying the value of the 39 Articles as a bulwark against Rome, you are inevitably striking a blow at their retention in the Anglican Church, and this consummation, I suppose the Christian Remembrancer and Guardian, the most able Anglican publications would accept with much equanimity.

I cannot predict whether your work will attract the notice of any of our theologians I hope it will, for controversy though unpleasant as a dose of medicine, like medicine does great good.

I am, Most truly yours John H Newman

The Bishop of Brechin

TO H. A. WOODGATE

The Oratory Birmingham April 6. 1868

My dear Woodgate

I conjecture you called on seeing dear Badeley's death in the Papers. The day before I last saw you here, I had heard of his having had a serious stroke which had the effect of calling Hope Scott from Hyères. I said nothing about it not knowing whether I was at liberty to do so, as people often conceal such things. And I waited before going to see him, till he should be better. And he did gradually mend — when, at the end of a fortnight, he suddenly had

[1] *An Explanation of the Thirty-Nine Articles*, two volumes, 1867–8, written at Pusey's suggestion.

another stroke. And within, I think, the forty eight hours, on Sunday (yesterday) week, while Hope Scott sat by his bed, he had a third, which carried him off within an hour.

I had not seen him since that time I met you in St James's Park.[1] It then struck me painfully that he was aging or breaking — but no one else remarked upon him. I had thought him older than it seems he was.

It is a great blow to Hope Scott, to whom, and to his interests, and his family, Badeley had devoted himself. And it is a great and sudden blow to me.

Yours affectly John H Newman

The Revd H A Woodgate

TO MRS RICHARD SIMPSON

The Oratory April 7. 1868

My dear Mrs Simpson

You have taken most kindly a tardy offering. I had intended to offer you a copy of the first edition. By an accident it was not done. Then, as a second edition was coming, I thought I had better wait for it; as it would, for good or bad, contain some more compositions. This is the history of it. I would gladly have taken an earlier opportunity of asking your acceptance of some writing of mine, but I write so few things which with any gracefulness I can offer to a lady. But now I thought an occasion presented itself of showing, that, tho' so many years have passed, I have not forgotten, as I have not, that I have had the pleasure of knowing you.

My kindest remembrances to your husband, who does me honour in giving any song of mine a musical canonization[2]

Most truly Yours John H Newman of the Oratory

Mrs Simpson

WEDNESDAY 8 APRIL 1868   Eddy F.[Froude] called away by his brother dying

TO WILLIAM FROUDE

[8 April 1868]

. . . .

He [Robert Edmund Froude] showed me your letter to him, and said he did not quite understand what you said at the end of it. On reading it, I told him that I did not find a difficulty in it — that you showed yourself, as you ever did, thinking of others, not of yourself — that you could wish abstractedly that he was not about his brother's bed, but that you could not say no, to what seemed so natural.

[1] See diary for 25 June 1866.
[2] See letter of 3 Jan. 1869 to Simpson.

Then he said that he did not wish to be with him at the last. And it was evident he feared it. He alluded to Mary's death — of which I recollect quite fully your account. If it has remained on my imagination, of course it has upon his. And he certainly spoke as if he could not bear it.[1]

I should not think much . . .[2]

THURSDAY 9 APRIL 1868   I took the functions   [also Friday and Saturday 10 and 11 April]

TO CHARLES FRANCIS CUDDON

The Oratory Bm April 9. 1868

My dear Mr Cuddon

I thank you very much for the little book of Devotions you have given me, so suitable to this Sacred Season — and offer you my warmest acknowledgements for the very kind words with which you accompany it[3]

I am, Most truly Yours John H Newman of the Oratory

The Revd C. F. Cuddon

TO JAMES HOPE-SCOTT

The Oratory ⌜Good Friday⌝ [[April 10]] 1868

My dear Hope Scott

⌜How many trials are given you! If all is well, I hope to say Mass for you and Lady Victoria on Easter Monday⌝[4]

Ever Yrs affly John H Newman

TO BISHOP ULLATHORNE

The Oratory   Good Friday 1868

My dear Lord

In asking your Lordship at this time to confer the Subdiaconate on our Novice, Father John Norris, we beg to state that the Oratory undertakes henceforth to provide him with a Patrimony to the amount of £40 a year.

[1] Mary Froude died on 30 May 1864. See letter of 1 June 1864 to William Froude. Arthur Froude died on 9 April 1868.
[2] The copy ends thus. Froude replied on 9 April, 'What you had understood from my letter was exactly what I meant: though I should have expressed myself rather differently had I known about Eddy's feeling, what you tell me . . .' He also reported, 'Happily what Eddy saw of the closing scene of Arthur's life, painful as it was, had not that harrowing tragic aspect which was presented in poor little Mary's case . . .'
[3] Cuddon was a curate at St Patrick's, Soho Square.
[4] Mrs Hope-Scott had a son who died the day after his birth, 9 April 1868.

Begging your Lordship's blessing on us at this Sacred Season, I am

Your obt and affte Servt in Xt   John H Newman

The Bishop of Birmingham

TO WILLIAM FROUDE

The Oratory   Easter Day 1868

My dear William

Thank you for your long letter.[1] I am very glad Eddy was in time. Since it was to be, it was a relief to me to be told that the worst was over. At least I dreaded for you all a prolonged suffering, knowing how hard young lives die. Eddy gives a good account of you and his mother — but, as we get on in life, we can control our feelings and behaviour more — and then again there is the fear lest you should suffer more afterwards.[2]

I don't know Eddy as you think I do. It requires close attention and familiar intercourse to read anyone — and I am as likely as any one else to have but a surface view of him, though it is a view of a particular surface.

I am writing to him and to your wife. Say everything affectionate from me to Isy, and thank her for her letter.

Ever Yrs affly John H Newman

TO MRS WILLIAM FROUDE

The Oratory Easter Day 1868

My dear Mrs Froude,

This is a sorrowful Easter day for you — yet a joyful one too. Through the past week you have been like the Blessed Virgin under the Cross. What a great mercy it was he should die at home, and not in some wild foreign place among strangers. This is what makes a time of mourning so bright. You have landed him safe on the eternal shore — What could you wish better?[3]

At your leisure, when time has gone on, you will be able to tell me how you have been supported through so great a trial

Ever Yrs affectionately John H. Newman

P.S.   If all is well, I shall say Mass for him on Tuesday morning.

[1] That of 9 April, the day Arthur Froude died, at Chelston Cross, Torquay, aged 24. He was in the Royal Navy and had become a Catholic at 17.

[2] The two paragraphs that follow were copied separately, but belong to this letter. William Froude had been surprised at the force of R. E. Froude's feelings.

[3] Mrs Froude had written on 20 Feb., 'I thank God every year more and more, that we have had you for a friend. It is curious to me to see that — although my children are all so different, yet there is something in your writings which fits into their minds in a way that no other serious reading does. I read your books over and over again to Arthur, now that he is ill, and he is never tired of hearing them . . . . I cannot help feeling that . . . this quiet time at home, for thought and attention to his religious duties, will have been of great advantage to him.'

MONDAY 13 APRIL 1868   Mr Cornish and his wife called   cold days

TO EMILY BOWLES

The Oratory Easter Monday 1868

My dear Child

The best congratulations to you of this Blessed Season. It is a drawback to be told by you that you are not well — and Fr Coleridge confirms it. Please, let me know about you, when you have any thing to say; but I understand you to talk of coming down here.

Changes, awful from their greatness, seem coming on. Perhaps they won't in our time — for I am old enough to remember how much evil was expected from the first Reform Act, which did not come to pass. But, whether the evil comes sooner or later, it will come; and though, as an act of justice, I can but rejoice that the Irish Establishment is going, yet I am not sure that it will be on the whole a gain to the Catholic cause.[1]

You grieve me by what you say of L.S.[2] but I have no doubt you have done her, and will do her good. People, if at all clever, must have much self command and deep faith, not to be in danger of getting restless in this day.

I do not know whom you mean by Mrs Ph.[3] or what you mean by her going to see me. As to Miss Fitzgerald I know nothing at all about her, or her abode. She wrote some letters which from their simplicity and frankness struck me very much — and you confirmed my feeling — but she has not written to me since she was in Ireland. If she is what she appeared to be, her friends can but delay her progress towards conversion.[4]

There is no news here.

Ever Yrs affly J H N

TUESDAY 14 APRIL 1868   Lord and Lady Denbigh called?   Ambrose went to Brighton

---

[1] Gladstone was advocating the disestablishment of the Church of Ireland, and in 1869 passed it into law.

[2] The initials L.S. [Louisa Simeon] have been erased, but can be read. Emily Bowles wrote about her on 31 May, 'I had several long talks with L. Simeon before they left Town — and last week had a *very* nice letter from her. I wish she could marry — and so have some settled sphere for her great powers.'

[3] Emily Bowles has left a note that Mrs Phillimore was 'the widow of Mr John George Phillimore of Shiplake, who had been received into the Church. After a short, singularly exemplary Catholic life she died after a few days' illness.' Mrs Phillimore's husband, a learned jurist, died in 1865. She was Rosalind Margaret, younger daughter of the Judge Sir James Lewis Knight Bruce.

[4] Emily Bowles wrote on 31 May, 'Geraldine Fitzgerald reappears and vanishes still — but her cousin Miss Perry — an *outer* Sister at St Peter's Home has been received. She was appointed to look after G. and keep her straight. Is not this remarkable? and proves that your idea of G. is true. She communicated the Catholicity which is yet latent in herself.' Geraldine Penrose Fitzgerald, born on 27 Jan. 1846, became a Catholic in 1869.

Easter Tuesday 1868

My dear Child

I have seen your dear letter and passed it on to Miss Mitchell.

I have just been saying Mass for Arthur.

He has been called away at a happy season, and though it makes your Easter sorrowful, yet who shall say that the gates of Paradise do not open wider for elect souls at such a time of indulgence?

God grant us all to die as hopefully as he has died; but, ah, how many years you may have to run first! Yet, all through that time, and more and more, the thought of him will be a fount of consolation and refreshment to you; and when God calls you, as He has called him, one of your joys will be that you are going as to our Lord, so to him, Our Lord will not be alone. He takes away our loved ones as hostages, that we may be compelled, even by our earthly affections, to lift up our hearts to Him. Who shall say this is not religious, considering the Blessed Virgin, after His ascension, looked forward to meet Him, not only as her God, but as her Son?

Ever Yrs affly John H Newman

WEDNESDAY 15 APRIL 1868   Hopkins went for good about now

SATURDAY 18 APRIL   The Bishop called

MONDAY 20 APRIL   Canon Walker came and went   Ambrose returned from Brighton

TO RICHARD FREDERICK CLARKE

The Oratory Birmingham April 21. 1868

My dear Sir

I will gladly see you to-morrow, Wednesday, as you propose, at some time between four and six.[1]

---

[1] Clarke was a Fellow of St John's College, Oxford, 1860–9, and towards the end of this period was drawn increasingly towards Catholicism. 'About this time he was offered a salaried office in the University, some sort of pro-proctorial duties, to which was then annexed a preliminary declaration against transubstantiation. This was a difficulty to him. He wrote to Newman. Newman invited him down to Edgbaston, and gave him this advice: "If you still have any doubt about transubstantiation, you may make the declaration, which will mean no more than that you are no believer in the doctrine; if you have no doubt of it, of course you must refuse." Clarke did refuse, and converted the pro-proctorial velvet that he had bought into a waistcoat, which I have seen him wearing at St Beuno's, where he told me the story. In 1869 he took the step which changed all his fortunes. He was received into the Catholic Church at Farm Street, on 10 July 1869, by Father Henry Coleridge. Had he cared to go abroad, and be lost to the society of St John's College for a few months, he might have contrived to retain his fellowship, by benefit of the University Test Act of 1870. Clarke thought it the more honourable course to avow himself a Catholic from the first. Accordingly he left St Johns, and found acceptance at Trinity.' Joseph Rickaby, in the *Month*, (Oct 1900), p. 339.

Clarke was the last Fellow of a College to be forced to resign his Fellowship, on ceasing to be a member of the Church of England.

My only difficulty is my fear that I should have nothing to say worth coming for.[1]

I suppose the Oath of Supremacy is what it was — I A.B. do swear that I do from my heart abhor, detest etc . . . that Princes excommunicated etc etc . . . And I do declare that no foreign Prince etc hath or ought to have any *jurisdiction* etc Ecclesiastical or Spiritual within this realm.

1 I do not see how a Catholic, however loyal, can take this oath — for we believe the Pope's jurisdiction to be wherever there are baptized Christians; according to our Lord's words to Peter 'Feed my sheep.'

2. 'A person fast drifting towards Catholicism,' but 'not seeing his way to become a Catholic at once' either has some definite obstacle in the way of faith, as a distinct holding off from some particular doctrine or doctrines, or has a general and indefinite want of faith, a dim belief amid remaining doubt, such as to warrant or oblige him to *wait* till he has clearer views.

(1) If the former, that obstacle ultimately falls on the doctrine of the Pope's prerogatives — for if he believed that the Creed of the Pope could not be wrong, he would accept the difficult points in Catholicism on *faith* — in the Pope — Therefore, since he does *not* accept them, this shows that he does *not* apply the 'Feed My Sheep' to the Pope — or that he does *not* believe in the Pope's universal jurisdiction. But, if he does not, he *can* take the oath to the Queen's Supremacy.

(2) On the other hand, if, according to the latter supposition, he merely has not a clear view, and doubts which way the truth lies, though he inclines to believe Catholicism and thinks he shall do so, doubting in some sense every thing, doubting Anglicanism certainly, then I think he *cannot* swear to the Queen's Supremacy — for one cannot swear that that *is*, which we *doubt* as to its being or not being.

3. We give to the Pope and to the Church an authority above the law of the land in *spiritual* matters. If the State told us to teach our children out of the Christian Knowledge Society's books, and the Pope told us not to do so, we must disobey the State and obey the Pope.

Very faithfully Yours John H Newman

[1] Clarke asked on 21 April: '1 Whether a loyal Roman Catholic would be able with a good conscience to take the "Oath of the Queen's Sovereignty".

In the case of your answering the above question in the negative. 2 Whether, in your opinion, a person who is fast drifting towards Catholicism and is strongly inclined to believe that the Church of Rome is the true and only Church of Jesus Christ, but at the same time does not at all see his way at once to become a Catholic, would be justified in taking the said oath.

3 What the nature of the authority is which is denied to any foreign Prince Prelate etc. Whether it is an authority *above* the law of the land or which acts *through* it, or which is separate from and independent of it? Whether it is an authority which Roman Catholics generally would claim for the Holy See? — My reason for asking these questions is that they concern myself personally and immediately.' Clarke concluded 'I am in a most difficult position — and I may have to decide by Thursday afternoon.'

TO THOMAS HARPER, S.J.

The Oy Bm April 21. 1868

Dear Fr Harper

I am rejoiced to hear you are so much better — but fear you will not allow yourself to get well before you set to work.

Alas, I have done very little in what really is always an easy work, criticism, — but I send you what I have[1]

Yours most sincerely, John H Newman of the Oratory

WEDNESDAY 22 APRIL 1868   Mr Clarke came for an hour

TO W. J. COPELAND (I)

The Oratory Bm April 24/68

My dear Copeland

I have unfortunately mislaid the copy you sent me of the projected passage in your Preface. I hope you have got one, for I thought it very good.

As the first volume is now near publication, is it not well to get it ready? Perhaps you have no need of a Preface at all, but, if you mean to have one, one ought to have before one the *whole*, in order to judge of the effect of the particular passage.[2]

As I have read the Sermons already in print, (for the first time since I last published them,) I have been agreeably pleased with many of them — but many of them, which I used to think some of the best, I have been disappointed in — and especially in this way, that I could not understand what they were aiming at or what parties they were describing. Things are so different now from what they were. But if *I* do not recognize their truth, how will a younger generation? So that I have thought perhaps that Rivington will find it a bad bargain

Ever Yrs affly John H Newman

P.S.   How it was you did not receive till March 26 what I put into the post on March 15 is to me a great mystery.

TO W. J. COPELAND (II)

April 24/68   Evening

My dear C

Your letter has just come, since the inclosed was written.

1. It is good your talking of *my* trouble with the sheets, when you have so much, and all out of love.

[1] See letter of 14 Nov. 1868 to Pusey.
[2] See letter of 22 March to Copeland.

2. Nothing will be better than for you to draw up something *without* me, if you will take the trouble. I do hope you have a copy of your Paper. I can't fancy where it has got to.

3. I have *no* opinion about Parochial *or* Plain — 'Parochial and Plain' connects them all together — and Rivington is the better judge.

4. As to *my feeling* about the republication put it at the lowest, it is this, which even fierce Anti-Anglicans would understand. When certain persons think the Sermons would do good to the cause of religion (if they do, which I assume) I should act like the dog in the manger if I barked when they were about to be re-published, considering that in my heart that [sic] on the whole I think their effect will be good, and can thank God that I feel I can think this. If the alternative is put to me, had you rather *all* printed or *none* printed? I should think myself right in saying, *of the two* alternatives, the former. I say this, to make you master my feeling.

4. About your name appearing only in the Preface, not in the Title Page, I leave it quite to you.

5. The Preface should not be long, and if it is all as good as the two sentences you sent me, it will be very good.

6. I shall be here all next week, with *this* chance, viz a very holy person is dying at Stone — a remarkable woman — who has raised up something like 80 nuns, being herself a nobody — simply a servant originally. And I may be suddenly called to her Funeral. They wished me to preach the Funeral Sermon, but this I have declined.

I grieve about your brother

Ever Yrs affly John H Newman

The *type* of the Reprint is very keen and good

TO BISHOP ULLATHORNE

The Oratory April 24/68

My dear Lord

I feel your extreme kindness — but I intreat you most earnestly not to ask me to preach the Sermon.[1] I *really am not up to it.* I do most fervently hope you will let me say No. *There is only one person can do it.*[2] I said Mass for her today and yesterday, and on an earlier day in the week — and hope to do so tomorrow

Do forgive me Your faithful Servt John H Newman

---

[1] Ullathorne wrote on 24 April to say that Mother Margaret Hallahan was rapidly sinking, 'I ask you, as one whom she always regarded with great regard, and affectionate esteem, as one who can appreciate her great soul and great worth, to preach the funeral discourse . . .'

[2] According to a letter of 25 April to Ullathorne from Escourt, who had seen Newman, he meant to point to J. Spencer Northcote as the preacher. Ullathorne wrote on 26 April, 'he could not do it, for he is like her own son, and would break down.'

Mother Margaret Hallahan did not die until 11 May. Manning was to have preached at her funeral, but was prevented, and Ullathorne took his place at short notice.

TO MRS F. J. WATT

The Oratory, Birmingham. April 24/68

My dear Child,

I did not forget your wedding day — tho', as my days are almost spent to get ready letters for the Post, I had not time to write to you. Now I write on the Octave, which may be accounted the day itself.

I am glad to hear Mamma is coming — but I hope the weather will be better for her than it is just now. I trust she will bring better account of Phillipine.

The organ gallery is finished, and does very well. St. Joseph has now a real little chapel before his image — and we are making an altar there. You should come over for St. Philip's day with your husband to see it. We are putting for the present the great picture of the dispute about the Immaculate Conception which the Abbe Rogerson gave me above the organ gallery.[1]

Ever yours affectionately, J. H. N.

SATURDAY 25 APRIL 1868   Mr Blake in Bm[Birmingham]
SUNDAY 26 APRIL   Mr Blake to dinner

TO W. J. COPELAND

April 26/68

My dear C

As a memorandum I say that on Friday night the 24th I sent you some proofs to Trinity College as well as a letter — and tonight I send you some to Trinity also.

N.B. I calculate the 'plain Sermons' if printed in the same type (the *old* one) as the Parochial, would only make 540 pages whereas the Parochial were 400. Therefore it will never make *two* volumes (which would require 800 pages) but one thick volume.

Ever Yrs affly J H N

---

[1] This picture by Innocenzo da Imola is still in the church of the Birmingham Oratory. It was given to Newman in 1866 by John Singleton Rogerson, who from 1858 until his death in 1884, was the unofficial English Catholic chaplain in Paris. As he explained in a letter of 31 May 1866 to St John, Rogerson presented the picture to Newman 'as an expression of my admiration for his Letter to Pusey on the Dogma of Devotion to the Blessed Virgin.'

TO BISHOP ULLATHORNE

TO BISHOP ULLATHORNE

The Oratory Bm April 26. 1868

My dear Lord

I wrote to your Lordship last night, but I find my letter has not yet got to you, and therefore write again.

In your kindness you are wishing to put on me a sacred task to which I am quite unequal. I have had long experience of myself, and I know what I can do, and what I cannot. I cannot do every thing — I cannot do a thing because I wish it. I am a man for ordinary work, not extraordinary. Sometimes I have been forced to do what I knew I could not do, and, as I anticipated, have failed. I know I should fail in this; and how much it would distress me to fail on such an occasion! I assure you that the very thought of it is in the way to make me ill. I can stand many mental pains, but not that of straining myself to do what is quite above me.

I entreat you then not to think it any want of reverence towards dear Mother Margaret, or want of love towards her children, or disrespect towards your Lordship, or insensibility to the high honour done me, if I ask you most earnestly not to put on me a burden which my shoulders will not carry. Please, recollect too that I am not so young as I was — and am kept in health, by being kept in tranquillity

Your affte & obt Servt in Xt   John H Newman of the Oratory

The Rt Revd The Bp of Birmingham

TUESDAY 28 APRIL 1868   Copeland came for some hours.   Henry went to London with Miss Farrant

TO CATHERINE BOWDEN

The Oratory. Bm April 29. 1868

My dear Child

I rejoice at the news you tell me of yourself — and thank God for His great mercies to you — and earnestly pray that the good resolve which He has put into your heart may have its full accomplishment.[1]

It is a great trial that you should not have seen Mother Margaret — you have been so near seeing her, which makes it all the greater — but her image will be imprinted on the very walls of her convent, when she is gone and she will be the more present because she is absent. You could not have sought admission in any holier community, or one which has upon it greater promise or earnest of large service for the glory of God.

[1] Catherine, the third daughter of Henry Bowden, told Newman of her intention to enter Mother Margaret Hallahan's convent at Stone. This she did on 15 Dec. 1868, and died there in 1940. See letter of 25 Nov. 1868 to her.

Mother Margaret is still alive — in great suffering. I will not forget you — and with love to all of you I am

Ever Yrs affectly John H Newman

TO W. J. COPELAND

May 1/68

My dear C

We have no criticisms to make on your Preface — but, as far as we go, many thanks.

Is it worth while to let Rogers see it? he has an enstatic mind[1]

Ever Yrs affly J H N

SATURDAY 2 MAY 1868   Blake left   fine weather

TO MOTHER MARY IMELDA POOLE [?]

May 5/68

I have said 10 Masses for dear Mother Margaret, during the last 14 days

J H N

TO LADY CHATTERTON

The Oratory Bm May 6. 1868

My dear Lady Chatterton

I will gladly look at your MS, as you wish me — though I fear my perusal cannot be of any great service to it.

With my best regards to Mr Dering and your Niece

I am, Most truly Yours John H Newman

THURSDAY 7 MAY 1868   Mr Kennard came into the House

TO W. J. COPELAND

The Oratory May 7/68

My dear C

I have nothing to say to the Preface, except that it reads very well (if it is modest to say so).

[1] 'Keenly critical.'

I like your addition, and prefer 'would, one may be sure, desire to see altered or omitted,' to 'desire to alter or omit.'[1]

I direct this as you wish me, but send proofs by this post to Farnham.

Ever Yrs affly J H N

P.S. Of course there will be a table of contents for each volume in the beginning.

SATURDAY 9 MAY 1868   The Bishop called   E.Froude came

TO WILLIAM GOWAN TODD

The Oratory May 9/68

My dear Dr Todd

I would most willingly and gladly preach for you, if I did so for any one — but I have not preached in London since the year 1848, nor (I may say) out of my own Church from that time, except two or three times. It is not only out of keeping with our Rule to do so, but I have not strength for it, and not many weeks ever pass without my having to do the ungracious thing which I am doing to you. I hope you will excuse me on these pleas.

I quite feel for your Orphanage, for we have a boy's Orphanage also, and have had it about the same time — and, if it is a difficult thing to collect means for supporting it in London, I assure you it is still more so in a place like this[2]

Most sincerely Yours John H Newman of the Oratory

TO JOHN HUNGERFORD POLLEN

The Oy Bm May 10/68

My dear Pollen

How very welcome to me that your wife should think of me at such a time! I said Mass for her at once. And I will say Mass for the little child when he goes to Church, if you let me know when that will be.[3]

I hope I shall see you soon — in spite of your engagements. The first Vespers of St Philip are on the 25th, to-morrow fortnight. We act a Latin Play — the Phormio again. Three years have passed since we did it — a long time in the life of boys. After High Mass next day, we hope to adjourn to Rednall, if the weather is propitious.

I have been anxious about my health for a year past, but don't wish it

---

[1] See note to letter of 22 March to Copeland.
[2] Todd was in charge of St Mary's Orphanage, Greenwich, the Committee of which met at 17 Portman Street, London.
[3] Stephen Hungerford Pollen was born on 2 May 1868.

mentioned — because it will be misunderstood. I am perfectly well, — better than I have been for a long while, but I cannot subdue tendencies which make me anxious.

Thanks for your catalogue[1]

Ever yours affly John H Newman

MONDAY 11 MAY 1868   Mother Margaret died.   beautiful weather
TUESDAY 12 MAY   E.Froude went

TO MOTHER MARY IMELDA POOLE[2]

The Oratory May 12. 1868

My dear Sister in Xt

Your long sorrow is over — and now you may rejoice. Ad vesperam fletus, et ad matutinum laetitia.[3] The worst is over to your dear Mother, and now she either is in heaven or will be shortly. How much she will now be able to do for you, which with all her fervour she could not do here!

I suppose we *all* of us said Mass for her holy soul this morning; (five, I know, did — two are away.) and, please God, on Thursday I will do so too. I am sure you are not able to grieve — I, who knew her so little, nevertheless can do nothing but rejoice and thank God

Ever Yours most sincerely in Xt   John H Newman

WEDNESDAY 13 MAY 1868   Mr Kennard went

TO JAMES SKINNER

May 13. 1868

My dear Sir

I have not gone out of my way to seek Mr Kennard.[4] I never heard his name till he came here, and stated the difficulties he felt in the Church of

---

[1] Pollen sent Newman part of his *First Proofs of the Universal Catalogue of Books on the Literature of Art,* London 1870. See letter of 2 March 1870.

[2] This letter has no name on it and may have been addressed to Augusta Theodosia Drane, who wrote at once on behalf of Imelda Poole, the news of Mother Margaret Hallahan's death.

[3] *Psalm* 29:6.

[4] Skinner, who was Perpetual Curate of Newland, Great Malvern, wrote on 10 May, 'It is six and twenty years since we last met; but I can never forget your kindness, when, under the auspices of Robert Isaac Wilberforce, you honoured me with your acquaintance at Oxford.
The respect and love (if you will pardon me) in which I then learned to hold you, have never been shaken, for a day, until now.'
Skinner then complained that Newman had persuaded his Deacon-curate, Charles Kennard, that he ought to become a Catholic, without allowing him a due period of reflection. Skinner then quoted from a letter Kennard had just written to a brother curate 'Dr Newman has been excessively kind to me. I have ever to thank him for being, under God, the instrument of finally opening my eyes.'

England. They were such that it was perfectly plain to me that he could not honestly perform his duties as an Anglican Clergyman, and, since he asked my advice, I plainly told him so. We are taught by moralists that it is one of the primary duties of humanity, when a stranger asks the way, to show it to him. I was obliged to give him an answer, and had I told him he could return to you and lawfully take part in the duties of an Anglican parish, or partake of the Anglican communion in his existing state of mind, I should have violated the rule both of charity and of veracity. *I* did not make his state of mind: I found it. *I* could not change it, even if I had been called to do so. *I* did not intrude my advice upon him; he asked it. If you had been in my place, you would have so far have [sic] done just what I have done.

And further he opened the question of his position towards Catholicism. Had I found it was a new question to him, or that he was ill prepared to entertain it, I should have advised him to wait. But he has already waited a year, and is well acquainted with our doctrines. You must be so kind here again as to put yourself into my position, as I certainly wish to put myself into yours. With the views you express in your letter about the 'bondage to the see of Rome,' I quite understand your earnestness to hinder him from joining the communion of that see — but, 'they must give, who take' — and if you believed as *I* do, that that communion was the One Fold of Christ, and then considered that Mr Kennard knew what he was doing, and had convictions on the subject which have never been obliterated, I think you would have done as I have done.

Mr Kennard proposed to stay here till today (Wednesday) and then to return to Newland to meet his Father. I saw reasons (personal to himself) both for and against his being received into the Church before he left this house. On the whole, had it depended on me, I should have advised his reception, but when he said that he had rather first return, I at once acquiesced.

I respect you so much that I will not do more than direct your notice to an insinuation in your letter which I think you will yourself condemn. It has never been my way to aim per fas atque nefas 'to make a proselyte to my communion.'[1] But when a man comes to me and asks me plain questions, how can I answer it to God, if I conceal from him what I believe God has taught me?

Thanking you for the friendly things you say of me

I am, Very truly Yours John H Newman

THURSDAY 14 MAY 1868   Serj. Bellasis came.

[1] This was a phrase used by Skinner in his letter, who replied apologetically on 20 May and said his meaning had been misunderstood.

TO EDWARD HENEAGE DERING

The Oratory May 14. 1868

My dear Mr Dering

Thank you for the honour you propose to do me — which I gladly accept.[1]
Lady Chatterton's MS has come safely
With my best regards to her and to Mrs Ferrers

I am, Most truly Yours John H Newman

TO GERARD MANLEY HOPKINS

The Oratory Bm May 14. 1868

My dear Hopkins

I am both surprised and glad at your news.[2] If all is well, I wish [to] say a Mass for your perseverance. I think it is the very thing for you. You are quite out, in thinking that when I offered you a 'home' here, I dreamed of your having a vocation for us. This I clearly saw you had *not*, from the moment you came to us. Don't call 'the Jesuit discipline hard', it will bring you to heaven. The Benedictines would not have suited you.

We all congratulate you

Ever Yrs affly John H Newman

FRIDAY 15 MAY 1868 Bellasis went. Went to Rednall and back with Ambrose in his basket
SATURDAY 16 MAY Mr Kennard passed through Bm[Birmingham]

TO THE EARL OF DENBIGH

The Oratory May 16. 1868

My dear Lord Denbigh

It is most unfortunate that I was away when you called on Friday with M. de Charette and M. d'Azy. I had kept in the way the day before, since you said you were to be in Birmingham on *Thursday* — and on Friday I had business a few miles out, and was absent from 1 till 6. It was very kind in you to bring such distinguished persons — and I hope you will do me the

[1] Dering wished to dedicate to Newman the novel he was about to publish, *Florence Danby*, London 1868. It was 'dedicated by permission to the Very Rev. Dr. Newman.'
[2] Hopkins had decided to become a Jesuit. On 5 May 1868 Hopkins wrote in his Journal, 'Resolved to be a religious.' On 7 May he wrote, 'Home, after having decided to be a priest and religious but still doubtful between St. Benedict and St. Ignatius.' *The Journals and Papers of Gerard Manley Hopkins*, edited by Humphry House, second edition, London 1959, p. 165.

additional kindness, if you have an opportunity, of expressing my regret to them.[1]

Most sincerely Yours in Xt   John H. Newman of the Oratory

The Earl of Denbigh.

TO LADY CHATTERTON

The Oratory Birmingham May 17. 1868

My dear Lady Chatterton

I have read your pages with great interest.[2] What you say in the course of them about your own history has especial interest — and the collection of passages you bring together from infidel writers is appalling. Have you seen, (I suppose you have,) the Bishop of Orlean's exposure of French infidelity?[3]

I had not heard of the 'Pilgrim and the Shrine.'[4] The question is, what is best to do with such publications. To notice them is an advertisement of them. A work which goes so far in blasphemy as it, defeats its purpose — and frightens most readers, rather than persuades them — still certainly there are those whom it will unsettle, and those whom it will settle in utter atheism.

However, it is not such writers that will do Christians most harm; but hard-headed logicians, not popular in their subject, who argue things out in their own way, beginning with the beginning, especially if they address themselves to the young and mentally unformed. An evil time is before us. Principles are being adopted as starting points, which contradict what we know to be axioms. It follows that the only controversy which is likely to do good, is *philosophical*.

I propose to return your MS by tomorrow's post — as there is some difficulty in doing so on Sunday

With my best remembrances to Mr Dering and your niece

I am, Most sincerely Yours John H Newman of the Oratory

Georgiana Lady Chatterton

[1] Athanase Charette de la Contrie (1832–1911), was a colonel in the papal zouaves, who distinguished himself at the battles of Castel Fidardo and Mentana. M. d'Azy was probably a companion in arms.

[2] This was perhaps the manuscript of Lady Chatterton's *A Plea for Happiness and Hope*, a pamphlet privately printed at this time.

[3] Félix Dupanloup, *Lettre pastorale sur les malheurs et les signes du temps; l'athéisme et le péril social*, issued in 1866.

[4] *The Pilgrim and the Shrine, or Passages from the Life and Correspondence of Herbert Ainslie, B.A. Cantab.*, three volumes, London 1867, an anonymous but largely autobiographical novel by Edward Maitland.

The Oratory Bm May 17. 1868

My dear Lord

Our Latin Play is tomorrow week, the 25th.

Next day we have High Mass, and, if the weather admits, have an excursion to Rednall.

I have not liked to write to you before, thinking that, in your great sorrow, I might be intruding on you.

We should of course be much gratified by your presence at all, or any, of these separate celebrations.

If you came to Rednall, I would ask the Vicar General and Canon Estcourt to attend you. Or any how, will you let me ask them through you?[1]

Yr obt & affte Servt in Xt   John H Newman

MONDAY 18 MAY 1868   Mr Venables came to paint me for Lord Denbigh [2]

TO SIR JUSTIN SHEIL

The Oratory Bm May 18. 1868

My dear Sir Justin

The suggestion you made in your last letter about the boys going to Rednall on Sunday had already struck me; and we will try it. But I am not sanguine about its success. Putting aside the question of expense (as to which I thank you most heartily for your offer, but I doubt if it would be universally approved) I doubt whether it would be popular, after the first and second time, with the boys themselves — or with the masters, who like a quiet day at home. And then again, even though the little peasants in the street of Rednall are not encouraged to play at marbles by what they see going on in our field, I am not sure that the parson will not be down upon us, as parsons and others have been down upon us *here*, whenever the boys used their voices a little too loudly on the Sunday —[3] and as the law was actually attempted against us, I forget with what success, at St Wilfrid's near Alton Towers, many years ago.

However, I assure you I heartily wish success to the experiment and, for myself, for years I have had a larger plan, viz of building a Summer School house at Rednall, where the boys could be from May to October — say four months, taking out the Holy Days; but we have already thrown such large sums of money into the school, that we shrink back from spending more.

It gave me the greatest pleasure to find, that on the whole you are so well satisfied with us as to contemplate sending us other of your boys.

[1] Ullathorne's Vicar General was Michael O'Sullivan.
[2] This portrait is now in the possession of Mrs Humphrey Watts of Oxford.
[3] See letter of 8 June 1862 to F. H. Mylius.

I hope you are coming down for this day week, as Fr St John wishes to have some conversation with you about your two sons. That indeed he could have elsewhere, but *you should see Edward act before he leaves us*[1]

Most sincerely Yours John H Newman

Sir Justin Shiel K C B

P.S.   Since writing the above, we have received your letter. I am very glad to read its contents.

TUESDAY 19 MAY 1868   Mr Venables went in evening
WEDNESDAY 20 MAY   first representation of Phormio
FRIDAY 22 MAY   second representation of Phormio   weather still good

TO ROBERT ORNSBY

The Oratory Bm ⌜May 22/68⌝

My dear Ornsby

I ought to have written to you before now, but have had nothing to tell you.

[John] Simeon has already left us, and I suppose his father gets him a coach for the army, while he remains *at home*. We have two boys going to Oxford, next Christmas, as it stands. Of course we cannot *prepare* them for Oxford. I suppose you would not like to do so. Perhaps their entrance examination will be in October. At present their friends prefer that they should remain with us up to the time, in spite of our not preparing them, rather than go to a chance Tutor. It would be more comfortable to us to part with them now — but we cannot turn them off, both from gratitude to our friends and from love of *them*.

⌜I thought the University Charter would come to nothing — and this, I believe, is the case.[2] Stewart wanted me to write in behalf of it — but timeo Danaos etc.[3] What good could come from Disraeli? and the Irish Bishops from the first, tho' they were caught by his proposal, were determined to have it altered in a way which Disraeli could not allow. Robertson wrote to me, if I understood him, actually *against* the disestablishment of the Anglo-Irish Church.

It is a matter of simple justice to destroy what is a crying injustice and a great scandal. But whether it is a great gain to the Catholic cause is not so certain.⌝

Ever Yrs affly in Xt   John H Newman

---

[1] Edward Sheil was acting the part of Phormio.
[2] 'It became obvious to the press and the public that the negotiations [between the Bishops and the Government] were at an end when the official correspondence was published in the third week of May.' E. R. Norman, *The Catholic Church and Ireland in the Age of Rebellion*, p. 276, who adds 'The Ministers had never really been in earnest.'
[3] Letter of 15 March to Stewart.

The Oratory Bm May 22/68

My dear Canon Walker

I got Smith on the Pentateuch at once on your suggestion, and have been much interested in what I have read of it — but have not read enough to get into it as a whole.[1] Mr Beverley's work too has come, but with no supplemental chapter. Pray convey my acknowledgement to the *unknown* author.[2] It is a careful and severe examination of the theory of Darwin — and it shows, as is most certain he would be able to do, the various points which are to be made good before it can cohere. I do not fear the theory so much as he seems to do — and it seems to me that he is hard upon Darwin sometimes, which [sic] he might have interpreted him kindly. It does not seem to me to follow that creation is denied because the Creator, millions of years ago, gave laws to matter. He first created matter and then he created laws for it — laws which should *construct* it into its present wonderful beauty, and accurate adjustment and harmony of parts *gradually*. We do not deny or circumscribe the Creator, because we hold he has created the self acting originating human mind, which has almost a creative gift; much less then do we deny or circumscribe His power, if we hold that He gave matter such laws as by their blind instrumentality moulded and constructed through inumerable ages the world as we see it. If Mr Darwin in this or that point of his theory comes into collision with revealed truth, that is another matter — but I do not see that the *principle* of development, or what I have called construction, does. As to the Divine *Design*, is it not an instance of incomprehensibly and infinitely marvellous Wisdom and Design to have given certain laws to matter millions of ages ago, which have surely and precisely worked out, in the long course of those ages, those effects which He from the first proposed. Mr Darwin's theory *need* not then be atheistical, be it true or not; it may simply be suggesting a larger idea of Divine Prescience and Skill. Perhaps your friend has got a surer clue to guide him than I have, who have never studied the question, and I do not like to put my opinion against his; but at first sight I do not [see] that 'the *accidental* evolution of organic beings' is inconsistent with divine design — It is accidental to *us*, not to *God*

Most sincerely yours in Xt   John H Newman

[1] W. Smith, *The Book of Moses or the Pentateuch in its Authorship, Credibility, and Civilisation*, London 1868.
[2] *The Darwinian Theory of the Transmutation of Species examined by a Graduate of the University of Cambridge*, second edition, London 1868. Newman later received the 'Supplementary Chapter,' London 1868, which had a notice at the beginning, 'It has been suggested to the author that as the question at issue with Mr. Darwin is precisely the "Origin of Species," a direct investigation of that very point, namely, how species had its commencement, is needed to settle the question. . . .' Newman appears only to have read the preface to the book, and also this 'Supplementary Chapter.' The rest of his copy of the book is uncut. The author was Robert Mackenzie Beverley, now aged about 70, who, as a young man, had published attacks on what he called the corrupt state of the Church of England. He lived at Scarborough.

P.S. Why is not the principle of generation atheistic, if that of development is? Did we not know the *fact* that species and races are drawn out in succession from one couple, we might say that it was a theory inconsistent with the doctrine of creation. And à fortiori, it might be urged, 'here the *accidental* meeting and marriage of two persons, or the sinful intercourse, will oblige the Almighty to create a soul at any moment.' Therefore (not only not the body, but) the soul is *not* created, but is the accidental consequence of the human will, etc etc.

TO E. B. PUSEY

The Oratory Bm May 24. 1868

My dear Pusey

Thank you for your kind remembrance about St Athanasius.[1] I fear I cannot do any thing to the second part, and I do not recollect any serious misstatements. There were two or three wrong words in the first Part. I suppose I shall never do much, or any thing, more in that line of writing, much as I should like to do so.

I am sorry at your and the Bishop of B's [Brechin] discouragement — but any one in England would have confidently said beforehand how he would be received at Rome.[2] The central authority cannot *profess* to relax. E.g. thirty years ago the National System of Education was introduced into Ireland — Rome only *kept silence* — it is the utmost that could be expected of it. Again, take Maynooth and the Maynooth Oath — if Rome had been obliged to speak, it could only have disapproved — therefore it did not speak.[3] All such local matters it leaves to the local Bishops — it never acts without the local bishops. They ever have the formal initiative. It puts a veto on their proceedings, or does not, — but it does not originate — and, if it is *obliged* to speak, it speaks according to the strictest rule of ecclesiastical principle and tradition. In the late question about Oxford the Pope personally *wished* going to Oxford to be prohibited — and he *showed* his wish — but he was quite nervous about the result of the English Episcopal meetings, and St John who was at Rome last Easter year, while the decisive meeting was taking place, was distinctly told (I think by Cardinal di Lucca) that the Pope never acted without the local

[1] Pusey wrote on 11 May that the second volume of Newman's *Select Treatises of S. Athanasius in controversy with the Arians* in 'The Library of the Fathers' was out of print, and asked for any alterations he might wish made in it.

[2] Pusey wrote, 'I have taken up (secret) the old subject of making propositions on controverted subjects, with a view to ascertaining, whether a Congregation at Rome would pronounce an opinion.' He then referred to the visit there of Bishop Forbes of Brechin, 'Bishop Forbes has come back disappointed. They seem to put as the alternative, "If you believe in the Pope, you want no explanations, you have only to submit, if you do not believe in the Pope, explanations are of no use" However we can but try [.] Bossuet did not cut things off in this sharp way [.] But Bishop F. purposely did not consult any of the Cardinals etc, being so discouraged as for any hope, under the present Pope.'

[3] This oath, approved by a number of bishops at Maynooth in 1821, denied the indirect power of the Pope and stated that his infallibility was not an article of faith.

Hierarchy — then, *when* the Bishops had *decided*, the Pope came out with a tremendously strong Rescript.

Therefore I think it was a mistake if the Bishop of B. applied to the highest authorities at Rome — as much so, as it has been in certain Anglican Priests, or laymen addressing our English Bishops. The proper organs for negociation are local Bishops with local Bishops.

At the same time, I do not expect any thing would have come of that either, just now. The local Bishops are the proper channels of communication between the English people, or a portion of them, and Rome. It is their duty to soften difficulties not to increase them. I cannot deny that Archbishop Manning has done every thing in his power to increase them, not to soften them.

As far as I know the history of former attempts at reconciliation, may bear out what I have said. It must be recollected that *then* religion was national and political, to an extent in which it is not now. Bossuet represented, not only a local hierarchy, but a political power — Leibnitz in like manner was, I think, a sort of agent for Protestant governments. There were *then* constituted organs of reconciliation, which do not exist now. Were there any chance now of *bodies* being reconciled to Rome, Rome would take the extraordinary step of regarding the *case* of bodies — but it will not make concession to *individuals*. Concession and compromises are in their nature an abandonment of some advantage, of some *better* way. If Rome thinks that the celibacy of the clergy is the *better* way, it will not compromise with some one Monophysite Priest of the East who says 'I will sign Pope Pius's creed and conform, on condition you recognise my married life.' But it *would* compromise perhaps with a Patriarch, Metropolitans, Bishops with their flocks, who would renounce their error on condition of keeping their rites and usages. The Bishop of Brechin (I speak under correction) represented nothing tangible. He did now show a list of Anglican Bishops, 'Lordi,' Members of Parliament, country gentlemen, farmers and labourers, who, he could pledge himself, would one and all sign the Creed of Pope Pius and hold the latter decisions of Rome including the Immaculate Conception, on condition that they might hold that an Ecumenical Council was the one and only seat of Infallibility, till an Ecumenical Council determined otherwise — But, till some great end is answered, why should we suspend our ordinary rules?

I know this is a discouraging view to take, but I do think it is the true one. I don't deny, as you say, that the Pope is just now approachable only through a few men, such as Mgr Talbot (who has done a great deal of harm,) — but any other Pope, it seems to me, would act mainly in the same way as regards the Church of England. At Rome they will ever say, 'Do not come with your stipulations, but submit,' — *unless* some great expediency makes it a duty to relax the rule, just as St Athanasius etc did not insist on the homoüsion, though it had been made the symbol of orthodoxy at Nicæa.

I have answered incidentally your question about Bishop Forbes's learned and most interesting work.[1] It will excite very little feeling among English Catholics, except one of opposition. What *can* be done, when Ward has become proprietor of the Dublin Review, and Manning is the official counsellor of the authorities at Rome? These two facts are such remarkable *accidents*, that they seem to be providential. I do not see what can be done at present.

Lest I should be mistaken, I must add that I do think communion with Rome is *necessary* for a person being in the Visible Church. Indeed, did I not think so, I never should have left the Anglican Church[2]

Ever Yrs affectly John H Newman

The Revd E B Pusey D D

MONDAY 25 MAY 1868   third representation of Phormio
TUESDAY 26 MAY   High Mass — O'Sullivan singing it. Rednall party (more parents and old boys than ever before)   I remained at Rednall with Ambrose one night
WEDNESDAY 27 MAY   returned with Ambrose in his basket

TO EMILY BOWLES

The Oratory May 28/68

My dear Child

Some one has just told me you are very unwell. This is much more than what you said. I had hoped you would have been here before now. I said Mass for you this morning

Ever Yrs affly John H Newman

TO CHARLES H. KENNARD

May 28/68

To Revd C Kennard

I grieve much to hear of your distress.[3] We do not forget you and shall be very glad to see you, as you propose, on Saturday[4]

J H N

[1] *An Explanation of the 39 Articles.* Cf. letter of 6 April to Forbes. Pusey wrote, 'Do you think that Bishop Forbes' second volume on the Articles is likely to be kindly received among you?'

[2] Pusey replied on 13 Aug. about reunion, 'True that there are not political helps as formerly but there is a common foe, infidelity, and I trust a common faith. Separate we fight at a disadvantage.' See also letter of 16 Aug. to Pusey.

[3] Kennard wrote in an undated letter, 'I seem to be completely deserted by God. I am surrounded by those whom I have reason to love best in the world, and they tell me, that the Devil has got hold of me and though my intention perhaps is pure, yet that I am under a strong delusion – and then to add to my unhappiness my power of mental prayer is taken away, I have no desire for religious exercises, and Meditation seems an impossibiliy. . . .'

[4] Kennard came to the Oratory on 30 May, left on 2 June, returned on 27 June and was recived into the Catholic Church by Newman on 9 July.

TO JOHN P. KENNARD

May 28/68

To Mr Kennard (the Father)

Your Son writes to me in extreme distress. Is it not for the good of his soul that he should be received into Catholic communion? If you allowed him to come here, I would engage that he should not be received into our communion for a month — and no obstacle should be put in his way to his leaving us at any moment, just as when he was here before. I propose this, because I think he would be calmer here than any where else. At the same time of course I should *anticipate* that at the end of the month he would make up his mind to be received. I know he wishes to come, at least to talk to us.[1]

J H N

TO JAMES SKINNER

May 28/68

To Mr Skinner

. . . Mr Kennard, I understand, has waited a year with strong convictions in his mind that the Anglican communion is not part of the Catholic Church. This being the case, no one had a right to exact a promise from him to wait longer, his convictions continuing. It was all one with making him promise to commit a sin . . .

J H N

FRIDAY 29 MAY 1868   monthly examination of boys   I busy in the Sacristy

SATURDAY 30 MAY   monthly examination of boys   Mr Kennard came

SUNDAY 31 MAY   Whit Sunday   There have been now 4 months of beautiful weather. Hardly any east wind this year.

TO CATHERINE ANNE BATHURST

The Oratory   May 31/68

My dear Child

Thanks for your congratulations. We had beautiful weather — a number of friends from London — a Latin Play well acted — and a very successful dejeuner at Rednall. Every one pleased.

[1] Owing to being absent from home John Kennard only received Newman's letter on 4 June. He replied next day 'I am conscientiously obliged to decline the request which you make.' He had however already released his son from a promise to wait for three months. His son wrote to Newman that he felt it would be 'very dangerous' to remain without receiving Holy Communion for another two months as his father wished.

I wished you could have been with us. At present our anxiety is the Orphanage. It has grown to 50 boys — but it does not pay its expenses; and requires much more than it has in the way of establishment to make it really efficient. We want a master, and can't afford one. Perhaps Austin has told you that it is changing its site for a 99 years one.

I grieve indeed to hear what you tell me of yourself — but it is all a riddle what you say. I have never heard any thing from any one about you but from yourself, and you have told me nothing. I don't know whether you are still in connexion with the Dominicans, or with whom. I have not a dream who they are who have been unkind to you; nor what you mean when you say you cannot come to England — whether the vow forbids you or want of means.[1]

Thank you for thinking of us and talking of us — I wish you could see us by some new kind of photograph or electric wire

Ever Yrs affly John H Newman

TO OSCAR BROWNING

The Oratory Bm   May 31/68

Dear Mr Browning,

You must, I fear, think my silence for so long, after the receipt of your letter, very rude — but during the last week we have been keeping our yearly festival and its accompanying festivities — and they first took me up entirely, and then knocked me up — so that my letters are in arrears — and I have neglected yours in the number.[2]

I have been for years hunting for the sort of book you speak of — a manual explanatory of scholastic terms — The nearest approach to what I wished to find is a little Belgium [sic] book with this title — 'Lexicon quo Veterum Philosophorum et Theologorum Locutiones explicantur — Tornaci (Tournay) Casterman. 1849.'

But nothing, I suppose, serves so well for Dante as Ozanam's work — which I doubt not you know — though I do not. I am somewhat perplexed you do not allude to it — for, if it is insufficient for your purpose, I doubt whether you will find what you want.[3]

Excuse this very meagre answer to you and believe me,

Most truly Yours, John H Newman

The Revd O. Browning

---

[1] Catherine Bathurst was still at Bruges, occupied in good works.

[2] Oscar Browning wrote on 20 May that he realised a knowledge of the Schoolmen was 'almost necessary' for understanding Dante, and wanted a dictionary of their technical terms.

[3] A. F. Ozanam *Dante et la Philosophie Catholique au treizième siècle*, Paris 1840, second and third editions 1845 and 1855.

TO SISTER MARY GABRIEL DU BOULAY

The Oratory   Bm May 31. 1868

My dear Child

What can I say to console you better than what you must be saying to yourself, that your long sorrow is over, and that now after her intense sufferings, your dear Mother is at rest, or rather in Heaven.

If ever there were persons who had cause to rejoice and whose joy is but intermeddled with, not increased by the words of a third person you are they.

What can you all desire more than that your Communties should receive so special a Consecration as is granted to you in the agony and triumph of such a Mother?

It is a thought to raise and encourage you while you live, and is the augury of many holy and happy deaths

Pray for an old man and believe me Ever yrs affectly in Xt
John H Newman of the Oratory

TO THE EARL OF GAINSBOROUGH

The Oratory, Birmm May 31. 1868

My dear Lord Gainsborough,

I feel very much the kindness of your sending me the memorial of one whom no one could see ever so little without admiring and remembering.[1]

How great the blow has been to yourself, none can know but you and He who sent it.

He knows well what he does — and that he may send you also all needful strength under it

is the earnest prayer of yours most sincerely in Xt
John H. Newman of the Oratory

TUESDAY 2 JUNE 1868   Mr Kennard went.   I went with Ambrose to Rednall in his basket

WEDNESDAY 3 JUNE   came back with A.

TO RICHARD CHENEVIX TRENCH, ARCHBISHOP OF DUBLIN

The Oratory   Bm June 3. 1868

My dear Lord

I have just received your beautiful volume, with your autograph at the beginning of it.[2]

[1] Lord Gainsborough's wife died on 22 Oct. 1867.
[2] *A Household Book of English Poetry* selected and arranged by Richard Chenevix Trench, London 1868.

Let me thank you sincerely for it, and for your giving me a place in such high company

I am, My dear Lord, Very truly Yours John H Newman

THURSDAY 4 JUNE 1868   went with Ambrose to Rednall
FRIDAY 5 JUNE   Ambrose returned without me
SATURDAY 6 JUNE   walked back early
MONDAY 8 JUNE   E Coleridge and his wife called

TO R. W. CHURCH

The Oratory Brm June 8. 1868

My dear Church

Will you, that is, can you, tell me anything of your movements this late spring and early summer, that I may be on the look out for a time, when I might find you and Mrs Church at home, if I fell on you from the skies, that is, very suddenly? not that I would be so rude as not to let you know beforehand.

What a wonderful course of fine weather! we here have had four months of it already. We had hardly any winter; and I dread a wet July and August.

Edward Coleridge of Eton was good enough to call on me to-day with his wife. I have not seen him for, I suppose, 25 years — but I have known him for 50. He reminded me that I used to play the Tenor at Dr Lee's concert at Trinity, when I was an undergraduate which I had forgotten —[1] and that he had caught me in later years at Oriel giving Charles Marriott a lesson on the violin.

Ever yours affectionately, John H. Newman.

TO MARIE ALICE JONES

June 8/68

My dear Mrs Jones

I thank you very much etc . . . It is the record of a life in which every thing has been at cross purposes etc . . . There is a tragic character in Mr

Trench wrote on 13 April, 'When I remember a day very long ago, which Tom Acland enabled me to spend at Oxford I do not like to write *altogether* as a stranger. [See *Moz.* II, p. 128.

My purpose in writing is to ask whether you would do me the very great favour to allow me to include two short poems of yours in an English Anthology I am making . . .'

The poems included were 'James and John,' *Vv.*, p. 177, at p. 368, and 'A Thanksgiving,' *Vv.*, p. 45, at p. 383.

See also *Richard Chenevix Trench, Archbishop, Letters and Memorials*, edited by the Author of 'Charles Lowder' [Miss M. Trench], London 1888, II, p. 57.

[1] Thomas Lee, President of Trinity College, Oxford, 1808–24.

Jones's history so noble, yet the prey of feelings etc. . . . 'An enemy hath done this.'[1]

I understood you to ask whether your narrative should be made public. It is very well written. You have written it under obedience. *However*, before I could answer in the affirmative, I ought to see clearly some *object* to be gained by your doing so. The individuality of your case, which makes the narrative so real, in the same degree withdraws it from the number of those histories which serve as a lesson to others.

J H N

TO COVENTRY PATMORE

The Oratory   Bm   June 8/68

My dear Sir

Pardon me for giving you the trouble of reading another letter from me. It has struck me that, in the one which you have just answered, I so worded what I said, as to seem to call Mr Gladstone an experimentalist or empiric in politics. I had no thought of him in what I said — and have far too much respect for him, to like the appearance of having so spoken of him, I was thinking of the two great *parties*, Whigs and Conservatives since 1859, bidding against each other for popularity, and binding themselves with pledges which they would evade if they could.[2]

As you say in your letter, I grieve at the forbidding aspect which Catholics are at this time assuming in England

Very truly Yours John H Newman

TO THOMAS SHORT

The Oratory Birmingham Trinity Monday 1868

My dear Short,

It is fifty years today, since I was elected scholar of Trinity — and, as you had so much to do with the election, I consider you my first bene-

---

[1] Mrs. Jones, who was staying with A. L. Delerue, the priest at Spetchley, had visited Newman and left her manuscript with him, as she wrote on 4 June, 'whom I naturally wished to make acquainted with certain facts which I always believed to have resulted from his prayers, and which were so unhappily changed from their blessed promise by a severely used authority.'

[2] In his comment on this letter in Basil Champneys *Memoirs and Correspondence of Coventry Patmore*, London 1900, II, p. 80, Patmore thought it referred to a conversation: 'I never saw Dr. Newman but once, when I had a tête-a-tête conversation with him for about an hour. I was struck chiefly by his shyness and his extreme care to be exactly truthful in expression. Weeks after this conversation I received a letter from him written expressly to qualify, in some slight degree, some expression he had used about Mr. Gladstone.'

factor in Oxford. In memory of it, I have been saying Mass for you this morning.[1]

I should not have ventured to write to tell you of this — but, happening to mention it to William Neville, he said — 'Do write and tell him so — for *I* said Mass for him yesterday, being Trinity Sunday.'

This letter will at least show the love we bear to you and old Trinity, amid all changes. Take it as such,

and believe me to be, Affectionately Yours John H Newman[2]

The Revd Thos Short.

P.S. I never forget how kindly Wilson coached me some time before I went into the Schools for my examination.[3]

TUESDAY 9 JUNE 1868   went to Rednall with Ambrose in his basket

TO MRS JOHN MOZLEY

The Oratory Bm June 9. 1868

My dear Jemima

My doctor is just gone — I waited, before writing to you, till I saw him. He had not been for a month. Till then he had seen me every week, or (at least) fortnight, since last summer. He took a longer interval now, because he thought me better. Now after a month, he tells me I have no bad symptom. For this I should be thankful, and am — what keeps me anxious is that I am obliged to keep on with the acids — though I am to try a less quantity. I expect any one else would have had his inside eaten out by the quantity I have taken, but it seems to do me nothing but good. I was told of a person who took only once one of my doses, and it seriously disordered him. And I have to be very particular in what I drink at meals, and in part in what I eat. So that I am at present unfit for any place but home.

I have a promise of several years standing with Church to visit him in Somersetshire — and I don't like putting it off, considering the distance. If I effect it, I doubt whether I can go again from home this year. I bear in mind your kind wish — but, at my age, it is a great effort to leave home.

This has been an annus mirabilis as regards weather, at least here. From

---

[1] Short was a tutor at Trinity College, 1816–56, and a Fellow of his College from 1808 until his death in 1879. Newman met him on 26 Feb. 1878, when he visited Trinity, after he had become the first honorary Fellow of his College.

[2] Short replied on 10 June from Totnes, 'Many thanks for your kind and devout remembrance of me. I hope I shall bear it in mind for the remainder of my life. Will you give a similar message from me to W. Neville, to whose suggestion you tell me I owe your letter . . . I shall not fail to tell others of the kindly feelings which you both cherish towards my dear old College.'

[3] This was in 1820. John Wilson, a Fellow of Trinity College from 1816, became President in 1850 and retired in Dec. 1866.

the beginning of February, it has been beautiful — rain at nights, not in the day; no East wind; a clear lovely sky. This is the fifth month of it. I have had no cold through the winter — nor indeed (as I think) in the winter before it. I have not had a bad cold for at least 4 years. The acids, I think, are the cause of the improvement.

You do not say how you are. I hope John R. M. has got some place or other. Is Harry *settled* at Eton?[1]

Ever Yrs affly John H Newman

WEDNESDAY 10 JUNE 1868   back [from Rednal]
THURSDAY 11 JUNE   sang Mass   C.C. [Corpus Christi]   still bright sunny weather
SATURDAY 13 JUNE   Neve called.   R.Ward in the House
SUNDAY 14 JUNE   glass steadily at 70° in my room
TUESDAY 16 JUNE   Ambrose and I went to Littlemore and back (*without going thro' Oxford — going to Abingdon — and returning by Littlemore rail*)   Outhwaite passed through.

TO W. J. COPELAND

The Oratory Birmingham June 17. 1868

My dear Copeland

Will you tell some one about you to write me one line to say how you are — I am quite frightened by what I have heard of you[2]

Ever Yrs affectly John H Newman

TO MRS CRAWLEY

The Oratory Bm June 17, 1868

My dear Mrs Crawley,

I trust you will take kindly my sending you a Volume of Verses which I have lately published — and of which I beg your acceptance, though I know there are portions of it which you would rather see away. I do so, as the only way I have of expressing the great pleasure it gave me to see you and Mr Crawley — and my gratitude for your kindness.

It is a great pleasure to me to have seen Littlemore once again — and to see so many persons whom I have not seen for so long — and to see how beautiful the place looks. It will be a pleasant picture in my memory.[3]

[1] John Rickards Mozley was Professor of Pure Mathematics at Owens College, Manchester, 1865–85. In 1868 he married Edith Merivale, daughter of Bonamy Price. Henry Williams Mozley was an Eton master, 1865–97.
[2] Copeland replied next day that he had been suffering from rheumatic fever.
[3] See also letters of 18 June to Wilberforce and 25 June to Copeland.

Might I ask you to be so good as to give the inclosed photograph from me to Martha King, when you can do so conveniently.

With kindest remembrances to Mr Crawley, I am, most sincerely yours

John H Newman

Mrs Crawley

TO G. W. HUNTINGFORD

The Oratory Birmingham June 17. 1868

My dear Mr Huntingford,

I was so unready yesterday that I fear I did not acknowledge properly Mrs Huntingford's kindness in asking me to luncheon.

By way of setting myself right, will you ask her to accept from me a small volume which I send by this post.[1]

Thanking you for your various civilities, which were one chief feature in the happy hours I passed yesterday at Littlemore

I am, My dear Mr Huntingford Very truly Yours
John Henry Newman

The Revd G W Huntingford

THURSDAY 18 JUNE 1868   drought   rain wanted

TO HENRY WILBERFORCE

The Oratory Bm ⌐June 18/68⌐

My dear Henry

Thank you for your affectionate letter and invitation — but I can't accept it. It is not much more than a week since I refused one from my sister. I have real duties here which make it difficult to get away; I am on a strict regime, which I don't like to omit for a day — and I have an old man's reluctance to move. I have promised R W Church a visit for several years, and it must be my first.

I am gradually knocking off some purposes of the kind. ⌐When your letter came I was at Littlemore! I had always hoped to see it once before I died. Ambrose and I went by the 7 a m train to Abingdon, then across to Littlemore — then direct from *Littlemore* by rail to Birmingham where we arrived by 7 — just 12 hours.⌐ The man of Ross has a name for planting —[2] at least I have

---

[1] The autograph of this letter is pasted into a copy of *Vv.*, in which is written 'with best respects of the author. June 17. 1868'. Huntingford was the Vicar of Littlemore.

[2] John Kyrle, celebrated in Alexander Pope's *Moral Essays*, Epistle III, about the middle, 'who hung with woods yon mountain's sultry brow?' etc.

begun something in that way at Littlemore,[1] ⌜and Crawley has done as much again, and much more tastefully. Littlemore is now *green*. Crawley's cottage and garden (upon my 10 acres which I sold him) are beautiful. The church too is now what they call a *gem*. And the parsonage is very pretty. I saw various of my people, now getting on in life. It was 40 years at the beginning of this year, since I became Vicar. Alas, their memory of me was in some cases stronger than my memory of them. They have a great affection for my Mother and Sisters — tho' it is 32 years since they went away.⌝ There is a large lunatic asylum — separated, however, from the village by the rail road — so it is no annoyance, rather it adds green to the place — nor is the rail road an annoyance, for it is in a cutting. ⌜It is 22 years since I was there. I left February 22. 1846. I do not expect ever to see it again — nor do I wish it.⌝

I am so glad to find you are so pleasantly placed. It would give me great pleasure to see your wife and daughters — some one said Harry [Wilberforce] is with you — is he not at Ushaw? And say every thing most kind to your Sister in law, whom I should greatly like to see.[2]

Ever Yrs affly J H N

TO ROBERT BEVERLEY TILLOTSON

The Oratory June 19. 1868

My dear Tillotson

I heard yesterday that some Birmingham man had just written word that you were seriously ill, or worse. Your friends last autumn gave us a very different account.

In consequence I have been saying Mass for your welfare in soul and body this morning, and I pray God to forgive you all your sins and to do away with all their consequences, and to fill you with His heavenly Grace.

This requires no answer[3]

Yours affectly in Xt   John H Newman

---

[1] [[I had just begun planting at Littlemore, and Crawley]]

[2] i.e. Mary, the wife of William Wilberforce. Henry Wilberforce had retired to Woodchester, near Stroud.

[3] Tillotson replied on 7 July by means of Fr Hewit as amanuensis, 'I trust you will be assured of my warm and undying affection to yourself and all the fathers of the Oratory, and my gratitude for all the spiritual blessings and other favours I have received from you.'

TO HENRY WILBERFORCE

The Oratory Bm June 19. 1868

My dear H W

How long does your sister Mary stop with you? I was thinking whether I could not come some day *and return*, as I went to and fro to Littlemore.

Ever Yrs affly John H Newman

TO ASHLEY CARR GLYN

June 21/68

I will gladly accept with thanks your translation of Ozanam. As to what you say of yourself, I cannot believe you will be able to content yourself for ever with such shadows of religion as you speak of. It is my trust and prayer that some day, if I live, I shall hear from you again.[1]

TO PETER LE PAGE RENOUF

The Oratory Bm June 21. 1868

My dear Renouf,

I read your Pamphlet yesterday, and found it to have the completeness and force which I had expected in it.[2]

It is very powerful as an argument, and complete as a composition. I certainly did not know how strong a case could be made out against Pope Honorius. But with all its power, I do not find it seriously interferes with my own view of Papal Infallibility; and its completeness is in part due to your narrowing the compass of your thesis and is in part compromised by your devious attacks on writers who differ from you.

However, after all that can be said of you by opponents, I am glad you have published it.

1. I am glad you have had the boldness to publish on the subject, because I think it intolerable that one side of a question should be ostentatiously obtruded on us in the Dublin Review and elsewhere, as the one Catholic

[1] Glyn wrote on 19 June that he was suffering from 'a recoil from an attempt to embrace, what from want of a better word, I will call "Ultramontanism," and which the great majority of Catholics with whom I have come in contact seem to regard as alone legitimate.' He found himself drawn 'to the Coleridge theology and philosophy, and repelled by both the High and Low Church systems in the Established Church.' Glyn ended by asking if he might send Newman his translation of A. F. Ozanam, *History of Civilization in the Fifth Century*, two volumes, London 1868. He wrote in it 'Fr Newman — with the Translator's kind regards.' Glyn does not appear to have had any further contact with Newman. In 1871 he married Mary Louisa Duncombe and in 1875 he died.
[2] *The Condemnation of Pope Honorius*, London 1868.

Faith, and that unauthoritative writers should hold a pistol to our ear after the fashion of 'Your money or your life,' when there is another side with as real a right to be heard and to make converts, if it can, and with, in times past, as great a following of theologians; and because I consider this intolerable state of things is occasioning the loss of souls.[1] Though I myself consider the Pope's formal definitions of faith to be infallible, I rejoice to see a pamphlet which has the effect of reminding the world that his infallibility is not a dogma, but a theological opinion.

2. In one respect, however, you resemble the writer of the Dublin Articles, and it is the first of the points on which I shall criticize you; viz. you do not complete your theory. *He* is evidently afraid to complete *his*, lest, when carried out, it should appear, like Novatianism, to be constituting a Church within a Church, or, like the Evangelicals of this day, to be pronouncing that not all Catholic Priests 'preach the gospel.' Indeed, what else can he mean when he asserts or implies that large bodies of Catholics are in such sense heretics, as only to be saved by invincible ignorance? You on the other hand tell us that the Pope is not infallible, but there you leave us. Depend upon it, others will draw conclusions for you, if you will not draw your own. For Fr Ryder's statements this at least may be said, that they leave no question to be asked of him, and no difficulty which he has not at least treated.[2] This is what I mean above by your narrowing your thesis.

3. And I will mention another point, in which I think your argument is wanting, even on its own selected ground. Facts are disproved in two ways; by adverse experiments, and by adverse testimony. The supernatural facts, which the Church teaches, are for the most part only open to objections under the latter head, because they *are* supernatural. We cannot prove or disprove by experiment the contrast which faith holds to exist between the states of a soul before and after baptism. The obvious exception to this rule lies in the proof of the doctrine of infallibility. Thus you have in your particular subject a peculiarity, which, for the sake of clearness, you should, I think, have insisted on. The offhand answer which will be made to you is, that you do not take into account the development of doctrine. This objection is important; it touches the second of your two heads of argument, — for instance, your argument from St Cyprian's opposition to St Stephen; but it does not touch your first. No theory of doctrinal development can touch the fact, if it be a fact, that Pope Honorius formally taught heresy.

4. When I said you went out of your way to give opponents a handle against you, instead of strictly keeping to the point of your argument, I meant your pronouncing that 'the arguments used by the first apologists of Pope Honorius cannot have been sincerely believed by their authors:' p 7 — that Baronius 'invented an abjuration;' p 12 that he and Bellarmine used 'disrespectful language of an Ecumenical Council,' p 9 when they seem to have

---

[1] Cf. letter of this day to Glyn.
[2] Cf. letter of 1 Jan. 1868 to Russell.

been only using a reductio ad absurdum; and that Fr Perrone has 'asserted an untruth' under the mask of 'contemptible quibbling' p 24.

And now, if I am not tiring you, I will tell you why you do not touch, or very slightly touch, my own view of the subject; and I suppose what I hold is in fact what many others hold also.

1. I hold the Pope's Infallibility, not as a dogma, but as a theological opinion; that is, not as a certainty, but as a probability. You have brought out a grave difficulty in the way of the doctrine; that is, you have diminished its probability, but you have only diminished it. To my mind the balance of probabilities is still in favour of it. There are vast difficulties, taking facts as they are, in the way of denying it. In a question, which is any how surrounded with difficulties, it is the least of difficulties to maintain that, if we knew *all about* Honorius's case, something would be found to turn up to make it compatible with the doctrine. I recollect Dr Johnson's saying, 'There are unanswerable objections to a plenum, and unanswerable objections to a vacuum, yet one or the other must be true.'[1]

2. Again, any how the doctrine of Papal Infallibility must be fenced round and limited by *conditions*. The gift must be defined, and the circumstances of its exercise. Even Ward excepts 'obiter dicta;' and what are and what are not such, have to be determined. Pighius himself would not say that the Pope was infallible in his Table Talk or in the compliments he pays to the French Soldiery.[2] If we make his own intention the test, still we have to find out the intrinsic notes determining the fact of his intention. The Editor of the Raccolta decides that Leo X did *not* mean the Sacro-sanctae to be an Indulgence, *because* it gains for the reciter the forgiveness of his defects in saying office.[3] Mgr Sarra, in his book on Indulgences, which Fr St John has lately translated, asserts in like manner that, when the Pope in certain forms of Indulgence distinctly declares that he remits guilt, he really does not mean to do so, for such doctrine would be against the Catholic Faith.[4] This then is one large condition, which all Ultra-montanes acquiesce in and exercise, whether they will or no, viz — that, when the Pope uses words which, taken in their obvious meaning, are uncatholic, he either must not be intending to speak ex cathedra, or must not mean what he seems to mean. But, if this be so, Ultra-

---

[1] 'There are objections against a *plenum*, and objections against a *vacuum*; yet one of them must certainly be true.' *Boswell's Life of Johnson*, edited by George Birkbeck Hill, revised and enlarged 1934, I. p. 444.

[2] Albert Pigge (1490–1542), in *Hierarchiae Ecclesiasticae Assertio*, Cologne 1538, VI, maintained that the authority of a General Council was derived from the Pope, and that no Pope had been a heretic. He dealt specifically with the case of Honorius.

[3] The prayer beginning 'Sacrosanctae et Individuae Trinitati' was meant to be said after the recital of the divine office. 'And as this grant is not properly an Indulgence, but rather a compensation for, or a supplying of the defects committed in the recitation of the Office, it follows that it is not suspended during the Holy Year like the other Indulgences.' *The Raccolta*, translated by Ambrose St John, London 1857, p. 331.

[4] Domenico Sarra *Il Domma delle Ss. Indulgenze dichiarata a' Fedeli*, Rome 1867, translated *The Doctrine of Indulgences explained to the Faithful*, London 1868. In Chapter VI the point Newman mentions is explained. The remission of guilt spoken of in certain papal bulls is only that consequent on dispositions caused by the wish to obtain an Indulgence.

montanes and Gallicans differ only in the number and stringency of the conditions to which they subject the Pope's Infallibility. Bossuet, I suppose, would receive a definition of the Pope, to which the Bishops of the Universal Church had *afterwards* bonâ fide assented; Fr Perrone does not contemplate the Pope's making any statement obligatory on our faith, on which the Bishops of the Universal Church had not *first* been bonâ fide consulted.[1] If you prove on the one hand that Pope Honorius committed himself to a heresy, I can prove without difficulty on the other, that the Pope, in violation of Fr Perrone's condition, acted without consulting his natural advisers

Ever Yrs most sincerely John H Newman[2]

TO GILBERT SIMMONS

The Oratory, Birmingham   June 21. 1868

My dear Sir

I am sorry I have not answered your letter sooner, but I have not been master of my time.

I have no doubt at all what ought to be said to your questions. As to your vow, of course some inquiry would be necessary before it could be determined whether or not it would be binding — but, if it is, you can fulfil it as well in the Catholic Church as out of it — but you do not introduce the subject of it into your questions.

1. As to your promise to your Superior, you cannot be bound to anything morally wrong. Now if you are convinced that the Roman Communion is the Church of Christ, you cannot without sin remain out of it. No promise to commit sin can possibly be binding.

2. This clear principle is an answer to your second question also — viz whether gratitude to him for his kindness can keep you against your convictions in your present position.

3. I do not know how I can answer your third question about reparation — though of course it is both natural and right you should do any thing you can to lessen the pain which your sense of duty obliges you to cause him

Every thing depends on *your conviction* that the Roman Communion is the Church which our Lord and His Apostles founded. No man can give you this

---

[1] J. Perrone, *De Locis Theologicis* II, De Romano Pontifice, Chapter IV.

[2] Renouf replied on 30 Aug. and excused himself for the delay which was due to incessant travelling as an Inspector of Schools. He went on, 'I hardly know what to say. It is quite certain that I should never have dreamed of writing at all upon Pope Honorius if others had been content to hold the view of Papal Infallibility which you hold. There are several passages in my pamphlet which, as they have been understood, do not correctly express my meaning. The passage about Perrone which you refer to should have run thus, "P. does not perceive that under this quibbling etc a falsehood is asserted" Perrone is not the author of the argument he merely repeats what ever so many others had said before him. For Baronius my respect and veneration are almost unbounded and when I talk of his inventing an abjuration I no more mean to question his honesty than I would that of any of our contemporaries who hearing that Dr Pusey had received communion from the Pope's hand should write that Pusey had abjured Anglicanism.' See also letter of 30 Nov. to Renouf.

conviction; God's grace alone. Be sure what you are doing; do not act on impulse or mere liking; but, if God gives you a conviction that we are in the fold of Christ and you are not (and this I of course hold) let nothing keep you back.[1]

Very truly Yours John H Newman

MONDAY 22 JUNE 1868   I went to Rednall   rain came at night
WEDNESDAY 24 JUNE   The weather recovered itself, and was as brilliant as before but not so warm

TO W. J. COPELAND

Rednall June 25/68

My dear C

We have been greatly concerned to hear of your serious illness — and now my only fear is that you will go to work too eagerly for your safety. It is unfortunate that, instead of pushing on Volume 4, they have nearly finished Volume 6. I can't think why — whereas Volume 4 wants a good 100 or 150 pages. I am still astonished they should make plain Sermons 2 volumes not 1. It will be not more than 440 pages altogether — which is only 40 more than volume 2, whereas two volumes of 220 each will be ghosts.

I heard of your illness from Crawley, and your letter, tho' bad, was a great relief. But rheumatic fever has sequels, and you must, as of course you know, be very cautious. I wish you took care of yourself, half as much as I am careful for Number 1.

Ambrose and I went suddenly to Littlemore — I wanted to see it once before I died. We went straight to Abingdon — then by fly to Sandford — Walked about the place — and back from Littlemore straight to Birmingham. We did not go through Oxford. We had 5 hours there, but not time for every thing. It was a most strange vision — I could hardly believe it real. It was the past coming back, as it might in the intermediate state.

I was rejoiced to see Littlemore so green — tho' very few of my *street* trees remain — I wonder any have lived through the dangers of road commissioners and boys' knives. Crawley's is a really pretty place — the Church is greatly improved — and the Vicarage is very nice.

We saw Mrs Palmer, young Humphries and his second wife (a Boswell) — old Mrs Humphries and her daughter — Martha King — Charles Pollard's

---

[1] Simmons, born in Lancashire on 13 Nov. 1846, appears to have been studying for the Anglican ministry at St Paul's Mission College, Dean Street, Soho, of which the wealthy and eccentric George Nugee was principal.

nephew — Mr Whitlock — We could not walk about much — the day was so hot. We did it all between 7 and 7 o'clock.[1]

Now do *take care* of yourself, for that is the point

Ever Yrs affly John H Newman

SATURDAY 27 JUNE 1868   Kennard came *a third time*   I returned from Rednall

TO WILLIAM MONSELL

The OratoryBm June 28/68

My dear Monsell

I was at Rednall when your letter came, and by a most unusual chance your letter was not forwarded to me. I despatched two telegrams to you as soon as I got here last evening.

Can you come next Sunday? If you write about it, put on your letter 'to be opened.' I have had so many things to talk to you so long, that I fear I have forgotten a good many of them — I wish to know your view and account of all things. What a miserable thing it is that we have not a Paper — and that the Westminster and Register have it all their own way.[2]

Ever Yrs affectly John H Newman of the Oratory

The Rt Honble Wm Monsell M P

TO GILBERT SIMMONS

The Oratory, Bm June 28. 1868

My dear Sir,

I quite understand your state of mind — it is very natural, and quite right and conscientious. If you put it to me, not only as a Catholic Priest, but as a private person, whether it is your duty to be a Catholic, I have but one answer. It is the duty of every one whom God enlightens to see that the Catholic Church, that is the Church in communion with Rome, is the only true Church, the one fold of Christ, and Ark of Salvation; though I believe great numbers are in invincible ignorance, therefore are not answerable for not doing what they have never known they ought to do. They are saved in their ignorance, but their ignorance does not avail those whom God calls by His grace.

But when the question is asked *who* are those who are called, and *when* are they bound to act upon it, of course caution is necessary in dealing with individuals. I have long determined, though I find it difficult to keep my rule, not to

---

[1] Mrs. Palmer was the schoolmistress, Boswell had brought Newman's library from Littlemore to Maryvale. Martha King he had prepared for confirmation. See *Trevor* II, p. 461.

[2] Manning's *Westminster Gazette* and the *Weekly Register* supported the extremist line, and at the end of 1868 the *Tablet* came into the hands of Herbert Vaughan.

give definite advice to any one I have not seen. How do I know you are not a person who have taken up a fancy to-day, and will give it up to-morrow? There is nothing in your letter like this, and I am not supposing it — but there are those who have come to the Church with but an imperfect idea of its teaching and its usages, and when they knew it better have, like the disciples at Capernaum (John vi) left it again. Again very young persons, without any fault of theirs, are sure to have great changes (*naturally*) in their religious opinions, and therefore unless your present convictions are from *supernatural* grace, you will be sure to change. From the tone of your letter I think they *are* from supernatural grace, but no one can pronounce but one who knows you personally. You do not tell me your age, and I know nothing of your religious history. Judging from my imperfect knowledge, I should not think it right for you to be received without your having personal intercourse with some Catholic first. Is there any chance of your being able to come this way? Or do you know of any *convert* whom I could trust? Let me hear from you again[1]

MONDAY 29 JUNE 1868   I went to Rednall

TO W. J. COPELAND

Rednall   July 1/68

My dear C

I should not be at all surprised at Rivingtons' leaving out the dedication through carelessness.[2] They are careless printers. Within the last 2 months, in printing the *Appendix* of Verses to my second Edition, though it regularly went through the Press and I revised it, they deliberately left out the last 4 out of the 20 pages, and *so* it was published before I knew of it.

I am very glad you have had your eyes about you. There is probably no date to the *dedication* of volume 3, but it is appended to the *Advertisement* which follows. I have written to Wm Neville to look and send it to you.

Volume 6 never had a dedication — for this reason, that, after Number 90, I thought no dedication of mine could be a compliment. I had been condemned by ecclesiastical authority, without a word said in my favour, though Jelf came to me, on the beginning of the row about it, from Archbishop Howley to say that, if my friends would consent not to move, nothing should be done on the other side.[3]

I dedicated the Sermons on subjects of the day to you, not as any favour to you, but as the dedication expresses, to thank you for taking my part.

Every Yrs affly J H N

---

[1] Conclusion and signature have been cut out.
[2] i.e. that of Volume III of *P.S.*
[3] As to this understanding see letter of 16 Oct. 1864 to J. D. Coleridge, and *Apo.* pp. 90 and 138–40.

THURSDAY 2 JULY 1868   cold north wind
FRIDAY 3 JULY   returned from Rednall

TO GILBERT SIMMONS

The Oratory, Birmm July 3. 1868
My Dear Mr Simmons

I shall be very glad to see you whenever you come — and thank God for having put such *good* desires into your heart[1]

SATURDAY 4 JULY 1868   Monsell came, and Mr Lloyd of St Edmund's to dinner
SUNDAY 5 JULY   but the fine weather continuing
MONDAY 6 JULY   Monsell went.
TUESDAY 7 JULY   Mr Rymer came to examine

TO WILLIAM MONSELL

July 7/68
My dear Monsell

I send you one of the Papers I spoke to you about. I don't want it back

Yours affly John H Newman

TO LE COMTE DE MONTALEMBERT

The Oratory   Bm July 7. 1868
My dear Comte de Montalembert

I have received the letter which you have been kind enough to send me through Father Hyacinth. I shall rejoice to make the acquaintance of so distinguished a person.[2]

---

[1] Again conclusion and signature have been cut out.

[2] On 3 July Hyacinthe Loyson, at this time a discalced Carmelite, sent a letter of introduction written by Montalembert to Newman on 29 June. It began 'I am sure you will be satisfied to make the personal acquaintance of Father Hyacinthe, although I am afraid that his ignorance of the english language will not allow you to enter into intimate conversation with him. If you could, you would at once recognize in him, not only the worthy and eloquent successor of Lacordaire in the french pulpit, but a man completely completely [sic] identified with yourself, in everything related to the honour of the Church and the interests of truth.'
Already on 23 June Loyson had written to Newman that he was coming to England 'surtout pour vous voir et pour m'entretenir avec vous de plusieurs graves sujets qui me préoccupent, et pour lesquels vous me serez, j'en suis sûr, d'une grande lumière et d'un grand service.' On 3 July he explained that his visit was postponed, and evidently in reply to a letter from Newman insisted, 'Je tiens infiniment à vous voir, et s'il faut vous dire toute ma pensée, vous êtes la personne avec qui je désire le plus converser en Angleterre.' He also said they could converse in Latin, or by means of an interpreter, and that he was filled with sadness 'en voyant la marche que suivent les affaires ecclésiastiques.'
Loyson came on 12 Sept.

As to the little book, which I ventured to send you, not knowing your address, I told my Publisher to send it for you to Messrs Le Coffre. I write by this post to him to bid him send a copy to the place from which you write to me.[1]

Mr Monsell, who was here a day or two since, gave me on the whole a good account of your health, though he did not speak very confidently. I hope your recent publication may be taken as a token that the good news is not unfounded.[2]

I have received from your Publisher another volume of your works, which I prize very much, and beg to offer you my deep acknowledgements for the gift[3]

Believe me to be with the truest respect Monsieur le Comte

Sincerely Yours in Xt   John H Newman of the Oratory

TO HENRY WILBERFORCE

The Oratory Bm ⌐July 7. 1868⌐

My dear H W

I return with thanks Mozley's letter. ⌐It rejoices me to think that you are at last in harbour in a quiet home and with a pleasant garden. My time is fully occupied here even with daily matters. Lately I have had all the Sacristy matters on my hands⌐ — have had to analyze all the details of the work — apportion it among four or five helps, and write out and post up the duties of each. The School always takes up time — and now the Orphanage is becoming in size a second school. ⌐And, during the Vacation now coming on us, I must be at home for every one else is going away. Besides this, since, now for a year, I am taking medicine twice or thrice a day (with vast benefit but still without such a change of constitution that I can dispense with it) I feel it very difficult to leave home.⌐ When I go to R. W. Church, (I say 'R W', for did I say to (the Anglican) 'Church' it would be like Burnham Wood going to Dunsinane)[4] I hope to take you on my way, if you will receive me.

⌐When I saw Dornford's death in the paper⌐ I wrote to Rogers for some intelligence about it. He wrote to some person near Dornford. From both their letters I could see that they had no very near sympathy with his fortunes — and I really think I lamented him more than any one in his immediate

---

[1] Montalembert noted on the autograph of Newman's letter 'Je l'ai reçu *Verses on various occasions.*' His publisher was Lecoffre, 90 rue Bonaparte, Paris.

[2] Montalembert's recent publication was evidently an article on the disestablishment of the Church of Ireland, to which Loyson referred in his letter of 3 July, 'L'Irlande et L'Autriche,' *Le Correspondant*, (25 May 1868).

[3] This was the ninth volume of the Works of Montalembert, *Oeuvres polémiques et diverses*, Paris 1868. On the cover is written 'Hommage de l'Auteur' and inside Newman has added 'from the Author.'

[4] *Macbeth* V, ii, 24. Wilberforce had settled at Stroud, which was on the way from Birmingham to Church's rectory at Whatley in Somerset.

neighbourhood.[1] ⌐I ever liked him, though I laughed at him — he did not pro-
voke dislike— he was rather overbearing than irascible —⌐ but T. Mozley, I
fear, is right in saying that he was neither beloved nor is regretted. ⌐Alas —
alas — perhaps it is that my sympathy lies in my being old like him and in
going the way he has gone — omnes eodem cogimur[2] and one's old friends are
falling on every side.⌐

Ever Yrs affly John H Newman

WEDNESDAY 8 JULY 1868   Mr Simmons *Simmonds* came
THURSDAY 9 JULY   Kennard received

TO JAMES SKINNER

[9 July 1868]

My dear Sir

You ask of me whether you have 'correctly described the line of persuasion
which I pursue in my search for souls to win them away from their place in the
Church of Christ.'[3] Surely you cannot intend me to answer so strangely worded
a question, which is after the pattern of the well known logical catch 'Have you
or have you not the wickedness to disagree with me in opinion.'

I have no intention of entering into controversy with you. I can only
express my sincere regret that what I called the key to my view of the matter
between us has been made by you to open a door on which I see written up 'No
thoroughfare'

J H N

FRIDAY 10 JULY 1868   Simmons received
SATURDAY 11 JULY   Simmons left   attempt at rain
SUNDAY 12 JULY   glass up again to 74°   in the early morning in my room

TO EDWARD BELLASIS

12 July 1868

You see the Jesuits complain of the London University's *French* books —
vide *The Month* for July.[4] They and the Downside Fathers publicly protested
some years back against the London University *Philosophy* —[5] and you tell
me that Father Weld thinks, as indeed I think, they don't care a rush for us[6]

---

[1] See letter of 2 Feb. to Rogers.
[2] Horace, *Odes* II, iii, 25. Tom Mozley succeeded Dornford as Rector of Plymtree.
[3] Having learned that Kennard was now in Birmingham, Skinner wrote on 8 July a long
reply to Newman's letter of 28 May.
[4] See 'The Catholic Colleges and the University of London,' the *Month*, (July 1868), p. 14.
[5] See letters of 1 Dec. 1858 to Ornsby and 25 Jan. 1859 to Weedall.
[6] For the context of this letter see that of 25 Jan. 1868 to Bellasis.

MONDAY 13 JULY 1868   Kennard left.   Mr Rymer left for Oscott
TUESDAY 14 JULY   Monthly Examinations began   still fine
WEDNESDAY 15 JULY   Dr Russell passed thro'
THURSDAY 16 JULY   Simmons came for good   drops of rain
SATURDAY 18 JULY   the boys went   Mr Rymer left for good

TO WILLIAM LEIGH, JUNIOR

The Oratory Bm July 18. 1868

My dear Mr Leigh

As to your questions, I think you should keep yourself to one subject at a time, as far as you can. I mean, as far as you can do it without tiring yourself, for it may easily happen that you want some relief, and then you might take up a second subject profitably. For instance, as to the subjects you mention you might give yourself to Latin for as long a time as you could without fatigue, and then you might take up some light historical work, or some French or Italian poetry.

As to Latin; your mode of studying it should be different from a boy's — a boy cannot be trusted with cribs — but a grown man has discretion. You might get one of 'Dr Giles's Keys to the Classics —' (Cornish 297 High Holborn) say Ovid's Metamorphoses or Livy Book xxi. Cæsar is very dull; perhaps if you read it with Louis Napoleon's Life of Cæsar, you would be able to get on with it, but that depends what taste you have for military affairs. If I were sure you would not say it was too hard (I don't think it need be) I should recommend a play of Terence. One can't put them uncorrected in to the hands of boys, but in themselves they are more interesting than any other classical works. They are very well edited by 'The Revd James Davies of Lincoln College' published by 'John Weale, 59 High Holborn, 1858.' Take the Adelphi or the Phormio. There is a good translation of Terence, I think, in Bohn's Series.

As to your boy, the new 'Public School Latin Primer' is better than the Old Eton Grammar. But you should inquire of the School he is going to, what Grammar is used in it — else, the poor little fellow will be at a disadvantage.

Very sincerely Yours John H Newman of the Oratory

The Oratory Bm July 19. 1868.

My Dear Mr MacColl

I fear I can do nothing for you. The Dominicans in England know nothing about their brothers in Italy, and the Italians will be very unwilling to tell. I had great experience of this in the Achilli matter. It took months to move even Cardinal Wiseman, and, except that Campbell anyhow would have hurried me into a trial, one might impute it simply to the Cardinal, that there was any trial at all. Months were lost in idle efforts — though at length I made some progress in getting evidence of notorious facts.[1]

I am afraid I cannot doubt matters are very bad in Italy, as you say. But, for that reason, I believe I do not like to substantiate what not unfairly may be taken by strangers as the outcome of their own way of going on. No one makes more ruinous confessions of the state of the Italian Priesthood than St Alfonso Liguori — and I do not know how one can wish for a continuance of a state of things, which seems hopelessly bad. Everything I have heard of the regime of the Bourbons makes me rejoice in their overthrow, and I trust they will never be restored. A distinguished Roman Prelate, who was here last year, said that a new generation will be brought up without any religion at all. He did not see any hope for Italy — and he said the Pope had very few supporters.[2] I suppose things *must* be worse before they are better — and this reconciles me to what else would be insupportable, the sacrilege and blasphemy which prevails there. It is difficult to balance [evils][3] but there is something more revolting in 'holding the truth in unrighteousness'[4] than in persecuting it.

As to Mr Meyrick, from the tone of his letters, as they appear from time to time in the Papers, he must be a most unpleasant man.[5]

Most truly yours John H Newman

MONDAY 20 JULY 1868   glass 80° in corridor at 7 PM   weather more brilliant and warm than ever

[1] MacColl, who had spent the winter of 1867–8 in Italy, was writing in favour of the disestablishment of the Church of Ireland. On 30 May 1868 he wrote to Gladstone, 'I also wish to show, from my recent experience in Italy, that the policy of our Bishops with respect to the Irish Church is the counterpart of the policy of the Court of Rome in Italy — a policy which is driving the whole Italian nation into infidelity.' *Malcolm MacColl Memoirs and Correspondence*, edited by G. W. E. Russell, London 1914, p. 27. MacColl wanted further information.
For Wiseman's negligence over the Achilli Trial see letters of 11 Nov. 1851 to Badeley and 26 Nov. 1851 to W. G. Ward.
[2] This was Mgr. Nardi. See diary for 23 Aug. 1867.
[3] The copyist has omitted a word here.
[4] *Romans*, 1:18.
[5] Frederick Meyrick was the author of a number of anti-Catholic pamphlets, and supported reform movements on the Continent which were opposed to the Catholic Church. *DNB* describes him as 'a clever disputant' who 'hindered his ecclesiastical advancement by his controversial zeal.'

TUESDAY 21 JULY   In evening John Norris admitted as a triennial

TO H. P. LIDDON

The Oratory Bm July 21. 1868

My dear Mr Liddon

I wish we had been more careful to preserve the Authorship of the Tracts. What is some perplexity to me is that, unless I am gravely mistaken, I sent back to Mr Keble the great bulk of the remaining copies of his Tracts about (say) 10 or 12 years ago, at a time when the Rivingtons wanted the stock removed from their premises. I considered it really mine, in as much as I had paid for the printing, but I thought it best to send it back to him. Where is it?[1]

Mr Keble wrote Number 4 'Adherence' etc[2] and I have somewhere the Manuscript in his hand-writing. |Number 40, Richard Nelson, Number 3 | Numbers 52. 54. 57. 60 Four Sermons on Four Holy days. |and Number 89 on the Mysticism of the Early Fathers. I don't think he wrote any others.

I cannot help hoping that I have answered your question fully

Very sincerely Yours John H Newman

The Revd H. P. Liddon

WEDNESDAY 22 JULY 1868   John went.   Ambrose went   In my room 79°

TO ROBERT WRIGHT BRUNDRIT

The Oratory Bm July 22. 1868

My dear Mr Brundrit

I thank you for the paper you have sent me. The mistakes are certainly laughable. I suppose the person responsible for them has found them out by this time.

Very truly Yours John H Newman

THURSDAY 23 JULY 1868   Wm[William] went, to join Ambrose for Switzerland   rapid fall to 66° 8 A.M. but dry still   (*up to this time still, the weather still fine*)

---

[1] See letter of 28 Jan. 1854 to Rivington.
[2] *Adherence to the Apostolical Succession the Safest Course. On alterations in the Prayer-Book.*

TO EDWARD BELLASIS

23 July 1868

As to the London University all we want is *fair play in books* on all subjects — viz., that there should be a choice — and this might be the subject of a pamphlet — but you should get a person to write it who knows the *workings* of the University The Jesuits know it best — but they will be too cautious or timid.

TO W. J. COPELAND

The Oy Bm July 23/68

My dear Copeland

I am glad to hear from you, tho' you don't say how you are, or how this hot weather has suited you. The glass in our Corridor has stood at 80° at 7 PM. and in my room at 79° in the morning. Today it has fallen to 71° but no signs of rain.

I can't help thinking there are three sheets of different volumes which have not come to me. I noticed one of them at the time. The other two I sent and send last night and tonight.

Ambrose and William have set off for Switzerland, and the School is in Vacation. Else, we are as usual

Ever Yrs affectly John H Newman

P.S. The *point* is whether the Sermons *sell*. You say they have had a 'hearty welcome —' does that mean 'sale'?[1]

I think in the proof I sent yesterday I left out (Epiphany) (Septuagesima) before the *text* of the Sermons.

SATURDAY 25 JULY 1868 Sudden attack of diarrhoea sent for Carter — *on my bed* attempt at rain — went off

SUNDAY 26 JULY confined to my bed

MONDAY 27 JULY confined to my bed. better in evening glass got up to 78 not oppressive

---

[1] Copeland wrote on 1 Aug., 'Rivington advised me very early of the sale of 1000 of the 1st volume. I find the little bookseller in our town here has sold 18, and my impression is that the sale is satisfactory, and that the Sermons will reach from their tempting aspect and low price, many persons of a different class, from those whom they reached before . . .'

TO H. P. LIDDON

The Oratory Bm July 27/68

My dear Liddon

There is no doubt whatever that Number 13[1] is John Keble's — and I can't make out why I omitted it; for I know the fact quite well.

Very truly Yours John H Newman

TO HENRY WILBERFORCE

The Oy Bm ⌜July 27/68⌝[2]

My dear Henry

I am under an attack of diarrhœa, a very unusual complaint in my case, and it affects my head, so that I cannot think. Also ⌜the subject [[you write about]] is so very wide — a book ought to be written upon it — till then two disputants are working in different media, and have no common principles. I have long wished to make at least a first essay, — but I despair from the difficulty of the subject and my scant time. I have begun it again and again — and either other duties came in the way and cut it short, or else I felt I had not got hold of the end of the skein and was not likely to unravel it. Don't mention it, but I have written my *first* book, it is on Assent — then would come Certitude ⟨Book 2⟩ — then Proof ⟨3⟩.⌝ I am really quite at a loss what to recommend — if I say any thing, it leads to other questions, and those to others, till one cannot tell the ultimate resolution of the matter. ⌜As to what I have done, I cannot tell whether it is a Truism, a Paradox, or a Mare'snest. Since it certainly *may* be any one of the three, the chance of its being any thing better is not encouraging.

I consider there is no such thing [[(in the province of facts)]] as a perfect logical demonstration; there is always a margin of objection — even in mathematics, except in the case of short proofs, as the propositions of Euclid. Yet on the other hand it is a paradox to say there is not such a state of mind as certitude. It is as well ascertained a state of mind, as doubt — to say that such a phenomenon in the human mind is a mere extravagance or weakness is a monstrous assertion which I cannot swallow.⌝ Of course there may be abuses and mistakes in particular cases of certitude, but that is another matter. ⌜It is *a law of our nature* then, that we are certain on premises which do not touch ⟨reach⟩ demonstration. This seems to me undeniable. Then what is the faculty, since it is not the logical Dictum de omni et nullo, which *enables* us to

---

[1] *Tract XIII, Sunday Lessons. The Principle of Selection.*

[2] [[This letter is evidently an answer to statements not stated in it; so far it is obscure in drift. There is not much in it]] See letter of 8 Aug. to Wilberforce who was corresponding with William Froude.

be certain, to have the *state of mind* called certitude, though the syllogism before us is not according to the strict rules of Barbara and Celarent?[1] I think it is φρόνησις which tells us *when* to discard the logical imperfection and to assent to the conclusion which ought to be drawn in order to demonstration, but is not *quite*?⌝ No syllogism can prove to me that nature is uniform — but the argument is so strong, though not demonstrative, that I should not be φρόνιμος but a fool, to doubt. Now the φρόνησις may be easily biassed by our wishes, by our will. This is even the case in mathematics and physico-mathematics; as the Dominican opposition even to this day to the Copernican system may be taken to illustrate. So again in History etc. a cumulative argument, though not demonstrative, may claim of us, i.e. by the law of our nature, by our duty to our nature, i.e. by our duty to God, *an act of certitude.* ⌜Paper logic, syllogisms, and states of mind are incommensurables. It is obvious what room there is for the interference of the will here. None are so deaf as those who won't hear.⌝

Now I know that to say all this and no more, is to open the door to endless disputes. The only thing to be done is to rest the whole on certain first principles, and to say if you can't take my first principles, I can't help it. But to find the first principles is the difficulty.

St John says 'He that believeth in the Son hath life — and he that believeth not the Son, hath not life.'[2] *I* say I see no difficulty here, *another* says the idea is absurd. What are we to do, when we thus differ in first principles? 'Qui vult salvus esse, ita de Trinitate sentiat.'[3] No *man*, certainly, has a right to say this — but why may not God say it? And, if my φρόνησις assures me that there is such evidence for God having said it (evidence qualis et quanta) that I am *bound in duty* to believe it, why must I not believe both the doctrine and the fearful sanction of it? If a person tells me that his φρόνησις does *not see* the existence of such evidence as is sufficient, that is another matter; but I am arguing against the *principle* that φρόνησις is a higher sort of logic — whereas even mathematical conclusions, i.e. the issues of *extended calculations*, require to be believed in by the action of φρόνησις; for how can I be sure, how can I be sure, I tease myself by saying again and again how can I be sure, that here or there my logical vigilance has not failed me? I have not got every step in every course of mathematical reasoning necessary for the conclusion, clearly before my eyes at once. And we know what command nervous persons are obliged to exert over themselves lest they should doubt whether even they see or feel; or whether they know any thing at all. ⌜Should not I be an ass if I did not believe in the existence of India? Yet are there not scores of persons who have evidence of a quality and quantity indefinitely higher than mine? for I have not been there, and they have. I should think myself a fool if I said 'I have some doubt about the existence of India,' or 'I am not certain about it,⌝

---

[1] Mnemonic terms for the syllogisms of logic.
[2] *John*, 3:36.
[3] Athanasian Creed.

or 'I *reserve* the point.' ⌐I *am* certain, YOU my good Sir, are certain too — you confuse two things quite distinct from each other, [[(when you say you are not certain)]] want of completeness in Barbara and Celarent⌐ which is a scientific rule of the game, ⌐ — and a habit of mind; — a calculating machine and a prerogative of human nature [[and human act]] —an objection is not a doubt — ten thousand objections as little make one doubt, as ten thousand ponies make one horse; though of course a *certain amount* of objection *ought*, as my φρόνησις tells me, to weigh upon my decision, and to affect my existing belief [[(tho' how much and what character of objection in each particular case my φρόνησις and that alone determines.)]]. A great deal of confusion arises from the *double* sense of a lot of cognate words — e.g. 'conclusion' means both the proposition drawn from two premisses, and the state of mind in which I find myself after reviewing the argument, the relation of my mind to a thing expressed in a certain proposition; and this *helps* the real intellectual mistake made by sceptical thinkers.⌐

The key, however, of the position, in the controversy which is before us, is this — to gain that on either side is the victory — whether you may or may not rationally keep your mind *open* to change on a point on which your φρόνησις has already told you to decide one way. Here I say there is a difference between science and religion, between religion of nature and the Catholic religion — but it would take too long a time to explain, and indeed I have not yet worked the whole matter out in my *mind* to my own satisfaction. I should ask, does not nature, duty and affection, teach us that a difference is to be made between things and persons? Ought I to be as open to listen to objections brought to me against the honour, fidelity, love towards me of a friend, as against the received belief that the earth is 95 million miles from the sun? Again ⌐there is a truth which no natural reason can gain, *revealed*. God may put His own *conditions* ⟨(in His prescient providence)⟩ on the development of that truth — and,⌐ (though at first sight paradoxical) ⌐He may make one of those conditions ⟨(thus foreseen)⟩ to be a slowness to receive more truth — (I don't mean of course a slowness to be taught, but a slowness to see that He is teaching). This condition[1] may be necessary on conservative reasons, from the extreme difficulty to human nature of retaining what is supernatural, so that, if we took in new truths too quickly, we might lose the old. Thus it might have been injurious to the thorough reception, the accurate complete mapping out of the doctrine of the Incarnation, if the Immaculate Conception B M V and her other prerogatives had been too readily received — or again the doctrine of man's free will and responsibility, one of the characteristic doctrines of Christianity, might never have made its way against the fatalism and recklessness of heathen times, if St Austin's doctrines of grace and original sin had been taught too early. And thus I resign myself to many things said and done now by good men, which, though they have in them the leaven of prejudice and

---

[1] [[This condition (which He foresaw and reckoned upon in making His revelation, or determined by the measure of the grace and light He gave,) may be necessary]]

uncharitableness, are based on a wish to keep simply to what they have received.⌐ However, this is one of those subjects which in the beginning of this letter I said were too large for a letter. One thing I must add, as having omitted. ⌐When I am asked why I *cautiously and promptly* exclude doubts, I answer I do so because they *are* doubts, I don't see the need of excluding objections. The mind is very likely to be carried away to doubt *without* a basis of objections *sufficient* in the judgment of the φρόνησις to justify it. The imagination, not the reason is appealed to. How could God exist without beginning? In reason this is no objection, for reason tells us that *something* must have been without beginning. But to the imagination it is an overpowering difficulty. To an half educated man I should say, strangle the doubt — don't read the book which so affects you. This is not bidding him not to listen to reasons, but to insufficient reasons, to false reasons, which are a temptation to him.⌐ The rule 'strangle doubts' is a rule of the confessional, not a point of dogmatic theology.

⌐As to Aristotle's ἀναποδεικταὶ ἀρχαὶ[1] I accept it without scruple, as a general truth — but in the particular case if I say, 'When A and B differ you may begin to doubt,' surely I mean, (and should explain myself to mean, were I asked,) '*In those things in which* they differ, begin to doubt —' The agreement of Murchison and Lyell in great and broad geological truths,⌐ they being both deeply read geologists, ⌐is a second reason for trusting them over and above their scientific proficiency, and my trust in them so far is quite consistent with my remaining in doubt about the point in which they differ, viz whether the changes in the crust of the earth were catastrophes or[2] like the changes which make a young man an old one.

And ⌐as to prayer, usum non tollit abusus. God has given His friends a privilege — that of gaining favours from Him. A father says to his child going to school, 'Now mind you write to me once a week.' And he rewards him in various ways, if he is obedient in this respect. We are God's children — we are not grown men —⌐ Saints would worship God solely because He is God — ⌐we all must love Him for Himself, but, considering what we are, it is merciful that He has made hope, as well as faith and love, a theological virtue.⌐ But this is but a poor and scanty exposure of a wonderful paradox.

As there may be some things in this letter, which I have not till now put on paper, please, keep it. I am sure I don't know what others will think of it. I only know, it is plain common sense to me. If you have any thing to say upon it, write.

Yours affly John H Newman of the Oratory

H W Wilberforce Esqr

P.S.   I am very glad to hear what you say of yourself in the second part of your letter. I have mislaid the first part and cannot tell, if there is any thing that I have not answered.

---

[1] 'indemonstrable first principles.'
[2] [[or gradual]] Sir Roderick Murchison held the latter view.

TUESDAY 28 JULY 1868   better   still on my bed
WEDNESDAY 29 JULY   some relapse   *at 8½ P.M. the glass at 80° in my room.*

TO L. J. CIST

The Oratory Bm July 29. 1868

Dear Sir

I have pleasure in complying with your wish. You may do what you will, with the following list of dates

Yours faithfully John H Newman

L. J. Cist Esqr

P.S.   As to my writings I have given a list of them down to 1864 in my History of Religious Opinions, or Apologia.

Febr. 21.	1801 —	born in Old Broad Street, City of London
May 1.	1808 —	sent to Old Ealing School near London
Decr	1816.	matriculated at Trinity College Oxford
about Xtmas	1820.	took B A degree
April 12.	1822.	elected Fellow of Oriel College
	1823.	took M A degree
	1825	appointed Vice Principal of Alban Hall
	1826	Tutor of Oriel College
	1827	Public Examiner for B A degree
	1827	Whitehall Preacher
	1828	Vicar of St Mary's
	1830.	Pro-proctor
	1832	Select Preacher
	1833	Oxford Tracts ⟨Tracts for the Times⟩ began
	1836	took degree of B D
	1838	Editor of British Critic
February	1841.	appearance of Number 90. resigned the British Critic. Stopped the Tracts.
	1843.	Resigned living of St Mary's
Sept [Oct.] 9.	1845.	received into the Catholic Church

TO ROBERT CHARLES JENKINS

The Oratory, Birmingham July 29th, 1868.

My dear Mr. Jenkins,

I am under the stress of a complaint common in this season, and it has so pulled me down, that I have not been able to go to the Library for any means of throwing light upon your question. So I have employed one of our party here, a good theologian with a keen eye for books and their contents.[1]

As I anticipated, he says that he can find nothing explanatory of the history of the 'Mysterium Fidei'; and the utter ignorance on the subject of the writers he has met with, and their confession of perplexed ignorance, is a strong reason for considering such immemorial tradition to be Apostolic. Theologians consider the form of consecration to lie in the first 4 or 5 words of the larger form as it runs in the Canon — and I should consider that our Lord used the words 'Mysterium Fidei' with other words — and that St. Peter had preserved them in his form of the Consecration, though not an essential part of it.

I am puzzled to find out your difficulty in the Placeat. *After* the Sacrifice is concluded, the Priest says in that Prayer 'O Holy Trinity accept this sacrifice which I have offered to you.'[2] — trum sacrificium acceptabile *fiat*,' and the Server replies, 'Suscipiat Dominus Sacrificium de manibus tuis etc.'

Your photograph is a very interesting one, and I thank you for it. Over and above its interest as so venerable a remains of antiquity, as a photograph it is remarkably good. On first looking at it, I thought it was from the South

THURSDAY 30 JULY 1868   better

TO W. J. COPELAND

July 30/68

My dear C

I do not like to plague you, yet I can't but be anxious about you after so serious an illness, and wish to know how you are going on. It is in its consequences time afterwards, that rheumatic fever is so formidable — and I trust your catching it will be your last imprudence as regards it. You have no one to keep you in order — you have no tie to your house — you go about your parish for a truer home, you go to great distances, rapidly too, on calls of duty or for the sight of friends. And I know of old how difficult you are to keep in order. I wish I could turn myself into a musical snuff box saying all this in verse and song and you obliged to wind me up every day. This hot weather ought to be good for you, but for the danger of chills.

For myself I have got one and it has taken the shape of diarrhœa, a most uncommon complaint with me. Ambrose and William are in Switzerland, and I hope recruiting (themselves, not soldiers.)

So the Bishop of Winchester has had another stroke[3]

Ever Yrs affly John H Newman

[1] Jenkins asked for explanations of a phrase in the words of consecration in the Roman Canon, and of the prayer 'Placeat' said before the blessing in the old Roman rite.

[2] Two or three lines are missing here, the page having been cut for the signature on the reverse side. Newman proceeds to quote the 'Orate Fratres' before the Preface.

[3] Charles Richard Sumner, Bishop of Winchester since 1827 had a first stroke on 4 March 1868. He resigned his see in Aug. 1869.

TO EDWARD HENEAGE DERING

The Oratory Bm July 31. 1868

My dear Mr Dering

I thank you for your volume, which I shall read with great interest — and I am glad to find you are getting established at Wootten Hall.[1]

You must be so very kind as to let me say I cannot avail myself of your most friendly wish to stay with you there. It is against our rule and tradition to do so. I never leave home except for the sake of my health under medical orders, or for some very grave reasons. This has been my rule for 22 years. This year I have refused my sister, whose home I have not been at since 1848. I do not recollect stopping at a friend's house but once, and that was in 1852, when the late Cardinal Wiseman bade me do that or travel for my health.

Repeating my thanks for your true kindness

I am My dear Mr Dering,

Most sincerely yours John H Newman

TO MRS HENRY J. LYNCH

July 31. 1868

Madam

Pained as I am at your letter, I am not at all surprised that, under the view, which you there express, of the difference between Mr Lynch and us, you should write to me as you do; but you would not write so at all, under our own view of it.[2]

You think we have committed an injustice to Mr Lynch; *we* on the contrary are fully conscious and certain, not only that we have not done him an injustice, but that we actually did him a positive service at a time when he and his needed a service done to them.

You think, in your own words, that we have broken engagements given solemnly in my name, ratified under my own hand, and confirmed by our solemn act; *we* deny this entirely and altogether.

Much then as I enter into and respect your feelings, I consider your letter, in itself, to contain *calumnies* against us, though you do not intend it to do so, and I hereby give it my first and my last reply.

I am very sorry to have so to write; sorry that I should appear to you in the character in which you present me to myself; sorry to have to say to you in

---

[1] At Henley in Arden. The volume was E. H. Dering's novel, *Florence Danby*.

[2] Mrs Lynch wrote on 29 July a 'solemn appeal' to Newman to 'see justice done' to her and her husband in regard to the estate of Rathtarman. See letters to Lynch in 1866 and to William Williams in 1867.

turn, as I do, that we have thought and done to My Lynch nothing but kindness, and have received from him in turn nothing but misrepresentation and persecution.

Thus much is quite plain, viz. that no good can come from a correspondence, in which you could only speak about us as you have heard of us from others, and we on the other hand should speak under a clear sense of our own straightforwardness and uprightness, confirmed, as it has been, by the judgment both of lawyers and of ecclesiastical authorities.

I have the honour to be Madam Your obedient Servt
John H Newman

TO JAMES SKINNER

Copy   July 31. 1868
Revd Sir

You will not, on second thoughts publish my letters *without my leave,* as in your letter of the 29th you propose to do. Not that I am at all dissatisfied with them, but you never would have got me to take the trouble to write them, had you not introduced yourself to me on the plea of a former acquaintance with me. Putting aside all other reasons, the way you took to gain them makes them *private*.[1]

If you do so unbecoming an act, I shall not in the least be surprised at your committing the second impropriety of not publishing them *all, entire* and *verbatim*; for instance, at your suppressing *this*, with which I close the correspondence

J H N

TO HENRY WILBERFORCE

The Oratory July 31 /68

My dear H

I am better — and I trust getting well.

You will understand that I am so personally interested in the subject on which I wrote to you, that I shall not be satisfied with so bare an acknowledgment, as you give me of it in your letter of this morning

Ever Yrs affly John H Newman

[1] See letter of 13 May to Skinner. He wrote on 29 July that he assumed the right to publish his correspondence with Newman, since Kennard's conversion has been publicly announced in the newspapers. On 1 Aug. Skinner wrote that he would respect Newman's request in regard to his side of the correspondence, but reserved the right to publish the letter he himself had sent.

SATURDAY 1 AUGUST 1868   Dr Evans back — *began to say Mass again*

TO EDWARD BELLASIS

Aug 1/68

I have my own subject, one I have wished to do all my life, one which I fear would not interest you and —— at all, one, which, if I did, I should of course think it the best thing I have done, being on the contrary perhaps the worst. I have the same fidget about it, as a horseman might feel about a certain five feet stone wall which he passes by means of a gate every day of his life, yet is resolved he must and will some day clear — and at last breaks his neck in attempting. It is on 'Assent, Certitude, and Proof' I have no right to look to having time to do anything — but if I have, it must be this.

TO MISS HOLMES

Aug 1. 1868

My dear Miss Holmes

I take advantage of a business letter to Mr Wegg Prosser to inclose a line to you. I have not written to you, — because I had nothing to write about. Since you are anxious about my health, you will be glad to know that I am well as I always am, and have suffered nothing from this wonderful summer. It gives me great pleasure to hear from you that you are turning your thoughts to London and making up for lost ground, though I am much afraid, using the liberty of one who has known you so many years, that you have not the power of drudgery and steady perseverance to succeed. And the effort will be more difficult with every new year. It would be the best of penances for you to bind yourself to one plan and one object. But sick people always dislike that remedy which is best suited to their case — so at least my Doctor tells me.

Yours affectly John H Newman

TO H. P. LIDDON

Aug 1 1868

My dear Mr Liddon

I believe the copyright both of the Tracts and of the Lyra Apostolica to be mine, *so far as this*, that Keble strictly made me a present both of his Tracts and his Poems for the purpose of those two works of mine. Nor had he any thing to do either with the printing bills or the sale receipts of either Tracts or Lyra, till I gave him the Lyra.[1]

The case was different with Pusey; he always paid for the printing and received the profits of sale of his own Tracts.

When I became a Catholic, there was a large unsold stock of Tracts which had cost me personally a large sum of money, and which still remains on my hands, the sale since that date having been very slow. I always intended, if the stock was ever run out, to give up whatever formal right I might have to Mr Keble's Tracts to Mr Keble, though I did not *expect* that would happen in the course of his life or of mine. After some years, on second thoughts I sent, or certainly intended and gave directions to send to him, the remaining copies of the current editions of his Tracts, though I had paid for the printing. I cannot tell what was actually done, both because it is many years ago and also because it was, as I believe, when I was in Ireland, or going to and fro between this place and Dublin, at a time of confusion and change.

The case was different with the Lyra, a small work, indivisible, with a small stock; and consequently in 1845 or 1846 I asked Keble to accept even the copyright of it. He took it, and from that time, as far as I know, he paid the bills and received the profits. I cannot say I ever intended to give the copyright to his executors; that, however, was a point the decision of which I had put out of my hands. It was natural on his death that it should revert to me, the only surviving writer out of the six, and the original projector of the work. It was due to the memory of the past.

I suppose that *legally* the copyright neither of the Tracts nor of the Lyra is my property, or any one's else; for I have given Keble no sum of money in purchase either of his Tracts or his Poems; nor (I need hardly say) did he give me any thing for mine. I believe that legally my Tracts and Poems are my property, and his Tracts and Poems are his. I believe I could hinder the Lyra being sold, as it is now sold, with my Poems included in it. How the de facto possessor of the Lyra goes on selling my Poems I am not bound to explain. Perhaps long possession gives a legal title; but I am regarding the matter as a moral question.[2]

You will understand from this that I make no claim at all on Keble's Tracts, and wish you by all means to republish them, as you propose to do

Yours very truly John H Newman

The Revd H P Liddon

---

[1] Liddon wrote on 30 July asking Newman, as owner of the copyright, for permission to republish Keble's *Tracts for the Times*. Cf. letter of 21 July to Liddon.
[2] The de facto possessor of the *Lyra* was John Mozley. Liddon sent this present letter to Thomas Keble junior, who replied on 7 Aug. that he considered Newman to hold the copyright of the *Lyra Apostolica*. See last note to letter of 13 Sept. 1866 to Thomas Keble. Thomas Keble junior was glad of the opportunity now given 'to put straight . . . a matter which my own awkwardness in great measure set wrong,' in 1866. See letter of 10 Aug. 1868 to Liddon, who wrote how painful it would be to many that any slight should be offered to Newman in connection with the memory of Keble.

TO SIR JUSTIN SHEIL

The Oratory Bm August 1, 1868

My dear Sir Justin,

I inclose the Master's Report of your two boys, and the Examiner's Report of Marks in the competition for the Norfolk Prize, with the names of other boys who have gained prizes.[1]

After all, we could not manage the Sunday expedition to Rednal. The Omnibus was bespoken, but new difficulties arose at the last minute.[2]

We consider that Edward has shown a desire to improve greater than would appear from that part of the Report which is Mr Challis's. It must be considered that we know him for longer and better than Mr Challis.

I hope you and Lady Sheil and family bear well this hot weather. We are not provided here with Oriental appliances to meet it. — tho' I suppose any how the heat of Persia is a match for any remedial measures.[3]

I am, My dear Sir Justin Most truly Yours
John H Newman of the Oratory

Sir Justin Sheil K C B

SUNDAY 2 AUGUST 1868   began to say Mass again.   Dr Evans called   first oppressive day.   At 8½ PM glass at 80° in my room
MONDAY 3 AUGUST   oppressive   Henry went for his holyday

TO W. J. COPELAND

The Oy Bm Augst 3/68

My dearest Copeland

I grieve to think you should consider it necessary to follow up so carefully any thing I threw out. Certainly I am puzzled to think I could have seen those sheets, for particular reasons, but directly you say I am wrong, Res finita est — and I have no doubt or trouble about it. Also, I don't wish to give you any trouble in inquiring at Rivingtons' about the sale. You have amply satisfied me by saying that already 1000 have been sold of volume 1 — for my own anxiety was, lest the experiment should be a failure, and Rivington lose by it. Your information then is to me very gratifying.

I rejoice you have so many people about you to keep you in order — and that my Musical Snuff box is unnecessary.

You are making a very long journey this hot weather — While it lasts, even

[1] The Norfolk prize, given by the Duke, was an annual one for books to the value of £20, and open to the senior boys.
[2] See letter of 18 May to Sheil.
[3] Sheil had been the British minister in Persia, 1844–54.

the Land's End will be dry — but will not Cornwall be damp as soon as a change takes place?

I am convalescent, thank you, and more — but I do not pick up strength as quickly as I did.

The hill behind our Cottage at Rednall is on fire — and we are watching with anxiety the progress of the flames. A high wind would be a very serious event —

I heard from the two tourists[1] from the neighbourhood of the bel Alp yesterday, and they are soon to go on to Zermatt under the Matterhorn. They are rather afraid of a spell of bad weather.

Edward Caswall is glad to hear so good an account of you. This is a terrible season for his brother in Yankeeland — but it *may* be the very thing for him. I have heard nothing of *your* brother lately.[2]

Ever Yours affectionately John H Newman

The Revd W. J. Copeland

P.S.   I certainly *wish* an index of dates at end of volume 8. But then will it not be a defect that the dates of 'Sermons for the Day' are not inserted in their place?[3]

TUESDAY 4 AUGUST 1868   Stanislas F.[Flanagan] came

WEDNESDAY 5 AUGUST   Dr Evans called.   Began dusting the books of the Library (not done since Long Vacation 1865)   a sudden shower and thunder

TO EMILY BOWLES

August 5/68

My dear Child,

I wish I knew how you are, especially in this hot weather. Has your beautiful book sold well?[4]

Ever Yrs affly John H Newman

---

[1] i.e. St John and Neville. Newman kept a copy of a testimonial he wrote for them: 'Ego, Joannes Henricus Newman, Præpositus Congregationis Sancti Philippi Nerii apud Birmingham in Angliâ
Testor
filios meos, Ambrosium St John et Gulielmum Neville esse Sacerdotes dignissimos Sanctæ Ecclesiæ Romanæ Catholicæ, et eos humillime commendo charitati et fraternitati Parochorum Reverendissimorum in Helvetiâ degentium.
Joan. H. Newman Congr. Orat.
Dabam die Aug 6 1868.
[2] Henry Caswall was in America. Copeland's brother was the invalid George.
[3] All the dates were inserted at the end of *S.D.*
[4] See letter of 4 Feb. to Emily Bowles.

The Oratory Bm Aug. 5. 1868

My dear Fr Coleridge

You ask me what I precisely mean, in my Apologia, Appendix p 26, by saying, apropos of Anglican Orders, that 'Antiquarian arguments are altogether unequal to the urgency of visible facts.' I will try to explain.[1]

1. The inquiry into Anglican Orders has ever been to me of the class which I must call dreary; for it is dreary surely to have to grope into the minute intricate passages and obscure corners of past occurrences, in order to ascertain whether this man was ever consecrated, or that man used a valid form, or a certain sacramental intention came up to the mark, or the report or register of an ecclesiastical act can be cleared of suspicion. I[2] never have been able to arrive at any thing higher than a probable conclusion, which is most unsatisfactory except to Antiquarians, who delight in researches into the past for their own sake.

2. Now on the other hand what do I mean by 'visible facts.' I mean such definite facts as throw a broad antecedent light upon what may be presumed in a case in which sufficient evidence is not forthcoming. For instance

(1) The apostolical Succession, its necessity, and its grace, is not an Anglican tradition, tho' it is a tradition found in the Anglican Church. By contrast — our Lord's divinity *is* an Anglican tradition — every one high or low, holds it. It is not only in Prayer book and Catechism, but in the mouths of all professors of Anglicanism. Not to believe it, is to be no Anglican, and any persons[3] in authority, for 300 years, who were suspected to doubt or explain it away, were marked men, as Dr. Colenso is now marked. And they have been

---

[1] Coleridge wrote on 4 Aug. that he was preparing a paper on Anglican Orders. 'There is a passage at the beginning of the paper in which something is said of "moral" considerations of likelihood or the reverse — e.g. that it is *primâ facie* unlikely that there would be a true succession without a prevailing belief in the Priesthood and the Sacrifice among the clergy themselves, and the people. It has occurred to me to quote your expression "antiquarian arguments are altogether unequal to the urgency of visible facts" — and then came the desire to ask you whether you would put down in three or four sentences what you mean by "visible facts".'

Newman wrote in *Apo.*, p. 341; (first edition, Appendix, p. 26):

'And, as to its possession of an episcopal succession from the time of the Apostles, well, it may have it, and, if the Holy See ever so decide, I will believe it, as being the decision of a higher judgment than my own; but for myself, I must have St. Philip's gift, who saw the sacerdotal character on the forehead of a gaily-attired youngster, before I can by my own wit acquiesce in it, for antiquarian arguments are altogether unequal to the urgency of visible facts.'

Coleridge went on to suggest that Newman might reply in a short letter, which 'would give you an opportunity of saying what would put an end to those floating rumours of which I told you some time ago,' i.e. that Newman held Anglican Orders to be valid.

See also *Ess.* II, pp. 76–89.

[2] When his letter was printed in the *Month*, (Sept. 1868), pp. 269–71, Newman began this sentence, 'On giving myself to consider the question, I . . .'

[3] Pages three and four of the autograph are missing at this point, and the text is that printed in the *Month*, until the words at the beginning of number (3) 'administration of the other sacraments.'

so few that they could be counted. Not such is the Apostolic succession; and, considering the Church is the *columna et firmamentum veritatis*,[1] and is ever bound to stir up the gift that is in her, there is surely a strong presumption that the Anglican body has not what it does not profess to have. I wonder how many of its bishops and deans hold the doctrine at this time; some who do not, occur to the mind at once. One knows what was the case thirty or forty years ago by the famous saying of Blomfield, Bishop of London.[2]

(2.) If there is a true succession, there is a true Eucharist; if there is not a true Eucharist, there is no true succession. Now, what is the presumption here? I think it is Mr. Alexander Knox who says or suggests that, if so great a gift *be* given, it must have a custos. Who is the custos of the Anglican Eucharist?[3] The Anglican clergy? Could I, without distressing or offending an Anglican, describe what sort of custodes they have been, and are, to their Eucharist? 'O bone custos,' in the words of the poet, 'cui commendavi Filium Meum!'[4] Is it not charitable towards the bulk of the Anglican clergy to hope, to believe, that so great a treasure has not been given to their keeping? And would our Lord leave Himself for centuries in such hands? Inasmuch then as 'the sacrament of the Body and Blood of Christ' in the Anglican communion is without protective ritual and jealous guardianship, there seems to me a strong presumption that neither the real gift, or its appointed guardians, are to be found in that communion.

(3) Previous baptism is the condition of the valid administration of the other Sacraments. Even when I was in the Anglican Church, I saw enough of the lax administration of Baptism among high Churchmen, though they did not of course intend it, to fill me with great uneasiness. Of course there are definite persons whom one might point out, whose baptisms are sure to be valid. But my argument has nothing to do with *present* baptisms. Bishops were baptized, not lately, but as children. The present Bishops were consecrated by other Bishops, they again by others. What I have seen in the Anglican Church makes it very difficult for me to believe that every now and then a Bishop was not a consecrator who had never been baptized —[5] Some Bishops have been brought up[6] as presbyterians, others as dissenters, others as low Churchmen, others have been baptised in the careless perfunctory way so common; there

---

[1] I *Tim.* 3:15.

[2] Blomfield remarked 'that belief in the Apostolical succession had gone out with the Non-Jurors. "We can count you," he said to some of the gravest and most venerated persons of the old school.' *Apo.*, p. 31. Blomfield also thought that testimonials for Holy Orders need not be refused to one who held that the Ministry had no authority except from the law of the land. Alfred Blomfield, *A Memoir of Charles James Blomfield*, London 1863, II, pp. 6–8.

[3] When he reprinted this letter in *Ess.* II, pp. 109–11, Newman altered this to read: 'I think it is Mr. Alexander Knox who says or suggests that, if so great a gift *be* given, it must have a rite. I add, it if has a rite, it must have a *custos* of the rite. Who is the *custos* of the Anglican Eucharist?'

[4] Terence, *Phormio* II, i, 57–8.

[5] In the printed texts altered to, 'What I have seen in the Anglican Church makes it very difficult for me to deny that every now and then a bishop was consecrator who had never been baptised.'

[6] In the printed texts 'in the north' has been added here.

is then much reason to believe that some consecrators were not Bishops, for the simple reason that, formally speaking, they were not Christians. I think there is a great presumption then that, where our Lord has not left a rigid rule of Baptism, He has not left a valid Ordination[1]

By the light of such presumptions as these I interpret the doubtful issues of the Antiquarian argument, and feel deeply, that if Anglican Orders are unsafe, with reference to the actual evidence producible for their validity, much more unsafe are they when considered in their surroundings

Most sincerely Yours John H Newman.[2]

THURSDAY 6 AUGUST 1868   break up of weather.   At 6 A.M. began a steady rain Stanislas left suddenly

FRIDAY 7 AUGUST   beautiful weather — rain and sunshine   glass kept up at 70°

TO HENRY JAMES COLERIDGE

The Oratory Bm Augst 7/68

My dear Fr Coleridge,

I have no objection to my letter's being published, but I should like to see it in proof — and should wish you to say if you want any thing altered or omitted. I shall have pleasure in seeing your article, if you have time to send it me[3]

Most truly Yours John H Newman of the Oratory

SATURDAY 8 AUGUST 1868   went into room next mine — my carpet taken up etc.

TO HENRY WILBERFORCE

The Oratory Bm Augst 8/68

My dear Henry

I return your letter. I think it ought to touch him.[4] It is very well written,

---

[1] In *Ess.* II, p. 111, this sentence reads, 'But at least there is a great presumption that where evidently our Lord has not provided a rigid rule of baptism, he has not provided a valid ordination.'

[2] Coleridge replied on 6 Aug., 'I hardly know how to thank you enough for your letter. I have shown it to Fr Whitty, who says it must be published, and that it will do immense good.'

[3] i.e. Coleridge's article in the *Month* for Sept. on Anglican Orders, 'Anglican Sacerdotalism,' at the end of which Newman's letter was printed.

[4] i.e. William Froude, whom Wilberforce was trying to persuade of the truth of the Catholic claim. See end of letter of 20 Aug. to Mrs William Froude.

and is religious as well as argumentative. *I* could not take the religious line with him — you, as being his aequalis, can. He is always afraid of bringing out his views to me, *though he tries*. But, though he feels the pain of doing so in writing to you, still he does it. I don't recollect his ever putting to me so pointedly his difficulty about *two* modes of reasoning, that of common sense and that of religion; though I have often used with him the saying of Aristotle, which you virtually use, that it is the same fault to demand demonstration of an historian as to be content with probabilities from a mathematician.

I am very weak, though the attack is quite over — and, in my weakness, of course I am thrown back in other respects, and am all wrong for the time. But I am allowed now to return to the cider, and that is doing me good. But I find my hand shakes, and I cannot well write

Ever Yrs affly John H Newman

TO H. P. LIDDON

The Oratory Bm Aug. 10. 1868

My dear Mr Liddon,

I thank you exceedingly for the trouble you have taken for me with respect to my possession of the Lyra Apostolica.

I did not mean to say, that in 1845–46, I distinctly limited the transference of the work in my own mind to Mr Keble's lifetime. I simply did not contemplate the event of his death. If, however, the question had been asked me, 'Supposing you survive Keble, supposing you survive all the writers, what is to become of the book then?' I think in that case, from my love to Keble, Williams, Froude, Bowden, and R. Wilberforce, all my dearest friends, whom I have never forgotten, whom now every day I commemorate before, or in my Mass, I should have said, 'O let me, while I live, at least have this keep-sake from them.' And such was the spirit of my letter to Mr Thos Keble junior in July 1866. I sincerely thought I should be gratifying him by the request I was making, and I was suprised to find it was otherwise.[1]

And now I want no transference of copyright. It may go back to Mr Keble's representatives on my death. If any thing suggest itself to you as necessary to secure this, besides leaving a memorandum to that effect, I will do it.

Nor do I wish to put any obstacle of course in the way of Keble's and William's [sic] poems being collected from the volume and published separately.

---

[1] See letter of 9 Sept. 1866 to Thomas Keble. Liddon wrote on 8 Aug. that he had corresponded with Thomas Keble Junior in order to clear up the misunderstanding of 1866, and as a result the latter had written the letter of 7 Aug. quoted in last note to letter of 1 Aug. 1868 to Liddon. Liddon asked Newman to agree that from Keble's death the copyright of the *Lyra Apostolica* had been his, and in the next sentence Newman does so.

I am surprised from Mr Thos Keble's letter to see how large the balance of sale was during his uncle's last years. I suppose, however, it had accumulated.[1] What I propose to do with such profits as fall to me is to ask to be allowed to offer them in the shape of books to the Library of the Keble College. I should select such books as those of our great School men and Theologians, from Alexander Hales to Benedict the 14th — and Greek Office books whether edited by Greeks or Roman Theologians, such as Goar's Euchologium. But you must tell me, if you see any objection to this.

God bless us all Most sincerely Yours
John H Newman

The Revd H. P. Liddon

P.S.   Will you convey the substance of this letter to Mr Thos Keble, thanking him for his letter.[2]

TUESDAY 11 AUGUST 1868   Thunder — rain   called on Mrs Hardman and Mrs
Bretherton and the Bishop.   glass fell to 66°

TO HENRY WILBERFORCE

The Oratory Bm ⌜Aug. 12/68⌝

My dear H W

⌜Thank you for the trouble you have taken in copying my letter,[3] and for the encouragement you give me, which I sorely need. I know any how, that, however honest are my thoughts, and earnest my endeavours to keep rigidly within the lines of Catholic doctrine, every word I publish will be malevolently scrutinized, and every expression which can possibly be perverted sent straight to Rome, — that I shall be fighting *under the lash*, which does not tend to produce vigorous efforts in the battle or to inspire either courage or presence of mind. And if from those who ought to be my friends, I cannot look for sympathy — if, did I do my work ever so well, they will take no interest in it, or see the use of it, where can I look for that moral aid which carries one through difficulties? where for any token that Providence means me to go on with my work?

I don't think that my various occupations here are the cause of my doing so little. I was full of household work when I wrote my Anglican difficulties

---

[1] Thomas Keble Junior wrote to Liddon in his letter of 7 Aug., 'Mr Mozley sent me a balance of £60 due to the publication at the time of my Uncle's death . . .'

[2] Liddon replied on 12 Aug. that John Keble would have been delighted at Newman's wish to link himself 'with the memories of the past' by the 'keep sake' of the *Lyra Apostolica*, and Keble's nephew regretted that he had not followed his own first instinct in the matter. Liddon added that Newman's gift to Keble College Library 'would be very welcome to those of us who think that the Apologia has done scarcely less than the Christian Year towards bringing all that they love and revere in Mr Keble before the eyes of his countrymen.'

[3] That of 27 July.

and Catholicism in England —[1] but I was not encompassed then by a host of ill wishers, and I was younger. Now it tires me to be a long time at one matter, and from fatigue I cannot write things *off*. Also my present subject is one which can only gradually be thought out.

As to my engagements here a Superior *must* have them. We are very few Fathers, and each has his work — one has the jail — another the Orphanage — two have the School — another has the Parish — another the Poor Schools. The great *domestic* works, the care of the Library, the Sacristy, the Accounts, necessarily in great measure fall to me, at least at intervals. Now I am at the Library. The Oxford matter, correspondence and accounts, took up an untold mass of time — and tired me, so that they wasted more. And now that I am getting so old, I want to go through all my correspondence etc etc — which will be close employment for some years.[1]

Every Yrs affly John H Newman

TO HENRY JAMES COLERIDGE

The Oratory Bm Aug. 13. 1868

My dear F. Coleridge

I should be *very sorry* if my letter about the London University appeared.[2] It was written to show privately. Then Serjt Bellasis wished it sent to the Times. I consented *because* he wished it. The Times would not insert it. I have no call to put myself forward in such a matter. I have never recognized, I have never endorsed, the London University. I inclose a letter to Bellasis, (which be so good as to direct,) telling him how averse I am to my letter being published.

I have corrected and return my letter on Anglican Orders. I am sorry to make so many corrections, but hope you will allow them.

And I return your own Article.[3] It is clear, forcible, and good. Its fault is that it is short. It ought to receive an answer, but I suppose it won't.

Most sincerely Yrs John H Newman

FRIDAY 14 AUGUST 1868   engaged in dusting my own books *engaged this time in dusting books of Library* Miss Munro here about this time   and Miss Smith and Miss Slinger from Cheltenham (*this is at least the 3rd time*)

[1] In 1850 and 1851.
[2] The letter of 25 Jan. 1868.
[3] 'Anglican Sacerdotalism' for the *Month* of Sept.

The Oratory Bm Aug 14. 1868

My dear Pollen

I hope you and Mrs Pollen are at some distance from London just now —
but, as you *may* be there, or may be able to help me even if not, I write this.

You will smile to know that for a month I have been advertising in vain
for a cook. Tell me how to get one — Is there not some institution in London,
whence cooks issue? Can't you put me in the way? She must be a Catholic of
course. I give no particulars, for what I want to know is, *where to go.*

I hope your wife is well, and all of you.

Ever yrs affly John H Newman

P.S.   William is with Ambrose in Switzerland — Bel Alp — Zermatt.

The Oratory Birmm Aug 15. 1868.

My dear Boy

Your letter to Fr Henry has deeply grieved me, as much as it has startled
me. I had seen very little of your Father, but he was so kind and winning, that
I wished to know him better, and am pained on my own account, as well as
when I think of your dear Mother and all of you. I don't forget at all what her
last words were, when she parted from me in the Spring; and with what
anxious feeling she said them; and I look upon your Father's reception as an
answer to her prayers. What a great, ineffable consolation to her in this her
great trial![1]

Say all this to her from me, and with my kindest thoughts of her, your
sister and yourself

I am, Yours affectionately John H. Newman

P.S.   Please God, I shall say Mass for your Father, living or dead, to morrow
morning

The Assumption 1868.

Master Henry Vincent Higgins

---

[1] Matthew James Higgins, 'Jacob Omnium' was taken ill after bathing, and died six days
later, on 14 Aug. He was received into the Church before he died.

The Oratory Aug. 16. 1868

My dear Challis,

We shall rejoice to see you on Tuesday, and a room shall be ready for you. For myself unluckily I go to Town Tuesday morning, perhaps only for a few hours, perhaps for the week. But, if I come back, I shall have to go up again before the week is over. I am obliged to go this week, as I am expecting Fr Hyacinth from Paris the week after. Can you talk French? if so, you will be very serviceable

Most truly Yours John H Newman

TO MRS MATTHEW JAMES HIGGINS

The Oratory, Birmm Aug 16. 1868

My dear Mrs Higgins

I hope you will not think me intruding on you at this moment, when you are in such deep grief. It is not as if I thought you could fancy that the lines I am sending you require any acknowledgment — else, of course I should not write a word.

Why I write is to congratulate you, as I do with all my heart, on the great mercy God has shown you, in showing mercy to your dear husband. What a most consoling thought! I often think what a consolation it must be to a parent, on losing a little child, to know that she has first made him a Christian and that his salvation is secured — but how much more rare is it to be able to praise God for having had power given one, by prayer and by example, to convert a husband! What a wonderful grace too, that he is now taken away in what I may call his baptismal innocence — in the fresh fulness of those great gifts which the Sacraments convey! These are thoughts which will be more and more consolatory to you day by day — and will bear you up and strengthen you against and amid the keen natural sorrow which your great bereavement causes you.

For myself I will only say that I felt deep regret on my own account at hearing of the loss of one whom, little as I had the opportunity of knowing him, I so loved and respected; and that I said Mass for him 'living or dead,' this morning — To morrow morning, please God, I shall say Mass for *you*, and for *his soul*.

I wrote to your son last night

Ever Yours most sincerely John H. Newman

Mrs Higgins

TO MRS JOHN MOZLEY

The Oy Bm August 16. 1868

My dear Jemima

I rejoiced in the hot weather — it was one of the 'old' summers — that is, one of the only two I recollect such, 1818 and 1826. It was the change that dished me — the glass fell 10 degrees — and I was seized with a shivering, and then with diarrhœa, a very unusual complaint with me. It pulled me down, but that was little, and I am recovering from it, but the mischief was that it threw me back in more serious ways, and my doctor said I was in a state which sometimes happens after fever, completely disorganized or out of sorts — and I have not yet come right, though I am much better. I am very thankful that I am as well as I am, but, if the necessity of going on with my medicine is to be a test, I am not better than I was a year ago. I with difficulty keep a great enemy at bay, but I trust I do so.[1]

P.S.   Copeland has been seriously ill of rheumatic fever. I am very anxious for him.

TO JOHN HUNGERFORD POLLEN

The Oratory Aug. 16/68

My dear Pollen,

What good people you are! I am likely to be in London for an hour or two on *Tuesday* morning — and if you drop me a line giving me Francatelli's direction (or any other person,) I will call on him about the Cook, if he does not live very much out of the way.[2] Direct to me at 'The Paddington Terminus Hotel.' I *may* be kept in Town the night, if so, I shall (if all is well) run down to Pembridge Crescent to take tea with you about 7 that evening; or, if you dine at that hour, to eat some of your pudding, since I shall have dined.

But pray don't stop at home; my movements are so uncertain

Ever Yrs affly John H. Newman

P.S.   Mr Higgins died a Catholic. Don't tell I am coming to London — else, people say Why did you not call?

---

[1] Conclusion and signature have been cut out.
[2] Charles Elmé Francatelli was the manager of St James's Hotel, 1 Berkeley Street and 77 Piccadilly.

The Oratory Bm Aug. 16. 1868

My dear Pusey

I can have no possible objection to your introducing any statements on controverted points in your letter to me, if only you say (what I suppose *you* would say too) that you know I hold that, *supposing* the *Church* declared and defined those controverted points in one particular way, i.e. defined that the Pope speaking ex cathedrâ was infallible, or that the Augustinian or the Dominican view of Predestination was not the true one, or that St John by a special privilege was preserved from venial sin, I should receive such doctrine as part of the original faith.[1]

I think you would say this too, only you would define the Church differently; you would say that it included the Greek and Anglican communions. But I suppose you *would* allow that, if the Latin, Greek, and Anglican Communion, met together in solemn council, *did* define either of the above points in one way or the other, it was thereby to be received as a part of the Apostolic faith. *If* you could say as much as this, you would not indeed conciliate some people — but you would hold the same principle as we do — you would but differ about a matter of fact, serious as that fact may be. No one could then fairly accuse you of private judgment, for you would be [but] submit your credenda to a power beyond you.

As to individual proselytism, you must recollect that we only feel and do what you feel and do towards Dissenters.[2] By what right have you converted from Dissent, as you say, 32 out of 40 Bishops of the Anglo-American Church? By the same right we have converted a number of men who are now among our Priests — You write to the Westleyans and try to co-operate with them; but I am sure you would make a Wesleyan, whom you met with, a good Anglican, if you could. I am not aware that Manning and Ward convert individuals, any more than I should, in order to weaken the Anglican Church, but from love to the soul of the individual converted, as *you* would feel love for the Wesleyan.

By the bye, the position of the Wesleyans is remarkable. They are narrow-minded, self-sufficient, and conceited — but they seem to me to be more likely to make a stand against infidelity than any religious body in England.

[1] Pusey, who was planning his *Is Healthful Reunion Impossible? A Second Letter to the Very Revd. J. H. Newman, D.D.*, Oxford 1870, thought of introducing into it propositions on controverted points, in view of the imminent Vatican Council, which he hoped the authorities in Rome might accept. He wrote on 13 Aug. asking whether he should insert them in his *Letter to Newman*, 'But would it in any way commit you? . . . But would its being addressed to you 1) call out any expression from you or 2) in case of your silence in any way compromise you.'

[2] Pusey spoke of the spread of infidelity in France and Italy as a reason for reunion. 'We should mutually strengthen one another if united. Yet the individual proselytism which Manning and Ward think the only way would not (humanly speaking) arrive at what we hope for, because we are gaining from the Dissenters. Out of 40 Bishops of the Anglo-American Church, 32 were born in some sect, and so, we are told, Priests and people in proportion. So, almost whatever number the Roman Church might gain from us, if we gain in the same proportions, we should still remain unassimilated.'

The Anglican Low-Church are poor bodies — and the Anglican communion is too much divided to do much. As to ourselves, I would not dare to take any view of God's purposes to His Church and through His Church in past times or future — but I sometimes think that as the Ark of Noah did not hinder or destroy the flood but rode upon it, preserving the hopes of the human family within its fragile planks, so has it been with the Catholic Church — she rode upon the barbarian deluge, saving the history and literature of the past, the true religion, and the tradition of the primitive ages from being swallowed up, but she did not withstand it, as (e.g.) for an instance St Leo repulsed Attila, and influenced Genseric. And so now, I am prepared for a break up of religion every where, as far as establishment goes, nay as far as consistent profession, but still, as in France and England, so in Italy there will be a remnant, the purer in that it is smaller. I am prepared to believe what you say of the wretched state of Italy. You were a bad Catholic, if you breathed a word hinting it ten years ago, but now the very men who so stupidly denied it, now preach it openmouthed. That close despotic system does not suit this age of the world, and, however dreadful sacrilege and blasphemy are, I cannot weep that there is a prospect of its being broken up.

I don't forget next Saturday[1]

Ever Yrs affly John H Newman

MONDAY 17 AUGUST 1868   engaged in dusting my own books etc   Ignatius went away?
TUESDAY 18 AUGUST   went to London to Rahn, and back   Miss Munro left   (Challis came from Morville)[2]

TO MRS JOHN HUNGERFORD POLLEN

The Oratory Aug 18/68

My dear Mrs Pollen

Don't think of answering this — I write to express with more heart than my telegraphic message of 3 PM could my true grief at having disappointed kind friends and disappointed myself by not coming to you this evening.

But I told your husband my coming was uncertain and that I should have to get back if I could. Still I am hurt to have broken a quasi engagement. I am sure, however, you will forgive me

Ever yours most sincerely John H Newman

P.S.   I saw Franconelli, and was pleased with him.[3]

WEDNESDAY 19 AUGUST 1868   got back altogether into my own room

[1] Pusey was born on 22 Aug. 1800. For his reply see at 24 Aug.
[2] Morville Hall, Bridgnorth.
[3] Francatelli. See letter of 16 Aug. to Pollen.

TO HENRY JAMES COLERIDGE

The Oratory Bm Aug. 20. 1868

My dear Fr Coleridge

I quite understood your kind reason for wishing me to see the Article on Anglican Orders. And I don't think that any thing you say in it will be thought mine *in sentiment* by Pusey, though my letter follows.[1]

As I said, I think it a forcible article, and *not* unfair to Pusey and only too short — and it demands an answer

Most sincerely Yours John H Newman

TO MRS WILLIAM FROUDE

The Oratory Bm Aug. 20. 1868

My dear Mrs Froude,

I was very glad to have a letter from you — and, though I could not expect that your sufferings would be less than you describe, I am relieved to find that you are able to speak of them. Of course no one but yourself knows what the bereavement is — except Him who has willed it and can support you under it —

I wish, if you are equal to it, you had some change, as Isy [Froude] has — I am glad she is enjoying this beautiful summer.

Is it not shocking that, Irish people being what they are, we should have burned into them such a hatred of us? From every thing I hear, I don't think there is such a peasant class in the world. Every one says the same. Fr Flanagan (who was with *us*) has a parish of I forget how many, not a small one.[2] Every one, except two or three, were at his Easter duties — and there seems hardly a crime committed from the beginning of the year to the end. Every where they hate the English — and are hostile to the landlords, more or less; at least to the landlord system, and what can be more audaciously cruel and insulting than the conduct of such men as Mr Scully?[3] Whatever bitterness there is in them, we are the cause of it, and whether we ever can undo what we have done, is more than any statesman can say.

If I saw much of Eddy, I should use him as a youth can be of use to an old man, — as a whetstone or steel for my knife. I want to know what raw

---

[1] Coleridge wrote on 17 Aug. that he wanted his article 'Anglican Sacerdotalism,' in which Pusey was attacked, to be seen by Newman, since his letter would be printed at the end of it in the *Month* for Sept.

[2] Flanagan was parish priest of Adare, County Limerick.

[3] William Scully, a landlord in Limerick and an apostate Catholic, treated his tenants with extreme harshness. On 14 Aug. he went with police to evict a number of them personally. Shots were fired and policemen killed and wounded.

material (he) has to say to many a manufactured article (mine) which I think genuine and sound, but cannot be sure of

. . . .

It is an anxious thing, but very interesting to me, to know what comes of Henry Wilberforce's letters. . . .[1]

Ever Yrs affectly in Xt   John H Newman of the Oratory

TO MISS M. R. GIBERNE

The Oratory Bm St Bernard's Day 1868

My dear Sister Pia

I was going to write today to you to congratulate you on tomorrow, when I hope to say Mass for you, when your letter comes.[2] I grieve indeed to hear you have got a 'knock on the head' — what does it mean? I trust you are prudent.

Dr Pusey is not converted, nor Hamilton.[3] The Anglicans are in sad confusion — no one knows what tomorrow may bring forth. The Evangelicals have raised a fund of many thousands for prosecuting Ritualists, Puseyites etc. They begin with Bennett — Pusey has challenged them to take himself. He says he will give up his preferment if it is proved in ecclesiastical court against him 1 that Anglicans may not hold the Eucharistic Sacrifice — 2. the *Objective* real presence — 3 the duty of adoring the host.[4] If he gives up his preferment, he goes a good way towards leaving the Anglican Church. If he leaves the Anglican Church, what is he to join? This, I suppose, has given rise to the report. I should not despair of him, if English Catholics did not make it a point of *faith* for him to believe in the infallibility of the Pope. This bothers him. *Of course* if the Ecumenical Council *defined* the Pope's Infallibility, that would be another thing, (not that I think it will) but, as things are, it is quite open to hold the Pope not infallible — but the Archbishop, Ward, etc etc. are clamorous on the point, and, while they are creating much uneasy feeling among lay converts, and unsettling their minds, they are hindering the chances of such as Pusey joining the Church.

---

[1] This sentence is preserved only in *Harper*, p. 183. Cf. letters of 27 July and 8 Aug. to Henry Wilberforce.
[2] The feast of St Jane Frances de Chantal, Foundress of the Visitation Order, which Miss Giberne had joined, was on 21 Aug.
[3] Walter Kerr Hamilton, the High Church Bishop of Salisbury from 1854 until his death in 1869. In his charge of 1867 he raised a storm by defending strongly the doctrines of the Real Presence, the Eucharistic Sacrifice and priestly Absolution.
[4] The Protestant 'Church Association' had begun a prosecution against W. J. E. Bennett, the extreme ritualist Vicar of Frome for his Eucharistic doctrine, chiefly as he had stated it in a public letter to Pusey. Pusey made great efforts to be included in the suit, but this was refused. Bennett was acquitted by the Court of Arches in 1870, and the judgment confirmed on appeal by the Privy Council. Liddon's *Pusey*, IV, pp. 217–18.

I have not forgotten your question — your letter containing it is on my Table — and I meant to answer it the next time I wrote. You must recollect that the Church has not put forth any authoritative interpretation of Scripture, and doctors differ very much, and allowably, in the senses they affix to particular passages. Thus e.g. the greatest Fathers explain 'My Father is greater than I' of our Lord's Divine Person — but the more modern rule is to interpret it of His human nature.[1]

St Thomas in his Catena Aurea thus quotes the Fathers on Matt. I. 19.

Pseudo-Augustine. 'Joseph says, shall I proclaim it or overlook it? If I proclaim it, I am running into the guilt of cruelty, for by Moses' law she must be stoned.'

Ambrose. 'St Matthew has beautifully taught us how a righteous man ought to act, who has detected his wife's disgrace.'

Jerome. 'How is Joseph thus called 'just', when he is ready to hide his wife's sin?'

Chrysostom. Being 'just', that is, kind, merciful, he was minded to put away privily her who according to the law was liable, not only to dismissal, but to death.'

Glossa. He sought it privily, being unwilling to disgrace her.

Augustine. Joseph with great mercy spared his wife, in this great crime of which he suspected her. On the other hand

Jerome. *'or*, Joseph, confident in her purity, *covered in silence* that mystery, which he could not explain.'

Rabanus. 'He beheld her with child, whom he knew to be chaste. Because he had read 'Behold, a virgin shall conceive etc' he did not doubt that this prophecy should be fulfilled in her.'

Origen. *'He sought to put her away, because he saw in her a great sacrament, to approach which he thought himself unworthy.'*

The hot weather is now over — but we have had a summer never reached except in 1818 and 1826 in my time. I had some diarrhœa, but am well now. — Otherwise, I cannot leave off my medicine for the complaint which I am threatened with.

God bless you and preserve you

Ever Yrs affly in Xt   John H Newman

TO HENRY WILBERFORCE

The Oratory Bm ⌈Aug. 20/68⌉

My dear H W

I never have met with an explanation of the word 'Positivism.' For myself I explain it by the contrast which Comte makes between it and other stages

[1] *John*, 14:28.

of intellectualism. These stages are, The Supernatural or Theological, the Metaphysical, and the Positive. In the first every phenomenon is referred to an unseen Being, in the second to some ideal entities — causes, forms etc — in the Positive we are content to take phenomena as facts, and from observation, to find their general laws. It is a positive philosophy in opposition to theories.[1]

He abjures Atheism because it is a kind of Metaphysics. It dogmatically denies an intelligent cause, and dogmatically assigns causes short of it. But the Positive Philosopher has nothing to do with causes.

As time went on, I believe he considered religion *necessary* for the mind — but it was all subjective. I believe he instituted a worship, a rite, to the Aggregate of humanity, the Auto-Man. Religious books would be necessary on this score — and nothing could be better than those of the Middle Ages. He had a great admiration for the Medieval Church — it educated the world in the only possible way for his own truer and purer system — what could be wiser than Papal infallibility? What more beautiful and salutary than the practice of confession?

As to the 'Imitation' in particular nothing could be better, if it suited a mind. Tastes differ — there is G. Eliot in the Mill on the Floss found the 'Imitation' so cold, so dreary that it could never constitute the religion of a woman, which requires something of passion — but I suppose that writer would say 'Qui potest capere, capiat.'[2]

I fear you expect from me what is far above me, and what I cannot do. But if I could suggest one or two thoughts which those who come after me can make use of, it is enough.

⌜Only think of Anderdon cutting me dead in Oxford Street two years ago! Father Neville was with me — and is clear or clearer of the fact than I. He held his eyes fixed on the ground and not by chance. *Don't mention this*⌝[3]

Ever Yrs affly J H N

TO MRS F. J. WATT

August 21. 68.

My dear Child,

I suppose you have long since given over your collection — but, as I have found some stamps I had put aside for you, I send them.

I hope you are well again, and your husband

Ever yours affectionately   John H. Newman

---

[1] 'In its original and narrower sense, the system of the French thinker Auguste Comte, which confined intellectual inquiry to observable ("positive") facts and their relations, and eschewed all consideration of ultimate issues, including those of philosophy and theology.' Definition in *The Oxford Dictionary of the Christian Church*, edited by F. L. Cross, London 1957, p. 1094.

[2] *The Mill on the Floss*, Book IV, Chapter iii, 'A Voice from the Past.'

[3] William Anderdon, an old friend of Henry Wilberforce, and under many obligations to Newman, was in 1866 and until he joined the Jesuits in 1872, Manning's private secretary.

SATURDAY 22 AUGUST 1868   Austin went away   my eye bad. *my eye lid swollen*   sent for Carter who not at home, sent for Jordan.   could not say Mass   A fire in my room!   much rain and cold wind

SUNDAY 23 AUGUST   did not say Mass

MONDAY 24 AUGUST   did not say Mass   Thomas (Pope) went away   Henry, Edward and I alone here.

TO E. B. PUSEY

The Oratory Aug. 24/68

My dear Pusey

I am sorry to say that the Month will be at you again in a few sentences in September. The ground is, which I think unreasonable, that you have not yet answered certain questions of fact which contradict what you have said in print.[1]

I should not notice it, except that a letter of mine follows it quite unconnected with it, and which the Editor would not have inserted if he had thought any one *would* connect it with it. Thus I happened to know about the Article — for the Editor wanted my judgment whether the proximity would make readers connect me with the *matter of the Article*. I thought not — and told him so — though I told him also that I was sorry any thing was said in the Article against you — tho' I had no right to interfere with him.

As to my own letter, the *matter* of it will pain you — but I did not know how I could help it. I was asked the *meaning* of a sentence of mine in my Apologia, and in this letter I have given it.[2]

When I spoke of the Wesleyans as I did, I meant simply to speak of them as withstanding infidelity and upholding our Lord's divinity — (tho' Adam Clark, I think, was *not* quite orthodox in his belief of it).[3] — I did not mean as arguing etc, but as presenting a mass of persons living on and in the notion that there was a Divine Law, a Judgment, a revelation, a vicarious sacrifice, a necessity for grace, that our Lord was God, and that there was a Trinity of Divine Persons. I do not know, out of our own pale, where to look for such a *concordant* body of living, professing, acting witnesses to these Truths. At the same time, I confess I know nothing of their internal state — and they may

---

[1] Pusey objected to the Swedish Orders and the *Month* maintained that 'There is no ground of complaint urged against them by him, which does not exist *in principle*, in the case of the Anglican ordinations'. Pusey replied on 26 Aug., 'I probably shall not see the writing in the Month, as I no longer read it. I read it and the W.R. [*Weekly Register*] as long as I hoped that they were accessible by me.'

[2] Letter of 5 Aug. to H. J. Coleridge.

[3] Pusey wrote on 21 Aug. 'I am so glad that you think so well of the Wesleyans, but it is pure Lutheranism, without the doctrine of the sacraments, which Luther professed [.] But since they have at least not the Body and Blood of Christ, it is well that they should not think they have. However, they are in earnest, and have, though a naked Gospel, in its outlines a true one. But conceit is but a bad earnest for the future.'

Adam Clarke (1762?–1832), Wesleyan preacher and theological writer; 'on the person of Jesus Christ, while maintaining his divinity, he denied his eternal sonship.' *DNB*.

not in fact be what I believe them to be. The Baptists and Independents seem to me to be divided in religious opinion, and unreliable — The Church of England has three schools — but the Westleyans, *as far as they go*, seem to me homogeneous.

As to your instance of a lady perplexed about the Immaculate Conception, of course, she never ought to have been received, unless she confronted the fundamental doctrine that she must believe what the Church (the Roman Communion) taught, whatever it might be, as being the word of God *through* the Church.[1] There is not unfrequently a hasty reception, partly by the fault of the receiver, quite as often by the fault of the received. People come with the most earnest sollicitations, declare that they have believed in no Church but the Roman for a long time, that, if they are not received, they shall fall into hopeless scepticism or infidelity, and implicitly throw the responsibility of this result on the priest who refuses to receive them. Perhaps he still tells them to wait — they do — and then they come again with the same story, and he is perplexed beyond measure what he ought to do. And at length he receives them. Sometimes all goes on well — and they become really devout and steady Catholics: and he thanks God that he has done right — but sometimes they turn out ill.

I have no right to be sanguine about any thing, but I think an avowal from you, such as you propose, in which you may expressly include me, if you choose, saying that both of us hold one and the same principle, viz to receive not only what 'the Church' *has* defined, but what it *shall* define (tho' we differ about the fact, what *is* the Church,) in matters of doctrine, — that such an avowal will open the eyes of many of us about you, who think you make your own interpretation of Scripture and the Fathers the ultimate foundation of your creed[2]

Ever Yours affectly John H Newman

TUESDAY 25 AUGUST 1868   said Mass up stairs

[1] In reply to Newman, Pusey wrote, 'I did not mean to blame individual proselytism, only to regret that Mg [Manning] and W. [Ward] speak of it as the only way. They, as you know, not only think organised reunion hopeless, but Mg even deprecates it, if it could be, as if we should only be a source of weakness to the Church. It is not his converting, but his deprecating organic reunion as wrong

. . . .

In illustration, I have been lately answering a letter of a poor lady, who has been excommunicate (as she says) for two years because she did not believe the Immaculate Conception. She had heard that I was joining the Church of Rome, and asked me how I got over the difficulty of the Immaculate Conception. I wrote to her, as you would, that it was inconsistent to acknowledge the Church of Rome to be alone the Church, and not to accept her decrees.' See note to letter of 28 Aug. to Pusey.

[2] Pusey began his letter of 21 Aug., 'Kindest thanks for your remembrance of me on Saturday. It will be very easy to mention that which is a common principle of both [of us], that the decision of the Church is final and infallible and that she is the judge of evidence. We held it in those old happy times, and (tho' some of yours I think censured me), it has been my habit, even amid this controversy, to believe implicitly all which the Church believes though I do not know it, while of course I believe explicitly all which I know that she believes.'

The Oratory August 25. 1868

My dear Sir Justin

Your son Edward has been with us, I think, at least as many as seven years; in the absence of our Secretary, I cannot speak for certain.

In all that time his conduct has been unexceptionable in all important matters — nor has he ever committed any serious offence against discipline.

And I know no boy whose school life has given clearer evidence of improvement year after year.

I have ever taken great interest in him, and he has my best wishes that our own experience of him may also be the experience of all others to whose care he may be committed

I am, My dear Sir Justin, Sincerely Yours John H Newman

To Sir Justin Sheil K C B &c &c

FRIDAY 28 AUGUST 1868   Dr Jordan left me.   Went out first time

TO MISS MUNRO

The Oratory Aug 28/68

My dear Miss Munro

I am sorry I do not see you so soon as you proposed.

I do not think it any thing wrong to wish not to get well — so that you simply put yourself into God's hands, and do not so wish from crossness or despondency. At the same time I grieve to hear you speak as if you thought that God really was determining it that way for you. I was deeply concerned to hear as much as you have told me about yourself lately as before — and have kept you in mind ever since, as one who needed that special strength from God which to those who need He always gives.

How can you doubt the fallibility of a director, when you have before now given me such clear proofs of the fallibility of such superiors? So far from thinking it wrong in you to doubt their infallibility, I should think it a very great mistake in you to begin to think them infallible. I have always thought that you did more than you ought to do, and that your happiness and also your duty lay in being still

God bless you

Ever Yours affectly John H Newman of the Oratory[1]

---

[1] Miss Munro has written on the autograph, 'The Cardinal's fatherly kindness came out most during the last few years of his life when he could hardly write — and I was ill from nerves and heart.'

Aug 28/68

My dear Pusey

Your letter has come. The inclosed may be useful to any one who is editing Keble's works — but I don't know to whom to send it.

My own letter in the Month is in explanation of my words about English Orders, 'Antiquarian considerations do not sustain the stress of visible fact.' The Article itself is on Bishop Forbes's Exposition of the 39 Articles.[1]

I think they go out of the way to speak of you, and I said so. My own letter is *not addressed* to the Month

Ever Yrs affly JHN

P.S. Is the lady who addressed you Miss Forbes? if so, I think she *is* mad. I only know her through her letters.[2]

TO MRS WOOTTEN

Friday Aug 28/68

My dear Mrs Wootten

Thank you for all your kindness about my eye. I consider it well now, and return what you lent me.

I did not forget the day so sacred to you in memory[3]

Yrs affectly John H Newman

TO W. J. O'NEILL DAUNT

The Oratory Bm Aug. 29. 1868

My dear Sir

I will gladly put the intentions of yourself and Colonel Scott on the prayer list of our Confraternity of the Precious Blood, and on our own. And, if all is well, I will say Mass for your and his intentions on the 4th.

I am sorry to hear the anxiety you are in about your Son. Personal trial is often the only way in which young men learn wisdom, which they might have gained cheaply and at once if they would only profit by the experience of others. But generally the trial and the wisdom comes sooner to them than we

---

[1] Cf. letter of 6 April to A. P. Forbes.

[2] Pusey said on 26 Aug., 'I suspect that the lady about whom I wrote, [must] be a little out of her mind; her letters seemed excited.' Newman thought this must be Helen Douglas Forbes. See letters of 4 Oct. 1864, 28 April and 9 May 1865. However on 31 Aug. Pusey wrote: 'After all, there can be no breach of confidence about the Dowager Marchioness of Queensberry [.] For she wrote to me on the ground of the report that I had submitted to the Roman Church, asking me how I got over the difficulty of the Immaculate Conception; so it was no intercourse which anyone could censure.' Caroline Margaret Clayton, widow of the seventh Marquis of Queensberry, became a Catholic apparently in 1862, and remained one.

[3] The anniversary of the death of her husband, John Wootten, on 26 Aug. 1847.

think — and I trust it will not be long before your Son learns at least so much as this, that those who love him well are better guides for him than himself.

I trust and pray that God will hasten this time

Most truly Yours in Xt   John H Newman of the Oratory

W. J. O'N. Daunt Esqr

TO JAMES LAURENCE SHEPHERD

The Oratory Birmingham Aug 29. 1868

My dear Fr Shepherd

I understand that your Translation is *prose* — so that literal, not poetical words are necessary.

1. I should be inclined to render the word 'Fumosa,' Grimed, or Begrimed, or Smoke-grimed, or Smoke-stained.

2. Gallicanus cothurnus is the Gallic *pomp* or pompousness (of language.) You might also keep the metaphor and say 'the Gallic strut' except that the word is not grave enough — though Dr Milner I think speaks of 'the Episcopal Strut' in a good sense. 'Gallic inflation' gives the meaning.

3. As to gnosis, I do not know the passages you refer to and cannot translate it without knowing the context. 'Haurior gnosim', as far as the words go, might be translated 'to drink or imbibe the spirit.'[1]

I wish my answers were more satisfactory

Sincerely Yours John H Newman

MONDAY 31 AUGUST 1868   Austin returned

TO AMBROSE ST JOHN

⌜The Oratory Bm Septr 3. 1868⌝

My dear A

I trust that by the time this gets to Brighton, you will have got back safe. If W. [William] comes by 8 o'clock, I will add the news of it, but I don't expect him till tomorrow or you in Brighton, recollecting how we tired ourselves two years ago, by not sleeping in London. We don't want you till over the 6th as you may have taken for granted.

I have little to tell you. Gaisford has invited Challis to Offington; so he is going tomorrow. He has given Darnell notice he is leaving him at Christmas. He said that Darnell would tell him nothing either about work or pay — and then the thought of Beccadelli, Ernest Charlton etc. mansit altâ mente repostum.[2]

---

[1] Shepherd made a number of translations that were never published.

[2] *Aeneid*, I, 26. Challis was working under Darnell, who ran a tutoring establishment, at which were these boys, previously of the Oratory School.

⌐My inflamed eye was in some respect a worse affair that my first indisposition. It did not keep me so long from saying Mass but it confined me to my rooms longer — and brought me down sadly. Now, however, I am picking up. I have dusted and arranged all the books in my own room — and I have rummaged out all the school letters etc from the beginning, and arranged them in packets. I should like to go on to set right the archivium — but, if W. [[William]] comes, I shall fall idle, and go to Rednall. I have not been there since you left — what with illness and work; and have been, and am, in bad spirits. I am getting on with my Opus, [[Essay on Assent]], but, ungratefully, I have got down hearted about it, as if cui bono? Challis has been looking at it, and, though he is complimentary, what he really thinks I cannot tell —⌐ if he stayed till you come, I should get you to pump him. He would let out to you familiarly. ⌐I have not touched the violin since I saw you, except Last Sunday, when I drew such doleful sounds from it, that I left off at once.⌐

Austin is back, but, I suspect, goes on Saturday again. He has been serving Mr Delarue's mission — that is his recreation, very imprudently.[1] ⌐The first stone of the new Schools was laid by Henry with great eclat yesterday —⌐[2] Miss Farrant has lost her brother. John [Norris] has been to the Isle of Man and returns better by the end of the week. Renouf is going to answer Ward.[3] I send you a packet of letters

Ever Yrs J H N

TO E. B. PUSEY

The Oratory Bm Septr 4. 1868

My dear Pusey

I wonder whether I ever wrote to you on the *previous question*, when you think of drawing up statements for the authorities at Rome.[4] If I do now, don't suppose I am doing more than giving you information according to my own measure of knowledge — and if I have already done so, excuse the repetition. I may be wrong in my impressions, but I think it best to state them, even tho' I seem to be giving you advice (which I don't mean) rather than putting the state of things before you, such as I conceive it to be.

I don't think then that at Rome they will attend to any thing which comes from one person, or several persons, however distinguished. If the Archbishop

---

[1] A. L. Delerue was the priest at Spetchley, near Worcester.

[2] i.e. a new building for the parish school at the Oratory.

[3] 'Mr. Renouf on Pope Honorius', *DR*, (July 1868), pp. 200–33. Renouf replied with *The Case of Pope Honorius reconsidered with a view to recent Apologies*, London 1869.

[4] On 31 Aug. Pusey wrote about the propositions he was drawing up, in view of the imminent Vatican Council, 'Do you mind looking at the inclosed propositions as to 1 Invocation of saints 2 Purgatory 3 The seven Sacraments They are the most finished which I have Of course I would not quote you, to any even of the most intimate of my friends. But I should like to know what you think of them'.

of Canterbury were to say 'I will become a Catholic, if you will just tell me whether what I have drawn up on paper, is not consistent with your definitions of faith,' the only question in answer would be, 'Do you speak simply as an individual, or in the name of the Anglican Church?' If he said, 'As an individual,' they would not even look at his paper.

Therefore, I do not think the Bishop of Orleans etc could get the Bishops of an Ecumenical Council to listen to any proposition from you, as such. The initial step would be an Address to the Council signed by a great show of names. Say you could present a petition from three or four Bishops of the Church of England, 50 Professors (Fellows of Colleges would count as such) 200 clergy stating that they, the undersigned, with certain congregations of the Church of England, say 150, were desirous of coming into communion with the Holy See, that they were willing on the question of the Anglican orders to submit to the decision of the Council, and that they presented statements of some of their articles of belief, in the hope and belief that they would be found consistent with the definitions of former Councils, including the Council of Trent, and that in the sense of those statements they accepted what was there defined; moreover, that they received the doctrine of the Immaculate Conception B.M.V. provided so-and-so was to be reckoned a right explanation of it, I think your cause must be taken up. But I think you will be putting yourself to bootless trouble, if you draw up statements which are to be presented in the name only of half a dozen, however eminent.

You will say perhaps that the conditions which I have set down are simply impossible — both the number of signatures and the admissions to be made in the Address — Of course I grieve if this should be the case — but consider how full a Council is of work, and whether it can be expected to go out of its way except for some great end. The reconciliation of the Church of England would be such an end — but then you must bring proof that it *is* the end of the conversion of a certain number of individuals. It must be recollected too, that such an Address as I have supposed cuts off the subscribers to it from the existing Establishment, and, if it were listened to, would gain that attention for *its own* sake, from the actual bodies of men it spoke for, not as leading to the reconciliation of the Church of England. But not only a Council, but the ordinary ecclesiastical bodies at Rome, have not time except for great objects. All large systems fall into routine — and at Rome the Sacred Congregations go by rule, by precedent, by law, by reason, but not by that fine attention to individuals, particular cases, actual combinations, which is implied in the Φρόνησις, ἀγχίνοια, σύνεσις, and γνωμοσύνη[1] of Aristotle. In this age of the world individual greatness and self-action is superseded by routine. The routine at Rome is the routine of 1000 years — nay Rome, except in the case of some great Popes, has never shown any great gift of origination. It has (I believe surely) a divinely imparted instinct and a promise of external guidance, as regards *doctrine* — but while it listens to practical plans brought before it,

[1] 'Practical wisdom, readiness of mind, understanding and good judgment.'

it does not go and hunt for them. Cardinal Barnabò says that only three countries give him trouble — viz. the Turks much, the English more, and the French most. That is to say, routine won't do in those countries. Under these circumstances it is a great thing for him to have an Archbishop like Manning, who makes every thing easy to him, by doing his best to work by routine and to *make* routine work in England. As I have said before to you, the *local* authorities are they who should encourage any aspirations in England towards unity — and the Archbishop has taken the opposite line.

Here is another disadvantage to you — The French Bishops are not the natural organs for your Address—and the natural questions which would be asked at once would be 'Why does not Dr Pusey apply through the Bishops of England?'

However, that the Bishop of Orleans etc are willing to take up your cause is a great point. Could you through Döllinger interest any German Bishops for you. The Archbishop of Mayence is a great man — and, though an ultramontane, is far from narrow in his notions and measures.[1] But Dollinger would tell you all about Germany. Professor Reusch (I forget his name, he is Professor of Exegetics) at Bonn is also a moderate man —[2] Your knowledge of Germany would almost be a reason for your going there on this matter, if Dollinger gave you any encouragement. The state of religion ⟨(*Protestants*)⟩ there is so sad that they look with yearning towards England, are very kind to me, and I am sure would listen to you. But all depends on your being able, even if confidentially, to show them a list of educated people and congregations who *on given terms* would enter into communion with them. *Are* there such terms?

You know, *I* deeply despair that terms *could* be named between you and them. The more I think of it, the more sure I am that unsurmountable difficulties, (i.e. at present unsurmountable) would show themselves. E.g. you can't belong to two communions at once — but, if you cannot promise in the name and for the Church of England, how can you be in communion with Rome without separating from the Anglican Church, how in communion with the latter without coming short of the former?

Still, my feeling of these obstacles is no reason why I should not give you as much information as I can.

I have made some remarks upon your papers. I think you cannot escape the word 'meritum' as belonging to the Saints (and to the just) — nor can you speak of 'tanquam per sacramenta;' and I doubt whether you can use 'poenitere' for 'poenitentiam agere.'

Ever Yours affly John H Newman

[3] Wilhelm Emmanuel von Ketteler, Bishop of Mainz from 1850 to 1877, defended the Church against the encroachments of the State and was the leader of social Catholicism in Germany. He was an inopportunist at the Vatican Council.

[4] Franz Heinrich Reusch, Professor of Old Testament at Bonn from 1861, was excommunicated in 1872 for refusing to accept the Vatican Definition, and became an Old Catholic. When in 1878 that body abolished clerical celibacy he resigned all his offices in protest.

TO R. W. CHURCH

The Oratory. Bm Sept 5. 1868

My dear Church

I hope you and Mrs Church enjoyed your visit to Aosta etc, tho' I fear you found it very hot, and the inns indifferent — not that I know the country.

For myself I enjoyed the hot weather, but the change was too much for me. The glass fell 10 degrees, and I had an attack of diarrhœa — and was picking up when I was seized with inflammation in the eyelid which pulled me down more. I was thrown out and thrown back in other respects — and am now getting straight. All this has made it difficult for me to go to you. I am unwilling to give up the idea, and yet I fear I must. It will come to that I fear — yet I should like to know your engagements. Not that I want to bind you — of course not, but if I get much better, I might perhaps write to ask you, 'Are you at home? have you room for me for two days?' Yet I hardly think I shall.

Copeland passed through this place lately in his way to Buxton — He alarmed us a great deal with his rheumatic fever — but he told me that he had quite got over it and (apparently) its apprehended consequences, and is likely to be better than he was before it. Buxton has done him good.

Whenever you chance to write, tell me if you know anything about the health of Charles Cornish, of whom I heard a bad account some time ago.

I have nothing to tell you, and therefore conclude by calling myself,

Ever yours affectionately, John H. Newman

TO W. J. COPELAND

The Oratory Septr 5/68

My dear Copeland

I write lest you should think me wanting in gratitude for your two letters — but I have nothing to say. I rejoice that you are so well. St John and Neville have got back, and have had a most successful time as regards health. They have been living 7000 feet high and it has done so much for them that next year you should go there. No proofs. I am well now

Ever Yrs affly J H N

You have turned Fr Hyacinth into F. Felix the Jesuit. He has not appeared yet.[1]

---

[1] In his letter of 29 Aug. Copeland referred to Hyacinth Loyson's expected visit to Newman, but called him, by mistake, Felix, thinking of the French Jesuit, Celestine Joseph Félix (1810–91). Both were well known as preachers at Notre Dame, Paris.

SUNDAY 6 SEPTEMBER 1868   went to Rednall
MONDAY 7 SEPTEMBER   William returned from Switzerland just about now
WEDNESDAY 9 SEPTEMBER   Fr Ambrose returned and came over to Rednall?
SATURDAY 12 SEPTEMBER   came in from Rednall and found Fr Hyacinth just come

TO SIR JOHN SIMEON

The Oratory Bm Sept 13/68

My dear Sir John

Fr Hyacinth, the Carmelite, is here — you must know him by name. The Duke of Northumberland invited him to Alnwick, if he came to England. He has written to know if he is there now. The answer comes tomorrow or Tuesday morning.[1]

Fr Hyacinth wishes to see Pusey, who is at *Chale*, and he talks of attempting it, if the Duke is not at Alnwick. Now I wish you to know him ⟨(Fr H.)⟩, I think you would like him — and it struck me whether he could come to you for a day, if he went to Pusey. Are you at home? is your house not overflowing with guests? I know it is a busy time with you — tell me, as soon as you can, whether, if he visited the Island, you could receive him or not.[2]

Say every thing kind from me to Lady Simeon — your daughters, and your boys, if at home.

Ever Yrs affly John H Newman of the Oratory

P.S.   Perhaps you could telegraph to me, if a Station is near you. If he comes to you, you will find he can speak freely and from his heart.

MONDAY 14 SEPTEMBER 1868   Fr Hyacinth went   Bellasis passed through

TO AMBROSE PHILLIPPS DE LISLE

The Oratory, Bm Septr 14. 1868.

My dear Mr de Lisle

I think you must know by name Father Hyacinthe, the Carmelite, who has preached the Advent Sermons in Notre Dame, and the Lent at Rome. If you do, you must know also what an interest he takes in the state of England and in the prospect of its becoming Catholic

He is now on a visit of a day or two at the Duke of Northumberland's at Alnwick, and thence passes to London. I know he would like to make your acquaintance, and I am sure you would like him — he has been here for a day or two.

---

[1] Hyacinth Loyson had met the sixth Duke of Northumberland in Rome.
[2] Chale, and Simeon's house, Swainston, were in the Isle of Wight.

I hope then I am not taking a liberty in telling you that he is returning to London, and that, if you are at home and disengaged, he would like much to pay his respects to you. He takes the greatest interest in the Union movement, though I do not know him well enough to pronounce that in all respects you would approve his view of it

Most truly Yours John H Newman

TUESDAY 15 SEPTEMBER 1868   went to Rednall with Ambrose?

TO JAMES HOPE-SCOTT

The Oratory ⌜Sept 15/68⌝

My dear Hope Scott

⌜I think you are not at Abbotsford, but I write on the chance of it.

If you *are* there, I think (unless your house is full or there is other acci-dental reason) you will like to see Fr Hyacinth, the celebrated Paris preacher, who is till Thursday (I believe) with the Duke at *Alnwick*

I ought to have written yesterday, but I thought it *impossible* you should be at Abbotsford. Don't let me put you out. If you find it convenient you had better telegraph to him. I have told him I am writing to you, but gave him little hope of you being at Abbotsford.

He has been here for a day or two and I like him extremely⌝

Yrs affly John H Newman

TO SIR JOHN SIMEON

The Oratory Bm Septr 15. 1868

My dear Sir John

Thank you very much for your telegram. Fr Hyacinth had a letter from the Duke yesterday, and went off to him at once. I wished him very much to see you. He stops at Alnwick for only a day or two, and it is uncertain where he goes next. I shall by this post send your message after him, and shall be very sorry, if he does not come to you. I am sure you will like him.

Ever Yours affectly John H Newman

TO HENRY JAMES COLERIDGE

Rednall Sept 17/68

My dear Fr Coleridge

An Anglican clergyman has written me an answer to my Letter to you — and wishes to publish my letter in answer to him, with his.

Are you disposed to have them both in the Month? Unless you can get them in in October, I don't suppose you will think it worth your while. For he will anticipate you.

Direct to me at the Oratory[1]

Most sincerely Yours John H Newman

TO SIR JOHN TAYLOR COLERIDGE

Rednall, Sept 17, 1868.

Dear Sir John Coleridge,

I must begin by apologizing for my delay in acknowledging your letter of the 10th. Owing to accidental circumstances, my time has not been my own; and now, when at length I write, I fear I shall disappoint you in the answer which alone I can give to your question.[2] It almost seems to me as if you were so kind as to wish me to write such an account of my visit to Mr. Keble as might appear in your Memoir, but, as I think you will see, my memory is too weak to allow of my putting on paper any particulars of it which are worth preserving. It was remarkable, certainly, that three friends, he, Dr. Pusey, and myself, who had been so intimately united for so many years, and then for so many years had been separated, at least one of them from the other two, should meet together just once again; and for the first and last time [[in their lives]][3] dine together simply by themselves. And the more remarkable, because not only by chance they met all three together, but there were positive chances against their meeting.

Keble had wished me to come to him, but the illness of his wife, which took them to Bournemouth, obliged him to put me off. On their return to Hursley, I wrote to him on the subject of my visit, and fixed a day for it. Afterwards, hearing from Pusey that he too was going to Hursley on the very day I had named, I wrote to Keble to put off my visit. I told him, as I think, my reason. I had not seen either of them for twenty years, and to see both of them at once, would be more, I feared, than I could bear. Accordingly, I told him I should go from Birmingham to friends in the Isle of Wight, in the first place, and thence some day go over to Hursley. This was on September 12, 1865. But when I had got into the Birmingham train for Reading, I felt it was like cowardice to shrink from the meeting, and I changed my mind again. In spite [[then]] of my having put off my visit to him, I slept at Southampton, and

---

[1] The letter of Rev. T. W. Mossman, was published in the *Month*, (Oct. 1868), pp. 417–21, followed by Newman's reply of 17 Sept. to him.

[2] On 10 Sept. Coleridge, who had undertaken Keble's biography, wrote: 'Towards the end of his life occurred the incident, which every one must feel to be so remarkable and interesting — the meeting under his roof, of yourself and Dr Pusey with him. I am very anxious to be able to give an authentic account of this . . .'

[3] These three words, and another below, were inserted in pencil by Newman in his presentation copy of Coleridge's *A Memoir of the Rev. John Keble*, Oxford and London 1869, where his letter was printed, pp. 516–19.

made my appearance at Hursley next morning without being expected. Keble was at his door speaking to a friend. He did not know me, and asked my name. What was more wonderful, since I had purposely come to his house, I did not know him, and I feared to ask who it was. I give him my card without speaking. When at length we found out each other, he said, with that tender flurry of manner which I recollected so well, that his wife had been seized with an attack of her complaint that morning, and that he could not receive me as he should have wished to do; nor, indeed, had he expected me; for 'Pusey' he whispered, 'is in the house, as you are aware.'

Then he brought me into his study, and embraced me most affectionately, and said he would go and prepare Pusey, and send him to me.

I think I got there in the forenoon, and remained with him four or five hours, dining at one or two. He was in and out of the room all the time I was with him, attending on his wife, and I was left with Pusey. I recollect very little of the conversation that passed at dinner. Pusey was full of the question of the inspiration of Holy Scripture, and Keble expressed his joy that it was a common cause, in which I could not substantially differ from them; and he caught at such words of mine as seemed to shew agreement. Mr. Gladstone's rejection at Oxford was talked of, and I said that I really thought that had I been still a member of the University, I must have voted against him, because he was giving up the Irish Establishment. On this Keble gave me one of his remarkable looks, so earnest and so sweet, came close to me, and whispered in my ear, (I cannot recollect the exact words, but I took them to be,) 'And is not that just?' It left the impression on my mind that he had no great sympathy with the Establishment in Ireland as an Establishment, and was favourable to the Church of the Irish.

Just before my time for going, Pusey went to read the Evening Service in Church, and I was left in the open air with Keble by himself. He said he would write to me in the Isle of Wight, as soon as his wife got better, and then I should come over and have a day with him. We walked a little way, and stood looking in silence at the Church and Churchyard, so beautiful and calm. Then he began to converse with me in more than his old tone of intimacy, as if we had never been parted, and soon I was obliged to go.

I remained in the Island till I had his promised letter. It was to the effect that his wife's illness had increased, and he must give up the hopes of my coming to him. Thus, unless I had gone on that day, when I was so very near not going, I should not have seen him at all.

He wrote me many notes about this time; in one of them he made a reference to the lines in Macbeth: —

> 'When shall we three meet again?
> When the hurley-burley's done,
> When the battle's lost and won.'[1]

---

[1] *Macbeth*, I, i, 1. For an account of the visit to Keble written at the time see letter of 13 Sept. 1865 to St John.

This is all I can recollect of a visit, of which almost the sole vivid memory which remains with me is the image of Keble himself.

I am, dear Sir John Coleridge, Yours faithfully,
John H. Newman.[1]

TO W. J. O'NEILL DAUNT

The Oratory Bm Septr 17. 1868

My dear Sir

I have not forgotten your question about the passage in Acts ii but am not sure that I understand the very point which you wish cleared.

You shall tell me if I have mistaken it, after you have read what I have to say about it.

When the fiery tongues at Pentecost fell upon the Apostles' heads, were these the Holy Ghost in a bodily form?

If the question is, Was the Holy Spirit *incarnate* in the form of fire, I answer, No. It is true that some of the Fathers compare the miracle to our Lord's coming in our nature, but they cannot be taken to speak literally.

Our Lord speaks of '*Water* and the Holy Spirit —' St John Baptist of 'the Holy Spirit and *fire*.' I should look on the passages as parallel — and call the miracle at Pentecost a transitory *Sacrament*. It typified and conveyed the Divine Gift.

Now, if so, as to the *outward sign*. I do not see we need say, it was material fire, because the words run, 'tamquam ignis.' But I do not see why it should not have been literally fire.

As to the *invisible grace*. In these later times it is usual to say that the Third Person of the Blessed Trinity resides in the soul by means of His *grace* — but it is still a theological opinion maintained by great divines (and I suspect the old opinion,) that His Presence in the soul is not merely His grace but *Himself*. I should say the same here. The descent of the Holy Spirit upon the Apostles may be understood of his actual Personal Presence in their souls, or of a special grace making them and qualifying them to be Apostles.[2]

Most truly Yours John H Newman

---

[1] Coleridge replied on 20 Sept. asking if he might print Newman's letter in its entirety. He also said: 'I will add a fact, which Mary Anne Dyson, who is staying with me, tells me: that dear Mrs Keble had had apprehensions of the effect of the meeting on him [Keble]; and sent for Mrs Wilcox that evening or the next day into her room, to say how happily it had passed — and what pleasure it had given him.'

[2] Cf. *Jfc.*, Lectures VI-VIII, and C. S. Dessain, 'Cardinal Newman and the Doctrine of Uncreated Grace,' the *Clergy Review* (April and May 1962), pp. 207–25 and 269–88.

TO THOMAS WIMBERLEY MOSSMAN

Rednall, Sept. 17, 1868

My dear Sir,

I feel intimately with what sincere desire of holding the truth, and the whole truth in religion, you write to me, and I gladly recognise the respectful terms in which you speak of the Holy See and the Catholic Church; and, though the conclusion of your letter sounds controversial, I do not suppose you really wish a formal disputation between us, for it stands to reason, that, if it is the duty of a writer to meet all comers who take exception to anything he has put into print, to such a one life would be but one continual controversy.

And you doubtless have cleared me from any charge of wantonness in professing the opinion which is the occasion of your writing to me. In the Appendix to my *Apologia*, I inserted a passage on Anglican Orders. A sentence in it was thought by a friend (lately) to need explanation; I could not in frankness and honesty avoid giving it.[1] As to that sentence itself, and the whole paragraph in which it occurs, I wrote it with much reluctance and pain, and as a matter of sheer duty. In the volume in question, I was bringing out my whole mind on the general subject of which it treated. I wrote, and against the grain, many passages which I knew would be unpalatable to excellent persons of my communion. I did not wish to hide anything. I had been accused of hostility to the Church of England; I was obliged to say just what I thought of its spiritual claims, and primarily about its Orders. I knew well what distress I should cause to persons whom I loved; nay, what sorrow and even resentment I should excite in many who wished me well. It was most impolitic in me, when I was defending myself from odious charges, to offend those who were to be my judges. But I could not help that; I was bound to say what I thought, whatever came of it; for, if I was touching upon tender points, they were as momentous in themselves as they were sacred in the minds of the Anglicans who maintained them.

Ever since that time, I have been treated with remarkable gentleness and sympathy by Anglican publications, and I have been grateful to them. I had in some sense recovered my *status* in the minds of their readers, and I felt that, by writing the letter on which you have animadverted, I was diminishing the good will of those who wished to be my friends. But here again I could not help answering a plain question when it was asked me by those who had a right to ask it; and my only regret is that which your letter suggests to me, that I have not been as clear as I wished to be in the answer I gave.

My reason for saying that I have been deficient in clearness is this — that you have misunderstood the point of my argument; it is from the nature of the case what Mr. Davison calls a *cumulative* argument, that is, an argument

---

[1] See letter of 5 Aug. to Coleridge.

lying in a cumulation of presumptions, and this you have not taken account of.[1]

Such presumptions, and such a cumulation of them, cannot tell against a demonstration. A fact no one can deny is equivalent to a demonstration. Had every Catholic writer admitted Anglican Orders for three hundred years, had there never been a question about them, in that case no combination of presumptions would have availed against such a prescription. The *onus probandi* would have been with those who after so long a time started a question about them. Again, to me the word of the Pope *ex cathedrâ* in favour of Anglican Orders, or of an Ecumenical Council, would be equivalent to such a demonstration; and no convergence of probabilities would have availed against it. On the other hand, when a fact is not thus undeniably patent, or has yet to be proved, or to be determined definitively in any other way, then such presumptions tell; and the more of them there are, the greater is their combined force; and that combined force would only be lessened, not destroyed, even granting that each separate presumption admitted of a substantial diminution.

1. As I expressly stated in my letter, I only gave *instances* of my full argument in the three special presumptions which I insisted on. I thought I had thus given enough to illustrate the obscure sentence in my *Apologia*. I might, indeed, as a fourth instance, have argued that 'Caesar's wife should not be suspected,' and '*Qui s'excuse s'accuse*:' the very fact that elaborate arguments are necessary in proof of the validity of Anglican Orders, being a *primâ facie* argument against it. Again, I might have urged, as a fifth instance, the fact that no other religious body had distinctly recognised their Apostolicity. I might have added other presumptions, especially the important one of the length of time during which the Anglican Church had stood aloof from every other religious body; so much so, as to show that it has practically given up the very idea of the visible union of Christendom.

2. Each of the presumptions alleged ought of course to have some intrinsic force, greater or less, if it is to be available; but it would be a mistake to fancy that by merely weakening one or other of them we destroy the collective force of them all. It does not suffice, for instance, to diminish (as you think you can — as I think you cannot) the cogency of my argument against Anglican Orders, drawn from the circumstances of the Anglican Eucharist, by referring to the circumstances of the Arian Eucharist in the fourth, fifth and sixth centuries, or to the knots of infidel Priests, here and there, now and then, in the last 400 years; for suppose you are able to do so, still, if you do not demolish it utterly, something of force in the argument is left, such as to preserve for it its place in my whole bundle of sticks, each of which (I might for argument's sake allow) you could snap in two, if taken separately from the rest.[2]

---

[1] John Davison, *Discourses on Prophecy*, second edition, London 1825, pp. 19–35.
[2] To Newman's argument against Anglican Orders in his letter of 5 Aug., 'Would our Lord leave Himself for centuries ... without protective ritual and jealous guardianship?' Mossman replied on 12 Sept. by citing Catholic behaviour in the Milanese before the Reformation and in France before the Revolution, and also the fact of the possession of valid Orders by the Arians.

On this subject I will quote a few sentences from the work of Mr. Davison, to which I have already referred. He is speaking of the proof of Christianity; but the principle he insists on belongs to moral evidence generally: —

'In treating of any single branch of the Gospel evidences, the result of such separate argument must always be taken with a reference to the other proof in reserve.

Though some kind of proof be incapable of accession by an extended cumulative reason, the proof of religion is not of that nature, but one which gathers light and strength by the concentrated force of all its moral evidence. The whole of it therefore must be laid together, and the aggregate of the concurrent proofs will close the investigation.

It is in the way of (a) vicious manner of reasoning to represent any insufficiency of the proof in its several branches as so much objection; to manage the inquiry so as to make it appear that, if the divided arguments be inconclusive one by one, we have a series of exceptions to the truth of religion, instead of a train of favourable presumptions growing stronger at every step.

Allowing that the remainder of the proof, in favour of the Gospel revelation, upon each of these points, (miracles, prophecy, etc.) after they have been fairly stated and examined, is only such a probability as any man may choose to admit, ... when these several inducements to one and the same conclusion of belief are drawn into each other, the joint amount of them, derived as they are from such different sources, is a collection of moral proof, which we cannot properly describe as being less than that of a cogent and conclusive demonstration.' — *On Prophecy*, Edition 2, pp. 24–30.

This is the nature of the argument which I used against Anglican Orders. Not, indeed, that I pretend to have demonstrated in it their invalidity; but, considering there is no proper historical or other demonstration of their validity, but at best only probable facts and arguments, I wished to point out the great weight of antecedent probability existing against it, which indisposes bystanders to acquiesce in it, and which has a logical claim to be met by a preponderating evidence in its favour, if it is an object to gain their acquiescence. Instead, then, of isolated parallels, if they are really parallels, from the history of the fourth or the sixteenth century, from Syria and Asia Minor or from Lombardy and Spain, let me ask you to confine yourself to one quarter of Christendom, and to show me, if you can, any religious communion, of present or past time, which has eventually been on all hands acknowledged to be a portion of the Catholic Church on the strength of its Catholic Orders, which, nevertheless, has been for three whole centuries unanimously ignored by all the East and all the West; which for three centuries has employed the pens of its occasional and self-constituted defenders in laboriously clearing away, with but poor success, the aboriginal suspicions which have clung to it on the part of so many of the invalidity of those Orders; which, as if unthankful for such defence, has for three centuries persistently suffered the Apostolicity of those Orders, and the necessity and grace of such Apostolicity, to be slighted or denied by its Bishops, Priests, and people, with utter impunity; which has for three centuries been careless to make sure that its consecrating Bishops, and the Bishops who ordained the Priests who were to be consecrated, and those Priests themselves had been validly baptized; which has for three centuries neglected to protect its Eucharist from the profanations, not only of ignorance and unbelief, but of open sacrilege; — show me such a case — such a long-sustained anomaly and such ultimate recognition — and then I will allow that the recognition of Anglicanism on the part of the Holy See is not beyond the limits of reasonable expectation. Moreover, if that expectation ever were to be fulfilled, then, of course, I should gladly assent to the voice of Authority. I should either conclude that the Anglican Episcopate had been able to bring forward irrefragable proofs of its Apostolical descent; or, if, on my examining what actually had been adduced, they seemed to my own private judgment short of decisive, then I should reflect that the Holy See had by a divine gift keener eyes in such a matter than I have, and could see in the evidence a conclusive force which I did not see myself.

Let me take an illustration parallel, though not similar. We are told, truly or not, that some Catholic countries in the western hemisphere are in a degenerate state. Now, supposing in the year 2200, it is found that a deplorable state of things has gone on in one of those countries for three centuries; that for all that time no sacrament has been administered to the Catholic population but baptism, and that, generally, by laymen; that the adult natives are by custom and on system unwillingly compelled to be baptized; that there are no catechisings or instructions, and, in consequence, no knowledge of Christian doctrine; that, on the contrary, either unbelief or a gross heathenish worship prevails among all classes; that Mass on festivals is ordinarily a scene of merry-making, feasting, and licentiousness; that the Priests universally keep concubines; that the Bishops, in spite of ecclesiastical prohibition, are Freemasons; and that they refuse the Holy See any oversight of religion, and drive away the Nuncios, Apostolic Visitors, or Regulars, whom the Pope sends out to them; and suppose, lastly, that in the said year 2200, though that country has never formally been put out of the Church, the Pope without another word ignores its Bishops and their Orders, and, disdaining to make any historical or antiquarian examination, sends some Vicar Apostolic or Cardinal Archbishop to begin a new succession and found a new Church — does such a proceeding of the Pope surprise me? Rather should I not be surprised if he acted otherwise? For I should argue, Who shall convince me that Priests and people, who were so careless of sacraments, rites, and doctrines, have cared to be exact in their Ordinations?

Do not suppose that I am comparing the condition of things among Anglicans with such a detestable state of society; I have already said that the cases, though parallel in the present question, were not similar. What I mean to insist on is, that there are cases when the Holy See does not feel itself bound to inquire into the records of a local Church for proof of the validity of its Orders, but blots it out from the Christian *orbis terrarum* on account of its notorious delinquencies. And I mean to say that Anglicanism presents one of these cases. Believe me, I love Anglicans too well, and know too intimately the depth and sincerity of their zeal, to have any pleasure in thus speaking. Nor will I ever deny the services which have been rendered by Anglicanism to the cause of morals and religion, nor the beauty of its domestic aspect; — as little will I deny that, bitter and mischievous as has been its opposition to the Catholic Church, still by its grand defences of the fundamental truths of revelation, and by the relics of Christian antiquity which lie embedded in its teaching, it has done her a real, though an unwilling benefit.

So much on the nature of my argument itself; now, as to the particular facts in history which you urge as parallel to those ecclesiastical shortcomings which are the ground of my separate presumptions, I think it sufficient to notice the case of the Arian Eucharist, which you consider your strongest point.

The Arians certainly had continuity and establishment; they lasted three centuries, and it was a union of Church and State. But was there any sacrilege in their Eucharist, such as that of which I have spoken as prevailing in the Anglican Church on the supposition of the validity of its Orders? I think not.

As to the Arianism of the fourth century, it certainly originated in Bishops and Priests. Its stronghold was in the State and in the Episcopacy; but still, in what sense in the Episcopacy? I answer, its genuine and pronounced upholders were but a handful of Bishops — you may count them. The semi-Arian Bishops were numerous, but for repudiating a symbol decided on by an Ecumenical Council. The rest of the Bishops — that is, the majority — were either deficient in controversial science, or cowards, who succumbed to the dictation of the State, without in their hearts denying the true faith. The priests and people all through Christendom were for the most part zealous for the Catholic doctrine. What, then, there was of sacrilege, was confined to a few Bishops scattered to and fro in high places through the empire, who perhaps never said Mass.

Next, as to the Arianism of the Gothic races in the fifth and sixth centuries. The Arian Goths could not be sacrilegious towards the Eucharist, because they had it not. They had it not, because they had not valid baptism. They had their own form of words for the rite; they baptized according to that form all Catholics whom they could catch; and they were baptized themselves with the true form on their entering the Catholic Church.

You are quite at liberty, since you wish it, to publish this letter with your own. I should not have wished it myself, but now I shall take the same leave of sending both to a Catholic periodical.

With very sincere respect, I am, My dear Sir, most truly yours,

John H. Newman

The Rev. T. W. Mossman.

SATURDAY 19 SEPTEMBER 1868   came in from Rednall   Stewart came in his way to Ireland

TO W. J. COPELAND

Rednall Sept 19. 1868

My dear Copeland

Keble wrote the Review of Walter Scott in the British Critic, as well as that on Gladstone — I can't tell, if he wrote any other.[1]

I speak without book, but I suspect that I must have preached that Sermon originally with a different text.[2] Is it the one for Trinity Sunday in Volume *one* — which picks out bits of the Creed from different parts of Scripture? If on going into Birmingham, I can throw light on this question, I will add a a line.

I am sorry you are leaving Buxton so soon — and that you do not speak so strongly of the good which it is doing you as at first

Ever Yrs affly John H Newman

The Oratory Saturday evening
I think I sent proofs to you at Buxton from Rednall on Thursday and Friday

TO MRS MATTHEW JAMES HIGGINS

Rednall. Sept. 19. 1868.

My dear Mrs Higgins

Though your most kind letter to me on the 4th did not require an answer, and indeed it is almost an intrusion on you to send one, yet I have wished, ever since I received it, to thank you for letting me know, by the very fact that you wrote to me and by the tone of your letter, how graciously God was supporting you amid your profound desolation — for desolation, the word we use in Holy Week for the special anguish of the Blessed Mary, is the only word which touches the case of one who lies under the weight of your special affliction.

The occasion I have found for writing to you without the need of an

---

[1] Copeland had been asked by Thomas Keble Junior whether John Keble wrote in the *British Critic*, (Oct. 1839), pp. 355–97, 'Gladstone's Church and State,' or any other articles in that periodical. Keble wrote, (Oct. 1838), pp. 423–83, 'Sir Walter Scott,' a review of his *Memoirs*, reprinted in John Keble, *Occasional Papers and Reviews*, Oxford 1877, pp. 1–80. Keble also wrote, (April 1841), pp. 411–40, 'Papers of Bishop Warburton,' reprinted, *op. cit.* pp. 108–47.

[2] Copeland inquired on 9 Sept. about a sermon he remembered Newman preaching on *Heb.* 2:1.

apology is this. I write to say that, since tomorrow is the Feast of the Seven Dolours, I intend, with God's help, to offer up the Holy Sacrifice for you.

With my truest and most respectful sympathy I am,

Sincerely yours in Christ   John H. Newman

Mrs Higgins

TO E. B. PUSEY

Rednall Sept 19/68

My dear Pusey,

As to the Weekly Reg. [Register] I never read it. It has slandered me worse that it has slandered you or any members of the Anglican Church. But such treatment is only one specimen of its vulgar tone, which is intolerable. Did it not give out the lie that your book was on the Index? And now it says every thing provoking it possibly can about the General Council. It lives by war. It is distinctly of the 'war party.' Its bread would go, if it did not keep up controversy in the bitterest spirit.[1]

As to the question of Anglican Orders, I think the real point is, with whom the onus probandi lies. Anglicans say to us 'You have not demonstrated that our Orders are invalid —' We say 'You have not demonstrated to our satisfaction that your Orders are valid.' When I was with you, then I thought we had such a fair case for our Orders, that it seemed right to act upon it. Now I think them, (since at best only probably valid,) seriously unsafe. But this to me is certain, that the Roman See never will acknowledge them, unless the proof for them rises much higher than it does at present — or, than it can rise much higher — e.g. on the point of Intention. Again, were not both Tait and Jacobson baptized by Presbyterians or Dissenters?[2] Where then is the proof of the validity of its administration? Now supposing the baptism of either was invalid, they cannot ordain *priests* (as *we* believe) and if any so-ordained priests were consecrated ever so carefully he would not be a Bishop. I think I once told you how Dr Bramston, Vicar Apostolic of London, was

---

[1] The *Weekly Register* had announced that the Eastern bishops were invited to the Council, but not the Anglican ones, which was true. On 8 Sept. an Apostolic Letter 'to all Bishops of Churches of the Eastern Rite not in Communion with the Apostolic See' invited them to the Council. On 13 Sept. an invitation was sent 'to all Protestants and other non-Catholics' to return to the fulness of Catholic Faith and to Catholic Unity.' Cuthbert Butler, *The Vatican Council*, I, pp. 93–6. Pusey wrote on 14 Sept. a letter printed in Liddon's *Pusey*, IV, pp. 158–9: 'The *Weekly Register* puts me quite out of heart as to any negotiations. For the Roman Curia has prejudged the question as to our Orders (at least if the *W.R.* is right) by inviting Nestorians and other heretics, because they own their Orders, and not our Bishops, because they are laymen. To refer the question of our Orders to it, then, is simply a way of having it decided for us that we and all our sacerdotal or episcopal acts are one great sham, indeed of owning it ourselves. . . .'

For the slanders against Newman cf. letter of 6 April 1867 to Hope-Scott.

[2] A. C. Tait, Bishop of London, Archbishop of Canterbury in Dec. 1868, and William Jacobson, Bishop of Chester 1865–84, had been a Presbyterian and a Nonconformist respectively.

re-confirmed, and re-ordained, though both Sacraments had been administered in the Catholic Church, because some question was raised about the exactness of his baptism.[1]

I don't think there is any the slightest possibility of our authorities ever acknowledging Anglican Orders — Nay, even though they were valid, I am not sure they need, or would. The Nicene Council ignored the orders of the Egyptian Meletians — according to the plain meaning of the words of their Epistle (Socr. [Socrates, *Church History*] 1.9) without any distinct question being raised as to their validity. I suppose there would be a tacit conditionality in such re-ordinations, which the Church, not the Ordinal used, would supply.

I can't tell whether the Church could supply for such informalities as may have occurred in the Anglican Ordinations. As an Anglican, I used to say that the Pope and Roman Church *could*, according to its own rules. Certainly we hold the Church's intention can do many things. Thus, if a real Priest thought he had faculties for hearing confessions, and by some accident had not — e.g. the time for which he had them having expired, and if he and his people gave and received absolution in good faith, then it is considered that the absolutions are valid. 'The Church supplies.' But this is an act of jurisdiction — to what extent it could supply in the case of a Sacrament, as Ordination, is another matter, and I cannot answer the question off hand.

You will ask me, as you indeed have in your letter, if the question of Anglican Orders, did it come before Rome, is so sure to be given against them, what could I mean by advising you to have recourse to Rome on the point? But observe how things stand, and what I said — I said if a *large body* of Anglicans presented themselves to Rome, and asked recognition, I think so still — When I was at Rome 20 years ago, both a Jesuit (foreign) and secular Priests were surprised to hear from me that Anglican Orders were doubtful. Not that they had studied the subject, but it was the tradition they had imbibed. But what more than any thing has turned the minds of Catholics against the probability of it is their increased knowledge of the indifference of Anglicans to the question. The intercourse with England, the knowledge of English history, has greatly advanced in Rome during these 20 years. And, knowing the course of Anglican Church history, they naturally ask, and I ask, can a true child be so careless of his parentage, as the Anglican Episcopacy has shown itself of its own? Solomon said 'Give her the child' where one of the two women showed tenderness for it; and so, well may the Pope say, 'If I am a father, where is my honour?'[2] Take the circumstances of this time. There is certain knowledge that an Ecumenical Council (say for argument sake of the Latin Church) is to be convoked. The Anglican Communion from the East and the far West, besides its English dioceses, is represented at Lambeth in solemn Pan-Anglicanism. Is it possible they should not indignantly demand admission into the Ecumenical Council, if they really duly estimated their

---

[1] See letter of 11 Aug. 1865 to Simeon Wilberforce O'Neill.
[2] 1 *Kings*, 3:27; *Malachi*, 1:6.

own ordinations and consecrations? A last chance is given them of wiping out the indifferentism of 300 years. Instead of doing any thing of the kind they speak of themselves as if the centre of the Ecclesiastical Universe, and fling some words, I forget what, at that very Majesty, which you say ought to acknowledge them.[1] Can you be surprised after this that you are ignored? Why, you have had long centuries to reverse the past in, and is there to be no statute of limitation, as that which invalidates a tradesman's account, if not presented to the debtor, after which Esau must in vain lift up his voice, and cry out 'Bless me, even me, O my Father?'

Even now, I am not sure that, if the whole Anglican Episcopate, as a body, preferred the claims of their Orders to the Holy See, and demanded judgment, their request would not be heard, and *impartially* entered into. It is a last chance. But of course such a supposition is the wildest of imaginations.

Ever Yrs affly John H Newman

P.S.   Father Hyacinth, the Archbishop of Paris's preacher wished much to call on you at Chale. He was going to Sir J. Simeon's but now he has gone up to Alnwick.

I hope you will not think I have written violently[2]

MONDAY 21 SEPTEMBER 1868   went out to Rednall   Kept Stewart till October 6 to coach the boys[3]

WEDNESDAY 23 September   came in from Rednall in afternoon to see F. Rogers who took tea with me

TO WILLIAM MONSELL

Rednall Bromsgrove Septr 23/68

My dear Monsell

We find it impossible, consistent with the due care of individual boys, to have batches for their first communion — if our school were larger, perhaps we might do so. The times we choose are Holy Thursday, Corpus Xti, and the Immaculate Conception — sometimes St Philip's day, or Whitsuntide. And two or three go together — and are put for a little while into retreat. We have

[1] At the end of the First Lambeth Conference, in Sept. 1867, the Bishops issued unanimously an Encyclical Letter or Pastoral, which included the following paragraph:
'Furthermore, we entreat you to guard yourselves and yours against the growing superstitions and additions with which in these latter days the truth of God hath been overlaid; as otherwise, so especially by the pretension to universal sovereignty over God's heritage asserted for the See of Rome; and by the practical exaltation of the blessed Virgin Mary as mediator in the place of her Divine Son, and by the addressing of prayers to her as intercessor between God and man. Of such beware, we beseech you, knowing that the jealous God giveth not His honour to another.' The *Guardian*, (2 Oct. 1867), p. 1048.
[2] See letter of 5 Oct. to Pusey.
[3] See letter of 30 Dec. to Bedford.

a retreat for all the boys the three first days of Holy Week, and they all make their Easter on Holy Thursday. That seems far the best time for Gaston, if he comes to us after Christmas — but I do not see any objection to his making his first communion at Christmas at home before he comes to school. There are advantages both ways.

I do not doubt we shall find him as well prepared in other things, as in his knowledge of religion — and we shall be very glad to have him.[1]

My letter in the Month will get me into some controversy. I was obliged to insert it, for the report has been strong that I believed in the validity of Anglican Orders.[2]

I am glad to hear so good an account of the Irish Elections — here, we somewhat dread, apropos of the Elections, an attack on Catholic Houses. Murphy is here again[3]

Ever Yrs affly John H Newman of the Oratory

The Rt Honble Wm Monsell M P

P.S. Father Hyacinth has been here, and talked of making his way to you. He left for Alnwick, but I have not heard from him since he went.

TO BISHOP ULLATHORNE

Rednall Sept 23. 1868

My dear Lord

Perhaps you knew at the time that Mr Ivers came to us some time ago, to talk about our putting the Chaplaincy of the Jail and of the Asylum into your hands.

It appears he did not come from your Lordship, or from the Vicar General but he showed us, as the V.G. signified to me on a former occasion, that it would be far more convenient, if Jail, Asylum, and Workhouse were under the care of one Priest, than if the present dislocated state of things continued.

We certainly feel this, and, on Mr Ivers's proposal, though we could not absolutely give him any answer while our Fathers were scattered about, we told him, that, subject to your Lordship's approval, we should be quite ready to make Jail and Asylum over to him

We have now had our meeting on the subject, and have come to the conclusion which we announced to Mr Ivers by anticipation.

In so concluding, we have acted under the belief that we were doing what

---

[1] Monsell's son, Gaston came to the Oratory School on 13 Feb. 1869.
[2] Letter of 5 Aug. to H. J. Coleridge.
[3] William Murphy was the anti-Catholic lecturer. See letter of 19 June 1867 to Mrs John Mozley. In the General Election of the autumn of 1868 one of the issues was the disestablishment of the Irish Church. Disraeli made some attempt to arouse 'No-Popery' agitation. However the Liberals increased their lead in Ireland, and Protestant dissenters combined with Catholic electors against those who took the Orange Protestant line.

would be acceptable to you as well as desirable for ourselves. But of course the decision rests with your Lordship.

Begging your Lordship's blessing, I am, My dear Lord,

Your obt and affte Servant in Xt
John H Newman of the Oratory

The Bp of Birmingham

P.S. We talked to Mr Ivers of making over the chaplaincy to him on Michaelmas Day.[1]

THURSDAY 24 SEPTEMBER 1868 went out to Rednall Challis slept at Oratory. I did not see him.

TO J. H. WILLIS NEVINS

Rednall, Bromsgrove Septr 24/68

My dear Sir

I would gladly assist you to the best of my power, as I think I understand your difficulty.[2]

I wish I knew the priests of the Archdiocese better than I do. If I did, I am sure I should be able to mention many, any one of whom would suit you. But I am scarcely ever in London, and have no means of speaking of more than a few.

I think Mr Yard would suit you — he is an elderly man, a recent convert, had great experience in directing souls even before he became a Catholic, and is very gentle and pleasant in his manner. I do not know his whereabout — he used to have a confessional in the Oblate Church in Bayswater — but the Directory will tell you.[3]

I should also mention Mr Lockhart, of the Order of Charity, whom I have known since, 25 years ago, he lived with me at Littlemore.

Also I should name to you Canon Oakeley of Islington, and Mr Garside of Summers Town [sic], if I knew what their state of health was.

Also Mr Macmullen of Chelsea, who is a thorough Englishman.

I will also mention a priest whom I can hardly be said to know, but of

---

[1] Michael O'Sullivan was the Vicar General. Ullathorne replied on 24 Sept. that he had no knowledge of what had been said by his subordinates, and he asked the Oratorians to continue to serve jail and asylum until further notice.

[2] Nevins, aged 21, had become a Catholic in May 1868. He wrote on 23 Sept. that 'the person who received me is not such a one as understands that English Catholics and Italian are distinct things. Now I am an Englishman in all senses of the word . . .' He asked Newman to recommend him a director in London. He wrote on the notepaper of 'Equity and Law Life Assurance Society, 18 Lincoln's Inn Fields.'

[3] George Beckwith Yard was living at 4 Kildare terrace, Bayswater, near to the Oblates of St Charles.

whom I have heard much said, as being full of kindness and good sense, Mr Gilbert Talbot of St John's Wood.

If I can be of any further use to you, pray let me know. I will not forget you at Mass[1]

Very truly Yours John H Newman of the Oratory

FRIDAY 25 SEPTEMBER 1868   R. *Robert F.* Wilson called on me, I being away

SATURDAY 26 SEPTEMBER   came in from Rednall

MONDAY 28 SEPTEMBER   returned to Rednall

TUESDAY 29 SEPTEMBER   H. N. Mozley came to Oratory for Social Science Association[2]

THURSDAY 1 OCTOBER   came in from Rednall

SATURDAY 3 OCTOBER   Stewart went. Lord Houghton and Mr Evans called[3]
H. N. Mozley went to Derby

MONDAY 5 OCTOBER   went to Rednall.   H.N.M. returned from Derby

TO E. B. PUSEY

The Oratory Oct 5. 1868

My dear Pusey

Most unfortunately, in moving to and fro between this place and Rednall, I have mislaid your last letter — and do not recollect more than one or two parts of it.

One was, I think, about the beginning of the controversy about intention. You know, I am sure, more about it than I do — all I know is that Catharinus wrote in favour, I think, of the external intention — what made him write I don't know. Was he not a Dominican? I think the Dominican Serry either wrote on the subject, or edited Catharinus's book.

Has not Benedict some thing about it in his 'Synodus Diocesana.' I suppose that *practically*, whatever be the doctrinal doubt as to the external or internal intention, all our Bishops and Priests must require and make the

---

[1] Nevins thanked Newman on 25 Sept., and said he would go to Canon Oakeley. Nevins also said, 'I believe firmly in the Catholic Church, I should have become an infidel had I remained a Ritualist, but truly Priests ought to be very careful how they deal with converts, it is painful to see the spite that certain Catholics bear against those who's view on matters that are not "de fide" differ from their own. Italian-English-Catholics talk about the "Spirit of the Church" and it is not enough to believe what is declared "de fide" but one must *believe* what has not yet been declared a dogma of faith, and if one reasons against this, one is told, oh! you are only a nominal Catholic. Now these men hinder many who would otherwise have joined the fold . . .'
    Nevins left the Church after the definition of Papal Infallibility in 1870, but returned two years later. See letter of 26 Nov. 1872 to him. He eventually became an Anglican again.
    [2] The Social Science Association met in Birmingham from 30 Sept. until 7 Oct.
    [3] Lord Houghton wrote on 2 Oct., 'I cannot leave this vicinage without trying to see you. I propose to call on you to-morrow . . .' See also letters of 12 Oct. 1868 to Hope-Scott, and 18 Feb. 1869 to Rogers.

internal intention, our rule being that, as regards the Sacraments, we must always take the 'tutior pars.'[1]

As to high Church baptisms, which was another point of which you spoke, of course, I had such wholesale baptisms, as Hook found at Leeds, in my mind, but not those only. I believe that, with the most earnest desire to administer the rite validly clergymen have been foiled by the child's cap — I know what difficulty I had in getting the cap put back, and how cross the nurse was, and how my baptisms were talked of in consequence — and I know the anxiety which has been felt by friends on thinking of their baptisms afterwards, lest such and such a child should not have been baptized. One of my most intimate friends, now one of our priests, having taken duty for a high church-man (high and dry) friend and being sure that from the cap he had not baptized a child, wrote to his friend afterwards. His friend answered that there was no need to do any thing — for he himself made it a point to put as little water as possible, lest he should be supposed to hide the spirituality of the rite. Another, now a member of a strict order of Regulars, so carelessly baptized as a parish priest, (quite unconsciously) that his friends came to me at Littlemore to say 'We wish you would speak to A.B. We are quite sure his baptisms are not valid.' He was quite a follower of yours and mine, and, I suppose, believed every word of your Treatise on Baptism.

Ever Yours affectly John H Newman

WEDNESDAY 7 OCTOBER 1868   H N M [Mozley] went
SATURDAY 10 OCTOBER   returned to Bm [Birmingham] for good   Woodgate called at Rednall after I had left.

TO W. J. O'NEILL DAUNT

The Oratory Bm Oct 10. 1868

My dear Mr Daunt

I write a line to thank you, as I do most heartily, for your letter of the 30th of last month. It grieves me to hear that you have been so ill. I am older than you, and need your prayers, and will pray for you, as you wish, in the hope that you will not forget me.

Your argument seems a very good and striking one

Most sincerely Yours John H Newman of the Oratory

W J O'N. Daunt Esqr

[1] The Dominican Ambrosius Catharinus in *De Intentione Ministri*, Rome 1552, maintained that an external intention on the part of the minister of a sacrament, sufficed for its validity, i.e. the mere intention to perform the ceremony. Later the Dominican, Hyacinth Serry wrote a defence *Ambrosii Catharini Vindiciae de necessaria in perficiendis Sacramentis Intentione*, Padua 1727. Benedict XIV in *De Synodo Diocesana* VII, iv, rejected this view, but allowed that it was speculatively tenable.

TO E. E. ESTCOURT

The Oratory Oct 11/68

My dear Canon Estcourt

I am very sorry I missed you and Mr Capel, when you called the other hand [day?]; still for the purpose of your visit, I could not have said any thing impromptu, as it was one which required careful consideration.[1]

The destitution of educated converts, especially if they have had Anglican orders, has been a deep distress to me ever since I have been a Catholic, and I rejoice that you and others are turning your minds to the subject.[2]

No means which promise to relieve it are to be put aside — but the chief advantage of the one you propose is as I think, that it will show sympathy with the persons in question, and draw attention to their sacrifices.

Few men, comparatively speaking, have a talent for composition, except in that general way in which it is made a part of general education — and few again like the extreme drudgery or are capable of the minute accuracy of editorial work. Some plan is wanted which will not only relieve one or two converts, but will encourage those many advanced Anglican clergymen and others, who see nothing but temporal ruin for themselves and families, nothing but helpless idleness, instead of their present various usefulness, in their becoming converts to the Catholic Church. I know that the Holy See never originates plans for local necessities, of which from the nature of the case it can know nothing; but it seems to me that the subject of your letter is as deserving the notice of authorities at Rome though it does not bear immediately upon the aggrandisment of the Chair of Peter, as some other matters which are watched there with a keen interest.

This is no argument why you should not pursue so charitable an object, so far as you can, yourself — if your plan promised well, but till at Rome they cast their eyes on our actual position here, I despair of much being first done by ourselves in any plan. However you wish me to consider yours on its own merits, and, so considering it, without saying that my difficulties cannot be overcome, I hope you will not be unwilling to let me state some of them.

You must not only then have good writers and editors, but you must have useful subjects to write upon, and good works to edit; else the contributions raised might be used more advantageously for their main end than in printing and publishing. When I was an Anglican, I used to grudge the subscriptions asked of me by clergymen for the publication of their Sermons in aid of some charitable object; for I used to say I had rather give my guinea wholly to

---

[1] Estcourt, encouraged by Mgr Capel, wanted to form a society for the publication of Catholic books of history, theology and controversy, both in order to meet a want and so as to give employment, especially to converts. They had called at the Oratory on 5 Oct.

[2] Cf. letters of 28 Nov. 1845 to Hope-Scott, 5 April 1846 to Badeley, 5 Aug. 1846 to Mrs Bowden, 10 Oct. 1850 to Northcote, 23 March 1851 to Henry Wilberforce, 7 April 1851 to Allies, and 28 April 1851 to Cullen. See also letter of 10 Feb. 1869 to Harper.

that object than fritter the greater part of it away in printing what I should never read, and which would only take up room on my bookshelves.

I am not comparing with such trashy Sermons the volumes which you contemplate; but still we must recollect that 20 years ago Mr Dolman attempted a Catholic Library of such works as Sir Thomas More's which soon came to an end from its being proved that valuable as they were, [they] were interesting rather to Antiquarians than to the public.[1] I do not mean that no works of that character, such as (according to Sir F. Palgrave) Gascoigne's would have a claim of the public,[2] but that before you go further in the matter you should have in your hand a sufficient list of works which will be read and valued for their own sake, for which competent editors can be obtained, and which will give so wide relief to converts as to answer your primary object in publishing.

The third great question is what sums are likely on any understanding to be collected.

Excuse these remarks if there is any thing abrupt in them

& believe me etc J H N

MONDAY 12 OCTOBER 1868   Austin and Edward went over to St Wilfrid's for the day

TO JAMES HOPE-SCOTT

The Oratory Bm ⌐Oct 12/68⌐

My dear Hope Scott

⌐I fancy that Fr Hyacinth fell in with the Duke of Nland [Northumberland] at Rome. Also with a lady he called 'Lady Bruce.' I do not know her correct title — whom he was much pleased with, and was to meet at Alnwick. I find from Lord Houghton, who was here the other day, that he somehow fell into *his* hands after he had been with the Duke — and Lord H. took him to the Archbishop of York and whither he went then and how he got home to Paris I don't know.[3] So he seems to have seen none but Protestants except ourselves. At one time he was going to see Pusey in the Isle of Wight, and Sir John Simeon in that case would have lodged him. Also I wrote to Mr de Lisle, but he was away. He does not know one word of English. I liked him very much — he is a simple warm-hearted man — and feels intensely the narrowness which is doing so much harm to our interests.

[1] Dolman published such works as Rock's *Church of our Fathers* and Lingard's *History of England*. By 1858 he had exhausted his capital and tried to form his business into a limited liability company, but was forced to retire to Paris.

[2] One of the works Estcourt suggested for publication was the *Dictionarium Theologicum* of Thomas Gascoigne (1403–58), the manuscript of which was in the library of Lincoln College, Oxford. According to Estcourt Sir Francis Palgrave, Master of the Rolls, had refused to publish it as being a controversial work.

[3] William Thomson, Archbishop of York 1862–90.

I wish you could give a better account of Lady Victoria [Hope-Scott] — We will not forget her.

For myself I am very well, thank God.⌐ Not the hot weather, but the change to cold gave me two short attacks of different kinds, and brought down my strength — but I have picked up again — and ⌐my doctor today told me that, except for grey hairs, I look younger now than I did twelve years ago when he first knew me professionally.

So another remnant of crumbling old Europe has gone in this Spanish affair. Whether young Europe will be as good is another matter — but it is no use crying over the dead, and it is no pleasure to live amid ruins. They are nearly all cleared away now.[1]

A friend told me yesterday that he had met abroad an intelligent man who said to him, 'Now mark my words, Sir, and write them down. I have long studied the politics of Europe, and can prophesy. You will find that this Spanish revolution has been done by the friends of order to bring on a crisis. It will be the first step to a great re-action, and Europe will gradually be restored to its old legitimate state.' If so the friends of order[2] have done a very wicked thing — for my informant, a Spaniard by birth, is full of the enormities of the Spanish liberals and the deplorable religious state of the peasantry⌐[3]

Ever Yrs affly John H Newman

TO WILLIAM PHILIP GORDON

The Oratory Oct 13. 1868

My dear Fr Philip

Thank you for your announcement. I will let our Fathers know of it, as you wish, and will gladly say Mass for you in a few days — just at the moment my intentions are bespoken[4]

Your affectionately John H Newman

The Very Revd Fr Gordon

---

[1] In Sept. 1868 the Bourbon Queen Isabella II was driven into exile, and power was in the hands of military politicians. It was, however, decided that Spain must remain a monarchy, and in 1870 Amadeus of Savoy became king.

[2] [['friends of order']]

[3] [[(N.B. Fr Hyacinth had said to me that the French minister of Marine has [had] lately told a friend of his (Fr Hyacinth's) that war between France and Prussia was inevitable, and, I think he said, immediate. Sept 1. 1873)]]

[4] W. P. Gordon was elected Superior of the London Oratory on 12 Oct., in succession to T. F. Knox.

TO WILLIAM PALMER

The Oratory Oct 13. 1868

My dear Palmer

We shall rejoice to see you, as you propose, on Saturday. I hope you will bring a good account of yourself, and of your present hosts, to whom I beg to send my kindest greetings by you, and of whose health I did not have the best of reports from Hope Scott the other day[1]

Ever Yours affectly John H Newman

WEDNESDAY 14 OCTOBER 1868 Mr Jones came into the House

MEMORANDUM, CONSULTOR PREVIOUS TO THE COUNCIL?

Oct. 14. 1868

This morning came the Bishop's letter inclosing that from Cardinal Caterini, conveying the Pope's intention (consilium mentis suae) of naming me (referendi) one of the Consultores Concilii, i.e. qui operam suam in institutis commissionibus, quarum singulis Pater Cardinalis praeest, alacriter impendunt.[2] Nothing is said of any *particular* Commission, or *who* besides belong to it, (of course). The Cardinal adds '*Si* Newman oblatum honorem acceptum habere velit,' he must go to Rome before the end of the year — '*Quicumque* vero sit hujus epistolae exitus,' he wishes the Bishop to let him know.[3]

---

[1] Probably the family of Lord Henry Kerr at Huntlyburn, near Abbotsford.

[2] Ullathorne sent on 13 Oct. a letter he had just received from Cardinal Prospero Caterini, Prefect of the Congregation of the Council, asking whether Newman would agree to be a consultor of one of the commissions that was preparing the business of the Vatican Council.

Cardinal Caterini's letter, from which Newman quotes, explained that the Pope had, for this purpose, summoned to Rome ecclesiastics distinguished for their knowledge of theology and holy lives, 'in order that, under the title of consultors, they may zealously employ themselves in the commissions appointed, each of which is presided over by a Cardinal.' Ullathorne was asked to let Newman know the Pope's intention to include him among the consultors, 'unless you have anything worthy of notice to the contrary.' 'If Newman is disposed to accept the honour offered him, he should come to Rome before the end of the year. In any event, whatever be the result of this letter, you will oblige me by sending me an answer.'

When sending Caterini's letter, Ullathorne wrote to Newman, 'I may state to you that the English Bishops were requested by the Holy See to nominate a theologian to proceed to Rome. But as the Bishops cannot conveniently meet to make a nomination at present. [sic] And this invitation to yourself is a totally distinct thing.'

[3] The question of inviting Newman as a consultor was being discussed in Sept. both at Rome and among the English bishops. For Manning's circular apparently designed to exclude Newman see Frederick J. Cwiekowski, *The English Bishops and the First Vatican Council*, Louvain 1971, p. 73, and *Purcell*, II, pp. 422–3. Patterson wrote privately on 17 Sept. to Neville wanting to arrange for Newman to be invited to the Council. Neville wrote back very forcefully to dissuade him. See also letter of 15 Nov. to Clifford.

The reasons for going are

1. The *chance* of my being placed in a commission, and with others, such, that I could do some good.

2. The good that it might do our Oratory, both as in itself a sign of favour, and if I returned a Bishop in partibus.

On the other hand

I premise. 1 That the Holy Father contemplates the *possibility* of my declining, and writes through the Cardinal to our Bishop to *sound* me.

2. This, while delicate towards myself, also leaves it open to pay me a compliment, even though it were *wished* that I should decline it.

3 It is quite a distinct appointment, from that of being Theologian for the English bishops, of which the Bishop speaks, and, as he says. That would be a high appointment; but this, considering that I should be merged in a number of consultors, and perhaps have to consider subjects quite beyond my knowledge and foreign to my experience, is scarcely more than a compliment.

I consider, then, that little or no good, and much harm, would come of accepting it.

1. I put my state of health first, because it is not only a sufficient reason in itself, but because it is the reason for declining which I should assign to the Bishop.

2 I may have but a few years to live, certainly only a few of mental vigour, and I might be spending them operosè nihil agendo.

3. I break off the work which I am now upon, and may never be able to take up the tangled threads of it again.[1]

4. I lose the chance of the arrangement of my letters and papers of past years, which require so much elucidation and can only receive it from me.

5 I have a warning, in the time I lost at Dublin, of what will come of my throwing myself into a work foreign to my talents, and among strange persons.

6. I have never got on intimately with ecclesiastical superiors. It arises from my shyness, and a sort of nervous continual recollection that I am bound to obey them, which keeps me from being easy with them, speaking my mind without effort, and lucidly and calmly arguing with them. I never could make my presence *felt*.

7. I never have succeeded with boards or committees. I always have felt out of place, and my words unreal. My part in the Synod at Oscott in 1852 is always in my mind as a bad dream.

8. I cannot speak any language but my own.

There are some things I *can* do — others that I *can't*. I should, by accepting this invitation, lose my independence and gain nothing

J H N

---

[1] i.e. *A Grammar of Assent.*

TO BISHOP ULLATHORNE

The Oratory. Oct 15. 1868.

My dear Lord,

I thank you for your letter and for the sight of the Cardinal's, which I now return.

I hope you will understand the deep sense I have of the Holy Father's condescension in thinking of me as one of the Consultors previous to the Council, and also of the delicacy towards me of the Cardinal in the mode of his reporting to you that most gracious thought of his Holiness.

I say the delicacy, because by the words, 'Quatenus nihil observatu dignum habeas,' and 'Sit [Si] velit Newman oblatum honorem acceptum habere,' he allows your Lordship privately to consult me, and anticipates the chance of my declining, without any direct communication being made from me to his Eminence in answer.

I have then availed myself of his, and indeed your Lordship's, permission to consider the matter carefully on its own merits by my best lights; and the result of my deliberation has been to decline the honour (which I hereby do) wishing to do so in the way most expressive of my true and humble gratitude for so great an act of favour on the part of his Holiness.

I decline it 1. because of the state of my health, which requires at present a careful and continual watching which I could not observe except at home. 2. And next, because, though health and life are of course not to be thought of in comparison of a great religious end, still no great religious end would be promoted by my presence at Rome for an august and momentous solemnity, for which I am not fitted either by my talents or by my attainments.

No one would gain by my being there, and I am not at all sure I should not lose my life.

I am, my dear Lord, begging your Lordship's blessing, Yr affte & obt Servt in Xt

John H Newman of the Oratory[1]

The Rt Revd The Bp of Birmingham

SATURDAY 17 OCTOBER 1868   F W N [Newman] came for a few hours.   Palmer came. G. Ryder came

SUNDAY 18 OCTOBER   to dinner besides those in house Renouf.   Wingfield at Edgbaston

MONDAY 19 OCTOBER   Palmer went — G. Ryder went

---

[1] Newman on 15 Nov. sent a copy of this reply to Dr Russell of Maynooth, who commented on 16 Nov., 'It is all that could be desired: and I am sincerely rejoiced that the special honour has been done you. I am very glad of it [the invitation] as a just tribute to yourself: and I am particularly happy in the knowledge of the good effect which it will have among those "who are without."' See also *A.W.*, p. 266.

TO EDWARD BELLASIS

The Oratory Oct 23. 1868

My dear Bellasis

Thank you for your letters. As to Edward, I certainly am nervous about him. You know, as I do not, his diffidence and shyness — but even, if this were overcome, which he does not feel himself, I have not confidence that the excitement might not suddenly be too much for him, and that he would not break down. You know this took place in the case of Pope's poor boy — After the first night he broke down — Baker was set to learn his part — but it obliged us to omit one day of representation — and luckily by the third day he picked up again, and acted. Then we substituted for the missing day the day *after* the third. And Baker was not wanted.[1]

This is the worst of a play — we have only tried one for 4 years. On one of them it failed altogether — on another one of the three days failed, in both cases by illness of the actors.

Of course, we have thought of doubling the parts — but first we have not boys for such a plan, next it is hard to make a boy throw himself with spirit into a part, nay to get it by heart, unless he is sure of acting it.

Again we are short of actors, so that we cannot afford duplicates.

I think I shall on the whole, from what you say and I feel, give it against Edward.

When you were here last, a stranger came, or I should have spoken to you about the London University affair — nothing indeed of consequence; when you come again I hope not to forget it.[2]

I gave your message about Mr Masfen. The boys are almost well now. I have not heard of them for the last day or two

Ever Yrs affly John H Newman

TO MRS JOHN CHIPPENDALL MONTESQUIEU BELLEW

The Oratory Birmingham Oct 23. 1868

Dear Mrs Bellew

I have never forgotten you or your sister — you have both of you been in my mind ever since I saw you. I rejoice and praise God at the news you tell me

---

[1] This was on the occasion of the Latin Play at the Oratory School in 1866, when Archdale Tayler Pope took the part of Phædria in the *Pincerna*. He died a month later. In May 1869 Edward Bellasis played Gelasimus in the *Aulularia*.

[2] See letter of 25 Jan. 1868 to Bellasis.

about yourself and those dear to you. Thank you for writing me so long a letter.[1]

As you so kindly speak of my having been of use to you, I know you will not forget me in your prayers, for I am now an old man and my work seems almost over.

I send you by this post a little book, as you wish.

On All Saints Day my intention is engaged — but I will say Mass for you, please God, on the Vigil

Most sincerely Yours John H Newman of the Oratory

Mrs Bellew

SUNDAY 25 OCTOBER 1868 the Bishop called I preached in morning
WEDNESDAY 28 OCTOBER Kennard came?
THURSDAY 29 OCTOBER sang high Mass[2]

TO HENRY JAMES COLERIDGE

The Oratory Octr 29/68

My dear Fr Coleridge

Fr Ryder has shown me your letter. I need hardly tell you the report about my behaviour at Littlemore is false from beginning to end[3]

But I cannot deny it in print, till it gets into print — Else, qui s'excuse, s'accuse. Moreover, it will have the effect of lugging in a sort of gratuitous insult to my Anglican friends, after the manner of the story of a gun — which, being a good story, the tellers brought into all dinner parties, by saying 'Hark! did not you hear a gun go off? well, whether or not, talking of a gun, I recollect etc etc' Then came the story.

If I had not said too many words to you on the subject already, I should add that, if I set a precedent of answering before accused, I should have to write infinite letters, and should become 'querulous for ever' – and this would be infra dig.[4]

The Revd Fr Coleridge S.J.

[1] Mrs Bellew, who, with her sister, had visted Newman fifteen years previously, wrote to say that she and her family were about to be received into the Catholic Church. Her husband was one of the most popular of London preachers, and gave up more than a thousand pounds a year by becoming a Catholic.
[2] Feast in England of the Venerable Bede, which was kept at Birmingham Oratory with a high mass.
[3] On 28 Oct. in a letter to Ryder Coleridge told him of a story he had heard from an Anglican source about Newman, 'that he has been to Littlemore (very likely) but "*he went to the service and stayed to the end*" — Now can you without much trouble get me leave to contradict this or explain it. It is said "one old woman waited for him, having recognized him, and she went into the Church and spoke to him".'
[4] Conclusion and signature have been cut out.

FRIDAY 30 OCTOBER 1868   Mr Tevie?   and Mr Stevens at dinner
SATURDAY 31 OCTOBER   Mrs Higgins and daughter in Bm [Birmingham] till Tuesday next
SUNDAY 1 NOVEMBER   preached in morning

TO E. B. PUSEY

The Oratory Bm Nov. 1. 1868

My dear Pusey

Thank you for the books — your Addresses, and for Philip's great work, for such it is, if long diligence and trouble make a work great. Thank him for it, please, expressly for it comes to me from him, though through you.[1]

I have found your letter. As to Dr Wiseman's baptizing after you, if it be the case I think it is, he especially wanted *not* to baptize (even conditionally.)[2] It was a sort of fancy (I may say) he had — to *accept* Anglican Baptism. At Rome they were very slow to allow (even conditional) baptism to be administered — but I am afraid I must say the lady changed her tone and contradicted herself — and after giving a most satisfactory account of your baptism, said just the reverse: hence her word could not be taken. In the case of Burder, now a Cistercian Abbot, there was *no* baptism even conditional. Dr Wiseman took the witness of persons present, when, from being a Dissenter, he conformed to the Church of England with baptism. Since that time, i.e. in 1852, the Synod of Oscott has, I think, made one general rule, and we are bound without asking any question to baptize converts conditionally.[3]

The old stories are certainly repeated by us, and different grounds taken against the Anglican Orders —[4] but this is the case because we do *not* think those old stories *have* been *entirely* invalidated, and we *do* go from one ground to another, because we *do* think *some* suspicion remains under every head — and that the whole case against them lies in the sum total of those separate suspicions.

---

[1] The books were E. B. Pusey's *Eleven Addresses during a Retreat of the Companies of the Love of Jesus, engaged in Perpetual Intercession for the Conversion of Sinners*, Oxford 1868, and *Sancti Patris nostri Cyrilli Archiepiscopi Alexandrini in XII Prophetas*, Oxford 1868, edited by Philip, E. B. Pusey's son. Both gifts were inscribed 'with kindest love.' The pages of *Eleven Addresses* are uncut.

[2] A note has been written on the autograph 'Isabella ⟨?⟩ Young in 1842?'

[3] The first Provincial Synod of Westminster held at Oscott in 1852 decreed: Cum magis invaluerint causae quae animos vicariorum apostolicorum, ineunte hoc saeculo, impulerunt, ut decernerent, omnes post annum 1773 natos, et inter protestantes baptizatos, conversos ad fidem, esse baptizandos sub conditione, hanc regulam absolute innovamus, praecipientes, omnes a protestantismo conversos esse baptizandos conditionate, nisi ex indubiis probationibus certissime constet in ipsorum baptismo omnia rite fuisse peracta, quoad materiae et formae applicationem.' Decretum XVI 7.

George Burder, who was an Independent, became an Anglican before he went up to Oxford. He became a Catholic in Jan. and a Cistercian in June 1846.

[4] In his letter of 14 Sept., (Liddon's *Pusey*, IV, p. 158), Pusey spoke of this, and asked how the question of Anglican Orders could be decided by those who had shown such animus. Cf. letter of 19 Sept. to him.

Don't you imply that Manning was the *Jesuit* candidate for the Arch-bishoprick? Really this was not the case. Clifford was their man — but both he and Dr Grant of Southwark whose names were given in to the Pope with Dr Errington's, ruined their chance by *declining* in *favour* of Dr Errington. It is a sad story — Dr E. is a most saintly man — but he had taken an extreme rigorous line some years before, when he was the Cardinal (Wiseman's) Coadjutor, and had offended the Pope. The Chapter of Westminster stuck up for him, and sent in his name, and the two others, whom they mentioned, Clifford and Grant, were on his side too, and each declined to be Archbishop. Then the Pope was displeased, and determined to take some one else — and the choice lay between Manning and Dr Ullathorne. The latter was under-stood to be the candidate of Propaganda, but the Pope chose Manning, who had become a dear friend of Cardinal Wiseman's and had ingratiated himself with the Pope.[1] Lord Clifford, Dr Clifford's father, had been a great ally of the Jesuits — and the son had been brought up almost under their shadow, though he was not in one of their Schools. As far as the Jesuits go in England, they take a moderate line — they backed up the Rambler — they have been some of my best friends. That there is a party of them at Rome, the party of the Civiltà Cattolica, who take an extreme part I know — but from what I hear the great body of them are opposed to the organization and special privileges of that Editorial Staff, as *such* — and though I dare say they agree with its opinions, I don't think they like or sympathise in its violence, bigotry and dogmatism.[2]

Ever Yours affectly John H Newman

The Revd E B Pusey DD

MONDAY 2 NOVEMBER 1868   sang Black Mass

TO MALCOLM MACCOLL

The Oratory. Birmingham. November 4 1868

My Dear Mr MacColl,

I thank you sincerely for your Pamphlet. It is very able and forcible. I hope it will be widely read. I think already I have observed use made of it in speeches at the Hustings.[3]

Very truly yours, John H. Newman.

The Rev. M. MacColl.

[1] For the story of Manning's appointment as Archbishop of Westminster see *Butler*, I, pp. 257–306.

[2] The *Civiltà Cattolica*, a fortnightly review edited by Jesuits in Rome, followed the extremist line.

[3] *Is there not a Cause?* in favour of the disestablishment of the Church of Ireland.

FRIDAY 6 NOVEMBER 1868   snow lying a day or two
SUNDAY 8 NOVEMBER   preached in morning

TO JAMES LAURENCE SHEPHERD

The Oratory Bm Nov. 8. 1868

My dear Fr Shepherd

Your handsome and valuable volumes have just come. I thank you very much for so splendid a gift. The collection of hymns would in itself be a treasure, if there were nothing more.[1]

Most sincerely Yours in Xt   John H Newman of the Oratory

MONDAY 9 NOVEMBER 1868   Marshall and E. Coffin in the house, for the marriage

TO WILLIAM MONSELL

The Oratory Nov 9. 1868

My dear Monsell

I do not know whether you recollect that, when you and Mr Fullerton charged yourselves with the duty of executing Lady Olivia Acheson's charitable intentions towards us, you thought it expedient for legal reasons that the deeds of our property here should be placed in your lawyer's hands. This was done, and they have been ever since in the keeping of Messrs Ward and Mills.

It is now going on for seventeen years since Lady Olivia's death; and, as we naturally wish to have possession of our deeds, it has occurred to us to inquire, as I hereby do, whether the reasons for your holding them, to which I have referred, are still in force, or whether you think you could prudently let them come back to us.

We have so clear an evidence of your and Mr Fullerton's friendly feeling towards the Oratory, in the trouble you and he took in our behalf, on the occasion of Lady Olivia's bequest, as to be sure that, should your answer be in the negative, it will be so given from the legal necessities of the case, and not from any want of considerateness towards our wishes[2]

I am, My dear Monsell, Yours ever affectionately
John H Newman of the Oratory

The Rt Honble Wm Monsell M P

[1] These were evidently the first two volumes of Shepherd's translation of Guéranger's *Liturgical Year*. See letter of 23 Feb. to Shepherd.

[2] See letters of 15 Oct. 1854 and 1 Dec 1854 to St John. The deeds were now returned to the Oratory.

TUESDAY 10 NOVEMBER 1868   Bessie Phillipps married to Mr R. Pope[1]

TO R. W. CHURCH

The Oratory Bm Nov 14 1868.

My dear Church

Thank you for your sermons — they are on the most interesting subject of the day — and I am sure I shall be pleased with them; certainly I am, with what I have already read of them.[2]

Whenever there is a vacancy in a Professorship of History, I look out for the chance of your filling it. But you are very unlucky. Twice the Anti-Gladstone party has been in, when there has been a vacancy at Ch Ch [Christ Church].[3] I should have preferred for you Modern History, as being more your line — I had hoped you would have got it instead of Bernard.[4]

The Conservatives have made very good, that is, very clever appointments. I suppose the Dean of Cork represents the Broad Church, while McNeil is the Low, and Mr Bright the High.[5] From the little I have seen of Dr McGee, he will be a great accession to the intellectual power of the Bench — but probably, as a Bishop, his time will be taken up with other matters than the scientific controversies of the day. Perhaps, however, he is rather a generous, forcible orator, and [than?] severe thinker. Every one speaks as if Mill was invincible — and had carried all before him — but there must come a re-action.

Ever yours affectly John H. Newman

TO W. J. COPELAND

The Oratory Bm Novr 14. 1868

My dear Copeland

I am glad to find you give a good account of yourself; but I am sure you cannot take too much care of yourself this winter. I dread your 'running up' to

---

[1] Elizabeth Agnes Phillips, who now became the second wife of Richard Pope, was a daughter of Mrs George Phillips, who became a Catholic with her children in Aug. 1851, and died in 1857, just after she had established a small hospital in Birmingham, with the help of the Oratorians.

[2] *Sermons preached before the University of Oxford*, London 1868; Church discussed 'the relations between Christianity and the ideas and facts of modern civilised society.' p.v.

[3] H. L. Mansel was appointed by Lord Derby Professor of Ecclesiastical History at Oxford in 1866, and two years later was succeeded by William Bright, appointed by Disraeli. A Canonry at Christ Church was annexed to the Professorship.

[4] This was a mistake, as Church pointed out in his reply on 19 Nov., for Montague Burrows, appointed Chichele Professor of History at Oxford, in 1862.

[5] The Dean of Cork was William Connor Magee (1821–91), recently appointed by Disraeli Bishop of Peterborough. In the last year of his life he was made Archbishop of York. Hugh McNeile (1795–1879), a strongly anti-catholic Evangelical, became Dean of Ripon in Sept. 1868.

London, 'running down' to Cheltenham, — 'running over' to Danbury. You must learn to settle down — and be as stationary as I am.[1]

Thank you for all the trouble that you are taking in my behalf. As to the dates of the Sermons I cannot divest myself of the idea that it will be uppish to give them, though I should like it abstractedly. As I said to you, it seems to turn the Sermons to a different purpose as being historical.

If any of the Sermons on Subjects of the Day are to be published, the question does not press.[2] Would not Rivington be in a position now to decide whether any of those Sermons would answer? As being dedicated to you, I should like them republished, but they are on the whole so different (e.g. the two last) from the Parochial and Plain that [it] is a question whether they can be mixed up with that series.[3] I see my text for my last sermon is 'Man goeth forth etc.' This was my text of the first Sermon I wrote (for St Clement's) in 1824 and taken accordingly. The evening had come. Altogether I am puzzled.

Ever Yours affectly John H Newman

P.S.   I am, I hope, going on well, thank you.

TO E. B. PUSEY

The Oratory Bm Novr 14. 1868

My dear Pusey

I am very glad you have finished your answer to Fr Harper.[4] It has annoyed me much to think that charges against you stood without that answer you could give — and I am not party of course at all, on the contrary I have again and again protested against the tone taken as regards you in the Month. And, strange to say, (for men view things so differently,) its conductors have not only wished to leave off attacking you, but consider they have.

Fr Harper has been very ill — his book quite knocked him up, and for a while he has been thought dying. Consequently he has not been able to write his second volume, on the Pope — for which he had collected materials — and the subject has got into the hands of Fr Botalla, a foreign Jesuit, who I am sorry to hear has taken an extreme line which Fr Harper would not have taken. I sent Fr Harper a number of objections to his published volume, principally about you, and I know he meant to use them in a second edition, or in his second volume, and I cannot help hoping he would have done you justice.[5]

---

[1] Copeland wrote on 12 Nov. that he had visited Woodgate at Danbury.

[2] The dates at which the sermons were first preached are included at the end of S.D.

[3] i.e. the two sermons preached at Littlemore, 22 Sept. 1842 and 25 Sept. 1843, 'Feasting in Captivity' and 'The Parting of Friends.'

[4] Pusey wrote on 13 Nov., 'I have I hope nearly got through my answer to Harper's allegations against me. Into his own book I do not enter.' Thomas Harper's book was Peace through the Truth, London 1866, in reply to Pusey's Eirenicon.

[5] See letter of 21 April 1868 to Harper.

Bennett's prosecution may come to an end — but surely Colquhoun and Company will go on, as they have pledged themselves, to you and Denison.[1] I wish you were able to get back to the Minor Prophets.

I am not going to Rome. The Bishop of Orleans ⟨(this is not known)⟩ at the beginning of the year asked me to be his theologian. And lately the Pope sent a message offering me to be a Consultor — I have begged off — and, as far as I can see, rightly.[2] I am not a theologian, and should only have been wasting my time in matters which I did not understand. I have ever more than inclined to hold the Pope's Infallibility — but as a matter of expedience, I wish nothing done at the Council about it. There is always a large party of Bishops who are alive to the question of such expediency — but they have not *facts* to produce. Definite, tangible evidence of the inexpediency of touching the question is what is wanted.

Ever Yours affectly John H Newman

P.S.   I congratulate you on Mr Bright being the new Professor. Of course I should have preferred Church, but that was not to be expected.

TO WILLIAM CLIFFORD, BISHOP OF CLIFTON

The Oratory Bm Novr 15. 1868

My dear Lord

Our Bishop has told me your very great kindness in making me your choice, when you had to name to the other Bishops some one to go to Rome from the Bishops as a Consultor in preparation of the Ecumenical Council.

It has been a great honour done me — and very gratifying to my feelings — and I write these lines to you to thank you for it, as I do with great sincerity. It is a fresh token of your unvarying kindness towards me

Begging your blessing on me and mine, I am, My dear Lord,

Your faithful friend & servant in Jesus Xt
John H Newman of the Oratory

The Rt Revd The Bp of Clifton

---

[1] Pusey wrote that the prosecution of W. J. E. Bennett, see letter of 20 Aug. to M. R. Giberne, put off making an appeal to the Vatican Council, 'while the question was whether we were tolerated,' in the Church of England. Pusey seemed to think the prosecution led by J. C. Colquhoun and the Church Association would come to nothing.
[2] See letter of 31 Dec. 1867 to Monsell and Memorandum of 14 Oct. 1868.

TO C. H. V. PIXELL

Nov 15/68

Dear Sir

I thank you by anticipation for the publication you propose to send me.[1]

I do not expect that the articles you speak of will interfere with the logical force of the argument to which you say they are a reply.

I agree with you most sincerely that it is desirable not 'to strive —' in the sense in which the Apostle so speaks — but it must be recollected that the very first and[2] principle of the Tract movement was 'Truth before peace —' brought out categorically [;] and the very motto of their high and dry opponents, the establishment men, the mild evangelicals and the amiable anti-dogmatists of the day was your present motto 'Beati pacifici —' If the first Tractarians had taken this divine beatitude as their only rule, perhaps Ritualism now would not exist; and if you carry it out yourself you will give up the prospect of converting the Wesleyans or Dissenters

J H N

The Rev C H Pixell

TO CHARLES RUSSELL

Private

The Oy Bm Nov 15/68

My dear Dr Russell

I think you may like to see my letter to the Bishop apropos of the Cardinal's to him. Please, return it[3]

Ever Yrs affly John H Newman

TO LADY SIMEON

The Oratory Novr 15. 1868

My dear Lady Simeon

I was on the point of writing to you to inquire about this new candidate, when your message came to me through Stephen. It grieves me very much to

---

[1] Pixell, who was Perpetual Curate of Skirwith, Cumberland, had already written to Newman on 21 Sept. in defence of Anglican Orders. He wrote again on 14 Nov. to say that he was having the *Union Review* for Nov. sent to Newman, for the sake of the first article 'Dr. Newman and the English Orders,' and for a letter on the same subject 'from a distinguished clerical convert to the Roman Catholic Church,' pp. 481–512, and 549–60.

[2] Word illegible. Pixell also spoke of the many both outside and within the Catholic fold, 'who do not believe and for the sake of these, is it well so to strive? "Beati Pacifici!"' See II *Tim.* 2:14 and 24, 'charging them before the Lord that they strive not about words to no profit, but to the subverting of the hearers.'

[3] See note to letter of 15 Oct. to Ullathorne.

hear that Sir John should be thus needlessly troubled. I take it for granted it will not endanger his seat, but needless expense is most annoying. What can be the meaning of it? Is it that the Conservative Clubs say, you shall pay for your victory as dearly as possible?[1]

I am glad to see Jack's name stand so high in the examination list.[2] He is a very good fellow really — and I think will always show himself so — His fault is a liability to a sort of wild excitement, which of course is very dangerous in a young man. But he is affectionate and true, and it is Fr St John's strong feeling and my own, that you can always depend on his honesty and openness, I hope and believe that Sir John will always be able to trust him. He ought to be older before he gets his commission — the failure of the Oxford scheme has spoilt that arrangement. I won't forget Sir John's wish about finding a travelling companion, but it is a difficult matter.

How dreadful poor Gaisford's loss![3]

Ever yours most sincerely in Xt   John H Newman of the Oratory

The Honble Lady Simeon

TUESDAY 17 NOVEMBER 1868   Election of Members for the New Popular Parliament? I did not vote[4]

TO THOMAS GRANT, BISHOP OF SOUTHWARK

The Oratory Nov. 23. 1868

My dear Lord

Fr St John has shown me your Lordship's letters to him. They lead me to say to you, that I entirely approve and concur in all that he has done in the matter to which they relate.

In what he said to the boys he made no mention of your name, nor any allusion to it. I cannot of course be so sure, that the boy, with whom your Lordship is confidential, may not have mentioned it. He who has spoken to you about others, may have spoken to others about you.

And he has misrepresented₁ Fr St John's words greatly and variously. Here again I am bound to submit to your Lordship, that he who has misrepresented his master, is not unlikely to have misrepresented his schoolfellows. For

---

[1] Sir John Simeon was the unopposed Liberal candidate for Parliament in the Isle of Wight, and the sitting member. At the last minute a Conservative candidate came forward but was defeated. Stephen was Sir John Simeon's son at the Oratory School.

[2] i.e. for a direct commission in the Army. John Simeon joined the Rifle Brigade.

[3] Thomas Gaisford's second wife, Emily St Lawrence, died on 6 Nov.

[4] This was the first General Election after the passing of the Second Reform Act in 1867. In Birmingham three liberals were elected by considerable majorities over two conservative contestants. See letter of 3 Dec. to Mrs John Mozley.

myself, I think he has used words in one sense, and you in your sollicitude [sic] for our welfare have interpreted them in another and worse.

We consider we have discovered him; but your Lordship may be sure, without our making you a solemn promise, that we shall be considerate and prudent in our treatment of him.

We have a grateful sense of your Lordship's wish to do us good; but you must not think ill of us, if we prefer our own way of finding out evil, if indeed evil there be, to any other way.

Begging your Lordship's blessing,

I am, My dear Lord, Your faithful servant in Xt
John H Newman of the Oratory

The Rt. Revd The Bishop of Southwark

TO E. B. PUSEY

The Oratory Novr 24/68

My dear Pusey

I never heard of any such person as your correspondent speaks of — and no one in this house ever heard of the name. Nor do I quite accept the account, though of course many persons become converts, of whom one hears nothing.[1]

As to Dalgairns's work, I have never seen it — and, though I hear it referred to every now and then, I never heard any opinion given about it.[2] But, as we are far more accustomed to hear if there is any thing wrong in a book, that [than] if they are good and useful, and, since I never have heard any one say that Dalgairns has said any thing temerarious, offensive to pious ears, etc etc I have always, and with reason, believed that it may be trusted, as at least teaching a probable and safe doctrine.

As to accidents, I have always considered that the word may be dispensed with — and the inclosed extracts from Fr Perrone seem to bear me out.

By the bye Perrone says, de Euchar. p 236, speaking of St Chrysost. ad Cæsarium, Theodoret etc 'Citati Patres naturæ et substantiæ nomine significant rerum naturales sensilesque qualitates.'[3]

Ever Yrs affly John H Newman

---

[1] Pusey enclosed a letter, not to be found, concerning someone in Scotland, and said 'the tale seems to be horribly suspicious.'

[2] Pusey wrote 'What is thought of Dalgairns' book on the holy Sacrament on its philosophical side [?],' i.e. J. D. Dalgairns, *The Holy Communion, its Philosophy, Theology, and Practice*, Dublin 1861. Pusey asked whether instead of the word 'accidents,' that of 'species' could be used because it 'does not commit to any philosophy.'

[3] Joannes Perrone, *Praelectiones Theologicae* VII., Rome 1843, Tractatus de Augustissimae Eucharistiae Sacramento I, Cap. ii. 2.

TO CATHERINE BOWDEN, SISTER MARY ALBAN

The Oratory Bm Novr 25. 1868

My dear Child

I congratulate you most sincerely on your approaching clothing.[1] If any thing would carry me away from my 'nido' here, it would be the claim which you and yours have on me for every the most affectionate manifestation of my interest in you and anxiety for your welfare; but the greatest thing I can do is to say Mass for you; and that I can do quite as well here as at Stone. So here I will remain, not thinking of you the less but the more because I am not bodily present with you and your brothers and sisters on the 15th.

Ever Yours most affectly in Xt   John H Newman of the Oratory
Sister Mary Alban

P.S.   Will you give the inclosed to Mother Prioress

TO WILLIAM EWART GLADSTONE

The Oratory Bm Novr 25. 1868

My dear Mr Gladstone,

Your are too great a man to condole with, so I will not presume to say a word on the issue of your contest in Lancashire, for which we have all been looking with extreme interest. Of course I can understand how personally you must suffer, but soldiers have the smart of wounds, though they are victorious at the end of the campaign.[2]

I have waited till now to thank you for your pamphlet, which I received so long before publication, as to make me believe it comes from yourself. It is most noble — and I can congratulate you with greater reason and more hearty satisfaction upon it, than I could upon a score of triumphs upon the hustings.[3]

---

[1] Catherine Bowden was to begin her novitiate with the Dominican nuns at Stone on 15 Dec.

[2] Gladstone fought the general election over the question of the disestablishment of the Church of Ireland. The liberals were returned to power with a majority of about 112, 'but in South-West Lancashire the Church of England was strong; orange prevailed vastly over green; and Mr. Gladstone was beaten. Happily he had in anticipation of the result, and by the care of friends, already been elected for Greenwich.' John Morley, *The Life of William Ewart Gladstone*, cheap edition London 1912, II, p. 191.

[3] This refers to Gladstone's *A Chapter of Autobiography*, written by 22 Sept. but only published on 23 Nov. In it he defended himself against the charge of inconsistency, for having supported the established status of the Irish Church in *The State in its Relations with the Church*, 1838, and now, thirty years later, proposing to disestablish it. He had been misled, among other things, by the success of the Oxford Movement in the thirties: 'An extraordinary change appeared to pass upon the spirit of the place. I believe it would be a moderate estimate to say that much beyond one half of the very flower of its youth chose the profession of Holy Orders, while an impression scarcely less deep seemed to be stamped upon a large portion of its lay pupils. I doubt whether at any period of its existence, either since the Reformation, or perhaps before it, the Church of England had reaped from either University, in so short a time, so rich a harvest.' p. 53.

It puts me in mind of him
  Who comprehends his trust, and to the same
  Keeps faithful with a singleness of aim,
  And, thro' the heat of conflict, keeps the law
  In calmness made, and sees what he foresaw.

etc etc.[1]

Believe me to be, My dear Mr Gladstone, with the greatest respect
Most sincerely Yours John H Newman

The Rt Honble Wm Gladstone M P.

TO JOHN O'HAGAN

The Oratory Bm Novr 25. 1868

My dear Mr O'Hagan

I am very sorry to hear of the additional trial which Judge O'Hagan and his children have — and beg to assure you and Mrs O'Hagan that I will lose no time in saying Mass for the soul of the dear relative you have lost, and that under such sorrowful circumstances.[2]

It pleases me very much to hear from you, and that you should be so kind to think of me at the time of your distress — and also what you say of the kind thoughts which you and others have of me. It is always a pleasure to me and a consolation to know that men whom I liked and valued so much have not forgotten me.

Yours affectionately in Xt   John H Newman

    Gladstone confessed, 'I for one formed a completely false estimate of what was about to happen; and believed that the Church of England, through the medium of a regenerated clergy and an intelligent and attached laity, would not only hold her ground, but would even in great part probably revive the love and allegiance both of the masses who were wholly falling away from religious observances, and of those large and powerful nonconforming bodies . . .' p. 54.

    Gladstone went on, 'And surely it would have required . . . a marvellously prophetic mind to foretell that, in ten or twelve more years, that powerful and distinguished generation of clergy would be broken up: that at least a moiety of the most gifted sons, whom Oxford had reared for the service of the Church of England, would be hurling at her head the hottest bolts of the Vatican: that, with their deviation on the one side, there would arise a not less convulsive rationalistic movement on the other . . .' p. 54.

    Thus the Church of England grew weaker and weaker, while Gladstone made the further mistake of underestimating the strength and progress of nonconformity. Those two mistakes led him 'into the excess of recommending the continued maintenace of a theory [the union of Church and State] which was impracticable, and which, if it could have been enforced, would have been . . . less than just . . . For I never held that a National Church should be permanently maintained except for the nation,' i.e. while the greater part concurred in establishment. p. 56.

  [1] Wordsworth, *Character of the Happy Warrior*, 39–40, 53–4.

  [2] John O'Hagan wrote at the request of his wife, whose mother, Mrs Thomas O'Hagan, had died a few weeks earlier. She was Mary Teeling, and was married in 1836. For several years before her death her reason had given way after the death of her eldest daughter. Her children had hoped that before the end she would recover her mind, but this had not happened.

TO W. J. COPELAND

The Oratory Novr 26. 1868

My dear Copeland

I am, as you may expect, exceedingly gratified by your letter. Of course I could not have expected it, and I consider it, I trust not presumptuously, as a token that I shall have done some useful thing in my generation.[1]

It did not surprise me to hear the Dissenters had bought my volumes. I have at various times had letters from men among them more or less influential, who had told me, that, without accepting my ecclesiastical principles, not a few fraternized with me as far as ethical and religious sentiments went. I have answered them, that I thought, as things are, the first step towards unity was a unison of feeling, and that if I were prospered to do any thing whatever towards laying that necessary foundation, on which higher strata of truth might be deposited at some future day, I should have received a great favour and mercy from the Giver of all good.

As to another volume, I fully feel with Rivington, that, if it is to be done, it must be done quickly. My great difficulty about Sermons for the Day is that it is dedicated to you — and I don't like to curtail it. Yet it is obvious that to print all the sermons in the Volume would be quite out of place. If you printed from 6 to 18 inclusive, it would be a defective volume — if you added some of my University Sermons as 4, 5, 6, 8 or the 4 Sermons on Antichrist in the Tracts, how could it be all dedicated to you? this is a great difficulty. From the 6 to the 18 inclusive would be in *octavo*, as originally, 238 pages.

As to the money, give me what you please. It will be *your gift* — and, as we have been trying to buy the fields on the *other* side of us, as well as the public house, at Rednall, it would go towards it[2]

Ever Yrs affly John H Newman

P.S. At present I can't at all call to mind the Sermon on Hebr 3.1.[3] I never saw Gladstone's conspectus, I think.[4]

[1] Copeland wrote on 24 Nov., 'I have seen Rivington who tells me the Sermons are selling so well that there is little doubt but that a supplemental volume from the "Sermons for the Day" would answer, and that a list of dates might be well appended to that: and that if published it had better not be far behindhand from the other eight volumes. . . . The Sermons are selling extensively among Nonconformists . . .'
[2] Copeland wrote that already from the sale of the *Parochial and Plain Sermons* up to the middle of July £1000 was due to him. Rivington 'says that when the 8th Volume is out he expects more sets will be sold as sets. As many as 3500 of the First Volume, including those he has sent to America. . . . Anyhow the Sermons seem taking their place as somewhat of an English Classic — and are a property. — And this makes me most anxious for your direction as to the disposal of the money . . .'
[3] See letter of 19 Sept. to Copeland, who spoke of a sermon on *Hebrews* 2:1.
[4] Copeland asked, 'Have you any where Gladstone's conspectus of the Movement in (I think) the Foreign and Colonial some twenty years ago?' This was 'Present Aspects of the Church,' the *Foreign and Colonial Review*, (Oct. 1843). See *Moz.* II, p. 427.

The Oratory, Birmingham, November 26th. 1868.

My dear Rogers,

Do you keep up your intimacy with Sir Francis Doyle? If so, do take an opportunity of expressing to him the great surprise and pleasure which it has given me to read in today's paper of the extraordinary compliment he is going to pay me at Oxford next week by lecturing on my Dream of Gerontius.[1] It is no matter of course whether he praises it or finds fault with it, (and I am sufficiently conscious how open it is to criticism to be sure that the praise it has hitherto had is the praise of partial friends) but the great compliment is his having thought it worthy of being made the subject of an Academical Lecture at all. But you will understand all that I mean without my saying more. It is curious that I should meet with this good turn from him, for, though I have met him so very seldom, and so long ago, I have always kept him in mind, and meant to ask you about him.

Gladstone's letter is a very noble one — but his friends will say it is sadly injudicious. In his concluding remarks he goes as far as the Syllabus on the particular subject of which he treats.[2]

Excuse my bad writing I have some rheumatism in my wrist.

Ever yours affectionately, John H. Newman

The Oratory Bm Nov 27/68

My dear William

I see in to-day's paper the death of Sir J. Harding. I don't suppose I ought to grieve — but I do grieve. Strange to say either last night or this morning I was thinking of him in Church — I think I said a Hail Mary for him.

[1] Sir Francis Doyle was elected Professor of Poetry at Oxford in 1867. The lecture on *The Dream of Gerontius* was published in his *Lectures on Poetry*, London 1869, pp. 91–124. On 30 Nov. Doyle wrote that he had heard from Rogers, and hoped that Newman would accept a copy of his lectures, which he later sent him. See also letter of 12 Feb. 1869 to Rogers.

[2] *A Chapter of Autobiography*, 'I can hardly believe that even those, including as they do so many men both upright and able, who now contend on principle for the separation of the Church from the State, are so determined to exalt their theorem to the place of an universal truth, that they ask us to condemn that whole process by which, as the Gospel spread itself through the civilised world, Christianity became incorporated with the action of civil authority, and with the framework of public law. . . . But Christ died for the race: and those who notice the limited progress of conversion in the world until alliance with the civil authority gave to His religion a wider access to the attention of mankind, may be inclined to doubt whether, without that alliance, its immeasurable and inestimable social results would ever have been attained.' pp. 58–9.

'As long as the Church at large, or the Church within the limits of the nation is substantially one, I do not see why the religious care of the subject, through a body properly constituted for the purpose, should cease to be a function of the State . . .' p. 60.

Rogers's reply is in *Letters of Frederic Lord Blachford*, edited by G. E. Marindin, London 1896, p. 275. Rogers remarked, 'One great weight which Gladstone has to carry in the political race is a *character* for want of judgment.'

I know it must sadden you, even tho' it be a relief, and I can't help sending you a line to say how I sympathise with you.

I recollect thinking in Chapel, 'He was nearly the only person who was kind to me on my conversion' (you were another). I met him in the street in London soon after it — He stopped me — shook hands with me — and said to me some very friendly and comforting words. It is the last time I saw him.[1]

Ever Yrs affecty John H Newman

W Froude Esq

TO THE HON. COLIN LINDSAY

The Oratory Birmingham Novr 27. 1868

My dear Sir,

I rejoice to hear from you, that, through God's mercy, you see your way to be received into the Catholic Church. I will gladly become the instrument of that mercy to you, as you propose.

Unless your being close to the Rail determines you to go to the Queen's Hotel, I should recommend the Plough and Harrow, Hagley Road — it is a quiet, highly respectable Hotel, close to our door. As it is not large, it would be well to secure a room as soon as possible; and, should you think it worth while to telegraph to me on receipt of this, I will proceed to do so. Meanwhile, I will try to get the refusal of a room without pledging you, which at this time of year will not be so difficult.[2]

I am, My dear Sir, Most truly Yours
John H Newman of the Oratory[3]

The Honble Colin Lindsay

[1] This was on 18 Nov. 1845. Sir John Harding went up to Oriel College in 1826 and was Queen's Advocate General 1852–62.

Froude replied on 2 Dec., 'Lady Harding will so much value what you said of her husband that I shall venture to send her your letter.' Froude also said that Harding had been out of his mind in his last years, and, 'He often used to break out against Rome and Romanism . . . but he was always indignant against all who had regarded your change as detracting in the least from the grounds of real friendship.'

[2] Lindsay, a son of the Earl of Crawford, was the first President of the English Church Union, founded in 1860 to defend Anglo-Catholicism in the Church of England. He resigned in April 1868 and was succeeded by Lord Halifax. On 26 Nov. Lindsay wrote from Haigh Hall, Wigan,

'As I am desirous of becoming a member of the Roman Catholic Church, I write a line to ask you to receive me, if you would do me such a kindness. I have been for upward of 6 months studying the question of the Supremacy, and I have arrived at the conclusion, that the Pope is the Head of the Church, and the Chief Pastor of the Flock.

I have therefore resolved to become, with God's help a *real* Catholic. —

As I have been somewhat before the public as the (late) President of the English Church Union, I would prefer being received away from my own home (which is Brighton): and also from this place, which is the residence of my Father. —'

Lindsay added that he intended to go to Birmingham to the Queen's Hotel, on 28 Nov., on which day Newman received him into the Church.

[3] On 2 Jan. Lindsay wrote to Newman, 'Before I submitted my convictions were intellectual, (i.e. after reading) now they are from within. I *feel* the truth now, which I did not, (or at

179

The Oratory, Nov. 29th 1868

My dear Henry,

Mr Kennard, the bearer of this, is a recent convert. I am sure you will be glad to know him.

While I am writing, I will ask you to return the book of your brother Robert, which you borrowed of me. I take it for granted you won't want it longer.

Ever yours affectionately, John H. Newman.

H. W. Wilberforce Esq.

TO PETER LE PAGE RENOUF

November 30. 1868

My dear Renouf,

I am sorry to find that your Pamphlet on Pope Honorius has not only been the subject of severe criticism, but has been the occasion of unworthy personalities on yourself.[1] This is very sad; but you have in a measure brought them upon yourself by certain personal reflections of your own upon previous writers in the controversy, especially upon the excellent Fr. Perrone. It is not surprising, as times go, that you have been paid back with interest.

I have a claim on you in this matter; because, as you must recollect on hearing of your intention of writing on Pope Honorius, I expressed to you my satisfaction at it. Not, indeed, that I myself take your view of his case. I have ever held the Pope's Infallibility, that is, held it as a theological opinion, the most probable amid conflicting historical arguments. But it is a great duty to consult for others as well as for oneself; and I welcomed the prospect of your Pamphlet, not only as expedient at a time when ecclesiastical history is studied less carefully than is its due, but especially because its publication is a virtual

least very faintly) before I was received. Before I was received I was inclined to run away. I had bought Gladstone's [A Chapter of] autobiography, which I read on my journey to Birmingham, and when I read his glowing account of the English Church, I began to regret my engagement with you. Being thoroughly convinced that the Pope was the Head and Source of Jurisdiction, and of the necessity of being in his communion, I resolved to lose no time. This was my reason for wishing to join the moment I saw you; and when you asked me "when I would be received", I answer "*now*". I have never regretted the step I took, for I know I have got the Truth.'

[1] See letter of 21 June 1868 to Renouf. The article 'Mr. Renouf on Pope Honorius,' *DR*, (July 1868), pp. 200–33, began 'When we say that the views advocated by Mr. Renouf are most untrue and mischievous, he will accept this as the greatest compliment we can pay him; but we must further give our opinion that his pamphlet is passionate, shallow and, pretentious.' There were also attacks on him in the Catholic papers, and a reply by P. Bottalla S.J., *Pope Honorius before the Tribunal of Reason and History*, London 1868.

protest against that narrow spirit, so uncharitable to the souls of men, which turns theological conclusions into doctrines of obligation.

I cannot be sorry then even now, that you have written on the subject, though I do lament some passages which you have unnecessarily introduced into your argument. This indeed I have told you before, viz., when I read your Pamphlet for the first time, on its publication. I write to you a second time about it in order to make to you a suggestion: — is not your best answer to the rash accusations which have been made against you, not simply to pass them over in silence, which you would naturally do, but to set yourself and your cause right with the public by withdrawing those superfluous animadversions on the living and the dead, which have so painfully grated on the ears of those who love and esteem you?[1]

I am, My dear Renouf, Yours affectionately
John H. Newman of the Oratory

TO W. J. COPELAND

The Oratory Bm Decr 3. 1868

My dear Copeland

I never for an instant supposed that any part of the Volume could appear without my Dedication to you — impossible — but the question was and is whether all the Sermons contained in it were to appear, or only some.

And I think it must be left to Rivington. He has two questions to decide — 1. whether he thinks certain of the Sermons will go down with the public. 2. Whether he is willing to run the risk of two volumes — for they are too many for one.

As to the Sermons, both of us, I suppose, should prefer that certain things which occur in them should not have been said — but on my part I have no difficulty in letting them be reprinted as they stand.

This [is] all I have to say. By the bye the first sermon I ever wrote (for St Clement's) had for its text 'Man goeth forth etc' as my last had[2]

Ever Yrs affly John H Newman

---

[1] Newman noted in his Journal on 30 Nov., 'I shall be selling out my newly acquired stock of credit in these Catholic Circles, if I publish this letter on Renouf's pamphlet upon Honorius, as I am thinking of doing.' *A.W.*, p. 267. Renouf replied on 15 Dec. that he would be 'deeply grieved' if Newman's letter were published, 'partly because, in itself, I do not think it does me justice; but chiefly because when read by the light of what others have said about me it would convey to the public a very incorrect view of your real ideas on the subject.' Renouf added that he would find it much harder to answer than the attacks of W. G. Ward and Fr Bottalla. See letter of 17 Dec. to Renouf.

[2] Copeland, writing on 1 Dec., wanted *S.D.* published complete, and said, 'If, as you propose, the *dates are to be added* of all the sermons, what will they, *the dates*, be without the *first* and *last* Sermon of this Volume the record of the "morning" and the "evening" of that mysterious "day's" work and labour, which had its sunrise in 1824, and its sunset in 1843.' The text of the first sermon in *S.D.*, 'The Work of the Christian,' and the last, 'The Parting of Friends,' was the same, 'Man goes forth to his work and to his labour until the evening.' *Ps.* 104:23.

TO MRS JOHN MOZLEY

The Oratory Bm Dec 3. 1868

My dear Jemima

I am very well, thank you — tho' I still take medicine and am on a regime; and do not yet consider myself safe. But I have had no cold, and certainly attribute it, not only to the shower bath which I have now taken for some years, but also to the cider, which among other great benefits has certainly acted as a tonic to my throat. I drink nearly a quart a day.

I have known little about the election here — we feared that the defeated black-country 'lambs' might have been paying us a visit in their rage — but Murphy's exploits in Birmingham last year have perhaps satisfied their strong passions — any how we have got off better than the Lancashire towns.[1] There were plenty of polling booths and no row except about the Town Hall. What a wonderful critical time it is — I did not vote, but my friends felt so much the protection which Catholics received from the Liberals last year, that they voted for Bright and Co. *I* should, had the issue of the contest been doubtful — but I did not wish to show extra-attention to them, and merely pay them a superfluous homage.

Had I my way I should prefer Disraeli's mode of settling the Irish question to Gladstone's (if Disraeli was in earnest) — and so, I think, would most men, but it seems to be impossible.[2] It is a very clever dodge Disraeli's going out at once — and it is a great question how Gladstone, not a man of special tact, will be able to get on with the Queen and House of Lords against him, and a strong opposition in the Commons, ably generalled and united. But I am a Gladstonite.

I wish John had a better season for his marriage.[3]

Ever Yrs affly John H Newman

The first sermon Newman ever wrote was preached at St Clement's on Sunday Morning 27 June 1824. The first sermon he ever preached was that at Over Worton, the previous Wednesday evening. Its text was 'Wait on the Lord: be of good courage, and He shall strengthen thine heart: wait, I say, on the Lord.' *Ps.* 27:14.

[1] Lancashire was the only part of England where trouble was caused during the general election by Protestant No-Popery candidates. In the Black Country, in new seats, where the Liberals were victorious, there were fierce fights between 'roughs.' A band, sent by the Conservatives, of Dudley 'lambs,' were defeated by the people of Cradley Heath, whom they attacked. For Murphy see note to letter of 23 Sept. to Monsell.

[2] Disraeli's policy was that of concurrent endowment for the Church of Ireland and the Catholic Church in Ireland.

[3] Jemima's second son, John Rickards Mozley, was about to be married to Edith Merivale, daughter of Bonamy Price.

TO CHARLOTTE WOOD

The Oratory Bm Decr 5. 1868

My dear Miss Wood

In answer to your question I have to say that the report is *not* true that 'I have received an invitation to be present at the approaching General Council;' and therefore I have not *declined* it.

I *have* been asked to go *at once* to Rome to take work in one of the commissions sitting there to prepare matter for it. This I have begged off.[1]

Jack Simeon is a very good fellow. He is honest, open, and straightforward — and such a boy, one believes, cannot go wrong. He is religious and affectionate. I am much gratified and pleased by your account of Eddie.[2]

But it is sad news about yourself — I am glad the worst is over and that you are getting well. People say it is a very unhealthy season. What we fear here is the scarletina for our boys. We had a fright three months ago — but it went off. Now they have it at Oscott, and I fear extensively. We have only a fortnight now to the Vacation — and it will be a relief when the boys are safe at home. But this anxiety about epidemics is the greatest of a schoolmaster's crosses. It is the only one over which he has no power; and, since the scarlet fever has re-appeared, it is perpetual.

I was so much annoyed that Sir John Simeon had a contest, that I am not properly joyful that he has succeeded[3]

Ever Yrs affectly in Xt   John H Newman of the Oratory

TO JAMES HOPE-SCOTT

The Oratory Bm ⌜Decr 7. 1868⌝

My dear Hope Scott

⌜Thank you for my letters [[⟨?⟩]]⌝. I am glad to hear about Lady Victoria — for whom I said Mass.

⌜There is nothing so sad, so piercing as to look over old letters. I have hosts — and am always hoping to begin the work of reading and destroying. I used to say, I will do it before I am sixty, and then I shall be ready for whatever God wills — now I say, I will do it before I am seventy.

There is one work of a literary kind I want to do, and then I shall cease

[1] See letter of 15 Oct. to Ullathorne.
[2] i.e. Edmund, younger brother of Jack, Sir John Simeon's eldest son. Miss Wood lived in the Isle of Wight, as did the Simeons.
[3] See letter of 15 Nov. to Lady Simeon.

writing. Extremum hunc Arethusa mihi concede laborem.[1] It is like tunnelling through a mountain — I have begun it, and it is almost too much for my strength — it is half theological, half philosophical — something to do with faith and certitude. Perhaps the tunnell will break in, when I get fairly into my work. When I have done it, if I am to do it, and done my letters of past years, then I shall say, Nunc dimittis.

I fear from the tone of your letter that you are not so well as you should be — but perhaps you are tried by the Duke's coming of age.[2]

Ever Yours affectly John H Newman of the Oratory

TO E. B. PUSEY

The Oratory Bm Decr 7/68

My dear Pusey

I send three numbers of the *Études* which were sent to me by some one unknown, at the time of publication. I know nothing about their being sent to you, or at least do not recollect

You are quite welcome to my numbers — as I have not any others but those three Thank you for your book and Keble's.[3]

Ever Yrs affly John H Newman

TUESDAY 8 DECEMBER 1868   I sang High Mass   a very warm December   a great deal of profuse rain — mostly at night

TO FREDERIC MILLS RAYMOND-BARKER

The Oratory Bm Decr 9. 1868

My dear Barker

I am very glad to hear from you, and, without wishing to controvert, will answer your question. I have at various times got up the evidence on the question of Anglican Orders — and always with the same result. I thought a good deal might be said for them, but in so extremely important a case I should have liked more — and in the case of the Sacraments we must go by what is *safe*. I had nothing to do with the article in the Month, and my letter was quite independent of it.[4] Probable evidence sometimes amounts to moral certainty — but sometimes it does not.

---

[1] Virgil, *Eclogue* X, 1.

[2] The Duke of Norfolk was born on 27 Dec. 1847 and succeeded his father in 1860. Hope-Scott, his brother-in-law, had had the chief responsibility for his estates during the minority.

[3] Keble's book was *Village Sermons on the Baptismal Service*, Oxford 1868, which Pusey published. It remains uncut except for the Table of Contents.

[4] See letters of 5 and 20 Aug. 1868 to H. J. Coleridge.

As to Hussey's Book, I have got it, but I cannot say I know it. It is very long since it came out.[1] The principles of argument on which such works are written are so different from those which I should follow myself, that it seems waste of time to get them up. I have set down my own principles in my Essay on Development of Doctrine.

As to the poor my own experience is that they could (humanly speaking) be converted in any numbers, if the well-to-do, who give away coals and blankets in winter, and in other ways have influence over them, did not stand in the way.

With every kind remembrance (for I take it for granted you are the Barker I knew and liked so well)[2] I am,

Most truly Yours John H Newman

The Revd F R Barker

THURSDAY 10 DECEMBER 1868   Mr Gainsford junior made a call on me [3]

TO RICHARD WARD

The Oratory Decr 14. 1868

My dear Richard,

Thank you for your letter — Gaisford told us of your success. It pleased us all very much, and I am sure your Father and Mother are pleased.

There is always, and must be, extreme uncertainty at Examinations — and the fact of getting a class, whatever that class is, is a proof of careful reading — and this is the great point.[4]

Ever Yours affecly John H Newman of the Oratory

R. Ward Esqr

TUESDAY 15 DECEMBER 1868   Katie Bowden clothed.[5]   Exposition — called on Mrs Robins — Mr Clarke made a call on me[6]

---

[1] Robert Hussey, *The Rise of the Papal Power traced in Three Lectures,* Oxford 1851.
[2] Raymond-Baker was Pusey's nephew, and went up to Oriel College in 1834. His wife, Elizabeth, daughter of William Hacket of Aylestone Hall, Leicestershire, whom he married in 1853, became a Catholic in 1867.
[3] In 1865 R. J. Gainsford asked Newman whether he would receive a visit from his eldest son, aged 23, William Dunn Gainsford, who had lost belief in the authority of the Church. This visit was not, it seems, effected until now. Newman's letter to him of 10 Nov. 1870 shows that he was doubting the fundamentals of religious faith. He eventually returned to the Church. See Index to this volume.
[4] This refers to R. Ward's success in Honour Moderations at Oxford.
[5] At the Dominican Convent, Stone. She now became 'Sister Mary Alban.'
[6] This was Richard Frederick Clarke. See letter of 21 April 1868. On 12 Dec. he wrote, 'During the last nine months God has been leading me on, in spite of my own unworthiness, towards the Catholic Church.' His way was not yet clear, and he wished to discuss his difficulties. See letter of 20 Dec. to him.

The Oratory Decr 15. 1868

My dear Copeland

I have a copy of 2nd Edition which I will send you; I send it you and not Rivington because it is an un-used copy, and you make like it for Mr Churton, supposing his copy is not so good.[1]

How is it that Rivington cannot find copies? When the Apologia came out, he remonstrated with me for putting against 'Sermons on the Day' 'out of print,' for he said he had still copies.

As to the copy right, *it is William Froude's* since 1853, and you must write to him, please, in my name and send him the necessary paper — i.e., Rivington must.

I think you should put two lines of Advertisement to the volume, saying that you are Editor.

And I think that, from the notice of the volume, contrariwise to what you have done in the case of the other volumes, you must keep my advertisement, and the Notes, e.g. at p 348. 378. 384.[2]

I hope you take care of yourself this damp weather

Ever Yrs affectly John H Newman

TO EDWARD HENEAGE DERING

The Oratory Bm Decr 15. 1868

My dear Mr Dering

Thank you for your little Tract, the translation of Mgr de Segur, which came to me just now.[3]

Of course it is a simple duty to abjure and denouce Freemasonry, because it is a Secret Society reprobated by the Holy See — but I doubt whether Secret Societies are dangerous in any country which is well and prudently governed. They say that Russia is a 'despotism tempered with regicide' and the Duke of Wellington in his correspondence says that even the conspiracy on Nicholas's accession was the work of secret societies. And so in like manner governments, which are not despotic, if they are bad, unjust, or slovenly and do-nothing, naturally give scope and vigour to secret societies. Hence the

[1] Copeland wrote on 12 Dec. that Rivington was prepared to republish *S.D.*, and thought it should be reprinted entire.

Copeland added, 'W R Churton tells me there is certainly a demand for the Volume which is constantly taken out of the University Library [Churton was curate at Great St Mary's, Cambridge], and snapped off as soon as it is returned. I gave him a copy which I picked up at Rivington's some time ago, which as it is the second edition I have begged again to reprint from, as the book is not to be had.'

[2] This was done. See Copeland's Preface to *S.D.* and pp. 308, 335, 340.

[3] This was a translation of Louis Gaston de Ségur's *Les Franc-maçons*, 1867.

Ribbon men, Whiteboys, Fenians etc etc of Ireland — but, however worthy of reprobation Freemasonry is, still, when we come to the matter of fact, what harm can it do in England, I don't expect its poison will be active or will spread, while we have a Free government, as we have.

As it is so near Christmas, I take the opportunity of offering you, Lady Chatterton, and her niece my best Christmas congratulations and good wishes.

Most sincerely Yours in Xt   John H Newman of the Oratory

E H Dering Esqr

TO SIR FREDERIC ROGERS

The Oratory, Birmingham, Dec. 15th 68.

My dear Rogers,

I hope I shall not bore you by writing by return of post, but it is my habit to do so of necessity, else letters so accumulate.

Not that I have anything to say. You have understood my suspicion. I thought you must be alluding to some definite transaction in which Gladstone took a part — and so you are. But I utterly forget altogether about his having anything to do with Isaac Williams' Candidateship. Indeed, those years are almost a blank in my memory, as regards any details of what happened.[1]

A popular assembly involves the necessity of a great deal of not-above-boardness. How can a public man get on, if he is to be the mark of any number of questions, and may not fence and parry? Hence a *habit* is created, and really the line separating allowable and blameable reticence is at times so faint, and so zig-zag, and the time it takes, the number of words, the length of correspondence, to give an exact and a full exposition of one's own meaning, and the work that has to be got through is so great, and the certainty of one's apprehension and malevolent interpretation of one's meaning after all is so clear, that I do not know how to wonder that the conduct of public men, and their treatment of others, should be rough and ready, or rather that among Parliamentary men, there should be even what some M.P. 30 years ago called (severely but plausibly) 'enormous lying'

Is not Lord Granville your Principal, and Monsell his sub?[2] I suppose you will like the former, and I trust you will like the latter who is a great ally of mine.

Ever yours affectionately John H. Newman.

[1] Rogers was corresponding with Gladstone in Dec. 1841 about the contest for the Professorship of Poetry at Oxford. He wanted a compromise that would prevent a defeat of the Tractarians and of the principles they represented. See *Letters of Frederic, Lord Blachford,* edited by G. E. Marindin, London 1896, p. 108; John Morley, *The Life of William Ewart Gladstone,* popular edition London 1912, I, p. 227; *Correspondence on Church and Religion of William Ewart Gladstone,* edited by D. G. Lathbury, London 1910, II, p. 266.

[2] Lord Granville was Colonial Secretary and William Monsell Under-Secretary for the Colonies in the ministry Gladstone had just formed. Rogers was Permanent Under-Secretary for the Colonies.

TO J. WALKER OF SCARBOROUGH

The Oratory Bm Decr 15. 1868

My dear Canon Walker

I am glad to hear from you, though I don't deserve your letter — for you are alluding to something I do not twig. I do not commonly see the Tablet now — and I don't know what is in it — but certainly I have written nothing there, nor have I heard of any thing in it which makes me understand your allusions.[1]

Did not I see Mr Trappes in your company some twenty years ago? I saw him about that time — and there were two — which confuses my memory for I have seen both. It seems very hard that such as he may not have their say, but are shut up. I have myself ever professed to hold the Pope's Infallibility as a theological opinion — but, as so holding it, of course I imply there are other opinions on the subject, and, though it would be no hard matter to me to accept it as a dogma, yet it isn't a dogma — and Dr A or B or Fr C. or D. cannot proprio motu make it so. For this reason I was glad of Renouf's pamphlet, tho' I suppose there were sentences in it which neither you nor I nor any one else would have been sorry to miss.

I had hoped that by Dr Errington's appointment to Glasgow there would have been the end of a great scandal — but I can quite understand his asking for tongs, shovel, and other implements, if he was expected to take the chesnuts out of the fire.[2]

Ever Yours very sincerely John H Newman

WEDNESDAY 16 DECEMBER 1868   Exposition.   Examination of boys

THURSDAY 17 DECEMBER   Examination of boys

[1] There were two brothers priests, Francis and Michael Trappes. One of them was evidently the author of a letter signed 'Investigator' in the *Tablet* of 5 Dec. Paul Bottalla's reply to Renouf's pamphlet, dedicated to Newman, *The Condemnation of Pope Honorius* (see letter of 21 June 1868), had been favourably reviewed the previous week. 'Investigator,' while asserting that he thought Bottalla's refutation was complete, ventured to defend Renouf on one small point. In the *Tablet* of 12 Dec. he was taken to task in letters both from the Reviewer and from Paul Bottalla. The *Tablet* had just passed under the ownership and editorship of Herbert Vaughan.

[2] The Holy See, through Manning, asked Archbishop Errington, Wiseman's deposed Coadjutor, to accept the office of Apostolic Administrator in Scotland, for the purpose of restoring the Scottish Hierarchy, in which he would become Archbishop of Edinburgh. Walker wrote to Errington on 20 Oct. 1868, in a letter preserved at the Oratory: 'I have never got rid of the suspicion and cannot that it was hardly a bona fide offer *on all sides*. If it were why should the correspondence be finally closed? Because you complained or stated that the pre-liminaries you required had not been executed or even set about? But that was reasonable if the preliminaries were not unreasonable. Was it because you suggested inaction till after the Elections? But that was indisputably prudent. Or was it, I wonder, that you took unnecessary alarm at the non-mention of your promotion in the last letter from Rome? . . .'

TO PETER LE PAGE RENOUF

The Oratory Dec 17. 1868

My dear Renouf

I am sorry you do not approve of my letter.[1]

I will say nothing at the moment, but shall ask you to be so kind *as to send my letter back to me*

Yours affectly John H Newman of the Oratory[2]

TO THE HON. COLIN LINDSAY

The Oratory Bm Decr 18. 1868

My dear Mr Lindsay

I have been very glad to hear from you that you are going on so well. Something, I see, was said about you at the meeting of the Church Union — but I take it for granted, nothing to pain you. Surely you gave Dr Pusey quite notice enough —[3] and for myself, had you waited ever so much, I cannot understand how a long argument on paper can meet and alter the growth and consummation of an inward change, the fruit of time. It seems to be all the difference which exists between the written tables of stone and the law written on the heart.

When fresh converts are in great anxiety, pain or other trouble, it is common to allow them to go to communion often; and therefore I do not doubt you are right in going twice a week. Some of them have said that they should not have known how to sustain the burden of the trial without such supernatural support. At the same time I think you should watch yourself lest the great gift should become common to you. There is not indeed such danger in persons of reflection and education like yourself, but I think it is the experience of several of our priests here, that it would have been better, if they had been less indulgent with their penitents in this respect. Our Father, St Philip, who was a great encourager of frequent communion, nevertheless kept a tight hand over his young penitents in this respect — and I cannot but see there are signs of re-action among English Priests, in the direction of reverting to the practice of rarer communions as was the custom forty years ago. In this matter you must be a rule to yourself.

---

[1] i.e. letter of 30 Nov. 1868 to Renouf, who replied on 19 Dec. 'Dearest Father, I return the draft of your letter. . . . Ever affectionately yours P le P. Renouf.'

[2] Newman made a note on his letter of 30 Nov. to Renouf: 'N B. January 2. 1869. Today's Catholic Papers report that Renouf's Pamphlet is upon the Index. This is the *first* notice of the fact, if it is a fact. He was not suspected till now — and therefore not at the date of the foregoing correspondence, J H N.'

[3] Lindsay had resigned in March 1868 both as President and as a member of the English Church Union. At a meeting on 15 Dec. a motion acknowledging his services but regretting his secession was passed. One speaker pointed out that he had resigned months previously. Pusey became a member of the Union in 1866, seven years after its foundation by Lindsay.

You have *no need* to make a general confession on your Confirmation — certainly not — and it is not usual — I never heard of a case — and I advise you *not* to do so, unless you *yourself* feel urged to do so.

As you mention Schools, I am led to send you our own Prospectus. St Philip has wonderfully warded off the Scarlet Fever from us again and again — and we ourselves take pains to keep it away, which they cannot take in a large school. We have between 50 and 60 boys — and have or have had among them the Duke of Norfolk, Lord E. Howard, Sir John Simeon's Sons, Mr Scott Murray's, Sir John Gerard's, Mr Hornyold's, Sir C. Wolseley, Sir Justin Shiel's, Serjeant Bellasis's, Mr Gaisford's etc etc Mr Towneley's, Lord Charles Thynne's, Sir Edward Blount's etc.

Most sincerely Yours in Xt   John H Newman of the Oratory

The Honble Colin Lindsay

P.S. Fr St John, our Schoolmaster, will be at Brighton in the Christmas Holydays, and will give you any information you want about the School. Should you send your boy to Oscott, I know it will be for some very good reason.[1]

SATURDAY 19 DECEMBER 1868 Bishop ordained in our Church John and Thomas Deacons

TO B. M. PICKERING

The Oratory Bm Decr 19. 1868

Sir

I thank you for the courtesy and considerateness shown in your letter, which I have this day received'[2]

I have a difficulty in answering your question. I have never, I think, (rather, I am sure,) done any thing to commit myself to the allowance that the copyright of the Essay you mention is *not* mine; but, whether it is or no a lawyer only can decide. This only I can say, that I was much surprised and displeased, when I found Mr Mawman (I think) in 1828 claiming it.

Dr Whately, who got me to write the Essay (and that on Cicero), told me before I wrote that he had made a bargain with Mr Mawman that his and Dr Arnold's publications in the Encycl. Metropol. should be their own property respectively, and gave me to understand that the case would be the same with

---

[1] Lindsay sent his son Leonard, born in 1857, to Oscott, and his youngest son, Claud, born in 1861 to Beaumont and Stonyhurst. See letter of 1 Jan. to him.

[2] Pickering wrote on 18 Dec., 'I have just purchased from the proprietors of the Encyclopaedia Metropolitana the copyright of your Life of Apollonius Tyanaeus and Comparison between Scripture and other Miracles,' and copies of them. He went on to ask whether he had a right to sell them, since Newman usually kept the copyright in his own hands. 'I would ask if I have a good and just title to it as (excepting only a few personal friends) there is no one to whom I should be more sorry to give just cause of offence.'

mine. I was paid a small sum for both. When it was published, and I found I should not be allowed to use it as my own, I wrote to Mr Smedley, the Editor, claiming it, and saying that there had been an understanding to that effect. He answered that 'understandings' did not go for much.[1] In consequence, when I was asked to write other articles, I refused to do so. I never thought it worth while to inquire how the law lay; and so the matter has rested from that time to this. Perhaps, for what I know, my having neglected to claim my right for so long a time has forfeited it. Also, when there was a reprint some 15 or 20 years ago, and I was asked whether I would make alterations in my article on *Cicero*, I did make them without any protest about the copyright. I was *not* asked to correct the Essay you write about.

This is all I have to say on the subject.

I am, Sir, Yours faithfully John H Newman

Mr B. M. Pickering.

P.S. I have found my letter to Mr Smedley of May 29, 1828. After saying 'My College engagements do not allow me to keep pace with the Encyclopædia' in answer to Mr Smedley's wish for Articles from me on the early Church, I proceed to express my feeling 'at hearing there was some hesitation in the minds of the Proprietors of the Encyclopædia concerning the right of the contributors to publish their papers in a separate shape. For myself' I say 'I have no present intention of exerting the right, supposing it to be one, as I certainly understood it was, when I sent Mr Mawman the Articles on Cicero and Apollonius. . . . This feeling is entertained by every Oxford contributor whom I have heard mention the subject.'[2]

TO RICHARD FREDERICK CLARKE

The Oratory Bm Dec 20. 1868

My dear Mr Clarke

Your letter of this morning gives me the opportunity of asking you for the name of that German (it begins with Sch) whose history (I think) of Philosophy, you said, was translated and used by Oxford men.[3]

I am struck from your letter with the difference of senses in which the word 'Liberalism' is used. You consider it designates a course of action, I a set of principles. You would call Gladstone a liberal, I an Anti-Liberal. You might call me a liberal, because I do not deny that under existing circumstance the abolition of tests is the advisable course; I should call myself an Anti-Liberal, because, in harmony with the Pope's syllabus, I should say that the best thing

[1] See *Apo.*, p. 388, 'Note on page 90.'
[2] See *Moz.* I, pp. 185–6.
[3] *Handbook of the History of Philosophy* by Dr. Albert Schwegler, translated and annotated by James Hutchison Stirling, Edinburgh 1867. Newman had a copy of the second edition, 1868.

of all is to have a Unity of religion in a country and that so *real* that its Ascendancy is but the expression of the universal mind.

Again, I think I observed another thing in your conversation, which startled me, tho' perhaps I mistook you. You seemed to think that the Rector of Lincoln[1] was true in saying that Catholics do not allow the philosophical mind to have free play to the same sense in which those who are not Catholics have free play — and you spoke as if in Catholics there must be a reserve, and that they began by belief: — so they may do in ordine historico or personali, (i.e. in the sense in which Anti-Lls [liberals] do so) but not in ordine philosophico, for reason, as St Augustine says, comes before faith — . Now I never could allow what you represented the Rector as saying

Most truly Yours John H Newman

MONDAY 21 DECEMBER 1868   H B[Bittleston] and Miss Farrant went to London.   I went to London to the Langham, going to Rahn the Dentist.

TUESDAY 22 DECEMBER   returned early to Bm [Birmingham] Ambrose went to Rednall

WEDNESDAY 23 DECEMBER   Eleanor Watt in Birmingham this week and two following

TO W. J. COPELAND

The Oratory Decr 24. 1868

My dear Copeland

Your splendid and welcome present has come safely. I was in London at the beginning of the week or I should have thanked you sooner.

I hope you are well. We send you all kind Christmas greetings. I send you a letter which ought to have gone to you long ago.[2]

Ever Yrs affly J H N

FRIDAY 25 DECEMBER 1868   I sang 5 o'clock Mass and preached

WEDNESDAY 30 DECEMBER   Ambrose went to Brighton   I in retreat

TO HENRY BEDFORD

The Oratory Decr 30th. 1868.

My dear Mr Bedford,

I feel very grateful to you for your letter. It is a great happiness to be remembered, as you remember me, so kindly and so long. It is one of the rewards I have received from going to Ireland, to have gained friends, who, in spite of absence, do not cease to think of me.

[1] Mark Pattison.
[2] This was a letter of 30 Sept. from Miss Mary Drury, asking to be allowed 'to make a few selections from passages in your "Parochial Sermons;" I am preparing a collection of Extracts from favourite authors . . .'

And now you have got a still kinder thought in your mind — and that is, that you will no longer have the merit of remembering me in spite of absence, but that you will come and see me. I hope you will fulfil this very good intention the next time you come to England. But give me the notice beforehand, for, though I am seldom away, yet it would be very annoying if for some reason or other there was a balk in our meeting from cross purposes.

It was a great pleasure to me to see Stewart — and he did us a great service while he was here.[1] Will you tell him, when you see him, if he has not heard of it, that his two youths have passed their Little go as well as their entrance examination?

I shall not forget what you say with so much warmth about my writings — I shall not, because I consider it a pledge that you do not forget in your prayers one who is now so old as to have especial need of them.[2]

> Yours, My dear Mr. Bedford, With great sincerity & affection
> John H. Newman of the Oratory.

H. Bedford Esq.

P.S.   Pray remember me most kindly to any of your good Priests whom I used to know.[3]

A happy new year to you.

TO B. M. PICKERING

The Oratory Bm Decr 30. 1868

Dear Sir,

I am puzzled equally with you —[4] Of course I do not like to give up a right, if I have one. I am quite ready to do this, if you will do so too: — to refer the question to the decision of any lawyer versed in the law of copyrights. I do not know what else I can propose to do. I cannot simply say to you that the copyright is *not* mine, for I don't know how the law stands — but I think it far

---

[1] See diary for 21 Sept. Bedford wrote that Stewart had given him 'such an interesting account of his visit to the Oratory, that I have serious thoughts of calling on you next Summer on my way to London.' Stewart himself wrote to Newman on 3 Jan., 'There is nobody here who does not remember you as well as if you had only left us yesterday. Indeed I was quite an object of interest when I came back from Birmingham for having had the happiness of spending a fortnight with you.

There is one person especially whom I have often heard speak of you with the greatest regard and that is Thomas O'Hagan the new Chancellor.' Gladstone had just appointed him Lord Chancellor of Ireland.

[2] Writing on 24 Dec. Bedford spoke of what Newman's writings had done 'to bring me into the Catholic Church, and to instruct and confirm me therein — to them, under God, I owe all that is really valuable, and so I venture to regard you as a spiritual Father and therein as my best friend.'

[3] Bedford was on the staff of All Hallows College, Dublin.

[4] On 28 Dec. Pickering replied to Newman's letter of 19 Dec. that he did not understand it. He wished to know whether he had a right to publish Newman's essays. Pickering now began to republish Newman's works, see letter of 17 April 1869 to him.

from improbable that the question would be given against me. Any how it ought to be settled

Yours faithfully John H Newman

B M Pickering Esqr

TO H. A. WOODGATE

The Oratory, Decr 30. 1868

My dear Woodgate

I have not seen Mr Meers, and I have no reason to suppose that he has been received into the Catholic Church. Hs is known to one of my friends here, Mr Bittleston — how I don't know, and at the moment I have not the means of asking him. I suspect Mr Meers must have written to Mr B. to tell him his mind was made up to become a Catholic. I don't think any of us knew him till now. I never heard his name mentioned.[1]

He was to have called on me last Thursday — he never came — that made us think his mind was not made up — and we have done nothing.

I can quite understand a man being in good faith a member of the Anglican Church — and I feel the greatest difficulty of attempting in that case to stir him from his position — for I might merely unsettle him, and lead him to give up the truth which he already has instead of embracing what is fuller truth. But, if Mr Meeres comes to me and I think his reasons and his dispositions such as they should be for conversion, I should certainly receive him into Catholic communion, because it is written — 'Freely ye have received, freely give — ' and, as I myself changed my place in order to save my soul, so I think another would run a grave risk of losing his, who, when he felt that our Church was the one Church of Christ, did not submit himself to it.

This principle applies to any thing which Mr Meeres may do, when a Catholic, in his late Parish. If, being an Anglican clergyman, he has used his influence, while he held a cure, to unsettle the minds of his people (I have not heard a word on this subject, except from you) he has committed a breach of

---

[1] Woodgate wrote on 29 Dec. about a complaint he had received from Robert Wylde, a curate of Henry Clarke, Rector of Northfield, with Bartley Green, near Birmingham. Woodgate stated that Wylde 'has had, as his fellow worker in the Curacy, Mr Meeres who has recently joined your communion, and was received by yourself, I believe, at the Oratory, of which he is at present a member or in some relation which recognises subordination to yourself as Head of the College.

Wylde's complaint is that Mr Meeres, since his departure continues to come into the Parish, especially his own District, Bartley Green, to take advantage of the acquaintance with the people which he had as their late Pastor to persuade them to leave their present communion for his.

Our loose abnormal system, or rather want of system, which has long prevailed in England has recognised attempts of this kind as not being beyond the limits of the rule to be observed in regard to proselytizing — that is if done by strangers who have no connexion with the place. But surely there is a wide distinction, to take no higher ground than those of delicacy or honour, in a former Pastor tampering with those whose former spiritual relation to him he has renounced.'

See letters of 5 and 12 Jan. 1869 to Woodgate.

trust — but it may be, that without any fault of his he knows those among his late flock, who ought to be Catholics for the same reason that he himself ought to be a Catholic — and surely he ought to value their souls as he does his own.

I am saying nothing that I would not reciprocate. If a Catholic Priest deliberately disbelieved in Catholicism, I could not desire him to remain in his pastoral office — if he declared he must become a Portestant to save his soul, I should think him wrong, but I could not resist him; if after leaving he tried to make others, whom he knew to be already in his own case and to fear for their souls as being Catholics, to become Protestants, I should think he had a deplorably misinformed conscience, but I could not complain of it.

From this, you will understand how I shall act with Mr Meers, if he comes to me. Should, however, I find that he is wishing to use his simple *influence* with his late people, their love for him, their respect for him, as the *instrument* of unsettling those who at present are good Anglicans, and are *not* in the state I have supposed, that is, not in his present state of mind, I shall certainly tell him he has no right to do so. If the *fact* of their knowledge of him, and affection for him, unsettles them and leads them to look towards his new communion, and at length fixes them in a firm faith that it is the house and only house of God, *that* will *not* be his fault — but will be a legitimate cause of rejoicing to him.

I am sanguine you will see the fairness of what I say. It is surely the way in which you would behave to the Wesleyans. Your friends have lately said with exultation that the greater part (I think) of the United States Anglican Bishops were originally dissenters, as showing the power and the prospects of Anglicanism.[1] You have no scruple, the rules of fair dealing being observed, in converting Wesleyans — I am sure you will not complain, though you may be pained, that we should convert Anglicans, salvâ regulâ simplicitatis et aequitatis.

As to Mr Clarke, I know how excellent a man he is, and I am sorry I cannot help giving him pain

Ever Yrs affectly John H Newman

P.S.   On reading over your letter again, I am glad to believe that I have said nothing you will not agree to. A happy New Year to you.

THURSDAY 31 DECEMBER 1868   Outhwaite came

TO MOTHER MARY IMELDA POOLE

The Oratory Decr 31. 1868

My dear Sister Imilda

I was very much touched by the point you and yours have made to remember my Day, and thank you and Sister M. Raphael [Drane] most sincerely for your letters. And now I have delayed writing to you, till I can wish

[1] See note to letter of 16 Aug. 1868 to Pusey.

you all in the highest and best sense of the words, a happy new Year. We are ever beginning the new Year every morning — but there is always something that goes to the heart when the first of January comes round, and the unknown future is specially brought before us. I did not need your notice to remind me of the contrast between your last year's Christmas and this — yet though it is all the difference between deep trial and triumphant joy, I will never believe that as time goes on, you will not feel a special consolation and gladness in the remembrance of those sacred months.[1]

It is as great, as it is an unmerited and unexpected mercy to me, that your dear Mother should have thought of me with such affection.[2] I am sure I need her prayers, and the prayers of all of you especially, now that each year, as it comes, is bringing me so very near, nearer perhaps than I think, to that solemn trial, which she has so triumphantly passed through, and which we must each of us in our turn undergo. May we have some measure of that preparation for it, which she had made for hers!

Will Sister F. Raphael kindly allow this to be an answer to her letter, as well as to yours?

Ever Yrs most sincerely in Xt   John H. Newman

TO THE HON. COLIN LINDSAY

The Oratory Jany 1. 1868[3]

My dear Mr Lindsay

A happy new year, in the best sense of the word, to you and all yours.

I think you have quite understood what I said about communion. I did not at all mean to discourage your communicating twice a week, as long as you yourself felt it to be right.

We will gladly receive your boy now — and shall quite understand the reason, should you and Lady Frances remove him at Midsummer.

The School meets punctually on Tuesday January 26. No particular clothes are necessary — but if you want information as to linen, our Matron, Mrs Wootten, will be happy to give it. Fr St John will call on you[4]

Most sincerely Yours in Xt   John H Newman of the Oratory

The Honble Colin Lindsay

[1] Mother Imelda Poole wrote on 27 Dec., that the previous Christmas, when Mother Margaret Hallahan was already suffering in her last illness, was 'most sorrowful,' whereas 'this year we feel it a consolation to think of the happiness which we cannot doubt she is enjoying.'

[2] Mother Imelda Poole wrote that Mother Margaret Hallahan's regard for Newman was 'something special. She instinctively felt that you understood her, and as many did not understand her — she felt a freedom of soul with those who did — and could shew her genuine self to them. You were one of those for whom she most constantly prayed and she took the most lively interest as you know in all that concerned you.'

[3] A slip for 1869.

[4] Cf. letter of 18 Dec. to Lindsay. He replied to this present letter next day that his wife wished to keep her boy at home, since he was unwell. Lindsay added, 'Besides we wish him to be a priest, and as he has shown an inclination to serve in the Sanctuary, we hope these

SUNDAY 3 JANUARY 1869   Mr Stokes called

TO CATHERINE ANNE BATHURST

The Oratory Jany 3/69

My dear Child

I had half hoped you would write to me — I had been saying Mass for you a day or two before your letter came — and not to speak of others, have given you a share in each of 23 Masses in the course of the year.

I am sorry indeed you are not to be in England — for England is your place — and you are never so useful as when you have a number of young women, girls and boys attached to you, not by vows, but by love.

My best Christmas greetings, and good wishes for the new year to you and yours — and especially to any of your party whom I know.

I will not forget your notice of having a shelter for a convert.

I have nothing to tell you here — we have two new Deacons, who soon will be Priests — and who are two new Preachers already — which is a great relief to us. You know several of us are getting old now.

The Duke of Norfolk has just come of age — on St John's day. It seems but yesterday he was a little child crawling on the floor at Abbotsford.

The Marquis of Bute is just received at Nice.[1] He is portentously rich, some say to the extent of £300.000 per annum

Ever Yrs affly John H Newman

TO MRS JOHN MOZLEY

The Oratory Jany 3. 1869

My dear Jemima

I congratulate you and John on J R's marriage —[2] and send you and him and all friends at Derby my best wishes for the new year. The weather is somewhat better now; else, it has been too wet for pleasant touring, and strange for Christmas.

feelings will develop in him. — I believe the School at Edgbaston is a *general* one for all classes and vocations.' See letter of 5 Jan. to St John. The boy, presumably Leonard, born in 1857, did not become a priest, but his younger brother, Claud, born in 1861, was ordained in 1895.

[1] The Marquis of Bute was received into the Catholic Church on 8 Dec. in London, at the chapel of the Sisters of Notre Dame, Southwark, by Mgr. Capel. Brought up a Presbyterian, he had been increasingly drawn towards the Church while at Oxford, and became a Catholic a few months after attaining his majority.

[2] John Rickards Mozley. See letter of 3 Dec. 1868 to Jemima.

There is always a question whether people should be prudent and wait — or marry at once. I have always been against long engagements; indeed they seem to me hardly religious, for they give opportunity for all the chances of the World, trouble and change, to intervene, and affections which from being mutual should grow, as it were, into oneness, to be balked and beaten back. But there is only a choice of difficulties and of blessings in the present state, and I suppose those who marry young must have to rough it.

I heard from Maria Giberne some little time since — and she told me, what I had not understood at the time, that about a year ago a window fell on her head and knocked her down — or something of the kind — she was opening or shutting it. You know, the common continental windows are very cumbrous. She had not got over the effects of it when she wrote

Ever Yours affectly John H Newman

Mrs Mozley

TO FRANCIS WILLIAM NEWMAN

The Oratory Jany 3/69

My dear Frank

A happy new year to you and Maria — thank her for her kind message and tell her how glad I am you can give so good an account of her.

If the proof of health lies in firmness of handwriting, *you* have nothing the matter with you. I thought the same of Hawkins, the Provost, when he wrote to me some time back. He used to say he should not live till 40 — now he is in his 80th or 81st year, and his handwriting is as perfect, as I am told his mind is active.

It seems to me wonderful that no society exists which can take upon itself the expenses of printing so important a work as an Arabic dictionary. The East comes into the scope of European interests more and more every year, and considering that Arabic is the classical language of Mahometanism, and is the normal form of the Semitic varieties, I cannot account for it.[1]

I have nothing at present the matter with me, and have only to be careful and to watch myself

Ever Yours affectionately John H Newman

F W Newman Esqr

[1] F. W. Newman's *Dictionary of Modern Arabic,* two volumes, was published in 1871.

TO FRANCIS WILLIAM NEWMAN

[1869?][1]

acquiesce thankfully in your way, if you prefer it.

I am amused at what you say about eyes being upon me — and can hardly understand you. If you mean that there are a number of curious eyes, Protestants especially, looking at me, I can believe it, though I don't know it. But if you fancy I am not free to take my carpet bag and go any where tomorrow, as far as subjection to any man or word of man goes, it is not so. No one on earth, from the Pope downwards, would have any ecclesiastical power whatever to hinder me from receiving £10.000 a year, if it were given me, and spending it entirely on myself. All I could *not* do, ecclesiastically, would be 1. to marry — 2. to give up saying daily office. But you yourself have lived a hardy life sufficiently to be able to understand, that I could not with *comfort* to myself indulge in what to *others* would be comforts — and that my chief or sole luxury if I indulged in any, would be that of buying books.

My best love to Maria, and accept the same yourself from

Yours ever most affectionately John H Newman

TO RICHARD SIMPSON

The Oratory Jany 3. 1869

My dear Simpson

I am sorry to say I have not managed to hear your music yet — though I hoped to have done so. Thank you for it, and for the compliment you have paid my Verses. I have tried it on the Violin, which was a poor way of getting hold of it. It promised to be very good — and I like the accompaniment especially and the harmonizing.[2]

You sent it me as a Christmas present, and I return my thanks, inadequate as they are, in company with my best and kindest wishes for the New Year, to yourself and Mrs Simpson.

I have never thanked you for the original Essay you sent me on the Philosophy of Shakespeare's Sonnets.[3] It is a very curious and interesting subject,

---

[1] Only the second sheet of this letter is to be found, and so it is without a date.

[2] Simpson sent Newman on 24 Dec. a copy of the music to which he had set one of the poems in *Vv.*, 'not as if it was worth any thing, but as showing how far I suck my inspiration, such as it is, from you.'

Simpson went on to say that he and Acton and Wetherell were planning to set up a new quarterly review, 'we intend this time to steer quite clear of any religious declarations whatever, and to make it only political and literary.' The *North British Review* was taken over and the number for October 1869 appeared under Wetherell's editorship.

[3] *An Introduction to the Philosophy of Shakespeare's Sonnets*, London 1868.

but it requires more knowledge of them and more of a fixed idea of Shakespeare as a living man and a definite person than I possess, to allow me to have any critical opinion upon it.

It is a happy thing to have a number of resources — When you are not making displays of ecclesiastical fire works, you can, like Cincinnatus or Cato, turn (as I am told) to gardening, to Shakespearian criticism, and to musical creations

Yours affectionately John H Newman of the Oratory

R. Simpson Esqr

TO HENRY WILBERFORCE

The Oratory Jany 3/69

My dear H W

My best and kindest Christmas greetings, and good wishes for the New Year, to you, your wife, and all of you.

I was amused at your saying you had not long letters from me now, considering my last, which you copied, frightened me when it came back to me in your handwriting, to think how many pages it took.[1]

As you have not said any thing about W. F. [Froude] I take it for granted he has not answered you.[2] If so, his silence arises from two causes. First it is so painful to him to write, that even when he has got himself to begin, he stops, puts his letter aside, and never takes it up again. Next, he sees things much more clearly than he can express them. And, when he puts his thoughts on paper, he is at once disgusted at there inadequacy to express his meaning, and so is led to give over. But I wish he would, because it is impossible so clever a mind should not see he could not carry out his views consistently, if he would but patiently attempt it.

As to my own essay, I have neither the patience to read nor the vigour to think; and how can I do any thing without thinking and reading?

I was not invited to the Council — but to be one of a few foreigners who were to be placed amid Cardinalitian Roman commissions or committees, to prepare matter on the subjects to be treated of in the Council. Such a work requires a strong memory for theological passages and a quick eye in turning over pages — and I have neither. Ignatius would be just the man for it.

I am much concerned at what you say of Wilfrid [Wilberforce].

Ever Yrs affectly John H Newman of the Oratory

H W Wilberforce Esqr

[1] Letter of 27 July 1868.
[2] See letter of 8 Aug. 1868 to Wilberforce.

MONDAY 4 JANUARY 1869 Mr Jones went and Outhwaite Challis came H W[Wilberforce] called — called on the Watts and Brethertons
TUESDAY 5 JANUARY Simmons went to his mother's deathbed.

TO AMBROSE ST JOHN

⌐The Oratory Bm Jany 5/69⌐

My dear A

⌐A happy new year to you. Yesterday morning I said Mass for the Future of each of the Fathers — on New Year's Day for the Future of our Oratory.⌐

I send you some letters. I have read Mr Dallas's. You see how parents feel the charge of want of truth.[1]

I have read [F.R.] Ward's letter. You could tell him that Sir John Simeon some time ago was inquiring for some one to go abroad with Jack [Simeon] — but I suppose it was a *Tutor.*

⌐Jones is gone to Morville. Challis is here. Simmons is called away this morning by the serious illness of his mother. Bateman convoyed 5 women to the Pantomime last night — and they had sausages for supper after it.

I suspect some one had been at the Lindsays —⌐ he said in his letter to me something of his son having a vocation, and our place not being adapted for vocations. I could not quite read him. He has lately been confirmed by his Lordship of Southwark.[2]

John comes back from Rednall today. I suppose you have filled up Bacchus's paper.[3]

⌐The Duchess of A. [[Argyll] is a good old soul but neither mincepies nor butter suffice me.

H Wilberforce was here yesterday⌐ in transitu for Rugby, and is to sleep here on his return.

Think of this plan — viz to place our Lady's image where the crib is. It can be seen from most parts of the church — and will be in a far better place there, for *devotion.*

Also I should like you to think of this, viz to put a temporary skreen across the Church starting from between the Sacristy door and St Valentine — to place the benches together a breadth of 24 feet — to place the nobs in *front* of these benches in the space 12 feet wide which intervenes between the highest bench and the rise of two steps — to put at the back of the new skreen a new

---

[1] John Henry Langford Dallas came to the Oratory School in 1865 and left in 1874.
[2] See last note to letter of 1 Jan. 1869 to Lindsay and cf. letter of 23 Nov. 1868 to Bishop Grant of Southwark, who had also written complaints to Rome about the Oratory School, in the spring of 1867.
[3] John Northcote Bacchus came to the Oratory School on 15 Sept. 1868 and his brother, Francis Joseph Bacchus, on 5 April 1869.

altar — I am afraid this would not give you a chapel for the boys; but it would give a chapel for the *poor school*, or for me to lecture in — and would *force* people to come up for the Sermon. This supposes of course the sacred heart chapel thrown open, and it and St Joseph's filled.

Thus: —

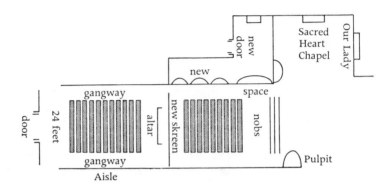

Also, I would, as in the sketch run a half aisle on the playground side, and throw it, by opening the arches, into the Church; this would add to the available space for hearing sermons, besides the Sacred Heart chapel.

William and I would bear the expense — the skreen would be wood and canvass, and moveable — so that, if it were a failure, it could be taken away, and every thing would be as before.

Your letter to Mrs Pope is quite right. I mean to call with it — I could not yesterday for H W came, and I had to go the Brethertons and Watts (N.B. she told me the time by means of the watch I gave her),[1] and today it rains so hard that it is impossible.

Bateman escorted 4 or 5 Ladies to the Pantomime last night.

We have had some beautiful days, at Brighton it must be lovely.

Ever Yrs affly J H N

P.S.   As to the Skreen, it should be canvass, and in portions — so that it could be used in bits for different purposes, if condemned as I intend to use it. If not used for the poor schools services the lower portion of the nave cut off would make a famous place for me to lecture in, especially as there would be a gallery.

[1] See Index to Volume XXI under 'Bretherton, Eleanor.'

TO H. A. WOODGATE

The Oratory Jany 5/69

My dear Woodgate

This is the anniversary of my sister's death in 1828.

I have learned some particulars about Mr Meeres; and will tell them as far as I can recollect a long story.[1]

A servant maid, called Elizabeth Taylor, nearly became a Catholic, when we were in Alcester Street, 20 years ago. She could not bear up against the opposition of her friends, and gave up the idea. Quite lately, she has sent for one of us, saying she was near death. She is at Bartley Green (if I give the name of it rightly) One of us, Mr Bittleston, accordingly went there, and in going fell in with Mr Meers, who joined him and talked with him about his own reception into the Catholic Church. *Afterwards* (if I understand rightly) he called at the Oratory — and saw Mr Mills, another of us, for an hour or two. After this he proposed to come to me for reception on December 24 — and, as I told you, did not come.

I have heard nothing more of any projected converts on his part in his late Parish; and, from the terms of a letter which came from him this morning from London, very much doubt if he is what you would consider 'tampering' with any one. If I understand his letter, addressed to Mr B. he is *not* going to be received immediately.

You may be quite sure that, if he came here, and showed that he was in a state of excitement and without a calm sense of what he was about to do, we should not receive him. At the same time great resolutions, great and cardinal changes, naturally excite a man. Empedocles ardentem *frigidus* Aetnam Insiluit;[2] but rarely can a man without emotion, without distress, without a spasm of heart, give up old friends, old scenes, old habits

Ever Yrs affly John H Newman

WEDNESDAY 6 JANUARY 1869 [and subsequent days]   very wet   damp   muggy

TO EMILY BOWLES

The Oratory The Epiphany 1869.

My dear Child,

Tell me something about yourself, how you are, where, and what you are doing. I have not heard from you for an age. How beautiful is Mrs Craven's

---

[1] See letter of 30 Dec. 1868 to Woodgate.
[2] Horace, *De Arte Poetica*, 465.

story in the Month! it is as beautiful as 'A Stormy Life — ' though so different — and I cannot pay it a greater compliment.[1]

Ever Yrs affly John H Newman

TO ALBERT SMITH

The Oratory, January 6/69

Dear Sir

I am glad you see your way more clearly. You are not bound to become a Catholic till you feel it your duty to be one, and then you are bound. There is no reason why you should not see Mr Mackonockie — it is better to consider all the difficulties in the argument for Catholicism before becoming a Catholic, than to let them come upon you after you are a Catholic.[2]

Yours very faithfully John H. Newman

Albert Smith Esqre

TO J. WALKER OF SCARBOROUGH

The Oratory, The Epiphany 1869

My dear Canon Walker

If I have not yet offered you the best wishes of this Sacred Season, let me do so now.

And I take the opportunity of doing so on my returning to you your letter and thanking you for the information it gave me.

Yours most truly John H Newman

TO GILBERT SIMMONS

The Oratory, Jan 8. 1869

My dear Child,

I am truly grieved at what you tell me. I know well what you must suffer, for I have been in like sorrow. If it is God's will to take your dear Mother, you will be able all your life to thank Him that He has enabled you to behave dutifully and affectionately to her. You have been a comfort to her, when she needed comfort.

---

[1] Chapters XXVII–XXX of *Anne Séverin*, the *Month*, (Jan. 1869), pp. 23–40. '*A Stormy Life*,' London 1867, was a novel by Lady Georgiana Fullerton.
[2] Cf. letter of 8 Jan. 1868 to Smith, who wrote on 4 Jan. 1869, 'I am almost quite convinced that the Catholic Church is the only true Church.' A clergyman friend begged him to see Alexander Mackonochie, the Anglo-Catholic Vicar of St Alban's, Holborn, before becoming a Catholic. Smith said that his sister had been received a year previously. He was to follow her example.

By all means stay, as you propose, till you see how things will be. I do not forget you, and I am sure others don't.

Yours affly in Xt   John H. Newman of the Oratory

MONDAY 11 JANUARY 1869   Challis went   no snow yet this season

TO CATHERINE ANNE BATHURST

The Oratory Jany 11/69

My dear Child

Your letter of the 5th has just come.

If God gives you the vows, I am sure it will be best for you, for you have prayed so earnestly on the subject, and so long.

Meanwhile I rejoice to hear from you that you are so happy in yourselves and in your Father Director[1]

Ever Yrs affectly John H Newman

TO WILLIAM MONSELL

The Oratory Jany 11. 1869

My dear Monsell

Ambrose is away — so I answer your questions for him.

1. We have no fever of any kind. In September, we had scarcely met when the two Bellasises were seized with scarletina — another boy showed symptoms — he was at once sent home with the wish of his parents — and the two B s removed at once from the premises. The illness of all three was very light. We sent round a notice to the parents of all our boys, knowing how anxious some parents are — but recommending them not to remove them. And the term passed, not only without fresh cases, but with unusual absence of illness. As I dare say you know, the fever has been every where. At Roehampton at the Sacre Coeur — Malborough [sic] school had to be dispersed etc We have always observed the simple rule of separating the suspected boy from the School before the complaint showed itself, and insisting on his absence for a considerable time after his recovery, and it has always succeeded.

2 Gaston may come in knickerbokers, if more convenient — and it will make no kind of remark. But trowsers are more usual

3 A room is ready for him under Mrs Wootten's charge.

4 She shall send you the outfit.

5. It being his first time of coming, he may have some licence as to the day. I suppose too it would be more convenient to you not to anticipate the meeting of Parliament.

[1] Catherine Bathurst was at Ghent, gathering Dominican tertiaries round her.

Are you at the Colonial Office or not? The Papers said Yes, and then kept silence.[1]

Though the light of Christmas is waning, it is not quite too late to wish you and Mrs Monsell the best blessings of the Sacred Season

Ever Yrs affly John H Newman

TUESDAY 12 JANUARY 1869   Dr Errington called, and Woodgate

TO MRS JOHN MOZLEY

Jany 12/69

My dear Jemima

Will you direct and send on the inclosed.

If you don't know the direction, you had better burn it.

A happy new year, if I did not wish it to you in my last

Yours affly John H Newman

P.S.   Woodgate was here just now, looking so ill and old as quite to shock me.

TO H. A. WOODGATE

The Oratory Jan 12/69

My dear Woodgate

I inclose a statement of Mr Bittleston, whom I naturally confide in more than in Mr Wilder [Wylde], without any disrespect to the latter, since I have known him, and he has known Elizabeth Taylor, before Mr Wilder perhaps was born, and all along to this day.

I think the said Taylor has prevaricated — She has an uneasy conscience, and one day wishes to see Mr Wilder, and another day Mr Bittleston.

Ever Yrs affly J H N

PS   The *drift* of the inclosed paper is to exculpate Mr Meeres as regards Elizabeth Taylor[2]

WEDNESDAY 13 JANUARY 1869   H Wilberforce came   Ambrose returned
THURSDAY 14 JANUARY   H W went [3]

---

[1] Monsell had been made Under-Secretary for the Colonies and remained so until Jan. 1871, when he became Postmaster-General.

[2] According to Bittleston's statement Elizabeth Taylor had received instruction with a view to becoming a Catholic, when the Oratory was at Alcester Street, i.e. about 1850. Her sister had become a Catholic then. Elizabeth Taylor had lately been ill at Bartley Green, and had asked to see Bittleston. Meeres had not had any special concern with her.

[3] See final note to letter of 25 Jan. 1856 to Caswall.

TO MISS HOLMES

The Oratory Jany 18. 1869

My dear Miss Holmes

So now at last I know your address.[1] You have not given me the opportunity of answering you for months. First you sent me a number of flying letters when you were travelling — so that I could not tell you I should be at Rednall, when you proposed to come here. Then, when you came, you never told me that you were staying here till the Sunday, and I thought you had past through and gone. Then you sent me a letter during High Mass saying you were going in an hour — and then off you went to the School in Cheshire, the exact locality of which I did not know. At last I know it.

I am extremely grieved to hear you are so ill. This is extraordinary and preternatural weather — and I have a dread of the north. Every hundred miles from the British Channel is so much worse a climate.

I doubt not that you are colouring your view of the Continent with your present sad indisposition — but I am afraid what you say is in substance true. For years and years our Catholic Newspapers told lies, and called one a bad Catholic, if one said Italy was in a bad state — but now when they can't help it, they turn round, and now abuse every one who says that the Italians are not the *only* parties in fault. As to the Temporal Power, that it is [sic] a distinct thing — but the *Governments* have been rotten — and the Roman Government is so still. And Providence seems to be making a sweep out — and it is the *only* way in which reforms *can* come to a Temporal Power, which is a Power of the earth as other Temporal Powers and may need reform as other such Powers, though *not* in Spiritual and doctrinal matters. God bless you

Ever Yrs affly John H Newman

P.S.   Even now you have not given me your *number* — so I think it safest to add 'The Ladies' School'

TO S. M. MACSWINEY

The Oratory Jany 18. 1869

My dear Mr Mac Swiney

I have the pleasantest recollections of you personally and officially — and know how zealously you have supported the credit of the University in your own Faculty. And I would gladly say this to Lord Dunraven and Mr Monsell as you wish me to do.[2]

---

[1] Miss Holmes has written in pencil on this letter 'High St Northwich or the Ladies School in the neighbourhood.'

[2] MacSwiney was proposing to apply for the post of Examiner in Practice of Medicine at the Queen's University in Ireland, and wished Newman to write a line of recommendation to these two members of the Senate, which made the appointment.

But I feel a delicacy of doing so except through Dr Woodlock — as I might otherwise seem to be interfering with matters which do not concern me. Will you then kindly do, what I dare say you have thought of doing already, — get a line on the subject from him?[1]

Most truly Yours John H Newman

TO WILLIAM MONSELL

The Oratory Jany 18. 1869

My dear Monsell

Of course I am exceedingly anxious lest I should not have said every thing that can possibly be said about the Scarletina.

It is simply true that we have *ever* escaped it. In the last 10 years we have had one, two, or three isolated cases — Gaisford's son, M. Cabrera's, and at different times three Bellasises. We have *at once* separated off the *suspected* boy, and he has had it mildly, and no others have caught it. We have observed a long quarantine and a thorough purification of every piece of clothing etc which touched him.

At this moment the complaint is all over England. It is in Birmingham and at Edgbaston — in a very mild form. At [Oscott][2] they had it in a very *bad* form. It turned to diphtheria, and a boy died and[3] But[4] they are not usually as careful there as we are. Several years back a boy died of it there[5] who had only that morning been removed into the Infirmary, and had hardly had medical attendance. So we were told at the time. We have an Orphanage here of about 50 boys. One or two had it last term. They were at once sent away, and the house has been purified — and the orphans not allowed to come here (to our Sacristy or House) for a month or six weeks after its appearance at the Orphanage — Even now we are doing our best that the boys of our School should not, for some time, come near any one of the orphans, e.g. in the Sacristy. We mean to cut off our boys from the fruit etc shop close at hand — and if possible keep them out of Church for a while.

I hope, please God, our efforts will be successful, as they hitherto have been — but I wish you to know just how things stand with us

Ever Yrs affly John H Newman

[1] MacSwiney who had not previously approached Woodlock, showed him Newman's letter. Woodlock said he could not consistently intervene with the Queen's University, but gave his best wishes to MacSwiney. On hearing this Newman said that MacSwiney might use his letter and promised to write to Lord Dunraven.

[2] Pieces have been torn out to erase words here and later. What is left and external facts reveal the word here erased.

[3] A word or two torn out.

[4] About three words torn out.

[5] These two words have been torn out, but sufficient is left for them to be deciphered.

TO CHARLOTTE WOOD

The Oratory Bm Jany 18 1869.

My dear Miss Wood

As to the Epistle to the Hebrews, I cannot give you information. You recollect it was not generally acknowledged as Canonical till the 4th or 5th century — so that comments would be rare. As to Latin, it would be absurd to give her the trouble of looking at the great work (folio) of Justiniani — who has written a *patristical* comment on St Paul's Epistles in two volumes.[1]

As to English, the best work, and the most instructive is St Thomas's Aurea Catena on the Gospels — which, as you must know, though not in the Oxford Library of the Fathers, was edited by me in English at Oxford, the translation being carefully done by friends of mine[2]

Traditions are unwritten — so, to ask for a list of traditions in written works is a contradiction in terms. However, for your purpose, you cannot name a better book that [than] the Faith of Catholics, Waterworth's Edition.[3] Also, such an inquirer as you are consulting for, ought to read the Catechism of the Council of Trent, (translation — small. the type small) for she will find then how little there is to startle her in the Catholic faith.

Thank you for your extract from the Times. I had seen it, and seen with satisfaction that we did every thing in the way of caution which is contained in it. Fever is every where and we long for some frost to kill it

Ever Yours affectly in Xt   John H Newman of the Oratory

TUESDAY 19 JANUARY 1869   Lord Edw[Edward] Howard called
THURSDAY 21 JANUARY   Janet Ogle called[4]

[1] Benedetto Justiniani (1550–1622), *In omnes Beati Pauli Epistolas Explanationes*, two volumes, Lyons 1612–13.
[2] *Catena Aurea, Commentary on the Four Gospels, collected out of the Works of the Fathers by S. Thomas Aquinas,* eight volumes, Oxford 1841–5.
[3] *The Faith of Catholics, on certain points of controversy, confirmed by Scripture and attested by the Fathers of the first five centuries of the Church.* 'Compiled by the Rev. Joseph Berington and Rev. John Kirk, third edition, revised and greatly enlarged, by the Rev. James Waterworth,' London 1846.
[4] Janet Ogle wrote on 15 Jan., 'I was very glad to get your note inviting me, as without that I dont know that I would have had the courage to venture.'

TO LADY SHEIL

The Oratory Jany 22. 1869

My dear Lady Shiel

I am very sorry to hear of Sir Justin's indisposition. We shall be very glad to receive Stephen We are making a little reduction, (but a small one certainly,) in his pension, which will be £70 instead of £80[1]

We will recollect his hint about not pushing him forward

Very truly Yours John H Newman

Lady Shiel

SATURDAY 23 JANUARY 1869   Simmons returned after losing his mother

MONDAY 25 JANUARY   Edward went to his sisters

TUESDAY 26 JANUARY   School recommenced — (with their new chapel)   *the room over the cloister a school chapel*

THURSDAY 28 JANUARY   (O'Brien of Dublin called with Montgomery?)

SATURDAY 30 JANUARY   Superior of Baltimore Sulpicians called [2]

SUNDAY 31 JANUARY   read the Bishop's pastoral against Fenianism.   through January very mild and profusely wet, and furiously windy

FRIDAY 5 FEBRUARY   Sunny bright days — I had no fire in them, till the evening

MONDAY 8 FEBRUARY   Duke of Norfolk called with his Sister

TO T. W. ALLIES

The Oratory Feb. 9. 1869.

My dear Allies,

I thank you for your goodly volume, which I was very glad to see; and like very much the choice of subjects, and the execution as far as I have been able to read it.[3]

It is very good news to hear such an account of your daughter, and I trust your and Mrs Allies's anxiety is at an end. It has been a very prolonged trial.

Our Bishop has courageously put himself against Fenianism, and there is a good deal of excitement among the Catholics here on the subject. He seems to me quite right, and I am glad of it, but some people are frightened, and I suppose he will have a little trouble in consequence.[4]

Yours affectionately in Xt   John H Newman

[1] Stephen Woulfe Sheil came to the Oratory School on 26 Jan. 1871, and left in July 1874.
[2] This was Joseph Paul Dubreuil, Superior of St Mary's Seminary, Baltimore, from 1860 until his death in 1878.
[3] T. W. Allies *The Formation of Christendom*, Part Second, London 1869, described the world in which Christianity appeared and the early history of the Church.
[4] Birmingham was one of the chief centres of Fenianism in England. Ullathorne's Advent

TO W. J. COPELAND

The Oratory Bm Febry 9. 1869

My dear Copeland,

My main, if not only real reason for wishing my Volume on Subjects of the day published was its dedication to you. I thought there were great difficulties in the way — and I wonder you have been able to overcome them. I am ready to receive the proofs, whenever Rivington sends them.[1]

You have had a great deal of trouble about them — and I wish you were out of the wood, and able to do your proper work — which is all suspended.

You say nothing about your health, or your Brother's.

Of course you have read the Memoir of Keble. It must have been a great pleasure, however sad a pleasure, to the Judge to write, and to have written it. I suppose he is the survivor of the circle in which he found himself at College and in which he has lived. He speaks of Tucker and another ⟨Turner⟩ as still alive; but there is nothing to show he was intimate with them. I suppose Turner is the man whom I recollect as Junior Proctor and as preaching the University Sermon in St Peter's one Lent. His text was 'I am that I am —' and he quoted Beveridge.[2]

I am very well — though I can't get confidence in myself

Ever Yours affectionately John H Newman

TO EDWARD THOMAS VAUGHAN

February 9, 1869[3]

Time was when, whether from my own fault or the fault of circumstances, even friends were hard upon me — but now even strangers to me personally

Pastoral had been devoted to the duty of obedience to civil authority, and greatly offended the Irish supporters of Fenianism, by denouncing it as an anti-Christian secret society. The Fenian *Universal News* attacked him as though he had said 'the Irish people' were the enemies of religion. In a new pastoral, read on 31 Jan. Ullathorne defended himself and made an appeal, which proved successful, to the Irish among his flock. See *Butler* II, pp. 141–4.

[1] Cf. letters of 14 Nov., 26 Nov. and 3 Dec. 1868.

[2] Sir J. T. Coleridge in *A Memoir of the Rev. John Keble, M.A.*, pp. 18–19, referred to John Tucker and William Henry Turner as being close friends of Keble at Corpus Christi College, Oxford about 1810. John Tucker (1793–1873), was a Scholar of the College 1810–20, and then a Fellow until 1853. For a time he was secretary of the Church Missionary Society at Madras. See *Moz.* II, p. 75. From 1852 until his death he was Vicar of West Hendred, Berks.

William Henry Turner (1796–1875), was a Scholar of Corpus Christi College, 1803–13, and a Fellow, 1813–36. He was Rector of Trent, Dorset, 1835 until death. Turner was Junior Proctor in 1817.

[3] This is part of a letter that Newman wrote to thank Vaughan for his article 'J. H. Newman as Preacher,' the *Contemporary Review*, (Jan. 1869), pp. 37–52, concerning the new edition of *P.S.* Vaughan spoke appreciatively of Newman's former influence at Oxford and of the deep religiousness of the *Sermons*.

are considerate and friendly; and, though I wish and trust to be influenced by the prospect of a higher praise or blame than any which comes from an earthly source, yet I may allowably take the approbation of honest and good men as a mercy from above, and beg Him from whom it is sent to reward them abundantly for their generosity.[1]

TO H. A. WOODGATE

The Oy Bm [9? February 1869]

My dear Woodgate

Thank you very much, but Judge Coleridge has sent me a copy of his Book.

It is wonderful he has been able to do it — as he says he can only work a few hours in the day.

I suppose he thought, if he took your Sermon, he could not refuse to take others — though of course its being a University Sermon made a difference — [2] but it is wonderful how a man of 78 or 79 could *compose*, i.e. put together, so many pages as he has done.

Ever Yrs affly John H Newman

TO MISS M. R. GIBERNE

The Oratory Bm Febry 10. 1869 Ash Wednesday

My dear Sister Pia

I wonder whether you have as mild weather in France as we have here. I am sitting without a fire from choice, nor have I had one, except in the evening, for nearly a week past. One does not know what it means. There may be subterraneous fires, which are doing their best to find a vent.

Thank you for all your prayers. I said Mass for you on the 28th and 29th January and should have written to you, had I not been busy.

Don't be annoyed. I am more happy as I am, than in any other way. I can't bear the kind of trouble which I should have, if I were brought forward in any public way. Recollect, I *could* not be in the Council, unless I were a Bishop — and really and truly I am *not* a theologian. A theologian is one who has mastered theology — who can say how many opinions there are on every point, what authors have taken which, and which is the best — who can discriminate exactly between proposition and proposition, argument and

---

[1] Vaughan replied on 12 Feb. that he wrote 'out of the fulness of a heart very thankful' for what he had gained from reading the Sermons again after many years. He only once saw or spoke to Newman, in August 1838 in St Mary's, but he reminded him of his friendship for his sister Mrs Phillips, and his niece Bessie Phillips, who had recently married Richard Pope.

[2] Woodgate appears to have asked Sir John Coleridge to include a sermon on Keble by Woodgate in his *Memoir*.

argument, who can pronounce which are safe, which allowable, which dangerous — who can trace the history of doctrines in successive centuries, and apply the principles of former times to the conditions of the present. This is it to be a theologian — this and a hundred things besides. And this I am not, and never shall be. Like St Gregory Nazianzen I like going on my own way, and having my time my own, living without pomp or state, or pressing engagements. Put me into official garb, and I am worth nothing; leave me to myself, and every now and then I shall do something. Dress me up and you will soon have to make my shroud — leave me alone, and I shall live the appointed time.

Now do take this in, as a sensible nun, and believe me

Ever Yours affly in Xt   John H Newman

TO THOMAS HARPER, S.J.

The Oratory Febry 10. 1869

My dear F Harper

I rejoice to hear so good an account of you, though I suppose you will work too hard now that you have begun again.

It has always been a real grief, and almost wound which I have carried about me, that married, and especially clerical married converts, have been so tossed aside, and suffered to live or die as they may. We have lost a vast deal of power and zeal, of high talent and devotion, which might have done much for the glory of God. And now, after 20 years of such neglect, our νέμεσις has come upon us in the person of Foulkes, one of them.[1] This is apropos of your Brother — Thank you for your offer, which we shall gladly take, and the boy too. Perhaps you know he does not satisfy us. We think his father spoils him — and, I grieve to say we cannot say we trust him — and we can say this of most of our boys. However, he has time to mend, and I feel sure your word will be of great use to him[2]

Yours most sincerely in J.Xt   John H Newman of the Oratory

The Revd Fr Harper S J.

[1] E. S. Ffoulkes became an Anglican clergyman in 1848, and joined the Catholic Church in 1855, influenced by Manning. He had just published a pamphlet *The Church's Creed or the Crown's Creed? A Letter to the Most Rev. Archbishop Manning*, London 1869, which showed that he was returning to the Church of England. He was formally readmitted on 5 June 1870. In his pamphlet he blamed the Western Church for admitting the 'Filioque' into the Creed under pressure from secular rulers, and for its use of the False Decretals. He thought Anglican Orders and Sacraments were valid, and that the primatial see of England was originally autocephalous. Also that English Christianity was as good or better than that of France, Spain and Italy. When Harper replied on 13 April to Newman's letter, he remarked how much he agreed with him as to married converts. See also letter of 11 Oct. 1868 to Estcourt.

[2] Samuel Brown Harper, an elder brother of Thomas, was at New Inn Hall Oxford, 1838–41, and took Orders. He was curate of Milton Abbas, Dorset, 1849–55, and became a Catholic. His son, Thomas Stanislas Harper, came to the Oratory School on 23 Jan. 1866, and left in July 1869.

The Oratory Febry 12. 1869

My dear Copeland

My awkwardness has misled you. To me personally it would be a great disappointment not to have that Dedication, not for your sake, but for my own. It is the poorest possible, but the only expression I have given of my love and gratitude towards you. Nor have I any sort of objection to the republication of any part of the Volume. I do not take the view of some things in it, which I did when I published it — but I think those things are perfectly harmless, and that the effect of the volume as a whole is what I now, as then, should wish it to be.

My sole delicacy is about the Rivingtons. They are going out in a new line, in publishing it. It is a history, not a collection of Sermons — it is a controversy. And I am only anxious that they should fully know what they are doing. Moreover, whether there is a chance of the volume having the effect of the former volumes.

But when you said that they had come into the project of publication, I felt that they *had* considered this thoroughly.

You will say, why, if so, did I begin my letter as I did? I cannot recall the train of thought which led to it, nor do I quite recollect what I said.[1]

All I know is that I have not the shadow of a difficulty in the volume being published, and that I positively wish the Dedication to be published, and very earnestly wish it. And shall be balked and put out if it is not.

· It is wonderful that Judge Coleridge at his age could publish so careful a volume, and with such interruptions from illness as he describes. Oxford is now a thing of the past — and I do not know where to look for any record of what it was — for Keble lived out of Oxford

Ever Yrs affly J H N

The Oratory, Birmm Feby 12. 1869

My dear Rogers,

I want you to do me a favour. Miss Whately, before publishing her Father's correspondence, wrote to me for any I had. I sent her all I could find with a very civil letter, and I sent her especially 4 letters (of 1834), two mine,

---

[1] Letter of 9 Feb. 1869. Copeland wrote on 10 Feb. that he had consulted Rogers who was strongly of opinion that *S.D.* should be republished unchanged, as the eight volumes of *P.S.* had been. Copeland did not wish *S.D.* republished simply for the dedication and decided after receiving Newman's letter, to write to Rivington to suspend operations.

and two his — saying that I should not at all wonder if she published his two without mine, but that if she published one of mine, I wished her to publish both. The book comes out, and she has published both of her father's, but only one of mine like a wild elephant between two tame ones.

I think she went to the continent, and left the finishing to others (I don't mean to Merivale) and hence the blunder. However so I am told it is.

Now I am making some new impressions of my 'History of my Religious Opinions (Apologia)' and I am tempted to put *all four* in an Appendix. This, however, is on the supposition that Whately's second letter puts me into a disadvantageous position, from which *my* second (and unpublished) letter extricates me.

What I want then is that you should read the four (which I will send you) and say whether I shall leave the matter alone, or publish the four. I shall not of course reflect upon Miss Whately.[1]

Miss Hampden has written to me to know whether I am the author of 'Elucidations of Dr Hampden's Theological statements.' So I suppose I am getting into a little war in another quarter.[2]

I have been much gratified by Doyle's lecture, which he sent me — and I have had a very nice letter from him — but I fear, tho' he says not a single syllable in his Lecture *positively*, that he has a shrinking from doctrine, however (what would be called) unsectarian — but I say this only to a friend.[3]

Ever Yrs affly John H. Newman

Sir F. Rogers Bart

SATURDAY 13 FEBRUARY 1869   Mrs Monsell came with her boy   profuse snow storm melting   East wind and north bright

TO HENRY JAMES COLERIDGE

The Oy Bm Febry 13. 1869

My dear Fr Coleridge

Your book came quite right, and I thank you for it — and have already availed myself of it.[4]

I did not acknowledge it at once, for you had already given me notice of its coming — and I had a great press of letters to write, besides our annual Audit on my hands

Most sincerely Yrs John H Newman

---

[1] See letter of 24 Sept. 1865 to E. Jane Whately. Rogers approved of the publication of the letters. See that of 18 Feb. to him and *Apo.* pp. 380–7, 'Note on Page 12.'
[2] This Newman managed to avoid. See letter of 26 March 1871 to Miss Hampden. See also letters of 16 May and 12 Sept. 1871 to H. Wilberforce and 7 Oct. 1871 to Miss Hampden.
[3] See letter of 26 Nov. 1868 to Rogers. Doyle wrote to Newman on 6 Feb.
[4] Evidently Coleridge's *Vita Vitae Nostrae Meditantibus Proposita*, London 1869.

TO HENRY TAYLOR

The Oratory Bm Febry 15. 1869

Dear Mr Taylor

I ought before now to have thanked you for the gift of your Pamphlet on Crime.[1] Pray accept my tardy but sincere acknowledgement for your recollection of me.

I wish my opinion on such a subject were worth any thing — but, as you may understand, I have lived too much out of the world to allow of that.

However, there is one principle which comes into your discussion on which I certainly have an opinion, and in accordance with your own; it is on the expedience of corporal punishment for certain offences

We have a boys' school attached to our House here; and we certainly find that the good old punishment of flogging, is, in due moderation as to severity and frequency, the most efficacious of all punishments, while it is the most prompt and summary, and the least irritating and annoying to the subjects of it. It is done and over — there is nothing to brood over, nothing to create a grudge, at least to English boys.

I am, My dear Mr Taylor, Very truly Yours John H Newman

H. Taylor Esqr

TUESDAY 16 FEBRUARY 1869   mild again   no fires till evening

TO SIR FREDERIC ROGERS

The Oratory, Birmm Feb 18. 1869

My dear Rogers,

Thank you for the trouble you have taken, which has quite answered my purpose. I have sent the letters to the Press. In my Apologia I quote from memory some of those words of mine in a letter to Whately, which he quotes against me in the Correspondence, viz 'strange office of an Instructor, viz. to make me think for myself'[2] — this is perhaps what you recollect — or perhaps you saw the letters when they were written — and your memory 35 years after retains some faint impression of parts of them.

However, I am not writing so much to thank you, as to ask you another service, if you can do it.

Some months since Lord Houghton was kind enough to call on me here.[3]

---

[1] Taylor, who worked in the Colonial Office, published a letter to Gladstone *Crime Considered*, London 1869. It led to a criminal code being prepared for the crown colonies.

[2] *Apo.* pp. 11 and 284: *Moz.* I p. 141.

[3] See diary for 3 Oct. 1868.

In conversation I said I had formerly met him in Wood's rooms. His memory was better than mine — he took me aback by answering 'Don't you recollect my writing "One Tract more" after Number 90, and I have still your letter thanking me for it.'

What was I to say? I recollect the Tract quite well, nay, I have seen the Title page of it lately — but had quite forgotten its Author.[1]

Now in these new Copies which I am having struck off I want to add a few lines acknowledging Lord Houghton's kindness — but I quite forget what 'One Tract more' was about. It is in our Library, I am sure, but I can't find it.

Perhaps you can recollect the Tract enough to enable me to say in a note 'I ought not to omit here the very generous protection ⟨defence⟩ I received at this time from the present Lord H., in a pamphlet entitled "One Tract more",' or the like.

But I don't like to say it, in total forgetfulness of the matter of his Tract.

If you can't help me, will you send this letter on to Church?[2]

Yrs ever affly John H. Newman

Sir F. Rogers

FRIDAY 19 FEBRUARY 1869   Mr Bellew called   green leaves out in the hedges   the almond blossom out

TO WILLIAM FROUDE

The Oratory Bm Feby 19. 1869

My dear William

Curiously enough I have just finished writing a letter on a work which runs pari passu with Hurrell's — Whately's 'Letters to an Episcopalian'. A high Churchman in London wants to republish it, but with Whately's name, and I can give him no authority for using it whatever, except my own witness of what was said at Oxford at the time, 1826. Even Hawkins recollects nothing about it. It is a very powerful work, and I should have liked Hurrell's letter to have helped me in determining the author, but it is more than unlikely, considering the book was published the very year when H was elected at Oriel.[3]

---

[1] *One Tract More or the System illustrated by the 'Tracts for the Times,' externally regarded,* by a Layman, London 1841, gave an account of the history of the Church of England and of the Tractarian Movement from an Anglo-catholic point of view. Newman's copy, which has on its fly-leaf, 'The Revd J. H. Newman with the author's respectful regards' is still in the library at the Birmingham Oratory.

[2] Newman inserted this note: 'To the Pamphlets published in my behalf at this time I should add "One tract more," an able and generous defence of Tractarianism and No. 90, by the present Lord Houghton.' *Apo.* p. 91.

[3] For *Letters on the Church by an Episcopalian*, which had a great influence on R. H. Froude, see next letter. William Froude wrote on 18 Feb. enclosing a letter from W. J. E. Bennett, Vicar of Frome, who asked for permission to reprint from *The Remains of Richard*

It is very kind in you thinking of writing to me on the subject of Mr Bennett's question, but I can have in any case but one answer. I think Hurrell's works, the more they are known, the more they will tend to spread those views which I now hold to be true — I mean, on the whole and on the long run — and it would rejoice me to know that what he did so long ago should bear fruit now. The case is the same with my dear friend Bowden's works, the probable usefulness of which just now has lately been brought before me.[1]

Of course I can claim no right in any way to answer Mr Bennett — but I shall be very glad, if you give him permission; and am quite ready to take the responsibility myself, supposing, if I understand you, you wish me to do so.

I think it a capital idea your notion of making over the copy right to Copeland I am afraid you have lately had some necessary trouble about mine.[2]

Palmer is the most able, authoritative, and patient of lionizers[3]

Thank Eddy [Froude] for his letter, and tell him I am trying to get time to inflict a few lines upon him — but necessary letters have the precedence.

Ever Yrs affly John H. Newman

TO H. A. WOODGATE

The Oratory Bm Febr 19. 1869

My dear Woodgate

I wonder whether your memory will serve you in a matter which happened in 1826.

In that year appeared 'Letters of an Episcopalian.' I have, at least twice, in print ascribed them to Whately, according to the general voice of Oxford at the time.[4]

A literary man in London thinks of republishing them now, in order to

Hurrell Froude II, Volume 1, Derby 1839, 'Remarks on State Interference in matters spiritual', pp. 184–269. Froude thought the question of republication should be considered 'by someone whose standpoint corresponds better than mine with that which the Publication, and the tenour of the "Remains" implies.'

[1] J. W. Bowden contributed to *Lyra Apostolica, Tracts for the Times*, and the *British Critic*, besides writing a *Life of Gregory VII*, as to which see letter of 28 Feb. to Copeland, and last note there.

[2] Froude, who had just transferred the copyright of *S.D.* from himself to Copeland, suggested that Newman should make over the copyright of Froude's *Remains* to Copeland as a natural companion to *P.S.*

[3] Froude wrote that his daughter Isy was in Rome with F. R. Ward and two of his children, staying in the house of William Palmer, who acted everywhere as their guide.

[4] See *Diff.* I, pp. 203–5; *D.A.* pp. 360–1; and *Apo.*, pp. 12–13, where Newman writes, 'The main positions of this able essay are these; first that Church and State should be independent of each other . . . and, secondly, that the Church may justly and by right retain its property, though separated from the State.' See also E. Jane Whately, *Life and Correspondence of Richard Whately*, second edition, p. 43 note.

serve the Church of England in the prospect of disestablishment; and wrote to me to know my *authority* for attributing them to Whately.[1]

I answered that I had *none* beyond the opinion of the day; but I referred him to Hawkins, Hinds and the Liverpool friends of Blanco White.

Hawkins answers that he not only cannot say any thing about the authorship, but he has no recollection of the book, has not got it, and has no note about it among his papers!

It is a very curious case, as I thought Hawkins would be sure to know something about it. But he does not even recollect the book.

Then it struck me that *you* possibly might recollect something about it.

Senior, Mayo, Tyler, would be sure to know something — but they are gone. Would *Pope* [,] W's brother in law? Could you get at him? I should not like my name to be introduced.[2]

The truth is the book is slap against the suppression of the Irish sees, in 1833, in which Whately had so great a hand. This I think is why he never owned the book; and it may be a reason why Pope would be silent about it.[3]

It is odd that no friend of W's has contradicted me, if I am wrong.

My correspondent, in order to sell the re-print, I suppose, wants to use Whately's name

Ever Yrs affly John H Newman

[1] A London doctor, G. Goddard Rogers, of 29 Grosvenor Street, a High Churchman, wanted to republish *Letters on the Church by an Episcopalian*. He had asked R. J. E. Bennett about the authorship and had been referred to Newman, to whom he wrote on 31 Jan. Newman told him to apply to Hawkins, who wrote that he could not remember the book. Later Dr Rogers met Hawkins in London and showed him a copy of *Letters . . . by an Episcopalian*. He still could not remember it, but thought it was not by Whately. Rogers informed Newman of this in a letter of 23 Feb., which he sent to Woodgate, writing on it 'You may like to see this. Let me have it back. JHN.' Dr Rogers later inspected the ledger of Longman the publisher, where dealings about the book had been with 'P. Bingham Esq.' Dr Rogers also discussed the matter with Manning, who had not been at Oxford when the book appeared, but thought it was not written by Whately. However, on 1 June 1869, Dr Rogers had an interview with Bishop Hinds, Whately's close friend, and wrote the same day to Newman: 'The whole matter is cleared up; for Dr Hinds affirms most positively the correctness of your statement in the "Apologia" that Whately wrote the "Letters on the Church." He is equally astounded with yourself at the Provost of Oriel's entire forgetfulness of the work; and he seems quite as sure that Dr Hawkins *read* it as that Dr Whately *wrote* it.

. . . .

On the part of Dr Hinds (whom I found a great invalid propped up on a couch) I am to send the *warmest remembrances* and inquiries after your health — He seemed quite pleased to set eyes on one who had been in communication with his "dear old friend."'

[2] Woodgate replied that there had been a thirty years' quarrel between himself and Whately's brother-in-law, but that they had lately made friends, and he would enquire of him if opportunity offered. Nassau William Senior and James Endell Tyler were dead, but Dr Thomas Mayo, Fellow of Oriel 1813–18, did not die until 1871. See also letters of 27 Feb. and 24 March to Hawkins.

[3] Whately had been made Archbishop of Dublin by the Whigs in 1831 and supported their suppression of Irish sees in 1833.

TO J. R. BLOXAM

The Oratory Bm Febry 21. 1869

My dear Bloxam

Thank you for your affectionate letter. I have a great weight of years now on me — and the birthdays of the old are mementos, not festivities — and belong to Lent, as is actually the case with mine. The 21st is the latest day on which Septuagesima possibly can fall — so that I never can have an Alleluia on my birthday.

There is a little mistake in my letter to Coleridge, as he has printed. I *saw* *Keble* on September 12 — he so puts it as if I saw him on the 13.[1] What you say of Beeding makes me say that, I was at that time very ill without knowing it — and went on ailing till next January when, in suddenly getting well, I at length knew how ill I had been.

I recollect well the breakfast at Magdalen, and wonder Judge Coleridge does not mention your name.[2]

And I wonder you are ever ill at Beeding — for I consider that part of the coast the healthiest in England — though certainly it is keen.

We have been very anxious lest the scarlet fever, which is so much about should get to our boys. At Oscott they had it fiercely at the end of the year — and now, on the boys' return since Christmas, it has broken out again there.

Ever Yrs affly John H Newman

The Revd J R Bloxam

TO MRS JOHN MOZLEY

The Oratory Febr 21/69

My dear Jemima

Thank you for your affectionate remembrances. I am very well thank you, and have been so long, so many years, without a cold, that I don't like to boast of it, lest I should have a reverse. We have all been very anxious lest the scarletina, which is so prevalent, should get among our boys; hitherto, we have been protected. Last November it broke out at Oscott, and the school was broken up — one boy died, and one theological student. Since Christmas it has

[1] When writing on 19 Feb. to congratulate Newman on his birthday, Bloxam spoke of Sir J. T. Coleridge's *Memoir of the Rev. John Keble*, and Newman's letter of 17 Sept. 1868, describing his last visit. After it Newman went on to visit Bloxam at Beeding. See diary for 19 Sept. and for Newman's illness, 17 Jan. 1866.

[2] Bloxam wrote that it was Newman who first introduced him to Keble. 'This introduction gave me the opportunity of inviting him to meet the Poet Wordsworth at a joint breakfast given by Frank Faber and myself on the morning after the Honorary Degree had been conferred on Wordsworth at the Commemoration. You I think were present at the Breakfast.' In the *Memoir*, Coleridge referred to the first meeting of Keble with Wordsworth in F. A. Faber's rooms at Magdalen, p. 248. The breakfast party was on 13 June 1839. See R. D. Middleton, *Newman and Bloxam, an Oxford Friendship*, London 1947, pp. 52–3.

broken out there again. At Roehampton, at a large girls' school one girl died, and another, whom Lady Herbert took home to London, gave it *her*. I am told she has had it badly — she had the Roman fever last year, caught by nursing a friend in it at Rome.

I am very sorry Janie is so unwell — she (and Edith)[1] should go to the Bel Alp — one of my friends was quite renovated, being a great sufferer from asthma, by going there for 6 weeks last summer. *I* had a very bad year in Switzerland, and could not make a fair experiment — but the change in him is wonderful. However, asthma is so capricious — his arises from indigestion or suppressed gout. Rose, who had the asthma very badly, could not sleep at Somerset House, when he was head of King's College, but was obliged to go off every night to his small parsonage near St Thomas's in the Borough.[2] As to Switzerland, I should consider it a simple penance to be for six weeks in the monotonous grim glare of those awful white mountains, which are well enough as sights, not as companions — but I believe the air is a wonderful medicine. You don't say any thing about yourself. Mrs Wootten keeps up, fragile as she has been for 30 years

Ever Yrs affly John H Newman

Mrs Mozley
Thank you and Janie for the pretty penwiper

MONDAY 22 FEBRUARY 1869   east wind began

TO MARIANNE FRANCES BOWDEN

The Oratory Febr 22. 1869

My dear Child

I was very glad to receive your good wishes yesterday and thank you for remembering the 21st. And today your and your Sisters' beautiful present has come. How could you know that it is just the thing which I wanted? But it is — I got two common ones when I was in Dublin, and have them still in use — but I wanted another, though I did not aim at one so beautiful as the one which you have sent me.

I hope you have still favourable accounts of Mary. Our Bishop spoke with great satisfaction to me of Katie some little while ago.[3]

John Simeon told me about Willie. They are in the same regiment.[4]

[1] Janie was Jemima's daughter, and Edith her daughter-in-law, wife of John Rickards Mozley.
[2] Hugh James Rose was Principal of King's College, London, 1836–8.
[3] Marianne's sister Mary, Mrs Victor Law, gave birth to her only child on 22 Feb. 1868 in India, and died there in 1870. Katie was now Sister Mary Alban at the Dominican Convent, Stone.
[4] Marianne wrote of her brother, 'Willie has joined his regiment the 97th at Aldershott.'

Thank you for your account of Papa. For myself I am very well, thank God — and since I remain here in clover, it would be strange if I were not

I hope Fanny's hand is not seriously hurt

Ever Yours affectly John H Newman

TO EDWARD FRANCIS COLLINS

Feb 23/69

My dear Sir

No apology was necessary for your letter — I have said mass several times for the good Nuns during the trial, and can quite understand that their sufferings must be greater than any but themselves can know.

Of course the prospect of great expenses is far from the least of these, and doubtless there are persons high in authority who will form a judgment on this point in a public point of view. As for me, who am so out of the world, and who have so little influence among Catholics, I am one of the last persons fitted to commence a movement which requires Bishops and the public press.[1]

J H N

TO W. J. COPELAND

The Oratory Febry 24/69

My dear Copeland

Do you recollect the Tract called 'One Tract more?' I have searched in vain for it. Can you tell me what the *line of argument* taken in it was? It was a generous defence of me by a friend of S. F. Wood's[2]

I hope I have not annoyed you by my shillyshally

Ever Yrs affly J H N

FRIDAY 26 FEBRUARY 1869 monthly examination of boys. H. W. [Wilberforce] passed thro'

---

[1] Collins, a Catholic journalist from Hull, who was now sub-editor of the *Tablet* under Herbert Vaughan, wrote to ask Newman's help for the Irish Sisters of Mercy at Hull. One of the nuns, Miss Saurin, who had been made to leave the convent, brought an action for assault, imprisonment, libel and conspiracy. An immensely long trial in Westminster Hall came to an end on 26 Feb. No scandal was brought to light, but practices of convent life were held up to mockery before Protestant England. To judge from the attitude of the Lord Chief Justice, Sir Alexander Cockburn, Miss Saurin had no real case, but the all Protestant Jury, while rejecting the charges of assault and imprisonment, found in her favour on the counts of libel and conspiracy, and awarded her £200 damages. See letter of 8 March to Emily Bowles for Newman's opinion.

[2] See letter of 18 Feb. to Rogers. Copeland replied on 26 Feb. that he remembered the name of the *Tract*, but had never read it. See also letter of 25 July 1869 to Copeland.

TO MRS HENRY BACCHUS

The Oratory Febry 26. 1869

Madam

I have great pleasure in complying with your request, and am,

Your faithful Servant John H Newman

Mrs Bacchus

TO WILLIAM MONSELL

The Oratory Febry 26. 1869

My dear Monsell

I hoped to have answered you before this. It grieved me exceedingly to hear the sad account Montalembert gave of his illness. I have begun to say a Mass for him once a week.

I wish I were enough of a Frenchman to be able to criticize or to form a judgment upon his Paper, which I return to you. That it is full of eloquence, full of instruction, and worthy of him, is plain enough. Nor do I see any thing to which malevolent Catholic opponents can object — but in this respect especially it is that my ignorance of French disqualifies me from having an opinion which is trustworthy. He does but state facts, and facts which it is impossible to gainsay. So I read him. And as to translation into English, you and such as you who live in the world, alone can judge of its expedience. I suppose his name would be quite enough to sell it.

All I can say is that I am obliged to you for giving me the opportunity of reading it.[1]

Rogers who wrote to me lately seemed to rejoice in having been brought across you at the Colonial Office

Ever Yrs affly John H Newman

The Rt Honble Wm Monsell M P

---

[1] Montalembert's paper was probably *Questions à soumettre au futur Concile*, in which, according to his biographer, he drew up the long series of complaints and grievances of which his soul was full. He wanted to see the masses kept within the Church, and felt that violent extremists had got hold of the publicity and were deluging people with sophisms, invective and falsehood. He wanted to make his voice heard, to show that not all accepted this monopolistic propaganda. R. P. Lecanuet, *Montalembert, III, L'Église et le Second Empire*, (*1850–1870*), Paris 1902, pp. 435–6. Montalembert's paper was never published.

The Oratory Febry 26. 1869

My dear Mrs Monsell

I know you have heard about your boy from others, yet I think it best to send you a line.

I am told that he is getting at home here, and is tolerably happy, considering the short time he has been with us; and I am in no anxiety about him. However, no one is perfectly acclimated to the atmosphere of a school except by degrees, and I am prepared to believe that we will have some ups and downs, but nothing of a very serious nature.

I hope he is punctual in writing to you, and am,

My dear Mrs Monsell Most truly Yours John H. Newman

Mrs Monsell

TO EDWARD HAWKINS

The Oratory Birmingham Febry 27. 1869

My dear Provost

I am just made acquainted with the fact that Dr Rogers has shown you a letter of mine to him. I ought to have been prepared for it for he showed me a letter of yours. But I was not; and wrote off to him the letter which he showed you currente calamo on receipt of his, to get the matter off my thoughts. I don't at all recollect how I worded it, but I hope I said nothing which you would not like to have read.[1]

My own feeling was that an intimate friend of another would be unwilling to ascribe to him, or allow to be ascribed, what he had not himself acknowledged to be his; and that this unwillingness might lead you to throw the onus probandi with a very good will on those who said the work in question *was* Whately's. Again, tho' I did not take the liberty of saying so, I felt the force of what I had often heard you say, and what you repeat to Dr Rogers, that you trusted to your notes more than to your memory, and I considered that you formed a judgment against the supposed authorship when you found nothing among your papers to confirm it.

But I shall not write more on the subject to Dr Rogers. He began the correspondence by asking me if I could throw light upon it — and I answered that I could not, but referred him to you, Hinds, Pope, and Dr Mayo.

I am glad of this opportunity of signing myself

Very affectionately Yours John H Newman

[1] See letter of 19 Feb. to Woodgate, and for Hawkins's reply, letter of 24 March to him.

FROM RICHARD HOLT HUTTON

'The Spectator' Office, 1, Wellington Street, Strand, London, W.C.
25th Feb, 1869.

My dear Dr Newman,

An idea, which originated I believe with the Poet Laureate[1] has been started, for organizing a Metaphysical Society in London, to which men of all parties from Archbishop Manning to Mr. J. S. Mill, might belong, for the sake if possible, of obtaining some basis of metaphysical science on which all metaphysicians might agree. I believe that Archbishop Manning, and I know that Mr [W.G] Ward, have agreed to be amongst its founders. It is proposed that the Duke of Argyll should be the first president, and that Dean Stanley, Mr Martineau, Mr Browning, Mr Tennyson, Mr Bagehot, Mr Knowles, Sir John Lubbock, and I believe several others should be among its first members. Mr J. S. Mill and others of the extremely Sceptical school of metaphysics would be invited to join. The object of it would be to meet some five or six or eight times in the year, to hear papers and discuss them on the fundamental questions of psychology and metaphysics — involving of course the metaphysical and physical questions at the root of natural theology, as to the spiritual or physical essence of 'force', the meaning of a 'law of nature', etc, — and to see if some assured basis of metaphysical science could not in this way be agreed upon. Every one is exceedingly desirous to get your co-operation; and I have been asked to request you to join us. We should desire to obtain also the help of any other Catholics of your metaphysical school you might think likely to be of use to us. I should add that the new Dean of St Paul's (Dr Mansel) is to be requested to join us, and also Mr De Morgan the Logician and Mathematician.

I cannot speak with too much emphasis of the value attached to your cooperation by all from whom I have heard anything on the subject. Mr Ward was talking to me yesterday about it, and though he has, I suppose, been very closely identified with a very different party in the Catholic Church, he spoke in the warmest way of the value of your aid. It would be a very great pleasure to me, if I should be able to promise your cooperation. I hope that the distance of Birmingham from London need not prevent you from frequently joining our discussions. Do you not think that questions of philosophy are really at the root of half the theological divisions of the world?

I cannot conclude without telling you how great a pleasure it has been, and is to me, to read the new edition of your old Oxford Sermons. It is more than a pleasure, often the highest of spiritual benefits.

Believe me, my dear Dr Newman, very faithfully Yours Richard H Hutton

TO RICHARD HOLT HUTTON

The Oratory Bm Feby 27. 1869

My dear Mr Hutton

Your letters are always so kind and friendly that it annoys me to think that I have no way of showing to you my gratitude for them. You will say that the acceptance of the proposal you now make me gives me an opportunity; and so it would, if I were younger, less engaged and better read.

Of course I am greatly flattered by the invitation conveyed to me from such eminent men; but I have a bad conscience mixed with the gratification as I really have no pretensions to receive such an honour. It has been my misfortune through life to have dabbled in many things, and to have mastered

---

[1] Alfred Tennyson.

nothing. I am not speaking as if I could not have done something if I had confined myself to one line; but I have in fact taken up nothing in particular, not history as Milman, not theology as Robert Wilberforce and many a Catholic Priest, not Christian Evidence as Butler and Davison. I have lived from hand to mouth, doing nothing but what I was forced to do, and in consequence at the end of my days it is a continual trouble to me that 'Vitam perdidi' not 'operosè nihil' but 'plurima festinanter agendo'[1]

I don't expect you will feel this as I do — but you will at least understand me when I say I am too *old* for anything of the kind. I am very well while I remain quiet at home and occupy myself daily in the details of home employments — but I have neither time nor strength for going abroad, and I never (I may say) leave home unless I am obliged. Moreover, I have lived so long out of the world that I have forgotten how to behave in it. I have said all this, lest you should think me disrespectful towards your invitation.

As to metaphysics, though it is so wide and so deep a subject, I dare say if I published anything more, and had the courage, it would be on some metaphysical point.[2]

Very truly Yours John H Newman

TO W. J. COPELAND

The Oratory Feby 28/69

My dear Copeland

I beg your pardon for the trouble I have caused you.[3] One thing I am perfectly certain of, however my words sounded, that I wrote, not to *settle* the matter, but to state my *misgivings* as being great. And what were my misgivings? I think, if I bring out my meaning, it is this — that Rivington and you would, by republishing that volume, be circulating what has a tendency to unsettle minds that believe in the Anglican Church. There are things in the volume which I should not indeed say now, but I have not any difficulty about republishing them, for I am sure that in their place and as a part of a whole, they look only one way. And for the very reason that I had no difficulty, I could not acquiesce in Rivington having no difficulty, *unless* he knew quite what he was about. But now that he has so carefully looked the matter in the face, I have no more delicacy in the matter — and shall be glad to receive the proofs as soon as he likes to send them.

[1] Newman adapts a saying attributed to Grotius on his deathbed.

[2] Hutton wrote on 28 March to express regret at Newman's refusal. 'If any *personal* influence could have made me embrace a faith to which I cannot see any way, it would have been your's.' He renewed his appeal two years later. See Newman's letter of 22 March 1871.

[3] Over the republication of *S.D.* See letter of 12 Feb. to Copeland, who wrote on 26 Feb. that Rivington did not think it would interfere with the sale of *P.S.*, and he understood it was '"historical and controversial" rather than parochial and practical.' Copeland thought Newman had been against republication.

As to Froude's Remains, I dare say I did not separate so distinctly as I ought two questions which stand apart, and which I meant should stand apart in my answer to W.F.[1] He asked me as in one sense Hurrell's representative, whether I should object to Mr Bennett's republication of about 100 pages of the Remains — and I answered, certainly not. I had two reasons. 1. because I thought that Hurrell, if on earth, certainly would have given leave. 2. because I thought that every thing that Hurrell wrote was more or less directly in favour of the 'Tendimus in Latium.'[2] Such was my answer to his first question — his second was whether he should not ask you to accept the Copyright — I thought this most natural and good — but I did not connect it with the first question, which might have been settled *without* it. What *you* would have to say in answer to Mr Bennett did not come into my mind — though, had I thought about it, I should not have thought there was so much difficulty in republishing the Remains than in republishing my Sermons on Subjects of the Day. I rejoiced in a use being put to the Remains, as I did in hearing that perhaps Bowden's Hildebrand was to be used against Ffoulkes. 'Non omnis moriar,' I thought.[3]

Ever Yrs affly J H N

MONDAY I MARCH 1869   Canon Walker came

TO WILLIAM MONSELL

The Oratory Bm March 2/69

My dear Monsell,

I saw Dr Evans today about your boy. He tells me he thinks he is even better than when he came. He had a cold last week, but that is getting well. We think he has taken an extra quantity of lolipops and alicampane — [4] which has not had a salutary effect. I believe Mrs Wootten is writing by this post to Mrs Monsell.

It is wonderful that Montalembert can keep up his energy when he is so disabled by illness. He thinks me a much greater man than I am. I would do any thing I could out of mere gratitude to him for his kindness — but, even if I had a connected large view to put forward, I could not write without any

---

[1] See letter of 19 Feb. to William Froude. Copeland was unwilling to take responsibility for the republication of Froude's *Remains*.

[2] *Aeneid* I, 205; i.e. towards Rome.

[3] Horace, *Odes*, III, xxx, 6. Bowden's *The Life and Pontificate of Gregory VII* provided an answer to points Ffoulkes had raised in his *Letter to Archbishop Manning*, e.g. as to the False Decretals. See letter of 10 Feb. to Harper.

[4] Elecampane was a sweetmeat flavoured with the root of the plant of this name.

excuse for writing — and how could any thing I wrote influence any members of the Ecumenical Council?

Gladstone's project seems clear, simple, and effective — but I suppose it will be pulled into bits in Committee[1]

Ever Yrs affectly John H Newman

WEDNESDAY 3 MARCH 1869   Canon Walker went.

TO HENRY BEDFORD

The Oratory, March 3rd. 1869.

My dear Mr. Bedford,

Thank you for your Lecture — which I am very glad to have in a separate form and from you, though I take in the Month.[2]

I quite sympathise with what you say of Vesuvius — It is the most wonderful sight I ever saw. We had to mount an exceedingly steep cone of 1000 feet, of mere ashes, which gave way under our feet, while masses of lava were coming down upon us. There was no stopping possible. We ran down on the contrary so fast as almost to lose our footing, and we heard of friends, ladies, who some days before had lost their footing actually and rolled down. There was a cone within a cone — and the upper one was hollow, and down we went into the crater. The sulphurs, issuing from the inside, were of the most various and beautiful colours, and my feet and hands were blistered. Your description recalled all to me, as my memory has not been refreshed since the time, 36 years ago.

Repeating my thanks, I am Most sincerely yours John H. Newman.

Henry Bedford Esqre

TO FANNY MARGARET TAYLOR

The Oratory March 3/69

My dear Miss Taylor

I grieve indeed at your bereavement, and thank you for the kindness of your telling me of it. I said Mass for your intention, that is, for your mother's soul, this morning. I always say and feel, one cannot lose a mother twice — It is a loss which stands by itself. I never wrote any lines about my own mother — those you refer to were about my Grandmother who died at 92.[3]

[1] On 1 March Gladstone introduced his bill to disestablish the Irish Church, which eventually became law on 26 July.
[2] 'Vesuvius in Eruption,' the *Month*, (Feb. 1869), pp. 138–54. For Newman's visit to Vesuvius on 10 April 1833 see *Moz.* I, pp. 385–87.
[3] Miss Taylor's mother, who never became a Catholic, died at the end of Feb. Newman's grandmother Elizabeth Good Newman (1733–1825) is referred to in *Vv.* IV 'A Birthday Offering', p. 13. See note there.

God will sustain and comfort you, and you will be able to bless Him and thank Him, (as indeed you do, but) with joyfulness, for what at first causes you such sharp suffering

Yours most sincerely John H Newman

TO MRS HENRY WILBERFORCE

The Oratory March 3/69

My dear Mrs Wilberforce,

I hope to send you by this post the Dream [of Gerontius]. Thank Henry for his letter, which quite answers my purpose.[1]

As to my moving from home, recollect I am an old man — and a journey is a great ceremony to me. I should rejoice to see you and your two girls, whose faces are as distinctly before me as if it were not near six years since I saw them. Was not St Germain's the last place I saw them at?[2]

Ever Yrs affectly John H Newman of the Oratory

MONDAY 8 MARCH 1869   Fortescue called about this time

TO EMILY BOWLES

The Oratory March 8/69.

My dear Child,

I was wishing to know how you were, and your letter comes giving a bad account of yourself. I know when any thing like bronchitis once has come, it returns. I had a touch some years ago — and was affected season after season. I appear to have got free from it by means of acids given me for another reason, especially cider, of which I drink a great deal daily. I suppose it acts as a gargle.

I inclose a letter for Miss F.[3] Poor thing, I never meant to say a word unkind about her.

Though the Convent case never should have come forward, I don't think much harm will come of it. Protestants have been able to make very little capital out of it. There has been no great scandal. On the other hand I fear there is a good deal of petty tyranny and injustice in the small places and out of the way corners of the Church, and authorities may be roused to put them on a better status. I can't forget of course what has happened to *you*.[4] Coleridge,

---

[1] Wilberforce wrote on 1 March giving his testimony that it was always taken as certain that Whately was the author of *Letters on the Church by an Episcopalian*. See letter of 24 March to Hawkins.

[2] See diary for 22 and 23 July 1863.

[3] Geraldine Fitzgerald. Cf. letter of 28 July 1869 to Emily Bowles.

[4] Emily Bowles had been a nun under Mother Cornelia Connelly but had left her in 1856, and there had been a long dispute over financial matters, not yet settled. For the Convent case see letter of 23 Feb. to Collins.

in introducing me into his speech, was (whether he thought of it or not) reversing his father's act towards me in that very court. And, strange to say, while a Coleridge, instead of being judge was Counsel, Cockburne, instead of being (my) counsel, was judge.[1]

I have seen various pretty sets of Verses in the Month — but I cannot find one with the title you give. Your 'Mariners' is very good — why have you not gone on with it?[2]

Ever Yours affectly John H Newman

THURSDAY 11 MARCH 1869   a cold week   glass fell to near 50   snow

TO CHARLES ORMSTON EATON

The Oratory Bm March 11. 1869

My dear Sir

We have no holidays at Easter. In the beginning of Holy week there is a retreat — and the boys attend the ceremonies on Thursday and Friday.

However, we do not object to such of our boys, as are asked for by their parents, going home for Easter week. If therefore, after this explanation, you still desire your nephew to be sent to you, he shall leave this place for Tolethorpe on Holy Saturday. We shall expect him back punctually on Low Monday April 5[3].

He is a good boy and deserves an indulgence — and perhaps the change of air for a week will do him good. I will take care your directions are observed, and will not forget your wishes about next Wednesday.

Most truly Yours John H Newman

TUESDAY 16 MARCH 1869   snow lying, then melting

[1] Sir John Coleridge, Solicitor General, was defending Miss Saurin. At the conclusion of his final speech he said: 'The greatest of living Roman Catholics — a man of whom neither here nor elsewhere I can ever speak without respect and veneration — Dr. Newman — has said —
"Nature amid the spheres hath sway;
Ladies rule where hearts obey."
[last lines of "My Lady Nature and her Daughters", *Vv.* XI, p. 37]
But that like other propositions, cannot be converted simply. . . .' Report in the *Guardian*, (3 March 1869), p. 247. Sentence in the Achilli Trial was given on 31 Jan. 1853. Sir John Taylor Coleridge was one of the judges and Newman's counsel was Sir Alexander Cockburn. See Volume XV.
[2] Emily Bowles was contributing articles on 'Early English Mariners' to the *Month*. The second, in the March number, appears to have been the last.
[3] Eaton, who lived at Tolethorpe Hall near Stamford, was the uncle of Joseph John Talbot Lamb (1857-81), who was at the Oratory School 1867-75.

TO MISS HOLMES

The Oratory March 16/69

My dear Miss Holmes

I grieve to hear you are suffering so much from the climate. Should I hear of any situation, you shall be sure to know. Thank you for your letter

Yours affectly in Xt   John H Newman

THURSDAY 18 MARCH 1869   warm again the buds persist in coming out

TO HENRY WILBERFORCE

March 18

When I began Saints Day Services, I read my lecture in the *Chancel* after, I *think*, the second lesson — and standing at the reading desk. I don't think I ever read from the Altar.

I never sat when reading it. I was in surplice because the Lecture was in the *midst* of the morning service.

J H N

Thank you for your two letters, I am in the midst of School work and so only send the above —

Yrs affectly A St J.[1]

FRIDAY 19 MARCH 1869   Fr Law of London Oratory called
SUNDAY 21 MARCH   *Palm*   Ambrose took the high Mass
MONDAY 22 MARCH   Fr Suffield came in the afternoon for the boys' retreat   Ambrose went for retreat to Rednall

TO MRS SPARROW

The Oratory Bm March 24. 1869

My dear Mrs Sparrow

I am very glad to find what I have said is satisfactory to you; and be sure that we shall rejoice to find ourselves able in any way to do anything towards the mitigation of those severe trials which a good Providence has sent you, and which you are meeting with so much courage.

I write again, however, because you have not understood me as regards William [Sparrow].

He pays us at present £100 a year. Of this £40 may be considered the worth of his board and lodging. This we do not charge him if he will assist us in the

[1] Wilberforce was writing his article 'F. Newman's Oxford Parochial Sermons' for *D.R.*, (April 1869), pp. 309–30. He asked St John to have this detail verified, see p. 319. St John sent Newman's own answer.

school, which reduces what he has to pay us to £60. Of this £60 we give him (£10 a term, that is) £30 as a salary for his assisting us. £30 remains which he will have to pay us actually in money. He will pay us £30 instead of £100. He will pay this sum for tuition money, to prepare for his examinations.

Very sincerely Yours John H Newman

P.S.   I hope you will excuse my fault, if I expressed myself a little obscurely in my former letter.

TO W. J. COPELAND

The Oratory Bm March 24. 1869

My dear Copeland

I expect to sleep in London March 31, this day week. And it strikes me to ask you whether you are likely to be at home on Thursday, (next day.) If so I would run down to you, and sleep at Farnham that day.

As I am so very uncertain a fellow, you must not put yourself out of the way in the least for me. If you say Yes, you must give me instructions how to get to Bishopgate Street (is not there your station?) whether by flying or by burrowing, or omnibus modis.

I think we may talk over many things, if the meeting comes off

With my best Easter greetings, I am, Ever Yrs affly
John H Newman

TO EDWARD HAWKINS

The Oratory Bm March 24/69

My dear Provost

I knew your age though I did not know your birthday; and hope you will long enjoy the vigour of mind and body which your handwriting and your wellreasoned Sermon betoken.[1]

As to my own testimony about the 'Letters by an Episcopalian,' my un-interrupted memory since 1826 is to the effect that you at that date led me to ascribe them to Whately — that you thought them his yourself — that Dorn-

---

[1] Hawkins replied on 23 March to Newman's letter of 27 Feb.:
   'I recollect nothing in your letter which I could dislike to read; and am only glad of Dr Rogers's inquiries having given me the pleasure of seeing your handwriting again, and a renewal of your kind expressions towards me. Not that I needed any fresh assurance of your unaltered feelings of kindness towards your old friends.
   As your letter was written on my *80th birthday*, it might very well be that my memory was much impaired; but I do not know that it is . . . At all events I cannot recollect at all the *book* or its *authorship*. I certainly should not wish to ascribe to Whately a book which he had not himself acknowledged, and especially on a subject which he had afterwards written upon at much length. . . .'
   In a postscript Hawkins wrote 'I send you by Book Post a copy of my last sermon which, tho' [you] may not approve of it, may interest you.'

ford thought you thought so — that you were not in the secret — that you showed Whately passages from his writings or letters or publications to show him you had found it out, and that he did not clear up the matter. This I did not say to Dr Rogers.

Also, I wrote to Woodgate on Dr R's writing to me on the point, and he makes answer, 'It seems incredible that Hawkins should have forgotten the book, which made so much sensation at the time. It is more likely that he is misled by the title, etc etc. The general impression in Oxford was that the book was Whately's.' Again he writes 'I believe there is no doubt about the authorship of the book.'[1]

Henry Wilberforce writes to me, 'I am much surprised to hear that any question has been raised as to the Authorship of the "Letters &c" The book was published the year I began my residence at Oxford. . . . I often heard the book talked about; I never remember any question or discussion as to its authorship; but it was always assumed by all parties to be by Dr Whately . . . I always supposed it to be, like the "Historic Doubts," virtually his acknowledged work'[2]

Thank you for what you tell me about your family.

With my best remembrance to Mrs Hawkins, I am,

My dear Provost affectionately Yours John H Newman

The Revd The Provost of Oriel

THURSDAY 25 MARCH 1869 Fr Suffield went. I celebrated

TO EMILY BOWLES

The Oratory Bm Holy Thursday Mar. 25/69

My dear Child

What can I have said to you, which has made you think that I 'lost' the copy of the *Month*? No such thing — some of our Fathers are anxious to see it as soon as it comes out, and they take it out of my room without scruple. Then there is a hunt-the-slipper to find it; and thus I come off second best. However, it re-appears in my room in due time, and it has so on the present occasion. And therefore I shall with thanks send your copy back to you.

Your verses are very good, the epithets especially. My only criticism arises perhaps from an idiosyncrasy, I don't like whole lines which have no rhymes. I say 'whole' because in the 'Common Metre' the whole line is split into two, and what does not rhyme is the middle of the line.

[1] In a later letter, on 27 March, Woodgate wrote that he had met Hawkins on Paddington Station 'and told him he was wrong about the authorship, which he did not seem disposed to dispute.'
[2] *Historic Doubts relative to Napoleon Buonaparte*, London 1819.

The way I have heard the London Oratory matter is, that the Jesuits wish to plant themselves next door to the Oratory.[1]

I think Coleridge's articles exceedingly good — well written; clear, graceful, and well reasoned — and courteous to opponents, no slight praise. His 'Scandal' Article is excellent — so is the one on Oxenham.[2] As to Dr Meynell, he was very provoking to the esprit de corps of a Jesuit, though whether he deserved the imputation of being on the verge of theological error, I do not know.[3]

Your Mariner Article reads very well, and is interesting. The fault of the *Month* is that it is tethered. I suppose a Jesuit publication must be — but certainly it came out well and strongly against Ward.[4] I am sure it is doing good. I am too busy to back it as much as I should like to do.

When you next write to L. Simeon, insert the inclosed

Ever Yrs affly John H Newman

TO LOUISA SIMEON

The Oratory March 25/69

My dear Louisa Simeon

Can I be of use to you?[5]

Most sincerely Yours John H Newman

FRIDAY AND SATURDAY 26 AND 27 MARCH 1869   Fr Ambrose took the functions   very cold   cold wind

SUNDAY 28 MARCH   Easter Sunday.   All covered with snow in morning — wild wind and snow storm in afternoon.

MONDAY 29 MARCH   cold stormy weather

[1] According to a note by Emily Bowles about this letter, there was an attempt or wish of the Jesuits to buy some property in Brompton.

[2] This refers to 'Reflections on a late Scandal,' a review of E. S. Ffoulkes's *Letter to Archbishop Manning*, and 'The Doctrine of the Atonement,' a review of H. N. Oxenham's *The Catholic Doctrine of the Atonement*, the *Month*, (March 1869), pp. 201–16 and 253–65.

[3] The *Month, ibid*, pp. 300–4, began an article 'Recent Pamphlets on Ontologism,' by severely criticising C. Meynell's pamphlet *Padre Liberatore and the Ontologists*, London N.D. [1868], notably for defending a philosophy which 'cannot but incur grave suspicion' after the Roman condemnation of Sept. 1861. Matteo Liberatore was the Jesuit who began the revival of Thomism.

[4] See the *Month*, (Nov. 1868), p. 514 and (Feb. 1869), p. 183.

[5] See letter of 29 April to Louisa Simeon.

TO W. J. COPELAND

The Oratory March 29/69

My dear Copeland

I am glad you can receive me.

I am at the Langham, and have an engagement at an uncertain hour on Thursday, and don't know the spaces to be traversed or the duration of ⟨times taken up in⟩ the traversing.

Now I suppose, if I manage to get my business over, and start from the Langham at 4, I shall get to Bishopsgate station at 5 — and if I get there by 5, I shall, as you say, get to Bishops Stortford by 5.50. I hope no blunder or misfortune will hinder this

We have indeed a forlorn Easter in point of weather

Ever Yours affecty John H Newman

TUESDAY 30 MARCH 1869   Ambrose went to Brighton

WEDNESDAY 31 MARCH   went to London (to the Langham), called on Pickering, Miss Bathurst at Kensington, Rahn dentist, Lady Rogers, dined at Rogers'.

THURSDAY 1 APRIL   called on Miss Munro, Miss Bowles — went to Rahn – down to Copeland's at Farnham, where slept

FRIDAY 2 APRIL   came back in London in midday — went to Rahn

SATURDAY 3 APRIL   with Rahn all morning — called on Lumley — came back to Bm [Birmingham]   Ambrose returned.

MONDAY 5 APRIL   Henry went to London to bring back Miss Farrant.

TO CHARLES SCOTT STOKES

[April 1869?][1]

My dear Mr Stokes

I dare say you have thought I ought to have written to you before now about John.

We gave his vocation a long trial, and at last came to the conclusion that certainly he was not intended by St Philip for the Oratory.

However, we did not like to act upon this decision without another trial — and therefore we have kept him about us a longer time, employing him in the School, as you allowed us to do, and giving him various extra work, which came to hand.

I need not say we have found him clever and useful — and we have done what we could to push him on in his books. However, we are still more convinced that an Oratorian life is not his vocation — and we have thought it better to tell you this — and to name the beginning of the Long Vacation, i.e. July 20 next, as the termination of his residence here.

[1] John Scott Stokes appears to have left the Oratory this summer or perhaps a year later. See letter of 26 April 1869 to Monsell, and also letter of 20 Nov. 1871 to him.

Of course this does not mean that, if he can get employment in London sooner, we should think of standing in his way.

TO HENRY WILBERFORCE

The Oratory ⌜April 5. 1869⌝

My dear Henry

⌜I have just seen your affectionate Article in the Dublin, and thank you for it.[1] It tells me things which I had quite forgotten. As to the Chancel of St Mary's, I think I read on the Gospel side of it — perhaps that is what you mean by the 'right.'[2] Also, though I don't recollect the particular time to which you allude and cannot recollect therefore my words, what I *used* to say was 'I can't be wrong if Keble and Rogers agree, and I will not change till then.' I took Keble and Rogers as being men of such very different minds, ages, and histories.[3]

It makes one sad to read the record of the long past.⌝

Your allusions to the Provost remind me of a letter that I lately had from him, which you may like to see. I inclose it — let me have it back[4]

Ever Yrs affly John H Newman

WEDNESDAY 7 APRIL 1869   Penny came and Dr ⟨?⟩ Purcell
FRIDAY 9 APRIL   Henry returned with Miss Farrant

TO MESSRS WILLIAMS AND NORGATE

The Oratory Birmingham April 9. 1869

Gentlemen

I have sent your letter by this post to Messrs Burns and Oates, and from them you will receive my answer to your question[5]

Your obt Servant John H Newman

Messrs Williams and Norgate

[1] 'F. Newman's Oxford Parochial Sermons,' *DR*, (April 1869), pp. 309–30. It contains much valuable information about Newman's preaching at St Mary's.
[2] Cf. letter of 18 Mar. to Wilberforce, who said of the Saints' day services in the chancel of St Mary's, Oxford, 'The vicar took his place on a level with them [the congregation], in the seat occupied by the Dean in his cathedral, on the right hand of the entrance from the nave.' *D.R., loc. cit.*, p. 319.
[3] On pp. 327–8 Wilberforce described how Newman had in Oct. 1839 confided to him his doubts as to whether he should leave the Church of England and become a Catholic, and how he had added, 'One thing I am sure I can promise you, that I shall never take such a step unless Keble and Pusey agree with me that it is a duty.' Cf. *Apo.* pp. 114 and 162.
[4] See letter of 24 March to Hawkins.
[5] This referred to *Callista*, about which Burns and Oates wrote on 12 April, 'We are now selling the ninth thousand.' They then advised, 'We think you would do well to accept Baron Tauchnitz offer of £20 for the Edition he proposes to print. We return Messrs. Williams and Norgate's letter.'

SATURDAY 10 APRIL 1869   Penny went.   Dr ⟨?⟩ Purcell went   very mild
SUNDAY 11 APRIL   The masses etc for the Pope.   very mild — no fire till evening
MONDAY 12 APRIL   went out to Rednall for 4 weeks or tomorrow

TO LADY CHATTERTON

The Oratory April 12. 1869

My dear Lady Chatterton

I ought long before this to have thanked you for the present of your beautiful Poem.[1] I think it is the nicest thing you have written. It is so graceful and the lines so musical.

And there are such poetical ideas in it — as that of the face of the Knight's effigy being a sort of sundial.[2]

Thank you very much for it, and, with my kindest remembranccs to Mr Dering and your niece believe me to be,

Most sincerely Yours John H Newman of the Oratory

Lady Chatterton

TO MARGARET DUNN

The Oratory April 12. 1869

My dear Child

I am glad to hear so good an account of you — and thank you for writing. If all is well, I shall say Mass for you tomorrow morning.

Experience is a very trying thing — but it brings with it great rewards. It is the way God leads us to heaven.

May He bless you and ever protect you through times of trial and times of consolation. Humble yourself when he gives you comfort — be grateful when he gives you pain. All things turn out well to those who love Him. Beg Him to give you the abundance of His grace.

Believe me Yours affectly in Xt   John H Newman

Miss Margaret Dunn

[1] *Lady May. A Pastoral*, London 1869.
[2] 'And, as a child, she knew when it was time
  In summer morns for school, because the knight
  In armour lying, on the altar tomb,
  Then seemed to smile with joy, as if he felt
  The morning sun that slanted o'er his face,
  And warmed, as Nelly thought, his hands upraised
  In ceaseless prayer. At noon he was in shade,
  And then she thought he frowned; for stern and sad
  The marble features grew. . . .' Part II, p. 8.

TO THE EARL OF GAINSBOROUGH

The Oratory April 12. 1869

My dear Lord Gainsborough

I return by this post Lady Blanche's Tale.[1] There is no doubt she has a talent for writing. Her pages are full of varied incident, and of tokens of a vivid imagination.

But I do not think the Tale in such sort rises up to the standard of her evident capabilities as to lead me to recommend its publication.

I conceive it does not do justice to her literary powers. It is one of those essays which men of genius make as preludes and exercises rather than as real works.

Writing of whatever kind, whether in serious or light literature, is an acquirement. It is gained by practice. Nothing great was ever done without an apprenticeship, and, though I doubt not the authoress has shown her literary tastes from an early time, and dare say this is not her first writing, nevertheless I think she must persevere still in the cultivation of what is as really an art as painting or music.

I have written very freely; but I have thought both you and she would wish me to do so. If I am hypercritical, recollect I have not a large acquaintance with the literature of the day, and might be more indulgent if I did but know what a multitude of tales are published which cannot compare in ability and composition to Lady Blanche's.

However, I have done my best towards forming a judgment, and you must be kind enough to make my peace with her, if you think me severe.

I am, My dear Lord Gainsborough Sincerely Yours in Xt
John H Newman of the Oratory

The Earl of Gainsborough.

TO E. B. PUSEY

The Oratory Bm April 12. 1869

My dear Pusey

I was away from home when your first letter came, and now I say something about both at once.[2]

As to Haddan's book, I don't expect it will alter people's opinions.[3] It will

---

[1] Lady Blanche Noel, Lord Gainsborough's eldest daughter. See also letter of 7 Aug.

[2] Pusey's first letter, of 31 March (according to a note by Copeland), is not to be found, but its subject is clear from what Newman proceeds at once to say. His second letter was one of 8 April.

[3] A. W. Haddan, *Apostolical Succession in the Church of England*, London 1869, which defended Anglican Orders, was about to be published. Pusey had evidently described it. Haddan sent Newman a copy of it early in July.

be strong to those who already agree with him, and will not affect others. At least most people I talk with seem to feel that no certain conclusion can be come to on the subject. I think we all feel that the case is like a boat with water in it. There must be a leak somewhere. Some men say that there are ten leaks — others fasten upon this or that. If A says that there is a leak here, he does not mean to *deny* the leak which has arrested the attention of B. And if ten persons each have their own leak, they are not 9 against 1 in every case (as you say) but they only think each that there is more certainty about their own. In the Achilli matter for which I was tried the Times after it was over said to this effect — 'There is nothing distinctly proved against him ⟨Achilli⟩ — but in a dozen places and times there is a *case* against him. It is hardly possible that he can clear himself from all of them. If he has been every where so maligned, he is a most unlucky man.'[1] This is the kind of feeling we have about Anglican Orders — not that we can directly disprove them, but that they are utterly untrustworthy. I do not mean to say that no one actually undertakes to disprove them — but that is done as a supererogation — in every case the suspiciousness is left. And in my own mind I do not think this feeling will ever be got over — and then if it remained in any degree, comes the practice of the Church of always going by the safer side in the matter of the Sacraments. In this point of view even those theological opinions, which are not the more common ones, still tell. I think Hallier mentions four opinions on the subject of invalidity of Orders — and one is that heresy in the Consecrators invalidates.[2] This, I conceive, would be recognized as practically of weight in a case in which, like this, you must go by the safest side. At least *conditional* Ordination would be a necessity in consequence of this opinion, though it be not the prevalent one — but in my own opinion conditional Ordination would not be thought of. It is the common practice, and it is hard to say when it was not, to ordain without any condition Anglicans, and for this I think the theological opinion I have mentioned is a sufficient warrant. Every one is at liberty to hold, that heresy invalidates ordination (as I think was observed in the instance of the Egyptian Meletians,) and no one would acquit the consecrators of Parker of heresy — and therefore any of our consecrating Bishops may treat Anglican Orders as invalid. It is on this account that I have long felt the controversy on the point to be so dreary — nothing makes progress — nothing effects any thing, any more than the buckets of the Danaid. You speak of being called on to 'submit the question to those who have prejudged.' That's just the point, it is prejudged — that is, *already* judged — and controversy does nothing. We consider the onus probandi is with Anglicans — and, even if we cannot disprove that's no matter — for it is the necessity of the Anglicans to prove.

---

[1] The reference is to the leading article in *The Times*, (26 June 1852), p. 5. See postscript to letter of 25 June 1852 to Faber.

[2] François Hallier *De Sacris Electionibus et Ordinationibus ex antiquo et novo ecclesiae usu*, second edition, volume III, Rome 1740, pp. 155–80.

If I can find any thing about St C. [Catherine] of Genoa I will write to you. I do not at present. You recollect the collection of passages in Bellarmine, from Bede etc. on the subject of the pœna damni *without* the pœna sensus. Those writers were before the 39 Articles. Of course, on the general subject, you know the passages in St Francis de Sales. I cannot help thinking that Bail in his Meditations says that the Pœna sensus is reserved for great sinners, not for consistent Christians — but I cannot find the passage.[1]

As to the Canon I think with you that Cosin is wrong in what he says about the Council of Trent.[2] I believe that the inspiration of Scripture is not *de fide* with us, though it is the general opinion. Also, when the Council says that God is Auctor utriusque Testamenti, I think it means 'of both Covenants.'[3] Our views of the inspiration of Scripture are any how much weaker than those common in the Anglican Church and among Protestants. In fact one explanation, which has never been condemned, virtually denies it, saying that some books are inspired antecedently, other posteriorly; e.g. the 2nd book of Maccabees is the latter. What is meant by a book being inspired afterwards, except that it is exalted into the state of a canonical book? Indeed it has seemed to me that all we had to believe was that the word of Scripture was *true* — but then came the question *in what sense* true? and the answer to this is, not in the letter, but in the mind of the inspired writer. Thus if Moses did not *mean* to say there was a universal deluge, his saying so grammatically would go for nothing — just as our Lord's seeming in Matt. xix to sanction selfmutilation or pulling out the eye etc goes for nothing, since the Church *interprets* His sacred words, and therefore too the words of Moses. Nay further, the whole of Genesis might be a compilation, and therefore not a single word inspired, and the inspiration would lie with Moses, the compiler.

There is a work on the Canon written by the late Mgr Malou (?) Bishop of Bruges. He is, I believe, of the Roman School. I think he says that the *Jewish* Canon was not finished in our Lord's time.[4] We are not allowed to send books out of our Library, or I would send it to you. Also you know, I suppose, Vincenzi's ⟨?⟩ (book) about 1845 at Rome upon the Deutero-canonical books.[5] I think Malou ⟨(or is it Stapleton? yes, I think so)⟩ says that even now the Church might pronounce the book of Hermas canonical, if it were a book of the Apostolic age.[6]

---

[1] See letters of 30 April and 13 May to Pusey.

[2] In his letter of 8 April Pusey wrote: 'I am more puzzled what sort of Eirenicon to propose about the Deutero Canonical books than about most things. I suppose that Cosin is wrong in saying that the Council of Trent laid down that all of Holy Scripture was to be received with equal affection etc.' Cf. *Denzinger-Schönmetzer* 1501–04.

[3] Cf. *S.E.* pp. 33–6, and *John Henry Newman On the Inspiration of Scripture*, edited by J. Derek Holmes and Robert Murray, London 1967, pp. 57–60 and 129–31.

[4] J. B. Malou, *La Lecture de la Sainte Bible en langue vulgaire jugée d'après l'Écriture, la tradition et la saine raison*, Louvain 1846, II, pp. 20–62.

[5] Aloysius Vincent Vincenzi, *Sessio Quarta Concilii Tridentini vindicata seu Introductio in Scripturas Deutero-Canonicas Veteris Testamenti*, two volumes, Rome 1842–4.

[6] Thomas Stapleton, *Authoritatis Ecclesiasticae circa S. Scripturarum Approbationem . . . Defensio*, Antwerp 1592, II, iv and v.

I speak under correction — but I think from every part of our Scriptures we should hold ourselves at liberty to prove doctrine

The post is so close upon me, I have no time to read this over

Ever Yrs affly John H Newman

TUESDAY 13 APRIL 1869   engaged all the time with my book on Assent

TO JOHN HAYES

The Oratory, Birmingham. April 13, 1869.

My dear Sir,

I saw the article you speak of in the 'Times', and felt flattered by the passage which referred to myself.[1]

The writer must have alluded in the sentence which leads to your question, to my 'Lectures and Essays on University Subjects,' which is at present out of print. In that volume there are several papers on English and Latin composition.[2]

It is simply the fact that I have been obliged to take great pains with everything I have written, and I often write chapters over and over again, besides innumerable corrections and interlinear additions. I am not stating this as a merit, only that some persons write their best first, and I very seldom do. Those who are good speakers may be supposed to be able to write off what they want to say. I, who am not a good speaker, have to correct laboriously what I put on paper. I have heard that Archbishop Howley, who was an elegant writer, betrayed the labour by which he became so by his mode of speaking, which was most painful to hear from his hesitations and alterations — that is, he was correcting his composition as he went along.

However, I may truly say that I never have been in the practice since I was a boy of attempting to write well, or to form an elegant style. I think I never have written for writing sake; but my one and single desire and aim has been to do what is so difficult — viz. to express clearly and exactly my meaning; this has been the motive principle of all my corrections and re-writings. When I have read over a passage which I had written a few days before, I have found it so obscure to myself that I have either put it altogether aside or fiercely corrected it; but I don't get any better for practice. I am as much obliged to correct and re-write as I was thirty years ago.

---

[1] 'The English Language,' *The Times*, (10 April 1869), p. 4, included this passage: 'If we were asked to name the three greatest masters of English style in the generation which is just closing we should point to De Quincy, Macaulay, and Dr. Newman. Their styles are very different, but each is superb in its way, and we believe that they are all the result of severe and laborious training, though they give the impression of innate and effortless grace. Dr. Newman at all events, has related in an interesting and instructive essay the various steps of that mental discipline which has made him such a consummate master of his native tongue.'

[2] *Lectures and Essays on University Subjects*, London 1859, 'Elementary Studies,' pp. 116–86; *Idea*, pp. 331–80.

As to patterns for imitation, the only master of style I have ever had (which is strange considering the differences of the languages) is Cicero. I think I owe a great deal to him, and as far as I know to no one else. His great mastery of Latin is shown especially in his clearness.

Very faithfully yours, John H. Newman.

The Rev. John Hayes

P.S. Thank you for what you so kindly say of me in old times.[1]

TO THOMAS HARPER S.J.

Rednall April 14/69

My dear Fr Harper

Your letter with your cheque for £17. 11 has just reached me and I thank you for it — you shall have a formal receipt from Bm [Birmingham] — but I think you will like a prompt acknowledgement.[2] Thank you for your sermon

Yours affly in Xt   John H Newman

TO AMBROSE ST JOHN

⌐Rednall April 15/69⌐

My dear A

Will you engage the room as inclosed.

I went to meet you at the bottom of the hill. You have escaped a whirlwind of dust.

⌐I am sadly discouraged about my book. All or much that I have done which I thought done[3] I fear must be done again

I don't grudge the trouble but the time and the throwing good time after bad⌐

Ever Yrs affly J H N

SATURDAY 17 APRIL 1869   returned to Bm [Birmingham]

---

[1] Hayes spoke of 'the cherished remembrance of having listened to your teaching from the Pulpit of St Mary's in my old undergraduate days.' He was matriculated at Magdalen Hall on 2 July 1834, aged 19, and was Vicar of Coalbrookdale, Salop, 1854–78.
[2] See letter of 10 Feb. to Harper.
[3] [[Finished]] i.e. *G.A.*

TO B. M. PICKERING

The Oratory Birmingham April 17. 1869

Dear Sir

I have received the copy of the last edition of my Apollonius Tyanæus etc which you have sent me.

On looking through it, an idea has struck me, which may or may not approve itself to you; but any how I will mention it.

The two subjects in the Volume, a Life and an Essay, do not hang well together.

I have *another* Essay (on Ecclesiastical Miracles) prefixed to the Translation of Fleury: it runs to 216 pages octavo. Turned into Encycl. Metr. type and size it would run to 171 pages perhaps. The first, (Encycl. Metrop.) Essay (on Scripture Miracles) makes 42 pages. The two together (in Metrop. type and size) make (42 and 171) 213 pages, and, turned into the type and size of Messrs Rivingtons' recent Edition of my Parochial Sermons, would run perhaps to 310 pages, which is less than the first 6 volumes, but more than the last two. Of course my calculations are rough.

Now what do you say to leaving out Apollonius Tyan. and making a volume of the two Essays?

As to Apollon. Tyan. it might form one out of half a dozen Essays on Doctrinal and Historical subjects, for a second similar volume.[1]

Very truly Yours John H Newman

B. M. Pickering Esqr

MONDAY 19 APRIL 1869   went out to Rednall   not good weather at Rednall

TO B. M. PICKERING

Rednall, April 22/69

Dear Sir

I have received your letter at this place today. It leads me to write as follows.

Sermons are not to be viewed in the same light as controversial or argumentative works. They are instructions, and no one would think of using them, without inquiring who wrote them and when. There was a difficulty

---

[1] From *The Ecclesiastical History of M. L'Abbé Fleury . . . translated, with Notes, and An Essay on the Miracles of the Period*, first volume, Oxford 1842, the *Essay* was taken to form the second part of *Mir.* For 'Apollonius of Tyana' see *H.S.* I.

Newman made a Memorandum on 20 May 1869: 'I sent to Mr John Rivington on May 2. 1869 a letter of Mr F. Rivington's of the date of March ⟨?⟩ 1857 in which he, on his own part and Mr Parker's of Oxford gave me the copyright of my Essay on Ecclesiastical Miracles in return for my letting the Rivingtons print small editions of Parochial Sermons volumes 2 and 5 In the same letter Mr F. Rivington declined to take a new edition of my Church of the Fathers.'

then in republishing my Parochial Sermons in this point, that I, a Catholic, could not print Anglican Sermons, and Anglicans could not be expected to read them, if corrected by me, a Catholic.

This difficulty does not hold as regards my Essay of Miracles. An argument is an argument all the world over. It would be no good, and I have no wish, to alter any intellectual deduction in it, though it tells against Catholics. If it did tell, it would not alter the fact to leave it out. I neither care then nor propose to alter the *substance* of a single sentence in my Essay. What I *should* wish to alter is the *wording*. I could not use the word 'Popish', or speak in a disrespectful tone of what I believe to be a divine system. Again, I might be tempted by the *addition* of a few words here and there, to explain and defend what still I did not withdraw from the original adverse criticism, whatever it was.

For instance, I have noticed that certain Scripture miracles are 'unworthy apparently of a divine origin,' but I add 'they are supported by the rest, as a few out of a number.' In like manner, after passages in which I mention some ecclesiastical miracles which are 'unworthy of a Divine Author,' I might be led to add 'but no Catholic is bound to believe them.'

You will find too that my other Essay on Miracles, written in 1842-3 when I was still an Anglican, modifies materially the conclusions of my first Essay — so that it would not much matter whether I altered Essay 1st or no, except for the sake of really improving it.

The only real alteration that it strikes me that I should be obliged to make, would be in one or two places, where I say that the Evil Spirit can work miracles — for Catholics do not allow this — but this, while it is a principle with Catholics does not impinge upon any Anglican principle. My difficulty would be of a literary kind here — viz how to alter it without damaging the composition and its logical run.

As to its taking the same *look* externally as the new Edition of my Sermons, it is so convenient a size and so handsome a type, that I am likely to use it for my acknowledged Catholic works. And it would be easy by a few words in a Preface to say distinctly that I had made alterations in the Essay. Nor, I repeat, do I think any one would care, if I had — because no one expects to agree with every thing a controversial argument contains, but men do like to agree point by point with what they use in religious teaching or for religious edification.

I do not think then the sale of the volume would be hurt by such alterations as I have suggested — on the other hand I really cannot think that the Life of Apollonius published with the first Essay would sell.

At the same time, in suggesting your publishing two Essays instead of one, I know I am adding considerably to your risk — and, if you can think of any way in which I could meet this, I should like you to tell me

Very truly Yours John H Newman

B. M. Pickering Esqr

SATURDAY 24 APRIL 1869   returned to Bm [Birmingham]
MONDAY 26 APRIL went out to Rednall

TO WILLIAM MONSELL

Rednall April 26/69

My dear Monsell

Lord Granville is to be applied to in behalf of one of our young Masters, John Stokes, for a writership at Ceylon. When he applied to me to write to you, I said that you had nothing to do with the appointments.

However, I write this that you may know, in case it is in any way brought before you, that Stokes is a very clever fellow, and I think would be liked. I am told there is no competitive examination — and so I suppose there will be plenty of Candidates.

While I write, let me remind you, what is not necessary perhaps, that, if you have a convenient opportunity, it would be a great kindness if you asked Lord Dunraven about his subscription (£100) to the Oxford Fund; — the question the circular asked him was, Would he have his money back? if not, was it to be kept for an Oxford Oratory, or for a Mission Church there?

Our Bishop says you have been talking to him about a projected work of mine on the Principles of Faith. By the way the Bishop spoke of it, I think he fancies it is on the question of the Infallibility of the Pope, or on the powers of a General Council etc etc. My purpose, if I ever fulfilled it, is of quite a different kind. It is on a metaphysical question — and for that reason there is a chance of my never finishing it — certainly not soon, for it requires more metaphysical and logical reading than I have. However, I mention the subject, to ask you to drop all mention of it. People are so jealous about me, that I could fancy myself quite bothered and hampered with external interference, tho' I am doing that which any one in the Church has a right to do[1]

Ever Yrs affly John H Newman

[1] A memorandum by Neville explains this paragraph:

'The Oratory, Birmingham. Thursday night April 22, 1869
Fr Ambrose St John came to me to-night to say that as I am going over to Rednall he would like me to tell the Father what the Bishop said to him to-day when he met the Bishop by accident and had to walk a short way with him.
First the Bishop asked after the Father — He said "Is Dr Newman writing anything?"
Fr Ambrose answered "Oh he is always writing something."
Then the Bishop said "Mr Monsell tells me that Dr Newman is writing a book." ⟨This is what afterwards became the Grammar of Assent⟩
To which Fr Ambrose said "He always has something or other in hand."
Next the Bishop said "Ah Mr Monsell told me that he is writing a book, a book about Faith or on the principles of Faith and I said to Mr Monsell "I think it is very unlikely ⟨?⟩ that Dr Newman would be writing anything (or ⟨?⟩ publish) anything (Fr Ambrose thinks the Bishop added 'on such a subject') without the Holy Father requesting him to do so, but, if the Holy Father did do so, I am sure that he (Dr Newman) would do it at once."
Fr Ambrose's impression is that the Bishop knew that he (Fr Ambrose) did not intend to let out what the Father may be about, and that the Bishop intended that he (Fr Ambrose) should tell the Father that it was ticklish ground and he is sure that his expression about his doubt about the Father writing was intended as a feeler.

Not sent.[1]   Rednall, Bromsgrove April 29. 1869

My dear Fr Coleridge

I do not like to have so kindly confidential a letter from you, without answering it as confidentially — but I reflect, what is anything I can say worth? I have hardly ever seen the Contemporary, and don't know how things go in the periodical world, and cannot presume to give advice. A theological review would be a great gain — whether it would pay is another matter — one step towards its paying would be to have known names to the Articles. The Contemporary has names has it not? Would your people like this?

For myself, I should have no difficulty in putting my name, *if* I wrote an article, but I have not any great expectation of writing much more. I am very well, but am overset, if I work many hours running, and cannot reckon on myself. Besides, it is almost a sacred duty to me to go through my letters and papers — there is much perhaps from others which ought to be burned, much which for the sake of others ought to be put into order. I used to say, This

Fr Ambrose added in pencil to my paper as follows:- On thinking over the conversation I am not sure the Bishop did not mean to express, "Well, if he is writing it must be because the Holy Father has desired him". This was no doubt the idea he wished me to carry away "I know what Newman is about or will be about better than you (Monsell) do". . . .
Note. I knew that the Father was desirous that it should not get about that he was engaged upon a book for he said that perhaps when the work had advanced a great way it might turn out that he had but found a mare's nest, and therefore that it would never appear, besides which he thought of having only five hundred copies at the very most printed for he said that as it would be a work not of general interest he did not like that expectations should be raised which would be sure to be disappointed.
As to what the Bishop had said I considered that the Bishop meant to intimate to the Father in an inoffensive way that the Father ought to shut up altogether and not bring himself before the public at all in any way — that for him to be writing a book was as treading on dangerous ground for I knew how persons having influence and about those having influence spoke of the Father, of the prospect of his some day finding himself upon the Index, of their close watch upon him, and of their boasting that if he continued to write they would sooner or later have the opportunity to get him on the Index, saying that a person could hardly go on writing for a length of time without at last affording some opportunity which could be laid hold of for bringing the Index to bear upon him.
Calling all the above and much else to my mind as I went to Rednall I thought it not un-likely, that there was the chance, that the Father might take the Bishop's words very gravely and discontinue his work. When then as happened I met the Father going to the Post and he asked me to turn back with him saying that he was taking some specimen pages for the printer I said nothing about the Bishop, thinking that if a portion were once out of the Father's hands he might consider his publishing or not beyond any body's interference. However, afterwards, when I told him about the Bishop, he laughed at my thinking that what the Bishop said could refer to such a work as he was then doing, but that the Bishop was off the scent, that he must be supposing him to be engaged upon something connected with the Temporal Power or the Infallibility of the Pope and then the Father reminded me of what was said about the time of the coming out to his Letter to Dr Pusey, and of the ominous sort of warnings and sayings in case he should venture to write a second letter relating to the Eirenicon.
                                              Wm. P. Neville'
Newman wrote on this memorandum 'shown to Monsell on occasion of his letter of May 1/71' See letter of 21 April 1871 to Monsell.
    [1] The letter Newman actually sent was that of 2 May. Coleridge's confidential letter is not to be found.

must be done before I am 60, and then I shall be all ready — now I say that it must be done before I am 70.

Now in great confidence I must be frank with you in answer to your confidence — and I wish you to *burn* what I am going to write.

I have ever received great favours from the Jesuits, and I have very good friends among them, and, as far as I know, and as I believe, no enemies. But, with many others, with most other thinking men, I dread their unmitigated action on the Church. Every religious body is good in its place; every religious body is dangerous, if it aims to engross the whole Church. The Jesuits, the Dominicans, the Franciscans, the secular Priesthood, the Colleges of a University, the Theological Faculties, are so many distinct and independent influences modifying each other, subserving the whole Church. But 'if the whole body is the eye, where is the hearing and smelling?'[1] Now from their wonderful system, and from their natural and commendable esprit de corps, the Jesuits tend (if I may use an undignified metaphor) to swamp the Church.

There is One that is wiser than we are, and has His times and seasons for all things. All of us may securely leave it to Him, to provide against any danger to the Church from her servants as well as her adversaries. He has once interfered and thrown you back; and, if you get too powerful, He will do so a second time.

However, that does not hinder it being our duty, each in his place, to act as he thinks God would wish him for the welfare of His Church — and the more a man feels the greatness of the services, which the Society has rendered to her, the more, from *gratitude* to it, will he fear for them such an increase of power as may be dangerous to them, because dangerous to her.

I cannot regard unmoved their present position. They are said to have the Pope in their hands — and the Civiltà seems to me, as far as I hear about it, to be hurrying on measures which I cannot contemplate without pain. Of course God will, as I have said, provide. Men cannot, not even the Pope, go further than He wills. He has laid down land marks from the beginning, which no one can pass. It may be His blessed will that the progress of religion should be checked for a time by bad counsel — it may be His will that the Church should only consist of the poorer and uneducated classes, and that, as in the beginning, the talent and learning and wisdom of the world should be excluded from the divine election. But I feel strongly that the action of men of influence at Rome at this time is doing all it can to bring this about.

Well, but one must act according to one's light. If a theological review was set up in England under the auspices of your Fathers, it would be an enormous improvement, as a theological Review on Ward's Dublin. In truth the two could not be mentioned in one breath. But if it aimed at inculcating as necessary to be believed what is not necessary, circumscribing the allowable liberty of the mind, at making certain political views as virtually de fide, at tying down Catholic action to what is obsolete and effete, and thereby at unsettling

[1] 1 *Cor.* 12:17.

the faith of Catholic youth and talent, and making a dreadful breach between society and religion, I could do nothing else but fold my hands and beg God to end the tyranny, and look for Him to do so.

I have never written or spoken like this to any other being — not even to any of my friends at the Oratory. I could not comfortably answer your question without bringing it all out. Pray burn it directly

Yours affectly John H Newman

TO LOUISA SIMEON

Rednall Bromsgrove April 29. 1869

My dear Louisa Simeon

I can fancy it was an effort to you to write your letter, and was not at all surprised that you delayed it.

For myself, though I asked you to write, and don't delay my answer, yet I am in a difficulty too, and my difficulty is that I have ever found it so delicate a matter to give advice without knowing well what I am about. I know I may do as much harm as good, or more, by rash advice, I mean by advising on general principles and not on the particular case.

I think you are right in saying that your difficulties arise from want of knowledge. It often strikes me how very different my own generation is from the present. We were gradually brought into the Church — we fought our way — all difficulties of whatever kind met us — were examined and overcome — and we became Catholics as the last step of a long course, with little difficulty because it was only the last difficulty of a series. But you find yourself a Catholic suddenly, so to say, just as you are plunging into a world of opinion and into a conflict of intellectual elements all new to you. You have no *will* to disbelieve, but that reason, the gift of God, which brought *us* into the Church, is yours as well as ours, and claims to have part in the work of grace, and it is according to God's ordinary Providence that it should have part. I have no doubt your case is not singular, though you are exposed to a trial from external circumstances greater than that of others, and though I do not speak from experience of others, for I am more frequently consulted by those who are approaching the Church than by those whose reason is disturbed in it.[1]

I wonder how far you know what is called Tractarianism — and, if you don't, whether a course of Tractarianism, so to say, would do you good. Here I cannot refer to books — but, when I get to Bm [Birmingham] I will look out some. Let me ask you a question, have you ever looked into my 'Parochial and Plain Sermons'? I am sorry to hear you are not well

Yours affectly John H Newman

[1] Sir John Simeon's house in London was a meeting place for literary and political society. His many friends included Tennyson, Jowett and Leslie Stephen. See also letter of 4 July to Emily Bowles.

Friday (I have just got your letter)[1]

My dear Miss Holmes

I am disengaged on Sunday from 10 to 2 — and from 4 to 5. Send up to me by the Porter and I will come to you at any time within those hours.

Did I come in tomorrow, I should have to attend a School examination — so it would be no gain

Ever Yours affectly John H Newman

TO E. B. PUSEY

Rednall April 30/69

My dear Pusey,

I fear Bellarmine's chapter is not to your purpose, or you would recollect it. It is the chapter in which he quotes the passages from St Bede and from the visions of various Saints testifying to the state of souls without any pœna sensus in some beautiful place, in prato quodam amoeno etc. I have quoted some of Bede's words in my Verses upon what I think I call 'refrigerium'.[2]

I will look when I go into Bm [Birmingham] for Sunday — but I don't think I can be mistaken, or you would know the chapter.

Also, I will try to find the passage in Bail in which (if my memory is not very wrong) he speaks of the pœna damni as the sole punishment of those who have lived a good life without mortal sin[3]

Ever Yours affectionately John H Newman

SATURDAY 1 MAY 1869   returned to Bm [Birmingham]

TO HENRY JAMES COLERIDGE

The Oratory May 2/69

My dear Fr Coleridge

Thank you for the kindness of your confidential letter; but I reflect, what can my opinion be worth?[4] I have hardly ever seen the Contemporary — and don't know how things go on the periodical world. A theological review would be a great gain — whether it would pay is another matter. Thirty years ago,

---

[1] On the autograph Miss Holmes has added in pencil 'April 30? 1869,' and also her own address 'at John Powell's Esqr Hagley Rd,' i.e. near the Birmingham Oratory.
[2] Vv., p. 210, 'Waiting for the Morning.' See letter of 12 April.
[3] See letter of 13 May to Pusey, when Newman sent the promised quotations.
[4] See at 29 April for the first draft of this letter.

the British Critic, a quarterly, selling 1200, did not pay. The Christian Remembrancer has lately stopped, a first rate Review in its way. A Catholic Review would not be likely to sell better than these Anglican ones.

But the Jesuits could supply an abundance of articles, and without being paid for them — and a wealthy society could bear a pecuniary loss. I have by me a calculation of a printer, many years back, which makes the printing of a Quarterly with paper £300 a year.

Names would increase the interest of the publication greatly.

There is no chance of my taking part in such a publication. I have so much to do already — and, though I am very well, I am soon overset by a spell of reading or writing.

I have no sympathy with an intolerant English Civiltà.

Ever Yours most sincerely John H Newman

TO BARTHOLOMEW WOODLOCK

The Oratory May 2. 1869

My dear Dr Woodlock

I am very glad to hear you propose to have a fresh Number of the Atlantis.

It is very difficult to me to promise any thing, tho' I should like to have an hand in the work.

Would you admit a very *dry short* article on the dispositions of the Calendar in the Proprium de Tempore?[1]

Most sincrely Yrs John H Newman

P.S. Some friend has sent me a clever publication 'The Carlow College Magazine.' I do not know to whom I am indebted.

MONDAY 3 MAY 1869   went out to Rednall
THURSDAY 6 MAY   Ascension Day   an inclement May
SATURDAY 8 MAY   went back to the Oy [Oratory] for good

TO SIR JOHN SIMEON

The Oratory May 8/69

My dear Sir John,

Thank you for the sight of your curious inclosure, which I return.[2] Persons like myself, shut out from the world, are apt to make great mistakes, when they attempt to interpret the words and deeds of those who live in it,

---

[1] Volume IV of the *Atlantis* appeared in 1863. After this, there was one more number, that of Feb. 1870, in which the first article was Newman's 'The Ordo de Tempore,' reprinted in *T.T.* pp. 383–402.

[2] Sir John Simeon wrote on 6 May: 'My friend Arthur Russell has given me a copy of a very interesting note of a conversation sent him by his brother Odo (our quasi minister at Rome) between himself and Cardinal Antonelli.

and I have too much experience of my own failures, when I have attempted to do so, not to feel that it is rash in me to play the interpreter of so great a diplomatist as the Cardinal, especially as I never saw him.

My notion is that he thinks the Council a great blunder — that things go on very well when a Pope and Secretary of State and a few others settle matters — but who can say what trouble a host of Yankee, French, Spanish, German, bishops well may give — 'We may have put our foot into it, and be

I think you would like to see it, and I should much like to have your opinion upon it. It seems to me as if the wily Roman had been playing with the ignorance of the Protestant, and yet it is strange that he should have committed himself in such a definite manner. . . .
What can be the meaning of it all? Can it be that they are going to venture on a theological coup d' état . . .'
In a postscript Simeon asked 'What is the meaning of Antonelli's sneers at the Jesuits' and wondered if there was a split between those responsible for the *Civiltà Cattolica* and the French Jesuits.
Neville made a copy of Odo Russell's note of a conversation:
'Copy of Conversation between Odo Russell and Cardinal Antonelli
Rome April 23. 69 Confidential
I asked Cardinal Antonelli and he said: "there is no necessity for the Council to proclaim a new dogma since the Infallibility of the Pope ex Cathedra has always been a dogma with us sincere Catholics"
I. Your Eminence means of course that the Holy Ghost presides over the decisions of Councils and that the Pope in Council becomes thereby infallible in the decisions he sanctions?
Ant. Not exactly, for the Pope stands according to our Catholic faith *above* Councils.
I. Pray explain — you told me the Bishops have the right of proposing measures — Well, if the Council passed a new law unanimously could the Pope object and decline to sanction it?
Ant. Of course, because like your Queen in Parliament the Pope has a Veto, that is the Pope's decision over-rules even the unanimous decision of Bishops in Council.
I. Then what is the use of the Council?
Ant. To discuss and reform questions of discipline, fasting meagre, mixed marriages etc. The Council has nothing to do with articles of faith or dogmatic questions — those the Pope settles and proclaims without the Council, according to his conscience which in those matters, has always been infallible.
I. The Civilta Cat. announces the proclamation of two new Dogmas — The infallibility of the Pope and the Assumption of the Virgin — they are then in the wrong?
Ant. The Jesuits are foolish and write about things we none of us can know! I don't know, they don't know what the Pope may be inspired to declare in the Council!
I. But assuming the Pope did proclaim a Dogma the Bishops objected to — what then?
Ant. That is impossible, because Articles of Faith are not matters of discussion. They come from God and cannot be subjects of discussion for a Parliamentary Assembly. The Council is a Parliament very like yours in England, for the discussion and reform of disciplinary questions. But Articles of Faith cannot be questioned or discussed. They come from God to the Pope, who himself has no choice: he must make the Will of God known to the Church as he is His Vicar. This has been since Peter the Apostle, *We* have always believed it because it is true and so it is foolish of the Jesuits to call an old Article of Faith, a *new* Dogma. They are mistaken!
I. May I then inform my Government that you disavow the Jesuits?
Ant. Certainly I do, and I have told all your colleagues so, and have sent the editors of the Civilta Cat. word that they write nonsense.
I. May I say that the Press is wrong and that the so-called new Dogma of the personal infallibility will not be submitted to the Council?
Ant. Certainly and it stands to reason — I ask you yourself — How could a Divine truth be submitted for discussion to men? The Pope need not ask the Council whether he is infallible since God has made him so. "Les Jesuites ecrivent des betises" when they propose to re-assert that which has always existed.
The tone in which the Cardinal and others speak leads me to think that in the opening ceremony of the Council the *Infallibility* will be laid down and asserted as a *fait accompli* and the Bishops will find themselves assenting to it by their sole presence in Rome.
Do you see what I mean?'
Odo Russell sent another account of this conversation to Lord Clarendon at the Foreign Office, on 1 May. See *The Roman Question Extracts from the despatches of Odo Russell from Rome 1858–1870*, edited by Noel Blakiston, London 1962, pp. 362–3.

unable to get it out. Therefore our great consolation is, that they are really worth nothing at all, and are an anachronism. All is settled already, and, if we want any thing new, all can be settled without them — nor do we wish them to pass this as a principle or dogma. It is already the fact and the truth, without a Council to settle it. It will be a great mistake and it is just the mistake of those Jesuits, who are notorious for maladresse, to be putting difficult things forward, rubbing them into people's faces, abusing every one who differs from them, when they should be simply and quietly *acted* on. This is not the day for new dogmas, but for practical work — but, since one must not speak disrespectful about any thing so sacred as dogma, it is best to say (as one can say) that it is an *old* dogma, ever held, and thus one can get the question of dogma out of the way — laudatur et alget.[1]

And then comes this Englishman with his questionings, having been primed for the purpose, and knowing nothing at all about the matter — into whose eyes it is very easy to throw dust, or in the words of Scripture "to answer according to his folly"[3]

I assure you the *unreal* answers which the Cardinal makes to his questioner, do seem to me like so much dust or chaff — but perhaps I have no right so lightly to estimate the utterances of a grave authority.

E.g. it is quite true, and Gallicans acknowledge it that without the Pope's confirmation the doctrinal decree of an Ecumenical Council does not stand — it is not Ecumenical without the Pope, but it does not *therefore* follow that the Council is confined to matters of discipline and cannot define doctrine *with* the Pope.

'Articles of faith not matters of discussion' — no, not when they *are* articles of faith — but *before* they are defined, they are discussed in two ways — 1. the testimony of the Bishops is asked and the authoritative declarations of the Fathers and former times. 2. the expedience of defining is discussed.

Of course the Jesuit party wish to pass the Pope's infallibility by some indirect act — but I do not think it will be successful. What has more chance is a condemnation of Gallicanism — but to this the French will make great opposition. There ever has been much that should not be in Councils — but we believe that, as a prophet says in Scriptures 'I cannot go beyond the word of the Lord,'[3] though he wished to do so, so it is with all the intemperate wishes of the members of Synodal bodies.

I believe many Jesuits are against the Civiltà, and its special privileges — but I fear that they may any moment be called to order.

What I have been saying pretty much agrees with your letter, if I understand you

Ever Yours affectly John H Newman

Sir John Simeon Bart M P

[1] Juvenal, *Satires*, I, 24.
[2] *Proverbs*, 26:4.
[3] Balaam, see *Numbers*, 22:18.

P.S. Your boy's fault is, as you say, want of power of application. But Fr St John hopes he may say that he is improving. He is very quick, and can do things very well, when he rouses himself.[1] For myself, thank you, as far as symptoms go, I am distinctly better.

I do not see how any one can doubt, looking at the matter dispassionately, that the Church now (as ever) in communion with Rome is the Church set up by the Apostles. Some persons believe it to be the Church *because* it is in communion — this proposition, that Rome is the centre of unity, I believe as a *doctrine*, taught by the Church, and indisputable — but, while I quite allow another to be brought into the Church on the ground that union with Rome is the logical differentia of the Church, I was not so brought myself but by the visible identity of the ancient Church and the present Roman communion. In the same way that I hold the See of Rome to be the centre of unity on the word of the Church, so I should believe that See infallible, if the Church so determined, and I believe a General Council is to be her Voice in determining — and I don't believe at all that a General Council can decree any thing which the Divine Head of the Church does not will to be decreed. I say this in consequence of one sentence of your letter.[2]

TO BARTHOLOMEW WOODLOCK

The Oratory Bm May 10. 1869

My dear Dr Woodlock

Thank you for your more than kind letter. I am glad you have so many promises. I hope Professor Sullivan will give you one. It was to him I surrendered the Editorship — has he given it up? His articles are always so able, and his name stands so high, that you must not let him escape you.[3]

Yours most sincerely in Xt   John H Newman of the Oratory

The Very Revd Mgr Woodlock

[1] Simeon wrote of his son Stephen at the Oratory School, 'He is sharp but none of my boys will ever do any thing. Idleness and general goodfornothingness does not skip a generation. Gout in a family is much less objectionable.'

[2] Simeon wrote 'Of course one believes that God is with the Church, and will not allow her to fall into error, but now the question arises what is the Church, and where is her voice to be found, whether as we used to be taught in a General Council, presided over by the Pope . . .'

[3] The final 1870 number of the *Atlantis* did not contain a contribution from W. K. Sullivan.

TO W. J. COPELAND

The Oratory Bm May 11. 1869

My dear Copeland

I now send you two sheets. There is a very curious false print 'original' for 'virginal —' we shall be said, I suppose, to be altering the text, if we set it right — yet 'original' is nonsense — and, if we altered 'immaculate' into 'miraculous,' I suppose we ought to be allowed to alter this.[1]

My note on 'Rationalism' was published in 1865. Tate's charge, which I have not seen, I suppose was an *answer* to it.[2]

The Rivingtons have asked for the names of the Authors of the Tracts. I have sent them the list, as far as I can recollect it, but have advised them to consult you and others.

Harrison will assist you to a certain point. In 1836 Christmas he accused me of Socinianizing, for (what I think afterwards was incorporated in my Prophetical Office) some remarks on the Apostles' Creed. After that I saw very little of him, but Pusey and Gladstone did.[3]

Mrs Wootten felt Mr Walsh's death very much — and at the time she was very ill herself — and has made us anxious about her strength.[4]

How very trying your brother's and sister's continued illness is — Caswall lately saw him and gave me an account of him

Ever Yours affectly John H Newman

TO MARIANNE FRANCES BOWDEN

The Oy May 13/69

My dear Child,

I don't know whether it is any use sending you the inclosed — I do so on

---

[1] 'O my brethren, make much of your virginal state, if you possess it, and be careful not to lose it.' *S.D.* p. 24. For the other change, in *P.S.* II, p. 142 see Preface to *S.D.* p. viii.

[2] Newman had just sent Copeland the new edition of *Apo.* He wrote on 4 May, 'I have read, you may be sure with what interest, your chapter on Liberalism and need scarcely say how strongly I sympathize with you in your distinct and telling refusal to whitewash the Liberals of 1845. — The Bishop of London's [A.C. Tait] Charge of Decr 1867, in its allusion to P's [Pusey] republication of Number 90 fully bears you out in all that you say.' See *Apo.* pp. 292–3. Tait's Charge was in 1866. He had been one of the four tutors who protested against *Tract XC*, and he now quoted from the XXXIX Articles as restricting Catholicism in the Church of England. This showed that his position had never altered. See R.T. Davidson and William Benham, *The Life of Archibald Campbell Tait*, London 1891, I, pp. 482–3. Copeland wondered whether A. P. Stanley's plea to Newman to modify his statement in *Apo.* had been made before or after Tait's Charge. See letter of 23 April 1865 to T. Arnold.

[3] Copeland hoped to visit Benjamin Harrison who would be able to give him details about the early history of the Oxford Movement. His disagreement with Newman was over the controversy with Abbé Jager, part of which was incorporated in *V.M.* I.

[4] Henry Walsh, the Oxford lawyer whom Newman first met in 1824, and who was a close friend of Mrs Wootten, had died.

the chance. Tell me something about Papa, Mary [Law], Katie [Bowden], and all of you

Love to Fan and Chatty [Bowden]. Ever Yrs affly John H Newman

TO ALEXANDER GOSS, BISHOP OF LIVERPOOL

May 13/69

Rt Revd Dr Goss

My dear Lord

I begin my answer to your Lordship's letter by acknowledging with much gratitude the extraordinary honour which you do me in the request you make of me, a mark of your consideration which is only in harmony with other special favours you have before shown me, and if I ask your leave to decline it, be sure it is not from any want of appreciation of your kind thoughts of me. If I could accept it you may be quite sure I would.[1] In truth your subject is not one to which I am equal either by experience or by study. Years ago I wrote on the denominational system for the upper classes when I was in Ireland — but with great difficulty — not as doubting its abstract desireableness, but as being unacquainted practically with the bearings of the question there and then. In consequence my lectures, as delivered disappointed people and made no impression. But the case of the poorer classes I have never considered and had no means of studying — and I really should not know how to write upon them.

And my existing engagements of various kinds are more than I can do justice to, since of course I am not so strong as I was — and to undertake any work in addition to them would be simply to abuse the kind confidence which has led you to wish to put it on me

These considerations I am sure will plead my forgiveness with you in making what otherwise would be an ungracious response to so flattering a proposal as you make me — and with that persuasion I subscribe myself

J H N

[1] Goss wrote on 12 May: 'Our Bishops when in London, decided to issue pastorals on the Feast of the Sacred Heart, in favour of denominational Education. . . . The object of my letter is to ask you if you will be good enough to write me such Pastoral. *You* can; *I* cannot. The subject is great and wants a masterly hand.'

Goss went on to say how much he regretted that Newman was not in Rome preparing for the Council, and how in a sermon he had 'stigmatized as an insult offered to the Catholic hierarchy of the world, the supposition that they were, without adequate examination, to proclaim the dogma of Papal Infallibility by acclamation . . .' Goss also said, 'Our press is in the hands of incompetent bigots, and if any man dares to speak honestly upon open questions he is denounced to Rome as a Gallican. No body dares to tell the Pope the truth.'

TO E. B. PUSEY

The Oy Bm May 13. 1869

My dear Pusey

It is too late to answer you now, even if I had any thing to say to the point. We have not got in the Library the 5th September Volume of the Bollandists — so I could not refer. The Bishop of Belley's account of St F's [Francis of Sales] conversations I fancied as good authority as Boswell's of Johnson's. I have written out the passages in Bellarmine — but of course you have observed them[1]

Ever Yrs affly John H Newman

P.S.   I have not heard from any quarter of any religious likely to write against you.[2] I think, if any did, it would be from the feeling, as I have said before, that, tho' you wished union, you wished to keep Anglicans in the Anglican Church more — and that your Irenicon had an arrière pensée.

I have just found this passage in the Life of Mother Margaret just published, showing the *animus* they impute to you.

'Many probably will be surprised to learn that she was far from liking the extravagant phraseology adopted in some books of devotion (about the Blessed Virgin). She intensely admired Dr Newman's celebrated "Letter", and was only deterred by timidity from writing him her thanks; but, when, as it was read aloud to her, the reader came to that page in which he enumerates,

---

[1] Pusey was searching for passages about Purgatory. For St Francis of Sales he had only found references to the Bishop of Belley's *Esprit de St François de Sales*. He also wanted passages from St Bernard mentioned at p. 127 of the Bollandist volume. Newman enclosed the passages he had promised in his letter of 30 April:

'Bellarmine de Purgator. ii. 7

Narrat Beda visionem valde probabilem, cui ipse fidem adhibere non dubitavit ... quoddam quasi pratum florentissimum ... in quo degebant animae, quae nihil patiebantur, sed tamen ibi manebant, quia nondum idoneae erant visioni beatae. Cui revelationi multas alias conformes adducit Dionysius Carthus. *et L. Blosius.*

... Erit locus ille mitissimum Purgatorium, et quasi carcer quidam senatorius atque honoratus.

... Scribit S. Brigitta animam quandam in Purgatorio nullam aliam poenam habuisse nisi dolorem ex desiderio dilatae felicitatis.

ii. 14

S. Bonaventura docet poenam damni in Purgatorio non esse majorem omni poenâ ... licet absentia Summi Boni ex se generat in amante summam tristitiam, tamen in Purgatorio mitigatur haec tristitia, et levatur magnâ ex parte propter certam spem etc Ista enim certissima spes affert incredibile gaudium

... Ex certis revelationibus constat aliorum poenam esse tam exiguam, ut nihil pati videantur.

Bail

S. Thomas en Meditation t. 5. p 246–7

Quelques âmes ... ne sont autrement punies que par le douleur qu'elles ressentent du délai et du retardement de leur félicité-etc S. Brigitte en cite un exemple etc.

There is a longer passage somewhere, but I can't find it. The whole Meditation agrees with St Francis as to the joy in suffering. Bail's book is well known and much recommended.'

[2] Pusey concluded his letter of 30 April, 'I am told privately that there is to be a personal attack on me in a R.C. book by a "Religious" It is a strange requital when I am employed on a strong Eirenicon from which I hoped good. "When I speak of peace, they are for war"'

in order to condemn, certain extravagant and preposterous expressions, *culled by a Protestant controversialist out of various foreign writers*, (some of them on the Index) she stopped her ears, and desired that they might be passed over in silence.'[1]

TUESDAY 18 MAY 1869   first performance of the Aulularia

TO MRS JOHN MOZLEY

The Oratory Bm May 19. 1869.

My dear Jemima

I was going today to write to you to send my congratulations to you and John on the day, when your letter comes.[2] I am sorry for the cause of your going to Whitby — but hope it will be a good thing for you as well as for Jane. You seem to me very early though — I have heard of it as one of the finest sea places in England, but for the summer months — Of course this sad weather may clear for you any day, considering how far the year is advanced, but it is a bad time to set out in.

I am sorry John R. and his wife have had to move, after having got into a nice abode near Bayswater, was it not? It is a great trouble; but if Sydenham suits her, of course that is every thing. I am always desirous to hear about Annie and Eliza — and if I ever was in Town for a day or two should attempt to find them out.[3] There was a chance at Easter of this being the case, and I should have called on Herbert [Mozley] to assist me, had it been fulfilled.

You will be glad to know that I have reason to hope I am better — all my bad symptoms are gone. I can't help having some little misgiving, for I had hardly any at all three years ago, when suddenly I found myself at the worst. But if I said so to my doctor, he would laugh at me. I have not taken those acids since the beginning of the year. They were directed only to counteract what was an effect, and could hardly touch the cause, which was my bad digestion. Perhaps however they gradually produced a permanent change in my constitution. However that may be, my doctor found a means of giving me steel which I have never been able to take since Dr Baillie gave it to me in 1818 —[4] and so it is, in a wonderful way, all bad symptoms are simply gone —

[1] *Life of Mother Margaret Mary Hallahan* by her Religious Children, London 1869, p. 320. Cf. letter of 13 July to Augusta Theodosia Drane. The reference is to *A Letter to Pusey*, *Diff*. II, pp. 113–14.
[2] Jemima was born on 19 May 1808.
[3] John R. was John Rickards Mozley, Jemima's eldest son. Annie and Eliza were the daughters of Newman's uncle Charles Fourdrinier.
[4] Cf. *Moz*. I, p. 101.

and now I have even left off the steel. And if I take cider, it is rather because I have bought it and like it than for any thing else.

Ever Yours affectly John H Newman

THURSDAY 20 MAY 1869   dreary weather.   candles at breakfast

TO W. J. COPELAND

May 20/69

My dear C

Read and send me back the inclosed, and tell me how it strikes you.[1]

I thought of saying

1. that I would be gladly be of use to him, if I could.

2. that, as my letters were not sorted, I had not the means of doing every thing I should wish to do, but would do my best.

3. that I did not think Keble ever wrote to me *confidential* letters — nor was with me on the terms on which he was on with his own contemporaries, such as Judge Coleridge.

4. that all letters which relate to the *Movement*, I consider to be *yours*, and that you are using them (I don't mean to mention your name) for your own object.

5. that, since I will do every thing I can for him, I beg he will lend me *my own* letters to Keble for you to see.[2]

Ever Yrs affly J H N

FRIDAY 21 MAY 1869   second performance of the Aulularia

TO LOUISA SIMEON

The Oratory May 24. 1869

My dear Louisa Simeon

I did not write to you again when I got back here, thinking there was a chance of seeing you on St Philip's day with Sir John [Simeon] — however, he is away — and we do not have him or you.

---

[1] George Moberly wrote on 18 May to say that he had been requested by Keble's executors to edit a selection of his letters. He asked Newman to lend him those he possessed.

[2] Copeland replied on 22 May, 'I think the matter is in safe hands with Moberly, and think also that you would do what is kind in saying what you have thought of saying, and doing your best to help him. . . . You know best how far you can except the letters which concern the movement. Anyhow the request gives you a fair occasion to ask for a sight of your own letters to K.'

Copeland added that Church had been invited by Messrs. Macmillan to write an account of the Oxford Movement.

George Moberly, who brought out Keble's *Miscellaneous Poems* in 1869, did not publish his letters. See letter of 5 July to Copeland. A volume *Letters of Spiritual Guidance and Counsel*, Oxford 1870, was edited by R. F. Wilson.

It is so much more to the purpose to speak than to write — What I suggested to you in my letter was, that you were not grounded in the *facts* of religious truth, as it is found in the world; but I cannot tell how to supply your want till I know whether I am right or wrong. If I recommended a particular book to you, I might from my ignorance, be giving you trouble to no purpose. Here we find ourselves in this world, with an instinct telling us that it is our duty to serve God, yet without the means of doing so as certain as the instinct is certain. As in the natural order of things a man would starve, if he did not find the means of living, so in like manner it is incumbent on us to look out for, to labour for, and so to gain the spiritual means, by which our souls may live — and this is the very end of our lives. Though then we should like, if we had our choice, that the way to arrive at religious truth were easy, yet it is not easy — and we must gain it as we can, and not be impatient or desponding — if we find obstacles.

I dare say you have said all this to yourself — but that is no reason why I should not say it — just the reverse, for in that case we run along one line and have the pleasure of mutual agreement.

Thank your sister for her letter and her very kind reference to my visit to Swainston. I am so glad to hear she is better.

Very sincerely Yours John H Newman

TUESDAY 25 MAY 1869 third performance [of the Aulularia] — before friends weather very bad

TO SIR WILLIAM HENRY COPE

The Oratory May 25. 1869

My dear Sir William

I feel the more than compliment you pay me in collecting together all I have written and though the particular compositions you write about have no great merit, I gladly would serve you, were it in my power, in your endeavour to get them. And I wish you had written to me, before you had taken as much trouble as you must have taken.

1. The only copy of my Article on Duncan's Travels which I have is bound up in a collection of 70 volumes of Tracts in our Library. The Number of the Review is headed 'The British Review and London Critical Journal. May 1824.' The Review of Duncan is Article 11 at p. 144. The Editor of the Review at that time was the Revd E. G. Marsh, incumbent of a chapel at Hampstead and late Fellow of Oriel. The publisher with whom I corresponded was Sealy. Our copy has no Title page — but in a Number of the year 1821, the Title Page is as follows:

'The British Review [and London Critical Journal]
Institia — ["— Fiat Justitia.—"] vol xvii London.   Printed for
Baldwin, Cradock and Joy, Paternoster Row   and
J. Hatchard and Son   Piccadilly. 1821'[1]

2. You are right about the date of the London Review. I had thought that
it was first published at the *end* of 1828; but I see that our Library copy, the
only one I know of, is dated on the back of the bound volume 1829. The
Article of the Theatre of the Greeks is mine.[2]

3. I trust I shall be able to send you a copy of the 'Suggestions' which was
never *published*[3]

4. I have but one copy of the letters of Catholicus, which appeared in the
Times in February 1841 and one is in our Library. I know of no others. The
letters were published all together by 'John Mortimer, 21 Wigmore Street,
1841,' under the title of 'The Tamworth Reading Room.'[4]

5. As to the Dissertatiuncula I have already expressed to Dr Russell my
great regret at not having a copy.[5] Do not scruple to ask me any other question

Very truly Yrs John H. Newman

WEDNESDAY 26 MAY 1869   Fr Suffield preached — the Bishop pontificated Dejeuné
[sic] at the Oratory

THURSDAY 27 MAY   Corpus Xti — I celebrated

TO HENRY WILBERFORCE

The Oratory Bm, C. Xti 1869

My dear H W

Will you tell me whether your friend Mrs Montgomery lives at Ifield Lodge,
Crawley — a lady signing herself what reads like 'Fanny Montgomery' has
written to me, who I think must be the person you know. Is she 'Honble' — I
have, of course, to answer her, and I wish to answer her correctly[6]

Ever Yrs affly John H Newman

P.S.   The best blessings for you all on this great Festival

[1] This article was not reprinted in Newman's edition of his works.
[2] 'Poetry with Reference to Aristotle's Poetics,' *Ess.* I, pp. 1–29.
[3] 'Suggestions on behalf of the Church Missionary Society,' *V.M.* II, pp. 1–17.
[4] *D.A.*, pp. 254–305.
[5] 'Dissertatiunculæ Quatuor Critico-Theologicæ,' *T.T.*, pp. 1–91.
[6] The hon. Fanny Charlotte Montgomery was a daughter of George Wyndham, first Baron
Leconfield. She married in 1842 Alfred Montgomery, a commissioner of inland revenue, who
lived at Crawley. Mrs Montgomery was the author of poems and novels, and was or became a
convert to Catholicism.

TO AUGUSTA THEODOSIA DRANE

The Oratory Bm May 28. 1869

My dear Sister M. Fr. Raphael

In thanking you for your kind and welcome letter, and the message to me which it contains from Mother Provincial, I take the opportunity also of acknowledging the receipt of the Copy which your Community has sent me of their Memoir of their dear Mother Margaret.[1]

As to that Memoir, it is not for such as me to panegyrize one so much above the ordinary level of faithful souls as was Mother Margaret, any more than it has been the purpose of the writer — but independent of the feeling of reverence which makes me unwilling to use many words about her, there is another reason which leads me, in writing to you to acknowledge the volume, to dwell more upon the volume itself than upon her to whose memory it is so dutifully dedicated.

My reason is this:- I do not think that any History would materially change the picture in my mind of Mother Margaret, as I had conceived it already, though it might add interesting and instructive details, and define and strengthen the outline. I felt her to be a wonderful woman, full of faith, devotion, and energy, and, by the force of these virtues, possessed of singular powers of influence. Her doings betokened her greatness. Also, I had heard from our Bishop of her severe and lifelong sufferings and penances. And I understood a good deal about her character from her mode of speaking in conversation. And, though I did not know of that habit of prayer which was the characteristic of her youth, and which is so enviable, yet, knowing what she was afterwards, I could not be surprised when I read about it in the Volume. What was most new to me in the Memoir, is (what ought *not* to be new to me) her singular tenderness towards myself, her sympathy and interest in one who in all his habits and circumstances, his ways of thought and his history, was so unlike what she was. While I feel something of remorse that I did not realize this in her lifetime, yet still how could I fancy that she could care about me more than she cared about a hundred persons like me, to whom her Christian charity would impel her to be kind? However, you must not take me to mean that I did not discern, and did not feel gratitude for, what I looked upon as simple charity; for in particular I always felt that some portion of the kindness which our Bishop has ever shown me, and the confidence he has placed in me, was owing to my being in the good graces of a Religious so holy, so straightforward, so revered by him as Mother Margaret. And here I must pay my thanks also to your present Mother Provincial, who, in the name of you all, and by the pen of the Sister to whom the composition of the Volume was committed, has had the courage to speak of me in terms, which many

[1] Imelda Poole succeeded Mother Margaret Mary Hallahan as Superior of the Order of Dominican nuns she had founded. For the *Life* of the foundress, see last note to letter of 13 May to Pusey.

others would not venture to use, though in their hearts they might agree with her.[1]

You see I have already passed, before I knew it, from Mother Margaret to her biography, and to the characteristic which strikes me as the principal merit of it, and a very great one, — and that is its boldness. The writer has felt that she could not fulfil the duty of severe loyalty to a great Servant of God, or the sacred claims of truth, and the wishes, as they certainly would have been, of Mother Margaret herself, unless she was very courageous in her narrative. And she has felt, that, if any one is bound to speak out without respect of persons or fear of what others might say, and as an example to others, it was one who had given up the world for Him who is the Truth, and especially who was a daughter and client of the free spoken St Catharine. And moreover she has had faith enough in the substantial sanctity and perfection of the dear Mother whom she has lost, to be sure that that Mother would lose nothing by having every one of her characteristics brought into the light, and that Almighty God does not need our managements and artifices, our observance of mawkish proprieties and tenderness towards weak scandalizabilities, in order to set off duly the creations of His grace.

It is a great encouragement and refreshment to the reader to have had placed before him something *real*; and, — useful as it may be for devotional purposes (which I am not denying) in the case of some minds, — certainly speaking for myself, I cannot abide the practice so common of cutting up a Saint into virtues and of distributing him into pigeon holes, which serves to destroy the special value of biography over didactic composition, and, without intending it, goes far to deny to Holy Church her perogative of being 'circumdata varietate.'[2] Whether Mother Margaret was a rose, or lily, or carnation, in our Lord's garden, I cannot tell; but she was either the one or the other, not all of them at once — not a generalization or idea of man, but a great work of God

After saying as much as this, I need not perhaps say more — however, if I must make a second remark, I should say with great sincerity that, while the Memoir is so bold and open — it is, in my opinion, composed with singular judgment; — not that I have read the whole of it, but I can speak confidently

[1] 'Among those present [at Bishop Ullathorne's consecration on 21 June 1846] were Dr, then Mr Newman, and his companions, who had but recently been received into the Catholic Church, and were then established at Mary Vale, or Old Oscott. This was the first occasion on which Mother Margaret met with one in whom, even before his conversion, she had always felt the deepest interest, and the friendship between them, once formed, remained unbroken to the day of her death.' p. 125.

'Some newspaper gossip on one occasion made very free use of Dr Newman's name, and drew from his pen a letter in which he made a noble profession of his unalterable attachment to the Catholic faith; Mother Margaret was so delighted at the terms in which this letter was conceived that she cut it out of the paper and kept it in a little leathern purse, which contained a few rare treasures, and which she always carried about her . . .' p. 247.

See also p. 280, and the passage quoted in letter of 13 May to Pusey: and C. S. Dessain, the *Month*, (Dec. 1965), pp, 360–67, '"Heart speaks to heart", Margaret Mary Hallahan and John Henry Newman.'

[2] *Psalm* 44:10. Cf. *H.S.* II, p. 229.

as regard the large portions which I have gone through. One sentence indeed there is, but only one, which, (to be open myself,) I will confess rather grated on my ear, as I read it. It is at page 307 — Mother Margaret said on Whit Sunday 'I am so fond of the Holy Ghost.' Did she not mean to speak of the Feast, the Devotion, or the thought of, that is, the thinking upon the Third Person of the Everblessed Trinity?[1]

Lastly, it is quite wonderful to me how so carefully selected and condensed a history could have been written and published with such speed.

Begging your good prayers ever, I am, My dear Sister M. F. Raphael

Most sincerely Yrs in Xt   John H Newman of the Oratory

SATURDAY 29 MAY 1869   inclement ungenial weather

TO CATHERINE ANNE BATHURST

The Oratory June 2/69

My dear Child

Thank you for your congratulations. I will gladly receive subscriptions for your object. And I hope you will head your Prospectus with the names of the Bishop of Ghent and our Archbishop.[2]

We had very bad weather on St Philip's day, but every one wished to be pleased — so it passed off well.

That evening I was to have dined with your brother, the dentist kept me waiting, and I did not get away from him till half past seven![3]

Ever Yrs affly John H Newman

TO EMILY BOWLES

The Oratory June 2. 1869

My dear Child,

I have been much pleased to read your graceful lines on 'Bluebells.'[4] They are natural and musical. Your March Number should have gone back to you long ago, but I have been so full of business, that it was delayed from day to day.[5] I hope this change of weather will be good for you.

---

[1] This passage remains unaltered in the second edition, p. 311, the Advertisement to which is dated 2 Oct. 1869.

[2] Catherine Bathurst was about to open a school at Ghent.

[3] Newman called on Catherine Bathurst in London on 31 March, and presumably was to have dined with her brother, Henry Allen Bathurst R.N., who became a Catholic in 1853, and who worked in the Admiralty Court.

[4] 'With the Bluebells,' the *Month*, (June 1869), pp. 530-1, a poem signed 'E.B.'

[5] See letter of 25 March to Emily Bowles.

Private.

— [1] wrote to me. I answered by saying how difficult I felt it to say any thing to the point without knowing more about her. I asked whether she was *grounded* in religious truth; since *we* had had that great advantage which she had not, of having battled our way through all intellectual difficulties into the Church.

She has not written again. I hoped to have seen her on St Philip's day here, with her Father — but he was from England.

Of this I made an excuse, and wrote again — saying I had hoped to see her, and saying something more. In my former letter I had asked whether she knew my Parochial Sermons.

Ever Yrs affly John H Newman

P.S.   I say all this to you that you may know where we stand.[2]

TO HENRY JAMES COLERIDGE

The Oratory Bm June 2. 1869

My dear Fr Coleridge

Serjeant Bellasis has mentioned to me your suggestion about some sentences of mine in my Letter to him about the L.U.[3] I hope you will not think it ungracious in me, but I do not see my way to come into it. I am very angry with the London University and dislike it intensely, but those feelings do not extend to its members and the persons before whom my Letter came treated me with great civility, and actually made an alteration in their established examination for Matriculation in consequence of what I said about it. They did not do all I wished, but they did enough to make me feel grateful to them — and I should not like to publish against them any part of a letter, which in a way was private and became their own property, as having been sent to them.

Don't think me unmindful of you, but believe me to be

Very sincerely Yours John H Newman

---

[1] The initials 'L.S.' have been erased, i.e. Louisa Simeon. See Newman's letters to her.

[2] Emily Bowles replied on 7 June that Louisa Simeon was very grateful for Newman's letters, but had no opportunity to answer them.

[3] Bellasis wrote on 28 May that Coleridge wished to quote in the *Month* from Newman's letter of 25 Jan. 1868 about the studies at London University. Bellasis thought Newman would not want use made of his letter against persons who had received it kindly. It was not inserted in the *Month*, (July 1869), 'Catholic Education,' pp. 1–21.

TO MISS HOLMES

The Oratory June 2. 1869

My dear Miss Holmes

I am pleased to find you are so well established, and now that the weather is improving, the Park will not be so trying to you.[1] We had a bad St Philip's day, as regards weather — but all friends were very kind. Miss Wegg Prosser spoke in the strongest terms of you as a Music Instructor

Ever Yrs affly John H Newman

TO J. WALKER OF SCARBOROUGH

The Oratory Bm June 2. 1869

My dear Canon Walker

I have long wished to know how you are. Write me a line to say that you are quite well again

Very sincerely Yours John H Newman

SUNDAY 6 JUNE 1869   Mrs Monsell here

TO J. WALKER OF SCARBOROUGH

The Oratory Bm June 6. 1869

My dear Canon Walker

I rejoice to have such a good account of yourself from you — and trust the ailment in your leg will come to nothing. When I tell you that my letter to you was one of 18 or more which I wrote that day, you will pardon its brevity.

I agree with you — it is a thousand pities that a clever man like Allies should sermonize in the way he does. We are reading him in the Refectory — and he always seems in the same place, prancing like a cavalry soldier's horse, without advancing, in the face of a mob. He has a noble subject, but I have not gained two ideas from his book — but I must not say so.[2]

I think Mother Margaret's Life bold and good — and am very much pleased and touched by the kindness of the passages about myself.[3]

Have you seen Pusey's answer to me? it is marvellously learned — but I don't see what we have to do with the 'activa conceptio' held or debated in the

---

[1] A note on this letter gives Miss Holmes's address as 7 Portsea Place, Connaught Square, London.
[2] This refers to T. W. Allies *The Formation of Christendom*, Part Second.
[3] See letter of 28 May to Augusta Theodosia Drane.

middle ages, when notoriously now, when the Definition of the Imm. Conc. [Immaculate Conception] is made, all divines say that the 'passiva' alone is intended.[1]

A friend has asked me whether it is too late now to bring out an answer to Ffoulkes — and I don't know the state of the religious public mind enough to answer him.[2]

I have not seen the Life of Lacordaire you speak of. Did not some Protestant write one?[3]

At last we have summer. We have lost Spring altogether

Ever Yours most sincerely John H Newman

MONDAY 7 JUNE 1869   She [Mrs Monsell] went to Rednall and back — Ambrose being at Rednall.

TO J. D. DALGAIRNS

[7 June 1869]

My dear Fr Dalgairns

I was accidentally told some time ago that you had written to Dr Northcote on the subject of Morris, and, though it perplexed me, I was glad to find his case in such good hands. I do not see any reason to take it out of them. I would willingly tell you if I had any names on the matter beyond those which I stated in the letter you have seen. You in London will be more able than another to ascertain how many are likely to contribute to the object and what sum will be sufficient; his friends then will be able to see their way more clearly. Of course you may say that I will be in that case one of the contributors.[4]

I grieve much to hear you still speak so poorly of your state of health. Time goes, as you say, very fast.

J H N

TUESDAY 8 JUNE 1869   Mr Campbell came
WEDNESDAY 9 JUNE   Diocesan Synod — dined with the Bishop

[1] See letter of 9 June to Pusey.
[2] This evidently refers to H. I. D. Ryder *A Critique upon Mr. Ffoulkes' 'Letter,'* London 1869, published in July. Cf. letter of 10 Feb. 1869 to Harper.
[3] Walker perhaps referred to B. Chocarne *The Inner Life of Père Lacordaire, O.P.,* Dublin 1867.
[4] J. B. Morris was without employment and in danger of starving. Dalgairns, who had seen a letter of Newman's to Wenham suggesting ways of helping him, wrote on 6 June, that he, Dalgairns had secured him help for another year. He wanted a larger sum to be raised among his friends, 'no name would be so powerful as the head of the undertaking as yours.'

The Oratory Bm June 9/69

My dear Pusey

It would be very easy to praise the great research of your book, but you would understand that such admiration was nihil ad rem. Also, what *is* ad rem, and what you in your love for me will not think nihil, is the thanks which I pay you from my heart for the affectionate words you use concerning me.[1]

But what you will wish to know is what I think of your argument. I saw our Bishop to-day, and he asked what I thought of your book. I said, I don't think he can have read your Lordship's book.[2] He will not believe that the Definition of 1854 contemplates the passive Conception, and he has brought a whole string of divines who have written on the *activa* Conceptio, which is a question as utterly gone by and dead as that universal belief of the early doctors that the sons of God who went in to the daughters of men were Angels. And why he will not believe what every Catholic says now, I can't understand. I can safely say I never heard any one interpret the dogma or the definition except of the Conceptio *passiva*, and it did not enter into my head that any one could take it otherwise till I heard Pusey say so. And are not the Catholics of the age the fit interpretors of the definition of this age? 'That is very extraordinary' said the Bishop — why I have said the same in my book. 'I wish you would send it to him' I answered — 'it will be one fact tending to convince him of what is as certain as the sun in the heaven. His work seems to me to be chasing a will of the whisp [sic]. However, I will tell your Lordship what I think would go a great way to satisfy him, viz. if at the Council some words were passed to the effect that the activa conceptio is an obsolete idea.'[3]

I have persuaded the Bishop to send you his book; and I wish you would send him yours, *if* you are giving away copies. If so, you should also send it to the Paulists of New York (Fr Hecker etc) to send to *their* Bishops. It would be a great thing, I think, if you set down definitely *what you want*. To say 'I want a disclaimer of the Conceptio Activa' *is* definite; but it ought to be coupled with your avowal that you do *not* object to the Conceptio Passiva. Else, there will be no quid pro quo. If you but felt you could say to the American Bishops who are going to the Council, 'We will profess we have no objection to the Conceptio Passiva, provided you disclaim the Conceptio Activa,' that would be a fair bargain.

As to promising that the Church will never increase its definitions, who

---

[1] *First Letter to the Very Rev. J. H. Newman, D.D., in Explanation chiefly in regard to the reverential love due to the Ever-blessed Theotokos, and the Doctrine of her Immaculate Conception,* Oxford 1869.

Pusey began his work 'My Dearest Friend,

First, let me thank you for the love shown in your letter [*Letter to Pusey*], a love which was such joy to my youth, and now is so cheering to my old age.'

[2] W. B. Ullathorne, *The Immaculate Conception of the Mother of God*, London 1855.

[3] See letters of 19 and 22 Jan. 1866 to Pusey.

can say that to the 'Spirit who bloweth where He listeth'?[1] A friend of mine said what sounds profane, but has a deep meaning. He said you wished 'to bind over the Holy Ghost to keep the peace.'[2]

Ever Yours, My Dear Pusey, Most affectionately, John H Newman

TO W. J. COPELAND

The Oratory June 10/69

My dear C

Rivington has been going at a great rate with the proofs. I inclose 2, and suppose there is only one more to come.

I am puzzled at the word 'Ember —' at p 397. What has it to do with the 'fruits of the earth?' I suppose there is no help for it.[3]

The index of Sermons and dates will soon be wanted. I shall look it through very carefully with the aid of my memoranda.

I send a batch of letters which, if you do not disapprove, I shall send to Moberly. But speak freely, if you think you want them yourself. I do not think they will be a loss to you, but you must judge[4]

Ever Yrs affly John H Newman

FRIDAY 11 JUNE 1869   R *Robert* F Wilson called on me in the evening
SATURDAY 12 JUNE   Mr Andrews came[5]   Mrs Wootten's second illness now

TO JOHN GEORGE MACCARTHY

The Oratory Bm June 12. 1869

My dear Mr MacCarthy

I am very glad to hear about you, after so many years, and thank you for reviving my plaisant [sic] recollections of you in so friendly a way.[6]

---

[1] *John*, 3:8.
[2] See letter of 22 March 1867 to Pusey, and for his reply to this present letter Liddon's *Pusey*, IV, p. 164.
[3] *S.D.*, sermon on 'The Parting of Friends.' 'We have kept the Ember-days for the fruits of the earth . . .'
[4] See letter of 20 May to Copeland. On 7 July George Moberly wrote to thank Newman for the letters of Keble he had sent, all of which he expected to publish.
[5] This was Septimus Andrews, who had been a master at Westminster School 1860–5, and Vicar of Market Harborough 1865–9. He had just become a Catholic, and having no private means, Lord Denbigh suggested to Newman that he might become, for a time, a master at the Oratory School. Andrews joined the Oblates of St Charles and was ordained in 1873.
[6] MacCarthy, a solicitor in Cork from 1853 to 1881, sent Newman a copy of his revised *The History of Cork, a Lecture*, Cork 1869, first published in 1856. The MacCarthy sept came from Cork. MacCarthy later became an M.P., worked to solve the Irish land question and became one of the Irish Land Commissioners.

There is a fitness in a MacCarthy writing the history of Cork. And your composition shows great research, and is characterized by a life and picturesque effect which is not always seen in antiquarian works.

Wishing you all happiness and hoping you will sometimes say a prayer for me   I am,

My dear Mr MacCarthy Sincerely Yours
John H Newman of the Oratory[1]

J. G. MacCarthy Esqr

TO JOHN HUNGERFORD POLLEN

The Oratory June 12 1869

My dear Pollen

I owe you a letter since May 26. I trust all has gone well with your wife and the little child.

In Easter week I was in Town for a few hours consecutive — and tried to get to you — in vain. Since you can't come here, I certainly should get to you if possible, whenever I was in London. But how seldom is that — and for how few hours when I am there. We had a bad day, but made ourselves very happy in Birmingham, our guests were so good as to be made happy easily.[2]

I have nothing to write about in our happy state of calm luxurious vegetation. The only drawback is that we are made for work, and therefore one has something of a bad conscience in standing all the day idle. Excepting this 'amari aliquid',[3] I am well content to be as I am. Say everything kind from me to your wife and believe me

Yours affectly in Xt   John H Newman

TO MR POPE

The Oratory June 12/69

Dr Newman incloses for Mr Pope a Postal Order for one Pound for the Idiot Child.

As they insisted at the Post Office on having a Christian name, it is drawn in favour of Mr J. Pope.

SUNDAY 13 JUNE 1869   most ungenial weather up to this time

---

[1] MacCarthy replied on 14 June, 'I am one of the thousands in nearly all lands who owe to you much of anything that is not bad in them; who prize your books as their best teachers . . .'
[2] i.e. on St Philip's feast, 26 May.
[3] Lucretius, *De Rerum Natura*, IV, 1134.

TO W. J. COPELAND

The Oratory June 14. 1869

My dear C

I don't know whether you are puzzled or not whether you should or should not give up those letters of Keble's to Moberly — but the delay in your answer gives me an opportunity of asking you how far you have clearly before you what the limits are, both of time and of consequences, which you mean to put to your history of the Movement. You should surely have this strictly before you. It was a movement with a definite object. What is the point of time at which that object is sufficiently attained for you to stop? Again, what limit do you put to collateral matters? is my leaving you to come in? If it is to be passed over sub silentio, then Keble's letters to me about myself may go to Moberly. Are the efforts and gatherings of the S.P.C.K. [Society for the Promotion of Christian Knowledge] to come into it? If so, letters which I have of Keble's on the subject must *not* go to Moberly.

I think this plan of Moberly's comes rather fortunately for you to oblige you to define the scope of your book. I will tell you what Keble's letters to me are about, and then you may judge *which* are for your purpose: — about Froude's Remains, about Peter Young, about Isaac [Williams] and the Poetry Professorship — about the British Critic — about Number 90 — about my own doubts and difficulties — about various Sermons of mine sent to him for criticisms — about his own writings etc sent to me — about Whig measures — etc etc.

It is curious, he criticizes rather gravely the 'Sermons on Subjects of the day —' and says that he and others think I speak magisterially in them. I am still anxious about the volume, though Rivington having no fears is a strong fact[1]

Ever Yrs affly John H Newman.

TUESDAY 15 JUNE 1869   Mr Campbell went   Austin went to his mother?

WEDNESDAY 16 JUNE   cold rain

THURSDAY 17 JUNE   fires in the evening

FRIDAY 18 JUNE   gas at boys' dinner   cold rain

[1] Copeland wrote on 19 June, returning Keble's letters and saying, 'There is no reason so far as I am concerned why you should not forward them to Moberly at once, for you are quite right in thinking they are not needed for what I am doing.'

TO GENEROSO CALENZIO

[18? June 1869]

Perjucundum est mihi, Pater Reverendissime, ex litteris tuis invenisse recordationem quandam mei superstitem esse in sanctissimo illo S. Philippi nostri domicilio Romano; — et gratias ago maximas et Tibi et Patri Carolo Rossi propter benevolentiam et Tuam et Illius, charissimi et optimi Sacerdotes, qui operis tui donatione vestrae erga me charitatis pulcherrimum ostenditur sequendum [?][1]

Opus illud eruditionis est planè singularis, et in Bibliotheca nostra unà cum Baronio, Raynaldo, Theiner, Laderchi, et caeteris Oratorianis Romanis Patribus locum suum jam proprium habebit.

Patres nostri, Ambrosio St John, et Henrico Bittlestone, quos tam benigne accepisti cum in Urbe essent, per me se tibi commendatos volunt et sui ut etiam mei coram Deo ad altare memineris.

SATURDAY 19 JUNE 1869   candles at our dinner

TO HENRY BEDFORD

The Oratory, Birmingham. June 19th. 1869.

My dear Mr. Bedford,

We shall be rejoiced to see you on the 26th. as you propose. You know, I believe, Father Pope — and perhaps some others, besides me.

Most sincerely yours, John H Newman.

TO JOHN EDWARD BOWDEN

The Oratory June 19. 1869

My dear John,

Thank you for your copy of Fr Faber's life.[2] As far as I have as yet made myself acquainted with it, it seems drawn up with great skill and judgment. I am very glad you have adopted the method, which, as far as it is possible, is in my opinion the true mode of biography — I mean carrying on the course of the narrative by letters

Yours affectly John H Newman

[1] On 11 June the Roman Oratorian Calenzio wrote that, at the suggestion of Carlo Rossi, he was sending Newman a copy of his *Esame critico-letterario delle opere riguardanti la Storia del Concilio di Trento*, which he had just published in Rome.

[2] John Edward Bowden, *The Life and Letters of Frederick William Faber, D.D., Priest of the Oratory of St Philip Neri*, London 1869.

TO MRS BUCKLE

June 19th. 1869.

My dear Mrs. Buckle,

Do not suppose I was unmindful of the notice which came to me, though I did not write to you.[1] Let me now offer you and Mr. Buckle my best sympathies. I don't like to say condolements, in the case of a soul who has dedicated herself to God and gained her crown. I had a great friend die in the same convent the year before last — and I doubt not your daughter's departure was as happy as hers. I said Mass for your daughter's soul the morning after the news came to me; and I hope she will requite me by her intercessions. And for you and Mr. Buckle, it must be a most consoling thought that there is one in heaven waiting for you and meanwhile helping you by her prayers.

Most sincerely yours in Christ, John H Newman.

SUNDAY 20 JUNE 1869   fires

TO W. J. COPELAND

The Oratory Bm June 20. 1869

My dear Copeland

If what you say is true to any great extent, it is a fatal objection to giving the dates.[2] The only one on my mind was one you have pointed out at p 69 volume vii The purpureus pannus begins at p 68 'The history etc' and ends at 'our pattern' p 70. I believe the rest is nearly verbatim as it was in 1825. Perhaps I have the autograph.[3] I believe volume viii, p 126 (Jeremiah) to be

[1] Mary Gertrude, daughter of Mr and Mrs William Hill Buckle, died in May 1869, aged forty-one years, after having been professed at the Convent of the Visitation, Westbury-on-Trym, fifteen years. Marianne Bowden died in the same convent in Oct. 1867.

[2] Copeland wrote on 12 June about Newman's list of dates of his sermons in *P.S.* and *S.D.*, (which, in fact, were the dates when the sermons were preached for the first time):

'Wonderfully as you have in many places anticipated yourself in various respects, there are passages in some of the very earliest sermons, which can scarcely belong to them as they stand. Several struck me in the Plain Sermons as they passed before me, and some have struck the reviewer in the "Saturday" of last week . . .' The *Saturday Review*, (5 June 1869), p. 748, said of *P.S.*, 'Their theology is nothing new: nor does it essentially change though one may observe differences, and some important ones, in the course of the Volumes, which embrace a period from 1825 to 1842. It is curious indeed to observe how early the general character of the sermons was determined, and how in the main it continues the same. Some of the first in point of date are among the "Plain Sermons"; and though they may have been subsequently retouched, yet there the keynote is plainly struck of that severe and solemn minor which reigns throughout.' This long review was by R. W. Church, see his *Occasional Papers* II, 'Newman's Parochial Sermons,' p. 452.

[3] Copeland continued 'However as you will be looking through the Index of dates as you say very carefully with the aid of your memoranda; you will be reminded of what has been rewritten or revised or retouched so far as to need some notice or comment. There are no doubt "variae lectiones" of more or less importance in the several editions. My own edition being the first I noticed many e.g. a fresh passage of some length on Rationalism in the Sermon on St Thomas's Day [*P.S.* II, 19–22] — and a passage which Burgon taxed me with having altered on St Simon and St Jude, on the "Roman Schools" [*P.S.* II, p. 390] . . .'

word for word (bating literary corrections) as I delivered it in 1830. I say so, because the Sermon was in my mind *all through* the movement. *Perhaps* I have the autograph of this. It is *almost* parallel to the passage in the 'Letter to a Magazine' (Tracts of the T. [Times] Number 82.) p xi 'Well and good etc.' tho' *that* says we *shall* succeed, yet *personally* the feeling is the same.[1] The passage p 252 on Religious Joy, I have no recollection about at all, and, as far as appears at first sight, was inserted in 1843.[2]

What you say of the 2 Sermons St Thomas and SS Simon and Jude is a difficulty. Besides, in that Second Volume, being a *series*, some were written *for* it in 1834-5, — and, unless I have marked to the contrary, were either not preached at all, or preached in type. I suspect, that on Self contemplation was never preached —[3] (It is marked 1835 — so it is not antedated.) — All this throws great difficulty in the way of publishing the dates, and at the moment I don't see my way out of it. Had the dedication of Volume 1. been dated in brackets, each volume would have been sufficiently fixed, and the only difficult one would have been the Plain Sermons, which is made up of old and new. I have given a conspectus of the dates of Sermons on the Day in the Apologia. They are all or nearly all late ones. What does the Saturday say about the dates?

Ever Yrs affly John H Newman

P.S.   I have looked tho' the MSS of all the St Mary's Sermons I can find, and find none of the Sermons we want. So I suppose the MSS have been destroyed.[4]

MONDAY 21 AND TUESDAY 22 JUNE 1869   preternaturally dark   fires and so for days
WEDNESDAY 23 JUNE   Austin returned
THURSDAY 24 JUNE   at 4 PM I could hardly see to read in my room

Copeland added, 'But there are passages in Volume VII, Sermon v, p. 69, and Volume VIII, Sermon viii, p. 126, and Sermon xvii, p. 252, all bearing date 1825, which are surely an advance upon that early period and seem to belong rather to the date of publication of the 5th Volume of Plain Sermons in 1843.'
The passage in *P.S.*, VII, pp. 68–70, speaks of the monastic movement of the desert fathers, which flowered as the early persecutions came to an end. The first page reference in Volume VIII, should have been p. 121. Copeland corrected this on 4 July. See letter of 5 July to him.
See Copeland's Preface to *S.D.*
[1] In *Tract* 82, in 1837, Newman wrote, 'Well and good . . . We know our place, and our fortunes; to give a witness and to be condemned, to be ill-used and to *succeed*. Such is the law which God has annexed to the promulgation of the Truth; its preachers suffer, but its cause prevails.' *V.M.*, II, p. 159.
[2] This was a passage about the Blessed Virgin. See letter of 5 July to Copeland.
[3] *P.S.* II, pp. 163–74.
[4] There exist Mss for sermons in *U.S.*, but none for the Volumes which Copeland republished.

June 24/69

My dear C

I send you 10 more of Keble's letters for you to inspect before I send them to Moberly

Ever Yrs affly J H N

Turn over

Without recollecting Keble's objection, I had myself when I sent the proof to you desired some change in the words (Sermons on Subjects — Sermon 3 p 32 old edition) 'at least in out ward appearance.' What I *simply meant* was this — that 'eating and drinking' was not in excess or with 'winebibbing —' therefore though He might seem to be a companion of publicans and sinners it was only 'in outward appearance.'

Would it be possible in the proposed preface to say that, 'since no alteration is allowable, what the author would have *liked* to have done in the passage was to insert the word "freely" —'

'The Son of Man had come freely eating and drinking, at least in outward appearance —'

N.B. I think Keble has made a maresnest of it — as if I held the heresy of the Docetæ.[1]

The Oratory June 25. 1869

My dear Louisa Simeon

I have delayed writing to you, both as feeling the risk of my disappointing and disturbing instead of aiding you by what I might say — and also because I found you had been so good as to take up my suggestion as regards my Oxford Sermons.[2] I thought they might for a while speak to you instead of a letter. I can never prophesy what will be useful to a given individual and what not. As to my Sermons, I was astonished and (as you may suppose) deeply gratified by a stranger, an Anglican Clergyman, writing to me a year or two ago to say that reading them had converted him from free thinking opinions, which he had taken up from German authors, or from living in Germany. I do not see how they could do so — but he said they did — and it was that, I think, which made me fancy it was worth while to recommend them to you.

You must begin all thought about religion by mastering what is the fact, that any how the question has an inherent, irradicable [sic] difficulty in it.

---

[1] The passage was altered in *S.D.*, p. 28, to read, 'The Son of Man had come, in His own words, eating and drinking . . .' See *S.D.*, p. viii, and letter of 25 July to Copeland.

[2] See letter of 29 April to Louisa Simeon. Newman omitted here from the draft, 'If medicine is an empirical art, how much more the science of souls.'

As in tuning a piano, you may throw the fault here or there, but no theory can any one take up without that difficulty remaining. It will come up in one shape or other. If we say, 'Well, I will not believe any thing,' there is a difficulty in believing nothing, an intellectual difficulty. There is a difficulty in doubting; a difficulty in determining there is no truth; in saying that there is a truth, but that no one can find it out; in saying that all religious opinions are true, or one as good as another; a difficulty in saying there is no God; that there is a God but that He has not revealed Himself except in the way of nature; and there is doubtless a difficulty in Christianity. The question is, whether on the whole our reason does not tell us that it is a duty to accept the arguments commonly urged for its truth as sufficient, and a duty in consequence to believe heartily in Scripture and the Church.

Another thought which I wish to put before you is, whether our nature does not tell us that there is something which has more intimate relations with the question of religion than intellectual exercises have, and that is our conscience. We have the idea of duty — duty suggest something or some one to which it is to be referred, to which we are responsible. That something that has dues upon us is to us God. I will not assume it is a personal God, or that it is more than a law (though of course I hold that it is the Living Seeing God) but still the idea of duty, and the terrible anguish of conscience, and the irrepressible distress and confusion of face which the transgression of what we believe to be our duty, cause us, all this is an intimation, a clear evidence, that there is something nearer to religion than intellect; and that, if there is a way of finding religious truth, it lies, not in exercises of the intellect, but close on the side of duty, of conscience, in the observance of the moral law. Now all this may seem a truism, and many an intellectualist will say that he grants it freely. But I think, that, when dwelt upon, it leads to conclusions which would both surprise and annoy him.

Now I think it best to stop here for the present. You must not suppose that I am denying the intellect its real place in the discovery of truth; but it must ever be borne in mind that its exercise mainly consists in reasoning, — that is, in comparing things, classifying them, and inferring. It ever needs points to start from, first principles, and these it does not provide — but it can no more move one step without these starting points, than a stick, which supports a man, can move without the man's action. In physical matters, it is the senses which gives us the first start — and what the senses give is physical fact — and physical facts do not lie on the surface of things, but are gained with pains and by genius, through experiment. Thus Newton, or Davy, or Franklin ascertained those physical facts which have made their names famous. After these primary facts are gained, intellect can act; it acts too of course in gaining them; but they *must* be gained; it is the senses which *enable* the intellect to act, by giving it something to act upon. In like manner we have to ascertain the starting points for arriving at religious truth. The intellect will be useful in gaining them and after gaining them — but to attempt to *see* them by means of the intellect is like attempting by the intellect to see the physical facts which are the basis of physical exercises of the intellect, a method of proceeding which was the very mistake of the Aristotelians of the middle age, who, instead of what Bacon calls 'interrogating nature' for facts, reasoned out every thing by syllogisms. To gain religious starting points, we must in a parallel way, interrogate our hearts, and (since it is a personal, individual matter,) our *own* hearts, — interrogate our own consciences, interrogate, I will say, the God who dwells there.

I think you must ask the God of Conscience to enable you to do your duty in this matter. I think you should, with prayer to Him for help, meditate upon the Gospels, and on St Paul's second Epistle to the Corinthians, unless the translation of it disturbs you; and this with an earnest desire to know the truth and a sincere intention of following it.

When you are disposed, write again, and, if you wish, I will answer you

Yours affectly in Xt   John H Newman

SUNDAY 27 JUNE 1869   Mr Bedford of Allhallows here all day   This week brighter and better[1]

TO MRS SPARROW

The Oratory June 28/69

Mr dear Mrs Sparrow

I write in a great hurry just to acknowledge your letter. When the other half note comes you shall have a receipt and the account shall be put right. I am very glad you have got so good a friend in the Duchess

Most sincerely Yours John H. Newman

TUESDAY 29 JUNE 1869   Fr Edward went to his sister

TO EMILY BOWLES

June 30/69

My dear Child,

Will you please have the inclosed put into the post? I suspect the sender wants Birmingham as the Post mark, and my writing on the direction, or may. And I know nothing of its contents.[2]

I hope you are well with this cold wind.

Ever Yrs affly John H. Newman

[1] See *A.W.* p. 267–8 for reflections in Newman's 'Journal' on 25 June 1869.
[2] When copying this letter in her 'Memorials of John Henry Newman' Emily Bowles wrote: 'I received a packet with the following note, characteristically discerning and defeating an underhand attempt to involve Father Newman in the disrepute of some pseudo-theological wrangle.'

TO HENRY JAMES COLERIDGE

The Oratory Bm June 30. 1869

My dear Fr Coleridge

Your new number has just come to me, and, as I know I sha'n't write you a line, if I delay, I take up my pen at once. You have had a good many capital articles lately, and I think you must be making way, especially from the tone of the Protestant Press. You saw the Spectator (I think) praised you lately. If you are to change your internal shape and drift, it must be on the ground that success is not tanti in your present line, not that you cannot gain it. I don't profess to give you that attention which I ought to give — I have so many interruptions, and our Fathers borrow my Numbers and then it is 'Hunt the Slipper' to get them back, and old men have, I suppose, a sort of impatience in reading new things — at least I find I read awhile, and then I get tired — and stop, when I have time before me. However, your review of Lecky was good, though I want to master it and have not — and the review of Thackeray —[1] It overcomes a great deal of jealousy and prejudice among Protestant writers, to find a Catholic sympathizing and taking an interest in Protestants and their literature — and you have lately been doing it, as you safely and fairly of course *can* do it. You do so in the said article on Thackeray and in other criticisms. In like manner you have said a word against 'Five years etc.' And your remarks on Pattison and Dr Gillow are in the same spirit.[2] What I have read of your Articles on Education I like very much — but from feeling that I have thought and written and read enough on the subject, and being just now full of other matters, I have not done justice to them.[3] As to Pusey, what you say in various parts of the Article is most true — but, perhaps from my fault, I wanted to be assisted by it, and have not been, in finding what the exact drift of his string of authorities is, and what it is worth.[4] I understood it to be to show that 'Immaculata Conceptio' is by tradition 'activa,' and that as such, it is by tradition 'condemned'. The answer to this, I suppose, is that the Church is not bound to receive a word in a certain sense in which in a former age it was used in the schools — the ὁμοούσιον gives us a stronger instance than is

---

[1] The *Month*, (June 1869), contained articles, 'On Thackeray's Place among English Writers,' and 'Lecky's History of European Morals.' Both these were praised in the *Spectator*, (5 June 1869), p. 685.

[2] The *Month*, (July 1869), severely criticised a Catholic work claiming to reveal the shortcomings of Anglican Sisterhoods, *Five Years in a Protestant Sisterhood and Ten Years in a Catholic Convent*. It also devoted eight pages to criticism of the pamphlet *Catholic Higher Education*, London 1869, by John Gillow, who had misunderstood Mark Pattison's *Suggestions on Academical Organisations*, Edinburgh 1869.

[3] Besides articles in earlier numbers, the July *Month* contained one on 'The Prospects of Catholic Education.'

[4] The July *Month* had an article on Pusey's *First Letter to the Very Rev. J. H. Newman*, entitled 'A Second Part of the Eirenicon.'

necessary for the Concept. Immac. for it was condemned at a large council 70 years before Nicaea. But perhaps I have not got hold of his sense.[1]

Ever Yours most sincerely John H Newman

THURSDAY 1 JULY 1869   dark and cold again
FRIDAY 2 JULY   I could hardly see to say mass   I could have borne a fire after dinner

TO E. E. ESTCOURT

The Oratory July 2. 1869
My dear Canon Estcourt

I send you, according to Mr Comberbach's directions, the list he gave some years ago of probable subscriptions to the Oxford Church. He was unable on my inquiring to give me any list of actual subscriptions, but he made over to me a sum of £187.4.3. For this sum I now send you a cheque, as he requests me to do, that is, for £190.3. which it has become by the addition of interest upon it, and the deduction of its share of the expenses incurred at Oxford, since it came into my hands. I date the cheque July 11, because my half yearly dividends will not be paid into my account at the bank till that day. Will you be so good as to let me have a receipt in due time?

I am, My dear Canon Estcourt, Yours very sincerely
John H Newman of the Oratory

Memorandum.

1864.	Decr. 7. Received from Mr Comberbach	187.4.3
	Interest at 3 per cent for four years from July 1/65 to July 1/69	22.8.9
		209.13.0
	Deduct, proportion of Expenses, viz lawyer's bills etc etc	19.10.0
		190.3.0

July 2/69 Cheque sent by me to Canon Escourt for £190.3.0

JHN.

[5] Coleridge replied gratefully on 1 July, and said that it was not intended 'to change our line or form,' at the moment. He did not think anyone quite understood Pusey's drift.

TO CHARLES MEYNELL

The Oratory Bm July 2/69

Private

My dear Dr Meynell

At length, on an auspicious day, I send you my sheets.[1] The printers have only sent the second this morning.

Your experienced eye will see if I have run into any language which offends against doctrinal propriety or common sense. Thanking you for your trouble,

Very sincerely Yours John H Newman

TO JAMES NARY

The Oratory Bm July 2. 1869

My dear Mr Nary

Fr St John has shown me your letter to him, and I think it best to reply to you myself, — the more so, because, as neither of us, I much regret, are able to give you the information you desire, I do not like to leave it to him to say so.

It was Fr Neville who was in treaty with Mr Carr and others for the ground which you speak of. It was not freehold ground. There was a great complication. I do not know how things stand at present, and consider that Fr Neville must not commit himself in a difficult question of law by speaking on the subject. Some time ago I asked Mr Hanley, whether, in behalf of the Catholics of Oxford, he would put himself in Fr Neville's place, but he did not feel that he could hope to raise the necessary sum.[2]

Very truly Yours John H Newman of the Oratory

[1] Feast of the Visitation. Newman had asked Meynell to criticise the sheets of *G.A.* There is a letter from Meynell, dated Monday, and written perhaps at Easter or Whitsun: 'Oscott
Dear Dr Newman
  If you think I can be of any use I send you my address for the next ten or twelve days
        13 George Street Wolverhampton
      I wish you heartily the joy of the season.
            Sincerely and respectfully Charles Meynell'
[2] For Neville's unfortunate purchase see note to diary for 10 Feb. 1867, and letters of the first part of 1867 to Clutton and 20 March 1867 to Hope-Scott and 21 March 1867 to Castle. Nary was the priest at Oxford and was trying to find a site for a church.

The Oratory Bm July 3 1869

My dear Professor Sullivan

Some time ago Dr Woodlock asked me for an article for a new Number of the Atlantis. I consented, but I asked how it was your name was not mentioned in connexion with the plan. Will you kindly tell me how this is? — Are you still Editor or not? Or how can any Number be successful which has not an article from you?[1]

Very truly Yours John H Newman

W. K Sullivan Esqr

The Oratory Bm July 4. 1869

My dear Child

I am truly annoyed about your Cross. When it came, I put it at once into a safe place — and then (as is often the case with me) the whole matter went out of my mind like a shot. I recollected nothing about it till your letter came yesterday — and now I cannot recollect where the safe place was. Sometimes I lose important letters in this way by what is simply over care. If I had let it lie on my Table, all would have been right. I will have a hunt for it, and send it to you, as soon as I find it.[2]

I forget whether I have written to you since you gave me an account of your evening party.[3] That Mr L. I believe to be a very clever man — but

[1] Sullivan replied on 11 July that he had not been asked to act as Editor of the Atlantis, probably because he was considered to be too busy, He had promised an article conditionally, if he could find time to write, but had been unable to do so.

[2] This refers to a small silver crucifix which Emily Bowles had sent to Newman to be blessed. See letter of 25 July.

[3] Emily Bowles described, early in June, a brilliant dinner and evening party at the house of Sir John Simeon, 72 Eaton Place: 'I was there last night, to a great assembly to meet Tennyson — whom I was very glad to see and know. Otherwise it was painful. Mr Lecky was there whose "Morals" [History of European Morals, London 1869] you have no doubt seen — and who is certainly a remarkable man — 25 — and looking like a lank-gawky, dreamy boy. He was introduced to me — but he came in late — and I did not say much. He said he was tired of hearing and reading strictures on his book. He is very interesting to me — pure minded and good evidently — having no belief — no ground of standing — no certainty of comparing — seeking God and finding Him only in glimpses — says conscience is the only guide — and wrongdoing only hindering self progress. I felt the greatest pain to see that soul — on the threshold of life — with a ship freighted out with such gifts — without compass or rudder. There were two girls friends of his, who say they would give the world to believe there was anything beyond this life — but have no belief. They read all these misbelieving books. Mr Palgrave's brother was there — the Layards — Sir R. Blennerhassett and Mr Gaisford — looking quite lost in his unhappiness. And poor Louy [Louisa Simeon] — looking so bright and noble — in the midst of all this throng of half-unbelieving protestants half unCatholic Catholics. Surely Sir John is not wise to drift into this seething mass of doubtful society — and take this child with him?'

from his books I am not over interested in him, and the noise he is making is enough to overset any person so young as he is. Miss F. wrote to me, and said she expected her faith to be much tried.[1] Her friends had told her that I was about to become a Protestant. I told her that, when pressed with stories against the Church, she ought to take that assertion as a specimen of their truth; that Protestants had been saying it before she was born, and would say it after I was dead — that they are sure to say that on my death bed I became a Protestant, as they almost say of Robert Wilberforce

Coleridge is too wise to be annoyed at my refusing to do what I could not (as at first he did not know) do honourably.[2]

Ever Yrs affly John H Newman

Miss Bowles

P.S. Thank you for posting my letter.

FROM CHARLES MEYNELL

Oscott Saturday [3 July 1869][3]

Dear Dr Newman

Because I send it back immediately by return of post please don't think I have not read it with the utmost care and interest. I felt squeamish when I saw it, thinking how much you gave me credit for knowing beyond what I know, but I determined immediately to put down this feeling as standing in the way of what you required of me. I was relieved at finding nothing for me to do.

Only one passage made me pause where it is said that nothing exists objectively except the *Individual*;[4] in the application of which statement to the doctrine of the Holy Trinity I remembered that Roscelin got himself into trouble; but I reflected that the Church never condemned the principle but only its wrong application. Then it occurred to me that St Thomas, according to Liberatore, held the same doctrine, and I quoted him as holding it in my pamphlet — 'F. Liberatore calls him a realist; but he admitted the fundamental doctrine of the conceptualists, that nothing exists, objectively, besides the individuals with that ratio of resemblance which is the foundation of the "universals"'.[5] I looked in St Thomas to find a passage, but could not find one to suit exactly, though I feel quite sure enough in my own mind. Well this will show that I am doing my duty.

I also remembered carefully your injunction as to silence.

Yours Respectfully Charles Meynell

---

[1] Emily Bowles also said: 'That provoking child, Geraldine Fitzgerald was carried by Miss Worsley to the Oratory and introduced to Fr Knox. I don't think it was nice — but when it was done she came to tell me, and ask my opinion. I said after thinking a little, that you had sent her to me, probably wishing me to be a friend and look after her welfare at first starting. And that you knew I lived close to Farm Street and far from the Oratory, so I concluded you would be received there. But that she was quite free.'

[2] See letter of 2 June to H. J. Coleridge.

[3] Newman has written on this letter in pencil 'first letter July'

[4] *G.A.*, p. 9.

[5] Charles Meynell, *Padre Liberatore and the Ontologists*, London N.D. [1868], p. 21.

The Oratory July 4/69

My dear Dr Meynell

I thank you very much both for your anxious attention to my sheets and for your despatch. I have altered the passage about 'individual.' What I relied on was the 'Sacro-sanctæ et *individuæ* Trinitatis —'[1] but I was aware that the word 'individual' was unsuited, if *directly* applied to the Holy Trinity or the Divine Being under the notion that the word stood for instances of an infima species differing only in number — which would be classing God with His creatures. I am glad you had not other things to remark.

If you will allow me to inflict on you the charitable trouble of looking at some other sheets, I am not certain that you will not suddenly light on a wasp-nest, though I have no *suspicion* of it — but when a matter has not been one's study it is difficult to have confidence in oneself

Yours most sincerely John H Newman

P.S. I ought before now to have thanked you for your Pamphlet, and said a word about it. I thought it very clever and very amusing, and that Fr Liberatori caught it — but I wish I knew enough on the main subject to have a right to an opinion.[2]

The Oratory July 4. 1869

My dear Pusey,

I can understand a Council making explanations, if some great good is to come from it, though they think them quite unnecessary; but not, supposing nothing to come of it. At the price of gaining the most important body of men who are represented by the Church Union, I think it would be little to say 'The immaculate conception is passiva,' but why should they do what they all feel to be unnecessary, if it is only to draw 'spinis de pluribus unam,'[3] without a chance of conciliating thereby those who have demanded it? As to the Greeks they can take care of themselves, better than Anglicans can take care of them. For myself, I have ever heard that their objection to the *definition* of 1854 was that 'they had ever held the *doctrine*.'[4]

I believe that in the middle age the question was not *cleared* — truth was

---

[1] A prayer to be said after reciting the breviary begins 'Sacrosanctae et individuae Trinitati . . .'

[2] See third note to letter of 25 March to Emily Bowles.

[3] Horace, *Epistles*, II, ii, 212.

[4] Pusey wrote at length on 20 June, wanting the Vatican Council to make a definition that would remove his particular difficulty concerning the Immaculate Conception of our Lady, and saying 'Greeks were as much startled as we.' See letter of 9 June to him.

therefore on neither side of the controversy — but, as time went on, a distinction has been made, and we see how much of the medieval question may be answered affirmatively, how much negatively.

So it was in the Ante nicene times as regards the doctrine of our Lord's Person. As far as words go, St Hippolytus omits our Lord's divine Sonship from his view of the doctrine. St Justin seems to arianize — others have to be piously explained; nearly all (if Bull is to be believed) speak as if they were ignorant of our Lord's 'invisible and immense' nature; St Basil was economically silent about the divinity of the Holy Ghost, and St Athanasius defended his act. Till a point is actually *defined* by the Church, there will ever be confusion. It does not follow that a truth was not held, that there *was* confusion.

As to the Immaculate Conception, I consider its tradition, (Quod semper) from the first, is contained in the doctrine '*Mary* is the *Second Eve*.'

As to 'all have sinned but one,' so in like manner Scripture says 'None followed the House of David but Judah only,' though Benjamin did also.[1] We must not tie down an author to his words when they look one way, as if they looked another. St Ambrose says that the text 'All have sinned' means that all have sinned *before their conversion*, but, as to those who deny a man 'abstinere a delictis' after conversion, 'non possum in eorum convenire sententiam'; St Chrysostom that Christ gives aid in baptism, and the Apostles to the already baptized. I put down the first instances that occur, but the principle is clear. In like manner that our Blessed Lady 'peccavit in Adamo, vendita fuit in Adamo,' (which Suarez maintains while he holds the Immaculate Conception) is quite enough to account for the Fathers' 'none are free from sin but one.'

As to the 'Quod semper etc' certainly one must explain one clause of it by another.[2] Universal reception is a more striking test than antiquity because it can be more easily ascertained. St Augustine uses it in the 'Securus judicat orbis terrarum.'

I did not say to Wilson that your writers were 'unauthoritative,' but irrelevant.[3] I meant what I have said above — that in the middle age truth and error were mixed together, as in the Ante nicene period.

I am *told* that our *American* Bishops are likely to play an independent part. The best way of getting at them is through the community of St Paul at New York — Father Hecker is their head. Perhaps you know him. As far as I know, he would do more for you than any one in America. I can write to him, if you wish. At the same time, I should not be acting as a friend, if I did

---

[1] I *Kings*, 12:20. Pusey referred to St Augustine's use of the text 'All have sinned' against the Pelagians.

[2] Pusey wrote: 'You people seem to me (except a certain number) to be drifting off from the "Quod semper," as if the practical teaching "ubique" was in itself an evidence of the "semper."'

[3] i.e. those quoted by Pusey in *First Letter to the Very Rev. J. H. Newman*. Pusey wrote that he had heard from R. F. Wilson, see diary for 11 June, 'that you think my quotations more or less of unauthoritative persons.'

not say, that I have not found any one (I think) who has not been repelled by what has been thought your hostile tone. I know how different this is from your intention. Since your new book came out, a priest who is more hostile to Ward, Manning etc than perhaps any one I know, has written to me about your part in the controversy in quite violent, and I know most mistaken, terms.[1] Men seem to think that you are not really seeking peace, but indoctrinating Anglicans how to accost, to treat with, to carry themselves towards, the Roman See — what points to make, what to concede, what not to concede — also, as saying to the Evangelical body 'You see, we don't agree with, and don't mean to give in to, the Romanists.' In a word, that your books are really controversial, not peace-making. You may be sure I take your part, — without any merit of mine, because I know how loving your heart is — but it has sunk deep into the minds of all Catholics. 'He has got an arrière pensée.'

Of our own Bishops, Dr Ullathorne of Birmingham, Dr Goss of Liverpool, Dr Clifford of Clifton, and perhaps Dr Brown of Newport, are the only ones, who are likely to profit by the gift of your book in the way you wish.

I am very sorry to send you so discouraging a letter — Fr Hecker would perhaps take another view — and I should be rejoiced if you thought I could do any good by writing to him.[2]

Ever Yours affly John H Newman

MONDAY 5 JULY 1869   gloomy thick weather

TO W. J. COPELAND

The Oratory July 5/69

My dear Copeland

Thank you for the copies of Keble. I am sending them on to Moberly.[3]

As to the list of dates, I am quite grieved you have been waiting for me, especially as by R's hurrying on the Proofs so, I suppose he wishes the volume out soon. I wish to do just what you and others think best. In all I have written, I have corrected later editions again and again, and I am not at all sure that many sermons are not altered in the later editions. Also, though I know on the whole what was altered in Sermons written early when prepared for publication, I am not a judge what the effect of the whole alterations will

---

[1] This was John Walker of Scarborough. See letter of 11 July to him.
[2] For Pusey's reply see at 23 July.
[3] These were copies of letters from Keble to Newman. Copeland wrote to Newman on 3 Sept., 'I find by a letter from Moberly that he is obliged to give up the Keble Correspondence "with regret," he says, "but with relief —" It was growing upon him to an enormous extent, and difficulties, as I always thought they might, were increasing every day.'

be on others. I should like some one, yourself or another, on knowing the whole state of the case, to make a decision.[1]

I think I recollect every paragraph in Volume 8 'Inward Witness' as written in the first draught or at least written long before the publication — but it is quite clear that 'the glory of virginity,' and one or two others *clauses* perhaps, p 121 were put in at a very late date.[2] As to the Sermon on Religious Joy, I have been reading it again, and (if I have marked it down in my list as an early Sermon) it has certainly been rewritten at a later date. The whole tone and style of writing is late.[3]

I have no list here of my Sermons. The one I made for you was from their *Numbers*, and then I referred to my Preaching Lists to see when those Numbers were preached. This was a long process, and I can't therefore do any thing definite till the *proof* of the list comes to me

Ever Yrs affly J H N

TUESDAY 6 JULY 1869   went to Rednall

TO EDWARD BELLASIS

Rednall July 7/69

My dear Serjeant

I have been writing to you continually but have never written.[4] I told Richard to write. I trust he is well up in his *general* literature now. And have given him some questions on the Merchant of Venice. They have not come in to me yet — but an Essay on Johnson's life which he has written is very creditable to him. Richard Pope says he is well up in his English History, and thinks he will pass creditably. As he has passed himself, *he* can judge. I get fidgetty because I am *no* judge. I wish some *London* graduate of the University (in London I mean) could be found to examine him. He has been working hard.

Tell Mrs Bellasis I won't forget her kind thoughts, if I come to London. I can't believe it is three years since I was at the Lawn.[5]

My book tries my head — but it tries me more to have it weighing heavy on my thoughts.

---

[1] Copeland wrote on 4 July that he did not think Newman's alterations in his sermons important enough to interfere with his giving the dates of their first preaching. In the Preface to *S.D.* Copeland noted the chief changes, and in the date lists, some sermons were eventually described as 'rewritten' etc.

[2] See second note to letter of 20 June to Copeland.

[3] See fourth note to letter of 20 June to Copeland.

[4] This letter concerns the sons of Bellasis. Richard was taking an external degree at London University. Newman wrote him a testimonial on 16 June: 'I hereby certify that Mr Bellasis has been for some years at our School, and that his conduct has been from first to last unexceptionable. John H Newman'

[5] The Lawn, Putney.

As to Edward, he slept with his window open — which has given both him and William bad colds. Colds are about. I will tell Ambrose your suggestions about his going home

Ever Yrs affly John H Newman

FRIDAY 9 JULY 1869   Wm [William] came out and returned   three bright days
SATURDAY 10 JULY   did not go back to Bm [Birmingham]

TO J. WALKER OF SCARBOROUGH

Rednall July 11/69

My dear Canon Walker

While my last letter was travelling about after you, Fr Ryder had to decide, and in a few days out came his Pamphlet. He was obliged to decide at once, the season was getting on so fast. The reason I was for publishing it is the vindication he makes of the Popes from the charge of dishonesty — which I think he does very well[1]

I hope he has sent you a copy, I shall see about it when I return to Bm [Birmingham]

For myself, I have not a dream of answering Pusey. It never came into my head. But you are hard upon him.

Ever Yrs most sincerely John H Newman
The Ory July 12/69

Just got your letter. Thank you. The Bishop was kind enough to send P. his book.[2]

TO CHARLOTTE WOOD

Rednall. July 11/69

My dear Miss Wood

I do indeed grieve at your anxiety, and have not forgotten you. Since no news has come fresh, it is my trust that the great apprehension which came upon you is passed away. I am very sorry you are so ill yourself

Yours affectionately John H Newman.

July 12   Your letter just come. I rejoice

MONDAY 12 JULY 1869   went to Oy [Oratory] and back.   gloomy
TUESDAY 13 JULY   again bright and very sultry

---

[1] H. I. D. Ryder, *A Critique upon Mr Ffoulkes' 'Letter.'* See letter of 6 June to Walker. In the second half of his pamphlet Ryder defended the good faith of the Popes in accepting the False Decretals.

[2] See letter of 9 June to Pusey.

TO AUGUSTA THEODOSIA DRANE

Rednall, July 13. [1869]

My dear Sister in Xt

I have not the Life here, we are reading it in the Refectory.[1] I rejoice to hear it has got so very soon to a Second Edition. It is a wonderful success, for I think it must principally have sold among Protestants. As to 'boldness', I think it bold not in one matter only but throughout. It dares in faith to show a great soul as she really was, knowing her Lord can plead her cause, and not squaring what is said of her by the feelings and opinions of readers. I think this is a great merit, being very conscious myself, in what I write, of wishing to persuade, instead of leaving the Truth to persuade of its own weight.

But as to your question — It never entered into my head, nor into the head of any one I have met with, to fancy any sinister meaning in your words about my Pamphlet; and I have not a dream what that meaning can be. I have no need to refresh my memory of them, for I have read them many times, and shown them to others; And as to the Dublin I have not seen it, but those who have, tell me that the words used are unintelligible, are like the growling of one who would find fault if he could, but can't — So I beg you not to alter a word for me, and as to the sinister meaning, I certainly shall not try to find it out, lest I should spoil my pleasure in the passage by an association however unfounded and ridiculous.[2]

The Spectator, which is a religious paper, bating one or two dreadful errors, spoke with great admiration of the Life from its own point of view, and I hear that there is a very favorable notice in the Saturday.[3] I look forward to dear Mother Margaret having as great a career of usefulness now that 'being dead she still speaketh' as in her life, tho' very different in its nature.[4]

Yrs affectly in Xt   John H. Newman

[1] *Life of Mother Margaret Mary Hallahan.* Augusta Theodosia Drane was preparing the second edition, which appeared in the autumn. Cf. letter of 28 May to her.
[2] The passage in Mother Margaret's *Life*, about Newman's pamphlet, *A Letter to Pusey*, was the one he quoted in his letter of 13 May to Pusey, referring to *Diff.* II, pp. 113–14. The reviewer of the *Life* in *DR*, (July 1869), p. 202, objected to what was there said, and as Augusta Drane wrote to Newman on 15 July, 'lectures me for not distinguishing between the phrases, *as quoted by Dr Pusey*, and as they stand in Originals . . .' The passage was not altered in the second edition except that in the phrase about preposterous expressions as to our Lady taken from 'various foreign writers (some of them on the Index),' the word 'one' was now substituted for 'some.' Second edition, p. 327.
[3] The *Spectator*, (26 June 1869), pp. 762–4; the *Saturday Review*, (10 July 1869), pp. 58–9.
[4] *Hebrews*, 11:4. Augusta Drane replied, 'We understand the book is selling among the Ritualists . . . The Protestant Reviews on it indicate that they have felt as if they had come in contact with a great soul.'

TO ARTHUR WEST HADDAN

Rednall July 14. 1869

My dear Haddan

Thank you for the promise of your Volume.

I am sure you have said nothing unkind of me.[1]

As to what you have written on the subject of Anglican Orders, doubtless it will confirm Anglicans in their belief of them; but, I venture to say, it will produce no practical effect on Catholics at all, here or at Rome.

Catholics consider that a reasonable doubt in the validity of Orders is sufficient for treating them practically as invalid; and it is the universal sentiment among us that, not on one only, but on many grounds, there is a reasonable doubt about the Anglican. Some think them certainly invalid, others think them very uncertain; others not improbably, others probably valid; but one and all hold that there is a reasonable doubt about them. They will never be recognized by Catholics.

I fear this will amaze you more than you so energetically tell me I have already done; but we must put away illusions, and take things as they are[2]

The Revd A. W. Haddan

THURSDAY 15 JULY 1869   went to Oratory and back with Wm [William]

TO CHARLES RUSSELL

The Oratory Bm July 15. 1869

My dear Dr Russell,

I am very glad at your news about Mr Bliss — How wonderful it is. I knew his Father and recollect his marriage, and he was one of the few persons who behaved tenderly to me at Oxford on my own reception.[3] I would

---

[1] Haddan, who had been Newman's curate for a year, 1840–1, wrote on 9 July that he was sending his *Apostolic Succession in the Church of England*, London 1869, 'its subject is English Orders, and therefore I *must* speak of yourself.' Haddan, who, in his book, did not mention Newman by name, added, 'I have not forgotten what I owe to you not for personal kindness only, but for things worth far more than that. And if I have tried to answer what (forgive me) did and does give me exceeding pain, viz. your letter etc about English orders [of 5 Aug. 1868 to H. J. Coleridge], it has been only because it lay straight in my way and could not be passed over. And the cause is good if the advocate is feeble.

I cannot help adding what I am sure you will forgive — that the more I think of the letter the more I am *amazed* that you should have written it . . . Yours very truly Arthur W. Haddan'

[2] The signature has been cut out and 'Yours very truly J H Newman' added in another hand. In a draft of his letter Newman spoke even more strongly of the unanimous opinion of Catholics against Anglican Orders.

[3] The eldest son of William Bliss, William Henry Bliss, had just become a Catholic. His wife was the daughter of Cecil Wray, on whom see Volume XI, p. 153. Newman perhaps confused W. H. Bliss's father with his uncle, Philip Bliss, who was Registrar of Oxford University, 1824–53.

gladly do any thing I can, but it will be a tough business. As to Dr Pusey, I fear it is just a point on which he would be peremptory — but I may be wrong.[1]

Ever Yours affly John H Newman

TO CATHERINE ANNE BATHURST

Rednall July 16. 1869

My dear Child

You must know what your line is so much better than I can do, that I hardly like to criticize a second time — else, I should tell you how much it disappointed me to find you were starting with so little apparatus of names and subscriptions.

I quite opened my eyes with surprise to find I was the only one who had to receive sums — first because my name by itself is likely to do you as much harm as good among those Catholics on whom you must depend. And then again people give money when the place of giving is close at hand, not when it is out of the way. Who will take the trouble to send post office orders or cheques to Birmingham? Depend upon it, London is the only place which can do you good.

But in like manner you must have subscriptions printed to begin your list, and to be samples of what other subscriptions ought to be or may be. The Bishop of Ghent should give something even though he does not pay till last, or *till* you get enough to *do* your work, Also, the Vicar General or the Curé or whoever it is who makes way for you. Also, since you are Tertiaries, and expressly *say* so in your Prospectus, you should name the Dominican Father or the Prelate whom you are under. I am sure all this is very necessary.

Please put down my name for £10 a year for 3 years. I will give more if you find you want it. You do not know the sort of Terms we are on with a great person like the Duke of Norfolk, or you would not think I could ask him. Recollect I have influence with no body[2]

Yrs affly John H Newman

[1] Bliss was an assistant at the Bodleian Library from 1866 to 1876. See letter of 2 Aug. to St John. Newman seems to have feared that Pusey, who was an *ex officio* Curator of the Library, would now wish Bliss to resign his post. Dr R. W. Hunt, Keeper of Western MSS. at the Bodleian, has kindly supplied the editors with this information: 'There is no evidence in our records that any difference was made on his [Bliss] becoming a Roman Catholic; rather the contrary. For on 11 June 1870 the Curators agreed that should W. D. Macray accept the living of Ducklington, Bliss should succeed him as Superintendent of the Catalogue of Printed Books. This arrangement was confirmed on 10 December 1870.' In 1877 Bliss was appointed by the Record Office a commissioner for examination and transcription of records in the Vatican Library, relating to English history, a post he held for over thirty years.

[2] Catherine Bathurst was starting a school in Ghent.

SATURDAY 17 JULY 1869   went back to Oy [Oratory]   Challis came

SUNDAY 18 JULY   glass up to 86 in shade

TUESDAY 20 JULY   Went to Rednall with Ambrose

WEDNESDAY 21 JULY   Woodgate with his 2 daughters and niece came to Rednall   *took tea at Rednall*

THURSDAY 22 JULY   went to Oy [Oratory] in evening to see Mr Husband

FRIDAY 23 JULY   returned to Rednall

TO MRS WILLIAM FROUDE

The Oratory Bm July 23. 1869

My dear Mrs Froude

I have had a spite against those velocipedes these 50 years, knowing what harm they did about 1820.[1] Make Eddy drop me a line when he is well again.

As to my movements, I may be away for a fortnight some time or other — but it depends on accidents.

Tell me, as soon as you can, when you and Isy are likely to come

Ever Yours affly in Xt   John H Newman of the Oratory

TO E. B. PUSEY

The Oratory July 23. 1869

My dear Pusey

I think the words of the Bull are these:- 'Quapropter si qui secus ac à nobis definitum est quod Deus avertat, præsumpserint corde sentire, ii noverint ac porro sciant se proprio judicio condemnatos, naufragium circa fidem passos esse, et ab unitate Ecclesiæ defecisse;' — words which are equivalent to an Anathema.[2]

I think it is very likely that at the Council or with its sanction, the doctrine will be added to the Creed of Pope Pius iv.

I have not seen the Dublin on your letter, nor am I likely to do so. It has generally been kinder to you than the Month. The latter has got a theory and is run away with by it.[3]

---

[1] The velocipede was an early form of bicycle, introduced into England in 1818. It had no pedals, and was propelled by kicking the ground.

[2] Pusey, who wrote on 19 July from Chale in the Isle of Wight, asked whether, if the Bull defining the Immaculate Conception of the Blessed Virgin in 1854 contained no anathema, the doctrine could be strictly a matter of faith. Newman quotes from the Bull, *Ineffabilis Deus*, 8 Dec. 1854. *Denzinger-Schönmetzer* 2804.

[3] Pusey wrote 'I hear the Dublin Review and Month are angry with me. I expected it, and was sorry to publish my Letter 1 to you without Letter 2 which is, please God the Eirenicon. This was not my doing.' The reviews of Pusey's *First Letter to the Very Rev. J. H. Newman* were in *DR.*, (July 1869), pp. 238–42, and the *Month*, (July 1869), pp. 92–9. Cf. Liddon's *Pusey*, IV, p. 165.

I heard to-day a very bad account of the Provost's health.[1] Perhaps you know a good deal more about it than I do

I am glad you have left Oxford for the sea breezes

Ever Yrs affly John H Newman

SATURDAY 24 JULY 1869   came to the Oy [Oratory]

TO THE EDITOR OF 'CHURCH OPINION'

The Oratory, Birmingham, July 24, 1869.

Sir,

A copy of your paper of this date has been sent me. I find in it some words attributed to me, in reference to the Authorized Translation of the Bible, which I never wrote.

There are, I believe, several clergymen of my name in the Church of England, and perhaps it is the writing of one of them; but, as this paper has been sent to me, I consider that the sender thinks the passage mine. And therefore I think it best to write to you on the subject.

Perhaps you would be so kind as either to state the Dr. Newman whose words were quoted, or to say you are authorized by Dr. J. H. Newman to state that they are not his.[2]

I am, Sir, Your faithful servant, John H Newman.

TO EMILY BOWLES

The Oratory July 25. 1869

My dear Child,

I have just found the Little Cross, which I have blessed and without any delay send to you.[3] I hope you are not in London this hot weather.

Ever Yrs affly John H. Newman

[1] Edward Hawkins, Provost of Oriel.
[2] This passage in praise of the Authorized Version turned out to have been written by Faber. See letter of 31 July, and also that of 2 Aug. 1869 to St John.
[3] See letter of 4 July to Emily Bowles.

The Oratory July 25/69

My dear Copeland

I declare I don't know how to alter the passage so as to please myself. The best would be simply to leave out the words 'at least in outward appearance —' (Sermon 3 p 32)

Or it might be, 'as if in outward appearance "a man gluttonous and a wine-bibber."'

Or 'had come freely eating etc.'[1]

Keble notices a misprint — Sermon 10 p 150. Have we corrected it in the new Edition? — 'keeps it level' should be 'keeps its level.'[2]

I have been accustomed for the most part to correct my successive editions very carefully. I have no doubt there are various differences in the Editions of my Sermons — but *for the most part* they should be literary — some are doctrinal. From what you imply, I suppose Rivington was for publishing the dates — his opinion is decisive.

How is it your letter is dated the 16th. I got it (I think) yesterday or the day before.

There is a *third* and much more perfect edition of my St Thomas in my Occasional Sermons published in 1857. I think it then became one of my best Sermons. I preached it in my church at Dublin as an Advent Sermon.[3]

Thank you about One Tract More — we found it at last in our Library.[4]

I grieve about the Provost. Woodgate too said he was looking very ill

Ever Yours affectly John H Newman

Avon Dassett. Nr Leamington Saturday, July 24th/69

Dear Dr Newman

I am so pleased with it.[5] It systematizes many random thoughts which I have had, and gives the account and reason of those incompatibilities, of which Mansel only stated the existence. And the illustrations make it easy to follow and pleasant to read. I hope you will pardon my praising it, which is an impertinence on my part, and not the business I have to do.

In order to save my modesty I have hit upon the following plan. I adopt the printer's method of putting Q's [Query] to the passages I wish to remark upon, and

---

[1] See postscript to letter of 24 June to Copeland.
[2] The correction was made, *S.D.*, p. 133.
[3] For the earlier editions of the Sermon on St Thomas see letter of 20 June to Copeland. The third edition was 'Dispositions for Faith,' *O.S.*, pp. 60–74.
[4] See letter of 24 Feb. 1869 to Copeland.
[5] i.e. *G.A.*, proof sheets of which Meynell was reading.

these Q's I wish to be considered exactly in the same light as you would consider the printer's — some of which may hit an oversight, while others are to be pooh-poohed, and others, perhaps to be laughed at, as only betraying the querist's own ignorance. But I will append notes to the passages Q'd to show why the crooked letter was affixed to them.

Qu. 1. *Ch. IV. p. 34.* 'I do not think it unfair reasoning thus to IDENTIFY the apprehension with its object.'[1]

Qu. 2. *p 43* 'A mystery is a proposition . . . or is a statement of the incon///vable;' Q Stet? (But I see the correction is intended to be expunged.)[2]

Qu. 3. *p. 45.* 'Whereas the PARALOGISM lies' etc Qu. Antilogy?[3]

Qu. 4. *p. 47* 'Our notions of things are never commensurate with the things themselves.' Q. *almost* never?[4]

Qu 5. *p. 49* 'The Supreme Being is rather to be considered a MONAD than a UNIT.' Q.Q[5]

Qu 6. *p. 49.* 'If I deny the possibility of two straight lines inclosing a space . . . I do so because a straight line is a notion and nothing more, NOT A THING OF WHICH I HAVE AN IMAGE, and an imperfect one' Q.[5]

Please pardon me, if I am in anything guilty of a usurpation and meddling in matters which do not belong to me in the remarks I am going to make.

Notes

Qu 1. I thought *identify* too strong a word in this place, and that more is said than is meant. The absolute identification of subject and object is Hegelianism. Of course this was not meant. But *even in thought* is there not always an antithesis between subject and object? between the act of apprehension and its object?

Qu. 2 explains itself

Qu 3. I don't know how the word paralogism is used in ordinary English, but the word is used, by Kant, exclusively to designate a halt conclusion — where the reasoning goes beyond its data (παρα) The incompatibilities you refer to he calls antilogies, which name they have retained. Please see if this distinction be worth anything.

Qu 4. Isn't it too much to say that our notions are *never* commensurate with things? Is not my notion of dirt, as, for instance, 'the right thing in the wrong place' commensurate with the thing thought about? And when we use, for the sake of emphasis identical propositions ('a man's a man, for a' that') — is it not of the very essence of such propositions that the thought should be commensurate with the things?[6]

Qu 5. The distinction between a monad and a unit is rather sharp. (I suppose a unit is one of many, while monad refers not to number at all, but to the absence of the note of divisibility. — A word or so within brackets to explain the distinction? Or do your own words sufficiently explain it, and it's only my own dulness?)

Qu 6. Should not the words 'not a thing of which I have an image' be within hooks? Because when I read it first, I referred the words 'and an imperfect one' to 'image'; but it is clear they belong to 'notion'

> 'Commas and points they set exactly right
> And twere a sin to rob them of their mite.'[7]

Now about the doctrine. Does it not imply or seem to imply, as it stands (because 'a straight line is a notion and nothing more') that, *absolutely speaking*, two straight lines may enclose a space? But the axioms concerning time and space are *necessary* axioms. Does not this seem to imply that necessary truth is only notional? And if necessary truth is only notional in one order of things, is it not equally open to say that it is only notional in another, and would not thus intrinsic morality be jeopardized? Perhaps all this criticism is premature: perhaps it is not pertinent. But I think it worth

---

[1] *G.A.*, p. 36.
[2] *G.A.*, p. 45.
[3] *G.A.*, p. 47.
[4] *G.A.*, p. 49.
[5] *G.A.*, p. 51.
[6] Meynell put a footnote to his letter: 'However there is a sense in which the proposition is plainly true. We don't know anything *fully*'.
[7] Pope, *Prelude to the Satires*, 161–2.

while to make it. For I remember that the Saturday Review considered that one of the weakest points in Mill's critique on Hamilton was his holding the view that 'if there were a universe in which whensoever two pairs of things were contemplated by the mind, the Almighty always created a fifth thing, in such a world two-and-two would make five!'

Please look at p 48 where I have ventured to correct the printer. 'Phocions or Ciceros' surely it ought to be — not Phocians.[1]

I am really quite horrified at the *sang froid* of these criticisms of mine. Pray say that you forgive me.

Yours Dear Dr Newman sincerely and respectfully Charles Meynell

P.S I see that there is another way still in which the passage at p 49 may be grammatically construed; so I give it up, and am glad I have called attention to it.

TO CHARLES MEYNELL

The Oratory Bm July 25. 1869

My dear Dr Meynell

I thank you very much for your criticisms, which will be very useful to me.

The only one which I feel a difficulty about is that about two straight lines inclosing a space. I cannot for the life of me, and never have, put it on a level with the Moral Law. Lines are our own creation — the Moral law is in the Nature of God Himself. The only thing which is not *ours* in reasoning is that 'if it is true that A is, it is not true that A is not.' But this foundation being allowed, lines are our own creation. They do not exist in nature. Who ever saw a line? it is an abstraction.

However, the next sheet will be my great difficulty — and I should not wonder if it was decisive one way or the other. You will find I there consider that the dictate of conscience is particular — not general —and that from the multiplication of particulars I *infer* the general — so that the moral sense, as a knowledge *generally* of the moral law, is a deduction from particulars.

Next, that the dictate of conscience, which is natural and the voice of God, is a moral *instinct*, and its own evidence — as the *belief* in an external world is an *instinct* on the apprehension of sensible phenomena.

That to *deny* those instincts is an absurdity, *because* they are the voice of nature.

That it is a duty to trust, or rather to use our nature — and not to do so is absurdity.

That to recognize our nature is really to *recognize God*.

Hence those *instincts* come from *God* — and as the moral law is an inference or generalization from those instincts, the moral law is ultimately taught us from God, *whose* nature it is.

Now, if this is a wasp-nest, tell me. If the Church has said otherwise, I give it all up — but somehow it is so mixed up with my whole book, that, if it is not safe, I shall not go on

Most sincerely Yours John H Newman

[1] *G.A.*, p. 50.

The Oratory July 26. 1869

My dear Woodgate

I hear on good authority that the poor Provost has a bad complaint on him, which requires a surgical operation, and, that, considering his age, an operation is impossible.

This accounts for what you said of him

Yours affly John H Newman

PS.   Bramston has been calling on me today. I was out. Where is he likely to be staying? He said he would call again — and my locality is so uncertain that I want to make sure that I shall be in, by writing to him first.

TUESDAY 27 JULY 1869   change of weather   Bramston called

FROM CHARLES MEYNELL

Avon Dassett July 26. 1869

Dear Dr Newman

There is no wasps' nest at all, in the sense you mean. And if you were to give up the work, I should grieve to the last day of my life that I ever, though in fear and trembling, expressed any opinion on the matter. I feel convinced that the book will do great good. And I have not the slightest doubt but that you are allowed to hold what you hold. If so then why did I say anything about my own hobby of Necessity? Because I wished to say everything about the matters submitted to me at the risk of being impertinent, rather than omit anything which might prove pertinent. In fact I wished to leave it to you to judge what was of use, and what was of none. What *I* think is of very little importance to anybody; but I thought it important, or might be important to say what others would say; and if I were mistaken there would be no harm done. If you had said: 'Ne sutor ultra crepidam', I might have deserved it, but I should still have thought that I erred on the right side. And still, if I say anything to no purpose (and I very probably may,) please take it as not said.

I consider that in matters of philosophy one cannot please everybody. If I take one view I am at war with one set of thinkers, if another with another. Coleridge said (or rather Schlegel said it first) that every man is born either a Platonist or an Aristotelian; at any rate every man is either one or the other. Be realist, like me, and you will get, or may get into hot water: be conceptualist, and I cannot promise you a better fate. The bother of the thing is that one must be either one or the other. Well: I am prosing. Isn't it enough that the Church allows you to say what you say, and that every moderate well-regulated mind will allow you to say it? They will say very likely: 'I cannot say it on my principles, because I don't see how it is reconcilable with certain primary truths of reason and [1] revelation; but *he* can say it, because he thinks it is reconcileable with such principles.' I say the Church is a good Mother and will condemn no man for his Logic. You do not hold as necessary and à priori some principles which I think are so: whereas if I denied these to be such, it seems, I should have to go on and deny all the others. I am sorry indeed that this is the case, for the love of approbation is very strong in me, and I would very far rather agree with than differ from you. But

[1] Perhaps 'or'.

this does not injure, in my eyes the real good that the book will do. Indeed it seems that I agree with the statements; though something is *implied* that the School to which I belong would not agree with. But does this matter? Still I thought it well to call attention to the fact.

Look please, if you have patience how I stand.

I used to hold, at the age of twenty, that all truth was derived from, and is an abstraction upon experience; and should have added that the only necessary truth, really, is that 'a thing cannot be and not be at the same time.' I think this goes a little *beyond* what you say to me in your letter; but I never heard, then or since that I am forbidden by the Church to hold this view, if I like.

Since then I read Cousin, Rosmini, Gioberti, Kant and others, and have also struck out a line of my own. And now I say:

That the principle of Contradiction itself would not be a necessary truth, if it were not for the element of *Time* that is brought into it. For Reason does not forbid me to hold that one thing may not become another thing; but only that it cannot be another *in the same time*. Kant's arguments had convinced me before I read Hamilton's approbation of them, that the intuition of time is à priori and necessary: because we cannot annihilate in thought the *scheme* in which all changes are possible, though we may so annihilate the changes themselves. So with Space. Hence the axioms of Time and Space are necessary axioms. I do not, cannot think it possible that, say in Sirius, two straight lines enclose a space. True I never saw a straight line. I suppose, as you say, that a straight line is an abstraction, from experience; but the element of necessity which attaches to Space, and to the axioms concerning Space, is not from experience, because everything which I experience is contingent. Time and Space account for most necessary axioms.

Then there is the principle of Causation. It is necessary. That things *have* causes, I know indeed by experience; but not that they *must* have causes; for this axiom carries me far beyond experience — to a First Cause, for instance, of which I have no experience. I find the same inexorable Necessity in aesthetics and morals. My conscience says: Do this: refrain from that: licet; non licet. But my reason tells me that some things must of necessity be done, and others, always, of necessity be refrained from. See then, how with me these things hang together. It seems if I gave an empirical account of Necessity in one order of things, I must do it in another. I could not then prove the existence of God by the Speculative Reason, which the Church Authorities (but I speak under correction) oblige me to do. The argument from design would indeed make believe that the world had a Designer — but I should want his attribute of Necessity, and therefore of Eternity; and should have only such a notion of His moral goodness, as the blurred beauty of this earth and certain aspirations in my vile personality would give me.

You will see that I do not agree with Dr Ward (though I have not yet told him so) that Necessity is a mere negation. Nor do I see how he reconciles this principle with another that he holds — that of synthetical judgments à priori. The principle of Causation is positive surely. The principle of contradiction is negative certainly —[1] save as to the positive element of Time, which it contains. My Necessity is positive; is God; for there is only One Necessary Being.

Well: how does this concern yourself? Really I don't know — ; but it may do so for all that. You might wish to know how you stand towards the class of thinkers which, in the main, I represent. You might possibly hit upon some way of pleasing everybody. Or you might make some other use of what I have said, that I have no conception of. Anyhow it can do no harm to say it

I hope that you will not find it necessary to answer this. But if you were to write a line and say that you would go on with the work, I believe my sleep would be sweeter in consequence, on the night after receiving such an assurance.

Yours Sincerely and respectfully Charles Meynell

[1] Meynell put a footnote, 'It is analytical of course.'

TO CHARLES MEYNELL

The Oratory July 27. 1869

My dear Dr Meynell

I am extremely obliged to you for the trouble you are taking with me, and I hope my shying, as I do, will not keep you from speaking out. Pray bring out always what you have to say. I am quite conscious that metaphysics is a subject on which one cannot hope to agree with those with whom in other matters one agrees most heartily, from its extreme subtlety — but I am also deeply conscious of my own ignorance on the whole matter, and it sometimes amazes me that I have ventured to write on a subject which is even accidently connected with it. And this makes me so very fearful that I should be saying any thing temerarious or dangerous — the ultimate angles being so small from which lines diverge to truth and error.

Be sure I should never hastily give over what I am doing, because I should have trouble in correcting or thinking out again what I have said — but if I found some irreconcilable difference, running through my view, between its conditions and what the Church teaches or has sanctioned, of course I should have no hesitation of stopping at once

So please to bear with me if I start or plunge.

In my next sheet, which perhaps won't make its appearance for some time, I fear there will be much crudeness — over and above the doctrine — perhaps faults of composition.

You interest me very much in what you say of your own opinions — and the history of them; and it is a proof to me that you will both understand and see the position of my own views better than I do myself.

Most sincerely Yours John H Newman

Thank you for altering Phoci*a*ns

WEDNESDAY 28 JULY 1869 went out to Rednall in the evening Ambrose and John went to Switzerland

TO EMILY BOWLES

The Oratory July 28/69

My dear Child

Miss F's direction is 19 Norfolk Square. She wrote to me lately, and seemed very happy. I am glad to find you confirm my impression[1]

[1] See letter of 4 July to Emily Bowles, which explains how Geraldine Fitzgerald had just become a Catholic. She wrote to Newman afterwards, 'Mama was the one I dreaded paining the most and the first few days were certainly dreadful, they used every means to bring me back and I could not have resisted in my own strength but God helped me and then your most kind letter came in the middle of it all and did me more good than I have any words to say, cheering me up and making me feel as strong as a giant, it gave me such heart and spirit. . . .'

Alas, I, rightly or wrongly, have long thought that Fr C's vocation lay in a different direction. I did towards him, what I doubt if I ever did to any one else — viz (before he had made his choice) to ask him to belong to the Oratory. (Only two persons did I ever mention this to.)[1]

I am very glad you are enjoying yourself so much. That coast is the best of all, I believe, for bracing air.[2]

Mrs Wootten is much better than she was — we are lightening her work; but that will make no difference to the boys' access to her.

As to Frederic, we have had many trials — but (if you were able to know what you can never know) you would understand that his matter is to us the most profound of all. We have before now been threatened, simply because the London Oratory received him — and, knowing what has passed here, I have always thought (though I have no evidence that it is so) that he was driven away (without fault of his) from the London Oratory, as he was from this. In the greatest perils St Philip has been a true Father to us[3]

Ever Yours affectly John H Newman

FRIDAY 30 JULY 1869   Woodgate and Bramston came over to dine with me at Rednall
SATURDAY 31 JULY   came in to the Oratory

TO THE EDITOR OF 'CHURCH OPINION'

[31 July 1869]

Sir

I thank [you] for giving me the opportunity of setting right what appears to be, (from what you say) a common misapprehension, as to the authorship of the passage on the Authorized Translation of the Bible quoted in Church Opinion of July 24

It is the writing of Dr Faber. It is contained in the Essay which he has prefixed to the life of St Francis [of] Assisi (Richardson 1853) p 116, and quoted as his in the Dublin Review for June 1853, p 466 note, from which you say that Archbishop Trench extracted it.[4]

I am etc J H N

SUNDAY 1 AUGUST 1869   I preached   Bishop called.   Dr Russell called and went on

---

[1] This paragraph refers to Henry James Coleridge.
[2] Emily Bowles was staying at North Berwick with the dowager Lady Downe.
[3] This paragraph refers to Emily's brother, Frederic Bowles, who had been a member of the Birmingham Oratory.
[4] See letter of 24 July 1869, and that of 1 April 1870 to Mrs John Mozley. Also that of 2 Aug. 1869 to St John. Richard Chenevix Trench, Archbishop of Dublin 1863–84, quoted the passage as coming from one 'who has abandoned the communion of the English Church,' in his *English Past and Present*, fourth edition, 1859, p. 33.

The Oratory Augst 1. 1869

My dear Serjeant

Did *you* send me the Examination List? I read that first, and rejoiced —
then I opened your first letter, and was confounded — then I bethought me
of your second letter, which the first had made me forget to open. So that, as
often, not second thoughts are best, but first and third.

All's well that ends well. Congratulate Richard. I have no doubt that he
(and Sparrow) did very well — and did us credit. Is it Lord Petre's son who
is in the second division?[1]

We don't know yet our two Fathers' destination.[2]

Ever Yrs affectly John H Newman

MONDAY 2 AUGUST 1869   Challis went away to Wild.   Lord Dunraven called

The Oratory Aug 2. 1869

My dear Copeland

The proof of the List is come —[3] but I have so defaced it with scribble,
that I am sending for another copy.

Of course many corrections are necessary. Meanwhile I have drawn it up
in another way, which, though not good for reference, has its advantages. So I
send it you for inspection. The doing it has enabled me to correct some
blunders and omissions which otherwise would have escaped me.[4]

Bramston has been here — and he and Woodgate came over and dined
with me at Rednall

Ever Yours affectly John H Newman

P.S.   I don't notice in what I send you the alterations in the course of
successive Editions. Might you not say, that the List is given in compliance

[1] See letter of 2 Aug. to St John.
[2] See diary for 28 July.
[3] i.e. the lists of sermons with their dates of preaching, at the end of *S.D.*
[4] Newman also sent a note:

'For the Printer   Aug. 4/69
As to the List of dates, There is an awkwardness in "When first preached" being over the
month and not over the year. Nor does the separation of month and year please me
    I have drawn out a specimen page, which I inclose, — and should like set up, and sent to
Mr Copeland
    As to the corrections in *type*, those I have made on the proofs.
                    J H N'

with the wish of various people — but it obviously requires explanations. Of course all of the Sermons were corrected carefully before publication — so that none of them are precisely as delivered — Again since various of them were preached over again several times, on each fresh delivery they would receive corrections, so that some of them were in that way gradually re-written, without set purpose of doing so. However, that the subjoined list makes as much allowance for such alterations as seems fairly required

TO AMBROSE ST JOHN

⌐The Oratory Aug 2/68⌐1

My dear A

Your letter just come. Bellasis and Sparrow are in the first Class of Passes. Sparrow now goes in for the honour examination.[2] Dr Russell was here yesterday for a few hours. He has been converting an Under Librarian of the Bodleian with 6 children.[3] The Tablet says I am employed on a work on Faith and Certainty. The Bishop came up yesterday and began upon my work. I said 'Oh people had been saying it these 19 years — ever since my Lectures on Anglican Difficulties — I wished I could do it' etc etc. However, he was not taken in and changed his subject. ⌐He spoke strongly against Ward. He said something strong about Mother Margaret's [Hallahan] contrasting Ward and me, as between a Priest saying daily Mass, and a layman who went to the Opera. He said the Oxford question must come up again. Lord Dunraven was here today. He says Lord Bute complains he has no money — his income is only £130.000 per annum. Lord Bute has taken no part in this Irish matter. The Duke of Norfolk went off to Paris with his Mother⌐ on the night about the Glebes ⌐and escaped the voting⌐.[4] Lord Adare is married to a Kerr and is gone to America for his wedding tour.[5] ⌐Bishop of Salisbury is dead aged 61.⌐ Challis went away today. 'Church Opinion' quoted Archbishop Trench and the Dublin, to prove I had written that passage about the Saxon Bible. On referring it turns out to be Faber's! and the amusing thing is the passage is actually quoted by John Bowden in Faber's Life —[6] which I was so far fetched as to say in a Letter (which the Editor of Church Opinion beyond

___

[1] This is a slip for 1869, repeated when Newman copied out the letter.
[2] At London University intermediate examination.
[3] See letter of 15 July to Russell.
[4] On 12 July, just before the third reading of the Irish Church Disestablishment Bill, the Lords, by a majority of seven, passed an amendment to provide glebes for Catholic and Presbyterian clergy. This was contrary to the decision of the Irish Catholic bishops, and opposed by most Catholic Irishmen. It was also contrary to the Government's pledges and the amendment in favour of 'concurrent endowment' was rejected in the House of Commons.
[5] The Earl of Dunraven's heir, Lord Adare, married a granddaughter of the sixth Marquis of Lothian, on 29 April.
[6] J. E. Bowden, *The Life and Letters of Frederick William Faber*, London 1869, Chapter X, pp. 394–5.

my intention *published*) that 'perhaps, as there were other Dr Newmans in the Church of England, the passage belonged to them, not to me.'

Ever Yrs affly J H N

⌐I say a mass for you every week.⌐ I have said two already.
It must be *Madan*.

TUESDAY 3 AUGUST 1869   the two de Hügels called[1]

TO THE EARL OF DUNRAVEN

The Oratory August 3rd 1869

My dear Lord Dunraven[2]

I think it plain that various facts, given in the volume you sent me, are simply unaccountable by any known physical causes — and must be attributed, as they are attributed in the narrative, to intelligent agents not in flesh and blood. Such agents claim them as their own work, and I do not know who there is to put in a rival claim.[3]

I take the narrative, as I find it, and cannot help thus speaking of it. And there is another impression I get from it, as it stands; and am obliged to own it; viz a very great desire to be at the greatest possible distance from the person in whom the whole narrative centres.

This second impression would be quite enough to make me shy of the matters narrated, quite apart from the question how I ought to feel as a Catholic towards them in consequence of the impression I have of their preternatural character.

However, to view them in that light: — Now first, any intercourse with the world of spirits is to be regarded at first sight as suspicious, even where the parties concerned in it are on the one side, pious Catholics, and on the other our Lady and the Saints. Confessors are accustomed to hear the report of such intercourse on the part of their penitents with much severity, and to discourage belief in it, and even when they are proved to be not delusions, they are accounted visions, not objective realities, as, for instance, cases of our Lord appearing in the Holy Eucharist, or of our Lady and the Saints appearing to shipwrecked persons or at deathbeds etc etc —

[1] i.e. Baron von Hügel and his convert wife, Elizabeth, daughter of General Farquharson, and not, as has sometimes been thought, their sons Friedrich and Anatole, aged seventeen and fifteen respectively. Baron von Hügel, an Austrian diplomatist, retired with his wife to Torquay in 1867. No doubt it was the William Froudes who encouraged them to call on Newman. Baron Friedrich von Hügel's only visit to Newman was in June 1876. Their correspondence before that date shows that he had not yet seen Newman.

[2] Lady Georgiana Fullerton preserved a copy of this letter, beginning 'My dear Madam.' It is printed in the *Month*, (May 1917), pp. 452–3.

[3] The volume sent to Newman was *Experiences of Spiritualism with Mr. D. D. Home*, by Viscount Adare, with Introductory Remarks by the Earl of Dunraven. Newman's copy of this privately printed book is still in the library at the Birmingham Oratory. Lord Dunraven was convinced of the genuineness of the experiences, and his son, Lord Adare, prepared the minute account of Home's séances.

However, there is one circumstance which would at once decide the question, as to whence the startling acts came — and that is, if they involved any contradiction of revealed doctrine, according to the text 'Though we or an Angel from heaven preach to you any other doctrine than that which you have received, Anathema sit.'[1]

Nor would it avail to exempt the preternatural communications from this judgment, though some of them were in their matter Christian and good — for we read of Satan being transformed into an Angel of light — and the woman who was possessed of a spirit of python testified strongly in favour of the Apostles, as the Demons did to our Lord as the Son of God, and Balaam even preached the truth, yet dealt in magic and was in league with God's enemies.[2]

For all these reasons, it is impossible not to regard these present manifestations with the greatest suspicion and fear.

Then again, it is remarkable how they resemble in their circumstances those manifestations of old, which are known to have been from an evil source. The Witch of Endor was a medium — so was the pythoness. In this connexion the words of scripture are very solemn — 'Nec inveniatur in te qui ariolos sciscitatur, et observet somnia atque auguria. Nec sit incantator, neque qui *pythones* consulat, nec divinos, aut quaerat à *mortuis* veritatem; omnia hæc abominatur Dominus' Lev. XX, 6.[3]

There is such a thing as forbidden knowledge, and I think it is generally understood that such was the subject of those books, which belonged to those who practised curious arts and which their owners burned on their conversion[4]

I know with what religious motives you have been led to tolerate or to sanction the present manifestations, but on carefully considering the narrations you have put into my hands, I do not see how I can speak well of them

Most sincerely Yours John H Newman

WEDNESDAY 4 AUGUST 1869   went early to Rednall

FRIDAY 6 AUGUST   returned from Rednall for good — for the Novena[5]

TO THE EARL OF GAINSBOROUGH

The Oratory Aug 7. 1869

My dear Lord Gainsborough

I hope you will make my peace with Lady Blanche [Noel] and pardon me yourself, for my silence since receiving your letter and its inclosure. I have

---

[1] *Galatians*, 1:8.
[2] 1 *Samuel*, 28; *Acts*, 16:16–21.
[3] The correct reference is *Deuteronomy*, 18:10–12.
[4] *Acts* 19: 19.
[5] In preparation for the Feast of the Assumption.

been away at our Cottage at Rednall, very busily employed — and I am ashamed on looking at your date, to see how time has gone.

The paper you inclose is a very beautiful one — very well written and very spiritual — and I need not say very just and true.

I seldom see the Saturday Review, I am sorry to say, and cannot guess whether they would take it. Perhaps the Editor would think it was not written with sufficient staidness and gravity. I should say it was too good for an article in a periodical — it is more like the speech of some bright affectionate heroine in a tale[1]

I am, My dear Lord Gainsborough Sincerely Yours in Xt
John H Newman

TO HENRY WILBERFORCE

The Oratory Aug 7. 1869

My dear Henry

Our Bishop has told me that your wife has been ill. I hope she is well now, and all is right

Ever Yours affecty John H Newman

P.S.   I fear the poor Provost is very ill.

SUNDAY 8 AUGUST 1869   I preached   a good deal of rain, and some evenings so chilly that I could have wished a fire

TO PETER LE PAGE RENOUF

The Oratory Aug. 9. 1869

My dear Renouf

Fr St John being away, I opened your letter to him. Fr Ryder has made the reference, which I hope you will find sufficient. I was glad to see your handwriting

Yours affectly John H Newman

TO W. J. COPELAND

The Oratory Aug 11. 1869

My dear Copeland

Drop me a line, if you come. I have nothing to take me away. My only known engagement being on Monday evening the 23rd, when Mrs Froude

[1] Cf. letter of 12 April to Lord Gainsborough.

calls on me in her way to the North. This has been, I should think, a trying summer for you. I hope you have had no uncomfortable symptoms.

I think myself lucky in such a haul. My Bankers are 'Birmingham Banking Co, Bennetts Hill, Birmingham, Private Account.'[1] We are still in correspondence with our Lawyer on the point you wanted me to settle, viz. Suppose I were gone, who would be my representatives? We cannot make out how *legally* to identify 'the Oratory.' It is not the subject of a charitable trust, and the Law ignores it. Hitherto, as I did at Littlemore, we have put our property in Joint Tenancy — but now we are told that Joint Tenancy does not secure us from the Legacy Duty of 10 per cent. So that our property might as well be in the hands of an individual of us. We should like to form a Trust under Chancery — but Chancery, I repeat, will not recognize 'the Oratory.'

As to the Sermons *adapted* to seasons, that must have been *very* frequent — but I doubt if it implied much change.[2]

Moberly's appointment is a very good one. His age is against him but the Diocese, I suppose, is not a laborious one[3]

Ever Yours affly John H Newman

TO MRS WILLIAM FROUDE

The Oratory Aug 11. 1869

My dear Mrs Froude

Monday the 23rd will quite do for me.

I should like nothing better than to come and see you, but first I have real engagements and duties here — and next I am never so well as at home — and the last time I went to the houses of friends, four years ago, I fell ill — and could only be a trouble to them.

And then I have the further difficulty — that, if I once went from home, there are so many friends whom I should like to see, and who would let me see them. And I am too old to go about.

As to my book, it is of that nature, that, till it is finished, it is not begun, and it *is not* finished. Therefore I don't like its being talked about.

Ever Yours affly John H Newman

---

[1] Rivington's statement showed that up to 1 July 1869 the volumes of *P.S.* had sold, 1, 3600, 2, 2900, 3, 2500, 4, 2300, 5, 2300, 6, 2100, 7, 2100, 8, 2000, 19,800 copies in all, for which Newman received £4 per 100, £792.

[2] Copeland wrote on 6 Aug. that the dates of a number of the sermons specially in *S.D.* did not correspond to the liturgical season attributed to them.

[3] Gladstone had just appointed George Moberly, aged not quite 66, Bishop of Salisbury.

TO CHARLES MEYNELL

The Oratory Aug. 12. 1869

My dear Dr Meynell

I send you with much trepidation my Asses' Bridge. Not that I have not many skeleton bridges to pass and pontoons to construct in what is to come, but, if I get over the present, I shall despair of nothing. Recollect, all your kindness and considerateness cannot alter facts; if I am wrong, I'm wrong — if I am rash, I'm rash — yet certainly I do wish to get at King Theodore over the tops of the mountains, if I can[1]

Most sincerely Yours John H Newman

The Rev C. Meynell D D

TO WILLIAM LEIGH, JUNIOR

The Oratory Aug 13. 1869

My dear Mr Leigh

I grieve indeed to hear your account of your Father. Please God, I will say Mass for him tomorrow. I have mentioned your anxiety to our community — and will take care that he is prayed for (without mentioning his name) in the meeting of the Confraternity of the Precious Blood.

Sincerely trusting he will be restored to you,

I am, My Dear Mr Leigh Most truly Yours John H Newman

SUNDAY 15 AUGUST 1869   preached

MONDAY 16 AUGUST   went with Wm [William] to Rednall and back — about painting and tank

TO EDWARD BELLASIS

The Oratory Aug. 17. 1869.

My dear Bellasis

. . . .[2]

I am made very sad just now, more than I ought to be, by a considerable hitch in the *revision* of my book. One point of my philosophy is objected to — and I don't see at the moment how I can go on. I cannot say what I don't

---

[1] The reference is to the expedition of British forces to Abyssinia in 1868. Meynell replied on 13 Aug., 'Let me take a little more time to think about this one, please; but I hope to finish with it before Monday. I read it all through at once greedily. But my mind is slow at taking in another's thoughts — I am like the animal on your funny seal, except that he is supposed to be *sure* as well as slow. And then I imagine all sorts of breakers ahead. However I trust that you have said nothing which it is unlawful to say. There is always this one great consolation, that I can do no harm, if I can do no good — except perhaps I might suggest groundless fears, which is not unlikely'

[2] The first two pages, half a sheet, of this letter are missing. The address and 'My dear Bellasis' are taken from a copy, which omits the first two pages.

hold. On the other hand to publish what would be merely the signal for controversy would do more harm than good. It is what I suppose is called the odium theologicum that men won't allow you to say 99 things which they cannot deny will do good, if the 100th is such, not which they can affirm is wrong, but perhaps may be taken up by some one else and carried out into excess which the writer never intended.

I have spent so much time and thought upon it, that it comes upon me as another of those great failures which have befallen me for many years, whenever I have attempted any thing for the Catholic cause

Ever Yrs affly John H Newman

FROM CHARLES MEYNELL

Avon Dassett Aug 16. 1869

Dear Dr Newman

Now I know that I can speak quite freely to you — that you will not only suffer me, but wish me to do so, I feel at ease.

Though it is not my business to do so, I shall first express the pleasurable feeling I experience in finding that your philosophy is not so empirical as I had anticipated — or rather feared. The recognition that 'even one act of cruelty, ingratitude, generosity or justice reveals to us at once intensivé the immutable distinction between those qualities and their contraries . . . pro hâc vice' —[1] the recognition, also, of 'original forms of thinking or formative ideas connatural with our minds without which we could not reason at all'[2] will abundantly satisfy the school of thinkers to which I belong. And if this element in your work does not stand out in prominent relief this is explained by the fact that you contemplate the mental organism not as it is in fieri, but as in facto esse. I feel very glad of this.

And now I will tell you that I do not think that in what you have written hitherto there is anything which could possibly be censured — I mean fall under any of the existing censures that I know of — but I fear for your Idealism. I am sure that very many persons would most strongly object to it, as dangerous in tendency, and possibly, if somebody, some disciple, relying on your authority went a little farther in this direction, it might bring your own work into disrepute as being unsafe on this head, and possibly into censure. This is precisely what happened to the Sulpitian philosophical course, which I used for ten years, and then, one fine morning, I got a little note from my bishop to say it was pronounced unsafe.[3]

The Cartesians were all idealists, I know; that is why I say, that I cannot believe the doctrine is condemned. Malebranche, it is true, is on the index; but other of his doctrines account for the condemnation; not his idealism. Still, it was only his Catholicism that prevented his agreeing with Berkeley. If there be no such thing as material substance, there can, of course, be no transubstantiation. You will say that you believe in the external world as firmly as I do myself. No doubt you do. You are not idealist pur et simple; but you are idealistic. They would call you hypothetical realistic. The theory which you hold, that of a natural suggestion which refers, by instinct, our sensations to an external object, is considered, by our modern philosophers, to be quite as indefensible as pure idealism. Perhaps you know this. If so I have not one word to say.

I held this once myself. I suppose I got it from some part of Reid (for Reid wavers between two views of sensible perception, one of direct immediate perception, and

---

[1] G.A., p. 65.
[2] G.A., p. 64.
[3] See note to Meynell's letter of 13 Oct.

another which is precisely your own): or else I got it from Brown. Anyhow I gave it up: and I remember, that while holding it I was uncomfortable about it in my mind. Our sensations, I said, are merely subjective; but we refer them to an object by the principle of causation. The object produces some effects constantly: these constant effects are *qualities*: since it constantly produces them it is it's nature to produce them. What made me give it up at last was this thought (whether mine or somebody else's I don't know) that *there is no such thing as a sensation of resistance* — though a sensation always accompanies resistance. We are made aware of the object as an energy which opposes itself to *my energy*, an obstacle. My body — 'Corpus quod aggravat animam' — [1] is the first object, one which it is my nature to be brought into contact with, which I know: through that I know others. Suppose I had no sensations at all I should still be aware of objects as the obstacles to my activity: so I felt it was not true to say that what we perceive are sensations which we refer to an external cause. The cause itself immediately opposes, resists us, and we refer to it the various sensations which accompany this resistance. I held with you that we first know ourself as cause,[2] and then by analogy regard objects as counter-causes, and I afterwards learnt that this view was first taught by Maine de Biran — about whom I know nothing more. (It is difficult to write philosophy *currente calamo*; but I trust you will make out my meaning) Here is an element in your system, in what you say about the origin of our notion of causation which might correct your idealistic tendency. Again the idealism is not interwoven with your system. With little trouble, if you cared to do so, you might put yourself into harmony with the modern teaching on the subject of sense-perception.

I find myself writing in a shockingly dogmatic style; but please consider it only as the opening of my mind to you fully, as you gave me leave: so I go on.

I do not like *instincts* in philosophy,[3] and would apply Occam's razor to all of them, as asserted of intelligence. If this surprise you, I cannot help it. I know what I mean when I say that the brutes have instinct, because I have such myself quatenus animal. I wink my eyes e.g. instinctively i.e. spontaneously, because if it depended on me, I should forget to do it and should go blind. Instinct, I say, is not an intellectual act. I even hold that in animals, instinct and intelligence are in inverse ratio. The more intelligence an animal has the less instinct, because he wants it less. Bees and ants are full of instincts; but a dog has fewer, and man fewest. The intelligence which belongs to instinct is not in the subject of it but in the Author — ie in God. I do not then understand what is meant by saying that we refer our sensations to an external object by an instinct.

Now for some particulars:

(1) 'The tokens of creative skill need not suggest a want of creative power.' I failed to catch your meaning: are, or how are skill and power in apparent antagonism? p 1[4]

(2) 'Theology, as such is always notional'. Qu. 'dogmatical theology' — not moral p 2[5]

(3) 'Their highest opinion in religion is, generally speaking, an assent to a probability, as even Butler has been understood to teach' ie he has been *by some persons*, so understood, or misunderstood? (I fear you be quoted as endorsing an opinion which I venture to think you do not hold — that, according to Butler Christianity is *only* most probably true.) p 4[6]

(4) 'Its acts are often inaccurate, nor do we invariably assent to them' (said of Memory or Reason) p 4.[7] It does not seem to me that Memory really ever deceives us any more than perception. We are deceived in the *use* we make of what it presents to us, confusing and mistaking, and misreading: so likewise it is in the *use* of reason we err; reason itself is infallible. If Memory or reason really ever once *lied*, absolutely,

[1] *Wisdom*, 9:15.
[2] *G.A.*, p. 66.
[3] *G.A.*, p. 61.
[4] *G.A.*, p. 52. Meynell's references are presumably to the galley proofs.
[5] *G.A.*, p. 55.
[6] *G.A.*, p. 59.
[7] *G.A.*, p. 61.

how should we believe it another time. Perhaps your meaning is sufficient obvious; but I should make some explanation myself.

(5) 'That things exist external to ourselves is founded on an instinct' p 4[1] (See what I have said above)

(6) 'The human mind lays down' 'by an inductive process the great aphorism that there is an external world' p 5[2] I would like this statement to receive a qualification (or rather a caution) similar to the one about the Moral Law being an induction — viz *an external object* recognized in each act of perception, *immediately* to save yourself from idealism — if you can bring yourself to think so.

(7) 'We consider mere images on the retina to be infallible tokens of something real beyond them' p. 5.[3] It is not — or is it meant that the image on the retina is the object perceived? It resembles the object neither in shape nor size. The optic nerve is opaque and unsuited to convey such images to the brain — so says Reid. According to Aristotle all the senses are modifications of that of touch.

(8) 'It is a perplexity . . . that grave philosophers should speak of it as an intuitive truth that whatever is must have a cause.' p 6[4] Surely you do these writers less than justice: they would say, whatsoever *happens* must have a cause. And they would agree with you that the notion of causation is derived from experience. For instance Hamilton admits that we learn from experience that things have causes; but that whatsoever happens *must* have causes, he would say is not derived from experience; because experience only teaches us what *is the case*, not what must be. It is possible some one may have stated the axiom as you have put it; but it is incorrectly so stated. When they say it is *à priori* they only mean that the necessary element in it is à priori. Compare it with the law of gravitation and one sees the difference.

(9) 'Some philosophies teach a necessity of the laws of nature' p 8.[5] Seems to require some stronger rejection: it is pantheism.

(10) There is 'no unvarying law in nature' —[5] I can't help thinking that you mean *invariable*. It is a law that the sun rises and sets — when did it fail to do this? But of course it might fail, *by miracle*. It is not invariable, though it is unvarying.

I think that the style is, as you said, a little crude here and there, but provided it be clear (which it is) and not slip-shod (of which I don't find any instance) I would not do much towards altering it, because I think it rather a good fault in philosophy to be homely. You could hardly be more homely than Plato!

Sincerely and respectfully Your's Charles Meynell

TO CHARLES MEYNELL

The Oratory Aug. 17. 1869

My dear Dr Meynell

I only do hope I am not spoiling your holiday. You are doing me great service.

To bring matters to a point, I propose to send you my chapters on the apprehension and assent to the doctrine of a Supreme Being. If you find principles in that chapter, which cannot be allowed, res finita est. As to your remarks on the printed slips, let me trouble you with the following questions.

[1] *G.A.*, p. 61.
[2] *G.A.*, p. 62.
[3] *G.A.*, p. 63.
[4] *G.A.*, p. 66.
[5] *G.A.*, p. 70.

1. You mean that it is dangerous to hold that we believe in matter as a conclusion from our sensations — for our belief in matter is in consequence of our consciousness of resistance, which is not a sensation. Will it mend matters to observe that I don't use the word 'sensations' — but experiences? and surely resistance is an experience — but if we infer matter from resistance, therefore we infer it from experience

2. By instinct I mean a realization of a *particular*; by intuition, of a *general* fact — in both cases without *assignable* or *recognizable* media of realization. Is there any word I could use instead of instinct to denote the realization of particulars? Still, I do not see how you solve my difficulty of instinct leading brutes to the realization of something external to themselves. Perhaps it ought not to be called instinct in brutes but by some other name.

3. Am I right in thinking that you wish me to infer matter as a *cause* from phenomena as an *effect*, from *my own view* of cause and effect. But in *my own view* cause is *Will*; how can matter be Will?

4. 'Hypothetical realism,' yes — if conclusions are necessarily conditional. But I consider Ratiocination far higher, more subtle, wider, more certain than logical Inference — and its principle of action is the 'Illative Sense,' all which I treat of towards the end of the volume. If I say that Ratiocination leads to absolute truth, am I still an hypothetical realist?[1]

Most sincerely Yours John H Newman

TO WILLIAM MONSELL

The Oratory Aug 17. 1869

My dear Monsell,

In Fr Ambrose's absence in Switzerland, I opened your letter to him. Of course that symptom is uncomfortable, but I trust you need not be anxious. Before now, I have spit blood, — from my throat — Ambrose has lately several times spit blood, — from his throat — Mrs Wootten has for several years spit blood, — from her throat. At the same time no doubt you have reason to be very careful with him. I know of no great doctor — but things are so well understood now, that either in Paris or London you are sure to get good advice, if men are honest and outspoken. The goat's milk, I suppose, is of the same class of remedies as cod liver oil.

It will be sad if Gaston has to make a break in his studies — but of course his health is the first thing. I suppose you will be in London before the Vacation is out, and if a Paris and London physician agree together this way

---

[1] In the draft, which differs slightly from the letter as sent, Newman cancelled the following passage at the end:

'I think we have intellectual instincts — that is, instincts which brutes cannot have, e.g. take the case of calculating boys. By instinct I mean arriving at what to most men — naturally are conclusions, without media. Can I use any other word instead of instinct?'

or that, you can't be wrong. We used to hear of Dr Watson, now knighted, as a great authority in such cases — but I know nothing about it

Ever Yrs affly John H Newman

P.S.   If you have an opportunity, will you tell M. Montalembert I have been saying Mass for him once a week since February — and shall go on doing so.

TO THOMAS HARPER S.J.

Confidential   Aug 18/69
My dear Fr Harper

Will you kindly tell me whether the doctrine in the inclosed slip is allowable, and if it is allowable, then 2. whether it is advisable —, and if not, then 3 whether it may be published with a note to this effect. 'I speak thus under correction, and withdraw it prospectively, if it is contrary to the teaching of the theological Schola.'[1]

TO CHARLES MEYNELL

The Oratory Aug 18. 1869
My dear Dr Meynell

I send you by this post the MSS which I spoke of in my last.

On second thoughts I don't see how I can change the word 'instinct —' I have not indeed any where used it for the *perception of God* from our experiences, but in later chapters I speak of Catholic instincts, Mother Margaret's instincts, the instinct of calculating boys, in all cases using the word 'instinct'

---

[1] Harper replied on 20 Aug. '1. I can see nothing whatever that is not allowable in the inclosed slip.

2 I can see nothing whatever which it is not advisable to print.

But 3. in two points, so far as my very limited knowledge goes, I seem to discover ideas *new* to the general teaching of the schools. I use the epithet without meaning more or less than what it conveys.

α. The existence of an *intelligent principle* of whatever sort in brute animals; anything beyond the senses, and imagination, which in them is sensuous memory.

β. The idea that the sensuous impression, (e.g. "mere images on the retina,") is the immediate object of intellectual intuition; and not the external thing itself present by means of the sensation, and "intued" in itself. I am myself inclined to the latter theory, not only because of what seems to me the external authority in its favour; but because the opposite (though of course I may be wrong) seems without a sufficient reason to yield up important outworks to the idealists. I cannot see how the reflection of a camera obscura can become an *object* to the intellect. I fancy I can see how it may be a lens; so that the understanding (νοῦς) can intue the essence, not in its universality (object of its native force when disembodied) but with that "haecceitas" which limits to the object, which is the cause of intellectual activity in that direction. In other words the intellect is tied to the object which sense presents; but it looks out on the essence of the particular object so presented through the sensible modification which awakens its activity'

Harper ended that he looked forward to Newman's 'help and guidance on *the* question, which presents itself to the thinkers of the day.' In a postscript he added, 'I burn your note; as I think it is according to your mind.' See also letter of 25 Aug. to Harper.

to mean a spontaneous impulse, physical or intelligent, in the individual, leading to a result without assignable or recognizable intellectual media.

Would it do, if I kept the passage and put a note to this effect, — 'I speak thus under correction, and withdraw it prospectively, if it is contrary to the teaching of the theological Schola.'?

Yours most sincerely John H Newman of the Oratory

P.S. I don't recollect saying any thing about my Style.

TO MRS MATTHEW JAMES HIGGINS

The Oratory Aug 19. 1869

My dear Mrs Higgins

Gladly would I be of any service in my power to Mr Blackmore — and I trust he will be able to come here. I only regret that it is not in my power at this time to move from home.

There is a great movement going on, and doubtless he is one of those who are being drawn gradually but surely by the grace of our Dear Lord into the bosom of the Catholic Church.

We will not forget the intention of your Sisters

Most sincerely Yours John H Newman

TO AMBROSE ST JOHN

⌐August 19/69⌐

My dear A

I have no news for you — Yours to Wm [William] came yesterday. Fr Thomas has received John's. ⌐Poor Mr Moore, MP for Tipperary, who was so civil to me has died suddenly of inflammation of the lungs. Mrs Buckle has had an apoplectic stroke and Mr Buckle a second paralytic. I have settled with Creswell about the Tank with pipes, gutters etc it is to cost £42 and to be invisible; round, diameter 10 feet, depth 13. 5624 gallons⌐ of water — opening by a pipe on the lawn — ⌐to be finished in a month. Painting inside house begins in September and will last a month. Mule most amiable — has struck up a friendship with Austin's donkey.⌐ Cow out of favour in consequence. ⌐All that wretched Gip's puppies drown,⌐ I hear. ⌐Nero starving for want of bones — wont eat biscuit. Woodgate and Bramston dined with me at Rednall —⌐ they are my two oldest friends — ⌐I have know W. since 1819 and

B. since 1822. Copeland is¹ to Buxton.⌐ My £1300 has fallen down to £780. Sale of Sermons not so rapid. William Bellasis is leaving for some counting house. Edward [Bellasis] comes back for a while. Richard [Bellasis] comes here in a day or two to consult about going to Germany or not. Thomas Hoghton going for next term to Boulogne. Monsell spitting blood ⟨*Keep this to yourself*⟩ — Poor Morell asking if we want a mathematical Tutor.² Great chance of my book being dished, because I am an 'Hypothetical Realist.' Ignatius went for his holiday last Monday — Edward next Monday. We suspect that the Bishop as last year, does not mean to send a Celebret. Wm sent down to him at once about it — but none has come. Wm thinks the old one ought to be endorsed by him. Perhaps the engraving is dear.³ ⌐Mrs Wootten went away on Monday⌐ for a holiday. ⌐Mrs Knight came on Monday.⌐ I called directly, but she was out. She called on me then — and I was out. ⌐I have done nothing yet to Library or Congregation Room —⌐ I am so idle. Now I hope I have convinced you there is no news. Love to John. ⌐Please do not climb *by yourself* — and do not bathe in Tarns I rejoice to find the place suits you.⌐

Ever Yrs affly J H N

FROM CHARLES MEYNELL

Avon Dassett Aug 18th 1869

Dear Dr Newman

I would not at all mind making some little sacrifice of myself to be useful to you; but I don't feel that I have done it yet. I had arranged to go out fishing to-day: so this will not go to-night, I fear I was hurried last time and not clear.

If you use the word 'experience' as to sensible objects, you will certainly save yourself from idealism. The *idealist* maintains that we experience certain sensations, all of which, as being merely *subjective* facts, do not give the *objective* reality: That the soul is the subject of such sensations, and that God is their cause: and, since material substance is eliminated by the law of Parcimony (for God can cause the sensations, without material substance), this is the whole account of the matter. A hypothetical realist (I take it) is one who admits that we perceive nothing but our own sensations which are subjective, but he postulates an external object as an hypothesis to account for the sensations. He cannot *prove* the existence of such object. A natural realist believes that we immediately perceive the object, and therefore it requires no proof. Dr Johnson's 'Thus I prove it Sir,' — stamping on the ground is the vulgar expression of the doctrine of immediate perception. Resistance is indeed an experience. But I regarded (once) resistance as a sensation, till I saw that, although all sorts of sensations accompany resistance, yet there is no sensation properly speaking of resistance. It is the fact of a resisting object which makes us refer the sensations to it. As far as I know Hamilton first introduced the terms *cosmothetical idealist* (I suppose one who holds the

---

¹ The paper has been torn and 3 or 4 words are missing. Newman perhaps wrote 'unwell and has gone'

² J. R. Morell had been dismissed from his post as Inspector of Schools in 1864.

³ A Celebret vouched for a priest and enabled him to say Mass in places where he was not known.

theory of image-ideas: what does *cosmothetic* mean?) *hypothetical realist, natural realist*. I think I use his language in calling your theory as I understood it hypothetical realism.

I cannot but think instinct a bad and misleading word for the perception of sensible objects: what is the matter with 'perception' a good old English word? As for abstract ideas, I should call them *conceptions, notions,* if you like; and then for universal truths, *laws of thought and things,* if you wish to designate the faculty which considers them as intuition, you will follow the general usage, I think. Don't we call them intuitive truths? As to the term instinct for the intuition of particulars, as it misled me it might easily mislead others. But you say we call that instinct which leads the brutes to realize external objects. Perhaps we do. But that is because we are contented to put up with the loosest kind of knowledge about the brutes (I think). I do not call it instinct, but intelligence which makes a brute realize the object: the lowest act of intelligence seems sufficient for the purpose: but it is a great difficulty where intelligence leaves off and instinct begins.

Since writing the above I got your note of yesterday. It is clear that you use instinct in quite a different sense from that in which I use it. Instinct with me never comes in, except where intelligence, or reasoning would be insufficient for the purpose. I suppose I got my ideas about instinct from Paley and a paper in the Spectator. But we certainly do use the word in ordinary language in the sense that you use it in, for an act in which we grasp a conclusion without being able to assign the process by which we arrived at it.

Terminology is a great difficulty to every philosopher. It is my business, I conceive, to throw out observations and yours to despise or use them as you think fit; so never mind what I say.

The passage you mention doesn't I think require a 'prospective withdrawal,' as it does not contain anything directly against the teaching of the schools. But as there are so many persons, imbued with the modern doctrine of perception, who hold that, if we do not immediately perceive external objects, it is absolutely impossible to prove their existence, *I* should be careful not to seem to deny such immediate perception. They will say 'if the external object has to be proved, it cannot be proved and there's an end of it.' I know a priest (and he is by no means a fool) who holds that matter is nothing else than the action of God upon the sensitive faculty. Such a one would be pleased at this seeming denial of immediate perception. But the passage, as I read it first, seemed to deny such immediate perception. It seemed to say 'We conclude, we know not how, by an *instinct,* that the subjective sensations are caused by a real outstanding object. Then by induction, from particulars, we arrive at what we call the external world.'

You have misunderstood something which I said about the origin of our notion of causation: 'In my own view Cause is Will: how can matter be will?' you ask. I thought there was an element in your writings which might correct the seeming idealism of the passage we have discussed ie you held (I gathered) Maine de Biran's view of the origin of causation. We are conscious of self as an *energy producing effects,* as when I lift up my arm. Here is cause and effect. When I encounter an object (put my hand in contact with a wall) the witness of conscience is to this purpose, that an energy opposes itself to the energy of my will. There is a counter-cause, immediately perceived by me — acting upon me. Here I said is a recognition of the doctrine of immediate perception, which would correct the notion implied by the former passage which seemed to say that we are only conscious of certain subjective sensations, from which we *argue* that there must be a cause of such sensations; for we come into immediate contact, not with resistance, for resistance is an abstraction, but with *something which resists,* with an external object. Then, when you go on further to say that nothing can move matter but Will — that is (as I understand) that it is God who moves matter, as it is I who move my arm, I am still better pleased; and find no objection whatsoever. Do we now understand each other?

I do not understand perhaps what you say at the end of your antepenultimate note: 'Hypothetical realism: yes if the conclusions are conditional. But I consider ratiocination far higher *etc* than logical inference.' I write merely at a venture in saying that by no possible glorification of Ratiocination will you satisfy the *Philosophers,* if you hold that we *conclude* an external object. But the very next line in which you contrast Ratiocination with logical inference shows me that I must be misunderstanding, and am speaking before I have learnt my lesson.

When I read what I have written, it seems to me that there is a dogmatic tone about it which amazes me. You have been the occasion of my losing every sense of modesty. But I should have considered it a great piece of impertinence in me to criticize your style of writing!! But as you wrote 'I fear there will be much crudeness — over and above doctrine — and perhaps faults of composition' (speaking of a coming sheet) I wrote, I conceive, that it was impossible perhaps, to avoid crudity (by which I understood a certain homeliness of expression) in philosophy, and that it was a good fault. Well, if ever I do the like again snub me soundly.

I will begin with the M.S. and finish as soon as possible.

Sincerely and respectfully Yours Charles Meynell

TO CHARLES MEYNELL

The Oratory, Aug 20. 1869

My dear Dr Meynell

Pray forgive me if unknown to myself and unintentionally I have led you to think, quite contrary to *my* thoughts, that you wrote dogmatically. Just the contrary, and you are doing me a great service in letting me see *how* matters stand in the philosophical school.

Forgive too the treacherousness of my memory, though by 'composition' I meant the composition of my matter, the drawing out of my argument etc.

Nothing can be clearer than your remarks. Now let me say I had no intention at all of saying that I know, e.g. that I have a sheet of paper before me, by an *argument* from the impression on my sense — 'that impression *must* have a cause —' but it is a *perception* (that is, a kind of instinct.) I have used the word 'perception' again and again; that perception comes to me *through* my senses — therefore I cannot call it *immediate*. If it were not for my senses, nothing would excite me to perceive — but as soon as I see the white paper, I perceive by instinct (as I call it) without *argumentative* media, *through* my senses, but not logically *by* my senses, that there is a *thing*, of which the white paper is the outward token. Then, when I have this experience again and again, I go on from the one, two, three etc accompanying perceptions of one, two, three etc external objects, to make an induction 'There is a vast external world.' This induction leads to a conclusion much larger than the particular perceptions — because it includes in it that the earth has an inside, and that the moon has a farther side, though I don't see it.

Therefore I hold that we do not *prove* external individual objects, but *perceive* them — I cannot say that we *immediately* perceive them, because it is through the *experience* as an instrument that we are led to them — and though we do not prove the particular, we *do* prove *the general* i.e. by induction from

314

the particulars. I am sanguine in thinking this is in substance what you say yourself

Most sincerely Yours John H Newman[1]

TO JAMES LAURENCE SHEPHERD

The Oratory August 20. 1869

My dear Fr Shepherd

Pardon my delay in answering your questions. Now I do my best.

1. 'Bona spei.' I construe it 'subjects of bad hope' or those who have a bad prospect before them. Thus in Wisdom xii, 19 we find 'et bona spei fecisti filios tuos.'

2 'syrtium silentio.' Syrtis is used here as elsewhere for sand, or a sandy desert, the Syrtes being properly the sandy shallows of the African coast. Thus Horace Od.i.22 'Syrtes æstuosas.' And Prudentius himself Libycis in Syrtibus Ammon. Apoth. and Syrtium nardo. Cath.xi.65

3. I cannot think of any thing better than 'sevenfold' — for septemplicis. It expresses the idea.

4 I am sorry to say that the only instance I can think of the parallel you

---

[1] Newman's draft ran:
'In substance but very different in manner   Aug 20 1869
My dear Dr Meynell
Nothing can be clearer than your letter and I thank you for it. I am very sorry my memory is so treacherous — however, I meant *composition* of the matter. Your remarks were very kind.
Certainly I meant that brutes had a *perception* of the world external to them and that by an instinct. *Instinct* is the name I gave to the general faculty by which they perceived. I had no intention to blackball the word 'perception' on the contrary I have used it myself in various places. I think that the external world must be *proved* — that perception is the *ground* of realizing and holding the external world — that perception is a kind of instinct — and that it is not immediate, but through the medium of sense, sense not as a *proof*, but as an instrument.
But your letter opens a more anxious question. Do you really mean that the philosophical Schola would not allow it to be said that an external world is reasoned out as a *conclusion* from particular instinctive perceptions of particular objects? that it would not allow it to be said 'I perceive something external here, there, in a third, in a fourth place etc *therefore* I conclude it to exist when I do *not* see the phenomena indicating it, or the interior of the earth or the further side of the moon?
                                            JHN
And is the *reason why* this must not be said this, viz because a conclusion is logically doubtful? So too is logically doubtful to me that Great Britain is an island, but my illative sense is keener than any logical analysis which can represent it, and brings it home to me, that under the circumstances (i.e. under the existing premisses,) though they are not enough for the requirements of logic, I shall be a fool to doubt the conclusion to which they point. In like manner my illative sense carries me from particular perceptions to the *truth* of an external world, and that truth elicits an act of assent to it.
Again I have no where said that there are no physical causes — but only that we have no experience of them, i.e. taking cause as represented by willing and doing.'
The first paragraph of the postscript was cancelled in the draft.

desire is that of St Wulfhad and S. Ruffin sons of Wulfhere but I fear it is not much to your purpose[1]

Very truly Yours John H Newman of the Oratory

The Revd. Fr Shepherd O.S.B.

TO HENRY WILBERFORCE

Confidential　　　　　　　　　　　　　　　The Oratory ⌜Aug 20. 1869⌝
My dear H W

Had I not been so very busy, I should have answered your former letter, which made me very sad. ⌜It made me sad to hear you write as you did about your wife and about yourself, though I thanked you in my heart for your speaking out.

It is sad to hear any one speak as if his work was done, and he was but waiting to go — not sad, as if it were not *good to go*; but not good to be in the world still, with one's work done — for what does one live for except to work? And then my thoughts glanced off from you and came down on myself with dismal effect — for what am I doing, what have I been doing for years, but nothing at all? I have wished earnestly to do some good work, and continually asked myself whether I am one of those who are 'fruges consumere nati' —[2] and have, to the best of my lights, taken what I thought God would have me do — but again and again, plan after plan, has crumbled under my hands and come to nought. As to the Oxford matter, my heart sank under the greatness of the task and I think it would have shortened my life, still it was work and service — and, when it was shut up, though I felt for the moment a great relief, yet it came upon me sorrowfully as a fresh balk and failure. Upon its settlement, I took up to write a book on some questions of the day, (you know the sort of questions, about faith etc) and now (in confidence) I think this will be stopped after my infinite pains about it.[3] Our theological philosophers are like the old nurses who wrap the unhappy infant in swaddling bands or boards — put a lot of blankets over him — and shut the windows that not a breath of fresh air may come to his skin — as if he were not healthy enough to bear wind and water in due measures. They move in a groove, and will not tolerate any one who does not move in the same. So it breaks upon me, that I shall be doing more harm than good in publishing. What influence should I have with Protestants and Infidels, if a pack of Catholic critics opened at my back fiercely, saying that this remark was illogical, that unheard of, a third

---

[1] These were two Anglo-Saxon youths, said to be sons of a King of Mercia, and venerated at Stone, Staffs.

[2] Horace *Epodes*, I, ii, 27.

[3] [[N.B. This was not fulfilled in the event]]

realistic, a fourth, idealistic, a fifth sceptical, and a sixth temerarious, or shocking to pious ears? This is the prospect which I begin to fear lies before me — and thus I am but fulfilling on trial what I said in my Apologia had hitherto kept me from trying, viz the risk of 'complicating matters further.'[1] There was a caricature in Punch some years ago so good that I cut it out and kept it. An artist is showing to a friend his great picture just going to the exhibition — the friend says 'Very good, but could you not make the Duke sitting and the Duchess standing, whereas the Duchess sits and the Duke stands?' I cannot make a table stand on two or three legs — I cannot cut off one of the wings of my butterfly or moth (whatever its value) and keep it from buzzing round itself. One thing is not another thing. My one thing may be worth nothing, at the best — but at least it is not made worth something by being cut in half [[or turned inside out]].

You must not for an instant suppose that I am alluding to the acts of any one whose *opinion* I have wished to have upon what I have written — but *through* a kind friend I come more to see than I did, what an irritabile genus[2] Catholic philosophers are — they think they do the free Church of God service, by subjecting her to an etiquette as grievous as that which led to the King of Spain being burned to cinders.[1]

But as to your most anxious question. It is very cruel in Lord A. and cowardly. He might think it no harm himself, to give a woman too much champagne, but I call it a similar cowardice and cruelty. I dare say dear Agnes has spirit enough. I don't ask her to box his ears, unless she is very desirous to do so, but I think she should morally at whatever cost. Though he cut her afterwards, I think she should say what comes to 'You are cowardly and cruel — unmanly and ungentlemanlike — and I beg you never to talk to me in that way again — and to consider your ears boxed.' And depend upon it she would do more towards gaining Lady A. and making her a Catholic by such spirited conduct than in any other way. Have I said enough for your purpose?[3]

Yrs ever affly John H Newman

SATURDAY 21 AUGUST 1869   dark weather

---

[1] *Apo*, p. 263
[2] Horace, *Epodes*, II, ii, 102.
[3] The correspondence shows that the reference is to Viscount Amberley, eldest son of Lord John Russell, who, when his father became Earl Russell in 1861, received a courtesy title. Lord Amberley, who was born in 1842, married, in 1864, Katharine, daughter of the second Lord Stanley of Alderley. He lived near Chepstow and the Wilberforces near Stroud. He spoke bitterly of Christianity. 'Amberley held advanced views in religious matters, and in *An Analysis of Religious Belief*, London 1866, made a somewhat crude attempt to disengage the universal and permanent from the particular and transitory elements in religion.' *DNB*. Newman sent Agnes Wilberforce a copy of *G.A.* in March 1870, to help her in her battle. Cf. letter of 14 Sept. to H. Wilberforce.

FROM CHARLES MEYNELL

Avon Dassett Friday Aug 20./69

Dear Dr Newman

I have carefully read it, and have been deeply interested and delighted with it. I would say I endorse it with all my heart, if that were worth anything to you. For I must now retire again into my native littleness — as I feel that the work for which you wanted to use me is as good as at an end. If the pages you have submitted me this last time are to be the final test, it is finished as far as I am concerned, and may God bless it to do good, is my earnest prayer. I will pray, or rather I will say a Mass, so soon as I hear it is all ready for publication, for this object that God may bless the work.

I will tell you, as soon as I can, what I think of certain particulars. My remarks will almost all bear upon points of terminology. I see this matter will be a great difficulty, as the word 'instinctive' and 'instinct' occur in so many places. If you resolve to retain the word, I wish you could do so, without denying the doctrine of immediate perception of a *resisting object*. All the sensible phenomena are shifty and unsubstantial enough, but this it seems to me is hardly a phenomenon, and is certainly (I think) not a sensible phenomenon. But I seem to be, again, dictating. Pray use and despise me where it seems right to do so.

There is one passage (p 8) which seems (but perhaps I am wrong) to smack of representationalism —[1] what I suppose Hamilton calls cosmothetic idealism. According to this doctrine we do not perceive *objects*, but only and always *images of objects*. If then you say, But the image supposes the object? The answer is, 'How do you know that? If you never know the copy, how do you know that what you call the copy is a copy? Suppose the copy is the only reality, the reality itself.' Instinct, *our nature*, you think will cut this Gordian knot? Our nature cannot deceive us. But the voice of Nature (even the idealists allow) witnesses that we perceive the objects not the images. Descartes says that, before he became a philosopher he thought that the objects perceived were the real things. Reid says (in effect) that in this matter he finds the philosophers on one side and the vulgar on the other, and that he goes in with the vulgar. And Berkeley says that the very object of his speculation was to reconcile philosophy with unsophisticated nature. The philosophers say that we perceive only ideas (images) and the vulgar that we perceive the real things, but Berkeley himself says *the ideas are the real things*. But perhaps I am wrong in attributing representationalism to the passage, and perhaps wrong in supposing that you do not know all this better than myself.

One thing strikes me about the terminology. Thompson in his laws of thought calls a single object perceived a *perception* or *intuition*, and what you call notion he calls concept. However notion requires no change. But how would it do to use intuition for *facts* as well as *truths*? It suits the etymology of the word. Is this worth anything?

Yet another thing. I think it is customary to confine the word perception to sensible things (especially since the time of Reid). But at p. 8. you speak of the *perceptive power of conscience*. Would Moral sense do better? And at p. 9 of the perception of the supernatural and Divine Object.[2] In philosophy I should not use *perception* but intuition of divine things.

I should like to say something, if you would let me, on the subject of p. 20[10?] about the beasts, about which what you have written has so much pleased me.[3] But I must defer this. You will see that I have not yet retired into 'my native littleness'. I will do so soon I hope.

Ever sincerely and respectfully Your's Charles Meynell

[1] *G.A.*, pp. 103–4.
[2] *G.A.*, pp. 105–10.
[3] *G.A.*, p. 111.

The Oratory Aug 21. 1869

My dear Dr Meynell

Your intention to give up has shocked and dismayed me more than I can say — *shocked* me, because I fear I must have said something or other in writing which has scared you:- and *dismayed* me, for what am I to do?

I quite understand that you must feel it a *most* unpleasant responsibility (though of course I should not tell any one), and an endless work — for when will it be finished? It is enough to spoil your holiday, and to bother your Professorial work — and I really have not a word to say besides thanking you for what you have already done for me, and begging you to forgive me, if like a camel, when they are loading it, I have uttered dismal cries.

Well, now I am in a most forlorn condition — and, like Adam, I feel 'the world is all before me — '[1] whom am I to ask to do the work which you have so kindly begun? I shall not get any one so patient as you, and, alas, alas, what is to come is, for what I know, more ticklish even than what you have seen.

I have availed myself of all your remarks in some way or other, though I have not always taken them pure and simple.

Thank you for saying you will say Mass for me. It is a great kindness

Ever Yours most sincerely John H Newman

P.S.   I have not said what I feel most sadly, your language about your own littleness. If you are little, I must be less, because you are *really* teaching me. I should be a fool if I did not avail myself most thankfully of your remarks.

You know, any how, you have promised me some remarks on the MS.

Avon Dassett Aug 23d 1869

Dear Dr Newman

I read the proofs which I return without (I think) having anything to remark upon them.

Be sure that nothing you *could* say would scare me: you are too considerate to do harm in this way. It is my own fault, but partly my misfortune. For I am a poor, nervous, frightened creature, really. And when I talked of retiring 'into my own littleness' my head was giddy, and I felt squeamish, as I do when I have to preach to superiors and equals in the Oscott pulpit — or when somebody comes to me for spiritual direction so infinitely better than myself that I feel no power to speak and, if I obeyed my impulse, would rather fall down and weep at their feet. But it is a fault also in part — I believe a sneaking vanity, born of the fear of making a fool of oneself; for I observe that religious men have never this nervousness, but just act and speak straight on. And so I will try to do for the future. But I thought probably you might not want me any more. However, since it is otherwise, I will go through with it as I promised, and I trust without making a scene or sensation about it any more.

[1] Milton, *Paradise Lost*, XII, 646.

When I am at Oscott I shall be just as well able to work for you as I am here, for there are less distractions. You have not spoilt my vacation, which I have enjoyed very much. It is not so much the cessation from work which does me good as the *change of life* — and I have good friends here who make me as happy as they can.

Do you know of a statement of Sir W. Hamilton to this effect that sensation and perception are in inverse ratio; that where sensation is at its maximum, perception is at its minimum? In the *tongue* (I suppose) sensation is at its maximum, when tasting: but the tongue would be a very unsuitable member for perceiving the surface of a body. The muscles of the fingers, by which the mind is made aware of resistance in its different modes and degrees, render them the proper members as instruments of perception. This is a fact which connects the doctrine of perception with the Will. However, it is time to leave you alone, to your own judgment, on the subject of perception.

I want to make a remark or so about p 20 which you can use as you think fit.

How do the brutes get their knowledge of, shall we say distance, from sight? You say 'Not by sense, for they are transcending sense; not by reason' — then by instinct.[1] This passage supposes that reason and instinct exhaust the division. The Cartesians — at any rate Malebranche — denied *intelligence* to the brutes. I do not hold this view. — I consider it, and I suppose it is considered now-a-days as one of that great man's sublime paradoxes. But how then *do* brutes get distance from sight — learn the meaning of light and shade? etc. Intelligence is not equal to the requirements of the case: I grant it. It is said that in infancy men *learn* to see. Anyhow the adult whom Cheselden cured of total blindness from cataract said 'it seemed the objects touched his eye', and he had to learn to perceive distance.[2] But in animals, the struggle for life, does not admit of this education by experience. They would perish before the education was finished. Hence the newly-hatched brood of the wild duck, disturbed in their nest on the bank, plunge at once into the water; and the young plovers run about and 'do for themselves', as soon as hatched. I must hold then that intelligence in the case of, at least, some animals is perfected by instinct.[3] But I do not therefore deny intelligence to the animals. And as to instinct, as I think I said, I consider it, as far as the animals are concerned a very sorry sort of thing. I give God the credit of it all: the beasts do by this guidance they *know* not what. And those of them who have it at its maximum, as the bee and the ant, have intelligence at its minimum. My canary knows the nature of glass, and checks himself in his flight when he comes near the window, while a bee or blue-bottle will go banging his head against the pane for ever. Instinct, though in general it preserves life, yet often is the occasion of death. The instinct that directs a rat, or a snake to make for his hole, or a moth to make for the light is often the cause of death, where a little intelligence might have saved them. The loss of instinct in domestication, mentioned by Darwin, is instructive. The intelligence is improved by exercise, as our own is, and so many instincts are disused, as not being required. Our own education weans us from the animal guidance of instincts. So you see, with me instinct and intelligence are in smart opposition, and therefore I should not consider man's knowledge of objects as instinctive, like that of the brutes; nor even compare it with their instinct.

P 7. 'images them on these phenomena'. It might have been my dulness, but I didn't make out the meaning of the sentence in which these words occur until I read on. Does it matter?[4]

p. 8. Our sensations give 'no exact measure or account' of the things.[5] The account seems accurate *as far as it goes*. Qu. FULL account? sufficient account. Every sensation

---

[1] *G.A.*, pp. 110–11.

[2] In 1728 William Cheselden the surgeon published in *Philosophical Transactions of the Royal Society*, XXXV, 447, 'An Account of some Observations made by a young gentleman who was born blind . . . and was couch'd between thirteen and fourteen years of age.'

[3] Meynell made a note in his letter: 'I am speaking of course about the case in point as to judging distances. It would be superfluous to say that I do not deny instinct to animals.'

[4] Cf. *G.A.*, p. 103, 'we picture them to ourselves in those phenomena.'

[5] *G.A.*, p. 103, 'The phenomena , . . give us no exact measure or character of the unknown things beyond them . . .'

is a manifestation of the nature of the object as related to sense; but what it is, in itself, apart from its manner of affecting us of course we don't know.

(It is at this page I met with something that looked like representationalism)

I don't think there is anything to remark further on the MS. beyond what I said in the former letter.

Never mind thanking me. I told you I would make a sacrifice for you if it were called for; but I have not done it yet. I have enjoyed this vacation as much as any and more than some.

Ever sincerely and respectfully Your's Charles Meynell

SUNDAY 22 AUGUST 1869   Richard Bellasis passed thro'
MONDAY 23 AUGUST   Mrs Froude called in evening and
TUESDAY 24 AUGUST   came to Mass.   Dr Charlton called   smoky weather

TO THOMAS HARPER, S. J.

The Oratory Aug 25./69

My dear Fr Harper

I ought before now to have thanked you for your letter.[1] It quite answered my purpose and has been of great service to me.

Most sincerely Yours in Xt   John H Newman of the Oratory

TO JOHN NORRIS

26 Aug 69

My dear John

Your letter got to me this morning. I trust you will find the sea air of use to you. Of *course* the French wines will make you ill. You ought to be very particular in your eating and drinking. Why do you dine at a miserable Table d'hote? You should go to a Restaurant and choose your dinner. I knew well that Mr Leslie was not Colonel. It was Austin's mistake. We owe both him and his Father an apology; and you must make him a pretty one from me.[2] I have no news for you.

Alas, Lady Sheil is dead.[3] The weather is sultry here — and the smoke of the Town has poisoned the atmosphere, and fills the house. Edward went for his holy day last Monday. Sparrow was the last and lowest, but he did get honours.

All kind messages from the Fathers

Yrs affly J H N

[1] That in note to letter of 18 Aug.
[2] Charles Aloysius Leslie came to the Oratory School on 27 June. He was the eldest son of Charles Stephen Leslie, only son of Colonel Charles Leslie of Balquhain, N.B.
[3] Lady Sheil was the mother of ten children, several still very young.

TO SIR JUSTIN SHEIL

The Oratory Aug 26. 1869

My dear Sir Justin

I have been shocked and deeply grieved at an announcement in today's Times of the great loss you have sustained.

This letter of course requires no answer — but I have admired and respected Lady Sheil so much, as to feel how heavy the blow must be on the members of her home.

I will say Mass, please God, for the repose of her soul tomorrow morning — and without delay a second Mass for you

Most sincerely Yours John H Newman

FRIDAY 27 AUGUST 1869   fine   glass in corridor at 82°
SUNDAY 29 AUGUST   Herbert Duke dined here.   sudden change and chill

TO AMBROSE ST JOHN

⌐The Oratory Aug. 29/69¬

My dear A

Your letter of the 24th came yesterday. ⌐Alas Lady Sheil is dead.¬ I saw it in the paper. The two boys Stauffer are come — and we are patching up a modus vivendi for them.[1] ⌐Ushaw Duke is here, and dined here today. The men have commenced their work in the play ground, and in two months the cuttings [[of the railroad]] are to commence. This is a good fact, if you go to Arundel — but mind and only ask her *advice*.¬[2] Sir H. Pollen is to send his son at Christmas.[3] ⌐John writes word he is not better at Boulogne. Simmons goes to the Jesuits,¬ if they will take him, which I suppose they will. He goes to see Fr Provincial tomorrow. ⌐Would Sparrow do to take his place?¬ He is the last of the 3rd class — which they say is worse than no honours. There is a talk of R. Bellasis going with Wm B. [Bellasis] to Bonn or to Aix la chapelle. Dr Charlton has been here — I had never seen him before. He is very pleasant. ⌐Eddy Froude has got a bad knee from a bicycle,¬ and is laid up. ⌐I trust *you* have not been bicycling.

[1] Walter Robinson Stauffer and Isaac Hull Stauffer came to the Oratory School on 1 Sept.
[2] A new playing field was now rendered necessary for the Oratory School, in which the Duchess of Norfolk would be interested.
[3] Charles John Hungerford Pollen came to the Oratory School on 2 Feb. 1870.

Hope Scott has been unwell —⁷ perhaps only knocked up. The last fact that has turned up about that unfortunate Moon, which astronomers can't keep their hands off, is, that its surface is above boiling water temperature.[1]

Ever Yrs affly John H Newman

Renouf is bringing out his answer to Ward.[2]
The Poncias are at Boulogne Hotel Imperial.

TO MRS HELBERT

The Oratory Aug. 30. 1869

Dear Madam

I shall be very glad, if any thing that I can say shall prove for service to you, but I am very diffident as to my ability to assist any one whom I do not know and cannot converse with.

As to your present painful perplexity and confusion of mind, you must not be overdistressed at it. You wish to please God — you cannot remove it — you can but put yourself into His hands — and this you must do, and doubtless do. You can do your duty whether you are in perplexity or in clearness of mind, look up to your Lord and Saviour with confidence, being resolved with His grace to do His will under all circumstances — and then no harm can happen to you. He does not call you to join the Church till you know it is the Church — He has helped you hitherto, and He will help you still.[3]

---

[1] This was propounded at the meeting of the British Association for the Advancement of Science being held at Exeter.

[2] P. Le P. Renouf, *The Case of Pope Honorius reconsidered with a view to recent apologies*, London 1869.

[3] Mrs Helbert wrote on 29 Aug. from Havant, 'Will you pardon my asking your assistance in a time of much perplexity.

I have read "England and Christendom" The Temporal Mission of the Holy Ghost, Grounds of Faith [three books by Manning] and a Volume of Cardinal Wiseman's Essays, also "Palmer's History of the English Church" and have listened to arguments and counter arguments until I am bewildered, and know not who or what to believe. I have been advised to seek your help, and assured that you would not deem my writing to you an intrusion.

May I therefore venture to state my difficulties, and ask you to be so kind as to answer them for me?

1. The historical difficulty presents itself to me — How am I to prove to myself that the Roman Church is *the* Church to whom exclusively the promises of Christ appertain? and then how am I to answer those who would say that the Church as depicted in the Temporal Mission — 'all glorious without and within' is irreconcilable with the facts of History. Is History to be thrown overboard altogether? or how am I to account for the internal sores and divisions of Catholic Christendom? How to reconcile unity of faith with Arian and Jansenist heresies the latter unexpelled — with the doctrinal differences between Ultramontanes and Gallicans upon so grave a question as that of the Infallibility of the Pope, so that I am told one Catholic would accept the Syllabus as infallible, and another would say that there has been no infallible enunciation since the Council of Trent! And would it lessen the difficulty were the infallibility of the Pope dogmatically affirmed at the approaching Council? could such a dogma retrospectively be applied to such Popes as Honorius, Boniface, Eugenius and the Borgias?

2. The cultus of the Blessed Virgin. I found difficulties enough in my old religion but *this* seems like a new religion to be superadded, of still greater difficulty — If the doctrine of the Immaculate Conception, and of the Spiritual and corporal Assumption of Mary were not required to be accepted as matters of faith during 18 centuries, why is such a necessity imposed

I do not know the book called 'England and Christendom' — and I have not read Archbishop Manning's. There are very false opinions afloat about the Catholic Church — it is thought it does not allow of private judgment, but it allows of a great deal — and this is the reason you are perplexed by hearing different Catholics say different things. If you want to know what we believe, go to our standard authoritative books — if you wish to hear what individuals think, go to pamphlets, reviews, and the like. The archbishop is a deeply religious man, but he, like other men, exercises his private judgment and has his own views. He puts forth what he believes himself, and what in conscience he thinks good for other people. I should do the same myself of course. When a man is perplexed by a difference between different teachers, if he cannot solve the difficulty at once, it is his duty to say 'I believe what the Church holds and teaches.' He cannot be wrong in that — the differences cannot be about any thing important *because* they *are* differences. Catholics do not differ about any thing important. If any one says to you 'this is of authority or that —' 'the Pope, for instance, is certainly infallible,' you have to ask 'do you hold it as an article of faith?' and again, 'Do *all Catholics* hold it as a matter of faith?' and the answer will be sure to be in the negative. Therefore, *supposing* the Archbishop says that the Pope is infallible in formal teaching, he has quite a right to say so, as I have myself, but he never will say that it is part of THE FAITH, for the Church has never so pronounced.

I believe in the infallibility of the Pope myself — that is, as an opinion. I think there are very strong reasons for holding it — but I quite recognize the right of others not to hold it.

I think it could be made an article of faith by a General or Ecumenical Council; and if such a Council should so determine, I should formally *believe as certain*, what I now believe in my own private judgment *as an opinion*, viz that our Lord and Saviour so determined, and gave the privilege of infallibility to St Peter and his successors.

You will ask why this doctrine (in case it shall be so determined by the Church) was not known as certain before — well, but why was not the whole gospel known from the time of Adam, or of Moses, or of David? Why is it not known to all the world? It has been the will of God to give knowledge gradually; and, as the Angels desired to look into what they knew only in part about the mysteries of redemption, so is it with us who are the redeemed. Prophets too and righteous men desired in vain to see the things which we see.[1] At the same time the plan of redemption, which was determined from eternity, was revealed to chosen men from the beginning, as to Abraham — and so the full truths of Christianity were made known to the Apostles and afterwards to the

upon us now? or how without a divine revelation can that be affirmed as matter of faith, which we cannot possibly know or prove to be true? . . .'

Magdalene Helbert, who was the mother of four children, had (as she wrote in Oct.) been to see Manning, who had recommended her to consult Newman. Her husband disliked her consulting Manning, but was quite agreeable to her consulting Newman.

[1] I *Peter* 1:12; *Matthew* 13:17.

Church, but have become clearer and clearer, as time has gone on. If the Pope's infallibility were to be determined now, I should say after the event, that doubtless there were good reasons for its being done at this time and not sooner. And I can *see* such reasons; for instance, in the present state of the world, the Catholic body may require to be like an army in the field, under strict and immediate discipline. I tell you frankly, that, in *my own mind,* I see *more* reasons for wishing it may *not* be laid down, by the Council, than for wishing it should be; but I know that I am fallible, and I shall have no difficulty in accepting it, if the Council so determine — and then there will be a point of private judgment less — but till then it *is* a point of private judgment.

As to your not being able to see the splendours of the Church, as some persons represent them, I do not wonder — for 'the King's daughter is all glorious *within* —' the best of us have sin enough. The Bride of Christ is holy, but each of her children has a bad side as well as a good (if a good) and he wears his bad side outside. Do not forget the parable of the tares — of the net — and that 'many are called, few chosen.' Of course there is, and has ever been, an abundance of evil — and that in Popes as well as in others; and Popes have made great mistakes — and Popes have said and done heretical things — though they were not heretics, and did not say and do them *as* Popes. Pope Liberius, for instance, when he gave up St Athanasius, did it under constraint, when he wished to get back from exile, and was in the hands of the Arians. This was not an act of his *as Pope,* ex Cathedrâ, but as an individual, and an erring one.

Now the very reason I became a Catholic was because the present Roman Catholic Church is *the only Church* which is like, and it is very like, the primitive Church, the Church of St Athanasius — I have said this in print.[1] It is almost like a photograph of the primitive Church; or at least it does not differ from the primitive Church near so much as the photograph of a man of 40 differs from his photograph when 20. *You know that it is the same man.*

Very truly Yours John H Newman

P.S.   Pray write again if you think I can be of use to you.

FRIDAY 3 SEPTEMBER 1869   John returned   7 orphan boys brought about now *in the old poor school room*

TO WILLIAM MONSELL

Confidential   The Oratory Septr 3. 1869
My dear Monsell

Your question is a difficult one.[2] As far as I know, English Priests are not

---

[1] *Dev.* pp. 97–8; *Ess.* II, pp. 74–5. See also letter of 10 Sept. to Mrs Helbert.
[2] Monsell wrote on 31 Aug. from Château de Drouilly, Montoire, a letter marked *most confidential,* 'I have just come back from Orleans, where I have been staying with the Bishop

good at keeping a secret, unless, I suppose, made to an intimate friend — but whether one Bishop could be made to comprehend that what is said to him by another Bishop of a foreign country *is* said in strict confidence is more than I can say. Except Dr Clifford there is no one you could depend upon. Most of them would be echoes of the Archbishop. The two who *fret*, are the Bishops of Liverpool and Newport, but I do not know enough of them to say they could not be talked over.[1] As to the person you mention, I can only account for his unreliableness by considering that, being a monk, he has the instinct of obedience so strong that he never would go against the Pope's private wishes. I think him in his own heart opposed to any doctrinal definition — he has clear and good views — very angry with Ward — not at all partial to Manning — but I expect nothing from him. If it were not that I could not be sure he could keep a secret, I should say he is the man whom the Bishop of O. should correspond with — but I think he has no spirit, when it comes to the point.

As to the document you speak of, when you talk of my looking at it, I suppose you mean the *English* translation which I will gladly do.[2] I wish I were a French scholar. The best way, I think, of getting it printed secretly, would be for me to write in confidence to Longman, and to get him to put one of his printers upon it. *He* (Longman) would send the proofs to me (if that would do for you —; I could send them to *you*) and no one would know any thing about it. A Protestant Printer would look at such a pamphlet as a matter of course. Or *you* might write to Longman.

There is an Essay of the Archbishop of Malines, a Redemptorist, on the Pope's Infallibility — very moderate, as I thought, and good — and agreeing with Fr Ryders pamphlet — and the view I should take myself, though *I* don't want it *defined*.[3] But that is the view *on which* it will be defined, if it is. I don't know whether I am right, and write under correction of the

[Dupanloup] who is much alarmed at the efforts that are being made to get the personal infallibility of the Pope defined at the Council.

He wants to know which of the English Bishops he may speak to in confidence and rely upon to aid him in his efforts to defeat this project — Would you kindly let me know the names of those that answer this description. Dr Clifford of course would be one — What do you say of the Bishop of Birmingham?'

Monsell went on to say that he gathered various bishops would be asking for a definition.

[1] These were William Goss and Thomas Joseph Brown. The next sentence refers, of course, to Bishop Ullathorne.

[2] Monsell wrote, 'It is possible that I may have a French confidential document addressed to the Bishops given me to translate. Would you mind looking over my translation for me, and letting me know how I can have *secretly* printed a sufficient number of copies to send to the English, Irish and American bishops. The document seems to me very able and judicious and calculated to produce a considerable effect on the minds of those to whom it is addressed.' This, it is clear from the correspondence, was the memorandum drawn up in the name of persons alarmed at the talk of a definition of the personal infallibility of the Pope, and addressed to the Bishops of Germany. At the beginning of it they say of themselves, 'Still, they have resolved not to put their views before the public. They submit this Memorandum respectfully to the episcopate alone, and wish that in no case it should be given to the world.' It argued very strongly the inopportuneness of a definition. The original was in German, and Döllinger acknowledged the authorship. Monsell was evidently using a French translation. Cf. Cuthbert Butler, *The Vatican Council*, London 1930, I, pp. 112–13. Newman helped Monsell to get the pamphlet printed in English; see letters of 22 and 29 Sept.

[3] Victor Auguste Dechamps, *L'Infaillibilité et le concile général, étude de science religieuse à l'usage des gens du monde*, June 1869.

Bishop of O. viz those theologians, as the French, who deny the Pope's Infallibility and lodge the gift in the Church, *enlarge the subject matter*. Ultramontanes,
who uphold the Pope's Infallibility, *contract* the subject matter. Ward burns
the candle at both ends — upholding the Pope's Infallibility *and* enlarging the
subject matter. *This* it is that I dread — and, though there will be sharper and
deeper wits than mine to see prospective dangers, yet I should be sorry if,
while striving (perhaps in vain) to hinder the definition of the Pope's infallibility, men like the Bishop of O. allowed the *extended* subject matter to be
defined. What made the Archbishop of Malines plausible, was the safeguards
he made as to what Papal definitions were — I don't know what he said
about the subject matter. One of the most important points is this — whether
the Church is infallible *when not* evolving the depositum of faith. I should like
to maintain the negative — and I remove the great difficulty of dogmatic facts
by saying that a dogmatic fact is only doctrine *in concreto* — as the ὁμοούσιον
is in fact — but I fear the French theologians since Fénélon and Tourney,
think that condemnation of dogmatic facts cannot be justified in the theory
without allowing the Church a *province* of infallibility, *distinct* from the
development of the Depositum. Now see what an enormous power it will give
the Pope, if *he is not restrained even by the Depositum*. This, I doubt not, the
Bishop of O. sees — it is to my mind *the* thing to be guarded against.

I am sorry to say I cannot help you on the documents you ask for[1]

Of course you will let me know what they say about Gaston[2]

Ever Yrs affly John H Newman

MONDAY 6 SEPTEMBER 1869 Thos [Thomas] went for his holiday. Mr Bowen came
for Mr Husband's reception. *in our Chapel*[3] Bishop Baily called.[4] Copeland came
THURSDAY 9 SEPTEMBER Ambrose returned

TO SIR WILLIAM COPE

The Oratory Sept. 10. 1869

My dear Sir William

I hope I can answer your questions satisfactorily.

1. The Preliminary matter to the Translation of St Athanasius was never

---

[1] Monsell wrote, 'do you know of any book or article in a review containing a collection of
those facts which shew the danger to religion among the Teutonic races by exaggerating or
intensifying Papal authority?'

[2] Gaston Monsell was to be taken to see the doctor of the Prince Imperial.

[3] Charles Bowen was the priest at Atherstone, and Edward Husband, an Anglican clergyman, who lived there, wished to be received elsewhere. See letters of 11 March 1870 to Mrs
W. Froude, and 25 March 1871 to R. C. Jenkins.

[4] This was James Roosevelt Bayley, Bishop of Newark, who was on his way to the Vatican
Council.

put into form or published, though it was collected in the shape of rough notes.

2.   The preface to the translation of St Cyril of Jerusalem is mine — and the Preface and Notes, though not the translation, of St Athanasius's historical Tracts.[1]

3.   The Advertisements to the 3 first volumes of Tracts are mine.

4.   None of the Translations in Records of the church are mine — but the notes in brackets are mine. However I can't be *quite* sure that the translation, Number 24 is not mine.[2] Charles Marriott translated and published Vincent of Lerins — but whether he did this I do not know

5.   The few lines of Advertisement to 'Hermit Saints' is mine — St Edelwald and the *prose* part of St Bettelin are mine

6.   The review of the Ecce Homo in the Month is mine. I don't think I have written any thing else there — except the letters on Anglican Orders, the Preface to the French translation of the Apologia, and Gerontius.[3]

7.   I think it was an *address*, not a letter, to my Parishioners at Littlemore — but I will not be sure.[4]

8.   I wrote a Review of Keble's Lyra Innocentium in the Dublin 1846 which I forgot to insert in the list of Works in the Apologia[5]

9.   I am now printing a short article for a new number of the Atlantis.[6]

10.   In 1819 my friend Mr Bowden and I jointly wrote a 'Poem' I send it you, marking the passages, which are mine[7]

Most sincerely Yours John H Newman

Sir W. H. Cope Bart

TO MRS HELBERT

The Oratory Sept 10/69

My dear Madam

1.   As to the scandalous lives of some Popes, to which you refer, we not only allow but glory in, as showing the Divine Care of the Church, that, even in the case of those very men, the See of Peter spoke truth, not falsehood —[8]

---

[1] See 'The Oxford Library of the Fathers.'

[2] See *Tracts for the Times*.

[3] Sir William Cope was making a collection of Newman's writings. 'Ecce Homo' was in the *Month*, (June 1866); the letters on Anglican Orders, (Sept. and Oct. 1868); the preface to the French *Apo.*, (Dec. 1866); The Dream of Gerontius, (May and June 1865).

[4] This probably refers to the Address at the laying of the foundation stone of the church at Littlemore on 21 July 1835. See *Moz.* II, p. 114, and pp. 486–7, where it is printed.

[5] See *Ess.* II, pp. 421–53.

[6] 'The Ordo de Tempore in the Roman Breviary,' *T.T.*, pp. 383–402.

[7] *St Bartholomew's Eve*, Oxford 1819.

[8] Mrs. Helbert wrote on 1 Sept., thanking for Newman's letter of 30 Aug. She asked again about infallibility and the scandalous lives of popes.

As in Balaam, as in Eli, as in Caiaphas, as in Judas, God was glorified, so has He been glorified, in that respect in which the Pope is His appointed teacher, in Alexander VI and Leo Tenth. They have never spoken false doctrine. But as to the cases of Liberius, Honorius etc, they are doubtful. For myself I do not see that Honorius, any more than Liberius, spoke any heresy ex Cathedrâ. Others think he did. Therefore a definition of ex Cathedrâ is required. The definition given by Mr Renouf would be different from mine. You may be quite sure that if the Infallibility of the Pope was ever defined, this point also, what is ex Cathedrâ, would be cleared up. At present it is unsettled, because the Pope's Infallibility is unsettled.

When it is said that 'no Father favours the infallibility of the Pope,' I should ask what do you mean by Father? are the Popes themselves Fathers? and what do you mean by infallibility? it is a word; — define it. As to my own opinion, I think it a very remarkable fact in Church history, that even from the first the Roman traditions about *all* matters have gone *beyond* those of the Easterns etc — and it is remarkable too that St Irenaeus, a representative of East and West and as early as A.D. 120 — 200, — the disciple of St Polycarp the disciple of St John, — says, 'If you wish to learn, go for the tradition to Rome, the Church of St Peter and St Paul.' Also that in matter of fact there were continual collisions between Rome and nearly every Church, and that Rome was always in the right. (This *Bull* grants, I think.) *Why* did the Pope always interfere and (if you will) dictate, except that he had a tradition of his infallibility? and why was he always right, except that he *was* infallible?

2. I observe here by the way you say 'by what authority short of a divine revelation *or* the infallible utterance of the Pope.' Why do not [sic] omit 'infallible utterance of an Ecumenical Council'? Do you think that *any one* in the *whole* Church thinks the Pope infallible in *any other sense* than a Council is? do you think that the Pope's Infallibility is an *inspiration*? If so, it is quite a mistake. But to proceed to the prerogatives of our Blessed Lady. In a letter I wrote to Dr Pusey three or four years ago I founded all that the Church teaches about the Blessed Virgin upon the *tradition of her being the second Eve*.[1] This is as well ascertained a doctrine of the primitive Church as any one can be. Next, the Church in all times is the *interpreter* of Apostolic doctrine. Thus, take the question whether our Lord was ignorant in His *human* nature or knew all things that man could know from the first — the Fathers differ on the point till the 6th century, when the Church settles the question in favour of His *knowledge,* by her infallible interpretation of Apostolic tradition. Not till the end of the fourth century did the Church

---

Mrs. Helbert quoted Renouf's first pamphlet, *The Condemnation of Pope Honorius*, p. 28, 'if the infallibility of the Pope be proclaimed then the test of Catholic doctrine quod semper, quod ubique, quod ab omnibus must be abandoned, for not a single Father favours the Ultramontane interpretation of the promises made to St Peter.'

Mrs Helbert renewed her question about the doctrine concerning our Lady.

[1] *Diff.* II, pp. 31–44.

declare the divinity of the Holy Ghost, viz in the 2nd Council A.D. 381 etc. *Of course* it was ever held by implication, since the Holy Trinity was believed from the first — but I mean the bare absolute proposition 'The Holy Ghost is God —' and, as an illustration of what I mean, St Basil in the middle of the fourth century kept from calling Him God when his Arian enemies were on the watch; I say, kept silence on the point, and, when some Catholics found fault with him, St Athanasius took his part. The Assumption of our Lady is more pointedly and in express words held by all Catholics, and has been for a thousand years, than the proposition 'The Holy Ghost is God' was held by the Catholic world in St Basil's time. There has been a gradual evolution of the Apostolic doctrine or dogma, as delivered from our Lord to the Church. If the Assumption of our Blessed Lady were now defined at the Vatican Council, I should say that plainly it, as the Immaculate Conception, is contained in the dogma 'Mary the Second Eve —' I have drawn out this argument as regards the latter doctrine in my letter to Dr Pusey — as to the Assumption, if Mary is like Eve but greater, then, as Eve would not have seen death or corruption, so, while Mary underwent death because she was a child of fallen Adam and sinned in Adam, she did not see corruption because she had more than the prerogatives of Eve. This is my answer to your question 'How am I to receive as matter of fact, what is neither known, nor can be known or proved to be true?' What do you mean by *known*? we know by *faith*, as we know that there *was* a Blessed Virgin. How do you know that our Lord was born of a Virgin except by faith? Why do you not say of *it*, 'How am I to receive'? etc?

3.   I would as soon say that Christianity is not true, as say that 'the Church has nothing to do with history.'[1] It is a piece of fanaticism — and no theologian would put his hand to it. I say that 'history read with open eyes is fatal to' Anglicanism, Wesleyanism, Congregationalism, Unitarianism, to every thing but Roman Catholicism. That we have our difficulties I fully admit, and that there are historical points, which if left to oneself one should interpret differently. Of course; — there *are* points in which I must go by faith, not by my private judgment — But to say that history is fatal to Roman Catholicism is the saying of one who should recollect that those who live in glass houses should not throw stones at one which has only glass windows, and those of plate glass.

As to the divine foundation of the certitude of faith being not historical

---

[1] Mrs Helbert asked a third question: 'Will you kindly tell me *how History is to be dealt with*. I am told on the one hand that if faith in the Church has nothing to do with history, then just as reasonably might a man become a Plymouth Brother as a Roman Catholic. Nothing is more certain than that the great Catholic fathers *did* appeal to history in justification of their claims; and what becomes of the evidence of Christianity itself, if we are to dispense with history. . . . I am told that History read with open eyes is *fatal* to the Papal claims.

On the other hand I am told that the divine foundation and the certainty of Faith are not historical, nor is historical criticism the divine way to faith. I can see this — but then "Faith is *independent of history* and is secured to the world by a divine order and provision anterior to history, coexisting independently of it. . . ."' After this quotation, presumably from Manning, Mrs Helbert asked how she could decide between the two views, and not be entangled in historical uncertainties.

but from the grace of God, this is quite true, but irrelevant. It only means you cannot make an act of faith by your own strength, and that, when you make a saving act of faith, you believe in *God*, not in man, though you *come* to believe in Him *through* history, *through* argument. Private judgment *must* be your guide, *till* you are in the Church. You do not begin with faith, but with reason, and you *end* with faith. How are you to get into the way of faith, but by history or some other equivalent method of inquiry? You *must* have some *ground* of becoming a Catholic, or you will not make a good one. You cannot become *entangled* by pursuing God's way. Of course you can only examine according to your means of examining — and *the whole* of Church history *is* a maze or *may be* a maze — that depends on your qualifications — but there is such a thing as common sense, and God will bless common sense to your conversion. Pray write again

Yours very sincerely John H Newman

SATURDAY 11 SEPTEMBER 1869   went over to Rednall and back with Ambrose
SUNDAY 12 SEPTEMBER   orphan boy died of scarlet fever

TO E. B. PUSEY

The Oratory Bm Septr 12. 1869

My dear Pusey,

Thank you for the very handsome volume of Turrecremata. It will be a great addition to our Library.[1]

I will write at once to Fr Hecker — but what I think best, would be, if you would write me a letter, which I could inclose to him, for you would state what you feel better than I could.

For myself, I do not think any advance would be made towards such things as you have in heart without a *certainty* that there was a fit object for them. Since no one with us doubts the sense of the Decree of the Immaculate Conception, why should any one go out of his way to say 'It does *not* mean the active Conception,' which is a mere misapprehension of opponents, unless to do so is the *price* of bringing those opponents to be one with us?

And so with other things, — and I am quite sure that the Archbishop of Paris and the Bishop of Orleans, would just feel this and nothing else.[2]

Also, though no one can tell what God will do at the Council, yet I think the moderate party will have hard work enough in hindering some extreme

---

[1] This was a copy of a new edition of Cardinal Turrecremata's *Tractatus de Veritate Conceptionis Beatissimae Virginis*, London 1869, edited by William Stubbs, the new Regius Professor of Modern History at Oxford. It was a rare book written for the Council of Bâle, and Pusey thought it would lead to a reconsideration of the doctrine. Newman has cut his copy up to page 9.

[2] Pusey considered that he found greater understanding of his difficulties with Darboy of Paris and Dupanloup of Orléans than with English Catholics even when they were not extreme ultramontanes.

measures being carried, to have any time or spirits to attend to objections, which in their hearts they would consider fancy-objections, unless they know that by attending to them they were sure to gain souls who otherwise would remain in opposition. One American Bishop has passed thro' England in his way to Rome —[1] the difficulty is the *catching* them

Ever Yrs affly John H Newman

P.S.   The *one* question which is occupying people's minds is 'Will the Pope's Infallibility be determined?' *All* questions sink before that.

I did not forget your birthday[2]

TO BARTHOLOMEW WOODLOCK

The Oratory Septr 12. 1869

My dear Dr Woodlock

I was so busy I did not answer your letter, but I sent my MS, such as it was, to Fowler.[3]

Thank you for your Letter to the Bishops. I was glad to see it, and since that I have seen their resolutions.[4]

An Irish woman (a Dublin woman, I believe) wishes me to say for her that she is a person of respectability. If you find she calls on you, this I certainly can say on the report of our Fathers. She was under our spiritual care, while her husband was alive — and is well thought of. I believe she returned to Dublin, to hinder her children being brought up Protestants. Her husband's relations, all Protestants, would have supported her and them, if they could have effected this. Her name is *Mayhew*.

Ever Yours most sincerely John H Newman

MONDAY 13 SEPTEMBER 1869   M. Hogan came   Simmons went for good   de Vere came

TUESDAY 14 SEPTEMBER   M. Hogan and de Vere went.   Opening of School.   Challis came.

---

[1] See diary for 6 Sept.
[2] 22 Aug.
[3] This was Newman's article 'The Ordo de Tempore,' for the *Atlantis*, IX, (Feb. 1870).
[4] The Irish bishops' resolutions, passed at Maynooth in Aug., condemned mixed education and demanded 'a complete system of education based upon religion,' not only for schools but also for higher education.

The Oratory, ⌐Sept 14. 1869⌐

My dear HW

⌐How does the war between Agnes and the Paynim giant and giantess proceed?⌐ I am anxious to know.[1]

⌐I am saying a weekly Mass for your wife and the girls⌐

Ever Yours affly, John H Newman

WEDNESDAY 15 SEPTEMBER 1869 *Challis a master* ⟨?⟩

TO E. B. PUSEY

The Oratory Sept 16/69

My dear Pusey

I see by to-day's Times that some American Bishops and Fr Hecker leave America for Europe next Monday. I did not observe the vessel, and unluckily the Paper has left my room and I cannot recover it.

It is no use then sending to America — and I write to stop your volumes, if that can be.[2]

Whether the party will rush through England, nay or whether they have embarked for *Havre*, I do not know. I will do what I can to learn — and you shall know, if any thing has to be told.

I suppose it has not entered into your mind to go to Rome yourself. There would be no way like that to know just what the Bishops of different countries thought. I think you would find them all of one mind as regards the position of the Church of England — but still you would know, as you now do not know. I am quite sure that every one would be rejoiced to see you and that you would receive kindnesses on all hands.

Or is there any one else who could go instead of you? two would be better than one.

I don't think they would go out of their way except they were sure that by doing so they brought important people into the Church. They would want a quid pro quo.

Bishop Forbes would not do, because he is a Bishop — and it would be unpleasant to him — so at least I think.

I do really think one or two learned Anglicans would tend to soften the antagonism which exists in so many quarters[3]

Ever Yours affectly John H Newman

[1] See end of letter of 20 Aug. to Henry Wilberforce.
[2] i.e. copies of the new edition of Turrecremata. See Liddon's *Pusey* IV, p. 183.
[3] Pusey's reply of 17 Sept. is in Liddon's *Pusey*, IV, p. 182, 'I know what I should find at Rome — great individual kindness, of which I am unworthy, an exaggerated belief in my personal influence, great interest in the progress of truth, and conviction of the duty of individual submission.'

SATURDAY 18 SEPTEMBER 1869   Monsell came   Ignatius returned?

TO AGNES WILBERFORCE

The Oratory Septr 19. 1869

My dear Child

It was very kind in you to write.[1] I hope you will not have to do battle — but if you have, I am sure you will be prospered — and will do more good than you can anticipate. Such duties are not pleasant ones — but, depend upon it, you will be glad afterwards.

I want you and Caroline sometimes to say a Hail Mary for some work which I am at.

I rely on your telling me the result of the combat, if it comes off.

Your account of Mama is very good. I send her my best and kindest wishes and remembrances and am

Yours affectly John H Newman

P.S.   Fr Ambrose has been writing to Mama these many days, but has not done it yet from press of work, the School just opening.

MONDAY 20 SEPTEMBER 1869   Monsell went[2]

TO JAMES LYNAM MOLLOY

The Oratory Septr 21. 1869

My dear Molloy

It is a pleasure to me to hear from you, though I am much concerned at the present occasion of it.

---

[1] In answer to Newman's letter of 14 Sept. to her father. She wrote on 16 Sept. that she had not met Lord Amberley again, 'but when we go home I shall certainly follow your advice,' i.e. that at the end of letter of 20 Aug. to Henry Wilberforce.
[2] Newman made a rough note: 'Sept 20 1869
1.   On Honorius's acts being compatible with infallibility, even if past.
2.   Infallibility a fact — our *knowledge* of doctrine may develop, but facts are facts from the first.
3.   if defined, it needs be circumscribed. It must be so defined that it is not possible to say his addresses to the soldiers are infallible.
4.   against negative propositions, e.g. 'Si quis dixerit nullam habere protestatem directe vel indirecte' etc
5.   What is its field?
6.   What its tests?
7.   Why is it, if I believe the Pope's Infallibility I do not wish it defined? is not *truth* a gain? I answer, because it can't be so defined as not to raise more questions than it solves.
8.   analyze how it is that the converts are all one way.
9.   On expediency. We must not say that Pope or Council may do any inexpedient thing *after* it is done — but such a thing is possible — and we may say so *before* it.
10.   'Woe unto those thro' whom scandals come'

Please God, I will say Mass for your intention tomorrow. Your letter was too late today[1]

Most sincerely Yours John H Newman

TO MARGARET DUNN

The Oratory Septr 22/69

My dear Child

I think you ought to try the London Convent, if they let you. I have written to them.

Ever Yrs affecly in Xt   John H Newman

TO WILLIAM MONSELL

The Oy Sept 22/69

My dear Monsell

It would not be possible to send to the Times *before* sending the Pamphlet to at least the *English Scotch and Irish* Bishops. And it is difficult on a moment to decide about the Times.[2]

So I have thought it best to strike out the word 'Confidential' from the title page — which will enable you to send it to the Times or not *presently*, au besoin, as the Bishop says. First, however, it must go to the Bishops of England, Scotland, and Ireland. When this is done, it will come upon you to decide. I have not seen the Fulda manifesto in the Times — only an allusion to it.[3]

---

[1] Molloy had nearly been expelled from the Catholic University in Dublin at the end of 1857. He was now becoming famous as a song writer.

[2] This was the confidential memorandum addressed to the German bishops, which Newman was helping Monsell to get printed. See letter of 3 Sept. to him. It was printed by Spottiswoode and Co., but Longman's name did not appear on the front page, which ran:

'*Is it Opportune to Define the Infallibility of the Pope?*

MEMORANDUM ADDRESSED TO THE BISHOPS OF GERMANY

Respectfully offered in translation to the Bishops of the United Kingdom and its Colonies and to the Bishops of the United States'.

[3] This was the joint Pastoral Letter issued by the twenty German bishops after their meeting at Fulda in the beginning of Sept., 'a fine loyal manifesto, reminding their flocks that the Council would be an œcumenical Council, and therefore according to Catholic teaching, under the special guidance of the Holy Ghost, so that its decrees would come to Catholics with the like authority as those of earlier General Councils. They sought to calm the fears and misgivings sown in the minds of Catholics by the suggestions of "Janus", that there would not be free discussion at the Council, that the bishops would be intimidated and afraid to speak their minds, so that the freedom of the Council and the validity of its decrees would be questionable. . . ,' Cuthbert Butler, *The Vatican Council*, I, p. 113.

You must see that Mrs Conelly informs you, directly that the copies come to her, that there may be no delay.[1]

Ever Yours affectly John H Newman

P.S. I inclose a letter just come. I need scarcely say that Renouf has a great knowledge of books and is a good worker.[2]

FRIDAY 24 SEPTEMBER 1869 Edward returned?

SATURDAY 25 SEPTEMBER Dr Rymer called

TO THOMAS JOSEPH BROWN, BISHOP OF NEWPORT

Sept 26/69

My dear Lord

I feel very grateful to you for your kind and flattering importunity — but I could not accept the most honorable office which you propose to me.[3] If I went to Rome at all, it would be in the train of that great French Bishop who now for 18 months has been incessant in his most condescending offer to take me there

J H N

TUESDAY 28 SEPTEMBER 1869 Mr Keon and his wife called or yesterday Henry went for his holiday

TO CHARLES MEYNELL

The Oratory Sept 27. 1869

My dear Dr Meynell

At last I have more to send you, and you will receive with this 12 Slips.

I don't think I have yet thanked you yet for your last most friendly letter and selfdenying purpose. I hope these slips will not plague you.[4]

Mr Keon, who holds a high (legal ?) post in the Bermudas, called on me

---

[1] Presumably Mrs William James Connolly, the landlady of 45 Clarges Street, where Monsell lodged when in London, and where Newman stayed in 1861.

[2] Renouf was applying for the Keepership of Printed Books in the British Museum, then vacant, but was not successful. Monsell approached his superior in the Colonial Office, Lord Granville, who was one of the trustees.

[3] Brown wrote on 22 Sept. begging Newman to go to Rome as the theologian of one of the English bishops. He himself had been dispensed from attendance owing to his age, but would be tempted to go all the same, if no other bishop engaged Newman. Newman replied next day, excusing himself. Brown wrote again on 25 Sept., 'I am thankful for your letter of the 23rd, but I am not satisfied with it.

It was because I had been told that a French Bishop sought to engage you as his Theologus, that I sought to enable a Bishop of our own country to have your great services.' Brown again offered to go to Rome himself.

[4] Letter of 23 Aug. placed after that of 21 Aug. to Meynell.

just now with his wife. He is of Stonyhurst, but I met him at Oscott in 1846. He is going up to Oscott tomorrow to renew his recollections of it, and I ventured to tell him he might use my name to Dr Northcote[1]

Most sincerely Yours John H Newman

TO THOMAS JOSEPH BROWN, BISHOP OF NEWPORT

The Oratory, Birmm Sept. 28. 1869.

My dear Lord,

While I thank you for your very kind letter, I must not let you suppose that any such feeling at all is mine, and in any way influences me, as you seem to detect in me.[2] Of course no one knows himself but it did not come into my mind at all to think there was the slightest inconsiderateness in any one towards me, because I was not given an opportunity of going to Rome. Indeed I don't know under what title I should have been asked to the Council. It is not usual to go out of the way to take an unusual step without good reason. I do not know what use of any kind I could be at Rome, if I went there. I do not see how any one would be the better or worse for my going. There is nothing I could do there that others could not do — nothing which I cannot do at home, that is, I can say Mass and Prayers here for the Council quite as well as, or better than I could there. And therefore I hope, My dear Lord, you will give over your kind anxiety and will believe me

Your Lordship's faithful Servt in Xt   John H. Newman of the Oratory[3]

The Rt Rev. The Bp of Newport

TO MRS HELBERT

The Oratory Sept 28. 1869

My dear Madam,

It is most trying to be in the state of uncertainty and suspense which you describe — and not to know whether you belong to the Established Church or not — it is a great trial for any one — more for women than for men — but then you must recollect you have chosen a man's part — you have chosen to go by antiquity, by the Fathers, by history, and to ask answers to questions arising thence. In consequence you must not wonder that you are tried with

---

[1] Miles Gerald Keon was Chief Secretary to the Governor of Bermuda. See diary for 2 April and 7 July 1846, and letter of 13 July 1846 to J. M. Capes.

[2] Brown's letter of 27 Sept. began, 'Bear with my writing often. But I do feel that you have reason — too much reason — for deeming yourself undervalued, neglected, by some or all of our Bishops in England, I grieve thereat, and reproach myself, though it would not have been so, were I in more immediate connection with you . . .'

[3] See Newman's final letter on 3 Nov.

the wearisome suspense which arises out of this course. You cannot be sure that you would not have got out of your difficulties sooner, if you had not appealed to history — but, having done so, you will, I doubt not, bear your trial bravely — and depend on it, God will not leave you, but will give you the requisite aids, and all will end well.[1]

1. When I spoke of the necessity of your having a clear view what you meant by 'Fathers,' I referred to your *excluding* the Popes of early times from the list of Fathers. You spoke as if the words of 'the Fathers' had power, and the words of the Popes none, — but that Popes must necessarily be brought to the judgment-seat of 'the Fathers.' So I said, without assuming the infallibility of the Popes, that at least *they* were Fathers, or at least as good witnesses as *other* Fathers.

As to St Basil, he certainly was not fond of Pope St Damasus, and I think it very likely that some rude words came to him from the representatives of St Damasus — and there was a quarrel between St Basil's party at Antioch and the Pope's party — but what has that to do with the Pope's infallibility ex cathedrâ? St Paul rebuked St Peter — but that does not imply that St Paul did not acknowledge the words of our Lord, Flesh and blood have not received [sic] unto thee that I am the Son of God.'[2] 'The Son of God' is dogma — a wrong step in practice, such as St Peter's was in no sense a dogma. The words you quote 'Facessat invidia —' are St Jerome's, not St Basil's — and are in *favour of the Pope's infallibility*. If you had quoted the words that follow, you would have found that St Jerome is asking the Pope's opinion, and says 'whatever *you* say, I say.[3]

---

[1] Mrs Helbert wrote on 15 Sept. with further difficulties about papal infallibility and the doctrines about the Blessed Virgin, but concluded: 'I admit the force of your answer to my difficulty with regard to the position History should occupy in any religious enquiry, and the use as distinct from the abuse of private judgement. I notice that you respond to the assertion that "History is fatal to the claims of the Roman Church" with a counter thrust and assertion.

I feel my own utter inability to deal with such enormous questions, and to such as I, the point to be determined seems to be, *whose* view of Truth am I to adopt — whose interpretation of the Past? In most that I have written I am but a copyist — as my Husband says, I am like a Post office — a receptacle of letters and arguments — on either side — but thoroughly incompetent to judge between them! — I should be very grateful if you would direct me how to use my "common sense" aright — in arriving at a decision? more seriously how ought I to proceed in doing what in me lays, with God's help, to escape from this confusion and entanglement of mind?

. . . you know but little of the distress I am in . . . *How* do I know that the Roman Church is all she claims to be. . . . What justifies me in leaving the Church of my baptism? am I not perhaps led away by desire of change — love of religious excitement — self display into this enquiry or perhaps by a secret disbelief which questions all teaching?

I know and feel the danger of all this. I have been nearly four months without Holy Communion not deterred in the first instance by these doubts, but by others which led me to reject the words of Absolution when offered to me — and it was in this frame of mind that I first went to see Archbishop Manning. It is because of this miserable beginning that I misdoubt myself . . .

. . . Now I feel that you will understand my position better:- indeed though I am an utter stranger to you you do not seem such to me.'

[2] *Matthew*, 16:17.

[3] Mrs Helbert quoted from St Jerome, *Ep. XV Ad Damasum Papam*, 'Facessat invidia: Romani culminis recedat ambitio, cum successore Piscatoris et discipulo crucis loquor.' St Jerome continued, 'Ego nullum primum, nisi Christum sequens, Beatitudini tuae, id est cathedrae Petri, communione consocior. Super illam Petram aedificatam Ecclesiam scio.

The cases which you put about Popes Pelagius, Zozimus etc are far too vaguely stated for me to answer. They are stock passages in controversy — some of them are no difficulty at all — others have some difficulty. For instance, you say that St Basil condemned the *judgment* of the Pope about the restitution of Eustathius of Sebastea (Sebaste). What is a 'judgment?' I do not recollect the case. St Basil had a quarrel with Eustathius of Sebaste, who became an Arian of some kind, and I am sure the Pope did *not* take him up then. But it would not interfere with the Pope's infallibility, even though Eustathius managed to deceive the Pope, or though Celestius, the Pelagian, deceived Pope Zozimus—such mistakes are not doctrinal mistakes ex cathedrâ.

As to the history of Vigilius and Honorius, it requires going into at length before it can be proved that the Pope's infallibility was compromised — for myself, taking the history by itself I should say that it told very strongly against the Pope's infallibility, though I don't think it actually disproves it. I have no hesitation in saying this, because I have never urged you to believe the Pope's Infallibility. I think that infallibility a point which *can* be defined by an Ecumenical Council — but till it *is* so defined, I only hold it as an opinion — I do not think that history actually proves that he is *fallible* ex cathedrâ, but I think there are facts which taken by themselves look like his fallibility.

All this, my dear Madam, let me say is away from the point. What you are called on to believe is the infallibility of the *Church*. If the Church, in the ensuing Council, said any thing about Papal Infallibility, it will be so strictly worded, with such safeguards, conditions, limitations, etc. as will add as little as is conceivable to what is *now* held — it will be so explained and hedged round as not to apply to the case of Honorius etc. It will not be, what Protestants fancy it will be, a declaration that 'whatever the Pope says is infallible.' It will not make acts like Honorius's infallible. The accusation against Honorius is that he wrote to the Eastern Patriarchs two dogmatical epistles, which subsequent Popes and Councils declared to be heretical. Very well — then, if the Pope is declared in the approaching Council to be 'infallible ex cathedra,' *dogmatic epistles to the Eastern Patriarchs* will not be *enough* to be an ex cathedrâ act. See how tightly the *cases* of an ex cathedrâ decision will be restricted.

2. As to our Lady's prerogatives, the rule of the Church is never to decree any doctrine to be of faith but what comes by tradition; but the infallible Church, while she always appeals to tradition, is the true judge and interpreter of it, not you or I. And therefore certainly, I say this, let *no one make a Catholic of you*, TILL you can say with me 'I believe all that the Church formally teaches to be the very word of God, revealed by His Son, transmitted by Him to His Apostles, and committed to the Church after them.' This you

Quicumque extra hanc domum agnum comederit, prophanus est. . . .' Mrs Helbert confessed on 2 Oct. that she had taken her quotation from Robert Hussey, *Rise of the Papal Power*, Oxford 1851, where it was incomplete.

must believe. What the Church in Ecumenical Council declares or has declared is *final*; and this is the sacrifice which you must make of your reason

As to your question how our Lady can be immaculately conceived, *yet* it can be true that she sinned in Adam, you will find it explained in my Pamphlet. She sinned in Adam, but, *before* she actually came to be, the sin was taken off her. Thus a rebel's children and posterity may be disinherited. They all suffer in him by anticipation, but before the great-grandchild is born the forfeiture may be reversed, and *he* may actually come into the property from his birth.

The Holy Trinity becoming a Quaternity by the assuming of Mary is worthy of Dr Cumming himself.[1] It reminds me of Tom Paine, who says that besides the Holy Trinity, Christians worship a God called Providence.

I don't see any doctrinal harm in St Buonaventura's Psalter — (I believe it certainly is *not* his) except that it is in very bad taste. Profaneness is often nothing more than bad taste and extravagance. Look at the service for King Charles the 1st's day, till lately used in the Church of England, — it compares Charles to our Lord in a fulsome way. People used to call it blasphemous — I never could.

And now let me add for your comfort that you are not bound to leave the Anglican Church till you clearly see your way to do it — You are, I repeat, in God's hands — He will help you, strengthen you, console you, and bring you into the light. But you must not be impatient. He has His own time. As to Holy Communion, of course that is the great difficulty. If you really do not believe in the Anglican communion, I do not see how you can attend it — it is a mockery. But every soul stands by itself — and you are thrown on your private judgment as you never would have been, had not the so-called Reformers put everything into confusion. *You* are not to blame for this — it was their sin — but you are suffering for it — as I before now have suffered, but as God's mercy has brought me out of that miserable position, so will It bring you.

With my best wishes and prayers for this happy termination of your anxieties

I am, My dear Madam, Very truly Yours John H Newman

[1] Mrs Helbert had read that this was a consequence of our Lady's Assumption into heaven. John Cumming, minister of the National Scottish church in Covent Garden, was a strongly anti-Catholic controversialist. Mrs Helbert referred to his letter in *The Times*, (4 Sept), 'Light Wanted from the Council,' in which he attacked the *Psalter of St Bonaventure*, which turned the *Psalms* into prayers to our Lady. Cf. letter of 13 Aug. 1864 to W. J. O'Neill Daunt.

TO EMILY BOWLES

Sept. 29/69

My dear Child,

I am here next week, and shall be glad to see you. You must *bespeak* a bed at the Plough and Harrow, else, you won't get one. Shall I do so for you?[1]

Ever Yrs affly John H. Newman

TO WILLIAM MONSELL

Sept 29/69

My dear Monsell

Of *course* they would not know any thing about the Pamphlet at Longman's. All was confidential. The only person who knows about it is (in Longman's absence) 'T. Reader Esqr.' I wrote to him last night — and I am sure you will receive the Pamphlet as soon as it is hot pressed etc. But this always takes time. Of course it is very provoking. I wrote last night to say that, if delayed a few days, the use of the Pamphlet would be gone.[2]

The Bishop of Orleans's letter is excellent.[3] It will do great good. As to the Telegraph, it has sometimes struck me, that the way in which I naturally might be led to write, would be some strong published statement charging me, for praise or blame, with Gallicanism or quasi-Protestantism. But an anonymous leading article is not enough.[4]

[1] Emily Bowles was anxious to hear Newman's opinion about the controversy over papal infallibility and its definition. In her 'Memorials of John Henry Newman' she tells how Newman insisted that even if the doctrine were defined 'in the face of the utmost protest of a large minority to be of faith then you will know that it is by the overruling of the Holy Ghost. God *cannot* leave His Church.' Emily Bowles objected that she might cease to believe, and leave the Church. '"You will not," he answered calmly, "We all must go through that gate of obedience, simply as obedience. And mind, if the dogma *is* declared, you will find that it will not make the slightest difference to you."'

[2] See letters of 3 and 22 Sept. to Monsell, for the pamphlet, *Memorandum addressed to the Bishops of Germany*.

[3] This was Dupanloup's public reply of 25 Sept. to the Carmelite Hyacinthe Loyson's letter to the General of his Order, of 20 Sept., published the same day in *Le Temps*. In this he announced that he was leaving the Order because it was his duty to speak out, in spite of the intrigues of an all-powerful party in Rome, and as a protest against the harm the projected council would do. Monsell wrote on 24 Sept. to Newman: 'I am afraid Fr Hyacinthe's is a bad business. I suppose he is not a fool. If he be not one, he must have foreseen the effect his letter would produce. What strength it would give to Ward and Veuillot. What a blow it would give to the Bishop of Orleans. If this be so must he not intend to go further?' See Newman's letter of 1 Oct. to Loyson.

[4] In a leading article about Loyson's Letter, the *Daily Telegraph*, (28 Sept.), came the following passage: 'Neither by Protestants nor by Catholics is the name of Dr. Newman ever mentioned without honour; and to both there must be something strangely significant in the report, that, when invited to attend the Council, he excused himself on the plea that "the air of Rome did not agree with him." Possibly the story may be incorrect; or, possibly, Father Newman may have intended to convey no more than the literal meaning of his words; but the

There was a report that Fr Hecker certainly comes round by Bm [Birmingham] In case this be so, you had better send me a dozen or more copies of the Pamphlet at once.

Alas, two American Bishops came over three days since and have passed on (I believe) to the continent

Ever Yrs affly J H N

P.S.   I feel Lord Granville's kindness especially in taking up Renouf.[1]

THURSDAY 30 SEPTEMBER 1869   called with Ambrose on the Bishop about ordination of John and Thomas

TO HENRY JAMES COLERIDGE

The Oratory Bm Septr 30. 1869

My dear Fr Coleridge

Is it allowable to say 'There are *Three Objects* of Divine Worship, Father, Son, and Holy Ghost'? As the text is 'There are Three that bear witness etc' I should have thought it was, but I am not quite satisfied with the plural 'objects'.[2]

Your Month has just come, and the variety of its subjects seems excellent. You must pity me that I cannot say more, for really I am overworked, and have no time for any thing

Most sincerely Yours John H Newman

FRIDAY 1 OCTOBER 1869   Abbé Novello to dinner

TO HYACINTH LOYSON

September or October [1 October] 1869

My dear Father Hyacinthe,

You may think with what interest and sympathy I read your letter in the Temps.[3] You spoke from your heart, and I recognized in it the sincerity, the

very circumstance that attention is drawn to the double signification of the message, when coupled with the notorious fact that the well-known convert from Anglicanism has more than once excited the open hostility of Ultramontane leaders like Dr. Cullen, unmistakeably marks the attitude which he is supposed to have assumed.'
[1] See postscript to letter of 22 Sept. to Monsell.
[2] See *G.A.* p. 135; 1 *John*, 5:7. Coleridge replied from the Jesuit house in Mount Street on 2 Oct., 'I have put your question to two or three learned men here, and they all shake their heads at the "Three Objects". I don't know that they mean it could not be defended, but that it sounds bad.' See letter of 3 Oct. to Meynell.
[3] This was Loyson's letter of 20 Sept. to the General of his Carmelite Order, published the same day in *Le Temps*, and at once translated. The General appears to have told him to keep silence on the infallibility question. Loyson wrote '. . . If in exchange for my sacrifices [in entering the cloister] I am now offered chains, it is not merely my right, it is my duty, to

earnestness, the fervour and the power, which made on me so lively an impression when you were so good as to visit me in this place. That visit is to me a beautiful, a sacred remembrance; every association connected with it has been to me a source of consolation and encouragement. I rejoiced then to see, if I could have before doubted it, that there were priests and preachers at this day in Catholic France, worthy of Bossuet and his great compeers.[1]

But, as you may easily anticipate, I do not write merely to tell you how surely I recognized in your letter the generosity of mind which I discerned in your words, in your countenance, when you conversed with me here. Alas! I must say the word, those dear associations, which attach to my memory of you, have received a shock from portions, and from the circumstances, of that letter. However, I do not write to speak of its contents, in which there was much to pain me, but of this — viz., Why did you send it to the Temps? is not your doing so a pregnant fact? what have you to do with Protestants? The English papers of the high Anglican School cry out that in the honesty of your nature you are trusting those who are not even genuine Protestants, but, whether they know it or not themselves, are 'inimici crucis Christi.'[2] There is just one thing in which I claim to be your superior; I mean, in my knowledge of Protestants and Protestantism. Beware of them, my dear and Reverend Friend. You do not understand them. Even good Protestants are not trustworthy in matters of religion. They open the door to errors which perhaps

reject them. The Church is passing through one of the most violent, the most obscure, and the most decisive [crises?] of its existence here below. For the first time in three hundred years an Oecumenical Council is not only convoked, but declared necessary. These are the expressions of the Holy Father. It is not at such times that a preacher of the Gospel, even the humblest, can consent to keep silence . . . I raise, therefore, before the Holy Father and the Council, my protest, as a Christian and a priest, against those doctrines and those practices which are called Roman, but which are not Christian, and which by their encroachments, always more audacious and more baneful, tend to change the constitution of the Church, the basis and the form of its teaching, and even the spirit of its piety. I protest against the divorce, as impious as it is insensate, sought to be effected between the Church, which is our eternal mother, and the society of the nineteenth century . . . I protest above all against the sacrilegious perversion of the Gospel of the Son of God Himself, the spirit and letter of which are alike trampled underfoot by the pharisaism of the new law. It is my most profound conviction that if France in particular, and the Latin races in general, are given up to social, moral, and religious anarchy, the principal cause is not Catholicism itself, but the manner in which Catholicism has for a long time been understood and practised.' Loyson went on to appeal to the forthcoming Council, but if it were not allowed to be free 'I would cry aloud to God and man to claim another, really assembled in the Holy Spirit . . .' The *Guardian*, (22 Sept. 1869), p. 1050. See second note to Newman's letter of 29 Sept. to Monsell.

[1] Loyson visited Newman, 12–14 Sept. 1868. In reply to his letter renouncing his Order and denouncing the Church, Dupanloup had written a firm but gentle reply, reminding Loyson of the scandal he was causing and begging him to repent. Cf. letter of 29 Sept. to Monsell. On 27 Sept. the Sulpician, John Baptist Hogan wrote to Newman from Paris: 'It affords me much pleasure to inform you that the faith of our poor dear friend (Hyacinthe) in the Church and in the Church's Authority remains unshaken. Yet he still believes he has performed a great and painful duty, and professes his readiness to do it even now, if it remained undone.' Hogan explained that Loyson had kept his letter a secret from his friends, but they had since elicited from him 'a promise that he will neither write nor speak until the meeting of the Council.' It had not been thought advisable to urge him to issue a second letter. Loyson was particularly anxious to know what view Newman took of his action. See also letter of 7 Oct. to Miss Holmes.

[2] *Philippians*, 3:18.

they do not hold themselves. I am not accusing them individually and personally, but warning you. You see them in couleur de rose. There are Protestants who are nothing else than infidels — They will use you, and secretly smile at you; or if not they, then the Author of Evil, who uses them too. The Holy Apostle speaks of the depths of Satan — altitudines Satanæ;[1] keep clear, I entreat you, of any Protestant, even of good Protestants. Listen to your own brethren and to your Father. And now, if I have said what is not to the purpose, and seems to wrong you, then forgive me since I do not write in the spirit of censoriousness and dictation, but in love.

J H N

TO WILLIAM MONSELL

The Oratory Bm Octr 1. 1869

My dear Monsell

I return M. Cochin's letter.[2] I am writing to Fr Hyacinthe by this post, and on the point which he specified, viz the danger of Fr H's being caught hold of by Protestants.

I inclose the Printer's Bill.

Ever Yours affly John H Newman

P.S.   I am in a perplexity about Fr H. not understanding English. My letter is ready, but I shall inclose a translation by one of the Fathers

SATURDAY 2 OCTOBER 1869   Thos [Thomas] returned

TO W. J. COPELAND

The Oratory Oct 3/69

My dear C

I have compared and corrected the lists I inclose, as carefully as I can.[3]

It strikes me that those Sermons which are *composite* e.g. volume vii, 12 and 17, must in great measure have been re-written. And in a measure those, which, being written for one season, were afterwards either preached or at least published for another.

Also, it strikes me that the name 'Plain Sermons' is especially inappropriate to some of those in Volumes 7 and 8.

These are my thoughts. It is sad your weather has been so bad. I hope you will go to Buxton again. It will be pleasanter when there are fewer people.

Every Yrs affly J H N

---

[1] *Revelation*, 2:24.
[2] On 29 Sept. Monsell sent Newman a letter he had received from Augustin Cochin, who was a friend of Loyson. A kind note Newman had already written to Hogan about him had had a good effect.
[3] i.e. the lists of dates of sermons at the end of *S.D.*

St Mary's College, Oscott, Birmingham [2 October 1869]

Dear Dr Newman

There was a good deal to read over, *carefully*, or I had returned it yesterday. It is theological, and in that region you are an authority and I am none. But I will say the little that occurs to me. I was very glad to read it, as this portion especially seems calculated to do so much good. I do not remember to have seen the opponents of dogmatical religion anywhere systematically dealt with.

I see a query, in pencil, p 27 to the term 'modes' as applied to the Divine Personalities — but is not the term scholastic? Another at 'according as we view Him in one or the other of them' God 'is the Father, *or* the Son, or the Holy Ghost'.[1] I suppose this sounds like Sabellianism; but the Sabellian meaning is obviously excluded by the context — that 'the Father is all that is meant by the word "God", as if there were no Son, no Spirit'. If I were inclined to doubt, it would be about the propriety of the word *separately*, — in saying that the Father is *separately* God, or the Son separately God — considering that the Father is that God who is necessarily Father, Son and Holy Ghost. Of course the context forbids any misapprehension, by asserting that 'God is a living Monas — more really one even than an individual man'.[2] However, I suppose the poverty of language, or the poverty of our conceptions requires that what we say of God in one aspect has necessarily to be corrected by what we say of Him in another — as is said elsewhere in these sheets. (I admire the luminous school-dictum 'Omnia unum idemque sunt, ubi non est relatio oppositionis.')

I don't know why there is a pencil query p 25 at 'any more than there can be an inference without a conclusion'; or at p. 26, at 'the objects (of devotion) as *supernatural*'[3] — Perhaps it is marked as if implying that there could be no natural object of devotion i.e. the Sacred Humanity? Again '*arbitrary* prohibitions' at bottom of p 29[4] is marked, and indeed I cannot say that I know distinctly what is meant by the word. Perhaps these q's were only intended for your own guidance in the choice of language.

I remain Dear Dr Newman Sincerely and respectfully[5]

P.S. I dreamt last night that you told me you were unwell (absit omen!). — I suppose, because I find in my own case that mental exertion and health are almost inconsistent.

The Oratory Oct 3/69

My dear Dr Meynell

Many thanks for your notice. I had found out my blunder on reading the proof over again, and set it right. It is astonishing how difficult it is not to make mistakes.

My corrector here put you out; I meant to have rubbed out his pencil marks. 'Arbitrary prohibitions' are such as St Augustine's that we may not

---

[1] *G.A.*, p. 124.
[2] *G.A.*, p. 125. Newman avoided the word 'separately.'
[3] Newman apparently altered these passages.
[4] *G.A.*, p. 132, line 2.
[5] Meynell forgot to write his signature.

say God is in One Person as well as Three — and Fr Perrone's that we may not call St Anne 'God's Grandmother.' Perhaps another is 'Those Objects of Divine Worship' which I have altered into 'There are Three that give testimony in heaven.'[1]

Most sincerely Yours John H Newman

MONDAY 4 OCTOBER 1869   Miss Bowles came

THURSDAY 7 OCTOBER   Mr Craig to dinner?   beautiful and wonderfully mild weather glass steadily above 64

TO MISS HOLMES

The Oratory Octr 7. 1869

My dear Miss Holmes,

You are a punctual person — your first half of £5 Number 45758 has come safely. I hope you have not inconvenienced yourself to send it.

I don't think Fr Hyacinth had any right to do what he has done. He is a monk and under obedience. His Fr General has told him to go back into his convent in 10 days or he will be ipso facto excommunicate. See what a fix he is in. If he goes back, he stultifies himself — if he does not, he is put out of the Church. Again, why did he send his letter to the *Temps*? an extreme Protestant, if not an infidel paper. I much fear the Protestants are getting hold of him. He was here this time year, and is a simple-minded warmhearted man; but monks always get into scrapes, when they go out of their convents, because

---

[1] *G.A.*, p. 135. See letter of 30 Sept. to H. J. Coleridge.

Many years later Newman made a memorandum, which he left in a copy of *G.A.*, and perhaps intended to insert in a future edition of that work: 'May 6 1885

The writer who accuses me of insinuating, without venturing to confess to a denial of the doctrine of eternal punishment by means of an *obiter* quotation in a note from Petavius, charges me also, in my exposition of the doctrine of the Holy Trinity of attempting silently to take for granted as genuine the celebrated text of the Three Witnesses by the expedient of quoting it, but without quotation marks. Here again I have an observation to make.

He would have read me more fairly, if he had read me more carefully, and had mastered the drift of the passage in which the quotation occurs. In it I am engaged in showing how the doctrine was practically intelligible to all minds educated or not, and might be made the object of devotional exercises, though it be, as it is, a theological enunciation. For this purpose, it was necessary for me for the time to drop all theological terms, such as *essence, substance, person*, as imposed by the Church, as πράγματα, ὀνόματα etc. as used by the Fathers. How am I to do this. There is one Divinity, and there are Three Divine — Three Divine *what*? I must not use the term 'Person', what is to be my substitute? In the dogmatic language of the Church I can say 'Persons', but for the sake of ordinary Christians I am denying myself the use of the word. In the schools of the Church there was not this necessity, and the term Subsistence or Person was received. 'Cùm conaretur,' says St Augustine, 'humana inopia loquendo proferre quod tenet de Deo Creatore suo, timuit dicere tres *essentias*; non esse tria *quædam*, non potuit dicere. Quaesivit *quid* tria diceret; et dixit substantias (ὑποστάσεις) sive *personas*.' de Trin. vii, 4 (9).

In the same difficulty I could not avail myself of the pattern of the Schools. After much trial I at last thought of using what, whether St John's writing or not was (to a Catholic) a sentence of inspired Scripture. This I did; it did occur to me that objection might be made to me, but I thought it would be enough, by leaving out the quotation marks to intimate that I stood aloof from the historical controversy. Are the words forbidden me, because (supposing it) they are not St John's? I will never submit to such a tyranny.'

they are not men of the world — don't know what's what — mistake chalk for cheese etc etc.

Then again why should he *prejudge* the Council? What an insult to all the Bishops who compose it! and to appeal from the Church to our Lord in a matter of faith is sheer Protestantism. The Church is the *voice* of our Lord.

St Bernard did not speak his strong words to Pope in the Temps Newspaper.[1] That there are real grievances at Rome, which he has suffered from, I don't doubt — but he has managed to spoil a good cause.

Ever Yrs affly John H Newman

FRIDAY 8 OCTOBER 1869   Miss Bowles went

TO THOMAS GODWIN

Oct 8/69

My dear Godwin

. . .

As to your business matters, I cannot propose any thing to the Congregation, till I know more about them

I fear they are in a worse state than you think.

We would do you a service, if they admitted of it.

Call on your creditors, and get *on paper* from them what length of time they will give you to pay them in.

When you have got their answers, let us have a *full list of your debts* with the *length of time* they allow you.

Then we shall be able to judge and will give you an answer about the £100.

It does not do to live from hand to mouth.

Unless you come to some understanding with all your creditors, you will not see your way, nor we either.

Mr Collis spoke in the kindest way about you to Fr Ambrose, said he had confidence in you, and wished to do you a service. It is not prudent to quarrel with people.[2]

J H N

---

[1] Miss Holmes had no doubt referred in her letter to the words of St Bernard against the Romans, which Newman quoted in his sermon 'The Pope and the Revolution,' *O.S.*, pp. 297–8.

[2] Godwin, until 1854 a laybrother of the Oratory, had, since 1863, been running a milk shop in Monument Lane, nearby. He was in debt, and Edward H. Collis, who had already lent him money, considered his affairs not desperate, and was prepared to lend a further sum. The Oratorians appear to have guaranteed the repayment of this last, and also to have lent Godwin £100. He, in return, was to deal only in milk, and to present accounts each quarter, until the loans were repaid.

FROM CHARLES MEYNELL

St Mary's College: Oscott: Birmingham. Saturday [2? October 1869]
Dear Dr Newman

I write about something which I forgot in my last note. It may be a trifle not worth writing about: but that you will judge. I noticed that the Four Last Things were numbered not as Death, Judgment, Hell, Heaven: but as Death, *Purgatory* etc.[1] And the sentence appeared to quote the Catechism. I assume that the Fire of Judgment is Purgatory: but there might be some who would miss the sound of the old form: and might not the Judgment be something more than Purgatory? I only ask the question, and leave you to consider whether it be worth a thought.

Yours Respectfully and Sincerely Charles Meynell

FROM CHARLES MEYNELL

Oscott [7 October 1869]
Dear Dr Newman

I have plenty of time on Thursday's so can send it back at once, having carefully read it. I have almost nothing to say, for it is plainsailing in the open sea. But just, please, look at p. 44 (near top) 'His assents are really only inferences, and assent is a name without a meaning, the needless repetition of *an assent* '(of an INFERENCE?)[2]

Secondly and lastly. You have thought out the subject and I have not, *so I speak with great diffidence*; but is it so great a condemnation of the view which you refute to say that it makes assent useless, if it only be the double[3] of inference? (p 40 and *passim*) *Consciousness* is only the echo of *direct knowledge* — but do we say that it [is] useless to have the word '*reflexion*' and that it implies nothing? We are so constituted that there is always the thought that is echo of the thought knowledge and consciousness. But I don't admit, of course, the view which you condemn. You will soon see if there is anything in this, and if any qualification be necessary. I am glad it goes on so briskly, and look forward to the time when I shall see it as a whole, and not piece-meal

Yours Sincerely and respectfully Charles Meynell

FROM CHARLES MEYNELL

Oscott Friday [8? October 1869]
Dear Dr Newman

I see nothing except a slip of the pen, or press at p. 47 line 4, to correct 'and of course *he* can assent' for *we*?[4]

When I have nothing to notice but a slip like this I presume I may just draw attention to it in pencil on the margin(?) and so save myself a penny! for the postage of a letter.

Sincerely and respectfully Charles Meynell

[1] *G.A.*, p. 145. Newman made the suggested alteration.
[2] *G.A.*, p. 175.
[3] *G.A.*, p. 165.
[4] Cf. *G.A.*, p. 182.

TO CHARLES MEYNELL

The Oratory Oct 8/69

My dear Dr Meynell

Thank you for your criticism about the Echo. I certainly ought to have taken notice of it, and my only difficulty will be how to bring it in — You are ten times more likely to be right on such a point than I am — however, at present I don't follow you, though I will think about it. My reason is this, that consciousness or reflection on one's acts is an act different in kind from those acts themselves. Its object is distinct. If I walk, my eyes may watch my walking — If I sing, my ears listen to my voice and tell me if I am in tune. These are acts of reflection on my walking and singing are they not? but the original act is bodily, and the reflex act is mental. I assure you, I most deeply feel that I may be out my depth.

Most sincerely Yours John H Newman

P.S. By no manner of means ever dream of giving yourself the trouble, of writing one word by letter, when marks on the margin will do.

I am not sure, from what you said, whether you read the inclosed bits of theology. Please to cast your eye over them. I must have a theological eye upon them, and one of your eyes is theological, though the other is philosophical.

SATURDAY 9 OCTOBER 1869 Miss Farrant ill

TO WILLIAM MONSELL

The Oratory Octr 9/69

My dear Monsell

Your cheque has come all right, and I will send you the receipt, when I get it.

Fr Hyacinth has not answered me.

You will be pleased with our Bishop's Pastoral[1]

Ever Yrs affly John H Newman

TUESDAY 12 OCTOBER 1869 Walford came   Henry returned because of Miss Farrant glass 66 slept with my window open accidentally without harm.

WEDNESDAY 13 OCTOBER   Walford went

---

[1] See *Butler* II, pp. 49–50. Butler concludes his account of the Pastoral Letter thus: 'Ullathorne's preoccupation was to secure solidarity of Pope and episcopate; Manning's was to keep the bishops out of it.'

TO HENRY JAMES COLERIDGE

Octr 14/69

My dear Fr Coleridge

You will see something about Spirit Rapping in yesterday's Guardian p 1120 column 3. It has been in the Standard[1]

I sent the book last night. From what you said I felt you quite understood that no stories were to be *quoted* from it.[2]

Most sincerely Yours John H Newman

TO MRS JOHN MOZLEY

Oct 14/69

My dear Jemima

I grieve to say (tell Alfred [Mozley]) that I shall be busy all day tomorrow in examining our boys, and should not be able even to leave the room to see him. It can't be helped — but he must not have the trouble of coming up for nothing.

I have not seen Sir J Coleridge's supplement. Till I see it, I cannot tell, but my impression is that Keble proposed that Tyler should have the red gown, Hawkins the work, and himself the pay[3]

Ever Yrs affly John H Newman

FRIDAY 15 OCTOBER 1869 Lisle Ryder came. Renouf came   sudden change — glass down 10 degrees

SATURDAY 16 OCTOBER   Roe at Plough and Harrow

[1] The *Guardian*, (13 Oct. 1869). 'A remarkable letter has been addressed to the *Standard* by Mr. W. C. Faulkner, philosophical instrument maker. He states that for many years he has had a large sale for spirit-rapping magnets and batteries expressly made for concealment under the floor, in cupboards, under tables . . .'

[2] See letter of 3 Aug. to Lord Dunraven.

[3] After the publication early in 1869 of *A Memoir of the Rev. John Keble*, by Sir J. T. Coleridge, he received further material, notably two parcels of letters, one to R. H. Froude, the other to the Archdeacon his father. Some of these were inserted in the second edition, published later in 1869. Among them was Keble's reply to a letter from R. H. Froude announcing that the Provostship of Oriel was vacant, owing to the promotion of Edward Copleston to the Bishopric of Llandaff in 1827. Froude asked if Keble would offer himself for election. Keble replied, 'I must beg a few days for consideration before I answer positively; I feel Hawkins's claim to be a very strong one . . .' and ended his letter with the message: 'My very kind love to old Hawkins, and tell him I think we had better put the Provostship in commission; Tyler take the red gown, Hawkins the work and I the play. Qu'en pensez vous?' *op. cit.* third edition, Oxford 1870, p. 178.

The Oratory Octr 16. 1869

Dear Sir

I thank you for your extract from Bunsen's Life. I had not seen it before. As the year is not given, I cannot refer to any memorandums I may have made at the time of the good Pastor Spörlein's visit.[1]

I recollect nothing about it, not even his coming — but I dare say that the account is substantially correct. If a gentleman came with a letter from Baron Bunsen, of course I should have wished to show him civility. That was the reason why I asked him to breakfast, not (I am sure) to have a dispute with him. But it is not at all unlikely that he wished to learn, on his part, my sentiments. If I asked him, of course I should have asked others to meet him — and my friends were those who agreed with me in religious opinion — and many of them very likely were younger than myself. Moreover, if the Pastor Spörlein, said any thing which savoured of German Protestantism, I can easily fancy that young men would like to astonish him — also, it is very likely that, when they were gone, I should try to soften matters and to sooth the Pastor. Of course I should not be able to succeed, as I could wish.

The only thing I should deny in the 'lamentable story' is that directly or indirectly I was unkind to him, or ungentle. The real shock to him was, that, coming to Oxford as a School of Protestantism, he fell into what he would feel to be, and what we could not help, a cold bath[2]

Very truly Yours John H Newman

---

[1] In a letter of 6 Sept. 1841 to his wife Baron von Bunsen wrote: 'The other day, Spörlein, the good pastor of Antwerp, my fellow-traveller, arrived, on his pilgrimage to seek comfort in the Church and faith of this country. At Oxford he went to Newman, who invited him to breakfast, for a conference on religious opinions. Spörlein stated his difficulties, as resulting from the consistorial government being in the hands of unbelievers, while in the evangelical society, which he had been tempted to join, the leading members protested against every idea of church-membership. The breakfast party consisted of fifteen young men, whom Newman invited to an expression of opinion and advice, and the award (uncontradicted) was that "Pastor Spörlein, as a continental Christian, was subject to the authority of the Bishop of Antwerp." He objected that by that Bishop he would be excommunicated as a heretic. "Of course; but you will conform to his decision?" "How can I do that," exclaimed Spörlein, "without abjuring my faith?" "But your faith is heresy." "How! do you mean that I am to embrace the errors of Rome, and abjure the faith of the Gospel?" "There is no faith but that of the Church." "But my faith is in Christ crucified." "You are mistaken; you are not saved by Christ, but in the Church."

Spörlein was thunderstruck; he looked around, asked again, obtained but the same reply — whereupon he burst out with the declaration that "he believed in Christ crucified, by whose merits alone he could be saved, and that he would not join the Church of Rome, abhorring her for intruding into the place of Christ." One after the other dropped away, and Newman remaining with him alone, attempted an explanation, which however did not alter the case. I repeated this lamentable story as Spörlein had told it . . .' Frances Baroness Bunsen, *Memoirs of Baron Bunsen*, second edition abridged and corrected, London 1869, I, p. 376.

[2] There is no reference to Pastor Spörlein in Newman's diaries, although the guests at breakfast parties are frequently listed there.

MONDAY 18 OCTOBER 1869   Lisle Ryder went   Roe here.   dark at 6 A.M. suddenly

FROM CHARLES MEYNELL

Oscott Oct. 11. 1869

Dear Dr Newman

I went home on Saturday, and returned late yesterday evening: else you would have heard from me before.

First about the theological subject. I did *read* the parts you refer to, but I expressed myself doubtfully about them, because I didn't think my opinion was worth giving — I fear before I get to the end of these sheets I shall lose every vestige of modesty! I will tell you frankly that the expression 'The Father is *by Himself* God' sounded new to me when you first used it (for you know this is not the first time); but I deferred to you, and thought you had authority for saying it. When again I read that the 'Son and the Spirit are each *separately* God, *as if Each Other and the Father were not*'; and that the Father is all that is meant by the word 'God', I hesitated, but again deferred to you, thinking that doubtless you weighed your words, and had authority for saying it. At the same time I told you that if I doubted about anything it would be about these expressions.[1] I asked myself How is it true to say that the Father is separately or by Himself God, since God is Father, Son and Holy Ghost? Is God the Father *all* that I mean by the word God, as if the Son and Holy Ghost had no existence? I reflected, however, that the expressions were meant as an emphatic distinction of the Persons, and any false notion on the subject was forbidden by the context. But this morning I betook myself to find an illustration. I said: 'The three angles of a Triangle are one Triangle: but is each one of them a triangle, as if the other two had no existence?' I know that these illustrations are treacherous things:[2] so whether there be anything in this objection I leave you to judge. I next went to my books, and after some trouble lighted upon something like the matter in hand. St Thomas (Sum. I.I. Q. XXXI art. IV)[3] asks: Utrum dictio exclusiva possit adjungi termino personali. He does not forbid the proposition Solus Pater est Deus in the sense 'Ille, *qui solus dicitur Pater*, est Deus'. Please look at this article, and also at the *one immediately preceding*, and especially at the second objection and the answer to it.[4]

On the whole it seems to me doubtful whether you can say that each of the Three Divine Persons is, *by himself*, simply and absolutely God, *as though the Other Two were not*. But you will judge.

As to the philosophical matter, I used to consider consciousness as a special faculty, as Reid and other metaphysicians did, till I learnt Sir W. Hamilton's doctrine about it; which is this. He says that knowledge and consciousness are only different aspects of the same thing. All thought being the relation of subject with object, if I consider the object known, I have knowledge; if I consider myself as knowing the object, I have consciousness. In the examples you give to walk, or to sing — these are bodily acts, and of course, as such, are neither knowledge nor consciousness. But if I think of my walk or my song, it is knowledge, if I think that *I* am walking, *I* am singing it is consciousness. Or I might have consciousness only — as not thinking about *the walk*, but that it is *I who am walking* — but even then the *object* would be present *confusedly*; and so in knowledge there must be some confused sense, at least, of myself, and my act. Here then are two names for the same thing. But if you think that there is nothing in the objection as connected with inference and assent, couldn't you deal with it in a

[1] See Meynell's letter of 2 Oct. placed before that of 3 Oct. to him.
[2] Here Meynell inserted a footnote: 'I see already that the illustration is not to the point: for we do not call each one of the angles a triangle, as we call *each person* of the Holy Trinity God'
[3] A mistake for I, xxxi, 4.
[4] The answer to the second objection says we cannot properly say 'Pater est solus Deus' except in the sense 'Pater est Deus, qui est solus Deus'.

note? — if it be worth mentioning at all: for consciousness and knowledge are the same kind of thing; but inference and assent are, clearly, different kinds of thing

I don't think there is anything to notice in the present sheets, beyond a printers' error which I corrected

Your's Dear Dr Newman Sincerely and respectfully Charles Meynell

FROM CHARLES MEYNELL

Oscott Oct. 13. 1869

Dear Dr Newman

Is this of any use? Brancherau gives it as the characteristic of evidence that it is an equipoise of the active and receptive elements in thought.[1] He means that, no more is given in an evident judgment than is strictly warranted by the intuition (perception). Thus the judgment says 'I am hot or cold', because, in fact, 'I am, hot or cold' — says: 'Two-and-two make four', because we perceive that they do. You will see from this that he uses the term *evident* in the sense of self-evident: and also how in this case the judgment only rehearses, or echoes the statement of the case which is given in the intuition. He would not say therefore that it was *evident* that God exists, though he would say that it was certain.

I am not to be understood as disagreeing with what you say, because I put what appears as an objection. I may also say something that seems irrelevant; but there's a method in my madness, because you might make some use or other of what I say, which I do not know. Hence I went into the subject of the Hamiltonian view about consciousness being only another aspect of knowledge, and not a special faculty. But I have misgivings that I was incoherent in some parts of my last, and I thought as I folded it up, that it was a slovenly production. But I write sometimes under great disadvantages, and that is an excuse — to a certain extent.

I wonder if I made 'ado about nothing' in what I said about the 'separately, or by Himself'. This is a great trouble with me that I might be only suggesting scruples instead of being of any real use. But I can only do my best. Please don't think it necessary to answer this.

Your's respectfully and sincerely Charles Meynell

TO CHARLES MEYNELL

The Oratory Octr 19. 1869

My dear Dr Meynell

I rejoice to think that your task is coming towards an end. I send you four slips. Don't hurry yourself about them.

Thank you for your remarks on the Subject of the Holy Trinity. I altered one passage at your suggestion — as 'by Himself' is in the Athanasian Creed, (vid Garden of the Soul and Crown of Jesus,) I have left it

As to Hamilton, I did not at all mean to go to the question whether the act of consciousness was different in kind from the simple act, but that it was not a repetition of a similar act — because the objects of the two are distinct. 'This is a house' — house is the object of my act. 'I am beholding a house' — my beholding a house is the object of the act.

[1] Louis Branchereau (1819–1913), a Sulpician, whose *Praelectiones Philosophicae*, 1850, taught a mitigated ontologism, and were later censured at Rome. He was a close friend of Bishop Dupanloup.

I am quite ashamed to think what I have cost you in paper, pens, ink, stamps, and time

Most sincerely Yours John H Newman

Oscott Oct. 20th 1869

Dear Dr Newman

I don't find anything in these sheets to remark upon. I have no doubt that you are quite right as to the 'by Himself'. It would be absurd indeed to expect you should trust me about a matter, on which I had no confidence in myself; for I contradicted myself in my two notes, defending the expression in one and finding fault with it in the other. However consistency in objection is not looked for in a devil's advocate.

If you think that the Creed expresses in effect (it does not in fact) 'Pater, *per se*, est Deus', I give in. I thought it equivalent to the hypothetical cancelling of the other Persons, which I doubted about. Pray do not think I write this to persist in the objection, but merely to explain myself. I withdraw it altogether.

You will hurt my feelings if you say a word about postage stamps. I never missed them: I abound in these and note-paper; and am one of the richest persons in England, for the only things which I cannot afford to buy are those which I don't want. And as to time, I have given it with such good-will that I have not felt the loss, and shall be abundantly rewarded if you have borne patiently with my blunders and stupidity.

Your's Dear Dr Newman Sincerely and respectfully Charles Meynell

The Oratory Oct 20. 1869

My dear Madam

I shall be truly pleased to see you here, as you propose, when you come to Birmingham. I have always great difficulty in giving advice to persons I do not know, but especially by letter. One may do more harm than good.

I do not think you have read aright my remarks in the Apologia, on Dr Wiseman's article on the Donatists. I think I expressly say that it did *not* strike me and I had known it for years. What did strike me was a passage he quoted from St Augustine which contained a maxim going far beyond the purpose of the controversy — Securus judicat orbis terrarum — 'the Christian commonwealth judges without misgiving.'[1] That is the maxim, (as I also feel now,) on which all depends. The Christian commonwealth is one organized body — from time to time local disturbances rise in it — branches of it rise up separately from the rest, and claim to be heard in matters of discipline or doctrine — they appeal to the Fathers — so did the Donatists, so did the Arians, the Monophysites, the Protestants, the Anglicans — but the Christian State, Commonwealth, Kingdom judicat securus, has the right, the power, the

[1] In her letter of 2 Oct. Mrs Helbert referred to *Apo.*, pp. 116–17.

certitude of deciding the rights and the wrongs of the matter. How do we know that Pius ix is true Pope? Securus judicat orbis terrarum. How shall we know that the coming Council is a true Council — but by the after assent and acceptance of it on the part of that Catholic organization which is lineally descended, as one whole, from the first ages? — How can we interpret the decisions of that Council, how the Pope's decisions in any age, except by the Schola Theologorum, the great Catholic school of divines dispersed all over the earth? This is why I am a Catholic — because our Lord set up the Church — and that one Church has been in the world ever since — because in every age bodies have fallen off from her, and have shown in the event that that falling off was death — that they tended to lose all definite faith, *as* bodies, (I don't mean *individuals* in them, as Dr Pusey) but as bodies — the Arians came to nought, and the Donatists — and the Greeks show no signs of life, but remain shut up as if in the sepulchre of the past — and now the Anglican Church is gradually losing any definite faith, and is upheld only by the virtue and faith of its individual members. This is one of the great facts by which God meant the learned and unlearned to be guided — not by explorations into history, which are beyond most of us — not by comparison of the state of the Church with the claims of science and the theories and the needs of civil governments. Supposing upon Dr Temple's appointment,[1] Dr Pusey and others broke off from the Church of England, and set up a new communion with a new Episcopical succession, and supposing he (Dr Pusey) still said that he was one body with the Church of England — He might say so, if he would — but would any one believe it — would not every one smile, and say that it was a fiction, an imagination? who will call the Methodists one body with the Church of England? Why then not be honest, and say out, that the Church of England, in a parallel way, broke off from the Roman Communion in the 16th century? why not say out, that the Anglican Church is *not* one body with the Roman Church? Next then, I say, if they are two Churches, they cannot both of them be Christ's Church — which of them is the orbis terrarum — that organized, constituted body of which St Cyprian and St Augustine write?

As to majorities and minorities in the Ecumenical Council, the *final act* of the Council is always unanimous, or the dissentients speak out and leave the Council — as at Nicaea and Sardica. But, as above, I put the validity of the Council upon its reception by the orbis terrarum, of which Greece and England are no part. Sometimes years have passed before a Council has been generally received — e.g. the Third Council (at Ephesus) nay, the Nicene — and so again the Fifth — and, I may say, the Second.

As to the Archbishop's Sermon, it speaks to Catholics not Protestants — Protestants are sure to take it in the sense which to a Catholic is not conveyed in its words.[2] e.g. He makes the Pope say 'I am the sole *last* Supreme Judge

---

[1] The High Church party were strongly opposed to the appointment in the autumn of 1869 of Frederick Temple, one of the contributors to *Essays and Reviews*, as Bishop of Exeter.

[2] Mrs Helbert asked on 5 Oct., 'if you agree, or will all Catholics be bound to agree in the words of the Archbishop [Manning] respecting the Pope, in his Sermon of yesterday. He

of right and wrong —' now look at that little word 'last.' Any Protestant would think it meant that man had no *natural conscience* — but that the Pope *made* right and wrong — which every Catholic knows to be a wicked heresy — but the Archbishop knew what he was saying, and he says no such thing, and any theologian, the high authorities at Rome, will quite understand the theological force of his words. He says 'the sole *last* judge;' that is, to him is the *appeal* when men differ IN DETAIL. Supposing the question was whether the rules about stealing could be modified by the laws of the state, I mean, as to gravity of particular acts, or whether smuggling was always, or in what sense, a bad sin — or poaching — or certain cases of duelling — or whether usury was allowable, or under what circumstances, and Catholics differ, then the Pope would be to them the final appeal — and what he said would be received. There are other senses in which it is true of the *Church* — viz that she is infallible in greater questions of morals — that is, that she will *always be protected* from all acts seriously infringing on that moral law, which is the inward gift to man as man from God — but the Protestant interpretation of the Archbishop's words is what he did not in his own breast mean — and is therefore a calumny upon him

I am, My dear Madam Sincerely Yours John H Newman

THURSDAY 21 OCTOBER 1869   Fr Carbonel S J. came (not into house)

TO W. J. COPELAND

The Oratory Oct 21/69

My dear Copeland

Thanks for the immense trouble you are taking. Don't dream of running down here.

I am quite content with the word 'enlarged' put to the two Sermons in their place in the Index in Volume 2[1]

When I put 're-written etc' against a sermon, it means that the *first* edition of the *printed* Sermon was rewritten *from* the MS as preached on the day assigned. Thus Volume 3 Sermon 1 was printed as it was preached on July 19. 1829 — but Sermon 2 in the Volume was not printed (in 1836) as preached on May 9, 1830 but re-written for the purpose of printing.

Yes, 'Birmingham Banking Co etc' My volume gets slowly on — I am so done up with it, that I shall leave off for a few weeks, and go to Rednall.

makes the Pope say, "I am liberated from all civil subjection my Lord made me the subject of no one on earth . . . and I claim more than this, — I claim to be the Supreme Judge and director of the consciences of men; . . . I am the sole last Supreme Judge of what is right and wrong" —' This was from Manning's sermon on The Syllabus of Errors, delivered at the Pro-Cathedral Kensington on 3 Oct., and reported in *The Times*, (4 Oct.), p. 6.

[1] See *S.D.*, p. 412. Copeland at first intended to describe not only Sermon XXVII but also Sermon XXXI as 'enlarged.'

Your Preface is exceedingly good.[1] It is neat, clear, and comprehensive —
and, as before, very considerate towards me

Ever Yrs affly J H N

P.S.   I don't think any thing need be said about *level*, for it was a false print.[2]
I doubt whether you might not add a sentence to this effect. 'In volume iv
p 280 "miraculous" has been substituted, with the author's approbation, for
"immaculate" which he wrote by a mistake, which he has also made in a note
in the translation of the Treatises of St Athanasius p 241. Also, in the present
volume p [28] the clause "in his own words" has been inserted to meet a
criticism of Mr Keble's at the time of its first publication.'
What do you think?

TO JOHN RICKARDS MOZLEY

J R Mozley Esqr   Oct 21/69
My dear John

I see an able article in the North British which I take for yours[3]

If so, let me ask you a question I have years ago read Mill on Induction —
but it is difficult, at my time of life, to get into new ideas.

I fancied he ⟨ultimately⟩ grounded his analysis of it on the principle
'Nature is uniform in its operations' — so that one instance stood for any
number of instances. This axiom being assured, then a true induction is a
demonstration

Some, I believe, call this process, not induction, but analogy

Now I want to know whether it is considered generally that Induction
leads to incontrovertible or to probable conclusions

You say in the article in question 'All these writers thought it *impossible
to give general laws of induction* — it seems tacitly assumed by them etc that
probable reasoning did not admit of being reduced to *rule and form*. . . . It was
reserved for Dr Mill etc.' p 84

Do you mean that Mill turned what was thought hitherto merely probable
(inductive reasons), into demonstration — or that he gave rules for that which
was only probable, before and after him, viz inductive reasoning?[4]

J H N

---

[1] i.e. Copeland's preface to *S.D.*, where he also incorporated the remarks Newman makes
here in his postcript.

[2] See second note to letter of 25 July to Copeland.

[3] 'The Different Schools of Elementary Logic,' The *North British Review*, (Oct. 1869),
pp. 71–96, signed 'J.R.M.' See letter of 7 Nov. to Wetherell.

[4] J. R. Mozley replied on 24 Oct. that logicians generally 'would agree that induction can
from its nature only lead to probable conclusions, though that probability may be of all
degrees, and may in many cases amount to practical certainty.' As to Mill, Mozley meant
'merely that he had traced the rules by which men advance in the discovery of probable
truth . . . As to analogy, Mill makes it only a fainter kind of induction, so that a large assemblage
of analogies tending to one point would amount to an induction . . .'

FRIDAY 22 OCTOBER 1869   Fr Carbonel went

TO MARK PATTISON

The Oratory Octr 22. 1869

My dear Rector

I think you will allow me to introduce to your notice Fr Carbonelle (I believe I spell his name aright). He is a Belgian Jesuit, living in Paris. He has known Englishmen in India, and speaks English. He came here introduced to me by Henry Wilberforce, who is a great friend of his, and I have myself learned a good deal from him during the few hours which he passed here.[1]

I am glad of this opportunity of writing a line to you, and am,

My dear Rector Sincerely Yours John H Newman

The Rector of Lincoln College

SATURDAY 23 OCTOBER 1869   Duke of Norfolk called

SUNDAY 24 OCTOBER   John and Thomas ordained priests in our Church by Bishop. Renouf left and Roe.

MONDAY 25 OCTOBER   Mr Drury called

WEDNESDAY 27 OCTOBER   snow lying for some days in places   very cold

THURSDAY 28 OCTOBER   Sir John and Lady Simeon called   sung black mass for Miss Farrant   praesente cadavere[2]   Henry went to London

FRIDAY 29 OCTOBER   Woodgate and Mr Boyle called.   Eddy Froude came   Abbé Duclos to dinner[3]

SATURDAY 30 OCTOBER   Henry returned

SUNDAY 31 OCTOBER   E. Froude went

---

[1] Carbonelle wrote on 26 Oct. to Victor de Buck the Bollandist, that whereas Manning blamed his attitude to the Ritualists as holding back conversions, Newman approved of it, and said that a wrong use can be made of any thing. Carbonelle added that he was 'un admirateur enthusiaste de Newman,' and, 'Une chose m'a frappé particulièrement dans sa conversation; c'est l'extrême attention qu'il met à ne rien dire qui puisse offenser personne, bien qu'il exprime souvent sa pensée fort clairement. Malgré l'opinion contraire, je ne pense pas qu'on puisse dire autant de Mgr Manning.' (Bollandist Archives, at Brussels, information kindly furnished by James Jurich S.J.)

[2] Frances Farrant, the second of two sisters who devoted themselves to the poor near the Oratory, died on 23 Oct.

[3] Henri Louis Duclos (1815–1900), ordained in 1840 and well known in Paris as a preacher and writer of practical books on religion. He was a curate at La Madeleine, 1857–70, and then Curé of St Eugène.

TO BISHOP ULLATHORNE

The Oratory Nov 1. 1869[1]

I know nothing, and never have had, nor have, nor can have, the slightest suspicion, of Dr Manning ever at any time having suppressed any letter of mine written to Cardinal Wiseman, and containing matter which had an ulterior destination.[2]

John H Newman

[1] On 7 Sept. 1869 Manning had excommunicated Ffoulkes until he should retract his pamphlet *The Church's Creed or the Crown's Creed? A Letter to Archbishop Manning*. See letter of 10 Feb. 1869 to Harper. Ffoulkes retaliated in Oct. with a second pamphlet, *The Roman Index and its late Proceedings, a Second Letter to the Most Rev. Archbishop Manning*, London 1869, in which he published the correspondence between them. This second pamphlet was evidently very vindictive. There was (and is) no copy of it at the Birmingham Oratory, (cf. first note to letter of 6 Nov. to Mrs William Froude), but large extracts were published in the *Guardian*. Although Newman was not concerned in the controversy, Ffoulkes attempted to enlist him on his own side. The *Guardian*, (27 Oct. 1869), p. 1203 reported this as follows: 'We cannot, however, refrain from quoting the following passage bearing on the treatment which Dr. Newman received from the Roman *Curia* in the matter of the Hall which he proposed to open at Oxford, and for which he had actually collected a large sum of money. It is already well known that the underhand treatment which he experienced compelled him to abandon the undertaking in disgust and return the money to the various contributors; but we believe that the following incident is now made public for the first time.' The *Guardian* then quoted this paragraph from Ffoulkes's pamphlet:
'Whether your Grace knows anything of the remaining intrigue to which I shall allude, it is not competent for me to say: the intrigue or series of intrigues, namely, that has for so long doomed to comparative retirement and inaction one of the master-minds of his age: when from the genius with which God has blessed him, and the influence which he wields over countless multitudes in all communions — above all, for the crisis through which we are passing — he ought to have been raised aloft on a pedestal as the S. Bernard of Europe. Characters that it takes ages to produce, we should make the most of while we can: therefore, when they are condemned to unmerited obloquy year after year, of their mature prime, it becomes a national, if not a world-wide calamity. Now, I have seen and read a pamphlet written by one scarcely his inferior in ability, and full his equal in honesty, detailing this intrigue from beginning to end, and disclosing such conduct in some cases — in one case comparable with the behaviour of Lady Nottingham to Lord Essex — as would have made all concerned in it, however exalted their positions, colour crimson had it been made public. The noble nature that had been assailed stepped in between this pamphlet and the world, just as it was ready for circulation: a presentation copy gave him the first tidings of what was contemplated, and he replied by telegraph begging that it might be suppressed. Should your Grace desire that its contents should be made public after my pointed allusions, its author may possibly be induced to defer to your wishes.' (pp. 62-3).
According to the story, the Earl of Essex, when in favour, had received a ring from Queen Elizabeth, with an undertaking that she would pardon him any offence if he sent it her when in danger. Shortly before his execution in Feb. 1601 he sent it to the Countess of Nottingham, who retained it, instead of transmitting it to the Queen.
Ffoulkes was evidently alluding to Manning's assurance to Newman that all would be settled acceptably in regard to the delation of his *Rambler* article, when in fact Propaganda was expecting an answer from him. See letter of 7 May 1860 and notes there; the correspondence with Ambrose St John in May 1867, when he discovered that the matter had not been settled; and letters of 10 and 14 Nov. 1869 to Ullathorne.
The pamphlet to which Ffoulkes referred was William Palmer's appendix to the French translation of the sermon 'The Pope and the Revolution.' See Appendix to Volume XXIII, and Newman's letter of 26 Nov. 1867 to William Palmer.
[2] On 31 Oct. Manning wrote to Ullathorne that he had just heard a statement that Newman wrote Wiseman a letter which would have cleared him in the matter of the *Rambler* delation, and that he, Manning, intercepted it. 'As I never heard this or of any such letter till to-night, I conceive you know as little as I on the subject: but as no one can so easily know the facts, I would ask you to let me know whether you have ever heard such a statement.' *DR*, (April, May, June 1920), p. 214. Shane Leslie, *Henry Edward Manning*, London 1921, p. 279.

TUESDAY 2 NOVEMBER 1869   sung black mass

FROM CHARLES MEYNELL

Oscott Oct. 23d 1869

Dear Dr Newman

I like it very much, and (if that's worthy anything) I agree with it: but I don't know whether you would altogether agree with me. I used to distinguish between *direct*, and *reflex* certainty. The direct certitude was what I suppose you would call instinctive belief. The reflex I used to call scientific certainty. I justified the direct, instinctive belief, as a certitude quite as reasonable as the reflex. I said that a simple rustic in believing the reality of an external world, of the objects of memory, of the Sovereign Being, had, really, sufficient, good reasons of his belief, and that his reasons for believing would be found precisely the same as those of the educated, were they brought out by an analysis of the facts of consciousness. But I think that you have done better in limiting the term 'certitude' to designate the belief informed by conscious reasoning.[1] It seems, on the face of it, inappropriate to speak of a man, as having certitude who had never asked himself *why* he believes.

You have made it clear enough that certitude is not to be confounded with infallibility.[2] I have, however, always held that Reason (though it sounds strange to say until one has explained) is infallible — and that, I think, even according to the designation of 'a gift or faculty which relates to all propositions in a given subject matter'.[3] I distinguish, of course, between reason, and *reasoning* — our *use* of reason. The distinction seems to my mind so obvious to be made that I should not mention it, had not Simpson pooh-poohed it when I made it in the 'Rambler'.[4] I say that there is an end of all certainty if Reason itself be once supposed to be fallible. If a man incautiously uses in argument an illicit process, or undistributed middle, I can show that is not a deliverance of the reason; it only looks like one; it is a fallacy: I appeal to reason against this particular reasoning. I don't suppose that *you* deny this, but if not why can I not say — or can I not say, that I am infallibly certain of the primary deliverances of reason — *of things that are self-evident*? And if some persons have altogether confounded certitude and infallibility, is not this because to some extent these are identical? To be sure we must distinguish between the *guide* and the *guided subject*; but an infallible guide, guides infallibly; and so does reason, properly consulted. Hence you yourself speak of indefectible certitude as to the primary deliverances of conscience.

Hence though I do not quarrel with such expressions as the treacherousness of memory, or the deceptions of sense, used colloquially, I hold that strictly and philosophically speaking, sense and memory are infallible, because their trustworthiness can be tested by a primary deliverance of reason — the principle of contradiction. The only way in which memory could deceive me, since it is a representative faculty would

Ullathorne then called on Newman, who wrote for him this present letter. On a copy of it Newman wrote '(given to Dr Ullathorne who came up here to me on occasion of Dr Manning's letter to him)'

Manning wrote again on 1 Nov. to Ullathorne: 'Until to-day I have not been able to decide what it is my duty to do in respect to the accusation made on me by Mr. Ffoulkes in pp. 62, 63 of his Second Letter, paragraph 3, "Whether" etc.' Manning now felt he must 'require the production of the pamphlet there referred to.'

[1] *G.A.*, pp. 195–6 and 210–12.
[2] *G.A.*, pp. 224–7.
[3] *G.A.*, p. 224.
[4] 'The Limits of Thought,' the *Rambler*, (May 1860), p. 103.

be by *re-presenting* that which had never been *presented*: and the only way sense could really deceive me would be if I perceived that which I did not perceive, which is absurd.

Even in wrong reasoning, reason is right (though it seems a paradox). Thus when two astronomers argued — one 'that the moon revolves round her axis, because she constantly shows the same side towards the earth', and the other that 'the moon *does not* revolve round her axis, *because she shows the same side towards the earth*', the judges of the dispute decided that the *reasoning itself* was right, from the point of the two astronomers, though it issued in contradiction: the fault was in the data reasoned upon, which were insufficient. If a man goes wrong in reasoning it is because he has not consulted his reason sufficiently attentively, or because the data are wrong.

I fear I have written at unnecessary length. Please bear with my loquaciousness — a sign of premature old age?

Your's Dear Dr Newman Sincerely and respectfully Charles Meynell

P.S. Your appeal to the Athanasian Creed put out my 'theological eye'. If I had been prudent I should have left the theology alone.   C.M.

TO CHARLES MEYNELL

Nov 2/69

My dear Dr Meynell

By this post I inflict some more on you. Thank you for the encouragement you gave me in your last. As to your question about right reason etc, I wish I were a metaphysician to answer it — but I have the greatest difficulty in passing to the *in fieri* from the *in facto esse*.

I seem quite to concur with what you say about direct and reflex certitude

Most sincerely Yours John H Newman

TO THOMAS JOSEPH BROWN, BISHOP OF NEWPORT

The Oratory, Birmm November 3, 1869

My dear Lord

I thank your Lordship for your kind letter; but I am not able to say more than I have said already.[1]

There was an English Bishop, just ten years ago, who, without a word to me, (which would have settled every thing,) and in spite of the sacred direction, Matth. xviii, 15, denounced a writing of mine to the Authorities at Rome.

He it is, who has created a prejudice against me there, such, as to be my

---

[1] Bishop Brown wrote on 2 Nov., 'This is positively the last letter with which I am likely to bore you for a good while . . .' and went on to urge 'that you might do much more at the Council than you can do remaining in England. Besides prayer, you could lay before those who sought information the spiritual condition and requirements of England, far better than any other can — and your opinions would be more regarded. Your presence too would give confidence to our poor troubled Anglicans.' Newman wrote on Brown's letter, 'This is the last of many letters on the subject.' He had already written on 22, 25 and 27 Sept.

sufficient justification in acting upon those positive inducements, which lead me at this time to remain quietly in my own place at home.[1]

I am, My dear Lord, Your Lordship's faithful Servt in Xt
John H. Newman of the Oratory

The Rt Revd The Bp of Newport

FROM ARCHBISHOP MANNING

8, York Place W. Nov. 2. 1869.

My dear Newman,

The Bishop of Birmingham has forwarded to me the paper you wrote on the subject of my letter to him.[2]

Mr Ffoulkes's pamphlet has done this good, that we shall let the light in upon the misunderstandings of these last years.

It is my intention to obtain a copy of the Pamphlet referred to by Mr Ffoulkes at p 63 of his Letter: and to take any steps it may make necessary. I feel that I have no right to ask you to assist me in obtaining the Pamphlet: and Mr Ffoulkes may be in error in supposing that you know the Author, and may know how to obtain a copy for me.[3]

If you are not unwilling to do so, you would confer on me a real and kind service.

On Friday I hope to leave England; and as return is always uncertain, and may, at best, be distant, I leave with you the assurance that the friendship of so many years, though of late unhappily clouded, is still dear to me.

Believe me, always My dear Newman, Yours affectionately ✠ Henry E. Manning

TO ARCHBISHOP MANNING

Nov. 3 1869

My dear Archbishop

Thank you for your kind letter — I can only repeat what I said when you last heard from me.[4] I do not know whether I am on my head or my heels,

---

[1] Bishop Brown's delation of Newman's *Rambler* article 'On Consulting the Faithful in Matters of Doctrine,' in the autumn of 1859, led to his being under a cloud at Rome, which only began to be removed in 1867. And now Ffoulkes's accusations, as to the part in the episode played by Manning, could easily have involved Newman in further unpleasantness with the latter.

[2] i.e. letter of 1 Nov. to Ullathorne.

[3] i.e. William Palmer's appendix to the French translation of Newman's sermon 'The Pope and the Revolution.' Manning seems not to have pursued the matter of the accusation against himself. If he had, he would have involved both Newman and William Palmer in his bitter controversy with Ffoulkes. See letters of 6 Nov. to Mrs William Froude and 10 Nov. to Ullathorne.

[4] Letter of 2 Sept. 1867.

when I have active relations with you. In spite of my friendly feelings, this is the judgment of my intellect[1]

Yours affectionately in Christ, John H Newman

The Most Revd Dr Manning

TO E. B. PUSEY

The Oratory Nov 4/69

My dear Pusey

My own opinion is that mistakes were made — or rather than [sic] in one or two Bulls words were used loosely. 'Go to the Holy Land in remissionem peccatorum', is not much more than 'Go and prosper.'[2]

The Priest's prayer *after* the absolution *always* now is 'Passio etc etc . . . quidquid boni *feceris*, et mali *sustinueris*, sit tibi *in remissionem peccatorum* etc[3] just as St Augustine says that the Lord's Prayer is the means of remitting venial sins.

However, I am not a theologian. The best book, and it is a great authority, doubtless you know — it goes through all these subjects — viz the De Indulgentiis auctore F. Theodoro à Spiritu Sancto Ord. Carmel, Romæ 1743.

Ever Yrs affly John H Newman

TO MRS HELBERT

The Oratory Nov 5. 1869

My dear Madam

I meant fully to have noticed your question, but, as I wrote on, it went out of my mind. But from what I said you will conjecture what it would be. It would be very presumptuous in me to give an answer to such a question. I

---

[1] The reasons Newman gave in his letter of 26 Nov. 1867 to Palmer, against publishing his appendix, still held good. They were: 'It is disrespectful to the authorities at Propaganda, as reviving what they wish forgotten. It is inconsiderate to the memory of the dead [i.e. Wiseman]. And it will be a scandal to the Protestant public.

It is likely to bring me into a most unpleasant and serious controversy.' In his memorandum of 3 Dec. 1867 Newman developed this last point: 'I should have a very painful controversy, now that I had congratulated myself as having got to land at last — that I should have to bring out Dr Brown's conduct etc etc.'

[2] Pusey wrote, 'Can you tell me what is the explanation of those forgivenesses (so to speak) of future sin in the Bulls of the early Crusades, which look like forgiveness of future sin. I used to think that the Crusades being a holy war, death thus was a sort of martyrdom. The promise is to those who should confess duly and with contrition. But there would be forgiveness through the sacrament. Yet the *language* does not relate to temporal consequences of sin but absolution of all their sins'.

Pusey gave some examples, such as 'Accipite igitur viam hanc in remissionem peccatorum vestrorum,' Amort, *Historia Indulgentiarum* I, ii, 3.

[3] After giving absolution in the sacrament of Penance, the priest says, 'Passio Domini nostri Jesu Christi, merita beatæ Mariæ Virginis, et omnium Sanctorum, quidquid boni feceris, et mali sustinueris, sint tibi in remissionem peccatorum, augmentum gratiæ, et præmium vitæ aeternæ. Amen.'

never do — and should make great mistakes, if I did so in the case of any one I did not know well.[1]

What I say can only be what applies to all persons — I would say more, if I could.

What I can say is this — that, though Almighty God does not at once tell us what is truth and make us certain of it, yet we can always be certain what we ought to do. First then you may be certain that you are not bound to change your religious position till you see clearly that it is your duty to do so — nor are you bound to acknowledge the communion of Rome to be the true Church till you inwardly assent to it — nor must you suppose that God will not in His own time enlighten you on the matter.

What your duty is, is to trust in God, to wait and pray, and to act up to your light, as far as light is given you. Never distrust God, be sure that He loves you. This I have said before, and say again.

As to receiving communion in the Anglican Church, I don't see how you can do so, unless you have faith in it.

As to that book Janus, a man must be a strange Catholic to have written it, if what I hear of it is true.[2] A friend of mine here, observing that he quoted in one place a rare book, which he happened to see in one of our bookseller's shops, bought the book, and found it said nearly the *reverse* of what Janus said. For myself, though I have the book, I have not at this time an hour at my disposal to give to it — but, as far [as] I have looked at it or heard of it, it seems a very able book written with a great exaggeration and colouring of facts.

As to your other questions about direction, I say the same, 'Can you *believe* in it? —' And, as for Anglican orders, I think them exceedingly doubtful — and, were they ever so valid, the power of jurisdiction, that is, of validly pronouncing absolution, is not conveyed in them, but must come of a separate act of ecclesiastical superiors, i.e. superior to the Priest exercising the power.

I would gladly write more — but no one but myself knows how heavily just now my work presses on me, and how many letters I have to write.

Trust in God, be patient as a duty — *don't give up what you have* — but pray God to give you all He has to give, and to teach you His full will.[3]

Most truly Yours John H Newman

[1] Mrs Helbert wrote on 28 Oct. her disappointment that Newman had not answered her question, 'Whether (under the circumstances I mentioned) I should not return for a time at any rate to my former obedience, and 2ndly if you would direct me to a course of reading within my compass, upon the subjects you had kindly entered upon with me.' Mrs Helbert added that a clergyman who had been advising her 'tells me that I cannot expect light, or to be taught of God, whilst I am wandering further away from the appointed means of grace — that no one *could* uphold me in continuing to refuse absolution, unless the validity of our Orders be denied. What can I say to this.'

[2] Mrs Helbert continued: 'Meanwhile I have been thrown back a very long way by reading "the Pope and the Council" by Janus. If all that book says be true . . . how could I ever change my religion?' 'Janus' was the pseudonym used by Döllinger (with others) for his anti-Ultramontane letters in the Augsburg *Allgemeine Zeitung* early in 1869. They were soon published in book form and in English.

[3] Mrs Helbert wrote her last letter on 10 Nov. from the Anglican House of Mercy at Clewer, of which she was an associate: 'I have been frightened at my own hopelessness and cold and hard

Nov 6/69

My dear Child

I did not write to you, for I had nothing to say.

As to Mr Harris, his is the case, alas, of a number of good youths — but I do not know him and could do nothing for him. I mentioned your anxiety to Fr Edward, who knows him, and I know would help him, if he could. I know no one at Liverpool or I would gladly mention his name.

I have no difficulty at all in sending your Prospectus to Hope Scott, if you will send me one — but would not your brother Stuart do it better than I?[1]

God bless and prosper you

Ever Yours affectly John H Newman

TO W. J. COPELAND

The Oratory Nov 6/69

My dear Copeland

I don't quite understand Rivington's difficulty.[2] Volume 4 is printed from *his* last Edition, not Burns's. As to the Editions after 1845 of some volumes, I had nothing to do with them except giving leave. I never saw proofs. I never saw them when published. I know nothing about them. Of course he re-printed them from his own preceding Edition. They were small editions to make up sets.

You say 'subsequently to 1843' — why not to 1845?

Whether, through my stupid carelessness or not I cannot find pp ii, iii, iv, v, of the Preface — but, when I had it before, it read very well, and all you say in your letter now, reads like improvement. I can only grieve that what is certainly successful after many perplexities should have given you so much trouble.

I hope I have said all you wish me to say I think I understand all your alterations

Ever Yours affectly John H Newman

state — and at the risk I run of drifting nowhere.' She was doubtful about calling on Newman in Birmingham, which she had suggested. 'All my friends hope that my stay here may lead to my return to my former way of thinking and to Communion. . . . Pray do not think that this needs any reply.' Mrs Helbert became a Catholic before she died in 1874.

[1] See letter of 2 Jan. 1870 to Hope-Scott.

[2] Copeland wrote on 5 Nov. that Rivington was 'seemingly haunted by the thought of that 4th Volume and by the fact of there being two or three Volumes, of which the last editions were so late as 1851 . . .' Newman had published a corrected edition of *P.S.* IV. It was important to make clear that in the reprinted volumes there were no alterations subsequently to 1845, and this was stated in the preface to *S.D.*

TO MRS WILLIAM FROUDE

Nov 6. 1869

My dear Mrs Froude

I suppose Eddy [Froude] had not time to write to you from Liverpool. He seemed pretty well, but I doubt not his trip will quite set him up.

I had a great deal of talk with him — and was only sorry when he went.

As to the passage you cut out from a paper — it is a *melodramatic misstatement* — but I cannot help being amused at it.[1] There are those who have been taking matters with a very high hand and with much of silent intrigue for a considerable time, and such ways of going on bring with them their retribution. This does not defend the actors in that retribution, Ffoukes is behaving very ill — but he is the 'nemesis,' as they call it, of a policy, which I cannot admire. Nor do I like the new North British — but it too is the retributive consequence of tyranny.[2] All will work for good; and, if we keep quiet, Providence will fight for us, and set things right

Ever Yours affly John H Newman

TO E. B. PUSEY

The Oratory Nov 7, 1869

My dear Pusey

I send you some Proof and copy, which is yours, not mine. Perhaps G. and R. [Gilbert and Rivington] in turn have sent mine to you.

Also I send a little book of authority, taken from Theodore.

I forgot to say that Theodore treats your subject at pp 36 and 228 of volume 1. I suppose you have the book[3]

Ever Yrs affly John H Newman

[1] The phrase 'melodramatic misstatement' occurs in a reply by Ignatius Ryder on 29 Oct. to an inquiry from W. G. Ward about Ffoulkes's accusation against Manning. Ryder wrote: 'I have not seen Ffoulkes's *Second Letter* beyond the very copious extracts given in the *Guardian*. I have no wish to see more if it. I will not trust myself to say what I feel about the attempt to lug in Father Newman . . . .

I am authorised to say this much, that the story about the letter is a melodramatic misstatement. I believe that Father Newman was treated abominably; but I am not at liberty to enter into any details.' *Purcell*, II. p. 343.

Many years later, in a review of *Purcell*, Ryder wrote: 'The form the story of Manning's negligence took in the hands of Ffoulkes was the monstrous exaggeration that he had actually suppressed a letter of Newman's to the Holy Office. It is this version which Fr. Ryder . . . characterises as "a melodramatic misstatement", The letter was written after consultation with Dr. Newman, in answer to an interrogatory of Dr. Ward's, who must have forwarded it to Cardinal Manning in whose collection Mr. Purcell found it.' H. I. D. Ryder, *Essays*, edited by Francis Bacchus, London 1911, p. 284.

[2] See letter of 7 Nov. to Wetherell.

[3] See end of letter of 4 Nov. to Pusey.

The Oratory Nov 7. 1869

My dear Wetherell

Thank you for the copy of your Review.[1] It is exceedingly able and careful. The Articles on Gladstone, Saint Bartholomew, and Logic are especially good.[2] It has, to me, only one fault, but a serious one.

I don't want a Review to be religious, or even to profess Catholicity — but, did not I know the quarter whence it came, I should think it written by liberal Scotchmen, religious in a way, who looked at the Church as a fiction of past times.[3]

Most sincerely Yours John H Newman

TO MRS WILLIAM FROUDE

[8 November 1869][4]

My dear Mrs Froude

When I said 'melodramatic misstatement' I alluded, I find, to some facts stated by Mr Ffoukes, but not in the Devonshire paper.

What the paper says, viz that I stopped a Preface when published by telegram on receiving a presentation copy and that, because it would do harm, is true, but I don't wish it mentioned that *I* say so.[5]

Ever Yrs affly J H N

TO LE COMTE DE MONTALEMBERT

The Oratory Nov 10. 1869

M. le Comte

I ever think of you, if you will not think it rude in me to say so, as one, who from his youth has nobly given his life and all his powers to the service of

---

[1] On 16 Oct. Wetherell sent Newman a copy of the quarterly *North British Review* for Oct. It had been taken over as organ of the liberal Catholics, with Wetherell as editor, and this was his first number. Its new prospectus disclaimed connection with any particular religious denomination, but said it would be devoted to scientific study of religion, history and politics, and would support Gladstone. Among the chief contributors were Acton and Simpson. Wetherell wrote, 'You will receive a copy of the Review regularly, if you will kindly give it house room.' It came to an end in 1871.

[2] The article on Gladstone was a review of his *Juventus Mundi. The Gods and Men of the Heroic Age*. Acton wrote on 'The Massacre of St Bartholomew,' and also a review article on Janus, *The Pope and the Council*. For the article on Logic, see letter of 21 Oct. to J. R. Mozley.

[3] On 26 Sept. 1870 Newman wrote to Wetherell of the *Review*, 'It is wonderful in point of matter and conscientious hard work.'

[4] Dated by postmark.

[5] The 'Preface' was Palmer's appendix to the French translation of Newman's sermon 'The Pope and the Revolution.'

religion — who has had much to bear, and has from first to last known how to combine zeal for Catholic Truth and devotion to the Church with loyal obedience to her authorities. And it would be strange indeed, if, so thinking, I were not one of those many, who would show their gratitude to you, if they could[1]

And now, that it has pleased our Merciful Lord so heavily to afflict you, I do what I can for you, Monsieur le Comte, in your need in saying Mass in your behalf. This I have done every week since the beginning of the year, and I hope, with God's help to go on doing so.

It is an extreme honour to me that the Bishop of Orleans should wish to have me with him, and should speak to me through you. He is so great a man, that it is a serious trouble to me and a real distress, to feel that I cannot take advantage of so special and condescending a kindness — but there are reasons quite special which make it impossible. I hope Monseigneur will not think me ungrateful or perverse in making this reply.

It is very kind in you to have received so favorable the volume of Verses which I ventured to send you

> I am, Monsieur le Comte with great respect
> Your faithful Servant in Xt   John H Newman

The Count de Montalembert &c. &c.

[1] Montalembert wrote on 8 November from La Roche en Brenil: 'I am entreated by our great and good Bishop of Orléans to trouble you again with his most urgent wish and request to obtain your consent to accompany him as one of his theologians to the approaching general Council at Rome.

. . . .

Since the publication of the admirable address of the German Bishops assembled at Fulda to their people, the general situation of Catholic affairs has taken a more cheerful aspect. [See second note to letter of 22 Sept. to Monsell] Hope and confidence have re-entered many a soul weighed down by gloom and despondency when a very different spirit seemed to prevail in the future prospects of the Church militant. Much has been done in this direction by the unwearied efforts of the illustrious prelate; and he is now straining his last nerve with the hope of being able to cope successfully with those whom he so justly terms *les ignorants et les insensés*.

With the help of Cardinal Schwarzenberg, archbishop of Prague, in whom he has met with a most valuable and unexpected auxiliary, he confidently trusts to obtain from the Roman authorities that professor Döllinger shall be summoned to attend the Council. But he very properly deems that your absence from this great assembly would be universally looked upon as a mistake and a misfortune; and he therefore cannot make up his mind to be deprived of the honour and strength of your assistance amongst his official theologians.

. . . .

I am happy to have this occasion of thanking you for the valuable gift of your *Verses on various occasions*, which I have read with deep and frequent sympathy, particularly the *dream of Gerontius*. But I feel still more grateful for the blessing you have deigned to confer on me by the Masses which you have promised our friend Monsell to celebrate on my behalf.'

Montalembert ended by saying he could never recover from the illness from which he had been suffering for four years. His letter is printed in full in *DR*, (Spring 1949), pp. 134–5. He died on 13 March 1870.

TO BISHOP ULLATHORNE

The Oratory Nov 10. 1869

My dear Lord

I thank you for letting me see the Archbishop's letter to you.[1]

After thinking over what happened this time ten years carefully, I am fully sure, and could depose in a court of justice, that Cardinal Wiseman never wrote to me any letter down to the day of his death in answer to my letter to him of January 1860.[2]

Should you on the other hand be ready to depose that he did, that of course would astonish and shake me — but I do not think you will. My own belief is that your memory brings before you some letter not addressed by the Cardinal to *me*.

Next, some months after my letter of January 1860, Dr Manning wrote to me from Rome in the Cardinal's name to say, either that '*all was settled*' or that '*all would soon be settled*.'[3]

---

[1] On 31 Oct. Manning wrote his first letter to Ullathorne about Ffoulkes's accusation, that he had intercepted a letter of Newman's which would have cleared him over the *Rambler* article delation. On 1 Nov. and 2 Nov. Manning wrote three more letters to Ullathorne on the subject, all printed in *Purcell* II, pp. 343–5, from the copies Manning kept, which are still in the Bayswater archives. The letter Newman thanks Ullathorne for letting him see, would seem to be that of 3 Nov. (Manning left London en route for the Council, on 5 Nov.)

In his letter of 2 Nov. Manning had written, 'I remember telling you that I was in the English College when the Cardinal [Wiseman] received a letter from Dr Newman on the subject of the Article in the Rambler. It was no statement or explanation, but a request to know what passages were objected to.' This was Newman's letter of 19 Jan. 1860, quoted below in letter of 14 Nov. to Ullathorne. Manning's description of it failed to mention Newman's readiness to explain the passages, and it was on this point that the criticism of Manning's actions turned.

In his letter of 3 Nov. Manning wrote to Ullathorne: 'I am much obliged to you for your last letter.

It was in this country that I stated to you that the Cardinal had received a letter from Dr Newman while we were at the English College.

I did so when you were saying that the Cardinal had failed to communicate to Dr Newman any result of his endeavours to remove the effect of the Bishop of Newport's [T. J. Brown] delation of the article in the Rambler. I stated also that the Cardinal fell ill almost at the time he received the letter, and that so far as I remember I never heard him again speak of it.

During that time I wrote to Dr Newman asking in what way I could be of use. He may perhaps still have the letter.

I endeavoured more than once to remove from Cardinal Barnabo's mind the impression left by the Bishop of Newport.

This is all I know on the subject.

Mgr Searle tells me that no letter or statement, so far as he knows, on this subject, exists among the papers left by the Cardinal, Mgr Searle has gone over them all. . . .'

In fact, as Newman explains here and at the end of his letter of 14 Nov. to Ullathorne, Wiseman did speak again to Manning about the consequences of the delation of Newman. As to removing from 'Barnabo's mind the impression left by the Bishop of Newport,' Manning knew that Propaganda wanted from Newman the explanations he had offered to make, and that he was under a cloud in consequence.

[2] Newman was correct. See also his letter of 14 Nov. to Ullathorne.

[3] See letter of 7 May 1860 to Ullathorne and notes there.

I never heard a word of the matter after this letter of Dr Manning's, till Cardinal Barnabò spoke of it in the spring of 1867 to Fr St John[1]

I am, My dear Lord, Your Lordship's faithful & affectte Servt in Xt

John H Newman

The Rt Revd The Bp of Birmingham

THURSDAY 11 NOVEMBER 1869   fall of snow and lying about this time

TO MALCOLM MACCOLL

The Oratory, November 12th. 1869

My Dear Mr MacColl,

I should have answered you before this, had I not been so very busy. I will gladly send you another copy of my article, when I come upon one. As to Dr. Temple's appointment, it is a subject on which I don't see how a person can have an opinion, unless he is bound to have one.[2] So much can be said on either side, that, unless duty enjoined it, I should never be able to make up my mind. The only point I see is, that, if all Bishops but two have spoken of his Essay severely, it is an inconsistency in them to consecrate, unless he explains first, but perhaps they have not spoken severely, in Convocation as has been said.

It is quite a mistake that I am writing anything on such subjects as the Papers have said. It was originally given out as a piece of gossip, perhaps half with an unfriendly feeling on the part of some Catholics, who, having first spread their misstatement, next, when no book came out, follow it up with a second, viz that it had been suppressed for some reason or other. A lie is like a shuttlecock, which two battledoors can keep up with great success, if skilfully used, without its falling to the ground. The next move ought to be that it has been sent for to Rome etc etc.

I am writing a small work on a definite subject, but not directly on any subject of the day, but as an enquiry into certain logical principles, and I venture to say, that, after all the talk that has gone on about it, it will disappoint friends and opponents when it appears.

Very truly yours, John H. Newman

The Rev. M. MacColl.

P.S.   What I am writing is not a 'first part', but all I have to say, which is little enough.

[1] See the correspondence with St John in May 1867.
[2] See second note to letter of 20 Oct. to Mrs Helbert.

The Oratory Nov 13/69

My dear Child

Never mind your present distress — all will come right — trust in God. If you made up your mind after your letter to me in September to join the Convent, I think you should have done so at once — but it can't be helped now. Perhaps you did not, so make up your mind. All things turn out for good — You ought not to leave your present situation, where you find yourself so well placed, for any place in London. You wish to please God, and all will come right. If it turns out that you cannot go into religion now, perhaps God will fulfil the wish He has inspired at some future day. If it is God's will that you should take care of your parents, He will bless you in that pious work quite as much as if you were in a convent.

Trust in Him, and be troubled at nothing

Yours most sincerely in Xt   John H Newman

The Oratory Novr 13. 1869

My dear Fr Suffield

(Private) A friend wants me to ask you, whether you know any thing of Mgr Gonin's theological opinions as regards the expedience of now defining the Pope's Infallibility or making the denial of it a condemned proposition. I suppose he has some prudent reason for wishing to know, but he seems to be in a hurry[1]

Yours most sincerely John H Newman

The Very Revd Fr Suffield

The Oratory Nov. 14/69

My dear Lord

I have found the collection of papers on the subject of my Article in the Rambler in 1859. They are carefully done up chronologically.

1.   I have looked through them. There is not a word from Cardinal Wiseman. But I find my own letter to the Cardinal, and Dr Manning's to me. The distance between their dates is three months.

---

[1] Joachim Hyacinth Louis Gonin became Bishop of Port of Spain, Trinidad in 1863. He was, like Suffield, a Dominican, and, since he absented himself from the decisive votes at the end of the Council, an inopportunist.

2. As to my letter to the Cardinal, I should say in explanation, (1) that it was a *private* letter to him, not a letter to Propaganda. It was a preliminary step. I asked for information. (2) Much less was it an answer to a *judgment from Rome*, but to an *accusation from England*, (e.g. from Dr Brown and Dr Gillow.) Had any judgment come from Rome, its tone would have been different of course; but you brought me a verbal message from Rome running thus, 'that it was desired to *call my attention* to a certain paragraph (pointed out) in the Article, and to ask an explanation of it.'(3) My letter to the Cardinal was written under the belief, (the belief which I still hold) that the passage was carelessly and ignorantly translated;[1] I thought probably it was the handiwork of some student at the English College, who knew a little both of English and of Italian.

Hence I wrote as follows:-

'January 19. 1860. My dear Lord Cardinal, Our Bishop tells me that my name has been mentioned at Rome in connexion with an Article in the Rambler, which has by an English Bishop been formally brought before Propaganda, as containing unsound doctrine. And our Bishop says that your Eminence has spoken so kindly about me, as to encourage me to write to you on the subject.

'I have not yet been asked from Propaganda whether I am the author of the Article, or otherwise responsible for it; and, though I am ready to answer the question when it is put to me, I do not consider it a duty to volunteer the information, till your Eminence advises it.

'However, I am ready, without the question being asked of me, to explain the Article, as if it were mine.

'I will request then of your Eminence's kindness three things:- 1. The *passages* of the Article, on which the Cardinal Prefect of Propaganda desires an explanation. 2. A copy of the *translations*, in which his Eminence has read them. 3. The *dogmatic propositions*, which they have been represented as infringing, or otherwise impairing.

'If your Eminence does this for me, I will engage, with the blessing of God, in the course of a month from the receipt of the information, 1. to accept and profess ex animo in their fulness and integrity the dogmatic propositions implicated. 2 to explain the animus and argument of the writer of the Article in strict accordance with those propositions. 3. to show that the *English* text and context of the Article itself are absolutely consistent with them. . . .

I am &c. J H N

3. Dr Manning's letter to me is as follows:-
'Rome — April 29. 1860. My dear Newman, I have many times intended to write to you to ask if I could be of any use to you in this place. And now Mgr Nardi, whom you already know, gives me a commission to write in his behalf.

'The Austrian Bishops in Synod have determined to establish a Catholic University, and he is anxious to have the following etc. . . .

'. . . I hope you are well and all the Fathers etc etc . . .

[1] This was the case. See second note to Memorandum of 14 Jan. 1860.

'. . . Here I am waiting two months, and shall be kept etc etc
'. . . Pray let me hear, if I can do or say any thing for you.
'. . . Henry Wilberforce has been here, and fell ill etc etc . . .
Believe me &c &c H.E.M.

(*Postscript*) 'The Cardinal desires his kind regards to you, and tells me to say that he has thought it better to wait till his return, when he proposes to bring the matter of your letter to a termination, which will be acceptable to you.[1]

This, My dear Lord, is the first and the last that I ever heard from the Cardinal, directly or indirectly, in answer to my letter of January 19, 1860[2]

I am, Your Lordship's obt Servt in Xt   John H Newman

MONDAY 15 NOVEMBER 1869   Lord E Howard, Lord Denbigh and Mr Berkely called. Public meeting at Town Hall of Catholics about education[3]
TUESDAY 16 NOVEMBER   we went to High Mass at St Chad's and dined with the Bishop to see him off to the Council
WEDNESDAY 17 NOVEMBER   Sir H. Pollen in our House

FROM CHARLES MEYNELL

Oscott F.S. [Festum Sancti] CAROLI. Novr. 4/69
Dear Dr Newman

What you say in your note[4] reminds me of what I am too apt to forget that we are in two different grooves. Much of what I have said would have been unnecessary had I read your work as a whole instead of reading it piece-meal. I think of the abstract, while you have to do with the concrete. I look out for laws of thought, you for general rules to guide the mind in the application of them. When you speak of Certitude, I think of apodictical certitude, whereas yours is the practical certitude — 'certitudine prudente', Rosmini somewhere calls it. This difference sets me at a disadvantage; though I have done my best to throw myself into your line, and would say anything that occurred to me even at the risk of blundering. I spent a great deal of time last night in trying to find a weak point, without success.

So far as I know the philosophical hand-books make the objective truth enter into the very definition of certitude, so as to exclude the notion of a false certitude; whereas you contemplate the possibility — and indeed the fact of spurious certitudes; for is not prejudice a spurious certitude? But this seems to me only a difference of words arising out of the different subject matters, the one abstract, and the other concrete which you and the Metaphysicians have respectively to deal with. Metaphysics doesn't care about the merely general, and dislikes exceptions: its object is the universal and invariable. It looks for a certitude which shall lie at the base of science, and be proof against scepticism ie apodictical certitude, and discovers its criterion to be the law of contradiction. Whereas you speak, it seems, of the certitude, concrete and practical, which

---

[1] Newman quoted this postcript in his letter of 7 May 1860 to Ullathorne.
[2] Ullathorne replied on 15 Nov., 'The last paragraph extracted in your letter, or rather the postscript of Dr Manning's is the passage I have all along had in my mind, imagining erroneously that it was a note of Cardinal Wiseman's.
I thank you for the information, and will take the letter with me to Rome . . .' There Ullathorne presumably showed it to Manning.
[3] The Elementary Education Act of 1870 was in preparation, and the meeting in defence of denominational schools was attended by 4000 people.
[4] Letter of 2 Nov.

results when a prudent man has with due care and diligence examined the grounds of his beliefs on all kinds of subjects and justified them to himself. It is an essential inconvenience that there should be no internal criterion of this kind of certitude, such as the law of contradiction is to apodictical certitude; but there is at least the negative external one of general indefectibility, — if he changes it shows he wasn't certain. Now, if I haven't blundered, but have learnt my lesson correctly, I don't see that you are in contradiction with the Metaphysicians.

I must beg your pardon if I am wrong in asking you a question. Have you contemplated the case, or is [it] worth while contemplating, of a man who denies the existence of certitude? I met such a one once who referred me for his views to a criticism on yourself, in, I forget in what Magazine — perhaps McMillan — and of which I suspect he was the author. It was to the purpose that 'it was the very A.B.C. of scientific men that it is the greatest mistake to make up one's mind once and for all *upon any subject whatsoever religious or otherwise*'. He told me that if anything in the world was demonstrated it was the impossibility of perpetual motion, but that he was not prepared to say that even that was an absolute truth. What is to be done with a man like this? I thought of sending you the article, but concluded that you would have seen it.

The proofs you sent me last could not detain me long. I read them, as I have read the whole with the greatest relish, so you are wrong in calling it an *infliction*. All that I feel is my poverty to be of use and I feel the artificial position I have been put in which has made me write in such a style sometimes that I shudder to think of it. It seems to me that I am like that prophet whom an angel carried aloft by the hair of his head all the way from Judaea to Babylon.[1]

Dear Dr Newman Sincerely and respectfully Your's Charles Meynell

P.S. Look, please, at the date of this, and say a little prayer to my saint for me.

FROM CHARLES MEYNELL

Nov. 8, 1869.

Dear Dr Newman

The statement that an inference can *never* (absolutely) 'reach so far as to ascertain a fact'[2] seems to me a very important statement; and therefore, as it is not a general, but a universal statement, I shall do my best to pick a hole in it. (But pray be merciful if I blunder: consider I never thought of the question till this morning!)

By inference you mean, inference by a middle term, syllogistic inference? Our new logicians call a *conversion*, even an inference; and you would not deny, I suppose, that you can attain a fact by an inference from *opposition*: e.g. either Dick or Tom did it, and Tom did not ∴ Dick did, and vice versâ, I will not ask you therefore what you think of Leibnitz's enthymeme 'the compound exists: therefore the simple exists' (if you say '*notions these!*' put it in this way. The compound is a *fact* ∴ the simple is a *fact*.) I will not ask you, I say, about this, because it may be said that there is no third term here, by means of which I get at the conclusion, but on analysing the notion of the compound you find in it the notion of the simple: if so it is not a mediate, but an immediate inference.

But we are speaking (I presume) of *mediate* inference. Now if, here, the middle term be the expression of a notion, we shall not get beyond a notion in the conclusion; if *Caesar is a man, and all men are mortal, he is mortal*. But now, suppose, that the middle term be the expression, not of a notion, but of a fact, will it not get me at a concrete truth? Suppose I say 'This lock has been meddled with by somebody, for I find a *fragment of the wards* of a key in it?' is it not *absolutely certain* that 'it has been meddled with?' — If I saw a murder committed and that the murderer had blue eyes, whereas the prisoner has deep hazel eyes, it would not perhaps be absolutely certain that the prisoner was not the murderer: there might be a miracle, or a lusus naturae, — but if the prisoner was dining with me in Paris, when the murder was committed in London?

[1] *Daniel* 14:32–8 (Vulgate).
[2] *G.A.*, p. 278.

Or suppose I infer that this snake (coluber natrix) is a true serpent because it can distend the thorax, or that this other (anguis fragilis, blind worm) is not true serpent, because he cannot distend the thorax, do I not get at a concrete truth? If you say these classifications are but arbitrary and there may be another division, on another ground next year. True, but it is a fact that such or such is now the case: as, if you shoot a hare it is game, under one set of game-laws, or is not under another.

Well, that is all I can find to say. *I* should just say that by inference you mean ONLY *mediate inference* — is it not so?

Mind, I don't say I'm right by any means: I dare not say so: you'll see if there's anything in it

Your's Dear Dr Newman Sincerely and respectfully Charles Meynell

P.S. I am so eager to see the part about the 'illative sense', but I expect I shall be out of my depth.

Please look at p 83 near top 'All inferential processes require general notions'[1] Well: but remember the controversy between Descartes and Gassendi on this head. 'This proposition I think, therefore I exist, supposes' says Gassendi this major: 'that which thinks exists, and consequently implies a begging of the question.' To whom Descartes 'I don't beg the question, for I suppose no major. I maintain that the proposition: '*I think: therefore I exist*' is a particular truth which enters into the mind without the aid of any other more general, *and independently of all logical inference. . . . As for you, you think that every particular truth rests upon a general truth from which it has to be deduced by syllogisms, according to the dialectic rules.* Imbued with this error, you gratuitously attribute it to me. This is your constant method *etc*' (This is a translation of a free translation! But Cousin quotes the original passage) (Histoire de la Philosophie Moderne). C.M.

TO CHARLES MEYNELL

Novr 17/69

My dear Dr Meynell

Thank you for your two very good letters.

I have put a note on the passage, in consequence of one of them, in which I boldly say that 'If it isn't A, it must be B' is not reasoning, except materially.[2]

I quite agree with you that the deepest men say that we can never be certain of any thing — and it has been my object therefore in good part of my volume to prove that there is such a thing as *unconditional* assent.

I have defined certitude, a conviction of what is *true*. When a conviction of what is not true is considered as if it was a conviction of what is true, I have called it a false certitude.

You will be sadly disappointed in my 'illative sense' — which is a grand word for a common thing.

Ever Yrs most sincerely John H Newman

P.S.   I send a number of slips

[1] *G.A.*, p. 283.
[2] *G.A.*, p. 287, footnote.

TO B. M. PICKERING

The Oratory Novr 17. 1869

My dear Sir

I am very sorry you were so near me without my knowing it — I would gladly have asked you to accept our hospitality — and could have had some talk with you about the Essays on Miracles.

I had [been] far from forgetting I owed your letter. Your letter which required one from me has been on my table now since it came — but I have been so very busy that I could not look at my Essay which you sent me, or fix any time for revising it.

I have undertaken a small work on the subject of some logical questions which has taken up all my time, and I could not tell when it would be done. It is not done yet, but it is getting to an end — and, as soon as ever it is done, I will set to work on the Essays

I am, My dear Sir Very truly Yours John H Newman

TO W. J. COPELAND

The Oratory Nov 21. 1869

My dear Copeland

You must pity and forgive me. The last several days I have been in a sad way — examining our school boys — racing against printers — and full of letter writing. I am very sorry, I hoped to have written on Friday — but the letter man came, just as I had the paper in hand.

You are inclined to leave 'Fellow of Oriel,' and so am I. It is a puzzle certainly. It will be criticized — but I don't see what else can be done.

What do you think of leaving out 'Fellow of Oriel' and everything else. On the whole I think this will be best,

'By John Henry Newman B. D.'[1]

Again I say, excuse me

Ever yrs affly John H Newman

P.S. The Preface reads very well.

---

[1] Copeland asked on 18 Nov. 'What is to be done about the "Fellow of Oriel" on the title page. The word "formerly" as applied in the other Volumes to the "Vicar of St Mary's" is out of place here . . .' for Newman had resigned from St Mary's before *S.D.* was published, and there in the original edition he was described as 'Fellow of Oriel College, Oxford,' whereas in the original edition of *P.S.* he was 'Vicar of St. Mary the Virgin's, Oxford, and Fellow of Oriel.' 'Fellow of Oriel' in *S.D.* had, as Copeland wrote 'its history and its meaning in the fact of your resignation of the living previously to the publication of the Volume.' 'Fellow of Oriel' was omitted in the new edition of *S.D.*

TO MRS WILLIAM FROUDE

The Oratory Nov 21/69

My dear Mrs Froude

I have ever held the Pope's Infallibility as an opinion, and am not therefore likely to feel any personal anxiety as to the result of this Council. Still I am strongly opposed to its definition — and for this reason. Hitherto nothing has been ever done at Councils but what is *necessary*; what is the necessity of this? There is no heresy to be put down. It is a dangerous thing to go beyond the rule of tradition in such a matter. In the early times the Nicene Council gave rise to dissensions and to confusions which lasted near a century. The Council of Ephesus opened a question which it took three centuries to settle. Well, these Councils were NECESSARY — they were called to resist and condemn opposition to our Lord's divinity — heresies — They could not be helped. But why is the Pope's infallibility to be defined? even, if denying it were a heresy, which no one says, how many *do* deny it? do they preach their denial? are they making converts to it? Let us look to it lest a judgment come down upon us, if we do, *though we have a right to do*, what we ought not to do. We must not play with edged tools.

I am against the definition, because it opens a long controversy. You cannot settle the question by a word — whatever is passed, must be a half, a quarter measure. Archbishop Manning himself only aims at *condemning two propositions*, i.e. at a *negative* act. How will that *decide* the question? No — it only opens it. At Nicæa, and Ephesus, great questions were opened, only opened — they had, as I have said, been opened by heretics first. *Now*, the Bishops of the Church are called upon to take the first step in opening a question as difficult, and not as justifiable, as the question which those early Councils were obliged to discuss. This question will lead to an alteration of the *elementary constitution* of the Church. Our *one* doctrine, in which all doctrines are concluded, is, 'The Church's word is to be believed —' Hitherto 'the Church's decision' means that of the Pope and the Bishops; now it is proposed to alter this for 'the Pope's word.' It is an alteration in the fundamental dogma. Hitherto, I *personally* may be of *opinion* that the Pope is infallible by himself — *but I have never been called to act* upon it — no one has — and what is the consequence? that *the Pope* cannot act upon it. Hitherto, the Pope has always acted, (for greater caution,) with the Bishops — he has not gone to the extent of what he might do, supposing him infallible. But, define his infallibility, and he will act alone. Well — God will direct him — but what is this but throwing away one of the human means *by* which God directs him? It is making the system more miraculous — and it is like seeking a bodily cure by miracle, when human means are at hand.

I say, any decision will be a half or quarter measure — as the Councils of Ephesus and Chalcedon were such. It opens a very large question. Suppose you pass Dr Manning's condemnation — still the *positive* question will be left open — and a new controversy set open — first, what *is* the implied positive force of these negatives? — let this be settled, then comes the question in *what matters* is the Pope infallible? — after this — when, under what conditions, is the Pope infallible? when e.g. he writes a letter? Councils are formal things — and there is no need of drawing the line between their acts, or not much need, but a Pope is a living man, ever living, and it will be a great work to go through this question well. You have to treat it doctrinally — and then again historically, reconciling what you teach with the verdict of history.

Then again recollect that this doctrine is a retrospective doctrine — it brings up a great variety of questions about *past* acts of Popes — whether their decrees in past ages are infallible, or whether they were not, and which of them, and therefore whether they are binding on *us*.

If any thing could throw religion into confusion, make sceptics, encourage scoffers, and throw back inquirers, it will be the definition of this doctrine. This I shall think, even if it passes — because, though then the doctrine must be inwardly received as true, its definition may still be most unseasonable and unwise. I do not know that the Church is protected against inexpedient acts — though of course God overrules them — and also, when they are once passed, there is no good, and much disrespect and highmindedness, in finding fault with them. Paul iii alienated England. I don't think he acted wisely; yet in one sense it is God's act, because it was done

Ever Yrs affly John H Newman

P.S. Keep this; I may want it. I have never before put my thoughts on paper[1]

---

[1] Mrs Froude replied on 30 Nov., 'I feel it to be a matter of immense importance, — and I can understand and appreciate your having kept so quiet, — holding so strong a view as you do. — I am greatly relieved at one part of your letter, where you say — "I have ever held the Pope's infallibility as an opinion . . . " If *you* feel this, *I* may feel the same. — Both Isy [Froude] and I . . . have long had an undefined dread as to what was going to be put upon us, and your letter had quite comforted us both. . . .'

The Council opened on 8 Dec. Four days later Newman made a rough note: 'Decr 12/69
1. I have ever held the doctrine of the Pope's infallibility, but vaguely. *Why then not wish it defined* [?]
2 and more effectively, because vaguely[.] I doubt whether you do not lessen it by defining it
3 Because you put it in *limits*. As it is there is nothing, when he *has done* it which does not stand.
4. What riles so many Catholics, is to have to believe as a *whole* dogma, what they would grant in each separate act.
5 I doubt whether the Immaculate Conception and the Assumption, being *defined*, will ultimately increase *devotion*, or not rather limit it.
6. 'Quieta non movenda.' In the early Church they were *obliged* to define because of Arius etc.
7. But see what a large controversy they opened, — 2 or 3 centuries. There is another reason for not defining now, because you cannot do it at once. *This* is what I say in answer to 'If you believe why not wish it defined?'
8. The increase of scoffers — the throwing back of inquirers.
9. 'Save the church, O my Fathers, from a danger as great as any that has happened to it.'

The Oratory, Nov. 21st 1869.

My dear Mr. Jenkins,

I thank you for your letter and pamphlet —[1] though of course you would not wish me without protest to let you say that we substitute the Blessed Virgin for Christ etc. What would you say to me, if I published a pamphlet and said that you substituted Queen Victoria for Christ? I think you would consider me very unfair untrue and unkind.

After making this my Protest, I go on to assure you I like your letter better than your Pamphlet and was pleased to read it.

I don't think Dr. Manning has put on any 'spectacles' He says what he thinks, and knows what he is about. I cannot help thinking he holds that the world is soon coming to an end — and that he is in consequence careless about the souls of future generations which will never be brought into being. I can fancy a person thinking it a grand termination (I don't mean that he so thinks) to destroy every ecclesiastical power but the Pope, and let Protestants shift for themselves.

As to myself, I should say that I have never felt any difficulty in the Pope's infallibility as a theological opinion.

Most truly yours, John H. Newman.

The Oratory Nov 21. 1869

My dear Mr Lee

I thank you for your handsome volume, and the more so because I have not merited it. I see you have taken notice of my letters in the Month.[2] You may be sure that controversy is not pleasant to me, and there are many things I would keep quiet about, if I could — but so far I think I may say that, in what I said, I substantially represent every Catholic, who thinks, and would say, he has a right to an opinion. I don't see how you and we ever will agree together on the matter. The only compromise I can think of is a conditional

---

[1] Jenkins sent Newman *A Letter respectfully addressed to his Holiness Pope Pius IX in reply to his Appeal to the Members of the Reformed Churches*, Folkestone 1869, not published, in which he hoped to see unity restored by acceptance of the Christian faith as it was in the early centuries. On p. 15 he maintained that acceptance of the actual Roman Church would mean 'a new Creed and a new Gospel . . . the substitution of the Blessed Virgin for Christ.' Jenkins also sent his pamphlet *What do Popes say on their alleged Infallibility? A Letter respectfully addressed to the most reverend Archbishop Manning*, London 1869, which showed he thought of infallibility as a kind of religious omniscience.

[2] *The Validity of the Holy Orders of the Church of England*, London 1869. The copy presented 'from the author' is still in Newman's room. For Newman's letters to the *Month*, see 5 Aug. 1868 to Coleridge and 17 Sept. 1868 to Mossman.

ordination, to cover possible defects of the Anglican rite etc, possible defects, as Anglicans might allow perhaps. This plan has been mooted lately; and was thrown out to me by Dr Wiseman many years ago. But I more than doubt whether either you would accept such a proposal, or we grant it.

As to *my own* argument, Anglicans will not see its force till they understand and admit the *ground work* on which it rests. Macaulay's argument applies to Anglican Orders, not to ours because the question of their validity holds a different place in our respective systems.[1] Anglicans claim to belong to the Church because their orders are good: but we claim to have good orders because we are the Church. We rest the fact of our being the Church, not on our Orders, but on our uninterrupted visible existence, on the continuity of body, system, claim, profession, doctrine, the see of Peter etc etc. and we say that, since we are the Church, *therefore* God has watched over us to preserve our Orders from any material damage. But Anglicans *begin* by proving their Orders, without this prescription, which makes us careless about proving ours.

I am very sorry to receive so unfavourable an account of Mr Ostrehan's health. I think you told me before that he suffered in his eyes. You don't speak of Mrs Ostrehan — I live always in hopes of seeing her once before I die.[2] You are quite recovered, I hope, from your own illness

With my kindest regards to Mrs Lee, I am,

Sincerely Yours John H Newman

TO MARK PATTISON

The Oratory Nov 21. 1869

My dear Rector

Thank you for your kind intentions towards Fr Carbonelle. H. Wilberforce introduced him to me, as one of the writers in the Etudes a Jesuit publication at Paris, which takes the moderate side in Church matters. He has been in India, and was, I found, very well informed. He wished very much to know the state of Oxford. Some one had given him a letter to Dr Pusey. I knew that he would learn a good deal from seeing you, and I thought you would be pleased to have become acquainted with him.

I saw the sad accident to which you allude as happening in your College[3]

Very sincerely Yours John H Newman

The Revd The Rector of Lincoln

---

[1] 'He [Gladstone] will hardly tell as that the Church of England is the true church because she has the succession, and that she has the succession because she is the true church' Macaulay's *Essays*, 'Gladstone on Church and State.'

[2] Mrs Lee's mother, Mrs Ostrehan, was Newman's second cousin.

[3] A commoner at Lincoln College had recently died from the administering of chloroform prior to an operation.

MONDAY 22 NOVEMBER 1869 went out to Rednall to finish my book (on *Assent*)

TUESDAY 23 NOVEMBER Ambrose out to Rednall

WEDNESDAY 24 NOVEMBER and back

FRIDAY 26 NOVEMBER Wm [William] out to Rednall and back

SATURDAY 27 NOVEMBER went back by the train in rain Stanislas came to the Oratory
Gaisford for Oxford

SUNDAY 28 NOVEMBER snow

MONDAY 29 NOVEMBER weather too bad to go to Rednall Gaisford went? Montgomery to dinner snow

TO MALCOLM MACCOLL

The Oratory, November 29th 1869

My Dear Mr MacColl,

I cannot tell whether anciently books were condemned without their authors being allowed to defend them, but we must consider how few instances were possible, in the rarity of books then published, if we can talk of publication.

There was no public then: and if one wrote an heretical book, and his diocesan lived next door, one would naturally talk to him about it, and hear what he had to say. On the other hand the great multitude of publications in a day like this, not only preclude a personal treatment of them, but make another treatment imperative. A book is thrown upon the world with the best intentions, and yet may do a vast deal of mischief. There are wrong headed men who always have a good sense, though they use most erroneous language. Volat irrevocabile verbum,[1] with a substantive, definite meaning. The Church claims to pronounce infallibly when the legitimate meaning of a book is bad, and warns the faithful. I do not mean to say that the pronouncements of the Congregation of the Index are infallible, but that the duty and the power of determining the absolute sense of a book is quite intelligible. Whether it is exercised judiciously or not in a particular case is quite another thing, but for myself I have no doubt about the principle.

Some Catholic papers delight in putting in gossip about me. It is a great thing to set up a puppet in order to knock it down. There is just as much truth in saying I ever dreamed of writing on Faith or Rationalism, as in saying that any person in authority ever dreamed of hindering me; and that is, no truth at all.

I make it a rule not to notice these things except under special circumstances, for, if I said A, I must say B and C. The best answer to the present gossip will be the appearance of my little book, which will show I neither have been writing on Rationalism, nor have been stopped for [from] writing. The books is about 'Assent', and is a very humble affair.

---

[1] 'Et semel emissum volat irrevocabile verbum,' Horace, *Epist.* I, xviii, 71.

381

I heard that Archbishop Manning considers the day of judgment certain to come in a few years. Whether this is better than the above gossip about myself I know not, but it is an answer anyhow to your astonishment about his Pastoral.[1]

Very sincerely yours, John H. Newman.

TO J. H. MACMAHON

The Oratory, Birmm Nov 29. 1869.

My dear Sir,

I thank you for your considerate letter. There is no foundation for the report of my writing on Rationalism. It never came into my head to do so; and, were it true, much as I feel indebted to you for your very kind proposal about it, I should have thought it best to throw my book on the criticism (if it so happened,) of an indifferent or hostile reviewer and to have taken my chance.

However, it had been my intention before your letter came, to ask your acceptance of a little book, such as it is, which I am passing through the press, and I hope you will let me do so still.

Very truly Yrs John H. Newman

TUESDAY 30 NOVEMBER 1869 went by train to Rednall. Stanislas went snow bitter wind freezing hard hard frost

TO WILLIAM MONSELL

The Oratory Dec 3/69

My dear Monsell

Your letter of the 1st just come. I have seen Gaston and he is to bring me a letter before post time and I shall put it in our post box. And this ceremony he is to perform once a week. Fr Ambrose told him to write directly your letter came to him (Ambrose) and he promised to do so. After a while Fr A. asked him if he had written, as he promised, and he said he had. On my talking to him about it today, he said he wrote last Friday. When asked if the letter went, he said he could not be sure that it was not in his desk. So *perhaps* you have received a letter, *since* your letter to me was posted.

Fr Hecker is just here. He seems to have seen the French Address to the German Bishops — and said that it was very logical.[2] I shall give him the copies in confidence.[3] I should have guessed that Dr Butler would have taken

---

[1] *The Oecumenical Council and the Infallibility of the Roman Pontiff: A Pastoral to the Clergy*, London Oct. 1869. Manning not only argued for a definition, but maintained that 'judgments *ex cathedra* are in their essence judgments of the Pontiff, apart from the episcopal body, whether congregated or dispersed,' and that Gallicanism was more dangerous for Catholics than Anglicanism.

[2] See letter of 22 Sept. to Monsell.

[3] See third note to letter of 3 Sept, to Monsell.

an Ultra line.[1] Our Bishop and other English Bishops will, I think, be moderate. Mgr Maret gave me his book, thank you.[2] I am told Archbishop Manning's Pastoral gives up the notion of any decree or acclamation in favour of Infallibility, and wishes it negatively ruled by condemning the Gallican propositions

Ever Yrs affly John H Newman

SATURDAY 4 DECEMBER 1869   Stanislas called at Rednall?
SUNDAY 5 DECEMBER   stayed at Rednall   all this time very hard at my book
TUESDAY 7 DECEMBER   went back to Birmingham for good
WEDNESDAY 8 DECEMBER   Ambrose sang High Mass

TO WILLIAM MONSELL

The Oratory Dec 9/69
My dear Monsell

I have been at Rednall for several weeks — and I fear Gaston has not written home. I find he has lately had a cold and is on the sick list. I have asked Mrs Knight to write to you about him — indeed I believe he is going to write himself. Nothing is much the matter, I believe.

What a splendid letter to his Clergy is the Bishop of O's [Orleans]! I hope he has *thrown back* the movement.[3] We hear from Rome that there is no talk of bringing forward the Infallibility except perhaps at *last*. What I fear is that Manning will attempt, by *delay*, to gain over Bishops whom he cannot carry with him at once. But the Bishop of O. will have his eyes about him.

Ever Yrs affly John H Newman

[1] George Butler, Bishop of Limerick, Monsell's Irish Diocesan.
[2] Bishop Henri Louis Charles Maret, *Du Concile général et de la paix religieuse*, two volumes, Paris Sept. 1869. Maret, who was Dean of the Theological Faculty of Paris, maintained that the Church was a constitutional monarchy, that a General Council was supreme over the Pope, and that he was not personally infallible. He wanted General Councils held every ten years. In his letter to Newman of 9 Oct. Maret described the book he was sending:
'J'y traite de la constitution de l'Église et de la périodicité conciliaire, comme du moyen le plus puissant de l'accomplissement de la mission du christianisme dans le monde. Je ne dis rien de nouveau, dans une si grave matière, mais il me semble que, dans les circonstances si décisives où nous sommes, ces idées doivent être proposées et soumises à l'usage du Concile. Je reste dans les doctrines de Bossuet, un peu modifiées et développées dans leur conséquences.
Peut-être ce travail plaira, en Angleterre, aux hommes modérés . . .'
[3] *Observations sur la controverse soulevée relativement à la définition de l'infaillibilité au prochain concile*, 11 Nov. 1869. Dupanloup gave the reasons not against the doctrine, but against the opportuneness of defining it as an article of Faith. See Cuthbert Butler, *The Vatican Council*, I, pp. 124–5.

TO HENRY WILBERFORCE

The Oratory Decr 9. 1869

My dear H W

Private.   Can you tell me any of the qualifications of Mr Robert Walker to undertake the office of a Master in a school. I mean, not simply in classics etc for being an *Oxford* man he must have no deficiency there, but in power of teaching, temper etc etc Does he not stutter? We have no vacancy, but he has applied, and I should like to know.[1]

My book is not finished — when it comes out, I shall ask Agnes to accept a copy, if you think well. It will be very *dry*.

Ever Yrs affly John H Newman

FROM CHARLES MEYNELL

Nov. 18th 1869.

Dear Dr Newman

I have read the proofs, which I send back, with great interest and pleasure. I feel quite sorry I am coming to the end — I didn't find anything to remark upon in the proofs.

After I had sent my last letter I got to see, what you would have seen at once, that in all the instances I gave of inference, the middle term had to do simply with the law of contradiction. Well, I have learnt a great deal from you: I had no notion that an inference was such a leaky sort of thing!

I take for granted that you will remember that my attitude of critic is a secret. If the world knew what would they think of me! When I calmly reflect upon it I am amazed at myself.

Your's Dear Dr Newman Sincerely and Respectfully Charles Meynell

FROM CHARLES MEYNELL

Oscott Nov. 27 1869

Dear Dr Newman

I am very much pleased with it, and especially with the part about instinctive inference. I should never have objected to the use of the word *instinctive*[2] in this case, as it is the popular use of the word. But when applied to a philosophical subject like perception, I feared it might get you classed with a set whom you perhaps would not agree with, if you explained yourself.

As the subject is one which I have only thought of in a random way, I am afraid to write about it. But I might chance to suggest something.

Although the inference be instinctive, it is only instinctive in the sense that the process is not brought up to the surface of consciousness, for process you evidently suppose there is. It isn't like a young duck taking to the water. This being the case I want some theory about the matter. Can I not have one? When a musician strikes off a complicated group of notes, with such rapidity that I feel he cannot think separately

---

[1] Wilberforce replied that he did not know Walker's capabilities as a teacher, but he was 'an excellent fellow.' He had a bad stammer.

[2] *G.A.*, p. 260.

of each note, I say that is by the law of contiguity. Separate notions combine so as to make parts of a whole, and one note suggests the group. But this law is inadequate to meet the cases mentioned. I would wish to refer each phenomenon to some law of the mind.

I should like to know why women *intue* (as Dr Ward terms it) rather than reason;[1] according to the saying of Swift 'Woman is a creature which doth not reason, and poketh the fire from the top'. I hazard this reason, that it requires concentration to submit a complicated process to the consciousness in reflective acts, and it seems that concentration of the mind is stronger in men than in women. These pursue the train of direct thought in consciousness a little way, then through giddiness, or impatience drop the thread. 'There!' exclaimed a lady, after finishing an arithmetical puzzle: 'it's done, but for goodness' sake don't ask me how I did it!'. The swiftness of thought sometimes prevents our recovering the links in consciousness: and when we recover them it would take some time to repeat over the process. 'When', (I read in Thomson's Outline of the Laws of Thought) 'Captain Head was travelling across the Pampas of South America, his guide one day suddenly stopped him, and, pointing high into the air, cried out, a lion! . . . He turned up his eyes, and with difficulty perceived, at an immeasurable height, a flight of condors soaring in circles in a particular spot'. Beneath this spot, far out of sight of himself and the guide, lay the carcass of a horse and over it a lion. The process is obvious: but the flight and manner of the condors would suggest the lion by the law of contiguity; and so the recognition of the lion was instantaneous.

But I have already written too much, and whether to any good purpose I don't know. Perhaps in the sequel there may [come] some theory of the subject: perhaps, from the nature of the case there cannot be. At present I do not know how (and from what you say, now I read it again) it seems I cannot know, how one reasons from things to things.[2]

I can furnish a case parallel to the calculating boys losing their art by learning the educational modes.[3] A friend who plays beautifully by ear, on the pianoforte, refused to be taught, on the ground that he should lose *what he had got* by gift.

I apologise for this *talk*: but you know, you won't have to answer it, else I become a nuisance.

Your's Sincerely and respectfully Charles Meynell

P.S. From one sentence, where you essentially require media for ratiocination,[4] I should infer that, if the process of instinctive inference could be recovered in consciousness, it would fall under the ordinary dialectic rules. If so, I want no theory for this kind of inference, and it is only stupidity which has prevented my seeing this. But I am not sure that I understand.

Isn't Mother Margaret's name O'Hallahan — in the reference it is given M. Hallahan[5] (I haven't the book by me.)?

FROM CHARLES MEYNELL

Oscott Decr 9th 1869.

Dear Dr Newman

Had I seen this before, I might have spared you the infliction of my last lengthy note. It was a great gratification to read these proofs, and I hope the reading will

---

[1] Cf. *G.A.*, p. 331, 'to women more than to men.'
[2] *G.A.*, p. 330.
[3] *G.A.*, p. 336. Newman appears to have used this information. He wrote on Meynell's letter 'And men who have the gift of playing an instrument by ear, are sometimes afraid to learn by rule lest they should lose it.' This sentence immediately follows the one about the calculating boys. See also p. 333.
[4] *G.A.*, pp. 330–1. Cf. pp. 259–60.
[5] *G.A.*, p. 335. Newman was correct.

benefit my lopsided understanding. You know that you have been out of my depth for a long time, and all I have to do is to follow and learn my lesson.

I am not to understand, am I? that you admit the antecedent of those who argue that because 'experience only leads to probabilities, certitude is a mistake?' p. 105.[1] But pardon me if this be a stupidity of mine, or a hypercriticism. It is all that I have to say.

Your's Sincerely and Respectfully Charles Meynell

TO CHARLES MEYNELL

The Oratory Decr 10/69

My dear Dr Meynell

I always look with great interest for your letters, tho' I don't expect them. That of this morning I might, were I fidgetty, to understand wrongly, as if (since my book is on a subject which you say you have not considered as much as other subjects) you put it aside as a bad job, which you could make neither head nor tail of. But I do not understand it so — but thus — that all you can say, whatever there be in the book odd or bizarre, you have found nothing (except what you have noticed) which you conceive goes counter to what ought to be maintained on its subject matter — and my assurance of this, is, that in your present letter you have been kind and vigilant enough to point out the clause about probability.

This does not require any answer — but merely to show you how clever I am in interpreting your words and your state of mind regarding the book. You are getting to the end of the ixth chapter. There will be only one more. I wish it were done

Ever Yrs most sincerely John H Newman

P.S. I have referred to the passage, and found I have said that 'experience *logically* only leads to probabilities'.[2]

FROM CHARLES MEYNELL

Please, read first the *last* postscript. C.M.

Oscott Decr 11. 1869

Dear Dr Newman

As I am not particularly busy I will tell you about my last letter — I wrote it with a nervous fear that I was sadly boring you with letters (I should have felt this much more if you had answered all of them) — So I wrote briefly and I suppose was obscure. However thank you for putting the best construction on my words — whatever they were. I certainly did not put the subject aside as a bad job, but I wished to express that my mind is both slow — and I fear narrow, and when a larger view of a subject is put before it, takes some time to expand to it — I ought to have seen that it was no part of your subject to enter into my crotchets and answer my difficulties as to how men

---

[1] *G.A.*, p. 343.
[2] In *G.A.*, 'experience leads by syllogism only to probabilities.'

reason intuitively from *things to things*, but to deal with the *fact* in its relation to the subject of certainty and assent. I thought this narrowness of mind made me a very poor critic; nevertheless I might possibly find something to point out which a reader might misinterpret, and I pitched, but doubtfully, on the sentence about experience only giving probabilities. It is only in this kind of way that I flatter myself I may be still of some use. I try to read it as if I were an enemy, eager to catch you tripping, if I can: so that there may be nothing that any body can possibly take hold of to twist against your own sense.

And I wanted to say when the work was finished — but I may as well say it now — that I feel most painfully that I have sometimes overdone this function[.] And I wish you knew me better, that you might know how little, on some occasions, my letters have represented my mind, or rather my character. I should no more have dreamed of setting up my opinion against yours on a point of theology for instance than I should of flying; but I did so in my artificial character — no nor in a point of philosophy, if you knew the whole bearings of the case. I might hold a different opinion, of course, but I should never try to *force* mine against yours.

Don't think from this that I repent of what I undertook in St Chad's. I would do it again, if I were asked. Only it is natural perhaps that I should not wish to appear in a disadvantageous light.

I should speak very enthusiastically about the book if I were not afraid of wounding your modesty. I will say one thing however, and that is that it is very interesting reading, so that I should not be surprised if it became *popular* (you know what I mean)

As I am as it were taking my farewell (though I remember that there is a little more to come and am very glad of it) I have only to ask you to pardon my faults.

Your's Dear Dr Newman Very Sincerely and Respectfully Charles Meynell

P.S. You must, *by no means*, be at the trouble of answering this letter, nor do I see that it can any way require it. I wonder what it was in my letter that you considered to mean that I thought this or any other portion of the book 'odd or bizarre'. I said *my mind* was lop-sided. I thought the form of all reasoning was the Barbara, Celarent;[1] and now a larger view was put before me which I hoped might do me good. C.M.

P.S. I know now how I led you wrong. I wrote I have been out of my depth for some time — I didn't mean in reading the last proofs — but from the time when you shewed me that all reasoning wasn't shut up in the logical forms. This opened a new world to me, and I thought 'A pretty fellow I am to be making believe I am to be a critic, when it is my business rather to learn my lesson!' I like this part quite as well as any other, and am sorry to have conveyed a different impression, and given you the trouble of writing. C.M.

FROM CHARLES MEYNELL

Thursday [16 December 1869?]

I have only to remark that I don't much like the expression '*mental* sensation' at p. 112 line 35;[2] but perhaps this is a trifle. It seems 'sensation or sentiment' would do just as well without the mental.

Are there any *philosophers* (you do not *say* so, but perhaps it seem implied) who really teach that one must begin with universal doubt? p. 118.[3] This is the popular notion of Descartes' doubt; but Cousin, Balmez, and Dugald Stewart understand it differently — as only *hypothetical*, in order to find out some fact that it was impossible to doubt about — the *conscious self*. Reid says Descartes' system begot a sect of sceptical egoists. But Hamilton says he doesn't believe in their existence; that while Reid puts them in France, F. Buffier puts them in Scotland. He, Buffier, wrote before Hume.

---

[1] Mnemonic terms for the syllogisms of logic.
[2] This has not been traced; possibly *G.A.*, p. 344, 'Certitude is a mental state.'
[3] *G.A.*, p. 377.

But Hume only assumed the role of sceptic as a pretended disciple of Locke's philosophy. And it is easy to see that Hume is laughing in his sleeve, when he describes his situation as a sceptic calling himself 'some uncouth monster' — 'expelled all human commerce', apologizing for using such expressions as *tis certain, tis evident* 'which a due deference to the public ought perhaps to prevent.'

Fichte was an egoist, in a sense. He believed in all the facts of consciousness just as other people, only he gave a different account of them. In fact I don't know a thorough going sceptic in philosophy (but *you* may). There are plenty of sceptics *practically*.

I think any philosopher would see what you say, that scepticism, thorough-going, is a contradiction. How can a man be certain that there is no certainty? I dare say that you don't intend to charge any *philosopher*; but I think people will think you mean Descartes' philosophical doubt.

I write *in haste*; but I read it all most carefully and like it very much.

Yours dear Dr Newman Sincerely and respectfully Charles Meynell

FROM CHARLES MEYNELL

St Mary's College Oscott Birmingham Saturday [18 December 1869?]
Dear Dr Newman

I ought to have sent this yesterday, for there is really nothing to correct. But there is some hitch or other at the bottom of p. 124 and top of 125 — some correction which you seem to have begun and not finished.

Is it not said too absolutely that Man 'cannot change his nature or *habits* at will'? p. 126 (near the middle) You do not speak, it is true of *men* but of *man*. But in a note you refer to Callista, who says, 'Let me alone; such as nature made me I will be. I *cannot change*.'[1] I thought that when people spoke of the impossibility of changing from an evil course, they meant not impossibility — not even moral impossibility but only excessive difficulty. You will see if there be anything in this, or if it be only my squeamishness.

I was very thankful to read it, and very much interested. I said the Mass for it which I promised and I hope the work will do a great deal of good.

Your's sincerely and respectfully Charles Meynell

P.S Perhaps the passage referred to is sufficiently qualified by what follows after — 'or at least . . . the longer he lives the more difficult he is to change'

FROM CHARLES MEYNELL

St Mary's College: Oscott: Birmingham[2]
Dear Dr Newman

I read it and wrote 'Nothing to remark upon' in the margin, as you will see. Since then it has occurred to me that somebody might object regarding what you say of eternal punishment, that you evade a real difficulty by a metaphysical subtlety. Then is the notion of eternity a mere negation?[3] Is it not the negation of a negation which equals an affirmation; for *limit* is a negation, and endlessness the negation of that negation? That is what Fenelon says by way of proving that infinity is a positive idea.

[1] *G.A.*, pp. 399–400.
[2] Newman wrote in pencil on this letter '1870.' It was probably written early in Jan. because Meynell wrote on 9 Jan., 'I suspect that you have finished with the book, and that I shall soon be able to read it altogether.' See also Newman's letter 'of congratulation and thanks' on 23 Feb. 1870.
[3] *G.A.*, p. 422.

Is it *possible that the Apocalypse* can have been fulfilled in events unrecorded in history? But I don't know anything of that subject.[1]

You would I am sure be pleased if you could know with what delight I read it.

Your's Dear Dr Newman Sincerely & respectfully Charles Meynell

SUNDAY 12 DECEMBER 1869   Snow again

TUESDAY 14 DECEMBER   Exposition in our Church   much rain

TO ROBERT ORNSBY

The Oratory Decr 14/69

My dear Ornsby

You must put my silence as to your letters to the account of my extreme occupation, which for many months has swallowed me up, and to my much correspondence. This, I expect, will be the 20th letter I shall dispatch today. And my hand is so tired.

Mr Andrews is a gentleman in every way, and of course a good classical scholar. I doubt his mathematics — and have no means of testing his French. There is no reason you should not make an engagement with him, should you wish it.

I felt the kindness of you writing to me on Mr Dalgairns's death, and have ill requited it.[2] But, though my book is a small one, it has taken me an immensity of time. I always say that book writing is like child birth. At the close of my first work, 'the Arians,' I was all but fainting continually. My work on Development all but pulled me inside out. My Apologia was as keen pain, as it was obliged to be short pain — 'si gravis, brevis.' And now I suppose I have written this small work over ten or fifteen times.[3] I cannot count, — or at least great part of it. I used to say, I had written parts of my Essay on Justification fourteen times over.

I wish you gave a better account of Mrs Ornsby

Ever Yours affectly in Xt   John H Newman

TO J. F. SECCOMBE

The Oratory, Bm Dec. 14, 1869.

My dear Sir,

Unless I were so absorbed with work just now, I should have sooner answered you. And letters are so numerous. This is the 20th I shall be answering to-day.[4]

---

[1] *G.A.*, p. 446.

[2] William Dalgairns, Ornsby's father-in-law, had been a Fusilier officer in the Peninsular War.

[3] Newman first wrote 'ten or twenty times.'

[4] Seccombe wrote on 5 Dec. that he firmly believed in the existence of a true Church, but

I have long held the Infallibility of the Pope myself as a private or theological opinion — but I never have attempted to bring anyone into the Church by means of it, for I hold it principally because others whom I know hold it, as I may hold many doctrines which are not defined by the Church, as being pious to hold or agreeable to general sentiment.

But if I am asked to defend it logically and prove it — I don't profess to be able — and I don't expect it will ever be made an article of faith. It did not bring me into the Church. The Greek Church seems to me put out of Court, by the very fact you mention, its not claiming infallibility. Did Our Lord intend Councils to cease with the seventh? Why has not the Greek Church held a council these last 1000 years? In the Latin, there is a continuation of all the functions which went on in the early Church — there is no suspended animation. My own reasons for becoming a Catholic I have given in my Essay on Development of doctrine. Should I be able to find a copy, I will gladly offer it for your acceptance, if you think it may be of use to you — but, though I hold the Pope's Infallibility as most likely, and as having the suffrages of most people in this day, I cannot defend it in a set argument, and never would use it as the instrument of bringing inquirers into the Church.

I am, My dear Sir, Yours faithfully, John H. Newman.

P.S. I must apologise for making you direct my letter — but I did not know what else to do.[1]

TO EDWARD BELLASIS

The Oratory Dec 15/69

My dear Serjeant

I should have written before, had I not been so desperately busy. Thank you for all you say so kindly about the school, as you always do. Did we get to 70 boys we should be right — but we have not come to that yet.[2]

Tell me your style and title 'Edward Bellasis Esqr, Serjeant-at-Law'? You will still let me put your name, won't you, to the beginning of my book? I suppose it will be my last. I have not finished it. I have written in all, (good or bad) 5 constructive books — My prophetical office (which has come to pieces) — Essay on Justification — Development of Doctrine — University Lectures

could not decide between the claims of the Eastern Orthodox and the Roman Churches. He did not think he could become a Catholic without believing in papal infallibility, which he did not accept. While 'the Orthodox Church completely answers to every requirement of an infallible guide. And yet she alone, of all denominations of Christians does not appear to demand the submission of Englishmen!' See also letter of 2 Jan. 1870.

[1] Newman cut out Seccombe's signature and noted on his letter 'Could not read his name any how. So gummed on the cover his own writing etc.'

[2] Bellasis wrote on 9 Dec. that he heard from his son Richard, at Edgbaston, 'that your book is "in the Press".' Bellasis also said that on 4 Dec. the Duchess of Norfolk had remarked to him about the Oratory School, 'both you and I have much reason to be grateful to Dr Newman.'

(Dublin) and this. Each took me a great deal of time and tried me very much. This, I think, has tried me most of all. I have written and re-written it more times than I can count. I have now got up to my highest point — I mean, I could not do better did I spend a century on it — but then, it may be 'bad is the best.'

Your two boys have been ill, I am sorry to say, as well as yourself — but trust the South will at once set you up. Thank you for your pleasant account of William [Bellasis]

Ever Yrs affectly John H Newman

TO J. P. TAYLOR

The Oratory December 15/69

My dear Mr Taylor

I thank you very much for the extract you send me from the Congregational periodical. I had much satisfaction in reading it. Lately it has come to my knowledge that both Congregationalists and Wesleyans, while professing to repudiate my doctrines, have at the same time shown great interest and pleasure in reading my books.[1] The critique which you have brought to my notice, is an instance of this. It is written in a friendly and considerate spirit. I have pleasure in thinking that I am contributing to lay the foundation of principles which may tend as a first step to bring towards Catholic Truth the various separated communions of this country. To begin with doctrine of the Pope is to begin to build St. Peter's from the cross and ball. We must begin from the bottom — not even only from the foundations of the building, but from the soil in which the foundations must be placed — If I succeed merely in this, to contribute to the creation of a sound material on which the stone work of the edifice of faith is to be placed, I shall think myself highly blest, and to have done as much as I can wish to do

Very truly Yours John H Newman

J. P. Taylor Esqr

SATURDAY 18 DECEMBER 1869   boys went down
MONDAY 20 DECEMBER   Lord C Thynne and Lady Castlerosse called

[1] See letter of 28 Jan. 1868 to Henry Allon.

TO CATHERINE BOWDEN, SISTER MARY ALBAN

The Oratory Dec 20/69

My dear Child,

By the time you get this you will be professed and therefore I send you my best congratulations. I have already intended to say Mass for you tomorrow morning.[1]

I am at this moment writing against time, and every day is valuable to me — so I cannot come tomorrow. I would have come if I could. You are all my oldest friends. I have known your dear Father for 50 years. Your uncle was my first friend at Oxford when I was a boy of 16.

God bless you Ever Yours affectly in Xt
John H Newman

TO E. B. PUSEY

The Oratory Dec 20/69

My dear Pusey,

Fr Hecker is a German — he was a Redemptorist. He and others left that Order and set up a Community of St Paul in New York. They have great influence, though some persons oppose them.

Drs Bailly, Kenrick, Clifford, are at Rome. So ought Dr Goss to be — for he has set out — but he was very ill — and at one time meant to go by sea.

If you direct to the 'English College' for the English Bishops — and to the 'American' for the U.S. Bishops I think it will be safest. Dr Ullathorne is at the English College.[2]

I had heard nothing of T. Keble's former illnesses. I grieve to have your news. A happy Xtmas to you.

Ever Yrs affly John H Newman

WEDNESDAY 22 DECEMBER 1869   heavy snow fall

THURSDAY 23 DECEMBER   melting

[1] This daughter of Henry and niece of J. W. Bowden was making her profession with the Dominicans at Stone.

[2] Pusey wished to send copies of his *Is Healthful Reunion Impossible? A second letter to the Very Rev. J. H. Newman,* Oxford 1870, to some of the English and American Bishops. Lord Acton wrote from Rome on 8 Jan. 1870 to Gladstone: 'Pusey's new book may do some good, if anybody has patience to read it. I have distributed several copies.' *Selections from the Correspondence of the First Lord Acton,* edited by J. N. Figgis and R. V. Laurence, I, London 1917, p. 100.

TO W. J. COPELAND

The Oratory Decr 23. 1869

My dear Copeland

Your grand Turkey came yesterday. We all habemus et agimus gratias maximas, and send you all good wishes and congratulations of the season. I was much grieved to see Mr Parson's death in the Papers.[1]

I cannot get through my book. There are 10 chapters and I am wedged fast in the tenth

Ever Yours affectly John H Newman

SATURDAY 25 DECEMBER 1869   snow   melting
SUNDAY 26 DECEMBER   snow
MONDAY 27 DECEMBER   melting

[1] John Parsons, the Oxford banker

List of Letters by Correspondents

List of Letters by Correspondents

Abbreviations used in addition to those listed at the beginning of the volume:

A.	Original Autograph.
C.	Copy, other than those made by Newman.
Georgetown	Georgetown University, Washington, D.C.
H.	Holograph copy by Newman.
Harrow	Dominican Convent, Harrow, Middlesex.
Lond.	London Oratory.
Magd.	Magdalen College, Oxford.
Oriel	Oriel College, Oxford.
Oscott	Oscott College, Birmingham.
Pr.	Printed.
Pusey	Pusey House, Oxford.
Rankeillour	The Lord Rankeillour.
S.J. Dublin	The Jesuit Fathers, 35 Lower Leeson Street, Dublin.
S.J. Lond.	The Jesuit Fathers, 114 Mount Street, London.
Stone	St Dominic's Convent, Stone.
Ushaw	Ushaw College, Durham.
Upholland	Upholland College, Lancashire.

The abbreviation which describes the source is always the first one after the date of each letter. This is followed immediately by the indication of its present location or owner. When there is no such indication, it means that the source letter is preserved at the Birmingham Oratory. It has not been thought necessary to reproduce the catalogue indications of the Archives at the Oratory, because each of Newman's letters there is separately indexed, and can be traced at once.

After the source and its location have been indicated, any additional holograph copies (with their dates) or drafts are listed and then, enclosed within brackets, any reference to previous publication in standard works.

Lastly, when it is available, comes the address to which the letter is sent.

Correspondent	Year	Date	Source	Location, Owner, Address
Allcock and Milward, Messrs.	1868	5 Feb	D	
Allies, T. W.	1868	19 Jan	C	
	1869	9 Jan	C	
Allon, Henry	1868	25 Jan	Pr	Albert Peel, *Letters to a Victorian Editor, Henry Allon*, London 1929, p. 272
		28 Jan	Pr	Albert Peel, op. cit., p. 273
Bacchus, Mrs Henry	1868	26 Feb	A	University of Iowa Libraries, Iowa City
Badeley, Edward	1868	5 Jan	A	
		21 Jan	A	The Book Shop, 25 Sadler Street, Wells, Somerset
Bathurst, Catherine Anne	1868	31 May	A	Harrow
	1869	3 Jan	A	Harrow
		11 Jan	A	Harrow
		2 June	A	Harrow
		16 July	A	Harrow
		6 Nov	A	Harrow
Bedford, Henry	1868	30 Dec	A	All Hallows, Dublin. *Ad.* Henry Bedford Esqr/All Hallows College/Drumcondra/Dublin
	1869	3 Mar	C	
		19 June	C	
Bellasis, Edward	1868	25 Jan	C	
		12 July	Pr	'Some of Cardinal Newman's Letters to Ours', privately printed by the English Jesuits, 1892, p. 19
		23 July	Pr	ibid., p. 19
		1 Aug	C	
		23 Oct	A	
	1869	7 July	A	
		1 Aug	A	
		17 Aug	A	
		15 Dec	A	
Bellew, Mrs John Chippendall Montesquieu	1868	23 Oct	A	C. Stafford Northcote Esq.
Bloxam, J. R.	1868	21 Feb	A	Magd.
	1869	21 Feb	A	Magd.
Bowden, Catherine	1868	29 April	C	
		25 Nov	A	Stone
		20 Dec	A	Stone
Bowden, Henry Sebastian	1868	24 Jan	A	Lond. Vol. 15 *Ad.* H. Bowden Esqr/ The Oratory/Brompton/London SW.
Bowden, John Edward	1869	19 June	A	Lond. Vol. 15
Bowden, Marianne Frances	1869	22 Feb	A	*Ad.* Miss Bowden/40 Prince's Gate/Hyde Park/London W
		13 May	A	*Ad.* Miss Bowden/40 Prince's Terrace/Hyde Park/ London W
Bowles, Emily	1868	4 Feb	A	
		1 Mar	A	
		13 April	A	
		28 May	A	
		5 Aug	C	
	1869	6 Jan	A	
		8 Mar	A	
		25 Mar	A	
		2 June	A	
		30 June	C	
		4 July	A	
		25 July	C	
		28 July	A	

Correspondent	Year	Date	Source	Location, Owner, Address
		29 Sept	C	
Brown, Thomas Joseph,	1869	26 Sept	D	
		28 Sept	C	
			D	
		3 Nov	C	
			D	
Browning, Oscar	1868	31 May	A	University of Sussex Catholic Chaplaincy. *Ad.* The Revd O. Browning/Eton College/ Windsor
Brundrit, Robert Wright	1868	22 July	A	Upholland
Buckle, Mrs	1869	19 June	C	
Calenzio, Generoso	1869	18 June	D	
Capes, J. M.	1868	16 Mar	C	
			D	
Casolani, Dr	1868	12 Feb	D	
Challis, Henry William	1868	16 Aug	A	
Chatterton, Lady	1868	6 May	A	Oscott. *Ad.* Lady Chatterton/Old Square/Warwick
		17 May	A	Oscott
	1869	12 April	A	Oscott (Edward Heneage Dering, *Memoirs of Georgiana, Lady Chatterton*, 2nd ed., London 1901, pp. 166–7)
Church, R. W.	1868	27 Feb	C	
		31 Mar	C	
		8 June	C	
		5 Sept	C	
		14 Nov	C	
Church, Mrs R. W.	1868	5 April	A	Library of the House of the Resurrection, Mirfield, Yorkshire
Cist, L. J.	1868	29 July	A	Georgetown
Clarke, Richard Frederick	1868	21 April	A	S. J. Lond.
		29 Dec	A	S. J. Lond.
Clifford, William	1868	15 Nov	A	Clifton Diocesan Archives
Clutton, Henry	1868	4 Feb	A	Mr Owen Clutton
Coleridge, Edward	1868	4 Feb	A	
Coleridge, Henry James	1868	12 Jan	A	S. J. Lond
		6 Feb	A	S. J. Lond. (*Ward* II, p. 205)
		5 Aug	A	S. J. Lond. (*Ess.* II, pp. 109–11; the *Month*, Sept. 1868, pp. 269–71)
		7 Aug	A	S. J. Lond.
		13 Aug	A	S. J. Lond.
		20 Aug	A	S. J. Lond.
		17 Sept	A	S. J. Lond.
		29 Oct	A	S. J. Lond.
	1869	13 Feb	A	S. J. Lond.
		29 April	A	S. J. Lond.
		2 May	A	S. J. Lond.
			D	
		2 June	A	S. J. Lond.
		30 June	A	S. J. Lond.
		30 Sept	A	S. J. Lond.
		14 Oct	A	S. J. Lond.
Coleridge, Sir John Taylor	1868	17 Sept	Pr	J. T. Coleridge, *A Memoir of the Rev. John Keble* London 1869, pp. 516–9. (Liddon's *Pusey IV*, pp. 110–12; E. H. Coleridge, *Life and Correspondence of John Duke Lord Coleridge* II, London 1904, pp. 71, 158)
			D	
Collins, Edward Francis	1869	23 Feb	D	
Cope, Sir William Henry	1868	14 Feb	C	
	1869	25 May	C	

Correspondent	Year	Date	Source	Location, Owner, Address
		10 Sept	C	
Copeland, W. J.	1868	2 Jan	A	Pusey
		19 Feb	A	Pusey
		26 Feb	A	Pusey
		6 Mar	A	Pusey
		10 Mar	A	Pusey
		13 Mar (I)	A	Pusey
		13 Mar(II)	A	Pusey
		15 Mar	A	Pusey
		22 Mar	A	Pusey
		31 Mar	A	Pusey
		24 April(I)	A	Pusey (*Trevor II*, p. 453)
		24 April(II)	A	Pusey
		26 April	A	Pusey
		1 May	A	Pusey
		7 May	A	Pusey
		17 June	A	Pusey
		25 June	A	Pusey
		1 July	A	Pusey
		23 July	A	Pusey
		30 July	A	Pusey
		3 Aug	A	Pusey
		5 Sept	A	Pusey
		19 Sept	A	Pusey
		14 Nov	A	Pusey
		26 Nov	A	Pusey
		3 Dec	A	Pusey
		15 Dec	A	Pusey
		24 Dec	A	Pusey
	1869	9 Feb	A	Pusey
		12 Feb	A	Pusey
		24 Feb	A	Pusey
		28 Feb	A	Pusey
		24 Mar	A	Pusey
		29 Mar	A	Pusey
		11 May	A	Pusey
		20 May	A	
		10 June	A	Pusey
		14 June	A	Pusey
		20 June	A	Pusey
		24 June	A	Pusey
		5 July	A	Pusey
		25 July	A	Pusey
		2 Aug	A	Pusey
		11 Aug	A	Pusey
		3 Oct	A	Pusey
		21 Oct	A	Pusey
		6 Nov	A	Pusey
		21 Nov	A	Pusey
		23 Dec	A	Pusey
Cox, G. A.	1868	17 Jan	D	
Crawley, Mrs	1868	17 June	A	Arthur Kyle Davis Jr, University of Virginia
Cuddon, Charles Francis	1868	9 April	A	Dinand Library, Holy Cross College, Worcester, Mass.
Dalgairns, J. D.	1869	7 June	D	
Darras Joseph Epiphane	1868	20 Feb	D	
Daunt, W. J. O'Neill	1868	28 Mar	A	St John's Seminary, Camarillo, California
		29 Aug	A	The same
		17 Sept	A	The same
		10 Oct	A	
De Lisle, Ambrose Phillipps	1868	14 Sept	C	
Denbigh, Earl of	1868	8 Mar	A	

Correspondent	Year	Date	Source	Location, Owner, Address
		16 May	C	
Dering, Edward Heneage	1868	14 May	A	Oscott. *Ad.* E. H. Dering Esqr/ Old Square/Warwick
		31 July	A	Oscott. *Ad.* E. H. Dering Esqr/ Wootton Hall/Henley in Arden/ Warwickshire
		15 Dec	A	Oscott. *Ad.* E H Dering Esq/ Wootten Hall/Henley in Arden
Drane, Augusta Theodosia	1869	28 May	A	Stone
		13 July	C	
Du Boulay, Mary Gabriel	1868	31 May	C	
Dunn, Margaret	1869	12 April	A	
		22 Sept	A	
		13 Nov	A	
Dunraven, Earl of	1869	3 Aug	C	
Eaton, Charles Ormston	1869	11 Mar	A	
The Editor of Church Opinion	1869	24 July	Pr	*Church Opinion*, (31 July, 1869)
		31 July	D	
The Editor of the Sun Newspaper	1868	22 Jan	A	Newman Preparatory School, Boston, U.S.A. *Ad.* The Editor/ The Sun Office/112 Strand/ London W.C.
Estcourt, E. E.	1868	11 Oct	D	
	1869	2 July	A	Birmingham Diocesan Archives
			H	
Forbes, Alexander Penrose	1868	6 April	C	
Fox, Miss Ellen	1868	25 Feb	C	
		9 Mar	C	
Froude, Isy	1868	14 April	C	
Froude, William	1868	8 April	C	
		12 April	C	
		27 Nov	C	(*Ward* II, p. 207)
	1869	19 Feb	C	
Froude, Mrs William	1868	12 April	C	
		20 Aug	C	
	1869	23 July	A	*Ad.* Mrs Froude/Chelston Cross/ Torquay
		11 Aug	C	
		6 Nov	A	(*Ward* II, pp. 284-5) *Ad.* Mrs Froude/Chelston Cross/Torquay
		8 Nov	C	
		21 Nov	A	(*Harper*, pp.193-5; F.J.Cwiekowski, *The English Bishops and the First Vatican Council*, Louvain 1971, pp. 326-7)
Gainsborough, Earl of	1868	31 May	C	
	1869	12 April	A	Dr Donald F. Winslow Library, Philadelphia Divinity School
		7 Aug	A	The Stark Collection, University of Texas
Giberne, Miss M. R.	1868	9 Jan	A	
		11 Feb	A	
		20 Aug	A	
	1869	10 Feb	A	(*Ward* II, p. 281)
Gladstone, William Ewart	1868	9 Jan	A	British Museum Add. Ms. 44414 (John Morley, *The Life of W. E. Gladstone*, Book V, Ch. 10)
			D	
		25 Nov	A	British Museum Add. Ms. 44416
			D	
Glyn, Ashley Carr	1868	21 June	D	
Godwin, Thomas	1869	8 Oct	D	

Correspondent	Year	Date	Source	Location, Owner, Address
Gordon, William Philip	1868	13 Oct	A	Lond. Vol. 11
Goss, Alexander,	1869	13 May	D	
Grant, Thomas	1868	23 Nov	A	Portsmouth Diocesan Archives
Haddan, Arthur West	1869	14 July	A	Stark Collection, University of Texas
			D	
Harper, Thomas, S. J.	1868	21 April	A	S. J. Lond.
	1869	10 Feb	A	S. J. Lond.
		14 Apr	A	S. J. Lond.
		18 Aug	D	
		25 Aug	A	S. J. Lond.
Hawkins, Edward	1869	27 Feb	A	Oriel
		24 Mar	A	Oriel
Hayes, John	1869	13 April	P	*Mozr.* II, p. 476
Helbert, Mrs	1869	30 Aug	A	
		10 Sept	A	
		28 Sept	A	
		20 Oct	A	
		5 Nov	A	
Hester, G. P.	1868	15 Jan	D	
		12 Feb	D	
Higgins, Henry Vincent	1868	15 Aug	C	
Higgins, Mrs Matthew James	1868	16 Aug	C	
		19 Sept	C	
	1869	19 Aug	A	Paul C. Richards, Brookline
Holmes, Miss	1868	1 Aug	A	
	1869	18 Jan	A	
		16 Mar	A	
		30 April	A	
		2 June	A	
		7 Oct	A	
Hope-Scott, James	1868	15 Mar	A	Rankeillour
			H	1873
		29 Mar	A	Rankeillour
			H	1873
		31 Mar	A	Rankeillour (Robert Ornsby, *Memoirs of James Robert Hope-Scott,* London 1884, II, p. 233; H. Tristram, *Newman and his Friends,* London 1933, pp. 177–8)
			H	1873
		2 April	A	Rankeillour
			H	1873
		10 April	A	Rankeillour
			H	1873
		15 Sept	A	Rankeillour
			H	1873
		12 Oct	A	Rankeillour
			H	1873
		7 Dec	A	Rankeillour
			H	1873
Hopkins, Gerard Manley	1868	7 Feb	A	Campion Hall, Oxford. (Claude Colleer Abbot, *Further Letters of Gerard Manley Hopkins,* London 1956, p. 408)
		14 May	A	Campion Hall, Oxford. (Claude Colleer Abbott, op. cit., p. 408) *Ad.* Gerard M. Hopkins Esqr/Oak Hill/ Hampstead/ London N W
Huntingford, G. W.	1868	17 June	A	Canon F. J. Bartlett. *Ad.* The Revd G. W. Huntingford/Vicarage/ Littlemore/Oxford
Hutton, Richard Holt	1869	27 Feb	C	
			D	

Correspondent	Year	Date	Source	Location, Owner, Address
Jenkins, Robert Charles	1868	29 July	C	
	1869	21 Nov	C	
Jones, Mrs	1868	8 June	D	
Kennard, Charles H.	1868	28 May	D	
Kennard, John P.	1868	28 May	D	
La Serre, H.	1868	8 Jan	C	
Leahy, Patrick	1868	15 Mar	A	Cashel Diocesan Archives
Lee, Frederick George	1869	21 Nov	A	Mrs Bond, Clifton
Leigh, William, Junior	1868	18 July	A	Woodchester Priory
		13 Aug	A	Woodchester Priory
Liddon, H. P.	1868	21 July	A	Keble *Ad.* The Revd H. P. Liddon/at the Revd R. Porter's/ Kenn Rectory/Exeter
		27 July	A	Keble *Ad.* The Revd H. P. Liddon/Kenn Rectory/ Exeter
		1 Aug	D	
		10 Aug	A	Keble *Ad.* The Revd. H. P. Liddon/at Mrs Henry Porter's/ Holcombe/Dawlish/Devon
			D	
Lindsay, The Hon. Colin	1868	27 Nov	A	
		18 Dec	A	
	1869	1 Jan	A	
Linford, Roger	1869	16 Oct	A	
Loyson, Hyacinth	1869	1 Oct	C	
			D	
Lynch, Mrs Henry J.	1868	31 July	D	
MacCarthy, John George	1869	12 June	A	Messrs Feehan, Cork
MacColl, Malcolm	1868	19 July	C	
		4 Nov	C	(*Malcolm MacColl Memoirs and Correspondence*, edited by G. W. E. Russell, London 1914, p. 291)
	1869	12 Nov	C	(op. cit., p. 291)
		29 Nov	C	(op. cit., p. 292)
MacMahon, J. H.	1869	29 Nov	C	
MacSwiney, S. M.	1869	18 Jan	A	Miss MacSwiney, London
			D	
Manning, Archbishop	1869	3 Nov	Pr	(*Purcell* II, p. 346)
			D	(two)
Meynell, Charles	1869	2 July	A	(For these letters see Appendix to Dr Zeno, *John Henry Newman: Our Way to Certitude*, Leiden 1957)
		4 July	A	
		25 July	A	(*Ward* II, pp. 256–7)
		27 July	A	(*Ward* II, p. 257)
		12 Aug	A	(*Ward* II, p. 257)
		17 Aug	A	(*Ward* II, p. 258)
			D	
		18 Aug	A	(*Ward* II, pp. 258–9)
			D	
		20 Aug	A	(*Ward* II, p. 259)
			D	
		21 Aug	A	*Ward* II, p. 260)
		27 Sept	A	
		3 Oct	A	
		8 Oct	A	
		19 Oct	A	
		2 Nov	A	
		17 Nov	A	
		10 Dec	A	
Milbourne, Mrs	1868	17 Mar	A	Pusey
Molloy, James Lynham	1869	21 Sept	A	
Monsell, William	1868	27 Jan	A	
		9 Feb	A	

Correspondent	Year	Date	Source	Location, Owner, Address
		28 June	A	
		7 July	A	
		23 Sept	A	
		9 Nov	A	
	1869	11 Jan	A	
		18 Jan	A	
		26 Feb	A	Montalembert Archives, La Roche-en-Brenil
		2 Mar	A	
		26 April	A	
		17 Aug	A	
		3 Sept	A	
		22 Sept	A	
		29 Sept	A	
		1 Oct	A	
		9 Oct	A	
		3 Dec	A	
		9 Dec	A	
Monsell, Mrs William	1868	27 Jan	C	
	1869	26 Feb	A	
Montalembert, Le Comte de	1868	9 Mar	A	Montalembert Archives, La Roche-en-Brenil (*DR*, (Spring 1949) p. 131)
		7 July	A	Montalembert Archives (ibid., p. 133)
	1869	10 Nov	A	Montalembert Archives (ibid. pp. 135–6)
			D	
Mossman, Thomas Wimberley	1868	17 Sept	Pr	The *Month* (Oct. 1868), pp. 421–8
Mozley, Mrs John	1868	21 Feb	A	J. H. Mozley, Haslemere, Surrey
		9 June	A	J. H. Mozley
		16 Aug	A	J. H. Mozley
		3 Dec	A	J. H. Mozley
	1869	3 Jan	A	Oriel
		12 Jan	A	Oriel
		21 Feb	A	J. H. Mozley
		19 May	A	Oriel
		14 Oct	A	J. H. Mozley
Mozley, J. R.	1869	21 Oct	D	
Munro, Miss	1868	28 Aug	A	
Nary, James	1869	2 July	A	Birmingham Diocesan Archives
			D	
Nevins, J. H. Willis	1868	24 Sept	C	
Newman, Francis William	1869	3 Jan	A	Newman Preparatory School, Boston, Mass.
		at 3 Jan	A	incomplete
Norris, John	1869	26 Aug	A	
O'Hagan, John	1868	25 Nov	A	S. J. Dublin
Ornsby, Robert	1868	22 May	A	
			H	
	1869	14 Dec	A	
Palgrave, Francis Turner	1868	26 Jan	C	(Gwenllian F. Palgrave, *Francis Turner Palgrave, His Journals and Memories of his life*, London 1899, pp. 101–2)
Palmer, William	1868	13 Oct	A	
Patmore, Coventry	1868	14 Jan	A	S. J. Lond.
		8 June	A	S. J. Lond. (Basil Champneys, *Memoirs and Correspondence of Coventry Patmore*, London 1900, II, p. 80)
Pattison, Mark	1869	22 Oct	A	
		21 Nov	A	

Correspondent	Year	Date	Source	Location, Owner, Address
Pickering, B. M.	1868	19 Dec	A	
			D	
		30 Dec	A	
			D	
	1869	17 April	A	
			D	
		22 April	A	
		17 Nov	A	
Pixell, C. H. V.	1868	15 Nov	D	
Pollen, John Hungerford	1868	10 May	C	
		14 Aug	C	
		16 Aug	C	
		18 Aug	C	
	1869	12 June	C	
Poole, Mother Mary Imelda	1868	5 May	C	Stone
		12 May	A	Stone
		31 Dec	C	
Pope, Mr	1869	12 June	A	
Pusey, E. B.	1868	24 May	A	Pusey
		16 Aug	A	Pusey
		24 Aug	A	Pusey
		28 Aug	A	Pusey
		4 Sept	A	Pusey (Liddon's *Pusey* IV, pp. 154–6)
		19 Sept	A	Pusey
		5 Oct	A	Pusey
		1 Nov	A	Pusey
		14 Nov	A	Pusey
		24 Nov	A	Pusey
		7 Dec	A	Pusey
	1869	12 April	A	Pusey
		30 April	A	Pusey
		13 May	A	Pusey
		9 June	A	Pusey
		4 July	A	Pusey (Liddon's *Pusey* IV, p. 165)
		23 July	A	Pusey
		12 Sept	A	Pusey
		16 Sept	A	Pusey (Liddon's *Pusey*, IV, p. 182)
		4 Nov	A	Pusey
		7 Nov	A	Pusey
		20 Dec	A	Pusey
Raymond-Barker, Frederic Mills	1868	9 Dec	A	
Renouf, Peter le Page	1868	21 June	A	Pembroke College, Oxford (*The Life-Work of Sir Peter le Page Renouf*, 1st Series, Vol. IV, Paris 1907, pp. lxxxi–lxxxv; *Ward* II, p. 236)
		30 Nov	C	
		17 Dec	A	Pembroke College, Oxford
	1869	9 Aug	A	Pembroke College, Oxford
Rogers, Sir Frederic	1868	23 Jan	C	
		2 Feb	C	
		1 Mar	C	
		26 Nov	C	
		15 Dec	C	
	1869	12 Feb	C	
		18 Feb	C	
Russell, Charles	1868	1 Jan	A	S. J. Dublin
		15 Nov	A	S. J. Dublin
	1869	15 July	A	S. J. Dublin
St John, Ambrose	1868	12 Jan	A	
		3 Sept	A	(*Ward* II, p. 253)
			H	1875

Correspondent	Year	Date	Source	Location, Owner, Address
	1869	5 Jan	A	
			H	1875
		15 April	A	
			H	1875
		2 Aug	A	
			H	1875
		19 Aug	A	
			H	1875
		29 Aug	A	
			H	1875
Seccombe, J. F.	1869	14 Dec	C	
Segno, Alexander,	1868	6 Feb	D	
Sheil, Sir Justin	1868	18 May	A	
		1 Aug	A	
		25 Aug	A	
	1869	26 Aug	A	
Sheil, Lady	1869	22 Jan	A	
Shepherd, James Lawrence	1868	23 Feb	A	Stanbrook Abbey, Worcester
		29 Aug	A	Stanbrook Abbey, Worcester
		8 Nov	A	Stanbrook Abbey, Worcester
	1869	20 Aug	A	Stanbrook Abbey, Worcester
Short, Thomas	1868	8 Jun	A	Mrs Cremenini
Simeon, Sir John	1868	13 Sept	A	Sir John Simeon *Ad.* Sir John Simeon Bart M P/ Swainston/Isle of Wight/(if not there, to be opened)
		15 Sept	A	Sir John Simeon *Ad.* Sir John Simeon Bart M P/ Swainston/Isle of Wight
	1869	8 May	A	Sir John Simeon
Simeon, Lady	1868	15 Nov	C	
Simeon, Louisa	1869	25 Mar	A	
		29 April	A	Georgetown
		24 May	A	
		25 June	A	(*Ward* II, pp. 329–31)
			D	
Simmons, Gilbert	1868	21 June	C	
		28 June	C	
		3 July	C	
	1869	8 Jan	C	
Simpson, Richard	1869	3 Jan	A	
Simpson, Mrs Richard	1868	7 April	A	Public Library, Mitcham. *Ad.* Mrs Simpson/4 Victoria Road/ Clapham Common/London SW
Skinner, James	1868	13 May	D	
		28 May	D	
		9 July	D	
		31 July	D	
Smith, Albert	1868	8 Jan	C	
	1869	6 Jan	C	
Sparrow, Mrs	1869	24 Mar	C	
		28 June	C	
Stewart, James	1868	15 Mar	C	
Stokes, Charles Scott	1869	April	D	
A Student of Maynooth	1868	2 Mar	C	(*Ward* II, p. 335; The *Sower*, May 1924)
Suffield, Robert	1869	13 Nov	A	
Sullivan, William Kirby	1869	3 July	A	
Taylor, Fanny Margaret	1868	4 Feb	A	Maryfield, Roehampton
	1869	3 Mar	A	Maryfield, Roehampton (F. C. Devas, *Mother Mary Magdalen*, London 1927, pp. 83–4)
Taylor, Henry	1868	14 Jan	A	Bodleian Ms Eng. letters. C.1.
	1869	15 Feb	A	Bodleian Ms Eng. letters. C.1.

Correspondent	Year	Date	Source	Location, Owner, Address
Taylor, J. P.	1869	15 Dec	A	Lond. Vol. 15
Tillotson, Robert Beverley	1868	19 June	A	Paulist Fathers, New York
Todd, William Gowan	1868	9 May	A	
Trench, Richard Chenevix	1868	3 June	A	
Ullathorne, Bishop	1868	1 Feb	A	
		10 April	A	Oscott
		24 April	A	
		26 April	A	
		17 May	A	
		23 Sept	A	
			D	
		15 Oct	C	
			D	(two)
	1869	1 Nov	A	Oblates of St Charles, Bayswater
			D	
			H	
		10 Nov	A	
			D	
		14 Nov	A	
			D	
Vaughan, Edward Thomas	1869	9 Feb	Pr	*Ward* II, p. 346
Walker, J., of Scarborough	1868	22 May	A	Ushaw
		15 Dec	A	
	1869	6 Jan	A	
		2 June	A	
		6 June	A	
		11 July	A	
Ward, Richard	1868	14 Dec	A	
Watt, Mrs F. J.	1868	21 Feb	C	
		24 April	C	
		21 Aug	C	
Webb, Clara L.	1868	4 Feb	A	St John's Seminary, Camarillo, California
Wetherell, T. F.	1869	7 Nov	A	(Abbot Gasquet, *Lord Acton and his Circle*, London n.d., p. lxxxii)
			D	
Whitty, Robert	1868	31 Jan	A	S. J. Lond.
Wilberforce, Agnes	1869	19 Sept	A	Ushaw
Wilberforce, Henry	1868	18 June	A	Ushaw. (*Ward* II, p. 205)
			H	1873
		19 June	A	Georgetown
		7 July	A	Georgetown (*Ward* II, p. 207)
			H	1873
		27 July	A	Georgetown
			H	1873
		31 July	A	Georgetown
		8 Aug	A	Georgetown
		12 Aug	A	Georgetown (*Ward* II, p. 252)
			H	1873
		20 Aug	A	Georgetown
			H	1873
		29 Nov	C	
	1869	3 Jan	A	Ushaw
		18 Mar	A	Georgetown
		5 April	A	Georgetown (R. D. Middleton, *Newman at Oxford*, London 1950, p. 159)
...			H	1873
		27 May	A	Georgetown
		7 Aug	A	Georgetown
		20 Aug	A	Georgetown (*Ward* II, pp. 254–5)

Correspondent	Year	Date	Source	Location, Owner, Address
			H	1873
		14 Sept	A	Georgetown
			H	1873
		9 Dec	A	Mrs John Moody, Texas
Wilberforce, Mrs Henry	1869	3 March	A	Georgetown. *Ad.* Mrs Wilberforce/ Chester Hill/Stroud/Glostershire
Williams and Norgate, Messrs.	1869	9 April	A	
Wood, Charlotte	1868	5 Dec	A	
	1869	18 Jan	A	
		11 July	A	
Woodgate, H. A.	1868	6 April	A	St John's Seminary, Brighton, Mass.
		30 Dec	A	
			D	
	1869	5 Jan	A	
		12 Jan	A	
		9? Feb	A	St John's Seminary, Brighton, Mass.
		19 Feb	A	
		26 July	A	Philip Reidy of Worcester, Mass.
Woodlock, Bartholomew	1868	23 Feb	A	University College, Dublin
		4 Mar	C	
	1869	2 May	A	University College, Dublin
		10 May	A	University College, Dublin
		12 Sept	A	M. Tierney, University College, Dublin
Wootten, Mrs.	1868	28 Aug	A	*Ad.* Mrs Wootten

MEMORANDA, ETC.

	Date	Source	Subject
1868	4 March	A	A New Periodical
	14 Oct	A	Consultor previous to the Council?
1869	20 Sept	A	Inopportuneness of definition of Infallibility
	12 Dec	A	The same (in note to letter of 21 Nov. to Mrs W. Froude)

LETTERS TO NEWMAN

		From	Inserted before Newman's of
1869	25 Feb	Richard Holt Hutton	27 Feb
	3 July	Charles Meynell	4 July
	24 July	Charles Meynell	25 July
	26 July	Charles Meynell	27 July
	16 Aug	Charles Meynell	17 Aug
	18 Aug	Charles Meynell	20 Aug
	20 Aug	Charles Meynell	21 Aug
	23 Aug	Charles Meynell	25 Aug to Thomas Harper
	[2 Oct]	Charles Meynell	3 Oct
	[2 Oct]	Charles Meynell	
	[7 Oct]	Charles Meynell	8 Oct
	[8 Oct]	Charles Meynell	
	11 Oct	Charles Meynell	19 Oct
	13 Oct	Charles Meynell	
	20 Oct	Charles Meynell	20 Oct to Mrs Helbert
	23 Oct	Charles Meynell	2 Nov
	2 Nov	Archbishop Manning	3 Nov
	4 Nov	Charles Meynell	17 Nov
	8 Nov	Charles Meynell	
	18 Nov	Charles Meynell	
	27 Nov	Charles Meynell	10 Dec
	9 Dec	Charles Meynell	
	11 Dec	Charles Meynell	
	[16 Dec]	Charles Meynell	14 Dec to Robert Ornsby
	[18 Dec]	Charles Meynell	
	[Early in 1870]	Charles Meynell	

Index of Persons and Places

The index to Volume XXI contains notices of almost all the persons who occur in that volume, and the indexes to subsequent volumes notices of those who occur in them for the first time. These are not repeated, and so, for persons and places already mentioned in those volumes, reference back is here made by a (XXI) or (XXII) etc. inserted after such names.

References are given, in the case of persons mentioned for the first time in this volume, to *The Dictionary of National Biography* or *The Dictionary of American Biography*, and failing them, to Frederick Boase, *Modern English Biography*, or Joseph Gillow, *Bibliographical Dictionary of the English Catholics*; also occasionally to other printed works. Much of the information is derived from the correspondence and other material in the archives of the Birmingham Oratory, and from various private sources.

417